P9-ECL-636

DATE DUE

			PRINTED IN U.S.A.

PROFESSIONAL

SPORTS TEAM

HISTORIES

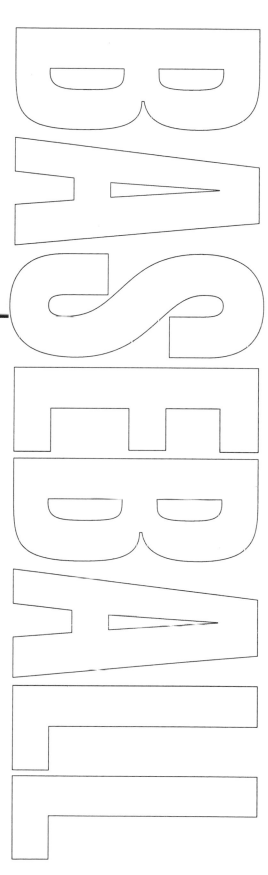

BASEBALL

BASEBALL

PROFESSIONAL SPORTS TEAM HISTORIES

MICHAEL L. LaBLANC, Editor

MARY K. RUBY, Associate Editor

Gale Research Inc. DETROIT • WASHINGTON, D.C. • LONDON

Riverside Community College
Library
4800 Magnolia Avenue
Riverside, California 92506

DEC '94

While every effort has been made to ensure the reliability of the information presented in this publication, Gale Research Inc. does not guarantee the accuracy of the data contained herein. Gale accepts no payment for listing; and inclusion in the publication of any organization, agency, institution, publication, service, or individual does not imply endorsement of the editors or publisher. Errors brought to the attention of the publisher and verified to the satisfaction of the publisher will be corrected in future editions.

This book is printed on acid-free paper that meets the minimum requirements of American National Standard for Information Sciences— Permanence Paper for Printed Library Materials, ANSI Z39.48-1984.

This publication is a creative work fully protected by all applicable copyright laws, as well as by misappropriation, trade secret, unfair competition, and other applicable laws. The authors and editors of this work have added value to the underlying factual material herein through one or more of the following: unique and original selection, coordination, expression, arrangement, and classification of the information.

All rights to this publication will be vigorously defended.

Copyright © 1994 by Gale Research Inc.
835 Penobscot Bldg.
Detroit, MI 48226-4094

All rights reserved, including the right of reproduction in whole or in part in any form.

Printed in the United States of America
Published simultaneously in the United Kingdom
by Gale Research International Limited
(An affiliated company of Gale Research Inc.)

No part of this book may be reproduced in any form without permission in writing from the publisher, except by a reviewer who wishes to quote brief passages or entries in connection with a review written for inclusion in a magazine or newspaper.

ISBN 0-8103-8859-6

10 9 8 7 6 5 4 3 2 1

STAFF

Michael L. LaBlanc, *Editor*
Mary K. Ruby, *Associate Editor*
George W. Schmidt, *Indexer*
Marilyn Allen, *Editorial Associate*
Michael J. Tyrkus, *Assistant Editor*

Barbara Carlisle Bigelow, Suzanne M. Bourgoin, Dean David Dauphinais,
Kathleen Dauphinais, Kathy Edgar, Nicolet V. Elert, Marie Ellavich, Kevin
Hillstrom, Laurie Collier Hillstrom, Anne Janette Johnson, Janice Jorgensen,
Denise Kasinec, Paula Kepos, Jane Kosek, Mark Kram, Mary P. LaBlanc,
L. Mpho Mabunda, Roger Matuz, Tom McMahon, Louise Mooney, Les
Ochram, Jack Pearson, Terrie Rooney, Mary Ruby, Julia Rubiner, Aarti
Stephens, Debbie Stanley, Les Stone, Gerald Tomlinson, Roger Valade,
Kathleen Wilson,
Contributing Editors

Kevin Hillstrom, Keith Reed, Mary K. Ruby, *Photo Editors*
Willie Mathis, *Camera Operator*

B. Hal May, *Director, Biography Division*
Peter M. Gareffa, *Senior Editor, Contemporary Biographies*
David E. Salamie, *Senior Editor, New Product Development*

Jeanne Gough, *Permissions Manager*
Margaret A. Chamberlain, *Permissions Supervisor (Pictures)*
Pamela A. Hayes, Keith Reed, *Permissions Associates*
Susan Brohman, Arlene Johnson, Barbara A. Wallace, *Permissions Assistants*

Mary Beth Trimper, *Production Director*
Mary Kelley, *Production Assistant*
Cynthia Baldwin, *Art Director*
Mark C. Howell, *Cover Designer*
Kathleen Hourdakis, *Page Designer*

Cover photo by arrangement with AP/Wide World Photos

Contents

INTRODUCTION

Professional Sports Team Histories is a multivolume reference series that chronicles the evolution of four major U.S. spectator sports: baseball, basketball, football, and hockey.

Baseball, the first of the four sports to achieve full professional status, evolved from the British game of cricket and other ball-and-stick games. The game's popularity grew dramatically during the Civil War, when a friendly ballgame represented one of the few recreational diversions available in army camps on both sides. The rise of professionalism in the sport during the 1870s only served to widen baseball's mass appeal.

Professional Sports Team Histories: Baseball traces the development of the sport's meteoric rise from a simple entertainment venue to its status as "the national pastime." By the beginning of the twentieth century baseball had already entrenched itself in the nation's psyche, with the game's early standouts becoming the first sports heroes. Despite the recent growth in popularity of the other three professional sports, baseball and its long and colorful tradition has retained its emotional hold on the nation's imagination.

With an extensive prose entry on each current team in the American and National Leagues, *Baseball* focuses on the formation and growth of each franchise and highlights the accomplishments of significant players and members of management. The volume also charts the various franchise moves and the period of expansion that began in the 1960s.

A Source of Convenient Reference *and* Interesting Reading

· **Informative historical essays,** many written by specialists in the field, offer an overview of each team's development from its inception through the 1993 season, with coverage of franchise moves, name changes, key personnel, and team performance.

· **A special entry on the history of the sport** follows the development of the game over the years and presents a thorough analysis of the factors that have led to changes in the way it is played.

· **Designed with a broad audience in mind,** the information in *Professional Sports Team Histories* is accessible enough to captivate the interest of the sports novice, yet comprehensive enough to enlighten even the most avid fan.

· **Numerous photos**—including shots of Hall-of-Famers—further enhance the reader's appreciation of each team's history.

· **Easy-to-locate "Team Information at a Glance"** sections list founding dates for each team; names, addresses, and phone numbers of home stadiums; team color/logo information; and franchise records.

· **Additional eye-catching sidebars** present other noteworthy statistics, interesting team-related trivia, close-up profiles of important players and management figures, and capsulized accounts of events that have become a permanent part of sports folklore.

Helpful Indexes Make It Easy to Find the Information You Need

Each volume of *Professional Sports Team Histories* includes a detailed, user-friendly index, making it easy to find information on key players and executives.

Available in Electronic Formats

Diskette/Magnetic Tape • *Professional Sports Team Histories* is available for licensing on magnetic tape or diskette in a fielded format. Either the complete, four-sport database or a custom selection of entries may be ordered. The database is available for internal data processing and nonpublishing purposes only. For more information, call (800) 877-GALE.

We Welcome Your Comments

The editors welcome your comments and suggestions for enhancing and improving any future editions of the *Professional Sports Team Histories* series. Mail correspondence to:

The Editor
Professional Sports Team Histories
Gale Research, Inc.
835 Penobscot Bldg.
Detroit, MI 48226-4094
Phone: (800) 347-GALE
FAX: (313) 961-6599

ACKNOWLEDGEMENTS

Professional Sports Team Histories represents the culmination of nearly three years' effort by a large and diverse group of people. The editors wish to acknowledge the significant contribution of the following individuals and organizations:

• The fine pool of sportswriters and historians who wrote the individual entries, especially Gerald Tomlinson, Mark Kram, Anne Janette Johnson, Jack Pearson, and Jay Pederson, for sharing their considerable knowledge of the subject matter. In cases where the writers have drawn on reference materials in addition to their own archival resources, we have included a Sources section at the end of the entry. These sources contain a wealth of additional information, and we urge the interested reader to consult them for a more detailed understanding of the subject.

• Mr. Mark Rucker of Transcendental Graphics of Boulder, Colorado, for assistance in securing photos of members of the National Baseball Hall of Fame and Museum. At the time this volume was in preparation, the contents of the photo archives of the Baseball Hall of Fame were in the process of being moved to a new facility and were unavailable for use. The staff of the Hall of Fame were kind enough to refer us to Mr. Rucker, whose extensive photo catalog covering the game's early years represents one of the finest private collections in the country.

• Mr. John Zajc of the Society for American Baseball Research (SABR), for assistance with team statistical records. The Society seeks to eatablish an accurate historical and statistical account of baseball from its origin; coordinate and facilitate the dissemination of baseball research information; and foster the study of baseball as a significant American social and athletic institution. For more information about the Society, its research projects, and numerous publications, contact:

The Society for American Baseball Research
PO Box 93183
Cleveland, OH 44101
Phone: (216) 575-0500

• The media relations departments of the various teams, for their valuable cooperation and assistance in providing photographs, historical materials, information on current players, and for directing us to local sports historians and sportswriters.

• Lauren Fedorko and Diane Schadoff of Book Builders Incorporated, for their help in securing knowledgeable and entertaining contributors of team essays.

• The talented and dedicated in-house Gale staff—especially Mary K. Ruby and the Contemporary Biographies and the Biographical References Group staffs; Keith Reed of Picture Permissions; Marilyn Allen, Mike Tyrkus, and Laura Standley Berger of the *Contemporary Authors Autobiographical Series;* Mark Howell and Cindy Baldwin of the Art Department; Patrick Hughes of PC Systems; MaryBeth Trimper, Dorothy Maki, Mary Kelley, and Eveline Abou-El-Seoud of Production; Don Wellman and Maggie Patton of Creative Services; and the entire Marketing and Sales departments—for their invaluable contributions to this series.

• The staff of the National Baseball Hall of Fame and Museum, for their assistance in the preparation of this volume. The Baseball Hall of Fame is an independent, nonprofit organization dedicated to the collection and preservation of information, records, and artifacts relating to the people who have performed outstanding services to the sport. The Hall is open to the public and features numerous displays, the National Baseball Library, and a gift shop. For more information about the Hall, its Museum, and its publications, contact:

The National Baseball Hall of Fame and Museum
PO Box 590
Cooperstown, NY 13326
Phone: (607) 547-9988

THE HISTORY OF PROFESSIONAL BASEBALL

Modern baseball evolved from various English bat-and-ball games, including cricket, that were popular in the early days of the Republic. At first the baseball games were amateur contests, but by the late 1850s commercialism had crept into the increasingly popular sport. By the late 1860s an all-professional team emerged, the Cincinnati Red Stockings.

Less than a decade later, in 1876, the National League was formed, replacing the earlier, shaky National Association of Professional Base Ball Players. The new National League fought off competing major leagues throughout the 1880s and early 1890s, operating briefly as a monopoly at the end of the century. This period of National League hegemony saw the dominance of teams from three cities: Boston, Baltimore, and Brooklyn.

In 1901 the American League, which had begun as the Western League, a strong but minor circuit, proclaimed its major league status. The National League protested but in the end was forced to accept the two-league structure of major league baseball. The first World Series, between Pittsburgh of the National League and Boston of the American league, was played in 1903.

For 60 years the two leagues remained eight-team circuits. Five cities were represented for many decades in both leagues—Boston, New York, Philadelphia, Chicago, and St. Louis. Among the great teams in the early days of the two leagues were Frank Chance's Chicago Cubs and John McGraw's New York Giants, both in the National League. Connie Mack's Philadelphia Athletics were usually strong contenders in the American League.

This was the so-called "deadball" era, in which a dozen home runs were almost always enough for a player to lead the league. The Black Sox scandal—the throwing of the 1919 World Series by the Chicago White Sox—rocked the national pastime and led to the appointment of Kenesaw Mountain Landis as the first commissioner of baseball.

In the early 1920s, two New York ball clubs, the Giants and Yankees, dominated their respective leagues. The Yanks continued their dominance throughout the decade, assembling in 1927 what is generally regarded as the greatest team of all time. In the National League the Pittsburgh Pirates and St. Louis Cardinals were usually at or near the top of the standings.

The Depression era saw various teams vying for leadership in the NL, while the Philadelphia Athletics and Detroit Tigers occasionally made inroads in the Yankees' dominance of the AL. When the nation went to war from 1942 through 1945, President Franklin D. Roosevelt gave professional baseball the "green light" to continue. The Cardinals and Yankees won five pennants between them, although as time went on, and more and more players entered miliary service, some unusual champions emerged—the ordinarily hapless St. Louis Browns in the AL in 1944 and the not-much-better Chicago Cubs in the NL in 1945.

Postwar baseball found the Yankees still winning with regularity, except in 1948 and 1954 when the Cleveland Indians nosed them out. In the National League the Brooklyn Dodgers finally began winning some pennants—only to have their Ebbets Field euphoria crushed when owner Walter O'Malley moved the Dodger franchise to Los Angeles in 1958.

That same year the New York Giants decamped for San Francisco. An earlier National League transfer had taken the Boston Braves to Milwaukee, and American League moves had sent the St. Louis Browns to Baltimore, the Washington Senators to Minnesota, and the Philadelphia Athletics to Kansas City.

Major league expansion began in 1961 with the addition of two clubs to the American League: the Los Angeles (now California) Angels and the replacement Washington Senators. In 1962 the National League expanded to ten teams, welcoming the Houston Astros and the New York Mets. Further expansion in 1969 was accompanied by the creation of two divisions in each league, East and West. Henceforth there would be not just a World Series to determine the major league championship, but prior to the World Series a League Championship Series in both the NL and the AL to decide the pennant winners.

In 1969 the "miracle" New York Mets (East) defeated the Atlanta Braves (West) for the NL title. The Baltimore Orioles (East) topped the Minnesota Twins (West) for the AL title. The "Amazin" Mets then went on to defeat the powerful Orioles in the World Series. Indicative of the new instability of franchises is the fact that none of those four teams was an "original" from the old 16-team

major league regulars. The New York Mets were a new ball club entirely. The Atlanta Braves had formerly been based in Milwaukee and before that in Boston. The Baltimore Orioles had replaced the old St. Louis Browns. And the Minnesota Twins were the former Washington Senators.

Nor had franchise transfers and expansion ended. Milwaukee, having lost the NL Braves, established the AL Brewers in 1970 by picking up the failed Seattle Pilots' franchise. The Pilots were a one-year phenomenon (1969), but Seattle, too, bounced back, introducing an expansion Mariners team to the AL West in 1977.

The Montreal Expos and San Diego Padres, both 1969 NL expansion teams, suffered the usual fate of such new entrants, finishing last in their divisions. The second-try Washington Senators folded in 1971 and were replaced by the Texas Rangers. The Toronto Blue Jays entered the AL East in 1977 in tandem with the AL West Mariners. In 1993 two more expansion clubs joined the National League—the Florida Marlins in the East and the Colorado Rockies in the West—bringing the total number of major league teams to 28.

In the Beginning

Probably very few people still believe that baseball was invented by Abner Doubleday, a 20-year-old future Army general, and that the first baseball game was played in 1839 on Farmer Phinney's lot in Cooperstown, New York. This charming and persistent myth, while never taken seriously by baseball historians, led to the choice of Cooperstown as the site of the National Baseball Hall of Fame and Museum and to many half-factual explanations of the origin of the national pastime.

Abner Doubleday, for his part, went on to West Point, became a career military officer, and in 1861, as an artillery captain, fired the first Union gun at Fort Sumter. This historic event reputedly led Branch Rickey, a true baseball innovator of the twentieth century, to say, "The only thing Doubleday ever started was the Civil War."

The modern game of baseball apparently evolved gradually out of old English games such as rounders, old cat, and town ball. The term "base ball" goes back to the eighteenth century. A surgeon in General George Washington's army saw soldiers batting balls and running bases at Valley Forge. There are clear parallels with cricket, too, a game popular not only in England but also in the United States.

An early baseball writer, English-born Henry Chadwick, used cricket terms to describe mid-nineteenth-century baseball games. Harry Wright, a pioneering baseball manager and entrepreneur, whose father was a cricket pro in England, found his own knowledge of cricket helpful in promoting professional baseball in America.

By the 1840s baseball had gained great popularity in and around New York City. In 1845 a group of New Yorkers met to establish a fraternal organization, the Knickerbockers, whose purpose was to arrange baseball games and at the same time to enhance their members' social standing. Alexander Cartwright, one of the members, drew up the proposed rules of baseball—rules that clearly foreshadow the modern game, although the pitching mound was only 45 feet from home plate, and the pitcher had to throw underhanded to the batter.

The Knickerbockers' first match game under the new rules was played against the Brooklyn Base Ball Club on October 21, 1845, at the Elysian Fields in Hoboken, New Jersey. Brooklyn's team, the loser by a score of 37-19, consisted mostly of cricketeers from that city's Union Star Cricket Club. The Knickerbockers' brand of baseball came to be called "the New York game" in contrast to the less popular and shorter-lived "Massachusetts game," which featured an asymmetrical diamond and allowed putouts by hitting the runner with a thrown ball!

Baseball was a gentlemen's game throughout the 1840s and well into the 1850s. The Knickerbockers tried to monopolize the sport, promulgating edicts and proclaiming their superiority, but often turning down match-game invitations in favor of games among themselves. Gradually teams

Trancendental Graphics

Alexander Cartwright

began to spring up throughout the East and Midwest. By 1854 New York was home to not just the Knickerbockers but also the Gothams, Eagles, and Empires. Across the East River in Brooklyn were the Eckfords, Atlantics, Putnams, and Excelsiors.

Soon there were teams as far west as Cleveland, Detroit, Chicago, and St. Louis. The National Association of Base Ball Players, established in 1858, helped to standardize the rules. The Association consisted of nominally amateur teams, but aspects of commercialism were becoming evident. As the popularity of the game grew, some teams began to charge admission and split the receipts. As early as 1859 the Excelsiors seem to have paid their star pitcher, Jim Creighton, a salary for his services.

During the Civil War baseball was a favorite pastime among the Union troops. On Christmas Day, 1862, a crowd of 40,000 Union soldiers watched two teams of their comrades play near Washington, D.C. In Confederate prison camps, baseball helped captured Union soldiers relieve the monotony.

This wartime dispersion of baseball further weakened the hold of the gentlemen's clubs on the sport, although most of the well-known clubs survived the war. The Brooklyn Eckfords, with Jim Creighton pitching, were the team to beat in 1862 and 1863. The Brooklyn Atlantics, starring shortstop Dickie Pearce and first baseman Joe Start, went undefeated in 1864 and 1865.

After the war, baseball spread rapidly across the nation. Every village and hamlet seemed to have a team. The great majority of players were amateurs, of course, but every year brought an increase in the number of salaried stars. In 1869 all ten players for the touring Cincinnati team received annual salaries between $600 and $1,400.

These Red Stockings, recruited by Harry Wright, earned their pay, winning 57 games, losing none, and tying one. By the end of 1870 there were at least five all-salaried ball clubs. This upset the gentlemanly amateurs, who walked out of the fall meeting of the National Association of Ball Players.

The pros quickly formed their own association, putting the word "Professional" before "Ball Players." The teams in this new National Association of Professional Ball Players were the Boston Red Stockings, Chicago White Stockings, Cleveland Forest Cities, Fort Wayne Kekiongas, New York Mutuals, Philadelphia Athletics, Rockford Forest Cities, Troy Haymakers, and Washington Olympics. The Kekiongas soon dropped out and were replaced by the Brooklyn Eckfords. Curiously, the Cincinnati Red Stockings, so successful in 1869, reverted to amateur status after a mediocre 1870 season.

The National Association of Professional Base Ball Players (1871-75) was the first major league. A player-run organization, it included the strongest teams of its day, but there were no regular playing schedules. Although the teams agreed to play each of the other teams in the circuit at least five times a season, they seldom did. Sanctions for

Trancendental Graphics

Harry Wright

violations by players and teams were minimal or nonexistent. Revenues were disappointing.

In the league's inaugural season the Chicago White Stockings were embroiled in a three-way race for the championship with the Philadelphia Athletics and Boston Red Stockings when Chicago's handsome new 7,000-seat Lake Front ballpark burned to the ground along with much of the rest of Chicago. The White Stockings were forced to play their remaining games on the road, faring poorly.

The Philadelphia Athletics won the title with a mere 22 wins, the same number as the Red Stockings, but the A's had lost fewer games than Boston. Harry Wright, Boston's manager, argued that more losses meant more games played and thus closer adherence to the league's rules. He felt his team deserved the pennant. Wright lost the argument, but his Red Stockings avenged their defeat over the next few seasons, taking the championship four times in a row through 1875 with such lopsided won-lost records as 39-8 and 52-18.

Birth of the National League

The very strength of the Boston Red Stockings helped to kill the National Association. In 1875 Harry Wright's star-studded team put together a 71-8 record, leaving little room for suspense. With Al Spalding (56-4) on the mound, plus the four top hitters in the league, the Red Stockings romped. Some of the league games, it was charged, were being fixed, and drunkenness, all too common among players, went largely unpunished. Fan interest declined. Attendance fell. Clubs began to abandon the league. The Keokuk, Iowa, club dropped out with a 1-12 record. The Brooklyn Atlantics withdrew after compiling a 2-42 mark. Four other teams with dismal records took the same route.

Because the National Association was a players' league, it was the players rather than the investors who reaped most of the rewards. Manager Harry Wright, an able businessman, made money. His star hurler was a shrewd operator, too, founding the A. G. Spalding & Bros. sporting goods company. Spalding started his business the year after he pitched Boston to its fourth straight pennant.

Wright and Spalding played important roles in establishing the National League, but the driving force behind the new venture was William A. Hulbert, president of the Chicago White Stockings. Hulbert, who had been a coal dealer in his youth rather than a ballplayer, was convinced there was money to be made in a league that subordinated players to owners. He presented his plan at a meeting on February 2, 1876, at the Grand Central Hotel in New York City. The new league would be called the National League of Professional Base Ball Clubs.

His substitution of the word "Clubs" for "Players" showed where the power would lie in the future. Hulbert's plan called for an eight-team league, central administration, binding contracts, paid umpires, and a regular playing schedule starting in 1877. Taken by surprise, the players caved in, signed the contracts submitted to them, and allowed the National Association of Professional Baseball Players to pass into history.

[Note: There is a "National Association" in existence today—the National Association of Professional Baseball Leagues, the governing body of minor league baseball. Founded in 1901, it has no connection with the old major league of 1871-75.]

The eight cities in the newborn National League—in order of their final standings in 1876—were Chicago, St. Louis, Hartford, Boston, Louisville, New York, Philadelphia, and Cincinnati. Al Spalding, hired away from Boston by the aggressive Hulbert, led the White Stockings to victory with a 47-13 won-lost record. Harry Wright, minus Spalding, could bring the Red Stockings home no better than fourth.

The owners earned modest profits or none at all, and although the league survived, a number of the early National League cities failed to make a go of it. Louisville, Hartford, Providence, Indianapolis, Milwaukee, Buffalo, Syracuse, Troy, and Worcester had all put in one or more seasons by 1881. In fact, the Providence Grays, managed by George Wright, Harry's brother, won the pennant in 1879. The Grays' star pitcher that year was 29-year-old John Montgomery Ward (47-17), who would loom large in the history of nineteenth-century baseball.

The gambling and game-fixing of the National Association was supposed to be a thing of the past, but it reared its head in the fledgling National League, too. In 1877 the Louisville Grays seemed to be a shoo-in to win the pennant. Their pitcher, Jim Devlin, was all but unhittable, and Louisville built up a lead in the standings that looked decisive.

But then, mysteriously, Devlin began losing. At the same time, infielder Bill Craver and outfielders George Hall and Al Nichols stopped hitting and started making errors. A Louisville *Cou-*

rier-Journal headline, "!!!—???—!!!," was followed by an investigation. Three of the four players admitted throwing games, with the result that Harry Wright's Boston Red Stockings won the pennant. All four players were banned from major league baseball for life, and Louisville dropped out of the league.

Rival Leagues and Rule Changes

As if thrown games and failing franchises were not enough, the National League faced another problem starting in 1882—a rival major league, then two more rival major leagues. The 1880s were a time of growing prosperity in the country, and professional baseball became a more appealing investment than it had been a few years earlier. The success of the NL attracted competitors. The American Association of Base Ball Clubs was established in 1882, recognized as a major league in 1883, and lasted through 1891.

The Union Association survived only one season, 1884, before being muscled out by its two rivals. The Players League, an attempt to put the ballplayers back in charge of their teams, also folded after a single season, 1890. Meanwhile, the dual-league arrangement that endured through most of the 1880s went over well with fans. Most clubs in the NL and AA made money. Both leagues increased the number of scheduled games throughout the decade so that by 1889 the NL was playing 132 games and the AA 140.

Throughout the 1880s, rule changes helped to shape the modern game. In 1881 the pitching distance was increased from 45 to 50 feet. In 1884 pitchers were allowed to throw the ball overhand. In 1887, with a new standard strike zone, batters could no longer request high or low pitches.

But a few other rule changes that year, such as a walk counting as a hit, were quickly rescinded. In 1888 the three-strike rule became permanent (replacing the unpopular four-strike rule of 1887), and the next year the four-ball-walk rule was fixed in place, along with the rule that a successful sacrifice would not be charged as a time at bat.

Between 1880 and 1882 Cap Anson's Chicago White Stockings dominated the National League. After the 1882 season Troy and Worcester were dropped from the NL and replaced by the New York Nationals (or Gothams, now the Giants) and the Philadelphia Phillies. The National Agreement of 1883 certified the American Association as a major league and required the reserve clause in both AA and NL player contracts.

The reserve clause, intended to halt the common practice of players "revolving," or jumping from team to team for better salaries, allowed owners to extend a player's expired contract for an additional year, presumably forever. Yet owners had no comparable restraints and could sell their players' contracts at will.

Some ballplayers and sportswriters equated the reserve clause with slavery. When the White Stockings sold Mike (King) Kelly to Boston for $10,000 in 1887, John Montgomery (Monte) Ward, a lawyer as well a New York Giants' infielder, wrote a scathing essay titled "Is the Base Ball Player a Chattel?"

The American Association had been accepted, albeit reluctantly, as a second major league (and the Union Association had not), but the National League and American Association owners were upset by the emergence of the Players League in 1890.

There had been plenty of friction before then between players and owners, but none so serious. Back in 1885 players led by Monte Ward had formed the Brotherhood of Professional Baseball Players. They tried collective bargaining with the owners and failed, whereupon the Brotherhood began recruiting players for a third major league.

The grass-roots appeal of this effort attracted many NL and AA stars. When the 1890 season opened, the eight-team Players League fielded strong teams in Boston, Brooklyn, New York, Chicago, and Philadelphia, with somewhat lesser entries in Pittsburgh, Cleveland, and Buffalo.

This city-for-city matchup between the NL and PL (except for Cincinnati-Buffalo) meant war, and Al Spalding of the senior circuit met the challenge. He lowered ticket prices, raided PL and AA rosters, brought lawsuits, intimidated the press, scheduled NL games to conflict with PL games, and in general tried to wreak havoc on the upstart circuit. He succeeded. The PL played classy baseball, attracted fans, won its lawsuits—and collapsed. The mutinous players, granted amnesty by Spalding, slunk back to the owner-controlled ball clubs.

Not only had the war over the Players League finished off the PL in one season, it also doomed the American Association. The AA, always weaker than the NL, lost out in the power struggle that followed the demise of the Players League. The AA struggled through the 1891 season but could not answer the bell for 1892. The National League, a major league monopoly from 1876 to 1881, became a monopoly again in 1892.

Boston, Baltimore, Brooklyn

The era of the one "big league," in which the 12-club National League monopoly reigned supreme, was not the financial bonanza most owners had expected. Baseball's magnates acted with a certain *hauteur,* but their bottom lines did not reflect their grandiose image of themselves. An economic recession hurt, as did the Spanish-American War.

Then, too, certain ball clubs were chronic losers, both on the field and at the gate (among them Cleveland, Louisville, and Washington), while a trio of others (Boston, Baltimore, and Brooklyn) began to take all the pennants. The Boston Beaneaters' manager, Frank Selee, led his team to four league titles.

The other pennant-winning manager in the "big league" period—the only other one—was Ned Hanlon, who directed the Baltimore Orioles to victory in 1894-96 and brought the Brooklyn Superbas home in front in 1899.

A split-season format was adopted in 1892 but proved unpopular and was dropped after the 1893 campaign, the season in which the distance from the pitching mound to the plate was increased to 60 feet six inches (as it is today). The dominant

ball club in both these years was the Boston Beaneaters, whose ace pitcher, Kid Nichols, went 35-16 and 33-13, and whose hitting star, Hugh Duffy, an outfielder, turned in batting averages of .301 in 1892 and .363 in 1893 (prior to his record-setting .438 in 1894).

Boston's quiet but hard-driving manager, Frank Selee, led his Beaneaters to back-to-back pennants again in 1897-98, once more with Kid Nichols pacing the mound staff and Hugh Duffy driving in more than 100 runs each season.

The Boston clubs of this decade were loaded with talent. In addition to Nichols and Duffy, the 1897-98 Beaneaters featured Hall-of-Famers Jimmy Collins at third base and Billy Hamilton in the outfield. Small wonder that they took the flag in 1897 with a .705 won-lost percentage and in 1898 with .685.

In 1894, 1895, and 1896 the Boston Beaneaters continued to do well, but the Baltimore Orioles did better. Baltimore's Ned Hanlon, a manager who looked rather bookish but who encouraged "hoodlumism" among his players and "winked at the evil" on the field, had a lineup of superstars—Dan Brouthers at first base, Hugh Jennings at shortstop, John McGraw at third base, Wee Willie Keeler and Joe Kelley in the outfield.

Even when the Beaneaters regained their pennant-winning form in 1897 and 1898, the Orioles finished a strong second. When Ned Hanlon moved over to Brooklyn in 1898, he stocked his team with top talent and led them to the title over second-place Boston.

Sustaining interest in a 12-team league posed a problem. The split season proved unpopular. In 1894 a Pittsburgh sportsman, William C. Temple, sponsored the first Temple Cup Series, pitting the league's first-place team against the second-place team with a $500 cup going to the winner of the best-of-seven contest.

After the first series, marred by fights, jeering, and reports of share-splitting between opposing players, the public greeted the playoff mostly with indifference. Following the 1897 season, Temple himself criticized the haphazard conduct of the classic.

The baseball owners, unchastened, simply scotched the series.

This was not a happy period for major league baseball, despite the booming bats occasioned by the 1893 increase in the pitching distance. In 1894 the pennant-winning Baltimore Orioles posted a team batting average of .343, while the fourth-place Philadelphia Phillies turned in a league-leading .349 mark. Boston's Hugh Duffy batted an astronomical .438, and Philadelphia's little-known Tuck Turner racked up a .416 batting average.

Pitching suffered badly for a while. In 1894, that unparalleled year of the hitter, the Phillies' Jack Taylor, for example, had a fine 23-13 won-lost record, but his ERA (fifth best in the league) was 4.08. Even the great Cy Young, whose lifetime earned run average was 2.63, saw his ERA balloon to 3.94 in 1894.

In time the pitchers developed ways to compensate. But the unprofitable 12-team "big league" monopoly dating from 1892 never found the key to success. At the end of the 1899 season the NL dropped four franchises—Baltimore, Cleveland, Louisville, and Washington—just in time to face the challenge of a new rival league.

Birth of the American League

Ban Johnson's timing was perfect. For six years Byron (Ban) Johnson, ambitious, aggressive, and dictatorial, had been president of the Western League, a strong minor circuit in the Midwest. In 1900, with the American Association dead, the U.S. economy in good shape, and a number of fine ballplayers (from Baltimore, Cleveland, Louisville, and Washington, in particular) looking for jobs, Ban Johnson made his move.

He changed the league's name from Western to American. He urged his friend Charles Comiskey, a Chicago native, to move his ball club from St. Paul, Minnesota, to Chicago, where it became the White Sox.

In 1900 the American League was still a minor league, still bound by the National Agreement. But Johnson, Comiskey, and others were deter-

Trancendental Graphics

Ban Johnson

mined to upgrade it to the major-league level, and rumblings that the old American Association might be revived spurred them to act quickly.

The AL owners hoped to gain equality with the NL without waging a baseball war, but that hope proved naive. As the American League prepared to establish franchises in Baltimore, Philadelphia, and Washington, the National League owners made it clear that they intended to fight.

At this point Ban Johnson, seizing the offensive, refused to renew the National Agreement and announced an AL franchise for Boston. American League raiders also went after top NL players, snaring, among others, the Beaneaters' superstar Jimmy Collins and the Phillies' Nap Lajoie. These moves, Lajoie recalled later, "got the American League more publicity in the winter months of 1901 than the National was accustomed to receive in an entire year."

The National League drew more fans than the American League in 1901—1,920,031 for the NL, 1,683,584 for the AL—but the totals were close enough to suggest that a dual-league plan for the majors made financial sense for everybody.

Nevertheless, the baseball war continued in the courts, with the NL trying to restrain or regain players, more than a hundred of whom jumped to the AL in 1901. Among their number was the Cardinals' great pitcher, Cy Young. Charlie Comiskey's Chicago White Sox, under manager Clark Griffith (a defector from the Cubs) won the first AL pennant, while the Pittsburgh Pirates took the NL title.

When the 1902 season also went smoothly and profitably for the upstart American League, the handwriting was on the wall. Most National League owners concluded they could live with a dual-league arrangement after all and agreed to negotiate a new National Agreement for 1903, recognizing the NL and AL as separate but equal major leagues.

The American League would be permitted to have a franchise in New York City—previously a bone of contention—and each league's schedules, rules, territories, and player contracts would be respected by the other.

A National Commission, created by the National Agreement of 1903, was charged with keeping the peace between the two leagues, and, headed by Ban Johnson and August (Garry) Herrmann, it did so admirably for many years.

In 1903 the Pittsburgh Pirates emerged as National League champions for the third straight year. Their shortstop, Honus Wagner, won the NL batting title for the second of eight times. In the American League the Boston Red Sox, paced by veteran hurler Cy Young, 28-9, captured the flag.

The 1903 season marked the beginning of a remarkably stable period in major league baseball. For the next 50 years the NL and AL teams would represent the same cities whose teams took the field in 1903. The National League had franchises in Boston, Brooklyn, Chicago, Cincinnati, New York, Philadelphia, Pittsburgh, and St. Louis.

The fledgling American League had franchises in Boston, Chicago, Cleveland, Detroit, New York, Philadelphia, St. Louis, and Washington. Not until 1953 (and the substitution of the Milwaukee Braves for the Boston Braves) did the lineup of cities begin to change.

Deadball Heroes, Black Sox Villains

Baseball, popular since its inception, gained ever increasing favor in the early years of the twentieth century. Although the World Series, first played in 1903, suffered a one-year hiatus when manager John McGraw of the New York Giants refused to have his team play the AL pennant-winning Boston Pilgrims, the Series returned in 1905. McGraw's ace pitcher, Christy Mathewson, marked the occasion by hurling three complete-game World Series shutouts.

Major league attendance more than doubled in the first decade of the century. The popular song "Take Me Out to the Ball Game" was introduced in 1908. This was an era of growing profits, few rule changes, and relative tranquility, except for the challenge of the assertive Federal League in 1914-15 and the "Black Sox" scandal that cast a pall over the 1919 World Series.

Optimism about the future of the game, along with advances in the use of structural concrete, led to a burst of stadium construction between 1909 and 1915. Shibe Park in Philadelphia, the first concrete and steel stadium in the majors, led the way, opening in 1909. It was followed by many other post-wooden, pre-bowl ball parks: Comiskey Park, Chicago, in 1910; the Polo Grounds, New York, 1911; Griffith Stadium, Washington, 1911; Fenway Park, Boston, 1912; Tiger Stadium, Detroit, 1912; Ebbets Field, Brooklyn, 1913; Wrigley Field, Chicago, 1914, and Braves Field, Boston, 1915.

This was the so-called deadball era. Baseball strategists favored the "scientific" style of play developed in the 1890s. Pitching, base running, and playing for one or two runs dominated the game. Home runs were rare. Pitchers' ERAs were low.

Even after the introduction of the cork-centered ball in 1909, there was no explosion of hitting. In 1905 first baseman Harry Davis of the

Philadelphia Athletics led the American League in home runs with eight. A decade later, in 1914, the Athletics' Frank (Home Run) Baker had upped the total to nine. In 1905 Christy Mathewson of the Giants led all major league pitchers with a 1.27 ERA. In 1914 the Red Sox's Dutch Leonard set a still-standing one-season record with an ERA of 1.01. Not until the 1920s did the "big bang" style of play, Babe Ruth's trademark, catch hold, upping batters' home-run totals and pitchers' ERAs.

Four of the eight ball clubs in the American League dominated the circuit for the first two decades. They were Boston, Detroit, Philadelphia, and Chicago—the only AL pennant winners prior to Cleveland's breakthrough in 1920. Boston won championships in 1903 and 1904 behind the pitching of Cy Young, then came back to take the flag in 1915, 1916, and 1918, when their mound staffs included Carl Mays, Babe Ruth, and Dutch Leonard. The Detroit Tigers, managed by Hugh Jennings, took three consecutive pennants, 1907-09, as Ty Cobb won the first three of his nine straight AL batting titles.

Connie Mack's Philadelphia Athletics won in 1905, 1910, 1911, 1913, and 1914. Pitchers Jack Coombs, Eddie Plank, and Chief Bender anchored the A's strong pitching staff. The Chicago White Sox triumphed first with their remarkable "Hitless Wonders" in 1906, then repeated in 1917 and 1919 with an outstanding team that is now forever linked with the greatest of all baseball scandals, the throwing of the 1919 World Series.

In the National League three ball clubs overshadowed the others during this period—Pittsburgh, New York, and Chicago—although Boston, Brooklyn, and Cincinnati each fought its way to the top once prior to 1920. The Pirates, after copping three crowns, 1901-03, came back in 1909 to win again. The New York Giants, under manager John McGraw, were always tough, and never more so than in 1904-05 when Iron Man McGinnity and Christy Mathewson were mowing down opposing batters. The Giants climbed to the top again in 1911-13 with Rube Marquard joining Mathewson on the hill. In wartime 1917, McGraw once more led his team to victory.

From 1906 through 1910 the Chicago Cubs were a true dynasty, winning four of five pennants, finishing second in 1909. The team was led by manager and first baseman Frank Chance, the "Peerless Leader," aided by second baseman Joe Evers and shortstop Joe Tinker, who rounded out the famous "trio of bear cubs." On the mound, pitcher Mordecai (Three Finger) Brown blew away hitters with practiced ease.

In the World Series the American League held its own against the older National League, winning two of the first three Series, including the surprising victory of the Chicago White Sox over the powerful Cubs in 1906. After the Cubs took two world championships in 1907 and 1908, and the Pirates one in 1909, the American League teams turned almost invincible, winning every World Series except one from 1910 through 1918. (The Boston Braves won in 1914.)

The Philadelphia A's took three out of four Series between 1910 and 1913. The Boston Red Sox prevailed in 1912, 1915, 1916, and 1918. During this period the AL gained the lead in World Series victories and has never relinquished it.

Two blips in the steady rise of major league baseball were the Federal League incursion of 1914-15 and the Black Sox scandal that came to light in 1920. The Federal League, billing itself as a third major league, competed for fans in four existing major league cities (Chicago, Pittsburgh, Brooklyn, and St. Louis) and in four minor league cities (Baltimore, Buffalo, Indianapolis, and Kansas City). In 1915 the Indianapolis ball club was packed off to Newark, even though the Hoosiers, with young Edd Roush in the outfield, had won the pennant in 1914.

The Federal League offered quality baseball, but there were inevitably legal battles with the organized baseball establishment. These ended in a complete but costly victory for the National and American Leagues. The Federal League, a strong, well-financed effort, died after two seasons.

Gambling had been a part of baseball for a long time, despite the owners' efforts to control it. But the prospect of actually fixing a World Series seemed far-fetched—until it happened. The underdog Cincinnati Reds won the 1919 Series, five games to three. But did they, really? There were immediate doubts about the honesty of the games, and a long investigation proved the doubts to be well founded. Eight Chicago White Sox players (the "Black Sox"), as the investigation showed, had conspired with gamblers to lose the Series to the Reds.

In the aftermath of this public-relations disaster, baseball's chastened owners abolished their in-house National Commission and named tough Federal Judge Kenesaw Mountain Landis as the new Baseball Commissioner, giving him sweeping powers.

Landis banned all eight of the Black Sox players from professional baseball for life. It was a draconian move, but it helped restore the image of the game. The two most noteworthy of the punished culprits were pitcher Eddie Cicotte and outfielder Shoeless Joe Jackson, both permanently derailed on their way to the Baseball Hall of Fame.

The Babe and the Big Bang

Modern baseball began, in a sense, with Babe Ruth. Today's staccato television replays of home run clouts stem directly from the Bambino's exploits. A first-rate pitcher, George Herman (Babe) Ruth was at the same time an awesome hitter.

In 1919 he set a home run record, 29 in a season, while pitching and winning nine games and losing five for the Boston Red Sox. Sold to the New York Yankees for the then-fabulous sum of $125,000, Ruth concentrated on his hitting—and in 1920 blasted 54 round-trippers for the Yanks.

The die was cast. The deadball style gave way to the "big bang." Rogers Hornsby of the St. Louis Cardinals, not previously noted as a home-run hitter, unloaded 21 four-baggers in 1921 and 42 (seven more than Babe Ruth) in 1922. It was a whole new ball game.

While Babe Ruth, the perennial, beloved cut-up, and other less charismatic sluggers such as Rogers Hornsby and later Hack Wilson of the Cubs and the Babe's teammate Lou Gehrig, were

Transcendental Graphics

Kenesaw Mountain Landis

making baseball fans forget the perfidy of 1919, the world beyond baseball was fostering a kind of giddiness, too. National Prohibition, far from keeping spirits of any kind in check, helped usher in the Roaring Twenties, a decade of rising wages, increased leisure, and entertainment as a growth industry.

Major league baseball was performance art at its best, even if manager Miller Huggins' potent New York Yankees sometimes made the American League pennant race a rout, and the durable John McGraw's New York Giants did the same for a while in the National League.

The Yankees of the 1920s won six pennants and three World Series. Early in the decade their pitching stars were Carl Mays, Bob Shawkey, Waite Hoyt, Sad Sam Jones, and Bullet Joe Bush.

At the end of the decade Waite Hoyt was still going strong, but the others had been replaced by George Pipgras and Herb Pennock. Urban Shocker, obtained from the St. Louis Browns, turned in a couple of fine seasons, 1926 and 1927.

The 1927 Yankees, arguably the greatest team of all time, had tremendous talent and few, if any, real weaknesses. Right fielder Babe Ruth batted .356 that year, hit 60 home runs, and collected 164 RBIs. First baseman Lou Gehrig hit .373, homered 47 times, and drove in a league-leading 175 runs. Center fielder Earl Combs matched Ruth's batting average, .356, while left fielder Bob Meusel hit .337 and drove in 106 runs. Tony Lazzeri played second base, batted .309, hit 18 homers (third in the league), and posted 102 RBIs.

The Yanks, who led the AL in all major offensive categories, finished 19 games ahead of the second-place Athletics and polished off the Pirates in four straight World Series games.

But the 1920s did not belong wholly to the Yankees. In 1920 manager Tris Speaker's Cleveland Indians won the pennant, with Speaker himself batting .388 and pitcher Jim Bagby posting a 31-12 record. In second place were the White Sox, their lineup still dominated by the soon-to-be-banned Black Sox players. The Yankees finished third, then won three straight pennants, but lost two of three "Subway Series" to the New York Giants.

In 1924 the Yanks dropped to second place as the Washington Senators, under kid manager and second baseman Bucky Harris, won both the AL flag and the World Series. The Senators, featuring Walter Johnson and new arrival Stan Coveleski on the mound, repeated in 1925, but were nipped in the Series four games to three by the Pittsburgh Pirates.

The Yankees reestablished their dominance in 1926-28, but fell victim in 1929 to the Philadelphia Athletics' mini-dynasty of 1929-31. For three seasons at the start of the Great Depression Connie Mack's Athletics enjoyed outstanding pitching from Lefty Grove, George Earnshaw, and Rube Walberg plus great hitting from Jimmy Foxx and Al Simmons. The A's won 104, 102, and 107 games over this three-year stretch, leaving the New York Yankees and Washington Senators in the dust. In 1929 and 1930 the A's also took the World Series.

In the National League John McGraw's Giants, after finishing second to the Brooklyn Dodgers in 1920, captured four consecutive pennants, 1921 through 1924, the first team to do so in the twentieth century. The Giants in the NL, no less than the Yankees in the AL, marshaled plenty of power at the plate.

Among the stars were future Hall-of-Famers Frankie Frisch at second base, Ross Youngs in the outfield, and Dave (Beauty) Bancroft at shortstop (through 1923). In 1922 and 1923 Casey Stengel patrolled the outfield. First baseman Bill Terry, also a Hall-of-Famer, arrived in 1924. Art Nehf was the Giants' most consistently successful pitcher throughout this victorious four-year span.

After the Giants' reign ended, the Pirates, Cardinals, and Cubs divided up the pennants through 1931, the Pirates taking two (1925, 1927), the Cardinals four (1926, 1928, 1930, 1931), and the Cubs one (1929). The Cards' new-found competitiveness was in large part the handiwork of Branch Rickey, whose pioneering farm system was beginning to pay dividends.

Up through Rickey's "Chain Gang," as critics called the Mahatma's minor-league hierarchy, came first baseman "Sunny Jim" Bottomley and outfielder Chick Hafey, each with a stop at Houston in the Texas League. The full fruition of Rickey's innovation, however, came later. During the 1920s the Phillies and Braves were consistently inept, while the Dodgers and Reds had winning seasons only sporadically. The National League, like the American League, was divided during the 1920s into perennial contenders and non-contenders.

In 1930 the hitters in the National League went on a binge. The Giants' Bill Terry batted .401 to beat out the Dodgers' Billy Herman at .393 and the Phillies' Chuck Klein at .386. Every regular in the Cardinals' lineup topped .300, with rookie outfielder George Watkins, a farm-system product, leading the parade at .373. Frankie Frisch and Chick Hafey drove in 114 and 107 runs respectively, but they were far outshone in that department by the Cubs' Hack Wilson who, in 1930, drove in 190 runs to set an all-time record. Chuck

Klein drove in 170 runs, ranking him second in the NL in 1930—yet putting him among the top ten players ever in season RBIs.

In the 1930 World Series the hard-hitting Cardinals fell to the Philadelphia Athletics, whose own best hitters, Al Simmons and Jimmy Foxx, had chalked up 165 and 156 RBIs in 1930 (still not enough to lead the AL—Lou Gehrig had 174). It was definitely the twentieth-century year of the hitter.

Bright Lights in the Depression

The stock market crash of October 1929 ushered in the Great Depression. Although the effects were not immediately apparent in the majors 1930 was a good year for baseball—the nationwide loss of jobs, incomes, and purchasing power had an inevitable impact over time.

By 1931 attendance and profits were dropping. Connie Mack's powerful and apparently dynastic Philadelphia Athletics were hurting badly. After three straight American League pennants, the A's drew only 400,000 fans in 1932, finishing second. Mack, needing cash, began selling off his great stars.

Al Simmons and George Earnshaw went to the White Sox, pitcher Lefty Grove to the Red Sox, catcher Mickey Cochrane to the Tigers, and, finally, after the 1935 season, Jimmy Foxx to the Red Sox. The A's sank in the AL standings.

Other teams, mainly the New York Yankees and, for a time, the Detroit Tigers, took over from the Athletics in the AL standings. Babe Ruth's skills began to erode, but Lou Gehrig continued slugging, and future Hall-of-Fame catcher Bill Dickey starred throughout the 1930s. In 1936 a young, fast, picture-perfect hitter, Joe DiMaggio, made his first appearance in the Yankee outfield.

Pitchers Red Ruffing and Lefty Gomez showed consistent winning form throughout the decade. The Yanks won the AL pennant in 1932, and then, after three years in second place, took four pennants in a row, 1936-39.

The Washington Senators, led by their play-ing-manager shortstop Joe Cronin, prevailed in 1933. The Detroit Tigers, powered by young first baseman Hank Greenberg, veteran second baseman Charlie Gehringer, and stars acquired from other teams—among them, Mickey Cochrane and Goose Goslin—captured pennants in 1934 and 1935. In 1935 Detroit won its first World Series since 1887.

The National League had no clearly dominant team through the 1930s, although the New York Giants took back-to- back pennants in 1936-37 and the Cincinnati Reds did the same in 1939-40. The Giants' standout performers in the decade were outfielder Mel Ott, who led the NL in homers in both pennant-winning seasons, and pitcher Carl Hubbell, who led the league in wins both years.

Pitching keyed the success of the Reds as the decade ended. Bucky Walters and Paul Derringer were noteworthy hurlers for the Reds, but the single most remarkable performance came in 1939 when Johnny Vander Meer pitched back-to-back no-hitters. Vander Meer was only 5-9 on the season (compared to Walters' 27-11 and Derringer's 25-7), but for those two sparkling games the left-handed "Dutch Master" was literally unhittable.

The St. Louis Cardinals' Gas House Gang captured the flag in 1934, but home attendance in that deep Depression year was a mere 325,000. Dizzy Dean won 30 games and lost only seven for the Cards, while his brother Paul went 19-11. First baseman Ripper Collins led the league in homers and placed second to Mel Ott with 138 RBIs.

The rest of the infield—Frankie Frisch, Leo Durocher, and Pepper Martin—turned in fine years as well. Outfielder Joe Medwick batted .319 and drove in 108 runs. The Gas House Gang capped the season with a four-games-to-three victory over the Detroit Tigers in the World Series.

Long-term futility had not yet set in for the Chicago Cubs, and during the decade they won the NL title three times, in 1932, 1935, and 1938. The mainstays of the Cubs' offense were second baseman Billy Herman, third baseman Stan Hack, and catcher Gabby Hartnett, with Bill Jurges steady at shortstop. Lon Warneke was the ace

Transcendental Graphics

George M. Weiss

their ball clubs. Cincinnati's Crosley Field introduced night baseball to the majors in 1936.

In 1939, in commemoration of the 100th anniversary of Abner Doubleday's supposed invention of the game, the National Baseball Hall of Fame opened in Cooperstown, New York. The first five inductees were Babe Ruth, Ty Cobb, Honus Wagner, Christy Mathewson, and Walter Johnson.

As the decade wound down, the Second World War started in Europe, and prosperity slowly returned to the United States. One glorious year of major league baseball, 1941, was followed by America's involvement in the hostilities overseas, the drafting and enlistment of ballplayers, the concomitant interruption of careers, and the gradual decline in the level of play through 1945.

Wartime Baseball

America entered the war after the Japanese bombing of Pearl Harbor on December 7, 1941. By that time the 1941 baseball season was history—and very memorable history. It was the year Ted Williams, playing his third season for the Boston Red Sox, batted .406, the last player to top .400 in more than half a century. It was also the year in which Joe DiMaggio hit safely in 56 consecutive games, another record that still stands.

In 1941 the Yankees won the AL pennant by a 17-game margin over the Red Sox, while the Brooklyn Dodgers, with a nearly identical record, took the NL title by a mere 2½ games over the Cardinals. The big noise for the Dodgers that year (in addition to their famous Sym-Phony band) was an aggressive, accident-prone young outfielder named Pete Reiser, who led the NL in hitting at .343. Brooklyn's other regular outfielders, Dixie Walker and Joe Medwick, chipped in with solid .311 and .318 averages, while pitchers Kirby Higbe and Whit Wyatt won 22 games apiece. Nevertheless, the Yanks proceeded to win the World Series, four games to one.

1941 was the last year of prewar baseball, but most major league rosters remained nearly intact

pitcher of the '32 and '35 campaigns; Bill Lee and Clay Bryant led the staff in '38. The Cubs succumbed in each of the three World Series, winning only two games (both of them in 1935) to their opponents' dozen.

Most major league ball clubs suffered financially during the Depression, but some of them suffered less than others. In the American League the Yankees went from strength to strength, as hard-driving executive George M. Weiss, following Branch Rickey's lead, built a productive farm system that promised future success for the Bronx Bombers. Tom Yawkey, owner of the Red Sox, spent money freely in attempting, without much luck, to build a contending team for Boston.

Hoping to attract the 1932 Summer Olympics, the city of Cleveland constructed its huge Municipal Stadium, the first of the publicly financed multipurpose facilities in the majors. In the National League the owners of the Cubs, Reds, and Dodgers continued to invest in the future of

Major League History

for 1942. The military draft had been in effect since 1940, however, and it had claimed Detroit star Hank Greenberg early, in May 1941.

The question of whether baseball would be played at all during a time of total war was answered by President Franklin D. Roosevelt in his so-called "green light" letter of January 1942 to Commissioner Landis in which he said, "I honestly think that it would be best for the country to keep baseball going." Ballplayers would be subject to the draft, though, and as the war went on a great many of them would serve in the armed forces.

But in 1942 manager Joe McCarthy's Yankees still had Joe DiMaggio, Charlie Keller, and Tommy Henrich in the outfield, Joe Gordon at second base, Phil Rizzuto at shortstop, and Bill Dickey behind the plate. Pitcher Ernie Bonham had an outstanding 21-5 season to complement the fine performances of Red Ruffing, Spud Chandler, and Lefty Gomez.

The Cardinals, who seemed to suffer less wartime disruption than other teams in the majors, welcomed a rookie outfielder to their ranks in 1942. He was Stan Musial, and he would help them capture NL flags in 1942, 1943, and 1944.

In 1945, with Hank Greenberg once more a Tiger, Stan Musial was just reporting for duty at the Bainbridge Naval Training Station in Maryland. In all, some 500 major league ballplayers served in the armed forces during World War II — including, eventually, Joe DiMaggio, Charlie Keller, Tommy Henrich, Joe Gordon, Phil Rizzuto, and Bill Dickey.

That was in the future, though. In 1942 a powerful Yankee ball club captured the AL pennant, but the NL champion St. Louis Cardinals proved too much for them in the World Series. The Yanks hung on to win the first game for Red Ruffing, then collapsed as the Cards took the next four in a row.

Johnny Beazley, a young St. Louis pitcher who was 21-6 in 1942 but never regained his form after the war, won two games for the Cards. Hitting honors for the winners were evenly distributed, with Stan Musial, Enos Slaughter, Terry Moore, Walker Cooper, and Whitey Kurowski among the standouts.

If 1942 was a fairly normal season, 1943 was not. Rosters were decimated. Severe cutbacks in nonmilitary transportation found major league teams taking spring training in such unlikely places as Cairo, Illinois (Cardinals); Bear Mountain, New York (Dodgers); Lakewood, New Jersey (Giants); Muncie, Indiana (Pirates); French Lick, Indiana (Cubs and White Sox); Medford, Massachusetts (Red Sox); and Asbury Park, New Jersey (Yankees).

A shortage of rubber, needed in the manufacture of traditional baseballs, led to the development of the "balata ball," using nonstrategic materials. The balata was a deadball disaster at first, but modifications made it somewhat livelier. By 1944 synthetic rubber brought the ball up to prewar standards. The quality of bats suffered at first, too, because of a lumber shortage and transportation problems. Night games were banned at New York ballparks for a while because it was feared the lights would silhouette ships for Nazi U-boats.

Through all these complications the teams played ball. The Cardinals, with many prewar stars still in the lineup (though not outfielders Enos Slaughter or Terry Moore), breezed to victory in the NL, while the Yankees, with a combination of regulars and replacements, won easily in the AL and went on to defeat the Cards in the World Series.

By 1944 the situation was improving on the battlefield but deteriorating on the ballfield—except for the Cardinals. The Cards still had Musial in the outfield, Kurowski at third base, Marty Marion at shortstop, the brother-battery of Mort and Walker Cooper, and Max Lanier on the mound. They won easily.

Over in the American League the impossible was happening. The St. Louis Browns, habitual losers, were staying even with the Yankees and Tigers and finally triumphing over both.

Browns' shortstop Vern Stephens led the AL in RBIs with 109, and the B-team got some good pitching from Jack Kramer and Nels Potter. In the all-St. Louis, all-Sportsman's Park World Series it was mostly (but not all) Cards, as Brownie first baseman George McQuinn drove in five runs to spark two wins for the underdogs.

By the last year of the war, 1945, no-names dotted the rosters. One-armed Pete Gray roamed the outfield for the St. Louis Browns. Stan Musial went to war, and the St. Louis Cardinals fell to second place. The Chicago Cubs—paced by first baseman Phil Cavarretta and outfielder Andy Pafko—edged out the Cards for first place in the NL.

In the AL, Hank Greenberg returned from the service for the last half of the season, and the Detroit Tigers climbed into the number-one spot, a game and a half ahead of the Washington Senators. Tiger pitcher Hal Newhouser posted an impressive 25-9 won-lost record with a 1.81 ERA.

Still, these were not impressive teams. When asked to pick the World Series winner in 1945, Warren Brown of the *Chicago Sun* reached a dour conclusion: "I don't think either one of them can win it." One did, of course—the Detroit Tigers, four games to three—and the hard-luck Cubs have not shown their faces in a World Series since.

Prosperity and Integration

When the war ended in late 1945, the United States was ready for big-league baseball (and minor league baseball as well, as proliferating leagues and soaring attendance soon showed). But a couple of tricky issues had to be faced. The first was the Mexican League affair. In 1946, the first postwar season, Mexican League promoters lured a number of major leaguers with high salary offers. When Baseball Commissioner A. B. (Happy) Chandler blacklisted the players, Danny Gardella, a Giants outfielder who had jumped to Mexico, brought suit, challenging the reserve clause. The owners thought it best to settle quietly rather than risk close judicial scrutiny of the reserve clause, and the defecting players were allowed to return without prejudice.

Another important issue facing organized baseball after the war was the long-standing ex-

clusion of blacks. Ever since the "gentleman's agreement" of 1876 there had been no black players in major-league baseball, although in the nineteenth century there been a number of blacks in the minors.

Branch Rickey of the Brooklyn Dodgers proposed to change that. He signed Jackie Robinson, a former football star at UCLA and an infielder with the Kansas City Monarchs of the Negro American League. Robinson played the 1946 season for the Dodgers' Triple-A Montreal Royals, performing well and earning a shot at the majors. In 1947 he batted .297 for Brooklyn, helped the Dodgers gain the NL championship, and won Rookie of the Year honors.

His success notwithstanding, it was a tough season for Robinson, who had to endure racial slurs, brushbacks, and other harassment without retaliating. He survived the ordeal and paved the way for other blacks, including, early on, Larry Doby (the first black in the AL), Roy Campanella, and Don Newcombe. By the 1950s there were a great many black ballplayers in the majors, among them Willie Mays, Ernie Banks, Monte Irvin, Hank Aaron, and Frank Robinson.

As black ballplayers became an increasing force in professional baseball, particularly in the National League, others forces were impelling change, too. The rapidly growing cities on the West Coast had been seeking major league status for some time, but when the 1950s began, the major-league city farthest west was St. Louis.

The first franchise move in 50 years—the Boston Braves to Milwaukee in 1953—did not change that situation, nor did the move of the feeble St. Louis Browns to Baltimore (1954) or the Philadelphia Athletics to Kansas City (1955).

But then, after the 1957 season, two franchise moves were made that rocked the baseball world in general and New York City in particular. The Brooklyn Dodgers became the Los Angeles Dodgers, and the New York Giants became the San Francisco Giants.

The U.S. economy expanded rapidly after the war, and consumers spent freely. Among the items they bought in ever-increasing numbers were television sets. The televising of major-league base-ball games had a devastating effect on the minor leagues, but the main impact on the majors was to increase the number of night games (sponsors preferred them) and to make international celebrities out of baseball superstars.

While all these financial, sociological, and geographical events were taking place in the national pastime, down on the diamond the New York Yankees continued to ride roughshod over their American League rivals—after the first post-war season, that is, and two subsequent interruptions by the Cleveland Indians.

In 1946 the Boston Red Sox romped to victory in the AL, with outfielders Ted Williams and Dom DiMaggio (Joe's brother), plus shortstop Johnny Pesky all among the top five hitters in the league. Pitcher Boo Ferris posted a 25-6 record and Tex Hughson went 20-11 as the Red Sox built up a 12-game edge over the second-place Detroit Tigers.

In the National League the St. Louis Cardinals bounced back after their dismal 1945 season and, with Musial and Slaughter once more in the lineup, took the NL flag by two games over the Dodgers and followed up by winning the World Series, four games to three, over the Red Sox.

The New York Yankees won every American League pennant from 1947 through 1964 except in 1948, 1954, and 1959. The Yanks were overpowering—too overpowering, many said, for the good of the league. Fans flocked to Yankee Stadium but not always to the ballparks of lesser teams. "Break up the Yankees" became a familiar cry of the day. Although the long reign on the Yankees saw players come and go, a small cadre of perennials existed.

Catcher Yogi Berra played his first game in pinstripes in 1946 and his last in 1963, spanning the great days of the postwar Yankee dynasty. Center fielder Joe DiMaggio, a regular since 1936, retired in 1951, the year Mickey Mantle arrived from Joplin of the Class C Western Association. Mantle retired after the 1968 season—completing a 32-year reign for the DiMaggio-Mantle duo in center field for the Yanks. Shortstop Phil Rizzuto

arrived in 1941 and departed in 1956. The next year Tony Kubek came up to take over that position for the next decade. Utility infielder Gil McDougald played regularly at one infield position or another from 1951 through 1960.

The premier Yankee pitchers of the early dynastic years were Vic Raschi, 1946-53, Allie Reynolds, 1947-54, and Ed Lopat, 1948-55, and of the later years, Whitey Ford, 1950-67.

The Yankees won every World Series from 1947 through 1954, except in 1948, when playing-manager Lou Boudreau's inspired Cleveland Indians captured the AL flag (by defeating the Boston Red Sox in a one-game playoff) and then proceeded to knock off the Boston Braves in the World Series.

The National League was much better balanced than the AL from the end of the war to the beginning of the expansion era. The Brooklyn Dodgers took the NL title six times—in 1947, 1949, 1952, 1953, 1955, and 1956—but except in the "Boys of Summer" seasons of 1953 and 1955 they eked out their victories by narrow margins. The Los Angeles Dodgers, keyed by many Brooklyn holdovers, won the pennant in 1959.

The great Dodgers of this period included infielders Jackie Robinson, Gil Hodges, Pee Wee Reese, and Jim Gilliam; outfielders Duke Snider and Carl Furillo; and pitchers Don Newcombe, Carl Erskine, and, later on, Sandy Koufax and Don Drysdale.

The Dodgers seldom fared well in their World Series encounters with the Yankees. The one exception for the Ebbets Field faithful was in 1955 when Johnny Podres tossed a final-game shutout to give Brooklyn the Series, four games to three. In 1959 the L.A. Dodgers faced the Chicago White Sox in the World Series and set them down handily on the pitching of Larry Sherry and the hitting of Gil Hodges and Charlie Neal.

Good as the Dodgers were, they could be had—and were, in 1948 by the Boston Braves, in 1950 by the Philadelphia Phillies' "Whiz Kids," and in 1951 and 1954 by the New York Giants. The Giants of the early Fifties were inconsistent but occasionally tough to beat, as in 1951 when pitchers Sal Maglie and Larry Jansen shared the league lead in victories with 23 each.

Outfielder Willie Mays joined the Giants in 1951, and in 1954 his .345 batting average led the league. Mays' 41 homers and 110 RBIs that season, though well below his personal highs, proved a big factor in the Giants' success. Pitcher Johnny Antonelli won 21 games, lost seven, and led the league with a 2.30 ERA.

The Giants lost the 1951 World Series to the Yanks but came back to pulverize the Cleveland Indians in four straight games in 1954. It was a particularly impressive performance for the Giants, because the Indians had won 111 games in the AL that year, a modern record. (The Cubs had won 116 in the NL back in 1906.)

The Milwaukee Braves were one of the Cinderella teams of the late 1950s. Nothing had been going right for the Braves in Boston, but with the franchise switch to Milwaukee in 1953, attendance skyrocketed—six times what it had been the Boston the year before.

The Braves did well, too, finishing second to the Dodgers. Not until 1957, though, did Milwaukee make it to the top of the heap, led by outfielder Hank Aaron and third baseman Eddie Mathews. The Braves' ace pitchers were Boston veterans Warren Spahn and Lew Burdette.

In the 1957 World Series, Milwaukee upended the mighty Yankees in seven games, with Lew Burdette winning three games, two of them shutouts. The Braves repeated as NL champions in 1958, but fell to the Yanks in another seven-game Series after leading three games to one.

The 1960 season, the last campaign before AL expansion, saw the Pittsburgh Pirates emerge unexpectedly with the NL pennant. Shortstop Dick Groat led the league in hitting at .325, while outfielder Roberto Clemente drove in 94 runs, as the Bucs topped the second-place Braves by seven games. Pittsburgh was not expected to defeat the Yankees of Mantle and Maris in the World Series, but a ninth-inning home run in the seventh game off the bat of Pirate second baseman Bill Mazeroski gave the Bucs their first world championship since 1925.

Expansion in the 1960s

During and after the Second World War, club owners and league officials of the Class AAA Pacific Coast League had tried hard to gain major-league status. After all, most of the cities in the PCL were large and growing—Los Angeles, San Diego, San Francisco, Oakland, Seattle. For the 1952 season the league obtained what was called an "Open Classification" with the idea of their eventually becoming a major league.

But the dream died over the winter of 1957-58 when Los Angeles and San Francisco were awarded franchises in the National League. The PCL reverted to Triple-A the next year. The two-team move to the West Coast did not expand the National League, which, like the AL, remained the eight-club circuit it had been since the turn of the century.

But expansion was in the air, partly because of Branch Rickey's proposed Continental League, envisioned as a third major league. National and American League club owners, fearing such competition, were spurred to offer franchises to potential major-league cities even if that meant enlarging their leagues. The AL was the first to take the plunge, adding two cities—Los Angeles (later California) and Minneapolis (called Minnesota)—to create a ten-team league.

The change was less simple than it sounds. The Minnesota franchise was that of the old Washington Senators, as were the Twins' players such as Harmon Killebrew and Bob Allison. A new Washington team was established, unhappily as it turned out, to take the place of the crew that had departed for Minnesota. These second-chance Washington Senators had scant box office success and in 1972 moved to Arlington, Texas, where, as the Texas Rangers, the team prospered on paper, though not on the field.

In 1961 the L.A. Angels finished eighth, the new Washington Senators tenth, and the Minnesota Twins (the old Washington Senators) seventh. Mired in the second division with these new entries were the Kansas City Athletics, themselves the old Philadelphia A's and new to the league in

1955. The strong, established ball clubs had a field day, the Yanks winning the pennant with 109 victories and the Detroit Tigers finishing second with 101. The Yankees' Roger Maris clubbed 61 home runs in this first year of expansion (shattering Babe Ruth's record), and his teammate Mickey Mantle slammed 54.

In the National League—still with eight teams in 1961—the Cincinnati Reds won the pennant but were pummeled by the Yanks in the Series. In 1962 the NL introduced its own two expansion teams, the Houston Colt .45s (later the Astros) and the New York Mets. These two teams finished in eighth and tenth place respectively, as the venerable Chicago Cubs, in one of their blue-funk periods, could manage no better than ninth.

The Mets, under manager Casey Stengel, won exactly one quarter of their games, ending with a 40-120 record but getting surprisingly strong support from their fans. Two recently arrived teams, the San Francisco Giants and Los Angeles Dodgers, finished one-two in the NL, both with more than 100 wins. The Yankees as usual took the AL flag, then nipped the Giants, four games to three, in the World Series.

From 1961 through 1968 each of the major leagues consisted of ten teams, although there were a couple of franchise shifts along the way. The Milwaukee Braves became the Atlanta Braves in 1966. The Kansas City Athletics became the Oakland Athletics in 1968. Both moves were acrimonious, with cries of bad faith from fans in the abandoned cities. But apart from these complaints, the ten-team leagues themselves were unwieldy, producing too many losers. A tenth-place team seemed to be not merely in the cellar but in a kind of newly constructed subcellar.

Another problem faced major-league owners in the early 1960s. The minor leagues, the training grounds for big-league ballplayers, had all but collapsed. After reaching their peak in 1949, the minors had been rapidly and severely eroded by the growth of television in general and of televised major-league games in particular. They were no longer supplying the talent the majors needed if they were to prosper.

Consequently, in 1965, following the lead of pro football, the major-league baseball owners initiated an annual free agent draft, which later became a semi-annual draft. Clubs would select eligible high school and college players, with the major league team lowest in the previous year's standings choosing first.

While many owners fretted over rising costs and a declining pool of talent (many fine athletes were opting for other pro sports), the players were generally doing quite well. In 1966 Marvin Miller, a labor negotiator, took over as executive secretary of the Major League Players Association. During his 17-year tenure, he negotiated five basic agreements, or contracts, raising players' salaries substantially and increasing pension benefits.

The mid-1960s marked the end of Yankee rule in the American League. Between 1961 and 1964 the Yanks won every AL pennant, still propelled by Mantle and Maris, still featuring Whitey Ford on the mound. But the old order was fading.

The Yankees won the World Series of 1961 and 1962 but lost those of 1963 and 1964. In the AL standings New York plunged all the way to sixth place in 1965 as the Minnesota Twins captured the pennant. The Twins did not represent a new dynasty, however, nor did any other AL ball club. The Orioles won in 1966, the Red Sox in 1967, and the Tigers in 1968.

Two National League teams—the Los Angeles Dodgers and St. Louis Cardinals—vied for dominance from 1963 through 1968. The Dodgers, under manager Walter Alston, relied on strong pitching from Sandy Koufax, Don Drysdale, and, in the later years, Claude Osteen and Don Sutton.

The Dodgers took pennants in 1963, 1965, and 1966 and won the World Series the first two of those years. In 1966 they lost to the red-hot Baltimore Orioles of Frank Robinson, Brooks Robinson, Boog Powell, and Jim Palmer. The Cardinals finished first in the NL in 1964, 1967, and 1968.

Like the Dodgers, the Cardinals had outstanding pitching. Curt Simmons, their aging ace, was gone by 1967, but the mound replacements for the Cards were formidable—Bob Gibson, Steve Carlton, and Nelson Briles. On offense they could

1994 REALIGNMENT

American League

Central

Chicago White Sox
Cleveland Indians
Kansas City Royals
Milwaukee Brewers
Minnesota Twins

East

Baltimore Orioles

Boston Red Sox
Detroit Tigers
New York Yankees
Toronto Blue Jays

West

California Angels
Oakland Athletics
Seattle Mariners
Texas Rangers

The NL produced some respectable batting averages (Cincinnati's Pete Rose hit .335), but over in the AL Carl Yastrzemski of the Red Sox won the batting title with an anemic .301, while Oakland's Danny Cater finished second at .290. The overall major league batting average was .237.

The other trend, the presence and performance of African-Americans and Latin Americans in the majors, was equally striking. In the brief 1960s era of ten-team leagues, MVP awards went to Maury Wills, Willie Mays, Roberto Clemente, Orlando Cepeda, and Bob Gibson in the National League; and Elston Howard, Zoilo Versalles, and Frank Robinson in the American League.

Baseball Becomes Big Business

True major-league expansion, as fans think of it today, began with the 1969 season. Baseball owners, taking their cue from the organizational plan of the National Football League, decided to add two more ball clubs to each of the two major leagues—a total of 24—and, more importantly, to split each league into two divisions, East and West.

In the 162-game schedule each team would play its own divisional rivals 18 times and teams from the other division 12 times. At the end of the season there would be a five-game playoff (later changed to seven games) between the divisional champions to determine the pennant winner in each league. The World Series would follow. The plan worked well and proved popular. Former tenth-place teams could now finish no worse than sixth.

The new teams in the National League were the Montreal Expos in the East Division (sixth place in 1969) and the San Diego Padres in the West Division (also in sixth place). The American League put both its newcomers in the West Division: the Kansas City Royals (fourth place in 1969) and the Seattle Pilots (last place, bankrupt, and out of the league after one season, to be replaced by the Milwaukee Brewers).

In 1977 the American League upset the six-team divisional structure by admitting two new

count on first baseman Orlando Cepeda, outfielders Lou Brock and Curt Flood, and catcher Tim McCarver. The Cards topped the Red Sox in the 1967 World Series. Bob Gibson won three games and Nelson Briles one, while Lou Brock collected 12 hits and stole seven bases.

Two trends were especially noticable during the 1960s—the widening imbalance between pitching and hitting and the growing presence and stellar performance of many black and Latino players.

The pitchers' ERAs and the hitters' batting averages went down in tandem. In 1968, the "year of the pitcher," Bob Gibson posted a 1.12 ERA; the overall major league ERA that season was a mere 2.98.

teams—the Toronto Blue Jays in the East and the Seattle Mariners (no connection with the Pilots) in the West. From 1977 through 1992 the skewed realignment stood: 26 major league teams, 14 of them in the AL, 12 in the NL. Then in 1993 the National League achieved parity—seven teams in each division—by adding the Florida Marlins to the NL East and the Colorado Rockies to the NL West.

Another organizational change was made in 1993, when club owners approved a plan to expand each league from two to three divisions, beginning in 1994. The new alignment (approved by a 27-1 margin by the owners, the only holdout being Texas Rangers owner George Bush, Jr.) brings with it a change in the playoff format: at the end of the season the three division leaders and a "wild card" team (the team with the best record not finishing first in its division) will compete in a quarterfinal series. The two winners of that series will meet in a semifinal round to determine which team will represent each league in the World Series.

Critics of the plan argue that the expanded playoff format is merely a gimmick devised by the owners and the television networks to increase revenues and will push an already-long season to the brink of November.

Proponents of the plan claim it will bring more fairness to postseason play, citing instances when second- and even third-place teams in one division might have better records than first-place teams in their weaker divisional counterparts. The new realignment also paves the way for future expansion.

Rules Changes

One of the few important rule changes in recent baseball history occurred in 1973 when the American League introduced the designated-hitter rule, which allowed a team to replace its (usually weak-hitting) pitcher in the batting order with a player whose sole function was to hit. The DH idea drew mixed reviews. The National League refused to go along with it, and, as one conse-

---

1994 REALIGNMENT

National League

Central

Chicago Cubs
Cincinnati Reds
Houston Astros
Pittsburgh Pirates
St. Louis Cardinals

East

Atlanta Braves
Florida Marlins
Montreal Expos
New York Mets
Philadelphia Phillies

West

Colorado Rockies
Los Angeles Dodgers
San Diego Padres
San Francisco Giants

---

quence, the DH rule was applied in the World Series only every other year.

But if baseball purists disliked this American League rule, they tended to dislike even more an innovation first adopted in the National League. When Houston built its Astrodome in the early 1960s, the intent was to have a natural-grass playing surface. Alas, the glare-producing glass in the dome had to be painted, the Bermuda grass died, and the Monsanto Chemical Company invented AstroTurf, a green "rug" to replace it.

This artificial playing surface caught on with a few owners of undomed stadiums as well as owners of the later domed stadiums in Seattle, Minnesota, Montreal, and Toronto. Artificial turf, like the DH, affected the nature of the game, but

Transcendental Graphics

Henry Chadwick

so, too, its defenders point out, did many other technical innovations and rule changes since the days of Henry Chadwick.

The expansion era saw some venerable individual records fall. Few fans thought Ty Cobb's total of 4,191 lifetime hits would ever be topped, but when Pete Rose closed out his career in 1986, he had collected 4,256. There were those who thought that Babe Ruth's career home run record, 714, was not only safe but practically sacrosanct. Yet when Hank Aaron hung up his spikes, he had blasted 755 round-trippers.

Ty Cobb's 892 career stolen bases set a record that held for decades. But Lou Brock later stole 936, and through the 1992 season Rickey Henderson had swiped 1,042. For years the Washington Senators' fast-ball pitcher Walter Johnson held the lifetime strikeout record of 3,508. The expansion era produced several pitchers who bettered that mark—though none so devastatingly as Nolan Ryan, who by the end of the 1992 season had whiffed 5,668 batters.

Other old records stood up—Joe DiMaggio's 56-game hitting streak, Hack Wilson's 190 RBIs in a season, and Ted Williams' .406 batting average in 1941—although Rod Carew of the Minnesota Twins posted a .388 batting average in 1977, and George Brett of the Kansas City Royals hit .390 in 1980.

Probably the most talked-about off-field phenomenon of the expansion era was the steep and steady rise of players' salaries. In 1965 the average major leaguer's annual salary was $17,000. By 1970 it had risen to $25,000. By 1976 the figure was up to $52,000, and 1980 saw it hit $185,000.

By 1986 the average salary had climbed to $412,000, and in 1993 it was more than a million dollars. Clearly, baseball owners would not have been paying such salaries if their operations were in the doldrums. But, even so, the increases seemed astronomical to many fans.

What was driving up salaries? A primary factor was the re-entry draft, included as part of the 1976 basic agreement between owners and players. No longer did the reserve clause theoretically bind a ballplayer to one team forever.

Now the required term was only six years. After that the player could opt for free agency and see what his services would bring on the open market. Often his services brought plenty, especially when one of the interested owners was a free-spender like George Steinbrenner of the New York Yankees.

Despite such gains by the players, most of them attributable to the skill and perseverance of Marvin Miller, uneasiness persisted, and it erupted in the baseball strike of 1981. This strike lasted nearly two months, wiped out the middle of the season, and resulted in a bizarre playoff scheme that pleased almost no one.

Nevertheless, major-league attendance continued to rise, television revenues poured in, and the national pastime, even with the increasing competition of professional football, basketball, and hockey, evolved into an enterprise so lucrative that in many ways it resembled show business.

This did not necessarily detract from the drama on the field. In 1969, the first year of divisional play, the "Amazin'" New York Mets captured the NL East title, swept past the Atlanta Braves in the new league championship series, and went on to defeat the mighty Baltimore Orioles in the World Series. The Mets won the pennant again in 1973 but fell to the Oakland A's in the Series.

The more consistent champs in the NL East in the early 1970s, though, were the Pittsburgh Pirates of Willie Stargell and Roberto Clemente, while in the NL West the Cincinnati Reds' "Big Red Machine" took five of seven titles between 1970 and 1976. Among the players powering the formidable Reds were Pete Rose, Joe Morgan, Tony Perez, and Johnny Bench. In the NL postseason showdowns between the Pirates and Reds, the Reds won each time except in 1971.

When the Big Red Machine began to falter in the late 1970s, the Los Angeles Dodgers, under manager Tommy Lasorda, were among the beneficiaries, finishing first in the NL West in 1977 and 1978 and then four times in the 1980s.

Pittsburgh and Philadelphia were the teams to beat in the NL East, and in 1980 the Phillies won their first World Series ever, defeating the Kansas City Royals, four games to two. The Phillies' preeminent heroes in this brief triumphal epoch were third baseman Mike Schmidt, first baseman Pete Rose (who starred at many positions in his long career), and pitcher Steve Carlton.

When the Phillies faded, the NL East title was up for grabs, and various teams captured it during the 1980s. Then in the early 1990s the Pirates, starting out with a superb but transitory outfield of Bobby Bonds, Bobby Bonilla, and Andy Van Slyke, won three NL East titles in a row.

Manager Earl Weaver's Baltimore Orioles took five of six American League East titles between 1969 and 1974, interrupted only by the Detroit Tigers in 1972. In 1971 the O's achieved the rare feat of having four 20-game winners in the same season: Dave McNally, Mike Cuellar, Pat Dobson, and Jim Palmer. The Orioles lost the 1972 World Series to the Pirates. Indeed, only once in those five years of success in the AL East did Baltimore gain the world championship, beating the Reds in 1970.

In the AL West it was a different story. Owner Charles O. Finley put together an Oakland Athletics' team that simply could not be stopped. Managed by Dick Williams and later Alvin Dark, it starred outfielders Reggie Jackson, Joe Rudi, and third baseman Sal Bando and featured outstanding pitching by, among others, Vida Blue and Rollie Fingers. The A's rolled past everyone, taking five straight AL West titles from 1971 through 1975 and three straight World Series in 1972, 1973, and 1974.

Then Charles Finley broke up the ball club. No comparably dominant team emerged in the AL West for another decade, when once again (much as the Pirates had surged back in the NL East), the Oakland A's fielded a powerful new ball club, this time managed by Tony LaRussa. The A's leaders on offense were home-run-hitting Mark McGwire at first base and Jose Canseco in the outfield.

As the expansion era progressed, trades and free agency made the building of new dynasties all but impossible. Solid teams quickly disintegrated. The brilliant Pirate outfield of the early 1990s was soon split asunder, with Bobby Bonilla going to the New York Mets in 1992 and Barry Bonds to the San Francisco Giants in 1993 (joining superstar Will Clark there). The McGwire-Canseco duo came unglued when the A's traded Canseco to the Texas Rangers for outfielder Ruben Sierra, pitchers Mike Witt and Jeff Russell, and cash.

A familiar cry at major league ballparks in days gone by was, "You can't tell the players without a scorecard." The average fan often could tell them, though, because the teams, like the leagues, were fairly stable. But rapidly changing rosters in the 1980s and 1990s made it difficult for even the most dedicated fan to know who was playing for whom at any given time.

Still, the history of major-league baseball is kaleidoscopic. The number of teams and players that have participated in the game since the National League's opening day in April 1876 makes baseball trivia a national pastime. In many ways change has been the norm rather than the exception. No doubt a major-league baseball game today would be almost beyond comprehension to a nineteenth-century gentleman who had played "the New York game" in an era when the purists were cricketeers.

And yet one of the strengths of baseball is its relative timelessness. The game does have continuity. Generations of ballplayers and fans come and go, but most of them understand, and understand in much the same way, the legacy of Ty Cobb, Christy Mathewson, Babe Ruth, Ted Williams, Willie Mays, Roberto Clemente, Hank Aaron, and other great stars of the near or distant past.

SOURCES

BOOKS

Allen, Lee, *The National League Story,* Hill and Wang, 1961.

Allen, Lee, *The American League Story,* Hill and Wang, 1962.

The Baseball Encyclopedia, 9th edition, Macmillan, 1993.

Carter, Craig, editor, *Daguerreotypes: 8th Edition,* The Sporting News Publishing Co., 1990.

Durant, John, *The Story of Baseball in Words and Pictures,* Hastings House, 1973.

Goldstein, Richard, *Spartan Seasons: How Baseball Survived the Second World War,* Macmillan, 1985.

Honig, Donald, *Baseball's 10 Greatest Teams,* Macmillan, 1982.

James, Bill, *Bill James Historical Abstract,* Villard Books, 1986.

Mann, Arthur, *Branch Rickey: American in Action,* Houghton Mifflin, 1957.

Murdock, Eugene C., *Ban Johnson: Czar of Baseball,* Greenwood Press, 1982.

Okrent, Daniel, and Harris Lewine, editors, *The Ultimate Baseball Book,* Houghton Mifflin, 1979.

Reichler, Joseph, *30 Years of Baseball's Greatest Moments,* Crown Publishers, 1974.

Ritter, Lawrence S., *The Glory of Their Times,* Macmillan, 1966.

Selzer, Jack, *Baseball in the Nineteenth Century: An Overview,* Society for American Baseball Research, 1986.

Tygiel, Jules, *Baseball's Great Experiment: Jackie Robinson and His Legacy,* Oxford University Press, 1983.

Voigt, David Q., *Baseball: An Illustrated History,* Pennsylvania State University Press, 1985.

Voigt, David Q., "The History of Major League Baseball," *Total Baseball,* edited by John Thorn and Pete Palmer, Warner Books, 1989.

—Gerald Tomlinson for Book Builders, Inc.

AMERICAN LEAGUE CENTRAL

CHICAGO WHITE SOX

One of the original teams in the American League, the Chicago White Sox (at first called the White Stockings) won the pennant in 1901, the league's first year. The owner of the Chicago franchise was Charles Comiskey, a former ballplayer who had purchased the St. Paul Saints of the Western League in 1895. When Ban Johnson established the American League at the turn of the century, he and Comiskey got permission to relocate the Saints to Chicago. They became the White Stockings, taking what had previously been the nickname of the National League's Cubs. A Chicago sportswriter shortened the name to White Sox in their second season.

After winning the pennant in their 1901 American League debut, and again in 1906 with the "Hitless Wonders," the White Sox fell on hard times for many seasons. Success returned with the approach of World War I as the Sox gradually assembled the team that would become the notorious, eight-men-out "Black Sox"—pitcher Eddie

Cicotte, outfielders Shoeless Joe Jackson and Happy Felsch, first baseman Chick Gandil, infielder Swede Risberg, and others. This was an outstanding team, although tainted and ultimately destroyed by scandal.

The White Sox finished a close second in 1920 before the news of their having thrown the 1919 World Series broke, after which—with many of their stars banned from the game—they went into a sustained decline, one that lasted almost 40 years. Even World War II, which skewed the standings and brought the doormat St. Louis Browns a pennant, failed to make much visible difference to the White Sox.

Finally in 1959, after a long climb under managers Paul Richards, Marty Marion, and Al Lopez, the White Sox reached the pinnacle once more. The 1959 team included infielders Nellie Fox and Louis Aparicio and pitchers Early Wynn, Bob Shaw, and Billy Pierce. It was a good ball club, but without dynastic potential. The Sox could not repeat as pennant winners, although they remained a first division team through most of the 1960s. In 1963, 1964, and 1965 they had superb won-lost records, but the puissant Yankees were too much for them in '63 and '64, and the Twins came on like thunder in '65.

When division play arrived in 1969, the White Sox took only one year to find the cellar, compiling a horrific 56-106 record in 1970. To try to reverse the skid, the Sox hired Chuck Tanner as their manager. Tanner brought the team briefly into contention just two years later, but they finished in second place behind the Oakland A's.

The 1972 team featured temperamental outfielder Dick Allen, who led the league in homers (37) and RBIs (113); knuckleball pitcher Wilbur Wood, who topped the league in wins (24-17); and Stan Bahnsen (21-16, a career performance for him).

In 1983, nearly a quarter of a century after their 1959 pennant, the White Sox finished first in the AL East under manager Tony LaRussa. They outdistanced the second-place Kansas City Royals by 20 games. But in the League Championship Series, the Baltimore Orioles of the AL East, after losing the first game, defeated the Sox in the next three games to go on to the World Series.

The White Sox settled it at lower levels in the standings until 1990, when they climbed from a basement finish in 1989 to a strong second-place showing under manager Jeff Torborg, who thereupon, alas, left to manage the Mets. His successor, Gene Lamont, led the Sox to two more second-place finishes in 1991 and 1992.

Early Success

The name Comiskey has been associated with the Chicago White Sox from the earliest days of the franchise, all the way back to the team's minor league days in St. Paul. When Ban Johnson, a sportswriter for the Cincinnati *Commercial-Gazette*, became president of the Western League—a revived minor circuit—in 1894, he already knew Charles Comiskey, the man who came to be called

Transcendental Graphics

Charles A. Comiskey

"Commy" or "The Old Roman." Comiskey had been in professional baseball since 1877, most recently as a playing manager for the Cincinnati Red Stockings. Commy had higher ambitions. Despite pleas to stay in Cincinnati, he bought the minor league St. Paul Saints of the Western League and installed himself as manager.

The team had originally been located in Sioux City, Iowa, but poor attendance forced a transfer of the franchise to St. Paul in 1895, partly to create a rivalry with twin city Minneapolis. The Saints were competitive but unprofitable, and league president Ban Johnson, along with owner Charles Comiskey, lobbied to move the franchise from St. Paul to Chicago, a city both men believed was big enough to support two professional ball clubs.

The transfer was approved, and the Chicago White Stockings of the new American League—still a minor league despite the change in name—took the field on April 21, 1900, after hasty construction of a ballpark at 39th Street and Wentworth provided them with a place to play.

TEAM INFORMATION AT A GLANCE

Founding date: April 21, 1900 (American League as minor league)
April 24, 1901 (American League as major league)

Home stadium: Comiskey Park
333 West 35th Street
Chicago, IL 60616
Phone: (312) 924-1000
FAX: (312) 451-5105
Seating capacity: 44,702

Dimensions: Left-field line—347 feet
Center field—400 feet
Right-field line—347 feet
Team colors: Silver and black
Team nickname: White Stockings, 1901; White Sox, 1902-present
Logo: Old English "Sox" in black with silver outline; letters step downward

Franchise record	Won	Lost	Pct.
(1901-1993)	7,228	7,127	.504

World Series wins (2): 1906, 1917
American League championships (5): 1901, 1906, 1917, 1919, 1959
American League West division first-place finishes (2): 1983, 1993
League/division last-place finishes (7): 1924, 1931, 1934, 1948, 1970, 1976, 1989

The minor league White Stockings won the pennant in 1900 with a team consisting mostly of one-time major leaguers, including second baseman Dick Padden and outfielder Dummy Hoy. Ban Johnson's plan to transform the fledgling American League into a major league gained the AL owners' approval, and when the 1901 season opened at South Side Park on April 24, 1901, the Chicago White Stockings became a major league ball club.

Also in the new, upgraded American League, were clubs representing Boston, Detroit, Philadelphia, Baltimore, Washington, Cleveland, and Milwaukee. That, in fact, was the order in which the teams finished, as the White Stockings repeated their minor league success of the prior year and took the pennant, holding on at the end of the season against the second-place Boston Somersets.

The playing manager of this landmark Chicago team was Clark Griffith, a pitcher from the uptown NL Cubs who decided to cast his lot with the AL White Stockings. Griffith had quite a year in 1901, going 24-7 to lead the team in wins. Pitcher Roy Patterson, the "Boy Wonder," lived up to his nickname in this, his rookie major league season, winning 20, losing 16.

In 1902 Roy Patterson had another fine year, 20-12, but Clark Griffith faded somewhat, and the

Few expected the Chicago White Sox of 1906 to win the American League pennant let alone the World Series. But there was no question that the Series would be a big event in Chicago that year. The Cubs were coasting to an epic first-place finish, having won an amazing 116 games and losing only 36.

Chicago fans would definitely be seeing the Cubs in postseason action, but they were astonished by the news that the challengers would be the White Sox, who squeaked past Clark Griffith's New York Highlanders and Nap Lajoie's Cleveland Naps by three and five games respectively.

For this all-Chicago Series the city went a little wild. Since there could not possibly be enough seats in either ballpark for all the interested fans, Western Union provided direct play-by-play telegraph service from the scene of action to two large gathering places, the Auditorium Theatre and the First Regiment Armory. Throngs gathered at these two sites to hear a baseball broadcasting first.

The first game was played at West Side Park, home of the Cubs, on a bitterly cold October day with snow flurries in the air. White Sox fans cheered as Nick Altrock limited the Cubs to four hits and bested the great Three Finger Brown, 2-1. After the Cubs' Ed Reulbach won a 7-1 contest at South Side Park the next day, defeating Doc White, the Sox came back with Ed Walsh, who threw a four-hit shutout to put the American Leaguers up two games to one.

The Cubs' Three Finger Brown then held the "Hitless Wonders" nearly hitless in game four, giving up just two hits and edging Altrock, 1-0. But the bats of the White Sox came alive in the next game when Fred Isbell's four doubles led a 12-hit Sox attack on Ed Reulbach and relievers Jack Pfiester and Orval Overall. The underdogs needed only one more victory to win the World Championship.

Fans clustered outside the confines of South Side Park for the sixth game of the Series, unable to get tickets. An enterprising youth climbed a telegraph pole and shouted down a play-by-play report of the action. The 19,240 folks who did get into the ballpark saw the home-park Sox jump off to a 7-1 lead and romp to an easy 8-6 win, this time with 14 hits. Left fielder Ed Hahn, a .227 hitter that season, collected four hits off the offerings of Three Finger Brown and reliever Orval Overall. Even the "Hitless Wonders" could hit one now and then.

White Sox fell to fourth. The team's batting leader in both 1901 and 1902 was outfielder Fielder Jones, a native of Shinglehouse, Pennsylvania. Griffith quit to manage the New York Highlanders in 1903. When the White Sox, under brawling, hard-drinking manager Nixey Callahan, a left fielder, dropped to seventh place that year, it was clear that changes were needed.

In June of 1904 Callahan surrendered the reins to Fielder Jones, a center fielder, who proved to have the right stuff. The White Sox rose to third place in 1904 and to second in 1905. Pitcher Big Ed Walsh, a rookie up from Newark of the Eastern League, was working on his spitball, going 6-3 in 1904 and 8-3 in 1905. He and the rest of the White Sox were ready for 1906.

Not that anyone could hit very well. Second baseman Frank Isbell led the regulars with a less-than-gaudy .279 batting average. The team as a whole batted .230 in 1906, nearly ten points below last-place Boston. They connected for a grand total of six home runs. They truly were the "Hitless Wonders." Fortunately, they got some very fine pitching from most of the staff. Frank Owen put in his third straight 20-win season at 21-13. Nick Altrock, enjoying his last good season, went 20-13.

Future Hall-of-Famer Ed Walsh, getting better every year, threw the spitter (his so-called "eel ball") for a 17-13 record, including 10 shutouts. Left-hander Doc White posted an 18-6 mark with a league-leading 1.52 ERA. Roy Patterson, nearing the end of his period as boy wonder, posted a record of 10-7.

The White Sox came up from the depths, nine games back on August 1, to win 19 games in a row and vault into the league lead. They held on to it, winning almost one third of their games by a single run, to nose out Clark Griffith's New York Highlanders by three games. Weak as the Chicago attack was, shortstop George Davis drove in 80 runs, good for third in the league, and second baseman Frank Isbell and first baseman Jiggs Donahue stole 37 and 36 bases respectively, ranking them among the league's top five in thefts.

In late August *Chicago Tribune* writer Hugh Fullerton noted that "it is a wonder how they score so many runs on so few hits ... the Sox take every advantage of misplays ... and dash daringly around the bases...."

The 1906 World Series proved to be one of those events that a generation of baseball fans never tires of recalling. The Chicago Cubs had won 116 games during the regular season—the most in baseball history—and were expected to annihilate the clawing, scratching White Sox.

The White Sox had pitching, of course, but so did the Cubs: Three Finger Brown and Ed Reulbach, for example. In this first subway series (before Chicago actually had a subway) the outcome seemed assured—until they played the games.

To everyone's surprise the hitless wonders took the World Series from the 116-game winners by a margin of four games to two, even managing to outhit the Cubs, .198 to .196.

White Sox to Black Sox

The hitless wonders remained mostly hitless in 1907 despite the addition of outfielder Patsy Dougherty, who was to carry the highest batting average on the club between 1907 and 1910. That Dougherty's team-best averages were .270, .278, .285, and .248 gives some idea of the lack of attack the White Sox pitchers had to overcome. Nonetheless, Ed Walsh upped his wins to 24 in

Transcendental Graphics

Kid Gleason (left) and Ed Walsh

1907, while Doc White led the league with 26 victories, and Frank (Piano Mover) Smith, 5-5 in 1906, contributed 23. The White Sox finished third. In 1908 Ed Walsh really turned it on, winning 40 games, losing 15, and posting an ERA of 1.42. No one else on the team did nearly as well—Doc White went 18-13—and the Sox again finished third. At the end of the 1908 season Fielder Jones called it a career, packing his bags for Oregon to embark on a new career in forestry.

On opening day, 1909, White Sox catcher Billy Sullivan was named to manage the ball club. His .168 batting average was pretty poor, but only a little worse than was usual for him. The big event for Sullivan (and baseball) that year was his patenting of a chest protector that made use of compressed air. It was the forerunner of the modern chest protector.

Early in the 1909 season the White Sox traded pitcher Nick Altrock to the Senators for Bill Burns, a pitcher who is remembered today for his role in the 1919 Black Sox scandal. By then he was retired from baseball, but he was more than willing to act as a go-between for the players and the gamblers. In 1909 Burns turned in a 7-13 record for the White Sox, a typical performance for him. Ed Walsh dropped from 40-15 to 15-11, following a month-long holdout at the start of the season. Needless to say, the Sox dropped a bit, too, down to fourth place.

The White Sox story of 1910 did not involve new manager Hugh Duffy, nor the sixth-place finish, nor the brief appearance in the lineup of Black Sox first baseman Chick Gandil. Instead, it involved the opening of Comiskey Park at 35th Street and Shields, hyped as the "Baseball Palace of the World."

The second all-concrete-and steel-stadium in the United States, the new ballpark was a happy compromise between the expansive architect and the tight-fisted club owner. The architect wanted style, the owner wanted function. The ballpark was a classic from the day it opened, July 1, 1910, until the day it closed 80 years later, when a new Comiskey Park opened across the street.

The White Sox of 1910 were a disappointment, finishing sixth, 35½ games off the pace. Ed Walsh's 1.27 ERA sparkled, but the still weak-hitting ball club (with a number of hitters in the high .100s) saw him record only an 18-20 season.

A fourth-place finish in 1911 ushered out Hugh Duffy as manager and reinstated old Nixey Callahan, back for three more tries at the brass ring. Callahan brought no improvement in the standings, although one of the key Black Sox players, pitcher Eddie Cicotte, was purchased from the Red Sox in 1913.

After the 1914 season, in which the Sox tied for sixth place, Charlie Comiskey bought second baseman Eddie Collins from the Philadelphia A's, giving the young, college-educated star a guaranteed five-year, $75,000 contract. Collins was worth it, but this bonanza (for those days) did not sit well with his lesser-paid teammates.

In 1915 Charlie Comiskey, frustrated by his team's lack of progress, decided to take a chance

Transcendental Graphics

Eddie Collins

on a rookie manager from the minors, 33-year-old Clarence (Pants) Rowland. The team already had some strength: Cicotte and Collins for sure, along with pitcher Red Faber, a rookie in 1914; catcher Ray Schalk and shortstop (later third baseman) Buck Weaver, both three-year veterans, and a newcomer for the 1915 campaign, outfielder Happy Felsch, up from minor league Milwaukee.

In late August the White Sox added another proven star, outfielder Shoeless Joe Jackson, purchased from Cleveland. A few days earlier they had acquired a top Pacific Coast League hurler, Claude (Lefty) Williams. The 1915 White Sox won 93 games, lost 61, and finished third in the league, behind Boston and Detroit. Pants Rowland had every reason to feel optimistic.

The following year brought the thrill of a genuine pennant race to Comiskey Park. The team occupied first place in early August, then fell behind the fired-up Boston Red Sox, but stayed in contention until the very end. Eddie Cicotte's 15-

Transcendental Graphics

Red Faber

7 and 1.78 did not quite match the 23-12 and 1.75 ERA of the Red Sox's Babe Ruth, but the Chicago pitching staff as a whole outshone Boston's hurlers.

Fred McMullin, a new utility infielder, contributed little to the pennant drive, but would achieve an unsavory fame in the coming Black Sox scandal. With all but one of the Black Sox players on the roster—Cicotte, Felsch, Gandil, Jackson, McMullin, Weaver, and Williams—the second-place White Sox of 1916 were a contentious but powerful ball club. Despite their bitter dislike of low-paying owner Charlie Comiskey and high-salaried second baseman Eddie Collins, they looked like a team with a future.

The White Sox captured the pennant in 1917. They won 100 games and lost 54, finishing nine games ahead of the Red Sox. Eddie Cicotte won 28 games and posted a 1.53 ERA to lead the league in both categories. Happy Felsch hit .308 and drove in 102 runs. Shoeless Joe Jackson's .301 was respectable, though not up to his usual par. The White Sox shortstop, rookie Swede Risberg, the eighth member of the Black Sox, was less than a first-year sensation, batting only .203.

No longer hitless wonders, the White Sox proved to be the best team in the majors, defeating the New York Giants in the World Series, four games to two. Red Faber won three of the games as a starter and lost one in relief. Eddie Cicotte went 1-1. Eddie Collins, Joe Jackson, Chick Gandil, Buck Weaver, and Happy Felsch all contributed to the offense.

The Scandal

The 1918 season was an unusual one. World War I intruded, and the "work or fight" edict scrambled rosters and affected the standings. The White Sox dropped to sixth place in a shortened season, and fans looked forward to a return to normalcy. What they got was the biggest furor in the history of American baseball, although it took a while to develop. In the meantime Chicago fans got two exciting years of pennant-fever baseball at Comiskey Park. The White Sox captured the flag in 1919, with Eddie Cicotte winning 29 games and losing only seven. Lefty Williams did well, too, posting a 23-11 mark.

The batting star for the White Sox was Shoeless Joe Jackson, who hit .351 and drove in 96 runs. This highly talented team, under rookie manager Kid Gleason—once a pitcher and no longer a kid—edged out Cleveland by 3½ games. They then sold out to gamblers in the nine-game World Series.

Ugly rumors were afloat as the heavily favored White Sox took the field against the Cincinnati Reds in the first game of the Series. Eddie Cicotte pitched and lost, 9-1. Lefty Williams took the mound in the second game and lost, 4-2. At a crucial moment in the fourth inning he walked three batters. Cicotte botched a couple of plays in the fifth inning of game four, and Happy Felsch made a fool of himself in the outfield in the fifth game. The Reds took the Series five games to three.

Cicotte was charged with two losses, Williams with three. Two of the three White Sox wins were chalked up by little left-hander Dickie Kerr, who was not in on the fix. Cicotte won game seven, 4-1. Few sportswriters saw anything bizarre enough about the Series to make an outright claim of conspiracy. Yet something was clearly amiss.

The betting odds shifted early and inexplicably in favor of the underdog Reds. Kid Gleason saw something wrong in game two and voiced his suspicions to Charlie Comiskey. Nothing happened. In fact, many of the conspirators got pay raises for the 1920 season.

They did well in 1920, too, and were in a tight pennant race with Cleveland and New York when a grand jury convened near the end of the season to look into allegations concerning the 1919 World Series. Eddie Collins enjoyed a .369 season in 1920, while three of the Black Sox—Joe Jackson (.382), Happy Felsch (.338), and Buck Weaver (.333)—had never played better.

For the first time in major league history (and the last time until 1971) a team had four 20-game winners on the pitching staff: Red Faber (23-13),

Transcendental Graphics

Ray Schalk

Lefty Williams (22-14), Eddie Cicotte (21-10), and Dickie Kerr (21-9). With three games of the regular season yet to play, eight White Sox players were indicted and suspended. Among them were Jackson, Felsch, Weaver, Cicotte, and Williams.

The Sox finished second, two games back. The eight Black Sox escaped criminal punishment when vital evidence disappeared, but the new baseball commissioner, Kenesaw Mountain Landis, barred them from the game for life.

At Home in the Depths

No team could lose so many stars at a single stroke and not suffer for it. The White Sox still had their great second baseman, Eddie Collins, and their fine catcher, Ray Schalk. On the mound they still had Red Faber and Dickie Kerr. These players continued to perform well. Collins hit .337 in 1921, and Red Faber posted a 25-15 record. Dickie Kerr went 19-17. But the team skidded all the way to seventh place. They did not recover quickly.

Earl Sheely, installed at first base, put in seven solid years for the White Sox, but he is largely forgotten, because the team wallowed in the second division throughout those years. Also largely forgotten is rookie pitcher Charlie Robertson and his perfect game against the Detroit Tigers on April 30, 1922. Among the Tigers who went 0-for-3 that day against the usually unimpressive Robertson were Ty Cobb and Harry Heilmann.

The escape from the second division came in 1936, after the team had finished in the cellar three times, in seventh place five times, in sixth place once, and in fifth place six times. During these years in the depths, managers and players came and went. Kid Gleason left after the 1923 season, to be succeeded by, among others, Eddie Collins, Ray Schalk, Lena Blackburne, Donie Bush, Lew Fonseca, and Jimmy Dykes.

Through the mid-twenties Eddie Collins continued to lead the offense, although veteran Red Sox outfielder and future Hall-of-Famer Harry Hooper put in three .300+ seasons.

Pitcher Ted Lyons arrived via Baylor University in 1923 to join Red Faber on the pitching staff. Lyons, also a Hall of Famer, served the White Sox for 21 years, racking up 260 wins against 230 losses. Despite the general ineptness of the team, Lyons won 20 or more games three times, in 1925, 1927, and 1930.

In 1927 the Sox picked up outfielder Carl Reynolds from Palestine, Texas, of the Lone Star League, where he had demolished Class D pitching. It was a long jump to the majors, but Reynolds made it, batting .323 in 1928, his first full year with Chicago. He starred for the White Sox through 1931, after which he drifted from team to team on his way to a career .302 batting average.

A third player of note—indeed, another Hall of Famer—arrived at the end of the 1930 season.

Transcendental Graphics

Ted Lyons

He was Luke Appling, a shortstop for Atlanta of the Southern Association. Appling started a bit more slowly than Reynolds, but he stayed longer (20 years with the White Sox) and set a number of records for American League shortstops, including the highest batting average for a season, .388 in 1936.

Charles Comiskey died in 1931. His son, J. Louis, took over the ball club. Although 1931 was a cellar-dwelling year for the White Sox, it was not their worst season during this barren era. That came in 1932, when the team lost 102 games under manager Lew Fonseca, finishing 56½ games back but, remarkably, not in last place, for the Boston Braves contrived to lose 111 games. Luke Appling led the Sox in RBIs with a modest 63.

Ted Lyons was the ace of the pitching staff with a 10-15 record and a 3.28 ERA. Obviously, these fellows needed some help. It did not arrive immediately. Meanwhile, the White Sox were

Transcendental Graphics

Luke Appling

losing fans to the nearby and relatively success-ful National League Cubs.

During the 1932 World Series, J. Louis Comiskey made an important deal with Connie Mack of the Philadelphia Athletics. The White Sox purchased third baseman Jimmy Dykes and out-fielders Mule Haas and Al Simmons. All three were quality players (Simmons was bound for the Hall of Fame), but the Sox still seemed to be bound for nowhere. Things began to improve, if only moderately, when Jimmy Dykes took over as manager in May 1934.

Dykes' won-lost record that season was 49-86, but the White Sox did have a few hitters. Al Simmons batted .344 with 18 homers and 104 RBIs. The new first baseman for the Sox, Zeke Bonura, hit .302 with 27 homers and 110 RBIs. Luke Appling, though no power hitter, checked in with .303. The pitching, by contrast, was abys-mal, as indicated by the staff's 5.41 ERA. Even Hall-of-Famer Ted Lyons could do no better than

11-13 with a 4.87 ERA.

The colorful, cigar-smoking, umpire-baiting Jimmy Dykes managed for 21 seasons in the ma-jors, never won a pennant, and never had a team finish higher than third. Yet he was considered an excellent skipper. His teams often did very well considering their middling talent.

The White Sox, under his tutelage, rose from the cellar in 1934 to fifth place in 1935, and then to third in 1936 and 1937. New outfielders Mike Kreevich and Rip Radcliff topped .300 both years. Pitcher Vern Kennedy surpassed all expectations in 1936, going 21-9. Zeke Bonura hit .330 in 1936 and drove in 138 runs. Luke Appling's .388 led the league, and his 128 RBIs contributed to the effort that finally lifted the White Sox out of the second division where they had been mired ever since the banning of the eight Black Sox players.

In 1937 Jimmy Dykes' partially revived team came in third again. Vern Kennedy tailed off to 14-13, but a young Texan, Monty Stratton, turned in a fine 15-5 record with a 2.40 ERA. Stratton went 15-9 in 1938, as the Sox fell to sixth place, but in the off-season the 26-year-old pitcher lost his leg in a freak hunting accident that ended his promising major league career and inspired a 1949 movie, *The Stratton Story,* starring Jimmy Stewart.

White Sox owner J. Lou Comiskey died on July 18, 1939, just before the first game of night baseball was played at Comiskey Park. The 1939 and 1940 teams had winning records, but they were good for only fourth place and a tie for fifth. Then in 1941 the Sox played even .500 ball, 77-77 and took third place.

Left-hander Thornton Lee, who had been with the club since 1937, posted a 22-11 won-lost record with a league-leading 2.27 ERA. Outfielder Taffy Wright, acquired the year before from the Washington Senators, put in an impressive year for the White Sox, batting .322 and driving in 97 runs.

Whether the team was truly improving, or whether Dykes's managerial skills were simply making things look better, became a moot ques-tion on December 7, 1941, when the Japanese bombed Pearl Harbor, and baseball went to war.

War and Losses

The tone was set on opening day, 1942, at Comiskey Park. A scant 9,879 fans showed up to watch the White Sox play the St. Louis Browns. The Browns won, 3-0. Ted Lyons was 41 years old; he pitched only on Sundays. Nonetheless, he won 14 games that year, lost six, and paced American League pitchers with a 2.10 ERA. The rest of the team did not fare quite as well.

Dykes, disgusted with their efforts, threatened to activate the coaching staff. "I'm serious about this. If my hitters don't show me something, you're going to see Dykes at third, Muddy Ruel behind the plate, Bing Miller and Mule Haas in the outfield." It remained just a threat, but the hitters never did show much. Neither did the pitchers. The Sox settled for sixth place.

They rose to fourth in 1943, fell to seventh in 1944, and edged up to sixth in 1945. What little stability there was on this wartime ball club came from Wally Moses in the outfield, Mike Tresh behind the plate, and a staff of struggling hurlers, among them Bill Dietrich, Orval Grove, and John Humphries. A promising young pitcher, Ed Lopat, arrived in 1944, but the front office under Grace Reidy Comiskey, hardly a font of baseball wisdom, traded Steady Eddie to the Yankees after the 1947 season.

Most teams welcomed back a few superstars from the military in 1946. However, with the exception of Luke Appling, who had gone off to war in 1944, there were no White Sox stars to take the place of the wartime players. Ted Lyons returned, but the ancient knuckle-baller was ineffective after the wartime layoff, going 1-4.

The team showed no improvement in 1946, and Jimmy Dykes quit as manager in late May. Ted Lyons seemed a logical man for the post, and he accepted it, perhaps foolishly, since the team needed a major transfusion more than a simple change of managers. The Sox dropped from fifth to sixth to eighth under Lyons, losing 101 games in 1948, 44½ games back.

They did little better under Lyons' replacement, Jack Onslow, a one-time catcher. The pitching staff showed glimmers of improvement, though. Left-hander Billy Pierce, 22 years old, came over from the Tigers. His record in 1949 was only 7-15, but he had many fine seasons ahead of him. Bob Kuzava also seemed to have a future, unlike young right-hander Howie Judson, who won a game against Detroit on April 21 and then proceeded to lose his next 14 decisions.

The batting star of 1949, until he broke his collarbone, was power-hitting outfielder Gus Zernial, up from Hollywood of the Pacific Coast League. Zernial would go on to hit 237 home runs in the majors, most of them for other teams since the Sox traded him after a couple of seasons.

Paul Richards and the Go-Go Sox

The dismal 1948 season had convinced the White Sox that a house-cleaning was in order. They fired general manager Les O'Connor and hired in his place Frank Lane, a highly regarded executive from the American Association. That same year Chuck Comiskey, a third generation White Sox owner, became an active participant in the ball club's fortunes. But it was the arrival in 1951 of manager Paul Richards, the "Wizard of Waxahachie," that really signaled the beginning of a new era in White Sox baseball.

Richards, an ex-catcher, worked his magic on the White Sox, turning them into a running, hustling ball club. This involved acquiring players who could run. One of these was the speedy Minnie Minoso, who came to the team in 1951 as part of the Gus Zernial trade. Minoso was a base stealer, leading the league in that category for three seasons in the early fifties.

Though they were not noted for stealing, the team did have some other spirited, aggressive ballplayers. Among them were second baseman Nellie Fox and shortstop Chico Carrasquel, both White Sox players since 1950.

A Richards-era acquisition with speed and base-stealing skill was outfielder Jim Rivera, who came over from the Browns in 1952. GM Frank Lane was known as "Trader" Lane, and the lineup

The 1959 World Series was the last postseason play for the Chicago White Sox in nearly a quarter of a century. Although the 1950s produced only one pennant, the decade is remembered by Sox fans as a kind of golden era, the period of the "Go-Go Sox." The team was exciting, with Chico Carrasquel and then Luis Aparicio at shortstop and as leadoff hitters. Nellie Fox was a fixture at second base after 1950. For most of the 1950s catcher Sherm Lollar and outfielder Minnie Minoso supplied what limited power there was at the plate. Jungle Jim Rivera put in eight seasons in the outfield. Other players came and went. The Go-Go Sox never had a steady third baseman, although Bubba Phillips had four good years, starting in 1956.

The Go-Go Sox were not hitless wonders—most of the regulars had respectable batting averages. Minnie Minoso's career mark was .298, for example, while Nellie Fox's was .288 and Hall-of-Famer Luis Aparicio's was .262. Still, there was one remarkable game against the Kansas City Athletics in 1959 that produced these astonishing totals after a seventh-inning Sox rally: 11 runs, 1 hit, and 3 errors. Left-fielder Johnny Callison got the only hit, as K.C. pitchers issued walk after walk and received less than scintillating support when the Sox batters did occasionally put the ball in play. Chicago won the game, 20-6. During the Go-Go years, the Sox got fine pitching from such hurlers as Billy Pierce, Sol Rogovin, Virgil Trucks, and Dick Donovan. Early Wynn and Bob Shaw, 22-10 and 18-6, were the top pitchers on the 1959 pennant-winning team.

Despite the team's clear strengths and fine record (in the shadow of the mighty Yankees), owner Bill Veeck spent the late 1950s trying to add some power hitters to the lineup. Specifically, he wanted Roy Sievers of the Senators and Ted Kluszewski, a Cincinnati veteran most recently with Pittsburgh. He got them, and changed the nature of the ball club. The sluggers brought no pennants to Comiskey Park, however. Throughout the 1960s and 1970s the White Sox were in contention a number of times, but not until 1983 (and again in 1993) did they finally climb back to the top.

of the Sox showed frequent changes during his tenure.

But the "go-go" was always there. Paul Richards' teams were consistent winners (although not pennant winners), finishing fourth in 1951, and third in each of the next three years. The premier pitcher during the Richards' era was Billy Pierce, whose best seasons were yet to come.

Before long Paul Richards and Frank Lane had run-ins with the Comiskeys—Richards argued with Grace, Lane with Chuck—and by the end of the 1955 season both were gone. The new manager, Marty Marion, kept the team in third place in 1955 and 1956, but the Comiskeys wanted a pennant, not third place, and they replaced Slats with the Cleveland Indians' miracle manager, Al Lopez.

Señor Lopez proved that his Cleveland suc-cess was no fluke. With the great Luis Aparicio replacing Carrasquel at shortstop and pitchers Dick Donovan, Billy Pierce, and Jim Wilson all having banner years, the White Sox moved into second place in 1957. The next year, newly acquired Hall-of-Fame pitcher Early Wynn lost more games than he won (14-16), but steady catcher Sherm Lollar upped his RBI total to 84, Nellie Fox led the league in hits (187) for the fourth time, and the Sox once again finished second.

Most sportswriters doubted that Al Lopez could push this good second-place team past the consistent pennant-winning Yankees in 1959. They knew he had accomplished such a feat with Cleveland in 1954, but they doubted that the Go-Go White Sox had sufficient power at the plate to unseat the Yankees with Mantle, Berra, and Howard.

If the 1959 pennant race surprised many people, so did the preseason brouhaha in which the feuding Comiskeys (Chuck's sister Dorothy owned 54 percent of the stock) gave Bill Veeck an opportunity to seize control of the Sox, which he promptly took. With sensationalist Veeck in charge, White Sox fans knew that cow milking contests, the reappearance of Eddie Gaedel (leading a Martian invasion), and other such promotional stunts would not be far behind.

One such promo was Al Smith night, intended to raise the spirits of the slumping left fielder. Any fan with the name Smith or a variation thereon (Schmidt, Smythe, etc.) was admitted free. With the stands thus full of his cheering namesakes, Al Smith dropped a fly ball, handing the Boston Red Sox a 7-6 victory.

The Yankees would win five more pennants in a row after 1959, but in 1959 they slumped badly. The White Sox's Early Wynn, in his nineteenth year in the majors, won 22 games, lost 10, and paced the team to a fairly easy first-place finish. The runners-up were not the Yankees but the Indians. Luis Aparicio stole 56 bases, Nellie Fox batted .306, and Sherm Lollar drove in a team-leading 84 runs once more. On the mound a former Tiger, Bob Shaw, had his best season ever, going 18-6 with a 2.69 ERA.

The Sox had no real sluggers during most of the season—Sherm Lollar's 22 homers led the ball club—but they had that go-go spirit. It carried them to the pennant but not to the World Championship. Los Angeles had won in the National League, and despite the best efforts of White Sox first baseman Ted Kluszewski, a late season acquisition from Pittsburgh, the Dodgers prevailed, four games to two. Big Klu, a slugger rather than a go-go player, slammed three homers and drove in ten runs in the Sox's losing battle against the remnants of the Dodgers' "boys of summer."

From Go-Go to So-So

Al Lopez had taken his team to the pennant as he had in Cleveland five years earlier, but this

Transcendental Graphics

Luis Aparicio

time the miracle had no encore. The Yankees were still the Yankees, and in 1960 the White Sox were relegated to third place. Over the winter Bill Veeck had added some power to the lineup, most notably first baseman Roy Sievers from the Senators and third baseman Gene Freese from the Phillies. Minnie Minoso was back after two years at Cleveland, and he, along with Sievers, proved to be the strength of the offense on this older, slower ball club.

The White Sox slipped to fourth in 1961 and fifth in 1962, but then experienced a mini-revival, still under manager Lopez, finishing second in 1963, 1964, and 1965. Bill Veeck was gone, having sold out when the team fell to last place in 1961. Chuck Comiskey was gone, having sold his minority share six months after Veeck's departure.

By 1963 only Nellie Fox was an on-field survivor of the 1959 pennant-winning White Sox regulars. Ron Hansen was trying, with limited success, to fill Luis Aparicio's shoes at shortstop. Tom McCraw, a career .246 hitter, was at first base. Pete

Ward, who started well for the Sox in 1963 and then faded in later years, held down third base. The outfield was negligible except for native Chicagoan Floyd Robinson, who put in seven good seasons for the Sox.

The three mainstays on the mound were Gary Peters, a 20-game winner in 1964; Juan Pizarro, 19-9 the same year; and Joe Horlen, 19-7 three years later. Al Lopez, complaining of a stomach ailment, resigned as manager in November 1965, and Eddie (The Brat) Stanky took over the reins.

Through 1967 the Sox stayed above .500, even though they finished in fourth place in Stanky's two seasons. Then they came unglued, hitting bottom in 1970 under a trio of managers. Divisional play (instituted the previous year) made sixth place the cellar, and the Sox's 56-106 record assured them of dwelling there.

The most familiar name in the regular lineup, regularly revamped during the skid, was Luis Aparicio, back at shortstop for the Sox after five seasons with the Orioles. Little Looie's .303 batting average led the team. On the mound in that grim year were a couple of capable pitchers with poor records, Tommy John (12-17), a White Sox staffer since 1965, and Wilbur Wood (9-13), a man about to turn his career around with four straight 20-win seasons.

As the 1970 season wound down, Chuck Tanner, who was distinguished mainly by having hit a home run in his first major league at-bat, was called upon to manage. His 3-13 record that year was ascribed to fate, and Tanner returned to guide the destiny of the Sox for the next five seasons.

Tanner's Tenure and Beyond

Chuck Tanner inherited a team with some strengths but many weaknesses. Over the winter of 1970-71 the White Sox's new GM, Roland Hemond, tried hard to improve the caliber of the team. Among his many acquisitions were second baseman Mike Andrews, pitcher Tom Bradley, and outfielders, Rick Reicherdt, Jay Johnstone, and Pat Kelly. The White Sox rose from the basement

Transcendental Graphics

Early Wynn

to third place. Wilbur Wood posted a 22-13 record with a 1.91 ERA. Third baseman Bill Melton, a four-year veteran of the Sox, led the league in homers with 33 and the team in RBIs with 86.

The White Sox challenged mighty Oakland late in the 1972 season in a campaign dominated by newly acquired superstar outfielder Dick Allen (.308 batting average, 37 home runs, 113 RBIs) and tireless knuckleballer Wilbur Wood (24-17, ERA 2.51). Reliever Terry Forster, in his second year, registered 29 saves. Allen, for whom the Sox, wisely or unwisely, had given up pitcher Tommy John, won the American League MVP Award, as Chicago finished a strong second to Dick Williams' Oakland A's.

They tailed off to fifth in 1973, fourth in 1974, and fifth in 1975. Veteran pitcher Jim Kaat, who came to the Sox in midseason 1973, chalked up a 21-13 mark in 1974 and 20-14 in 1975. In 1974 Dick Allen again took the AL home run title with 32 round-trippers. By 1975 Goose Gossage was coming into his own as an intimidating relief

---

Comiskey Park II

Starting in 1986 a great debate raged about what to do, or not do, about Comiskey Park. The stadium was structurally unsound and could not be repaired. There was talk of moving the franchise to St. Petersburg. There was talk of building a new stadium in Addison, a western suburb of Chicago.

Finally, a plan was developed to construct Comiskey Park II, a new facility across the street from the grand old South Side stadium. A bill to fund construction for the new ballpark passed the Illinois state legislature on June 30, 1988, by the narrow margin of 90 to 81.

Ground for the new stadium was broken on May 7, 1989, and the White Sox played their last game at Comiskey Park I on September 30, 1990. They played their first game at Comiskey Park II on April 18, 1991.

---

pitcher. But none of these individual achievements were enough to save Chuck Tanner's job. The Sox decided to gamble on old Paul Richards' managerial skills in 1976.

The Richards' magic was gone—not to mention Bill Melton and Jim Kaat. In their place the White Sox had signed first baseman Jim Spencer and outfielder Ralph Garr, among others. An undistinguished crew, the 1976 Sox finished last.

Bob Lemon replaced Paul Richards at the helm, and the 1977 team, with the addition of third baseman Eric Soderholm and outfielders Oscar Gamble and Richie Zisk, fought back throughout July and early August. The 1976 team leaders in home runs, Jim Spencer and Jorge Orta, had belted 14 apiece. In 1977 half the team did better than that: Oscar Gamble (31), Richie Zisk (30), Eric Soderholm (25), Chet Lemon (19), Lamar Johnson (18), Jim Spencer (18). This was quite a show of power, the exact opposite of the old go-go game of the 1950s. It almost paid off, but the Kansas City Royals and, surprisingly enough, the Texas Rangers finished ahead of the White Sox in the AL West that year.

The 1978 season did not go well at all. The Sox retreated to fifth place, and in midseason Larry Doby, a coach for the team, became the second black manager in the majors (he had also been the second black major league player, after Jackie Robinson). Don Kessinger, until then an active shortstop, was tapped to lead the 1979 effort, but he had his troubles, seemed to be miscast as a manager, stepped down, and 35-year-old Tony LaRussa saw the Sox through to another fifth-place finish.

There'll Always Be a Comiskey

The 1980s began with the White Sox about to rise up and Comiskey Park about to come down. The new skipper, Tony LaRussa, had shown his managerial skills at Knoxville in the Southern League and Iowa in the American Association, but in the majors he was better known as a part-time, weak-hitting infielder. That would soon change—but not in 1980.

The Sox boasted a few good players (Chet Lemon and Harold Baines in the outfield, for example) and a few promising pitchers (such as Rich Dotson and LaMarr Hoyt), but there were some holes, too. The team needed a first-rate catcher, for one thing. The 1980 White Sox finished at 70-90, in fifth place, 26 games back of league-leading K.C.

In the strike-shortened split season of 1981 LaRussa's White Sox, with old Red Sox pro Carlton Fisk now behind the plate, played solid baseball but failed to make the AL West Division Playoff. During the off-season the Sox picked up veteran outfielders Steve Kemp from Detroit and Tom Paciorek from Seattle.

The team finished third in 1982 with an 87-75 record. Designated hitter Greg Luzinski, purchased from the Phillies, paced the team in batting at .292, while Harold Baines led in homers with 25, and LaMarr Hoyt topped all AL pitchers in wins with 19. In December the Sox signed free-agent Seattle hurler Floyd Bannister to add to their impressive array of pitchers.

Wide World Photos

Carlton Fisk

The 1983 White Sox clinched the AL West championship on September 17 and went on to pile up a 20-game lead over second place Kansas City, the greatest margin of victory in league history. The record 2,132,821 fans who passed through the turnstiles at Comiskey Park were amply rewarded. The sportswriters called it "Winning Ugly," but ugly or not, the Sox's 99-63 record was their best since 1917.

Slugging outfielder Ron Kittle, up from Edmonton in the PCL, slammed 35 homers and drove in 100 runs to win AL Rookie of the Year honors. Harold Baines contributed 99 RBIs, Greg Luzinski 95, and Carlton Fisk 86. LaMarr Hoyt won 24 games to lead the league and take the Cy Young Award. Rich Dotson's 22-7 record and Floyd Bannister's 16-10 were their best efforts ever.

Good/ugly as the Sox were, only LaMarr Hoyt, with a five-hit, 2-1, victory, prevailed against the AL East champion Baltimore Orioles in the American League Championship Series. Floyd Bannister, Rich Dotson, and Britt Burns suffered successive defeats as the Sox scored only three runs in the entire four-game series. Baltimore went on to beat the Phillies in the World Series.

High hopes came to naught in 1984. The team looked about the same as in the previous year except for what on paper seemed to be some possible improvements—rookies Greg Walker at first base and Scott Fletcher at shortstop; the canny if aging Tom Seaver on the mound. But the on-paper prospects turned to ashes in the face of on-field reality, and the Sox plummeted to a fifth-place tie with the usually nonthreatening Seattle Mariners.

They bounced up to third in the standings in 1985, only six games back, with Harold Baines, Carlton Fisk, Greg Walker, and Ron Kittle leading the attack, albeit with modest batting averages (except for Baines' .309). The aces of the mound staff were Britt Burns, 18-11, and Tom Seaver, who finished at 16-11.

American League Central

The next three seasons, 1986-88, saw three fifth-place finishes. Tony LaRussa gave way to Jim Fregosi, who departed after the 1988 season in favor of Jeff Torborg. After a last-place finish in 1989, Torborg's White Sox made a strong comeback, all the way to second place, in 1990. Torborg left to join the Mets after the season ended, but his replacement, Gene Lamont, guided the team to two more second-place finishes.

A number of good young ballplayers came aboard in the early 1990s, among them first baseman Frank Thomas, third baseman Robin Ventura, and pitchers Jack McDowell and Roberto Hernandez. Another addition to the team was former Toronto Blue Jays outfielder George Bell.

Paced by the offensive onslaught of Bell, Frank "The Big Hurt" Thomas (41 home runs, 128 RBIs, .317) and Lance Johnson, whose 14 triples led the majors (.311 with 35 stolen bases), the 1993 White Sox coasted to a divisional title with a 94-68 record. Despite an ALCS playoff loss to Toronto, the team's strong, consistent play bodes well for the future.

SOURCES

BOOKS

Asinof, Eliot, *Eight Men Out: The Black Sox and the 1919 World Series,* New York: Holt, Rinehart and Winston, 1963.

Baseball Guide: 1980, 1987, 1991, 1992 Editions, St. Louis: The Sporting News Publishing Co., 1980, 1987, 1991, 1992.

Baseball Register: 1965, 1980, 1992 Editions, St. Louis: The Sporting News Publishing Co., 1965, 1980, 1991.

Brown, Warren W., *The Chicago White Sox,* New York: G. P. Putnam's Sons, 1952.

Ivor-Campbell, Frederick, "Team Histories: Chicago White Sox," *Total Baseball,* edited by John Thorn and Pete Palmer, New York: Warner Books, 1989.

Lindberg, Richard C., *Sox: The Complete Record of Chicago White Sox Baseball,* New York: Macmillan Publishing Company, 1984.

Lindberg, Richard C., *Who's on Third?: The Chicago White Sox Story,* South Bend, IN: Icarus Press, 1983.

Lindberg, Richard C., "Chicago White Sox: Second Class in the Second City." *Encyclopedia of Major League Baseball Team Histories: American League,* edited by Peter C. Bjarkman., Westport, CT: Meckler, 1991.

Mayer, Ronald A., *Perfect!: Biographies and Lifetime Statistics of 14 Pitchers of "Perfect" Baseball Games with Summaries and Boxscores,* Jefferson, NC: McFarland & Company, 1991.

Murdock, Eugene C., *Ban Johnson: Czar of Baseball,* Westport, CT: Greenwood Press, 1982.

Reichler, Joseph L., ed., *The Baseball Encyclopedia,* 7th ed., New York: Macmillan Publishing Company, 1988.

Thorn, John, and John Holway, *The Pitcher,* New York: Prentice Hall Press, 1987.

Veeck, Bill, with Ed Linn, *Veeck, as in Wreck,* New York: G. P. Putnam's Sons, 1962.

PERIODICALS

Baseball America, December 25, 1992-January 9, 1993.

Baseball Digest, October 1979.

Baseball Research Journal, 1975.

Sports Illustrated, October 17, 1983.

—*Gerald Tomlinson* for Book Builders, Inc.

CLEVELAND INDIANS

Once every generation or so, the Cleveland Indians win an American League pennant. Or at least they did through 1954. Since then the Indians have been unable to finish higher than second in the standings. Indeed, since 1968 they have never managed to come in better than fourth. Their seasons in the shadows have naturally kept attendance down, which was especially noticeable in Cleveland's cavernous lakefront ballpark, Cleveland (or Municipal) Stadium, whose seating capacity of 74,483 far exceeded that of any other major league facility. (The team opened its new stadium at the start of the 1994 season.)

Despite their difficulties, however, the Cleveland Indians (often called "the Tribe") are one of only four original American League franchises that have stayed in the same city continuously since the league's founding in 1901.

The Tribe's first real shot at an American League pennant came in 1908 under player-manager Napoleon (Larry, Nap) Lajoie. Led by ace pitcher Addie Joss and first baseman George Stovall, with Lajoie at second base, the team finished just half a game behind the Detroit Tigers, the margin resulting from a rained-out Detroit game that was not made up.

The Indians then settled back into mediocrity, albeit with a few fine players, until the World War I era, when a new owner and a new player-manager, Tris Speaker, put together several second-and third-place finishes around the big year, 1920, when the Indians won it all. The Tribe would come very close to winning again in 1921, 1926, and 1940, but not until 1948 did the coveted pennant once more fly in Cleveland, when another great player-manager, Lou Boudreau, led the way. The Tribe beat out the powerful Red Sox and Yankees and went on to take the World Series from the Boston Braves.

Throughout the 1950s, Cleveland had solid, contending ball clubs under manager Al Lopez. In a sense this was a golden age for the Indians, though dimmed annually (except in 1954) by Casey Stengel's indomitable New York Yankees. In 1954 the Tribe won 111 games, more than any American League team before or since, in overmatching the powerhouse Yanks. But then they fell to the New York Giants, four games to none, in the World Series.

The 1960s brought little happiness to Cleveland fans. Ditto for the 1970s and 1980s. For three decades, through the whole era of expansion and free-agency, the Tribe plodded through a succession of so-so seasons, seldom as truly terrible as the last-place 1991 Indians (57-105), but never better than the third-place 1968 team (86-75). Dedicated Cleveland fans became history buffs out of necessity, focusing mainly on the great days of 1920, 1948, and 1954.

The Lajoie Reign

The Forest City (a nickname that often puzzles outsiders) boasts plenty of baseball history and tradition, going back to the nineteenth-century Cleveland Spiders. But the history of the Cleveland Indians begins with the first game ever played in the American League—on April 14, 1901—Cleveland vs. Chicago, a game the White Sox won in extra innings.

American League baseball came to Cleveland when Ban Johnson, the founder of the circuit, approached local industrialist Charles A. Somers about bankrolling a ball club. Somers liked the idea, and the Cleveland Blues were born. They were not an immediate success on the field, finishing seventh in 1901 and fifth in 1902, the year Napoleon Lajoie came over from the Philadelphia Athletics.

So popular an acquisition was second baseman Lajoie that the team was renamed the Naps in 1903, a season in which the club's new namesake hit .355 to lead the league. The Naps finished a respectable (but distant) third that year. In 1904 Lajoie became player-manager, and, although his team slid to fourth, its won-lost record (86-65) showed that it had potential. In fact, the Naps were

in contention for much of the decade, challenging the leaders in 1906 and 1907, then coming within a whisker of taking the pennant in 1908.

These early Cleveland teams featured some genuine stars besides Lajoie. Nap was the lodestar, of course—a future Hall-of-Famer, batting .368, .355, and .381 in his first three seasons with the team and fielding, as always, with grace and consistency. Playing third base from 1901 to 1910 was Bill Bradley, who turned in his best season in 1902, when he batted .340 and tied for second in home run production with 11. George Stovall, a steady hitter without much power, held down first base from 1904 to 1911.

A Hall of Fame outfielder, Elmer Flick, toiled for the Blues/Naps from 1902 to 1910. He compiled a lifetime batting average of .315, winning both the batting and slugging titles in 1905. Flick, fleet of foot, stole between 24 and 42 bases each year.

On the mound from 1902 to 1910 was right-hander Addie Joss, whose lifetime 1.88 ERA is the second lowest ever. Joss won 160 games and lost only 97 in his career with Cleveland. Another pitcher of note during the years 1903 to 1909 was Bob (Dusty) Rhodes, 22-10 with a 1.80 ERA in his best season, 1906.

Everything seemed to come together for Cleveland in 1908. They won 90 games—the most for a Cleveland team until 1920—and lost 64. Joss (24-11, ERA 1.16) and Bob Rhodes (18-12, ERA 1.77) had superb seasons; little Heinie Berger, also a right-hander, chipped in with a 13-8 mark, the only winning season of his brief career; George Stovall had his best year, batting .292. But it was pitching that carried the day (or almost carried it).

Lajoie put in a subpar year at .289, as did third baseman Bill Bradley at .243 and catcher Nig Clarke at .241. (Clarke, by the way, is probably best known for his phenomenal day at bat in the Texas League in 1902, when, as a 19-year-old kid playing for Corsicana, he blasted eight home runs in eight times at bat as Corsicana buried Texarkana 51-3.)

On October 2, 1908, Addie Joss took the

TEAM INFORMATION AT A GLANCE

Founding date: April 14, 1901

Home stadium (until 1994): Cleveland Stadium
Boudreau Boulevard and Lake Erie
Cleveland, OH 44114

Home stadium, 1994—
Indians Park
2401 Ontario
Cleveland, OH 44115
Phone: (216) 861-1200

Team uniforms: Home—base color white, with dark blue and red trim
Road—base color gray, with dark blue and red trim
Team nickname: Blues, 1901-1902; Naps, 1903-1914; Indians, 1915—
Logo: Caricature of red-faced Indian with broad smile
and one red feather sticking up at back of head.

Franchise record	Won	Lost	Pct.
(1901-1993)	7,269	7,125	.505

World Series wins (2): 1920, 1948
American League championships (3): 1920, 1948, 1954

mound at League Park, Cleveland, against Chicago's Ed Walsh. It was a crucial game for the Naps. Walsh, who won 40 games that year, pitched a classy four-hitter and struck out 15. But Joss did even better, retiring 27 batters in a row, a perfect game.

The last Chicago batter, pinch-hitter John Anderson, sent a screaming line drive down the left-field line that curved foul at the last moment. He then hit a sharp grounder toward Bill Bradley, who was playing deep at third base. Bradley took the ball behind the bag and threw low to first base. George Stovall scooped it out of the dirt for the final out, ending the high drama and preserving Joss's perfect game—the fourth one in major league history.

The Naps seemed to have the pennant clinched, but they faltered at the finish, losing their last games to the White Sox and the St. Louis Browns and fading to second place.

Nap Plays, Others Manage

No one except Lajoie improved in 1909, and the Naps fell all the way to fifth place. Lajoie, who hit .324, felt that the burden of managing was hurting his play. In mid-season he surrendered the managerial reins to Deacon McGuire, a veteran catcher who had broken in with Toledo way back in 1884. McGuire had little success with the Naps, overseeing two fifth-place finishes before getting the ax early in the 1911 season.

Plenty happened while he was in charge, though. At the end of the 1910 season, Nap Lajoie and Ty Cobb were locked in a tight race for the batting title. On the last day of the season, the Naps played the Browns, and Lajoie went eight-for-eight—seven of his eight hits being bunts—as the Browns' third baseman continued to play too deep to field them. Cobb won the title anyway, by a microscopic .0007.

Years later *The Sporting News* proved beyond doubt that Lajoie did in fact outhit Cobb in 1910, but baseball commissioner Bowie Kuhn, invoking a kind of statute of limitations, refused to sanction changing the record books.

The 1910 season was notable for Cleveland in two other ways. They acquired 42-year-old Cy Young, the winningest pitcher of all time, from the Boston Red Sox, and the cagey old right-hander posted a 19-15 record for his new team, with a 2.26 ERA. It was his last winning season. They also acquired Shoeless Joe Jackson from the Philadelphia Athletics, a youngster who had played only ten games in the majors at that point but seemed a likely prospect.

Tragedy struck in 1911. Addie Joss, 30 years old, came down with spinal meningitis and died on April 14, two days after his 31st birthday. The loss hurt the Naps, although it seems doubtful that Cleveland would have had a contending team even with him. Seventeen games into the 1911 season, Deacon McGuire gave way to playing-manager George Stovall, who led the team to a third-place finish.

Two seasons later, under manager Joe Birmingham, they finished third again, and some thought they were on the road to contention. In addition to Lajoie and Shoeless Joe Jackson, the Naps had a couple of promising newcomers: shortstop Ray Chapman and catcher Steve O'Neill. On the mound were 20-game winners Cy Falkenberg (23-10) and Vean Gregg (20-13). But the dream turned to dust in 1914, as Falkenberg jumped to the new Federal League, Gregg was dealt to the Red Sox in mid-season, Lajoie's and Jackson's batting averages nosedived, and the team plummeted to the cellar.

That winter, Lajoie, who was nearing the end of his career, was released by Cleveland and picked up by the Philadelphia A's. During the 1915 campaign, Jackson was traded to the Chicago White Sox.

Pursuit of the Pennant

With Napoleon Lajoie playing for Philadelphia, the folks in Cleveland could hardly continue to call their team the Naps. It happened that Louis Sockalexis, an outfielder for the old Cleveland Spiders, had died in 1913. He was thought to be the first Native American to play major league baseball, so to honor him the team was renamed the Indians in 1915.

The new Indians were not mighty warriors. They finished seventh in 1915 and sixth in 1916. But a brighter day was about to dawn, heralded by the arrival of The Gray Eagle—Tris Speaker. Speaker was one of the best center fielders of his day, or any day.

Speaker's brilliant fielding complemented but did not overshadow his hitting. In his first year with the Indians, 1916, he led the league in batting at .386 (ending Ty Cobb's string at nine straight) and in slugging at .502. He also led in doubles, the third of eight times he would lead the league in that category.

In addition to Speaker, the Indians signed two significant new pitchers in 1916. One, Stan Coveleski, would eventually go to the Hall of Fame. The other, Jim Bagby, would put in half a dozen fine seasons for the Tribe.

In 1917 the team, under third-year manager Lee Fohl, jumped to third place, and in 1918 improved to second, only 2½ games behind the Red Sox. In 1919 they hung onto second place, this time 3½ games behind the pennant-winning White (or Black) Sox. Lee Fohl resigned in mid-season and was replaced by Tris Speaker, who continued to play center field while managing.

The 1919 season saw the addition of two more key players, outfielder Charlie Jamieson, a

| PROFILE | **Nap Lajoie: Baseball's First Superstar** |

The great figures of the game's early days, the stars of the dead-ball era, tend to be remembered today only as names or as black-and-white photographic images from the distant past. Napoleon (Nap) Lajoie is such a figure. But Lajoie, like the others, was a real person and a fascinating one. At the age of ten, he worked in a Rhode Island mill. He played sandlot ball and semipro ball. Offered a pro tryout, he was signed by the Fall River club of the New England League. His smooth fielding and .429 batting average (163 hits in 80 games) attracted the attention of the Phillies, for whom he played from 1896 to 1902, when in mid-season he was acquired by Cleveland.

He was, as J. M. Murphy says in the subtitle of his biography of Lajoie, "modern baseball's first superstar." In 1901 for Philadelphia the six-foot-one-inch second baseman led the league in almost everything: runs (145), hits (229), doubles (48), home runs (13), batting average (.422), and fielding average for second basemen (.963). No wonder the dazzled fans of Cleveland wanted their team called the "Naps."

Lajoie played for his namesake team for all or part of 13 seasons, managing it for five of those years. When he hung up his spikes in 1918 (his last two seasons were with Toronto and Indianapolis in the minor leagues), his lifetime major league batting average was .339, and he was the third player ever to collect 3,000 hits. He hit with commanding power in that dead-ball era. Hall-of-Fame pitcher Cy Young, looking back on the early days, said of Lajoie, "He'd take your leg off with a line drive.... Lajoie was the Babe Ruth of our day.... The kids followed him around, just as they hung after Ruth. He had color. He was great, old Nap."

Photo: *Transcendental Graphics*

.303 lifetime hitter, and pitcher Ray Caldwell, who would have a career season in 1920, then fade away. Jamieson, by contrast, continued to star for the Indians for nearly 15 years.

The 1919 Chicago Black Sox scandal—which involved allegations of game-fixing in the World Series—did not seriously affect the 1920 pennant race. Many of the World Series culprits—Swede Risberg, Happy Felsch, Eddie Cicotti, Lefty Williams—were still playing for the White Sox, and Chicago and New York remained the teams to beat. In 1920 the Indians beat them.

On August 16, with Cleveland leading the league by a few percentage points, the Yanks hosted the Indians at the Polo Grounds in New York. Carl Mays, the Yankees' submarineball right-hander, was on the mound when Cleveland's veteran shortstop Ray Chapman led off the fifth inning, crowding the plate, as always, leaning in to challenge the pitcher. Mays uncorked a fastball that hit Chapman in the left temple and rebounded like a batted ball. Chapman fell to the ground unconscious, his skull fractured. He died the next morning, the only player ever killed in a

Tris Speaker: The Gray Eagle

Called "Spoke" by his teammates, Tristram (Tris) Speaker, like Nap Lajoie, split his major league career between two ball clubs. He began in 1906 as a left-handed pitcher for the Cleburne team of the North Texas League. When Cleburne's right fielder fractured his cheek, the brash young Spoke announced that he was also an outfielder. And indeed he was. The Boston Red Sox picked him up in 1908, where he played through 1915. Traded to Cleveland, he put in one of the best seasons of his career in 1916.

Although Speaker's lifetime batting average, .344, puts him seventh on the all-time list, the Gray Eagle (called that because of his prematurely gray hair), is perhaps more often cited for his fielding. He played an amazingly shallow center field—possible for the speedy Spoke in the dead-ball era—and made unassisted double plays on short flies. He even did it once in a World Series game, the only player to do so. He sometimes acted as the pivot man on short-to-second-to-first double plays, playing the second baseman's part, and he was known to take pickoff throws from the pitcher. You might think he would give up a lot of extra base hits in functioning as a fifth infielder, but no. He was fast enough, and could react quickly enough, to get back on the sort of fly balls a center fielder is expected to handle. Speaker was inducted into the Baseball Hall of Fame in 1937.

Photo: *Transcendental Graphics*

major league baseball game. Two games were postponed—the one the next day and the one scheduled for the day of Chapman's funeral in Cleveland.

Stunned and weakened, the Indians brought up Joe Sewell from New Orleans to replace Chapman at shortstop. Sewell stayed with the Indians for 11 years and proved an asset right from the start, batting .329 for the 22 games he played in 1920.

On September 28 of that year a Chicago grand jury indicted eight members of the Chicago White Sox, who were immediately suspended for the World Series scandal. The Sox lost two of their last three games. This turn of events worked to the advantage of the Indians, who won both of theirs, with Ray Caldwell posting his 20th win on October 1 and Jim Bagby winning his 31st (to lead the league) the next day.

After two decades of play, the Cleveland Indians had finally captured their first pennant. Over in the National League, Brooklyn won the pennant, and in the best-of-nine World Series (the second of three such Series) the Indians prevailed, five games to two against Wilbert Robinson's Dodgers.

Stan Coveleski, 24-14 for the regular season, won three of those games, with an impressive

Series ERA of .067. The batting stars were Tris Speaker, Steve O'Neill, Charlie Jamieson, and outfielder Elmer Smith, who unloaded the first World Series grand slam home run. The fielding star was second baseman Bill Wambganss, who turned the only unassisted triple play in Series history.

The talented Tribe failed to repeat in 1921, although they finished a close second to Miller Huggins's Yankees. Third baseman Larry Gardner led the team in RBIs with 115. Indeed, Gardner, who is not much remembered anymore, led the Indians in RBIs for three straight years after his acquisition from the Philadelphia A's, driving in 79 runs in 1919 and 118 in 1920. Tris Speaker hit .368 in 1921, down from .382 the previous year. Stan Coveleski breezed along with a 23-13 record, but Jim Bagby dropped to 14-12 and Ray Caldwell to 6-6. Right-hander George Uhle, a 22-year-old native of Cleveland, picked up some of the slack with a 16-13 mark.

Transcendental Graphics

Stan Coveleski

Finishing Fourth

Under managers Lee Fohl and Tris Speaker—and under the ownership of Jim Dunn, who bought the ball club in 1916—the Indians enjoyed considerable success. In 1922 (the year Dunn died), however, they skidded to fourth; except for a good run in 1926, Speaker's last year as manager, they did not contend again, despite some respectable won-lost totals, until 1940.

Future Hall-of-Famers Tris Speaker and Joe Sewell continued to star, Speaker through 1926, Sewell through 1930, as did Charlie Jamieson, but the Indians' pitching declined in the late 1920s. Stan Coveleski, a mainstay headed for the Hall of

---

Game 5 of the 1920 World Series

The Baseball Encyclopedia calls the fifth game of the 1920 World Series "strange and memorable." Why so? For three reasons. First off: The New York Giants' spitballer Burleigh Grimes loaded the bases in the first inning. Up came Cleveland outfielder Elmer Smith, who had had a pretty fair season, batting .316 with a .520 slugging percentage. Smith saw a pitch he liked and unloaded the first grand-slam home run in World Series history.

Secondly: In the fourth inning, with two men on base, Cleveland pitcher Jim Bagby, a lifetime .218 hitter (with a regular-season career total of two home runs) belted a homer of his own—the first pitcher ever to hit one out in a World Series. It was a three-run shot and gave the Tribe a 7-0 lead.

The third incident was the most memorable of all: In the fifth inning—with Giants' runners at first and second—the batter, New York relief pitcher Clarence Mitchell, lined a drive toward center. Indians' second baseman Bill Wambganss caught the ball, stepped on second to double-off Pete Kilduff who had broken for third, then tagged out Otto Miller chugging in from first. It was the first and only unassisted triple play in World Series history. It made an instant hero and a long-term trivia question out of Bill Wambganss.

Fame, began to fade and was traded to the Washington Senators after the 1924 season. George Uhle had his ups and downs. So did Joe Shaute, a left-hander for the Tribe from 1922 to 1930.

The signing of right-handers Mel Harder and Wes Ferrell in the late 1920s seemed to augur prosperity for the thirties, but as the mound staff improved, the regular lineup seemed to deteriorate. Infielders came and went. One who came, stayed, and did very well, however, was first baseman Hal Trosky. In his first full season, 1934, Trosky collected 206 hits, including 45 doubles and 35 home runs. He scored 117 runs, drove in 142, and batted .330. Few players ever had a better rookie season. Trosky played for Cleveland until World War II. His best season, after that phenomenal rookie year, was 1936, when he drove in 162 runs to top Lou Gehrig and Jimmie Foxx.

There were two bright spots in the outfield, too. One was Earl Averill, who batted .331 as a rookie for the Indians in 1929. The "Earl of Snohomish" (nicknamed for his hometown in Washington) starred for Cleveland until 1939, putting up Hall-of-Fame numbers. Joe Vosmik joined the club as a regular outfielder two years later. Vosmik had a few great years, his best being 1935 when he batted .348, and led the league in hits (216), doubles (47), and triples (20). The Indians finished third that year, which was also one of Mel Harder's most successful. He won 22 games and lost 11.

League Park, called Dunn Field from 1916 to 1927, was home to the Indians from 1910 until July 1932. It was still a good ballpark in 1932, but Cleveland had decided to try to lure the Summer Olympic Games to the shores of Lake Erie. They laid plans for an enormous, circular stadium on the lakefront, a multipurpose facility seating upwards of 78,000 and intended mainly for track and field. Cleveland built it, but they (the Olympics) did not come.

It fell to the Indians to inherit the stadium—and for their fans to feel generally lost in it—until 1934 when once again they began to play all games except those on Sundays and holidays at smaller, more intimate League Park. That arrangement lasted until 1939 when lights were installed in Cleveland Stadium, making it the Indians' night-game ballpark as well. Finally, in 1947, the stadium by the lake became, and remained until 1994, the full-time, outsized home ballpark of the Indians.

There were four principal managers of the Indians in the late twenties and thirties. Roger Peckinpaugh took over in 1928 and lasted five-and-a-half seasons. An ex-shortstop, Peckinpaugh oversaw teams that were reasonably good but not good enough. Walter Johnson, the Big Train, replaced him 51 games into the 1933 season.

Johnson, a better pitcher than manager, also had limited success and gave way in 1935 to Steve O'Neill, the Tribe's old catcher. O'Neill, like his predecessors, delivered mostly fourth and fifth places finishes and, like them, got the hook. Oscar (Ossie) Vitt became the Indians' skipper in 1938, the year after managing a team that is reputed to have been the best ever in minor league baseball: the 1937 Newark Bears.

Feller and Boudreau

The Indians under Ossie Vitt came in third in 1938, third in 1939, and second—one game behind—in 1940. This improvement should come as no surprise, considering the young players Vitt inherited at Cleveland. First, there was Bob Feller, the right-handed fireballer from Van Meter, Iowa. Feller had arrived in 1936, a 17-year-old right off the farm. By 1938 he had matured to the point where he struck out 18 batters in one game and whiffed 240 in the season.

Lou Boudreau, a year older than Feller, was a rookie at Cedar Rapids in the Three-I League in 1938, but by 1940 he was the Indian's full-time shortstop. Another youngster, third baseman Ken Keltner, broke in with the Indians in 1938 and immediately established himself as a steady regular.

With Feller, Boudreau, and Keltner plus the solid nucleus of Mel Harder, Hal Trosky, Earl Averill, and Jeff Heath, the Indians were probably the third best team in the American League in 1938 and 1939. The Yanks won the pennant both years, their lineup ablaze with superstars: Lou Gehrig, Joe DiMaggio, Bill Dickey, Red Ruffing, Lefty Gomez. The Red Sox finished in second place both years, with a roster featuring Jimmie Foxx, Bobby Doerr, Joe Cronin, Lefty Grove, and, in 1939, Ted Williams. Given this competition, the Indians, while hardly content with third place, were surely not disgraced by it.

Then came 1940. The Yankees had lost Gehrig, the Red Sox suffered from shaky pitching, and at season's end the two teams vying for the league championship were Detroit and Cleveland. In early September the Indians—benefiting from excellent pitching by Bob Feller, Al Milnar, Al Smith, Mel Harder, and Johnny Allen—had a four-game lead, but then the Tigers swept a three-game series from them, and the Tribe stumbled through the rest of the month, eventually losing out to the Tigers by a single game.

The big news of the 1940 season turned out to be less the exciting pennant race (or even Bob Feller's opening-game no-hitter) than it was the "Crybabies" incident. By mid-June many of the younger players were fed up with the negative and sarcastic managerial style of Ossie Vitt. They banded together and demanded his ouster. Owner Alva Bradley, the dominant figure in a syndicate that had bought the club in 1927, refused to fire him.

When sportswriter Gordon Cobbledick broke the story in the *Cleveland Plain Dealer,* the players' revolt, according to Tribe historian Morris Eckhouse, "was bigger news than the fall of Paris to the Germans." But, disaffected or not, the team played on with Ossie Vitt at the helm and very nearly won the pennant.

Nonetheless, Vitt was gone in 1941, replaced by old Roger Peckinpaugh, under whose tutelage the Indians fell to fourth place. A highlight of the '41 season was the game on July 17 before a Cleveland crowd of 67,468, when Ken Keltner made two great stops at third base to help end Joe DiMaggio's record 56-game hitting steak.

The fourth-place finish spelled curtains for

Transcendental Graphics

Lou Boudreau

Peckinpaugh, and in 1942 the surprise pick to manage the team was 24-year-old shortstop Lou Boudreau. It was a good choice but, for the new skipper, bad timing. World War II was on, Feller left for the Navy, Hal Trosky retired, and the Indians struggled through the war years without much success, despite the arrival in 1943 of future pitching great Allie Reynolds.

Manager Boudreau had some fine years as a wartime player, winning the batting crown in 1944 with a .327 average. But things improved for the team only with the end of the war, which brought the return of Bob Feller, catcher Jim Hegan, and other war veterans, and, in 1946, the purchase of the Cleveland ball club by Bill Veeck, Jr., one of the great owner-promoters of baseball history.

Attendance in 1946 topped a million for the first time—although more because the war was over than because Veeck had arrived. But no one in baseball, then or now, disputed Veeck's talents as a hustler. According to baseball historian David

Q. Voigt, "Convinced that most fans were work-ing-class entertainment-seekers with unsophisti-cated tastes, Veeck offered ... many free attrac-tions like fireworks, prize nights, giveaways, and such extras as a red jeep for delivering relief pitchers to the mound. He saw women as potential baseball zealots, and catered to them shamelessly, using nylons, orchids, and a free baby-sitting service as lures."

Veeck, noting Branch Rickey's integration of the National League with Jackie Robinson, was the first in the American League to follow suit. He signed outfielder Larry Doby in 1947, then added Satchel Paige in 1948 and Luke Easter in 1949. He also stocked the Indians' minor league teams with outstanding black prospects.

Although fans streamed through the turn-stiles in 1946 and 1947, the Tribe made no upward strides in the standings, coming in sixth in 1946 and fourth in 1947. At the end of the 1947 season few sportswriters or fans realized that the stage had been set for the Indians' best season.

Heyday of the Indians

By 1948 Veeck had built not only a reputation for gimmickry but also a first-rate baseball team. The new-look Indians had Eddie Robinson at first base and Joe Gordon at second (in a trade that sent Allie Reynolds to the Yankees). These two new-comers joined veteran shortstop Boudreau and third baseman Keltner. The Indians knew they could count on Larry Doby and Dale Mitchell in the outfield. Starting on the mound, along with Bob Feller, were future Hall-of-Famer Bob Lem-on and one-season wonder (1948) Gene Bearden.

It was a formidable ball club—but so, once again, were those of Boston and New York. Cleve-land sped off to a good start with six straight wins. The Yankees stayed close, while the Red Sox sagged at the beginning. In July, Bill Veeck signed a legendary but ancient ballplayer—he was 42 years old—from the old Negro leagues, pitcher Leroy (Satchel) Paige. Critics complained that this was just another Veeck stunt, that poor Satch was

too old. They were wrong. Paige won six games, lost only one, and became—as Veeck no doubt anticipated—the biggest drawing card in the league.

Some immense crowds watched the Indians play at their capacious home park in 1948, includ-ing a record night-game turnout of 78,382 that witnessed Paige hurl a three-hit, 1-0 shutout against the Chicago White Sox. The pennant race went down to the wire. In fact, *at* the wire, the Indians and Red Sox were in a dead heat, and a one-game playoff was needed to determine the American League winner.

Boudreau named Gene Bearden, whose 2.47 ERA led the American League, as his starting pitcher. Boston manager Joe McCarthy unexpect-edly named an ex-Indian from the 1930s, Denny Galehouse, by no means the ace of his staff, to start for the Red Sox. Boudreau, the AL MVP, whose .355 batting average that year was second only to Ted Williams's, connected for two homers in the playoff game. Keltner chipped in with a three-run round-tripper, and the Indians could fly their first pennant since 1920.

In the World Series they faced the Boston Braves of "Spahn, Sain, and pray for rain" fame. The Indians lost the first game, 1-0, despite Feller's fine two-hitter. They won the next three, getting sharp pitching from Bob Lemon, Gene Bearden, and Steve Gromek. Feller came back in the fifth game, only to be shelled, thus suffering both Indians' losses in the Series. The Tribe took the final game behind Lemon, with Bearden in relief.

The Indians finished third in 1949 and fourth in 1950, but their decline did not stem from a lack of pitching. Mike Garcia joined the staff in 1949 along with Early Wynn, who came over from Washington. Nor did attendance suffer: 2,233,771 fans turned out in 1949. Nevertheless, the colorful Veeck era ended that season. The great promoter, needing cash for a divorce settlement, sold the club to a group headed by insurance executive Ellis Ryan.

The Boudreau era ended after the next sea-son, when Al Lopez was named the new manager of the Indians. The 1951 team responded by finishing a strong second. Wynn, Garcia, and

PROFILE

Rapid Robert Feller

Bob Feller was a rookie phenom who lived up to his promise. As a 17-year-old kid right off his family's farm southwest of Des Moines, Iowa, he faced the Boston Red Sox in an exhibition game on July 6, 1936. He pitched three innings and struck out eight of the bedazzled Bostonians. In his regular-season debut against the St. Louis Browns, he fanned 15 batters. Later in the season he whiffed 17 in a game against the Philadelphia A's.

Fans across the country took notice of Feller's astonishing start. Few doubted that he would be a part of the baseball scene for a long time, and he was, although (like many others) he missed three seasons during World War II. From 1938 to 1948 he led the American League in strikeouts seven times, fanning 348 batters in 1946, his personal high. He pitched ten shutouts that year and also posted his best ERA, 2.18.

But Feller could be wild. During those same years he led the league four times in walks issued. Considering his early effectiveness and his reputation as a strikeout king, it may come as something of a surprise to learn that his average number of strikeouts per nine innings, 6.07, is too low to rank him among the top 35 major league pitchers—a select company in which Nolan Ryan is first and Sandy Koufax second. Other, lesser stars who make the list are Tug McGraw, Denny Lemaster, and Al Downing.

Photo: *Transcendental Graphics*

Feller all registered 20 or more wins, while Lemon had an off year at 17-14. Except for veteran catcher Jim Hegan, the infield had no holdovers from the 1948 world champions. Luke Easter was now playing first base, Bobby Avila was at second, Ray Boone at shortstop, and Al Rosen at third.

The 1952 season was a replay of 1951. Again the Tribe had three 20-game winners. This time they were Wynn, Garcia, and Lemon, as Feller fell to 9-13. Larry Doby led the league in home runs with 32 (Luke Easter had 31), and Al Rosen led in RBIs with 105 (Larry Doby had 104). Both years the Indians lost to Casey Stengel's dynastic Yankees, in 1951 by five games, in 1952 by only two.

It was the same old story in 1953—a strong

second to the Yanks. Al Rosen had a career year, batting .336, hitting 43 homers, and driving in 145 runs. Cleveland's only 20-game winner was Bob Lemon. A pessimist might have seen a slight falling off in the Indians' play in 1953 and despaired for the 1954 season. Not to worry. The upcoming regular season would be a triumph.

The Winningest Season Ever

April 1954 gave no indication of the glory to come, for the Indians merely broke even. But in May they put together an 11-game winning streak and by June 1 were in first place, on their way to

Transcendental Graphics

Al Lopez

a 111-43 season. That kind of won-lost mark—a .721 percentage, a league record—would seem to be sufficient to bury any second-place team. But the second-place team in 1954 was the juggernaut from New York, the Yankees, and Stengel's men kept pace. In June and July the Indians went 41-17. Not good enough—the Yanks went 43-17.

The Indians, however, were not to be denied. They pulverized the second division teams, and on September 12, playing the Yankees in a double-header in Cleveland, they were in a position to clinch. A record (for a doubleheader) 84,587 fans crowded into Municipal Stadium to see if they could do it. They could.

Bob Lemon pitched a six-hitter, Al Rosen doubled home two runs, and the Tribe took the first game. Then Early Wynn pitched a three-hitter to win the nightcap. That gave the Indians an 8½ game lead—too great a gap for the Yankees to close, even though they went on to win a total of 103 games. Cleveland fans began to think of their team as invincible, but the World Series quickly

proved otherwise.

The National League champions were the New York Giants, managed by Leo Durocher. They had won 97 games, beating out the Brooklyn Dodgers, and although they had some superstars, including Willie Mays, the big gun for the Giants in the Series came off the bench. He was Dusty Rhodes, a part-time outfielder from Mathews, Alabama.

Rhodes won the first game for the Giants with a pinch-hit home run in the tenth inning. (This was after Willie Mays had robbed Vic Wertz, the Indians' first baseman, of an extra-base hit in the eighth inning by making an astounding over-the-shoulder catch of a 440-foot drive with two men on base.) Rhodes came back to tie the second game with a pinch-hit single in the fifth inning, and then, remaining in the lineup, added an insurance run with a homer in the seventh.

In game three Rhodes was inserted as a pinch-hitter in the third inning and drove in two runs to give the Giants a 3-0 lead. Durocher's men went on to win the game. Finally, in the fourth game, Rhodes rested, but the Giants romped anyway, jumping out to a 7-0 lead and winning the game 7-4 as an Indian comeback fell short. In support of Dusty Rhodes and his fellow hitters, the Giants' pitchers proved exemplary, while the Cleveland moundsmen, especially Bob Lemon and Mike Garcia, were hit hard. The shell-shocked Cleveland fans could only echo the Dodgers' familiar cry, "Wait till next year." Unfortunately for Clevelanders, next year never came. From 1954 to the present day the Indians have won neither a pennant nor a division title.

Colavito, But No Cigar

The Indians fielded some respectable teams in the late 1950s and 1960s, and they had some exciting players during those years. One of the players that Cleveland fans took to their hearts played his first few games for the Tribe in 1955, the year after that winningest season. He was Rocky Colavito, an outfielder who hit for distance rather than average, whose string of 238 consecutive errorless games testifies to his fielding ability, and whose throwing arm was not to be trifled with. On a couple of occasions he was used as a relief pitcher; his ERA for those 5-2/3 innings was a perfect 0.00.

But Colavito's fame and popularity rode on the home run ball. Although he led the league in home runs only once, he connected for 20 or more homers in 11 straight seasons and topped 40 three times. Cleveland fans adored the Rock. Still, the big news for the Indians in 1955 was not Colavito, who was still honing his skills at Triple-A Indianapolis. It was a sensational young left-handed pitcher, Herb Score, who won rookie-of-the-year honors and struck out a league-leading 245 batters while compiling a 16-10 record with a 2.85 ERA. Here was Cleveland's pitching star of the future, or so it seemed.

The Indians finished second in 1955, trailing the Yankees by just three games. They did nearly as well in 1956, a year in which the Yanks had no 20-game winners and the Tribe had three—Herb

Score, Early Wynn, and Bob Lemon. It was Bob Feller's final season and Rocky Colavito's first as a (nearly) full-time Indian (he played 35 games for San Diego in the Pacific Coast League that year).

The Rock hit 21 homers in 1956 (plus the 12 he hit on the Coast). Even so, in his first two seasons Colavito trailed teammate Vic Wertz in home run production. First-baseman Wertz, who never won over fans the way the handsome and personable Colavito did, was traded to the Red Sox in 1959. The Indians finished nine games off the pace in 1956, good for second place once again. But attendance dropped precipitously, as if the 1954 triumph had spoiled Cleveland fans for any more modest success.

In 1957, under their new manager Kerby Farrell (Al Lopez having departed to lead the White Sox), the Indians dropped to sixth, lacking even a 15-game winner. Wynn and Lemon, both bound for the Hall of Fame, were aging. Herb Score was the new ace. But on the night of May 7, 1957, Yankee batter Gil MacDougald smashed a line drive back at the mound. Score, off balance,

---

THE ROCK'S BIG DAY

Going into the game against Baltimore on June 10, 1959, Rocky Colavito had hit safely only four times in his last 30 times at bat. Nor were his teammates faring much better at the plate. General manager Frank Lane, "Frantic Frankie," as sportswriter Gordon Cobbledick called him, had ordered 25 tennis rackets to present to his ballplayers to show his contempt for their hitting ability.

In the first inning of the game on June 10, Colavito drew a walk. He scored when Minnie Minoso, breaking out of *his* slump, homered over the left-field fence. Rocky came to bat again in the third inning. He lifted a fly down the short left-field line, and it drifted into the seats for a 365-foot home run. Nobody paid much attention to that one, but in the fifth inning he drove an Arnie Portocarrero pitch 400 feet into the bleachers in left-center field. It was homer number two for the day.

Colavito came to bat again in the sixth inning, once more against Portocarrero, and this time he blasted a low fast ball into the seats in dead center field, 420 feet away. It was homer number three for the day.

Now, you might think the Orioles would pitch very cautiously to him the next time he came to bat. But no. In the ninth inning he faced reliever Ernie Johnson, who made the mistake of throwing a pitch right over the plate. Colavito rocked it high and deep into the left-center-field bleachers, 425 feet away. It was homer number four for the day.

The Indians won the game 11-8, and a teammate in the clubhouse shouted, "Now I suppose we gotta quit callin' you Joe D[i Maggio]. From now on you're Babe R[uth]." To which another player responded, correctly, that neither Joe DiMaggio nor Babe Ruth had ever hit four homers in one game. Lou Gehrig had done it. Willie Mays and Mike Schmidt would do it later. But on June 10, 1959, it was Rocky Colavito who did it—in consecutive times at bat and with increasing distance each time.

---

was struck in the right eye and seriously injured. He missed the rest of the season, then forfeited what might have been left of his career, damaging his arm by trying to return too soon the next year.

Outfielder Gene Woodling, acquired from the talent-laden Yankees in 1956, was Cleveland's only .300 hitter in 1957, batting .321. The handwriting was on the wall. Colavito stood on the brink of two stellar seasons, but the Indians as a team were in need of reinforcements.

They came in the form of 40-year-old Mickey Vernon at first base (for one season), veteran outfielder Minnie Minoso (for two seasons), and, on the mound, rookies Mudcat Grant and Gary Bell. The Tribe finished fourth. Colavito batted .303 (his best ever), cracked 41 home runs, drove in 113 runs, and led the league with a .620 slugging average.

The Rock did nearly as well in 1959, leading the league in homers with 42—and the team as a whole did considerably better, finishing a strong second to Al Lopez's White Sox. Pitchers Cal McLish (19-8) and Gary Bell (16-11) were at their best. This second-place outcome in 1959 is worth noting, because 1959 was the last time the Indians would stand that high at the end of a season for many decades.

Going Nowhere

From 1960 to the present day a succession of Cleveland managers have come, stayed for a short time, but not conquered. Birdie Tebbetts and Al Dark each put in four seasons. Tebbetts's best, 1965, saw the Tribe go 87-75 but end up in fifth place, 15 games out. Dark's best, 1968, was nearly identical in won-lost percentage, but the team finished third, 16½ games behind. The Cleveland stars of 1968 were pitchers Luis Tiant (21-9), whose 1.62 ERA led the league, and Sam McDowell (15-14), whose 1.81 ERA nearly matched Tiant's and whose 283 strikeouts topped the 280 of Detroit's 31-game winner Denny McLain.

After 1968, and the beginning of divisional play, a number of managers—Ken Aspromonte,

Frank Robinson, Jeff Torborg, Dave Garcia, Pat Corrales, and Doc Edwards—each presided for a couple of seasons or more over the lackluster Indians. There have been bright spots over the years. Three decades can hardly fail to produce some individual stars. But nothing the front office tried was successful in producing a winner, or anything close to one.

There was one terrific trade, in 1971, when Sudden Sam McDowell was sent to the Giants in exchange for Gaylord Perry. At the age of 30 McDowell's best years were behind him. At the age of 34 spitballer Gaylord Perry was in mid-career and at the height of his form. Perry won 24 games for the Indians in 1972 and 19 games in 1973. His brother Jim joined him in 1974, and they combined for records of 21-13 and 17-12. Yet even with Chris Chambliss on first base, Buddy Bell at third, and hot prospect (though not for long) Charlie Spikes in the outfield, the Tribe could not escape the miasma of fourth, fifth, or sixth place.

In the late 1970s and early 1980s, first baseman Andre Thornton brought some impressive power to the lineup, leading the team in home runs seven times, but the pitching staff was caught in a revolving door. Quite a few capable hurlers—Dennis Eckersley, Rick Wise, John Denny, Rick Sutcliffe—flashed by in those years but kept going.

Many Cleveland fans and a few sportswriters believed that their prayers for a new Rocky Colavito had been answered in 1980 with the arrival of outfielder Joe Charboneau. The kid came highly touted. But Charboneau proved to be a one-season wonder, with his 23 home runs, 87 RBIs, and rookie-of-the-year honors. He blazed like a comet and disappeared. That same season saw tall, right-handed pitcher Len Barker put in his best season in the majors, posting a 19-11 record for Cleveland. Neither performance helped much. The expansion Toronto Blue Jays alone saved the Indians from the cellar.

On May 15, 1981, early in that strike-shorted season, Len Barker thrilled a small, chilled crowd of 7,290 fans at Cleveland Stadium by pitching the twelfth perfect game in major league history. "I

Cleveland's All-Time All-Stars

This list is a composite drawn from a number of such lists over the years.

First baseman:	Hal Trosky, 1933-1941
Second baseman:	Nap Lajoie, 1902-1914
Third baseman:	Al Rosen, 1947-1956
Shortstop:	Lou Boudreau, 1938-1950
Outfielder:	Tris Speaker, 1916-1926
Outfielder:	Earl Averill, 1929-1939
Outfielder:	Joe Jackson, 1910-1915
Catcher:	Steve O'Neill, 1911-1923
Pitcher:	Bob Feller, 1936-1956

The list suggests that history stopped for the Indians in 1956. Even the most likely second or alternate choices do not modernize it very much: third baseman Ken Keltner; outfielders Charlie Jamieson, Larry Duby, and Rocky Colavito; pitchers Addie Joss, Mel Harder, and Early Wynn. Among recent Indians, only outfielders Andre Thornton and Joe Carter would be likely to make a third or fourth team. The clear choice for the all-time all-star manager is Al Lopez.

had total command," he said. "I could throw anything anywhere I wanted." His fastball zinging in at an average of 91 miles an hour, he struck out 11 batters in a sparkling 3-0 victory over Toronto. Barker's record for the full season was nothing special, eight wins and seven losses, nor was the record of the Indians, who, as usual, outshone only the Blue Jays in the nether reaches of the standings.

As the 1980s wore on, the Indians showed no signs of reviving. Although they finally won more games than they lost in 1986 under manager Pat Corrales, they finished no better than fifth. They could point with pride to a new power hitter, though, acquired from the Chicago Cubs in 1984—outfielder Joe Carter.

In 1986 Carter hit 29 home runs and drove in a league-leading 121 runs. He continued at that hot pace through the 1989 season, at the end of which the Indians traded him to San Diego for catcher Sandy Alomar, outfielder Chris James, and third baseman Carlos Baerga. Meanwhile, Cleveland held onto another outfielder, Joey Belle, a power hitter with great potential but worrisome volatility. Time would tell.

In 1992, with Belle, Baerga, and rookie Kenny Lofton looking good, the Indians had the satisfaction of moving into a tie for fourth place in the American League East, a gratifying finish since the team they tied was their old nemesis of the 1950s, the New York Yankees.

Disaster struck before the 1993 season, when relief pitchers Steve Olin and Tim Crews were killed and starter Bob Ojeda was seriously injured in a March 22 boating accident. The team never recovered from the shock, finishing in sixth place with a 76-86 record. Ojeda did make a courageous comeback late in the year, and Belle (38 homers, a league-leading 129 RBIs), Baerga (200 hits, 20 homers, 100 RBIs), and Lofton (.325, 70 stolen bases) shone. Indians' fans saw their last game in Cleveland Stadium; the team begins play in a new 42,000-seat park in April, 1994.

SOURCES

BOOKS
Baseball America's 1992 Directory, Baseball America, 1992.

Baseball Register: 1992 Edition, The Sporting News Publishing Co., 1992.

Cobbledick, Gordon, *Don't Knock the Rock,* World Publishing Company, 1966.

Eckhouse, Morris, "Cleveland Indians All-Time Teams," in *Baseball in Cleveland,* The Jack Graney Chapter of the Society for American Baseball Research, 1990.

Eckhouse, Morris, *Day by Day in Cleveland Indians History,* Leisure Press, 1983.

Eckhouse, Morris, "Cleveland Indians: Recent Wahoo Woes Overshadow Cleveland's Baseball Tradition," in *Encyclopedia of Major League Baseball Team Histories: American League,* edited by Peter J. Bjarkman, Meckler, 1991.

Ivor-Campbell, Frederick, "Team Histories: Cleveland Indians," *Total Baseball,* edited by John Thorn and Pete Palmer, Warner Books, 1989.

Lewis, Franklin, *The Cleveland Indians,* G. P. Putnam's Sons, 1949.

Lowry, Philip J., *Green Cathedrals,* Society for American Baseball Research, 1986.

MacFarlane, Paul, editor, *Daguerreotypes of Great Stars of Baseball,* The Sporting News, 1971.

Mayer, Ronald A., *Perfect!: Biographies and Lifetime Statistics of 14 Pitchers of "Perfect" Baseball Games with Summaries and Boxscores,* McFarland & Company, 1991.

Murdock, Eugene C., *Ban Johnson: Czar of Baseball,* Greenwood Press, 1982.

Murphy, J. M., *Napoleon Lajoie: Modern Baseball's First Superstar,* published as a complete issue of *The National Pastime,* Society for American Baseball Research, 1988.

Obojski, Robert, *Bush League: A History of Minor League Baseball,* Macmillan, 1975.

Reichler, Joseph L., editor, *The Baseball Encyclopedia,* 7th edition, Macmillan, 1988.

Reidenbaugh, Lowell, *Cooperstown: Where Baseball's Legends Live Forever,* The Sporting News Publishing Co., 1983.

Veeck, Bill, with Ed Linn, *Veeck, as in Wreck,* G.P. Putnam's Sons, 1962.

Voigt, David Quentin, *American Baseball: From the Commissioners to Continental Expansion,* Pennsylvania State University Press, 1983.

PERIODICALS

Baseball America, November 10-24, 1992.

Baseball Digest, January 1975.

Cleveland, December 1975.

Cleveland Plain Dealer, May 26, 1981.

Indians Game Face Magazine, 1990.

New York Times, August 17, 1920.

Sport, November 1951.

Sports Illustrated, May 11, 1959.

—*Gerald Tomlinson* for Book Builders, Inc.

KANSAS CITY ROYALS

The Kansas City Royals have brought a new era of baseball excitement to their hometown in Missouri. An expansion franchise that took to the field in 1969, the Royals have delighted Midwestern baseball fans with no less than six American League West divisional flags, two League Championships, and a dramatic 1985 World Series victory. Much of the Royals' success has laid waste to the conventional baseball wisdom about slow starts for expansion teams.

Within its first decade of existence, the club had established a mini-dynasty that challenged the mighty Oakland Athletics and New York Yankees for post-season laurels, and just past its tenth anniversary it sailed into a World Series.

Remarkably, through its first 25 years of existence, the franchise never finished in last place. In his book *Moments, Memories, Miracles: A Quarter Century with the Kansas City*

Royals, Steve Cameron called the Royals "the game's most innovative and successful expansion franchise," adding: "Championship flags are flying, a galaxy of stars have worn those blue and white uniforms and Kansas City has taken its second major league team utterly to heart. The city embraces bona fide baseball tradition."

The Royals' fine record of accomplishment has proven a sweet revenge for Kansas City fans. Residents of the Show-Me State endured almost fifteen years of lackluster professional baseball at the hands of the Kansas City Athletics and their flamboyant owner, Charles O. Finley.

Finley's decision to vacate Kansas City in 1968 brought an opportunity for the region to begin anew with a dedicated owner, Ewing M. Kauffman, and a team that was stocked with an abundance of talent from its earliest years. As James Rothaus noted in *The Kansas City Roy-*

als, the franchise began as "an exciting, growing team, with big dreams and high hopes," and it fulfilled those hopes while still a relative youngster in the American League.

Professional baseball came to Kansas City in 1955 with the arrival of the Athletics, formerly of Philadelphia. Back in the East the Athletics had won some early World Series championships under manager Connie Mack, but by the time the franchise reached the Midwest it was little more than a glorified farm team. In all the time the Athletics spent in Missouri—some 13 seasons—the team never earned a winning record.

To make matters worse, Midwestern fans were subjected to the whims of owner "Charlie O.," who invented outlandish promotional gimmicks such as a mule mascot, sheep grazing behind the outfield fence, and a mechanical rabbit built into the field. Cameron wrote that in Kansas City, "Finley was a disaster and a complainer, seeming always to be looking for a new home, a better deal, another city that would buy him off. And while all that unpleasantness continued year after year—threats to move the club to Louisville and heaven knows where else—Finley made the A's a laughingstock."

The eccentric Finley was not a completely hopeless case, however. By 1967 he had assembled a promising ballclub, with the likes of Bert Campaneris, Reggie Jackson, Sal Bando, and Jim "Catfish" Hunter in the ranks. This was perhaps the cruelest irony of all. Just as his team began to muscle out of the doldrums, Finley took it to Oakland, California. The Kansas City fans—who had found themselves the butt of jokes for years about their hapless team—were doubly humiliated by that team's departure. Hard feelings linger to this day, contributing excitement to any matchup between the Royals and the Oakland A's.

The departure of the Athletics had just a bit of silver lining to it. At least Kansas City had proven that it could support a major league franchise attendance-wise. Such proof is a valuable asset for a city trying to win an expansion team from Major League Baseball's finicky owners. Even as the Athletics packed to leave for the West Coast, Missouri Senator Stuart Symington went to work convincing the American League to award Kansas City a new franchise. Another key to luring an expansion team is funding. Symington called upon the region's top business leaders to invest in baseball and bring a new team to town. One man who responded to the plea was Ewing M. Kauffman.

The Business Of Baseball

Kauffman had been born on a farm in Garden City, Missouri, some 60 miles southeast of Kansas City. His family had given up farming while he was still a youngster, and he grew up in Kansas City, attending public schools and a local junior college. After a stint in the Navy, Kauffman returned home and founded Marion Laboratories, a pharmaceutical company. From a shoestring budget that eked a net profit of $1,000 in its first year, Marion Laboratories grew into a multi-million dollar pharmaceutical manufacturing and health care industry. Kauffman led it all the way, until in 1989 it merged with Merrell Dow, Inc. By that time, Ewing Kauffman was a very wealthy man.

In 1967 Kauffman hadn't the slightest interest in major league baseball—he was just acting for his community when he offered a million dollars toward the purchase of an expansion team. As the bidding for a franchise became more serious, however, he upped his interest to $7 million.

The American League awarded a new franchise to Kansas City in 1968—with a mandate to begin play the following year—and suddenly Kauffman found that he had competition for ownership of the team. He told Cameron: "It kind of irritated me because here I had shown interest and these people were trying to take a ballclub away from me that I really didn't know I wanted. But it brought out my salesman's desires and ambitions, so I got on a plane and

TEAM INFORMATION AT A GLANCE

Founding date: April 8, 1969

Home stadium: Royals Stadium
P.O. Box 419969
Kansas City, MO 64141

Dimensions: Left-field line—330 feet
Center field—410 feet
Right-field line—330 feet
Seating capacity: 40,625

Team uniforms: home—base color white, royal blue letters and trim
Road—base color sky blue, royal blue letters and trim
Team nickname: Royals, 1969—
Logo: Gold crown with letters KCR underneath

Franchise record:	Wins	Losses	Pct.
(1969-1993)	2,061	1,918	.518

World Series wins (1): 1985
American League championships (2): 1980, 1985
American League West division first-place finishes (6): 1976, 1977, 1978, 1980, 1984, 1985

called the other owners and told them why I would be the best person to give the club to."

Kauffman became the sole owner of the Kansas City Royals and outfitted his players in white-and-royal blue uniforms with a simple KC logo on their hats.

Fielding a brand new team can be a daunting enterprise, and Kauffman admitted that he knew very little about the sport in which he had just invested millions. Kauffman was a shrewd businessman, though. Unlike Finley, who exercised an iron hand over all of the Athletics' operations, Kauffman simply went out and hired seasoned baseball professionals to staff his front office.

First to sign was general manager Cedric Tallis from the California Angels. Tallis re-cruited Lou Gorman, John Schuerholz, and Herk Robinson to help with the expansion draft, scouting, and farm team development. The first manager of the Royals was Joe Gordon.

Tallis was an aggressive executive who told Kansas City fans to expect nothing less than a World Series from the Royals in short order. Then he began to build the team. The initial personnel came from an expansion draft held in October of 1968.

Each American League team had to make a certain number of its active roster members available to be selected by the new franchise. The Royals' first choice was righthanded pitcher Roger Nelson from the Baltimore Orioles. A near-*last* choice in the draft that day was the one everybody talked about. Unable to find a consensus amongst themselves about who to take, the Royals executives turned the decision over to Kauffman. Kauffman selected veteran relief pitcher Hoyt Wilhelm of the Chicago White Sox—a move that drew quiet fury from the baseball establishment in Chicago. Within days after the draft, Tallis had traded Wilhelm to the California Angels for catcher-outfielder Ed Kirkpatrick. Another post-draft trade brought catcher Buck Martinez from the Houston Astros.

Pumping Up The Roster

The best known of the first-year Royals was outfielder Lou Piniella. Cameron noted that "Sweet Lou" was "almost a household name before he had an official at-bat." A volatile and passionate player, Piniella was at the beginning of a career that would include 17 years in the big leagues as a player with a lifetime batting average of .291. He had the honor of producing the Royals' first-ever base hit when he smashed a double on Opening Day, April 8, 1969. The Royals went on to win their season opener against the Minnesota Twins.

The 1969 Kansas City Royals earned a 69-93 record in their debut season for a fourth place finish in the American League West. Piniella hit .282 with 11 homers and 68 runs batted in and was named A.L. rookie of the year. As Rothaus put it in his book about the team, "Kansas City fans were in love."

More trades strengthened the franchise even further. By the end of the 1970 season, Tallis had brought outfielder Amos Otis, shortstop Fred Patek, second baseman Cookie Rojas, and catcher Jerry May to Kansas City. In mid-1970 a new manager joined the club—a low-key, old-style baseball man by the name of Bob Lemon.

It was under Lemon that the Royals had their first winning season, in 1971, earning an 85-76 record for second place in the division. The Royals had come a long way fast, thanks to

Kauffman's financial generosity and Tallis's inspired trading that, to quote Cameron, "bordered on larceny."

Cameron wrote: "Tallis' trading spree was wonderful, obviously, but nobody in the Royals organization believed for a minute that they could build a World Series team simply by fleecing people every off-season." From Kauffman on down, the organization was dedicated to the tried-and-true farm system. Big money was spent on scouting from the outset, and the Royals dedicated themselves to building a team from young farm team players.

Kauffman took this notion to the extreme when he announced, in 1969, the formation of the Kansas City Royals Baseball Academy. The Academy—always a controversial idea during its brief run—hired natural athletes who had been passed over in the draft and gave them intense instruction in baseball fundamentals.

The cost of the enterprise, and its unproven track record, caused friction in the Royals' organization. Tallis and Gorman opposed the Academy and eventually lost their positions with the club.

The Royal Palace

By 1973 Kauffman was forced to disband the Kansas City Royals Baseball Academy. A costly construction strike at the site of the new Royals Stadium led to a $2 million loss for the team and forced a number of cost-cutting measures. Cameron thought the Academy might have proven itself had it lasted longer. "No less than 14 major-league players came from classes at the Royals academy, and 13 of them were, indeed, undrafted prospects who had been fine-tuned under a revolutionary type of instruction," the writer claimed. "The most remarkable story, clearly, was Frank White." White, a Kansas City native, won eight Gold Gloves and produced 2,000-plus hits in a long and storied career with the Royals.

A disappointing 76-78 season in 1972 ended with the team in disarray. Kauffman became dissatisfied with Lemon's managerial techniques, and, feeling that a young team like the Royals needed a younger skipper, Kauffman fired Lemon and hired Jack McKeon. Like so many of the Royals players, McKeon was promoted from the farm system, where he had won two straight pennants at the AAA level.

Unfortunately, McKeon proved unpopular with the players in Kansas City. The Royals won 88 games for him in 1973 for another second place finish, but they dropped to fifth in 1974 with a 77-85 record. Kauffman fired McKeon in July of 1975.

The managerial situation may have been frustrating, but fans still found much to be excited about in Kansas City. On Opening Night 1973, a capacity crowd endured bitter cold and snow to inaugurate Royals Stadium, a brand-new, state-of-the-art ballpark built exclusively for baseball. Royals Stadium replaced Kansas City's 1950s-era Municipal Stadium as the team's home. It was the first facility in the American League to feature artificial turf in both infield and outfield.

The new turf helped to shape the destiny of the Royals, according to Cameron. "Opposing teams were at a distinct disadvantage once the Royals got used to their turf and built swift, aggressive clubs to take advantage of it," the writer noted.

"Outfielders from Boston or Detroit would come to Royals Stadium and tip-toe around as though stepping through a minefield. They approached hopping balls as though they were live grenades, and for good reason. Slicing line drives to the corners turned into inside-the-park home runs, and hot shots over shortstop might scoot all the way to the wall."

Birth Of A Legend

Into this gleaming new ballpark walked a player for the ages: George Brett. The man who would become "heart and soul of the Royals for two decades and one of the most spectacular big-game performers in history," to quote Cameron, arrived from the minor leagues in August, 1973, as a temporary replacement for injured third baseman Paul Schaal.

A California native—and the second member of his family to make the major leagues—Brett began his career showing little of his enormous potential. He batted only .125 in 13 games with the Royals in 1973 and was sent back to the triple-A farm team in Omaha, Nebraska. Called up again on May 3, 1974, when Schaal was traded, Brett seemed ill at ease at the plate. He was batting around .200 at the 1974 All-Star break.

That momentary lull in the regular season proved momentous for George Brett. At the prompting of Royals hitting coach Charley Lau, Brett cut short a fishing trip during the All-Star break and returned to Kansas City for intensive batting instruction. The instruction continued before games and became a regular part of Brett's day.

Brett told Cameron: "I had this big, looping swing like Carl Yastrzemski, and Charley had to experiment until we found a way to get my hands into what he called the launching position. Once we got them there, it was more work to keep them there." Brett added: "I saw immediate results.... I owe everything to Charley Lau."

Brett blossomed into a hitting sensation, winning his first of three batting titles in 1976. His best year percentage-wise was 1980, when he flirted with .400 the whole season—despite injuries—and finished the year with a .390 average and another batting crown. Nor has age or injury taken much of a toll on rugged number 5, who won a third batting title in 1990.

Brett, who has said he'd like to be remembered "as a guy who always played hard and ran out every ball," is the only player in the history of baseball to win the batting title in three different decades. His success and the Royals' have been inseparable for a long time. He was truly *the* franchise player in Kansas City.

The Thrill Of Victory

Fortunately for Royals fans, Brett was surrounded by considerable talent by the mid-1970s. Outfielder Amos Otis, designated hitter Hal McRae, first baseman John Mayberry, and second baseman Frank White formed the nucleus of a potent and productive offense. As Cameron put it, "the Royals possessed some serious thunder and used it to seize all those championship flags that fly above the stadium."

Pitchers Steve Busby, Dennis Leonard, Paul Splittorff, and Larry Gura anchored the defense as the Royals moved from near-contender to repeating champions of the American League West. McRae told Cameron: "We ran through the American League like a bunch of wild men and kicked some rear ends. We had good pitching, a lot of guys who could hit the ball into gaps and run like hell—and everybody played hardball. We had some great teams."

The Royals began to gel when Kauffman fired McKeon midway through the 1975 season and replaced him with Whitey Herzog. Herzog and the Royals hoped to put an end to the Oakland A's domination of the A.L. West. Kansas City finally found that objective in sight in 1976 as the regular season progressed, but scrappy Oakland put up a fight. With a week to play, only four and a half games separated the Royals and the A's. Then Kansas City lost two straight games to Oakland in front of unruly California crowds.

In a move that seemed either desperate or just plain crazy, Herzog decided to start long reliever Larry Gura in the final game against Oakland in California. Gura pitched a four-hit shutout, and Amos Otis—who had been the victim of a bean ball just a week earlier—drilled a double and a two-run homer. At game's end the rejuvenated Royals filed into the team bus chanting "A.O., A.O." in honor of their comrade.

The Royals took the A.L. West championship of 1976 and advanced to the American League playoffs. When the division was finally clinched, two veteran Royals—Cookie Rojas and Freddie Patek—braved the October chill to plunge into the celebrated fountains at Royals Stadium for a victory swim. "Nothing will ever be as sweet as our first division pennant in '76," Brett told Cameron, "because we'd never been there before. The first one is extra special. And it was tough, really tough."

The Agony Of Defeat

Tougher still was a playoff series that pitted the Royals against the New York Yankees. New York won the first game, 4-1 after the Royals lost Otis to a broken ankle. Kansas City rebounded in the second game for a 7-3 win. The Yankees took the third game, 5-3. In the fourth matchup the Royals fought to a come-from-behind 7-4 victory. The series had stretched to five games, and in the decisive contest neither team seemed willing to exit gracefully.

Trailing in the eighth inning, Kansas City rallied to a tie when Brett hit a three-run home run. The tie held until the bottom of the ninth, when Chris Chambliss of the Yankees led off with a home run that barely cleared the right-field fence at Yankee Stadium.

Long locked in competition with the A's, the Royals now had a new nemesis in New York. The 1976 League Championship was just the first round in a series of tough pennant fights between the Royals and the Yankees in the late 1970s. Several times Kansas City romped in the American League West division, only to be sent home shy of the World Series by the team in pinstripes.

Probably the most disappointing finish occurred in 1977. The Royals earned a franchise-record 102 victories that year, including a stretch of 16 in a row and 24 out of 25. To this day Herzog declares the 1977 Royals the best team he has ever managed. Outfielder Al Cowens turned in a solid year with a .312 average and 112 runs batted in. Dennis Leonard won 20 games, Paul Splittorff 16. "This looked like just the team to stifle the Yankees," Cameron remembered.

It was not to be. In the 1977 League Championship Series—again versus the Yankees—the Royals won two of the first three contests and still lost the pennant. In the fourth game, John Mayberry had to be benched after two strikeouts and a couple of dropped throws as the Yankees won 6-4. Herzog fumed over the defeat, blaming Mayberry, who had indeed been suffering the effects of an all-night party.

Once again the series went to a fifth game. Splittorff drew the start in the clincher and carried a 3-1 lead into the eighth inning. The Yankees scratched a run from relief pitcher Steve Mingori, narrowing the lead to 3-2.

The ninth inning was a disaster for Kansas City. Herzog put Leonard in to pitch, even though Leonard had hurled a complete game just two days before. Leonard gave up a leadoff hit to Yankee Paul Blair, then walked Roy White and gave up two more soft hits to Mickey Rivers and Willie Randolph. Furious at the turn of events, Brett committed a throwing error, but by that time the game was decided. In their half of the ninth the Royals could not even the score, and New York held on to win the game 5-3 and the pennant.

Brett told Cameron: "The '77 team was the best we ever had. I still can't believe we didn't win that series with the Yankees. We had it and gave it away. It's never stopped hurting."

There Will Be A Quiz

The frustration seemed to dog the Royals into the 1978 season. Although the team won 92 games for another A.L. West division flag, the season was marked by dissension—a relatively rare event in Kansas City. First, Herzog openly faulted Mayberry for arriving at a playoff game in poor condition and let it be known that the popular first baseman would never take the field in a Royals uniform again. Mayberry's

contract was ultimately sold to Toronto at the very end of spring training in 1978.

Most Royals players and fans felt Herzog had acted rashly. Mayberry was popular, a good-natured team leader, and a fine hitter. His replacement, Clint Hurdle, never developed an equal stature with the club. Later in the same season, Herzog fired Charley Lau, another popular and respected Royal.

Nevertheless, Kansas City ended the 1978 season once again atop the American League West and once again in the League Championship Series against the Yankees. As Yogi Berra might have put it, it was *"deja vu* all over again" for the frustrated Kansas City franchise. In the first game the Yankees cruised to a 7-1 victory behind the hot bat of Reggie Jackson. The Royals rallied for a tight 10-9 win in the second game.

Game three was particularly disappointing, as the Yankees won 6-5 even though Brett hit three home runs. New York clinched the series in the fourth game on a sixth-inning homer by Roy White. For the third straight year the Yankees had topped the American League West at the Royals' expense.

Herzog felt that the one element missing for all those divisional championship Royals teams was a dependable late-inning relief pitcher. By the time that essential player showed up in Kansas City, Herzog had been sent packing.

In 1979 the Royals finally dropped from first place in the West Division, bowing to the California Angels with an 85-77 record. Herzog was fired at the end of the season and replaced by Jim Frey. It was Frey who led the team the year their much-needed reliever blossomed, and Frey who took his place in the dugout for the first Royals World Series.

The relief pitcher in question was a right-hander named Dan Quisenberry. He joined the team from the minor leagues in 1979 and did not seem particularly remarkable at first. Frey felt that Quisenberry might benefit from changing his delivery motion, and in the off-season the manager arranged for "Quiz" to work with noted underhand reliever Kent Tekulve. "The results were spectacular," Cameron wrote. "Quisenberry saved 33 games in 1980, becoming one of baseball's premier closers almost overnight."

Penant Fever

The 1980 season established the Royals once and for all as a dominant American League team. The man who moved them into the national limelight was none other than George Brett. Playing with nagging injuries, Brett nonetheless managed to keep his batting average above .400 half of the season. No one had batted .400 on a season since the heyday of Ted Wil-liams in Boston, so reporters flocked to Kansas City to see and talk to the hitting phenomenon.

"It was crazy," Brett told Cameron. "In a way, it was fun because I was hitting and we were winning, but eventually, everything got to be too much. Everyone asked the same things, day after day. 'What's it going to take to hit .400?' Every day. Then there were writers and TV people and magazines who'd ask to do something different. *People* magazine wanted to come to my house. A television crew asked about doing something at my house. It felt like half the United States was at my house."

At one point Brett separated himself from the media crush and refused to grant any more interviews. The injuries that kept him from 45 games in 1980 did little to dampen his swing

AP/Wide World Photos

George Brett

when he did play. He finished the season with a .390 average and his second batting crown.

Nor were his heroics confined to the regular season. As the Royals rode a 97-65 record into the 1980 American League playoffs, Brett and his teammates prepared to meet the Yankees yet again. "The whole thing with the Yankees was on our mind," he told Cameron. "You can't forget losing the way we did for three straight years."

The 1980 American League Championship Series opened at Royals Stadium on October 9, 1980. Larry Gura took the mound for Kansas City in the first game and demolished the Yankees, 7-2. The second game belonged to Dennis Leonard and Dan Quisenberry, who combined to produce a 3-2 victory for the Royals.

As the two teams travelled east to continue the series in Yankee Stadium, the Royals were tense and determined. A two-game lead was fine, but they would not celebrate until they had earned that pennant. After so many five-game disappointments against New York, no one predicted success prematurely.

Game three looked like a Yankees victory for the home crowd in New York. In the seventh inning, the Royals trailed 2-1 with two outs. Then Royals outfielder Willie Wilson stepped to the plate and stroked a double into the right-field corner. Yankees manager Dick Howser quickly called for a relief pitcher and brought the lethal Rich "Goose" Gossage into the game. With Wilson on second base and Gossage pitching, Royals shortstop U. L. Washington chopped a ball to Yankees second baseman Willie Randolph. It seemed like an easy infield play, but Washington somehow beat the throw to first to keep the rally alive. The next batter was George Brett.

Gossage was a fine reliever at the height of his powers in those days, but he had met his match in K.C.'s franchise man. Brett sent the very first pitch screaming across Yankee Stadium to the third tier of seats behind the right-field wall for a three-run homer. "It was prob-

ably the longest home run I ever hit," Brett told Cameron, "but what I remember most is how quiet the stadium got. And the reaction in our dugout. It was only the seventh inning, but everybody seemed to be out on the field.... It was like everyone forgot the game wasn't over yet." Two innings later it was over. The Royals held on to win, 4-2. Finally, after so many years of trying, they had won an American League pennant.

A Fight To The Finish

A three-game sweep is not necessarily beneficial for a team bound to the World Series. After winning their league championship, the Royals idled about in New York City awaiting the outcome of the National League series between the Philadelphia Phillies and the Houston Astros. The Phillies eventually won the N.L. pennant, and the Royals met their World Series opponents at Veterans Stadium in Philadelphia. Some members of that Royals team still feel that the days off hurt the team in the World Series.

On Tuesday, October 14, 1980, the Royals played their first-ever World Series game. Leonard got the start for Kansas City, and the Royals quickly leaped to a 4-0 lead. Unfortunately, Leonard ran into trouble in the third inning, and the Phillies scored five runs. Philadelphia added single runs in the fourth and fifth to lead 7-4. A Royals rally for two more runs in the ninth still fell short of the victory mark. Game One went to Philadelphia, 7-6.

Game Two of the 1980 World Series was another come-from-behind win for Philadelphia. It will probably be best remembered, though, for action off the field. Brett left the game in the sixth inning, suffering from painful hemorrhoids. Even as the Royals lost 6-4, Brett was jetting back to Kansas City for surgery to relieve the inflammation. It was an embarrassing problem, to be sure, but Brett did not dodge the veritable storm of media attention he received. He held a press conference and answered all the questions gracefully. Asked if he would be ready to start Game Three, he quipped: "Yes, I think my problems are all behind me."

When the World Series resumed in Kansas City on Friday, Brett was back in the lineup. He lost little time silencing his critics by stroking a home run in his first at-bat. Game Three was a tough struggle for both teams. At the end of nine innings the score stood 3-3. In the bottom of the tenth inning, Phillies bullpen ace Tug McGraw faced Brett with a man on base. Brett drew an intentional walk, placing runners at first and second. The next Royal batter, Willie Mays Aikens, hit a single that scored the winning run. The Royals had earned their first-ever World Series game victory, 4-3.

Aikens was a hero again with two home runs in Game Four as the Royals won 5-3 to tie the World Series at two games apiece. The Royals had the luxury of one more game on their home field before returning to Philadelphia. They hoped to build a commanding 3-2 lead in games, but their hopes were dashed in Game Five as the Phillies again came from behind in late innings to win 4-3. By this time critics were second-guessing Royals manager Jim Frey. Often during the regular season, Frey had brought Quisenberry into close games in the seventh or eighth inning.

The habit continued in the World Series with decidedly mixed results. Philadelphia slugger Pete Rose told reporters: "The guy [Frey] is giving us the World Series by letting us look at Quisenberry's delivery so much." Certainly that appeared to be the case in Game Five, when the Phillies took the lead only in the ninth inning.

The Series returned to Veterans Stadium, where Philadelphia closed it with a decisive 4-1 victory in front of a delirious hometown crowd. Rothaus wrote: "The Series was over, and Philadelphia was the winner. But the Kansas City fans knew they still had a tremendous group of champions in their city. They gave the Royals a welcome-home parade that rivaled Philadel-phia's victory parades. To the people of K.C., their team was still a winner."

Strike!

Baseball fans will always remember 1981 as the year shortened by a prolonged players' strike. The players walked out on June 12 and did not return until the first week of August. Since so much of the season had been lost, the Commissioner of Baseball decreed that the season would be considered two halves and that the division leader at the end of the first half would play the division leader at the end of the second half in a mini-playoff to decide each divisional championship.

The Oakland A's were leading the American League West when the strike began, but when play resumed the Royals took first place and held onto it until October. Thus the Royals earned the opportunity to appear in the divisional playoff against the A's.

The Royals were at a disadvantage from the outset of the mini-playoff. Their modest second-half 30-23 record was achieved despite severe difficulties with manager Frey, who was fired late in the regular season. The replacement manager, Dick Howser, did not arrive in time to put his stamp on the franchise. A resurgent Oakland snatched three straight games from Kansas City in the mini-playoffs. All the Royals could do was look to the future under a new skipper.

Howser turned out to be a well-liked manager in Kansas City. Cameron wrote that the former Yankee skipper's management style "was a testament to a stick-with-it game instead of what Howser considered short-term tricks and gimmicks. He was a guy who believed in identifying his best players and letting them perform, rather than hogging the spotlight with a series of show-time moves and stratagems."

Under Howser, the 1982 Royals put up a fierce fight for the divisional flag, bowing to the California Angels only in the last week of the

HISTORY	The Pine Tar Incident

It is known as the Infamous Pine Tar Incident, probably the most controversial moment of the 1983 major league baseball season. The scene of the "crime" was Yankee Stadium in New York City. The "criminal" was Kansas City's star hitter, George Brett. The "wronged victims" were Yankee manager Billy Martin and his team. Or so it stood for a brief moment on July 24, 1983.

Most batters use gloves to protect their hands from blisters. Brett, a future first-ballot Hall-of-Famer, batted bare-handed. In order to improve his grip on the wood, Brett, like many other batters, applied sticky pine tar to his bat handles. The procedure was no secret to Brett's teammates or his opponents. No one thought much of it until that fateful day in New York.

In the top of the ninth inning on July 24, Brett hit a towering two-run homer off Yankee relief pitcher Goose Gossage to erase a Royals deficit and put Kansas City ahead 5-4. Just after Brett rounded the bases, Yankee manager Billy Martin advanced to home plate to protest Brett's use of a "foreign substance" more than 18 inches up the handle of his bat. The umpires requested Brett's bat and used home plate—17 inches wide—to measure the amount of pine tar on the handle. Brett laughed at the whole procedure from his seat in the Royals' dugout.

Moments later, Brett was laughing no more. The umpires ruled his home run invalid and cancelled the two Royal runs batted in. An intense competitor under any circumstances, Brett charged from the dugout like an angry bull and had to be forcibly restrained by his teammates. As the melee continued on the field, sympathetic Royals players tried to sneak the tar-smeared bat out of the ballpark but were collared at the stadium exit.

The Royals walked off the field and lodged an official protest with American League president Lee MacPhail. Just three days later, on July 27, MacPhail issued a statement upholding the Royals' position and re-instating Brett's two-run homer. MacPhail noted that the home run should stand because Brett had not violated the "spirit of the rules." That Royals protest was the only one MacPhail upheld in his tenure as president of the American League.

The final three outs of the disputed game were played on August 18, 1983 before a Yankee Stadium audience of 1,245 people. Royals reliever Dan Quisenberry retired three Yankees in a row to bring Kansas City its long-awaited victory. And George Brett? Having been ejected from the original game for his shenanigans after the controversial ruling, he did not even have to show up at the park for that last half-inning. He watched it on television from a restaurant in Newark, New Jersey.

In 1992 Brett told reporters: "It's funny. I've got more hits than Babe Ruth and I played on a World Series championship team, but people will probably remember me for hemorrhoids and pine tar."

season. A highlight of that season was the performance of Willie Wilson, whose .332 average led the league. Quisenberry recorded a league-high 35 saves, and Hal McRae—having found a perfect niche as designated hitter—led the league in runs batted in, with 133.

All of the achievements in 1982 were accomplished by a team that was plagued by some 44 separate injuries to 22 different players. No one was prepared, however, for the psychological injury about to be inflicted upon the players and fans in Kansas City. In 1983—a season that saw the team slump to 79-83—four members of the Royals team were brought to court on drug charges. The four who entered guilty pleas to misdemeanor cocaine charges included pitcher Vida Blue, outfielder Jerry Martin, Willie Mays Aikens, and Willie Wilson. The cases of Aikens and Wilson were a particular blow to the Kansas City faithful—both players had contributed massively in the World Series year and in other seasons. Nevertheless, of the four convicted players, only Wilson returned to continue his baseball career with the Royals. Blue and Martin were released, Aikens traded to Toronto.

"Just Say No"

As a direct result of the drug scandal, Kauffman initiated a drug abuse awareness program through his Marion Laboratories. The owner told Cameron that from 1984 through 1991 "we taught over 100,000 kids the principles of self-management and social skills to resist cigarettes, alcohol and drugs. So yes, there was some good from the things our players did, but at the time it hurt me a great deal."

Howser began the 1984 season without Wilson, who was suspended until May 15. To make matters worse, Brett tore a ligament in his knee and missed the first six weeks of the season. Howser's lineup card on Opening Day 1984 contained only two players—Hal McRae and Frank White—who had started on Opening Day in 1983.

Half of the pitching staff consisted of first-year players, but this was not necessarily a liability. Two of those rookie pitchers were Mark Gubicza and Bret Saberhagen. In his book *A Royal Finish,* Alan Eskew wrote: "There's a century-old baseball adage that says you don't win with rookies, especially rookie pitchers. But the Royals were going to roll the dice with the rookies. Little wonder that preseason prognosticators were picking the Royals to finish fifth, sixth, or seventh, in 1984."

After 71 games of the 1984 season, the Royals were indeed in the cellar with a 31-40 record. As late as July 18 they were still 11 games below .500. Then, as if by magic, they turned around and began burning up the field. From July 19 until September 28, they won 44 and lost 25, outbattling the Minnesota Twins

Bret Saberhagen

and the Angels to win another American League West crown. The catalysts for this about-face were indeed the young pitchers, Saberhagen, Gubicza, and Danny Jackson, all of whom would blossom into full-fledged superstars the following year.

Rising From The Ashes

The 1984 American League Championship Series was a departure for the Royals in that they did *not* draw the Yankees as opponents. Instead they faced a gritty and determined squad from Detroit, the "Bless You Boys" Tigers. The Tigers swept the Royals 8-1, 5-3, and 1-0 for the A.L. pennant. This same Tiger team went on to win a World Series, while the Royals consoled themselves in Kansas City.

No one was particularly hurt by the outcome of the playoffs. The Royals had been picked to finish fifth or worse in their division that year and had proven every forecast wrong. Brett told Rothaus, "In a way, we should be embarrassed [by the sweep in the playoffs], but the way our young pitchers pitched, we've a lot to look forward to."

Brett was right. The 1985 Kansas City Royals were not to be denied. Down time after time in crucial situations, they battled back to stay in contention. This time all the laurels would be brought back to Royals Stadium for the faithful fans. Cameron wrote: "Let's not pussyfoot. The remarkable, resilient, relentless Royals of 1985 set a standard for baseball miracles which may never be matched."

It is quite difficult to repeat as division winner, but Kansas City had a long history of doing just that. Even so, the 1985 season held many chances for disaster. As late as July 21 the Royals languished in third place, seven and a half games behind the Angels. The Royals pitching was extremely strong, however—Saberhagen won the Cy Young Award for a 20-6 season, and veteran Quisenberry led the league with 37 saves. Brett won a Gold Glove at third base, and Willie Wilson and outfielder Lonnie Smith combined for 83 stolen bases. Still the divisional race was tight. The Royals did not clinch until October 5, but fittingly the decisive victory was a 10-inning, come-from-behind affair against the hated A's.

The American League Championship Series had been expanded to seven games, and for this longer playoff the Royals travelled north to meet the Toronto Blue Jays. Anyone who still had fingernails left after the regular season lost them completely as Kansas City teetered time and again on the brink of defeat. The Royals promptly dropped the first two games of the series in Toronto, 6-1 and 6-5.

In the third game, the Royals trailed 5-2 until Brett came alive and—in what Cameron called "nothing short of an audition for the Hall of Fame"—hit two home runs, doubled and singled, scored the decisive run, and nailed Blue Jay Damaso Garcia at home plate in a spectacular defensive play. Royals relief pitcher Steve Farr pitched four and a half innings of shutout ball, and Kansas City won, 6-5. All seemed lost in the very next game, however. Charlie Leibrandt took a 1-0 lead into the ninth inning, but he and Quisenberry could not hold Toronto. The Jays won, 3-1 and took a commanding three-games-to-one lead in the playoff.

That was the last winning the Toronto Blue Jays would do. The Royals shut the Jays out 2-0 in the fifth game, beat them 5-3 in the sixth game, and—against all odds—won the seventh game decisively, 6-2. As the jubilant Royals sprayed each other with champagne in the locker room after having won the pennant, Frank White summed up the situation perfectly. "Just a miracle a minute," the veteran second baseman said. Miracle season hadn't ended for the Royals.

Sweet Revenge

The 1985 World Series was a curious affair—a matchup between Missouri's two professional franchises, Kansas City and the St. Louis Cardinals. Locals called it the "I-70 Series," referring to the interstate highway that linked the two cities in separate parts of the state. In another curious coincidence, the St. Louis manager was none other than Whitey Herzog.

Cameron noted that although "there was a truckload of drama and heartbreak in the first five matchups" of the World Series, the contest inevitably came down to the last two games. Once again the Royals found themselves battling from the underdog position. They were stunned in the Series opener 3-1. In Game Two they held a 2-0 lead all the way to the ninth inning before St. Louis struck for four runs to win 4-2. Not only were the Royals suddenly down two games to none, but they had lost *at Royals Stadium* and now faced the prospect of a visit to St. Louis.

The change of scenery helped. In Game Three, Saberhagen got the win, allowing only six Cardinals hits while the Royals smacked 11, including a Frank White home run. It was Kansas City 6, St. Louis 1. The Cards roared back in Game Four, shutting the Royals out 3-0. Kansas City had struggled back from a three-games-to-one deficit in the League Championship Series. Could they do it again? Not without a little controversy.

The tables began to turn in Game Five. Royals pitcher Danny Jackson threw a five-hitter, and the Royals waltzed to a 6-1 victory. With the Series standing at three games to two, play shifted back to Kansas City's Royals Stadium. According to Cameron, Game Six of that matchup provided "heroics such as Kansas City fans had never witnessed."

The game stood scoreless through seven full innings. Then, in the top half of the eighth, St. Louis scored a valuable run on a two-out RBI single. The Royals did not score in their half of the eighth, and in the ninth they faced a brilliant Cardinal rookie reliever named Todd Worrell.

Worrell had struck out all six Royals he faced in Game Five, leaving little hope for a Kansas City rally. Rally they did, though. Royals pinch hitter Jorge Orta led off with a bouncer past first. The play looked like a clean out, from first baseman Jack Clark to the covering Worrell. Instead, first base umpire Don Denkinger flung his arms out in the "safe" sign. The Cardinals protested vehemently, but the call stood. The play so flustered the Cardinals that only moments later the bases were loaded with Royals and Dane Iorg hit a two-RBI single. All of Kansas City rejoiced. The Royals had stayed alive for a seventh game and had done it dramatically.

In Game Seven the Cardinals played as if the wind had been ripped from their sails. Saberhagen pitched a five-hit shutout for the Royals as the men in blue won 11-0 and took the World Series crown. Saberhagen made the national news for his nervy performance—and for the fact that his wife was having a baby even as he pitched the game. He was named Series Most Valuable Player as well.

Cameron wrote: "After all the pitiful seasons since major leagues came to Kansas City in 1955, Finley's sheep grazing beyond the right-field fence, the growing pains of expansion and eventually the anguish of coming so close in the playoffs and then the '80 World Series, the city at last became titletown."

A Devastating Loss

The triumphant Royals began the 1986 season with a World Series flag flying over their home ballpark, with a gutsy return to action by Dennis Leonard, who had undergone knee surgery, and with the news of the signing of a hot prospect named Bo Jackson. High spirits soon crashed, however.

Just two days after he managed the American League to an All-Star Game victory, Dick Howser discovered that he had a cancerous brain tumor. He was forced to step down as manager of the Royals in order to undergo surgery and chemotherapy. While his team struggled without him, Howser fought a valiant battle with the disease. He died in the spring of 1987.

Cameron wrote: "Firings and clubhouse squabbles are one thing, but the Howser tragedy tore at the heart of the Royals—from the top on down, from owner to bat-boys, pitchers to secretaries. Dick Howser's death rocked Kansas City, too, washing the community with a sense of loss and the feeling of being left without its baseball rudder. The man seemed to stand for everything the franchise believed, everything it had worked to achieve, and suddenly he was gone."

Howser's passing ushered in an era of managerial difficulties for the Royals. From mid-1986 until May of 1991 the position was in flux between Mike Ferraro (an interim manager while Howser was still alive), Bill Gardner, John Wathan, Bob Schaefer (another interim manager), and finally Hal McRae. Wathan, a long-time utility infielder with the Royals, lasted longest as manager during this period, serving partial seasons in 1987 and 1991 and full seasons in between.

The Royals failed to win the division through the period. Their best post-Howser showing came in 1989 with a 92-70 second-place finish, but in both 1990 and 1991 they finished in sixth place. The Kansas City Royals never dropped from the limelight, though. A new superstar had come to town in the person of Vincent Edward Jackson—better known as Bo.

Jackson Action

In a move reminiscent of Kauffman's Baseball Academy days, the Royals persuaded Jackson, a Heisman Trophy-winning football hero from Auburn University, to forgo professional football for a baseball career.

At first Jackson signed exclusively with the Royals and indicated that he would play only baseball, even though the Tampa Bay Buccaneers offered him far more to play football. "I'm always going to do opposite of what the public thinks," the young star said. Indeed, after just one season in the minor leagues, Jackson arrived in Kansas City on September 2, 1986, and hit a thunderous home run in his first big-league at-bat.

Cameron wrote that in Kansas City, "Bo was a one-man circus. He drew crowds like Elvis or Princess Di.... Bo was the Royals' biggest attraction ever. Never mind that Brett, a future Hall of Famer, shared the same dugout. George was ignored like a utility infielder whenever the Bo Show came to town."

Jackson's fame only increased when he announced in 1987 that he would play both baseball *and* professional football, and then joined the Los Angeles Raiders as a running back at the end of baseball season. The decision was not popular in Kansas City. Fans booed Jackson and pelted him with toy footballs, convinced that their star could not give his all to both sports.

Jackson confounded his critics and became a national hero as he blazed a path through two professional sports. In 1988 he became the first Kansas City Royal to hit 25 home runs and steal 25 bases in one season, and he was named Most Valuable Player of the 1989 All-Star Game after belting a 448-foot homer along with two other hits. Meanwhile, as a running back for the Raiders, he averaged 5.5 yards per carry and

was selected to the Pro Bowl.

Jackson's best year as a Royal came in 1990, when he averaged .272 with 28 home runs and 78 RBIs. Thanks to a popular "Bo Knows" advertising campaign for Nike shoes, the handsome Jackson became an internationally known media darling.

A serious hip injury sustained while playing football early in 1991 ended the Bo Show in Kansas City. Although medical opinion was mixed on Jackson's ability to overcome the damage to his hip socket—an injury known as a hip pointer—the Royals put their popular superstar on waivers. Jackson eventually saw limited action with the White Sox.

Cameron, for one, felt that the Jackson legacy in Kansas City was inflated by hype. "The bottom line," the author wrote, "when you talk to cold-hearted, objective baseball people, seems to be that Bo Jackson was occasionally a great player, but most often an ordinary one without instincts for the game or the desire to learn them. He was a sprinter in a marathon sport." Cameron added, "But you have to say this: It was a wild ride. For sheer entertainment, Bo was heaven in double-knits."

The Legend Lives On

The Bo Show notwithstanding, George Brett made history in 1990 when he earned another batting title with a .329 average. From a fresh-faced youngster of the 1970s, Brett had become the elder statesman of the Royals and mentor to such new Kansas City talent as third baseman Gregg Jefferies, outfielder Danny Tartabull, and slugger Kevin McReynolds. The latter player joined the Royals in a 1991 trade that sent Saberhagen to the Mets for three players.

The Saberhagen trade and the signing of high-priced free agents such as pitcher Mark Davis marked a shift in emphasis for the Royals. Known for a league-leading payroll, Kauffman's Royals have become aggressive bidders for free agent talent. The owner and his staff feel this is one means of keeping the team competitive in a changing baseball world. "We're in the Big Boys League now, and we have to play the Big Boys' games," Kauffman told *Sports Illustrated.* "If we hadn't entered the free agent market in a big way ... would we have kept the 2.2 million attendance? No. If we lose 500,000 at the gate, that's at least a $3 million loss. Either way, I lose money, but it's more fun to lose when you win."

Kauffman has not lost much money on his Royals over the years. From a financial point of view the team is a phenomenal success. The Kansas City market is one of the smallest in big league baseball, but the Royals were the first expansion team to draw two million customers in a regular season. Since 1980 the club has averaged 2.2 million in attendance every year, and season ticket sales are the envy of many a larger club.

Certainly the tradition of winning baseball has contributed to the fan support for the Royals, but stable and relatively generous ownership is the essential ingredient to the team's success. From 1983 until 1990 Kauffman shared ownership of the Royals with Memphis businessman Avron Fogelman, but more recently Kauffman has assumed full ownership again. The aging pharmaceutical magnate sometimes frets about what will become of his team when he dies—his first priority is keeping the Royals in Kansas City.

Fans have continued to flock into Royals Stadium in the 1990s. In the last week of 1992, Brett smacked his 3,000th career base hit, a milestone shared by only a handful of the greatest players. In 1993 a team stocked with youngsters, including hard-hitting Brian McRae, surged toward another West Division title under the management of Hal McRae. The two McRaes are father and son, and they provide yet another popular drawing card for the team.

Eventually the White Sox pulled away to take the crown, but the Royals finished a respectable 84-78, good for third place. Pitchers

Kevin Appier and Jeff Montgomery enjoyed banner seasons; Appier led the American League with a 2.56 ERA, and Montgomery tied for the league lead with 45 saves. An ineffective offense that finished last in the A.L. in runs scored and on-base percentage will need to be improved if the Royals seek to rekindle their pennant hopes in 1994.

As the Royals battled for the 1993 division title, reporters inevitably asked George Brett how long he would continue to play. Long retired from his duties at third base, Brett serves as Kansas City's designated hitter. More than once in 1993 Brett indicated that he might retire from baseball at year's end.

The idea filled him with ambivalence, however. "Every time I go 0 for 4, I want to retire," he told *Sports Illustrated.* "Every time I get three hits, I want to play. Every time I do something to help us win, I want to play. Every time I feel over-matched up there—that's a lot—I want to retire." And retire he did at the end of the 1993 season, driving a single up the middle in his last at bat for the 3,154th hit of his illustrious twenty-year career.

Brett's retirement will be greeted as a significant milestone in the history of the Kansas City Royals, a sign that time marches on and does not wait for even the greatest baseball champions. But just as time marches on, so do the Royals—at a pace that is sure to bring more World Series banners to gleaming Royals Stadium.

SOURCES

BOOKS

Cameron, Steve, *Moments, Memories, Miracles: A Quarter Century with the Kansas City Royals,* Taylor Publishing, 1992.

Eskew, Alan, *A Royal Finish: The Celebration of the 1985 Kansas City Royals,* Contemporary Books, 1985.

Rothaus, James, *Kansas City Royals,* Creative Education, 1987.

PERIODICALS

Sports Illustrated, April 23, 1990; April 1, 1991; June 17, 1991; April 20, 1992; June 21, 1993.

—Anne Janette Johnson

MILWAUKEE BREWERS

Some professional sport franchises may never have come into existence had it not been for the efforts and dedication of a single individual. In the National Football League (NFL), for example, the Green Bay Packers had Curly Lambeau and the Chicago Bears had George Halas. So, too, was it in major league baseball with the Milwaukee Brewers and Allan H. "Bud" Selig.

Back in the early 1950s, when baseball franchises were just beginning to hop around from city to city, the old Boston Braves pulled up the stakes on their Beantown tepees and moved to Milwaukee. The move thrilled Selig, a lifelong Milwaukeean and an incurable baseball enthusiast. He became more than merely an avid fan; he bought $24,000 worth of stock in the team, becoming its major public investor. The first years of the Milwaukee Braves were euphoric thanks to superstars such as Warren Spahn, Hank Aaron, and Eddie Mathews; in short order, the team won a Pennant and a World Championship.

Selig's joy as well as that of millions of other Braves fans sunk to the depths after little more than a decade, however, when the Braves, under new ownership, opted to move to Atlanta following the 1965 season. One of the more vocal opponents of the move, Selig initiated a project called "Go to Bat for the Braves" in an effort to convince the club's owners to stay in Milwaukee. It was a commendable, but futile toil.

But that was merely the start of Selig's quest. A year later, with the Braves long gone, he and Ed Fitzgerald—chairman of the board of Cutler Hammer and the future owner of the Milwaukee Bucks NBA basketball team—organized a group called TEAMS, Inc., an acronym for "To Encourage All Milwaukee Sports," with the primary purpose of seeking an expansion franchise for the city.

In 1967, after Selig and his group had cajoled the Chicago White Sox owners to play nine of their regular season games in Milwaukee, it was announced by the American League that two new franchises would be added to the loop's lineup. Selig and other TEAMS leaders felt that Milwaukee had an inside track on obtaining one of the franchises. The first of many disappointments they were to experience occurred when the American League awarded the two new spots to Seattle and Kansas City.

Two more years of struggle, rejection, and heartache were to follow. "Bud was the one who kept the effort and the fight together," recalled Milwaukee public relations guru Ben Barkin. "Without him, everything would have folded." Then in May of 1968, Selig and Milwaukee Circuit Judge Robert Cannon, another diehard baseball fan, were in Chicago for the announcement of plans for two new franchises for the National League. "We didn't believe that it could happen again," Selig said. "We were fighting for a franchise harder than anyone; how could they ignore us?"

But ignore the Milwaukee contingent they did, and the two new franchises went to San Diego and Montreal. "It was as dejected as I've ever been," Selig said. "For the first time, I was ready to quit." But, fortunately for Milwaukee baseball fans, Selig persisted.

In 1969 Selig and his group again thought they'd made the hurdle. "We made an offer to buy the Chicago White Sox from Arthur Allyn," Selig recalled, "and he accepted. We asked ourselves, what could go wrong now?" Selig's question was answered when Allyn changed his mind at the last minute, and sold the team to his brother. For years Selig put in thousands of hours and hundreds of thousands of flying miles to reach his goal, without a penny of compensation. In fact, the vast majority of expenses incurred, such as travel, hotels, phone calls, correspondence and so on, came out of his own pocket, all while he was running a completely unrelated automobile dealership business of his own.

Unexpectedly early in 1970, the solution came from two thousand miles to the west, when the newly formed Seattle Pilots became a bankrupt organization. In a whirlwind move, Selig and his group were able to purchase the franchise for $10.8 million. The final papers were signed on March 31, and the Milwaukee Brewers became reality. But incredibly, the season's opener, which would be in Milwaukee, was on April 7, only a week away.

Among other things, the new Milwaukee Brewers had to print and sell tickets, get County Stadium ready, and obtain uniforms for the players in only a few days. "It was chaos, madness," Selig remembered, "and it was the most wonderful week imaginable at the same time. We really didn't have time to get new uniforms; we just ripped off the 'S's' on the old Pilot's shirts and sewed on 'M's.'"

Selig, of course, became the club's first president and a director; other directors included Fitzgerald, Everett Smith, Roswell Stearns, and Carlton Wilson. Besides Selig, the team's officers were Judge Cannon, attorney Richard Cutler, and Marvin Milkes, who had been Seattle's general manager and who continued in that capacity with the Brewers as did Manager Dave Bristol and his entire coaching staff, Cal Coolidge, Roy McMillan, Jackie Moore, and Wes Stock.

On the field the new Milwaukee Brewers team bore little resemblance to its predecessor in Seattle, with only two key pitchers, Marty Pattin and Gene Brabender; infielder/outfielder Tommy Harper; and first baseman Mike Hegan, all of whom were carried over from the old club. Three rookies would go on to make major contributions to the new team, hurlers Bill Parsons and Skip Lockwood and outfielder Danny Walton.

Added to the staff by trades and other moves were hurlers Al Downing, Lew Krausse, and Ken Sanders; catcher Phil Roof; infielders Roberto Pena and Ted Kubiak; and outfielder Davey May. With all of the hoopla and grand expectations, though, all of these newcomers would

TEAM INFORMATION AT A GLANCE

Founding date: 1969 in Seattle, WA (as Seattle Pilots);
1970 in Milwaukee (as Brewers)

Home stadium: Milwaukee County Stadium
Milwaukee, WI 53214
Phone: (414) 933-4114
FAX: (414) 933-7323

Dimensions: left-field line—315 feet
Center field—402 feet
Right-field line—315 feet
Seating capacity: 53,192

Team colors: Blue and Gold
Team nickname: Pilots (1969); Brewers (1970—)
Logo: The lower case letters "m" and "b" positioned to look like a baseball glove.

Franchise record:	Won	Lost	Pct.
(1969-1993)	1924	2061	.483

go on to a 65-97 record, only one game better than the old Seattle Pilot's 64-98 in 1969.

Ticket prices for that first year in Milwaukee were $5.25 for mezzanine seats; $4.25 for boxes; $3.25 for lower grandstand; and all of $1.25 for bleacher seats. In the 25 seasons since the Brewers began play in 1970, more than 30 million fans have cheered the team on at County Stadium. The heroes have been many: Hall of Famer and all-time home run king Hank Aaron, who was with the team for the last two years of his illustrious career; another Hall of Fame inductee and one of the top relief pitchers of the game, Rollie Fingers; Robin Yount, Paul Molitor, and Jim Gantner, a threesome who have accounted for more hits than any other trio on any baseball team since the game began; and sluggers such as Gorman Thomas, Ben Oglivie, and Cecil Cooper.

A Less Than Stellar Start

The official return of major league baseball to Milwaukee occurred on April 7, 1970, as the Brewers took on the California Angels at County Stadium. The Opening Day lineup, the first ever for the Brewers, was Tommy Harper, 2B; Russ Snyder, CF; Mike Hegan, 1B; Danny Walton, LF; Steve Hovley, RF; Jerry McNertney, C; Max Alvis, 3B; Ted Kubiak, SS; and Lew Krausse, P. Unfortunately for the crowd of 37,237 at the home opener, the outcome didn't match the joyful mood: the Brewers were shut out by Angels starter Andy Messersmith, 12-0.

Milwaukee's first win would not come until April 11 in Chicago in an 8-4 decision over the White Sox. The Brewers' first win ever was credited to relief hurler John O'Donoghue. The team's first home victory would not come until

MILWAUKEE BREWER TEAM RECORDS

Most Games Won in a Single Season	1979 and 1982	95
Longest Winning Streak	1986-87	16
Highest Season Attendance	1983	2,397,131
Highest Team Batting Average	1979	.280
Most Team Home Runs	1982	.216
Lowest Team Earned Run Average	1971	3.38
Most Team Stolen Bases	1992	256

their sixth home game on May 6, with Milwaukee pitcher Bob Bolin fanning 10 in a 4-3 decision over the Boston Red Sox.

In June outfielder Davey May was acquired in a trade with the Baltimore Orioles. On July 18, in a 10-5 win over the Red Sox in Fenway Park in Boston, shortstop Ted Kubiak drove in seven runs, which remains a Milwaukee record. "Bernie Brewer"—69-year-old diehard Milwaukee fan Milt Mason—secluded himself into a trailer atop the Stadium scoreboard in late June, vowing not to come out until the team drew 40,000 fans for one day. He had to wait until August 16, more than two months.

Harper was only the fifth player in Major League history to hit 30 home runs and steal 30 bases in the same year; he had 31 and 38, respectively. Walton became the crowd favorite, especially with the newly named "Brew Crew" in the left field bleachers. Harper was selected as the team's Most Valuable Player (MVP), and he certainly deserved it, adding to those roundtrippers and stolen bases with a team-leading 82 runs batted in (RBIs) and a .296 average.

Marty Pattin, with a 14-13 won-lost mark, led the Milwaukee pitchers, while Krausse finished at 13-18. Pattin was voted Brewer Pitcher of the Year for the 1970 season. Overall, the Brewers' 65-97 record tied them with Kansas City for fourth place, a whopping 43 games behind division-leading Baltimore.

Prior to the beginning of the club's second season in Milwaukee, Frank "Trader" Lane replaced Marvin Milkes as director of baseball operations. Milwaukee won its first season opener 7-2 over the Minnesota Twins. The game was pitched by Marty Pattin, who would go on to lead the Brewers with 14 wins, 264 innings pitched, 169 strikeouts. In the latter two categories, he also led the league.

The Brewers lost their second game, then returned home to win their home opener 4-3 before 40,566 fans, which was to be their biggest crowd of the year. Newcomer Bill Parsons, a tall 6'6" player, would win Rookie of the Year honors, posting a 13-17 mark. Relief star Kenny Sanders set a new American League record for games finished with 77; led the league in games saved with 31; and, holding the most appearances with 83, was on his way to Fireman of the Year recognition.

Pattin, Sanders, Skip Lockwood, and another rookie, Jim Slaton, paced the Milwaukee club to 23 shutout wins. But on the other hand the Brewer team batting average of .227 was the lowest in the league. In May veteran outfielder Johnny Briggs was picked up in a trade with Philadelphia.

The team would go on to win 69 games, a four-game improvement on its first season in Milwaukee. In a major trade during the World Series, a move obviously intended to add some punch to the Milwaukee attack, Lane lived up to his name, engineering a blockbuster trade with

BREWER INDIVIDUAL RECORDS

Highest Batting Average	Paul Molitor	1987	.353
Longest Hitting Streak	Paul Molitor	1987	39 games
Highest Slugging Percent	Robin Yount	1982	.578
Most Total Bases	Robin Yount	1982	367
Most Extra Base Hits	Robin Yount	1982	87
Doubles	Robin Yount	1988	49
Triples	Paul Molitor	1977	16
Home Runs	Gorman Thomas	1979	45
Runs	Paul Molitor	1982	136
Runs Batted In	Cecil Cooper	1983	126
Bases on Balls	Gorman Thomas	1979	96
Stolen Bases	Pat Listach	1992	54
Games won	Mike Caldwell	1978	22
Highest Winning Pct.	Cal Eldred	1992	.846 (11-2)
Most Strikeouts	Teddy Higuera	1987	240
Shutouts	Mike Caldwell	1978	6
Saves	Dan Plesac	1989	33
Innings Pitched	Jim Colborn	1973	314
Consecutive Scoreless	Teddy Higuera	1987	32
Appearances	Ken Sanders	1971	83
Complete Games	Mike Caldwell	1978	23
Lowest ERA	Cal Eldred	1992	1.79

the Red Sox that sent Tommy Harper, Lew Krausse, Marty Pattin, and minor leaguer Pat Skrable to Boston for George Scott, Billy Conigliaro, Joe Lahoud, Ken Brett, and Don Paveletich.

For the season, outfielder Davey May led Brewer hitters with a .277 average and 65 RBIs, while Briggs held the most round-trippers with 21. Milwaukee finished sixth in the Division, 32 games behind Oakland. Sanders was voted the club's Most Valuable Player.

Became Part of the Eastern Division

Playing in the Eastern Division for the first time and in a season shortened by six games because of a player strike, Milwaukee could not fight its way out of the cellar and finished 21 games behind division-leading Detroit. An unusually cold and wet spring and summer led to a big drop in attendance: 600,440 was to be the lowest attendance figure ever for the Milwaukee club. Bill Parsons won the season opener 5-1, besting the Cleveland Indians, but then in the chilly home opener against Detroit, only 8,968 fans showed up. That total is easily the lowest ever for a Brewer opener.

Brewer manager Dave Bristol was given the ax in late May and was replaced by former Milwaukee Brave catcher and crowd favorite Del Crandall. Brewer pitcher Skip Lockwood got Crandall's managerial career off to an auspicious start, tossing a one-hit gem against the New York Yankees on May 30th. Earlier, in a 22-inning marathon against the Minnesota

Twins on May 12th, infielder Bob Heise set a club record by batting ten times.

Team individual leaders for the 1972 season included slugger George Scott, who topped the club with a .266 mark—edging out teammate Johnny Briggs by less than a percentage point—154 hits, 24 doubles, 88 RBIs, and four triples.

Briggs meanwhile pounded out 21 homers to pace the team and also led in slugging with a .455 performance. Jim Lonborg, with 14, and Bill Parsons, with 13, paced the hurlers, while Ken Sanders totaled 17 saves. Catcher Ellie Rodriguez improved to a .285 average in 355 at bats. Scott was voted team MVP, while Jerry Bell was selected as the team's Rookie of the Year.

Following the season, Jim Wilson was appointed director of baseball operations, replacing Trader Lane. In an off-season trade with Philadelphia, the club acquired the services of Don Money, Billy Champion, and John Vukovich, for Lonborg, Sanders, Ken Brett and Earl Stephenson.

Had First Taste of First Place

The Brewers' season opener of 1973 was delayed for four days after a 13-inch snowstorm had paralyzed the area. The wait was worth it as Bill Parsons, with help from Jerry Bell, shutout the Baltimore Orioles 2-0. Parsons allowed only one hit over seven and a third innings, but it was to be his only win of the season at home, as he succumbed to arm problems that had plagued him all year. He finished with a disappointing 3-6 record after winning 13 games in each of the two previous seasons.

In their most exciting season in their four year history, the Brewers put together a 10-game winning streak in June, taking 15 of 16 during the month and occupying first place as late as June 19th. The team's success electrified area fans as Milwaukee topped the million mark for the first time.

On the night they won their tenth straight, the exuberant fans and their screaming rattled a Red Sox pitcher to the point that he walked in three runs. The game marked the beginning of boisterous, deafening attacks on opposing pitchers by Milwaukee fans. Zealous fan Bernie Brewer was replaced by Bonnie Brewer, and together with team organist Frank Charles, a new festive atmosphere was installed at Brewer games.

The spirited play of rookies Darrell Porter, Bob Coluccio, and Pedro Garcia (the latter finishing second to Baltimore's Al Bumbry as league Rookie of the Year) sparked the team.

Davey May (.303) and George Scott (.306), led Brewer hitters, with May fashioning a 24-game hitting streak. Scott's .306 was actually the second highest average in the league, behind Rod Carew's .350. May, with 25 homers, and Scott, with 24, led in round-trippers, while Scott had 107 RBIs, a new club record. Scott and May each amassed 295 bases, tops in the league.

Johnny Briggs collected six hits on August 4 at Cleveland, still a club record. Scott and May were naturally voted as the team's co-MVPs, while Jim Colborn earned Brewer Pitcher of the Year and Garcia was named the team's Rookie of the Year. Colborn, who pitched a one-hitter against Texas, became Milwaukee's first to boast 20 games won.

After Milwaukee beat the Tigers early in 1973, Detroit manager Billy Martin made his now famous quip: "If the Brewers win with what they've got, I'm a Chinese aviator." Only a game below .500 as late as August 31, Milwaukee was hurt by lack of consistent relief pitching and fell to a 74-88 mark, fifth in the division and 23 games behind first place Baltimore.

Acquired Star Hitter Robin Yount

In the 1974 season the Brewers improved in the win column to 76, but it was their highest total ever and was also Crandall's best as manager. The dropoff in performances by veterans Scott, May, and Colborn, as well as second-year starters Coluccio and Garcia, prevented any further improvement.

Tom Murphy became the team's bullpen ace, adding 20 saves (second in the league) to 10 wins and a sparkling 1.90 earned run average (ERA).

At the time, it seemed like just another rookie making the team, but when 18-year-old Robin Yount was added to the roster during spring training, a Hall of Fame career was on its way. The slim, quiet Californian would go on to bang out more than 3,000 hits, a milestone reached by only 16 hitters in the entire history of the sport.

Steady Don Money played 87 consecutive errorless games at third base, and led the American league in total at bats, with 629. The popular Mike Hegan was re-acquired from the Yankees, and Deron Johnson was purchased from Oakland. On June 19 at County Stadium, Kansas City's Jim Busby pitched the first no-hitter against the Brewers.

In off-field moves, Jim Baumer was appointed director of baseball operations, replacing Jim Wilson, who had accepted the position of chief of the Major League Scouting Bureau. The club finished fifth in the division, 15 games behind league-leading Baltimore.

Billy Champion, with a 11-4 mark (good for a .733 winning percentage, the best in the league) and Ed Sprague, at 7-2, were surprises on the Brewer hill staff, while Slaton led in wins with 13. Money paced the team in hitting with a .283 average, while Scott led in RBIs with 82 and tied Briggs in homers with 17. Porter and Money were named to the All-Star team. Honey was voted the team's MVP, and Yount its Rookie of the Year.

On November 2, in a trade with the Atlanta Braves, the Brewers gave up May for the services of all-time home run king Hank Aaron. Aaron had played for the Braves for 21 years, 12 of which the team played in Milwaukee.

AP/Wide World Photos

Robin Yount

Improvement in Attendance

The largest opening day crowd in the club's history, 48,160, packed County Stadium on April 11, 1975, not only to usher in the new season, but to welcome home to Milwaukee all-time home run king Henry Aaron. The attendance at the game set the pace for the rest of the season as the Brewers were to go on to a 1,213,357 total, the team's highest ever.

In July Milwaukee hosted the Major League All-Star game. A total of 51,480 filled County Stadium to overflowing, with the National League coming out on top 6-3. The Brewers were represented at the game by Scott and Aaron. Milwaukee continued in 5th place, however, and dropped down under the 70-win total for the first time in three years.

"The Boomer," George Scott, enjoyed his best year ever, winning the league RBI crown with 109 and tying Reggie Jackson for the home run championship with 36. The big first baseman also led the Brewers with 176 hits and a .285 batting average and was an easy choice for the team's Most Valuable Player award. Pete Broberg, with 14 wins, led the hill crew, while Tom Murphy again was the team's top stopper, with 20 saves. Broberg was voted team Pitcher of the Year.

The squad got off to a good start in 1975, winning nine of 16 games in April and were still above .500 on July 1st. A nosedive in August and September, however, spelled doom not only for Brewer playoff hopes, but for Del Crandall's tenure as the club's skipper. During the final two months the Brewers were to win only 16 while losing 41. On the final day of the season the front office announced that Crandall's contract would not be renewed for the coming year.

Striving to get back on the winning track again, Milwaukee hired former Cincinnati coach Alex Grammas to replace Del Crandall. Grammas, who became the third Milwaukee Brewer manager, had a 10-year career as a player in the majors, with St. Louis, Cincinnati and Chicago, all in the National League. It was felt that Grammas's association with the "winning tradition" at Cincinnati would carry over to his performance as the new Milwaukee skipper.

After an excellent April for the 1976 season, during which the Brewers won 9 of 12 games, the team experienced a lackluster May, winning only 7 of 24. The team played fairly well through the summer before going into a fall swoon, losing 26 of 34 games in August and September. The Brewers finished at 66-95, 32 games behind the leader and a game and a half worse than they had managed in Crandall's last year.

First sacker George Scott won his fifth consecutive Gold Glove award, proving his talents were not merely swinging a big bat. Don Money and Bill Travers were selected to play in the All-Star game, and Travers was elected by his teammates as Brewer Pitcher of the Year,

winning 15 games and turning in a 2.81 ERA. After a fine 5-0 shutout win over the Yankees at County Stadium before an Opening Day crowd of 44,868, Jim Slaton went on to post a 14-15 mark for the year. No MVP was chosen by the team.

During the 1976 season the second member of the future Yount-Gantner-Molitor combo came aboard; 22-year-old Jimmy Gantner came up from the minors to hit .246 in 26 games at second. Three-year veteran Robin Yount, now all of 20 years old, became the youngest player in history to play in 161 games in one season. Sixto Lezcano topped the club in hitting, with a .285 mark, while Scott led RBIs with 77, homers with 18, and hits with 166.

In November of 1976, the Oakland A's third baseman, Sal Bando, who had become a free agent, was signed, not only for his bat, but for his "leadership abilities." The move was to be more prophetic than anyone then realized, as the likable Bando would 15 years later be named the team's senior vice-president in charge of all baseball operations. A month later, in major trades, the Brewers sent Scott and outfielder Bernie Carbo to the Red Sox for first baseman Cecil Cooper, then peddled pitcher Jim Colborn and catcher Darrell Porter to Kansas City for outfielders Jim Wohford and Jamie Quirk.

Began 1977 Season With High Hopes

The Brewers' second season under Manager Alex Grammas began with high hopes as the club won the Cactus League title for the first time ever with a 17-9 mark, then continued on during the regular season, posting an 11-6 record in April, the best in the league. An overflow crowd of 55,120, the largest home crowd for the Brewers up until that time, saw Milwaukee drop a tight 1-0 pitcher's duel to Baltimore's Jim Palmer; Bill Travers was the unlucky loser. After a hot start the team could not put together any semblance of a follow-up and finished with

Abner Dalrymple, Sam Weaver, John Anderson, Hugh Duffy—great names in Milwaukee baseball history? Most assuredly. They were key members of the two original Milwaukee Major League baseball teams. Despite what is generally believed, the Milwaukee Brewers are not the second Major League club to call Milwaukee home, following on the footsteps of the old Milwaukee Braves. They are the fourth.

The first club was also called the Milwaukee Brewers, and they played in the National League in 1878, two years after the league was formed. They finished last among six teams that year with a 15-45 record. Dalrymple, a left fielder, had a .354 batting average, the second-highest in the NL that year.

Weaver, one of only two pitchers on the club, had a 12-31 record, despite having a fine 1.95 ERA and 39 complete games. That number of complete games may seem like a tremendous figure by today's standards, but in those days most pitchers finished what they started. Tommy Bond of the league-leading Boston Red Caps, for example, won 40 games with 57 complete games. That 1878 Brewers team lasted only one year before folding.

Then in 1901, the first year for the new American League, Milwaukee was again represented as one of the eight teams. It was also known as the Brewers. The club's manager was future Hall-of-Famer Hugh Duffy, who was a player manager that year and hit a respectable .302. Duffy was one of the finest hitters of the era, and seven years earlier had put together an astonishing .438 average with 236 hits in only 125 games. First baseman Anderson was among the league leaders with a .330 average. Like the 1878 team, however, the club finished last with a 48-89 record, and after the season, moved to St. Louis, where it became the St. Louis Browns.

a disappointing 67-95 record, 33 games behind the first place New York Yankees.

At the plate, Cecil Cooper's first year as a Brewer was a winner, as he hit an even .300—only the second time a Milwaukee hitter had ever reached the figure—and banged out 193 hits and 20 homers. He earned the team's new Harvey Kuenn Batting Award for his efforts. Robin Yount began to give evidence of becoming one of the league's premier hitters, raising his average to a commendable .288, his highest ever. Don Money won the home run and RBI titles, with 25 and 83 respectively, on his way to earning Brewer MVP honors. Money and pitcher Jim Slaton were Milwaukee's representatives in the annual All-Star game.

On the hill, Jerry Augustine posted a 12-18 record to lead the team in wins; Moose Haas turned in a 10-12 performance to win Brewer Rookie of the Year plaudits; Slaton also won 10 for the club but was traded after the season to Detroit for outfielder Ben Oglivie; Bob McClure, picked up earlier from Kansas City, appeared in 68 games for the Brewers; and Bill Castro, now a pitching coach for the Brewers, led the 1977 club with 13 saves.

On June 17 Milwaukee picked up pitcher Mike Caldwell from Cincinnati for two minor leaguers, a move that was to pay big dividends a year later.

In November of 1977 the Brewers added another important link to their attack, acquiring outfielder Larry Hisle in the re-entry draft. The next day GM Jim Baumer and Manager Alex Grammas were given their walking papers, and Harry Dalton was named to replace Baumer.

MILWAUKEE BREWERS

Two months later, after a lengthy search, New York Mets Pitching Coach George Bamberger was announced as the team's new Manager.

Became One of Baseball's Best

The year 1978 marked the turnaround in Brewer fortunes as the club, after eight futile seasons, finally became one of the best teams in baseball. Milwaukee, in fact, became the talk of the baseball world as they zoomed to a 93-69 record, fourth best in all of baseball and 26 games better than their previous year's performance.

What was the reason? Newly acquired Manager George Bamberger (nicknamed Bambi)? The emergence of Gorman Thomas, Larry Hisle, Cecil Cooper, and Ben Oglivie as "Bambi's Bombers," power hitters supreme? Or was it the development of Mike Caldwell, Jim Slaton, and Larry Sorensen as big winners on the mound?

All of these things and more were factors in the Brewers' success. But most important was that the Brewers had, in one short year, transformed themselves from a perennial doormat into one of the most powerful and feared teams in the sport.

That 93-69 record, while being the fourth best in all of baseball, was also only the third best in the American League's Eastern Division, as New York, with a 100-63 record, and Boston, at 99-64, also had outstanding teams. The Brewers third place 93-69 mark was actually better than Western Division Champion Kansas City's 92-70.

The Brewer wrecking crew led the American League in home runs with 173 and topped the loop in six other major offensive categories. Against the World Champion New York Yankees, the Brewers swept all seven games played in County Stadium, and 10 of 15 overall.

Milwaukee pitcher Mike Caldwell won 22 games and lost only nine, with a sparkling 2.37 ERA. Black Mike, called that because of his ever present dark beard, was voted Comeback Player of the Year and topped the majors with 23 complete games. Had it not been for a fantastic year by Yankee starter Ron Guidry, Calwell's performance surely would have earned him Cy Young Award honors. His win total, number of complete games, earned run average, and six shutouts were all new Brewer records.

Second-year man Sorenson, at 18-12; Slaton (who had been re-acquired in the re-entry draft) at 17-11; Jerry Augustine at 13-12; and Bill Travers at 12-11 gave the team five starters with double figures in the win column, the only such quintette in baseball. A sixth Brewer starter, Moose Haas, started the season well, winning his first two games and fanning 14 Yankees in the second. A torn muscle in his arm ruined the rest of the season, however, and he had only a 2-3 record to show for his efforts.

Brewer hitters were led by Hisle's 34 round-trippers and 115 RBIs, Thomas's 32 towering home runs, and Cooper's .312 average, the highest to date for the team. Rookie Paul Molitor banged out a respectable .273 average, and Robin Yount continued to improve, posting a .293 mark for the year.

Don Money again was solid, also with a .293 average and steady play in the field, and Oglivie hit .303 with 18 homers. Hisle was voted team MVP; Oglivie won the Harvey Kuenn Batting Award; Molitor was easily Rookie of the Year for the team and was accorded the same honor by the league.

Amassing other awards, Brewer owner Bud Selig was named Major League Executive of the Year; Bamberger was voted Manager of the Year; Harry Dalton was picked as General Manager of the Year; and Money became the first Brewer ever to be voted into the starting lineup for the All-Star Game. Hisle and Sorenson also made the squad. The Brewers were selected as the top sports story in Wisconsin by both AP and UPI, and a total of 1,601,406 fans passed through the turnstiles of County Stadium, another Brewer record.

Achieved Best Record

Although they again fell short of their goal of winning a Division Championship, the 1979 Brewers won more games than any Brewer team had ever accomplished and put together a truly momentous season. That 95-66 record, good for a .590 winning percentage, for example, was and remains the best the Milwaukee club ever put together. (The Brewers would also win 95 games in their championship season in 1982, but that year they lost 67 games and thus had only a .586 winning percentage.) The total of 1,918,343 fans who filled County Stadium during the year was a new season record for attendance.

The team set several records that season. The Brewers had a winning record in every month of the season—13-9 in April, 15-14 in May, 16-10 in June, 19-10 in July, 18-12 in August and 14-11 in September-October—the first and only time that has happened in the club's history. Gorman Thomas set a new home run record of 45, which remains a Milwaukee high. Thomas also banged in a total of 123 runs, which broke the team's RBI mark, and remains the club's record.

Paul Molitor's .322 average was the highest any Brewer had ever attained up to that time. Cooper, Molitor, and Ben Oglivie each had 16-game hitting streaks during the year. But it was Sixto Lezcano, with a .321 average, 28 round-trippers, and 101 RBIs, who was voted the team's MVP and who also won Gold Glove Honors for his defensive play.

A low point in the season occurred in Baltimore on April 30, when outfielder Larry Hisle tore the rotator cuff in his shoulder, an injury that all but ended his career. The popular outfielder never completely regained his earlier form.

Mike Caldwell, with another fine season, won 16 while losing only six to pace the hill staff, with Jim Slaton at 15-9, Larry Sorensen at 15-14, and Moose Haas at 11-11 rounding out the starting five. Caldwell was voted as the team's Most Valuable Pitcher, while the Harvey Kuenn Batting Award went to Paul Molitor.

"Bambi's Bombers"

Entering the first season of the 1980s, "Bambi's Bombers," with what was felt to be the most potent batting attack in all of baseball, were the favorites to win it all. Milwaukee's hopes were dampened, however, during Spring Training when their popular manager, George Bamberger, suffered a heart attack that necessitated bypass surgery. Coach Buck Rodgers assumed acting managerial duties until Bamberger could return, which was not until June.

In addition to Bamberger's absence, a number of key Brewer players were also lost for a good portion of the season, due to injuries. Larry Hisle was never able to come back from his rotator cuff surgery the year before; Don Honey sustained ligament damage to his knee, and hurler Jim Slaton had shoulder injury woes. Each was out most of the year.

Opening Day was one of the high points of the year as Sixto Lezcano slammed a 9th-inning grand slam at County Stadium to lift the Brewers to a 9-5 win over the Red Sox before 53,313 happy fans. More club and individual records were broken during the season as Cooper banged out a .352 average, his highest ever and still the top mark a Brewer ever attained; Ben Oglivie walloped 41 homers, tying with New York's Reggie Jackson for the league lead; and Robin Yount amassed 82 extra base hits, including 49 doubles, which remains a Brewer record. Cooper had 219 hits and drove in 122 runs, on his way to being chosen Most Valuable Brewer and the recipient of the Harvey Kuenn Batting Award.

In July of 1980 195,657 fans poured into County Stadium for a four-game series against the Yankees, a four-game total that's still the highest in Brewer history. During the same summer the club unveiled its new electronic scoreboard in right field, with capabilities to show instant replay as well as animation.

Milwaukee led the major leagues in 1980 in home runs, with 203, in runs, with 774, in total bases, with 2,535, and in slugging percentage, with .448. For the second year in a row the club had three hitters with more than 100 runs batted in—Cooper (122), Oglivie (118), and Thomas (105). Brewer pitchers were paced by Moose Haas's 16-15 mark, with Mike Caldwell at 13-11, and Larry Sorensen and Bill Travers chipping in with 12 wins each. Haas was selected as the team's most valuable pitcher.

On August 16, 1980, 24-year-old Robin Yount became one of the youngest players in the history of the game to attain 1,000 hits. Only Detroit's Ty Cobb and Al Kaline reached the milestone at an earlier age. Although Milwaukee was blessed with an abundance of hitting, a depleted pitching staff led to a drop in their win total, down to 86-76.

In an effort to improve in this area, GM Harry Dalton pulled off a trade with the St. Louis Cardinals, picking up Pete Vuckovich and all-time save leader Rollie Fingers as well as catcher Ted Simmons, giving up Sixto Lezcano, Sorensen, Dave LaPoint, and David Green. In a later move, free agents Roy Howell and Randy Lerch were also added to the team.

Bamberger, who had returned as manager of the club on June 6, continued on until September, when he announced his retirement. Rodgers again took the helm, leading the club through the last 23 games. Overall, Bamberger's record for the year was 47-45, and Rogers's was 39-31.

Rollie Fingers's Pitching Prowess

After three solid seasons, the Brewers were favorites to win the American League East in 1981, and despite a strange, strike-shortened season, didn't disappoint the pollsters or their fans. Because of a mid-season player strike, the season was split into two halves, with the New York Yankees winning the first segment, the Brewers the second. It was the 34th time the Yankees participated in post-season action, while it marked the first appearance in playoff competition for the Brewers.

In a five-game series to determine the AL East representative, the Yanks won the first two games in County Stadium, but the Brewers fought back to take the next two in New York before the Yankees pulled out a 7-3 win in the finale. The New York club then swept three games from Oakland to earn the American League Championship, before bowing to the Los Angeles Dodgers four games to two in the 78th World Series.

Had the season not been split in two the Brewers would have been Eastern Division Champs, as their overall record for the year was 62-47, while the Yankees were actually third best, at 59-48. Baltimore had the second best overall mark at 59-46.

New Brewer stopper Rollie Fingers established his value immediately, earning a save in the 1981 season opener against Cleveland before an American League 1981 season high of 71,067 fans in Cleveland Stadium. Fingers, who came to be recognized by his handlebar mustache, went on to one of the finest records ever turned in by a relief pitcher on his way to winning both the Cy Young and the Most Valuable Pitcher Awards for the American League, the first time in history that the feat had been accomplished. Fingers's save total of 28 was the highest in both leagues. Incredibly, he did not allow an earned run in his 28 saves, spanning 41 innings. In his 47 total appearances, the Brewers were 40-7, an .851 winning percentage. Fingers's overall ERA was an eye-popping 1.04; in the second half of the season it was almost unbelievable, at 0.72.

Pete Vuckovich, after a slow start, went on to lead the Brewer staff with a 14-4 mark. His win total tied for high in the league, while his winning percentage, .778, was the best. Moose Haas, at 11-7, and Mike Caldwell, at 11-9, were also among the league pitching leaders.

For the fifth straight season Cecil Cooper

hit .300 or better, this time chalking up a .320 mark. Cooper also led the league with 35 doubles. For the fourth consecutive year, Gorman Thomas hit 20 or more home runs, this time in the shortened season, coming in with 21. Jimmy Gantner, playing in his first full season at second, led all pivot-men in the loop with participation in 94 double plays.

First AL Championship

After a long and often disappointing 12 years, the steady uphill climb for the Brewers finally paid off as the club won its first American League Championship in 1982. That drive to the top, in a very real sense, began on June 2 with the team in fifth place with a 23-24 record. At that time Brewers Manager Buck Rogers was replaced by batting coach Harvey Kuenn; supposedly just on an "interim" basis.

Under the popular Milwaukee hero, however (Kuenn was born and raised in Milwaukee, was a triple sport star at Milwaukee Lutheran High School, and a standout at the University of Wisconsin before going on to become one of the top hitters in baseball for the Detroit Tigers in the 1950s), Milwaukee won 72 and lost only 43, a .626 winning percentage.

The club swept to the top of the league with a 95-67 overall mark, the top record in the Majors. It also became the first team in League Championship Playoff history to win the Pennant after losing the first two games of a five-game series. The Brewers fought all the way to the seventh game of the World Series before losing to the St. Louis Cardinals.

Kuenn was awarded Manager of the Year and was also named as the Brewer's Manager for the following year—all thoughts of him being an "interim" manager had long disappeared. Kuenn's popularity was such that the team became known throughout the sports world as "Harvey's Wall-bangers."

In one particularly hot streak in June, when the team first moved into first place, the Brew-

BREWER PITCHERS		
15 or More Wins in a Season		
1. Mike Caldwell	1978	22
2. Jim Colborn	1973	20
3. Teddy Higuera	1986	20
4. Pete Vuckovich	1982	18
5. Teddy Higuera	1987	18
6. Lary Sorenssn	1978	18
7. Mike Caldwell	1982	17
8. Jaime Navarro	1992	17
9. Teddy Higuera	1988	16
10. Chris Bosio	1992	16
11. Moose Haas	1980	16
12. Mike Caldwell	1979	16
13. Billy Travers	1976	15
14. Lary Sorensen	1979	15
15. Jim Slaton	1979	15
16. Teddy Higuera	1985	15
17. Chris Bosio	1989	15
18. Bill Wegman	1991	15

ers tied a Major League record by bashing out 35 home runs in 15 straight games. The most feared offense in baseball led the Majors in eight batting departments, recording 216 home runs, 891 runs, and 2,605 total bases, all of which remain Brewer high marks.

The *Sporting News* Player of the Year, Robin Yount, led the AL in four key areas— 210 hits, 367 total bases, 46 doubles and a .578 slugging percentage, hitting .331 (only one point below Kansas City's Willie Wilson, who won the batting title with .332), on his way to AL MVP Award honors. He was also the team's MVP and the recipient of the Brewers' Harvey Kuenn Batting Award.

Yount became the first AL shortstop to ever lead the league in slugging and total bases in the same season, and the first to hit over .300 with more than 20 homers and 100 RBIs. He was one of only three players in the history of the game (along with Chuck Klein and Billy Herman) to collect more than 20 doubles, 10 triples, 20 homers, and 20 stolen bases in the same year.

The Brewers took both top AL individual awards, with Pete Vuckovich winning the league's Cy Young Award with a 18-6 mark. With the Brewers winning both honors, coupled with Rollie Fingers sweep the year before, Milwaukee became the only AL team ever to take both awards two straight years. Vuck was also voted the Brewers' Most Valuable Pitcher.

Other standouts during the season included Paul Molitor's 136 runs—the most in baseball since Ted William's 150 in 1949—along with a .302 batting average, 201 hits, and 300 total bases; Gorman Thomas's league-leading 39 home runs; Cecil Cooper's terrific stats of a .313 average, 205 hits, 32 homers, 121 RBIs, and 345 total bases; catcher Ted Simmons's rebound to 23 home runs, 97 RBIs, and an improved .269 average; Jimmy Gantner's fine .295 average, the highest he would ever hit in the Majors; and Ben Oglivie's 34 round-trippers and 102 RBIs. The threesome of Yount, with 210, Cooper, with 205, and Molitor, with 201, became the first three teammates to finish 1-2-3 in one season since the 1915 Detroit Tigers.

On the hill, besides Vuckovich's totals, Mike Caldwell was at 17-13, Bob McClure was 12-7, Moose Haas at 11-8, and Jim Slaton at 10-6. Newcomer Don Sutton, picked up late in August from Houston, finished with a 4-1 record but more importantly won the season finale against Baltimore to give the Brewers the Eastern Division crown. Almost forgotten was Rollie Fingers's continued contribution to the team's success, with 29 saves and a 2.60 ERA.

In other achievements, the Brewers led the league for the second straight year in double plays, and Yount won his first Gold Glove. Yount was voted into the All-Star game as a starter, while Cooper, Oglivie, and Fingers were also named.

The 79th World Series was dubbed "The Suds Series" because of the amount of beer production in the cities of Milwaukee and St. Louis. Even though the Brewers lost in the final game to the Cardinals, staunch Brewer fans, who set an attendance record for the year, showed their loyalty by turning out in thousands to greet the team in a special ticker tape parade. During the seven games of the Series, Caldwell won two games without a loss, and Brewer hitters were paced by Yount at .414, Molitor at .355, catcher Charlie Moore at .346, and Gantner at .333.

1983 Season Marked by Injuries

Injuries on top of more injuries plagued the 1983 season. Any chance the Brewers had to repeat as American League Champions fell by the wayside as eight different key players were lost for much of the season due to injuries, beginning with star hurlers Pete Vuckovich and Rollie Fingers during Spring Training. Vuckovich, who had won 18 games in 1982, appeared in only three contests during the year, finishing with an 0-2 mark, while Fingers was lost for the entire season.

Despite this, the Brewers still managed to win 87 games—a sixth straight winning season—and maintained their rank as one of the three top teams in the Major Leagues over the past six years. Brewer fans responded as 2,397,131 poured through the turnstiles at County Stadium, smashing the previous attendance record by more than 400,000; it remains a Brewer high.

Cecil Cooper, with his 7th straight .300-or-better season, the only time any Milwaukee Brewer has been able to manage that feat, turned in another super performance. In addition to his .307 average, Coop belted out 30 round-trippers and drove in 126 runs, the latter to tie for the AL lead, and still a Brewer record. The slugging first baseman again paced the club in total bases, this time with 336. Ted Simmons had his best season with Milwaukee, hitting

.308, collecting 185 hits, and driving in 108 runs, the first Brewer catcher ever to exceed 100 RBIs. Robin Yount's numbers dropped slightly, but the All-Star shortstop still hit a commendable .308 with 192 hits.

Paul Molitor again led the club in stolen bases with 41, and Jim Gantner had one of his most productive seasons, hitting .282 with 11 homers and 74 RBIs.

On the mound, Moose Haas compiled a fine 13-3 record, tops in winning percentage in the league; reliever Pete Ladd had 25 saves, and veteran Jim Slaton led in wins, with 14. Don Sutton recorded his 3,000th strikeout during the summer, only the 8th pitcher in the history of the game to do so.

For their efforts, Cooper was voted the team's MVP; Simmons earned the Harvey Kuenn Batting Award; Ladd was chosen as the club's Most Valuable Pitcher; and Tom Tellman, with a 9-4 record, was picked as the team's Rookie of the Year. The latter award was given out for the first time in six years. At All-Star time, the Brewers again had four representatives, Yount and Simmons, who were voted in as starters, as well as Cooper and Ben Oglivie. Following the season Harvey Kuenn stepped down as manager, with Rene Lachemann named to head the club for 1984. Milwaukee picked up catcher Jim Sundberg and outfielder Bobby Clark, the latter in exchange for Slaton.

A Sub-.500 1984 Season

For the first time in seven years, the Brewers fell to a sub-.500 campaign in 1984, and again injuries were to blame. Paul Molitor was out for virtually the entire season, playing in only 13 games, while Rollie Fingers was limited to 33 appearances and Pete Vuckovich was out for the whole year.

Brewer Opening Day pitcher Moose Haas got the club off on the right foot by posting a 7-3 win over Chicago and future Hall of Famer Tom Seaver on April 17 at County Stadium, but

from that point on it was all down hill. Under first-year skipper Rene Lachemann, Milwaukee fell into the American League Eastern Division cellar with a 67-94 record, a team record 36 and a half games behind the World Champion Detroit Tigers. Catcher Jim Sundberg was the Brewer's only representative at the San Francisco All-Star Game.

Don Sutton led the Milwaukee hill crew with a 14-12 effort, becoming the first pitcher in Major League history to record 100 strikeouts for 19 consecutive seasons. Fingers did manage to get in 23 saves and a fine 1.96 ERA, bringing his overall save total to 324, the most in baseball history.

Robin Yount paced the team in nearly all offensive departments, hitting .298 with 186 hits, 16 homers, and 80 RBIs. That 16 round-tripper total was the lowest for a home run pacesetter in club history. Yount was the natural choice for the team's Harvey Kuenn Batting Award, but teammate Jimmy Gantner was the surprising choice for team MVP.

Gumby had a solid season again, hitting .282 with 173 hits. Cecil Cooper suffered his first sub-par year with the team, with only 11 homers and 67 RBIs and a .275 average. A ray of sunshine was provided by newcomer Dion

BREWERS MANAGERS			
Career Records			
1. Harvey Kuenn	1982-83	159-118	.574
2. Phil Garner	1992	92-70	.568
3. Buck Rodgers	1980-82	101-78	.564
4. George Bamberger*		377-351	.518
5. Tom Trebelhorn	1986-91	422-397	.515
6. Del Crandall	1972-75	273-339	.446
7. Rene Lachemann	1984	67-94	.416
8. Alex Grammas	1976-77	133-190	.412
9. Dave Bristol	1970-72	144-209	.408

* 1978-80 and 1985-86

James, whose .295 average earned him Brewer Rookie of the Year plaudits. In late September Brewer GM Harry Dalton rehired the popular George Bamberger to head the club in 1985.

The Return of Bamberger

Brewer fans were hopeful that lightning could strike twice with their favorite manager, George Bamberger, back at the helm. The transplanted New Yorker had led Milwaukee to their first winning season ever seven years earlier, fashioning a 306-220 record over the three years he served as Brewer manager before stepping down in 1980.

But although the club did win four more games than it did in 1984 and moved up a notch in the standings, unfortunately that was all the improvement Bambi and his club could muster, finishing at 71-90, the second losing season in a row and 28 games behind the leading Toronto Blue Jays. And again, injuries took their toll, sidelining key players such as Cecil Cooper, Robin Yount, Ben Oglivie, Chuck Porter, and Randy Ready for lengthy stretches. At All-Star time, only two Brewers, Cooper and Paul Molitor, were named to the team, and both only as alternates.

During the year two Milwaukee rookies made impressive debuts, however, as Mexican-born Teddy Higuera put together a 15-8 record, the most wins ever for a Milwaukee rookie pitcher, while infielder Ernie Riles hit a commendable .286. Higuera was voted Milwaukee's Most Valuable Pitcher, and Riles was named the club's Rookie of the Year. Cooper, with a marked improvement to .293 and 99 RBIs, was named as the Brewer's MVP, while Paul Molitor, at .297, was an obvious choice for Comeback Player of the Year and Harvey Kuenn Batting Award honors.

Pete Vuckovich's comeback effort after more than two years of inactivity resulted in only a 6-10 mark. Rollie Fingers again led in saves, but only 17. Starter Danny Darwin, despite posting a disappointing 8-18 record, including 10 losses in a row, became the first Brewer hurler ever to toss a one-hitter, a two-hitter and a three-hitter in the same season.

New Faces in 1986

With 16 new names on the 1986 roster, "Be patient" was the theme Brewer leaders were asking the fans to accept. The club's pitching staff underwent the most drastic transformation, as by season's end only Teddy Higuera would survive from the 1985 crew.

Despite the team's 77-84 performance, their third losing year in a row, and a drop in attendance to 1,265,041, there were signs of better days ahead. To begin with, their win total was a six-game improvement over the previous year. But the new faces on the team offered the greatest hope.

Higuera's performance was outstanding, and it seemed as if the Brewers had come up with one of the top pitchers in all of baseball. His 20-11 record made him the first Brewer to win 20 since Mike Caldwell in 1978. His win total and 2.79 ERA were among the best in the league. He was voted not only the Brewer's MVP but its Most Valuable Pitcher as well, a combination that was a Brewer first. He was also the only Brewer selected to participate in the annual All-Star Game, and his 207 strike-outs were a Brewer record.

Newcomer Danny Plesac's 10-7 record, 2.97 ERA, and 14 saves earned him Brewer Rookie of the Year honors, while another Milwaukee rookie pitcher, Juan Nieves, had a 11-12 mark.

Robin Yount again led the club in hitting, with a .312 average, collecting his 2,000th base hit on September 6. Two acquisitions picked up over the previous winter made major contributions. Reliever Mark Clear, obtained from the Boston Red Sox, turned in 16 saves, while slugging outfielder Rob Deer, formerly of San Francisco, walloped 33 home runs and knocked in 86.

Two weeks before the end of the season Manager George Bamberger again retired, relieved by coach Tom Trebelhorn. Treb, who guided the club to a 6-3 record in the last nine games, was named the Milwaukee manager for 1987, the team's fifth manager. In post-season trades, in December the Brewers swapped pitchers Tim Leary and Tim Crews to the Los Angeles Dodgers for first baseman Greg Brock.

Best Season in Five Years

Under new skipper Tom Trebelhorn the Brewers put together their best season in five years, topping the 90-win total for only the fourth time in club history. Milwaukee was quickly dubbed as "Team Streak" by sportswriters as the team jumped out to a Major League record tying 13 straight wins on their way to a 17-1 record for the first three weeks.

Along the way hurler Juan Nieves recorded the Brewers' first no-hitter, a 7-0 win over Baltimore on April 15. Nieves finished 14-8 for the year. Robin Yount made a magnificent diving catch to record the last out in Nieves's classic, a catch that became the favorite of Brewer highlight films. During April Milwaukee had an 18-3 record, the best they have ever done in a single month.

But as quickly as the Brewers had risen, their fall was equally as unusual; the team dropped a record 12 straight and fell from the lead on May 13. Milwaukee limped into the All-Star break a game under .500, with only one player, Dan Plesac, named to the game.

Following that midsummer classic, Paul Molitor got red-hot, hitting in 39 straight games, the seventh-longest streak in the history of baseball and the best in the American League since Joe DiMaggio's record 56-game skid in 1941. Molitor went on to post some tremendous numbers, finishing with a .353 average—the highest ever for a Brewer—45 stolen bases (also a club record), 41 doubles, 114 runs, and a .566 slugging average. He also scored in 16 straight

200 or More Hits in a Season		
Cecil Cooper	1980	219
Cecil Cooper	1982	205
Paul Molitor	1991	216
Cecil Cooper	1983	203
Robin Yount	1982	210
Paul Molitor	1982	201

games, only two short of the Major League high, and stole second, third, and home in the same inning. He earned the team's Harvey Kuenn Batting Award for the third time.

Yount, who again hit .312, knocked in 103 runs, topping the 100 mark for the fourth time, and was selected at the Brewers' MVP. Rob Deer, who led the team with 28 round-trippers, tied a Major League record by hitting grand slam home runs in two consecutive games.

During one stretch in late summer, pitcher Teddy Higuera was almost untouchable, hurling a three-hitter on August 26 against Cleveland, winning 1-0; a one-hitter against Kansas City on September 1, winning 2-0; a two-hitter against Minnesota on September 6, winning 6-0; and going 32 consecutive innings without giving up a run. Higuera finished with a 18-10 record while chalking up 240 strikeouts, still a Brewer record. He was voted the team's Most Valuable Pitcher for the third straight year.

Chris Bosio also tossed a two-hitter during the year, beating the Minnesota Twins 1-0 on August 28 on his way to a 11-8 season mark. Billy Weg-man's top effort was a three-hitter on May 5 against California; unfortunately he was given little support and lost the game 2-0. He had a 12-11 record for the season. Dan Plesac led the relief corps, earning 23 saves and fashioning a 2.61 ERA.

Pale Sveum hit 25 home runs in 1987, the most for a Brewer shortstop since Yount banged out 29 in 1982. Rookie catcher B. J. Surhoff and newcomer Greg Brock each just missed the magic .300 mark by a point, while Bill Schroe-

Brewer All-Time Team

Fielders

1B	Cecil Cooper
2B	Jim Gantner
3B	Paul Molitor
SS	Don Money
OF	Robin Yount
OF	Gorman Thomas
OF	Ben Oglivie
C	Charlie Moore

Starting Pitchers

Teddy Higuera
Mike Caldwell
Jim Slaton
Moose Haas

Relief Pitchers

Rollie Fingers
Dan Plesac

DH

Hank Aaron

der, in 250 at bats, hit a surprising .332.

A total of 1,909,244 fans saw Brewer games at County Stadium during the 1987 season, the most since the franchise record of 2.4 million in 1983. Manager Trebelhorn got the club off running like never before, with Milwaukee totalling a team record 176 steals.

A Fight to the Finish in 1988

Although they didn't win the American League East title, the Brewers were in the fight right up until the end of the 1988 season, finishing tied for third place only a scant two games behind the leader. In one of the closest races in history—and a five-team race at that—the Red Sox finished with an 89-73 record, Detroit was

a game back at 88-74, Milwaukee and Toronto two back at 87-75 each, and New York only three and a half back in fifth place at 85-76.

The Brewers began the season with a 12-0 whitewashing over Baltimore in that city's opener before returning home to a crowd of 55,887 at County Stadium, the largest crowd in Brewer history. Tommy John and the New York Yankees spoiled the day for the huge throng, winning 7-1.

On May 28 journeyman pitcher Odell Jones nearly made baseball history for the Brewers as he tossed seven and a third innings of perfect ball and eight and a third before giving up a hit in a 2-0 win in Cleveland.

On June 8 Milwaukee acquired outfielder Jeff Leonard from the San Francisco Giants in exchange for infielder Ernie Riles. On June 12 Robin Yount became only the third Brewer to hit for the cycle as he accomplished the feat in a 16-2 win over the Chicago White Sox. Paul Molitor was voted into the All-Star Game as a second baseman, despite playing in only one game at that position during the year.

On August 28 against Detroit, manager Tom Trebelhorn inadvertently wrote Robin Yount's name in the lineup twice, leading to Yount's ejection from the game later. The Brewers rallied to win the contest 12-10. On September 3 shortstop Dale Sveum broke his leg in a collision with Darryl Hamilton, opening the door for rookie Gary Sheffield to move into the starting lineup. During the season a total of 1,923,238 passed through County Stadium gates, the third-highest total in club history up to that time.

The club got another fine performance from their ace, Teddy Higuera, who had a 16-9 record and a career best 2.45 ERA. Teddy lost out on the league's earned run championship by one one-hundreth of a point when Minnesota hurler, Allen Anderson, who had a 2.44 mark, declined to pitch in his final start to preserve his lead. Anderson's move was looked on with disdain by sports fans everywhere.

Higuera got help from newcomers Don

August, who had a 13-7 record in his first year with the team, and Mike Birkbeck, who had a 10-8 mark. Chris Bosio and Juan Nieves fell to only seven wins each. Bosio's 7-15 record included a team high 11-game losing streak. August was chosen as the club's Rookie of the Year. Middle reliefer Chuck Crim appeared in 70 games, high for the league, and Dan Plesac again led the team in saves, this time with 30, and was voted the Brewers' Most Valuable Pitcher. Bill Wegman finished at 13-13.

Molitor's .312 average and 41 stolen bases earned him the team's Harvey Kuenn Batting Award, and Yount's .306 batting and .465 slugging averages assured him team MVP honors. Yount was the only player in the American League to appear in all 162 games.

The 1989 Brew Crew

After two winning seasons under Manager Tom Trebelhorn, the Brewers finished with a disappointing 81-81 fourth place effort for 1989. For the third year in a row, however, home attendance topped 1.9 million, reaching 1,970,735, the club's third-highest total ever.

The Brew Crew, as the team had begun to be called, entered the American League Eastern Division race as the favorite, but injuries and inconsistent play caused the club to fall short of expectations. Milwaukee opened regular season play with five key starters on the disabled list—pitchers Teddy Higuera and Juan Nieves, and Paul Molitor, Dale Sveum, and Greg Brock.

Don August was picked for the Opening Day assignment against Cleveland there, and although he pitched well, lost to the Indians 2-1. For the Home Opener in Milwaukee, 54,301 showed up to see the Texas Rangers spoil the Brewers' day 6-4 in 10 innings.

Rookie hurler Jaime Navarro made his Major League debut on June 20, and although he didn't get a decision that day, went on to post a 7-8 mark with a commendable 3.12 ERA in his rookie year. Also called up during the sea-

son were power hitting outfielder Greg Vaughn and shortstop Bill Spiers. Dan Plesac was the only Brewer selected to play in the All-Star Game, but it was the third year in a row for the tall left-hander, a first for a Brewer pitcher.

After more than half the season, the Brewers started playing winning ball in August, moving from 12 games behind Baltimore to only a half game on August 21. Unfortunately, from that point on, Milwaukee lost six of seven on the road in Baltimore and Toronto to fall out of contention.

During the summer the Brewers announced their 20th Anniversary Team, as selected by the fans. It was: 1B, Cecil Cooper; 2B, Jim Gantner; SS, Robin Yount; 3B, Paul Molitor; OFs, Sixto Lezcano, Gorman Thomas, and Ben Oglivie; DH, Hank Aaron; C, Charlie Moore; and Ps, Mike Caldwell, Pete Vuckovich, and Rollie Fingers.

Robin Yount, with a .318 average, 195 hits, and 103 runs batted in, was chosen for his second American League MVP award, this time as an outfielder. It was only the third time (along with Stan Musial and Hank Greenberg) in Major League history that a player won the honor at two positions. Yount was also voted the Brewers' MVP for the third year in a row, as well as the recipient of the club's Harvey Kuenn Batting Award. Despite these honors, he was surprisingly surpassed as an All-Star player.

Chris Bosio led the club with 15 wins and a 2.95 era, his best year ever, and was voted as the Brewers' Most Valuable Pitcher. But Bill Wegman, who had won 13 the year before, was hurt most of the season and won only two games; Higuera had his worst season ever, winning only nine games; and Mike Birkbeck, who had won ten the year before, had an 0-4 record for 1989.

Chuck Crim again led the AL in appearances, this time with 76. Plesac, who set a new club record for saves with 33, brought his four-year mark with the Brewers to an even 100 saves and an overall 2.63 era. Spiers was the team's Rookie of the Year. Rob Deer hit only

.210 but again led Milwaukee in round-trippers, with 26, giving him 110 in four years with the Brewers.

Hopes for 1990 Dashed by Injuries

Despite their 1989 showing, the Brewers were predicted to fight it out with Toronto for the American League's Eastern Division crown. Early on the club did not disappoint as they won 12 of 18 in April to move into the lead, despite an Opening Day loss to the Chicago White Sox before 50,294 at County Stadium.

Demonstrating the power potential that they did have, Milwaukee bombed the Boston Red Sox 18-0 on April 16, the largest win margin in club history. From April 18-22, Brewer pitchers were responsible for 31 straight scoreless innings, another club record. Milwaukee remained in first place until May 15, then peeked back in again for a day on June 1, but from that point on fell to their first losing season since 1986. The reasons were the same: injuries.

Ace Teddy Higuera never returned to his dominating form, finishing with a lackluster 11-10 mark; Robin Yount, after his MVP season in 1989 and record setting salary contract, fell to an unproductive .247 average, his worst in the Majors; Don August fell to only six wins but an even more alarming 6.75 era; and both Jim Gantner and Paul Molitor suffered early season injuries necessitating rehabilitation stints in the minors, for both of them it was the first time back in the minor leagues in 13 years. Gantner got into only 88 games and Molitor 103.

On the plus side of the ledger, Milwaukee signed free agent veteran outfielder/first baseman Dave Parker prior to the season, and the Cobra turned out to be one of the club's highlights. Parker hit a solid .289, led the team in hits, with 176, and RBIs, with 92, earning Brewer MVP honors. He was also the only Brewer selected to play in the All-Star game.

Gary Sheffield finally began to live up to his billings, leading the team with a .294 average and also topping in stolen bases with 25. He was awarded the Harvey Kuenn Batting Award. Unfortunately, Sheffield continued to complain about virtually everything and became increasingly unpopular with the media and fans.

After leading the team again in home runs with 27, Rob Deer became a free agent and signed with the Detroit Tigers. Rather than resigning Deer, the team opted instead to pick up Houston free agent Franklin Stubbs. It was not the most successful of moves.

Trebelhorn's Last Season With the Brewers

The 1991 season was to be Trebelhorn's last as the Brewers' skipper. After a hard fought 5-4 Opening Day win in Texas against Nolan Ryan, with Mark Knudson on the hill, followed by an even more impressive 6-0 shutout victory by Chris Bosio in the second game, the Brewers settled to a 43-60 record by the 3rd of August: From that point on the club posted a higher winning percentage than any team in baseball, winning 40 and losing only 19. The hot finish, however, wasn't enough to save Trebelhorn's job. The club finished in fourth place, eight games behind Toronto.

On May 1 the Brewers and the Chicago White Sox fought a marathon 19-inning battle that lasted six hours and five minutes, the longest game in Brewer history. Paul Molitor was the team's only representative at the All-Star game in July, where he reached first on a catcher's interference at the plate, the only time that had ever happened in the mid-summer classic. On July 30 Molitor banged out his 2,000th base hit.

Detroit's Cecil Fielder crushed a 502-foot-long home run over the left field bleachers on September 14, the longest home run in Brewer annals. Another round-tripper of note: Jimmy Gantner set the major league record for homerless games at 1,762 before belting one off Oakland's Dave Stewart at County Stadium late in the 1991 season.

For the season, the Brewer offense was paced by a career-best .327 effort by Willie Randolph—a free agent who had been picked up earlier—and a solid .325 by Molitor. Second-year outfielder Darryl Hamilton chipped in with a surprising .311 mark, while outfielder Greg Vaughn led the club, with 27 round-trippers and 98 RBIs. After missing almost a year with leg injuries, Gantner came back to post a commendable .283 average, one of the best of his long career.

Bill Wegman, at 15-7, Jaime Navarro, at 15-12, and Bosio, at 14-10, led the starters, while Doug Henry became the club's stopper, replacing Plesac with 15 saves and an almost unbelievable 1.00 ERA. Teddy Higuera's woes continued, as the stubby Mexican hurler spent most of the year on the disabled list and won only three games. Molitor was voted as the club's MVP, Wegman as its Most Valuable Pitcher, and Henry as its Rookie of the Year.

Following the season, Randolph opted for free agency again, signing with the New York Mets, and then just prior to the 1992 season, perpetual malcontent Gary Sheffield was traded to San Diego for pitcher Rickie Bones and two minor league players.

The Brewers also reorganized their front office and field operations, naming Sal Bando as senior vice-president of baseball operations, Al Goldis as vice-president of scouting and planning, Harry Dalton as senior vice-president of special projects, and Bruce Manno, assistant vice-president of baseball operations. On October 9 Trebelhorn was dismissed, and then three weeks later, on October 30, Phil (Scrap Iron) Garner was named as the club's new manager.

A Pitching Resurgence in 1992

The 1992 season was for the Brewers' the best of times and the worst of times. After playing less than .500 ball and being far back in the pack for most of the season, the Brewers fought their way out of a jam with New York, Boston, and Detroit, then in an exciting chase through August and September caught and passed Baltimore and nearly overtook the champion Toronto Blue Jays.

With 160 games completed, the Brewers were still in the race, only two games out with two to play. But the Canadian club won its final two, and the Brewers dropped their pair to Oakland, and one of the hottest Pennant races in recent years was history.

The 1992 Brewers had a definite lack of long ball power, finishing last in the Eastern Division with only 82 round-trippers, the lowest total the Brewers had ever managed and not even half the total banged out by the Detroit Tigers (182). They more than made up for it on the basepaths, though, with a team record 256 stolen bases—far and away more than any other team in the entire league and more than any team in the AL East had ever totaled—and on the pitching mound, where the club's 3.43 ERA was the best in both divisions.

That latter ERA mark was down to 3.38 until the last two games of the season, which would have matched the all-time Brewer mark set two decades ago. During the club's stretch run in September, when they went 17-6 to pass up the Orioles, the team ERA was an astounding 2.17.

The Brewer hill resurgence was led by a young man who wasn't even with the team during the first two-thirds of the season, Cal Eldred. All the Iowa farm boy did after being called up from Denver in August was to post an 11-2 record, including 10 wins in a row (a new Brewer record also tied in 1993 by Chris Bosio), and a team leading 1.79 era.

Bill Wegman, who paced the club in the first half of the season, finished at 13-14 with a club-leading 261.2 innings pitched; Jaime Navarro continued to improve, leading the Brewers in wins with a 17-11 record; while Bosio had his top year with a 16-6 effort and those 10 wins in a row. Rickie Bones, obtained in the trade for

Sheffield, showed flashes of promise but could manage only a 9-10 mark. Ron Robinson, at 1-4 and a 5.86 ERA, and Bruce Ruffin, at 1-6 and 6.67, were major disappointments.

Also surprisingly effective were the Brewer cadre of relievers. Austin, with a 5-2 record and a 1.85 ERA; Mike Fetters with 5-1, two saves and a 1.87 ERA; Darren Holmes with 4-4, six saves and 2.55; Jesse Orosco with 3-1, one save, and 3.23; and even the deposed closer, Dan Plesac, with 5-4, one save and a 2.96 ERA, had a good year. Doug Henry had a poor 4.02 era and a 1-4 won-loss record, but did post a team leading 29 saves.

A total of 11 Brewers stole 10 or more bases during the campaign, something no other club had done since 1907. Brewer theft artists were led by Pat Listach, with 54, easily passing up Paul Molitor's old record of 45. Listach also hit a solid .290 and led the team in runs, with 93.

At the plate, the big story was Robin Yount's quest for his 3,000th hit, a feat that overshadowed a truly outstanding season by Paul Molitor. Playing a number of infield positions as well as being the club's primary designated hitter, Molitor led the Brewers in average with .320; hits, with 195; total bases, with 281; slugging, with .461; games played, with 158; at bats, with 609, runs batted in, with 89; and tied Darryl Hamilton in triples, with seven.

Moved into the third slot in the batting order for the first time, Molitor responded with the top RBI effort of his long career. His .320 average was fourth in the league. In addition to passing that magic 3,000 total and moving into 13th place in the all-time Major League hit parade, Yount also led the team in doubles, with 40, and was second on the team in total bases, with 217.

Filling the holes left by the departed Sheffield and the injured Bill Spiers, Scott Fletcher, picked up from the White Sox, and Kevin Seitzer, formerly of Kansas City, came through with .275 and .270 efforts, respectively, and both were more than adequate in the field. Fletcher in particular endeared himself to the fans and Brewer management with several late inning key hits to win games. While Hamilton again had a good year with a .298 average, Greg Vaughn's production was well under his 1990 marks, with a .228 average, 78 RBIs and 23 home runs.

A Frustrating 1993

After the surprising success of the 1992 campaign, Brewer fans were expecting big things in 1993. But after losing such key players as Molitor, Bosio, Fletcher, and Seitzer to free agency during the offseason, the Brewers entered spring training undermanned and disspirited.

To offset these departures, the club looked to their returning veterans as well as newcomers Kevin Reimer and Tom Brunansky and rookie first baseman John Jaha. But Milwaukee had too many holes to fill, and the Brewers struggled to a last-place finish at 69-93, 26 games behind the eventual World Champion Toronto Blue Jays.

The pitching staff, considered one of the team's strong points in 1992, faltered badly, particularly the relief corps. Only Graeme Lloyd and Jesse Orosco displayed any consistency out of the bullpen, as Henry and Holmes were unable to duplicate their success of the previous year. The starting pitching wasn't much better; Wegman was lost for much of the season due to a shoulder injury, Bones again wrestled with control problems, and yet another Higuera comeback failed.

Even Eldred struggled at times; though he did finish with 16 wins and a respectable 4.01 ERA, the second-year man was prone to giving up the long ball. One bright spot was the play of rookie Angel Miranda, called up from the minors during the season, who proved to be a capable starter and should secure a spot in next year's rotation.

The Brewers' weak offense served to magnify the shortcomings of their pitching. The team simply did not put enough men on base to get their running game in gear, and the free agent acquisitions supplied little punch to the lineup: Brunansky hit a dismal .183 before suffering a back injury, and Reimer contributed just 13 home runs, none after the All-Star break.

Veteran Brewer players also had their share of problems: 1992 AL Rookie of the Year Listach, troubled all season by nagging injuries, played in only 87 games, finishing with a disappointing .247 average; Spiers could manage only a .238 average in his comeback attempt; and Yount, though solid defensively, had a subpar year at the plate.

There was some good news, however. Jaha slugged 19 homers and drove in 70 runs after a slow start, and Surhoff, who also floundered early in the year, regained his stroke to finish at .274. Seitzer, reacquired midway through the year, hit .290 and stablized a somewhat shaky infield. But it was the Brewers' dynamic outfield duo of Vaughn and Hamilton who provided most of the offensive sparks. Vaughn blasted 30 home runs and added 97 RBIs, and Hamilton batted .310 while playing a superb rightfield.

With the promise of 1992 giving way to the disappointment of 1993, the Milwaukee front office realized that changes must be made if the Brewers were to regain their competitiveness, though the team's limited financial resources would probably prevent them from going after high-profile free agents or making any block-buster trades. Success needed to come quickly; with the team's poor performances on the field in the early 1990s, attendance has slipped, fueling rumors that the team may soon leave Milwaukee.

Yount, Molitor, Gantner: A Record-Setting Trio

In the history of any professional franchise, whatever the sport, the names of certain players invariably highlight the narrative. But seldom have any three players, over the course of their careers, done more for their team than the Milwaukee trio of Robin Yount, Paul Molitor and Jim Gantner.

The Milwaukee threesome banged out more hits while playing together on the same team longer than any three players on any team in the history of major league baseball. Yount's first year was in 1974, Gantner came up in 1976, and Molitor in 1978; thus they were together for 15 years before Gantner retired and Molitor joined Toronto. Only the Kansas City combos of George Brett, Hal McRae, and Frank White from 1973 to 1987, and Brett, White, and Willie Wilson from 1976 to 1990 played together for as long a period.

During the 1992 season, Yount, Molitor and Gantner obliterated the old three-teammate hit total of 6,200 that had been held by Brett, Wilson, and White, moving well into first place with a total of 6,401. (That total does not include the hits Yount or Gantner had in the seasons prior to 1978; it includes only the hits that they made in the years they were on the team after Molitor had joined them.)

In addition to the longevity factor, the names Yount, Molitor, and Gantner dominate the Brewer all-time offensive statistics. Yount ranks first on the club in games played, at bats, hits, home runs, runs, runs batted in, extra base hits, total bases, singles, doubles, triples, and bases on balls; is second in stolen bases; and fourth in batting average.

Molitor is first in batting average and stolen bases; second in games played, at bats, hits, runs, extra base hits, total bases, singles, doubles, triples, and bases on balls; third in runs batted in; fifth in home runs; and eighth in slugging. Gantner is third in games played, at bats, and singles; fourth in hits, runs, doubles, and triples; sixth in runs batted in and bases on balls; and seventh in extra base hits.

Yount, of course, has to be recognized as one of the greatest players in the history of baseball. He is one of only three players to be voted as the league's Most Valuable Player twice, each time for a different position (in

Yount's case, shortstop and center field). His 3,025 hits through the 1992 season not only guaranteed his future selection to the Baseball Hall of Fame but placed him in 14th place on the all-time major league hit list. His 10,554 official plate appearances rank eighth—only baseball immortals Pete Rose, Hank Aaron, Carl Yastrzemski, Ty Cobb, Stan Musial, Willie Mays, and Brooks Robinson have higher totals.

Of all of the thousands of shortstops over the 91-year history of the American League, only three others ever accounted for more total bases in one season than Yount had in his 1982 MVP year. He was the first shortstop in the history of the league to ever lead in total bases in a single year and the first ever to hit .300 while also clubbing at least 20 home runs and driving in 100. Brewer owner Bud Selig once commented, "I've had the pleasure of seeing some terrific shortstops, Ripken, Trammell, Smith, and I'll tell you, I wouldn't have traded Yount for any of them. There's something that none of the statistic sheets will reveal; that Robin Yount is first and foremost a 'team' player. Personal statistics mean very little to him. It's the performance of the team as a whole that's all important, and his teammates know this, too."

Paul Molitor, who joined the Brewers four years after Yount, also has some Hall of Fame-quality stats, and would have compiled even more had he not been so injury prone. Over his 15-year career with Milwaukee, Molitor had only six years in which he was able to play 150 games or more. His total games played for those 15 years is 1,856, which means he has missed 574 games, the equiv-alent to three and a half seasons.

Despite this, he has managed to hit .303 over his career, the highest career batting average a Brewer has ever attained. He has amassed 2,281 hits, including 33 leadoff home runs, the second-highest leadoff round-tripper total in baseball history. He hit safely in 39 straight games in 1987, the fifth-longest streak ever. His .353 average in 1987 was the highest ever for a Milwaukee Brewer. And, he was the first player in World Series history to bang out five hits in a single game. It is interesting to note also that it was not until 1978, when Molitor joined Yount and Gantner in the Brewer infield, that the team had its first winning season.

Gantner, the third member of this once-in-a lifetime trio, may not have put up the offensive numbers of his two partners, but he surely has nothing to be ashamed of, and in fact in 1984 was voted as the Brewers' Most Valuable Player. A lifetime .274 hitter, he has always been at his best in clutch situations and has one of the team's top averages with men on base. In his only World Series, he hit .333, with five of his eight hits for extra bases.

"Gumby," as he was originally dubbed by teammate Gorman Thomas, has also always been an outstanding and versatile defensive player, at home, at third base, and at short, as well as his normal second base.

The Business of Brewers Baseball

Late in 1990 Selig and the Brewers' management announced plans for the construction of a new stadium to replace venerable County Stadium. Unlike the many instances over the past few decades, where new facilities—such as those in Minneapolis and Baltimore—were built with taxpayer dollars, the Brewers said that they themselves would finance the design and construction of the new stadium.

As any baseball owner will readily tell you, the sport of the 1990s has become a big business, involving many of millions of dollars. The vast majority of a club's income comes from television. But while teams share equally in revenues generated by national broadcasting, each club keeps the revenues it makes from local programming. Thus a market such as Milwaukee, with its limited population, cannot hope to generate as much for the local franchise as can areas such as Los Angeles or New York.

Milwaukee's local television revenue for 1992 was less than $5 million; the New York

Yankees made more than $50 million. But players on the Brewer roster demand and get salaries as high as players on the Yankee payroll. So how can Milwaukee and other smaller markets hope to compete?

Under the league financial setup of the 1990s, they can't. But one way in which income can be increased in Milwaukee is through the addition of skyboxes, a concept that many fans do not grasp. For example, the best total attendance the Brewers can realistically hope for is in the 1.9 to 2 million range. At an average ticket price of $9, and an attendance of 2 million, roughly $18 million is generated.

The addition of 100 skyboxes, at $80,000 per year each, would bring in $8 million. That's an increase of nearly 45 percent in stadium revenue, with the same total attendance. Tearing down all or a portion of County Stadium to erect skyboxes is not feasible, for where would the team play during all of this construction? Hence the need for a new ballpark. Work will start on the new facility within the next two years, or the Brewers will not be able to remain in Milwaukee, team officials admit.

On the field, it appears that the Brewers club is in capable hands under Vice-President of Baseball Operations Sal Bando and Manager Phil Garner. Both are former major league ballplayers and have excellent credentials.

After losing much of the successful 1992 Brewer team and suffering through a poor 1993 season, how the club fares in 1994 will depend on many factors—-the free agent market and the ability of the team to sign their own free agents, such as Yount; the amount of players the club will lose to stockpile the two new teams in Denver and Orlando; whether young players such as Eldred, Listach, and Bones will improve; and finally, whether there will be a lockout in the spring.

Selig has always been extremely active in league affairs. For example, he is chairman of the Major League Player Relations Committee, co-chairman of the Joint Economic Study Group, a member of the Major League Executive Council and the Major League Ownership Committee, and a Trustee of the Baseball Hall of Fame.

On September 9, 1992, he was in effect named as the acting commissioner of baseball, replacing Fay Vincent. Selig assumed the responsibility when he was voted in as chairman of the Owners Executive Committee, which automatically placed him in charge of all Major League operations until a new baseball commissioner is named.

—Jack Pearson

MINNESOTA TWINS

Nobody would deny that the Minnesota Twins have experienced far more low than high points in their lengthy history, which extends back to a nineteenth-century incarnation as the Washington Nationals. That ill-fated National League team experienced rebirth as the Washington Senators—the direct forerunners of the Twins—one of the founding teams in the American League.

Yet, with two thrilling and record-filled World Series wins in less than five years (1987 and 1991), the Twins soared to great heights. Much of the credit for the sudden renaissance of the Twins goes to Manager Tom Kelly and General Manager Andy MacPhail. However, neither man held those posts during the early 1980s, when two stellar on-the-field performers made their major league debuts with the Twins—first baseman Kent Hrbek and center fielder Kirby Puckett.

In a sport where mid- and late-career trades are commonplace, Hrbek and Puckett have dedicated their talents for the long run to the one ballclub that helped foster them. The Twins, consequently, have been richly rewarded. Hrbek, a formidable power-hitter and one of the best first baseman in baseball, and Puckett, a five-time Gold Glove winner and eight-time All-Star player, came on board during an important transitional period for the Twins.

In 1981, the club was celebrating its 20th season in Minnesota under legendary owner Calvin Griffith. Back in the fall of 1960, Griffith had made the monumental decision to pull his beleaguered Washington Senators out of the nation's capital and reintroduce them in another city that, among other things, would contribute better payoffs at the gate. Now, 20 years later, the club had seen brilliant performances by the likes of Harmon Killebrew, Rod Carew, and Tony Oliva.

In 1965 the Twins had achieved their first 100-plus victory season in 88 years, though they finished the season with a heartbreaking 4-3 World

Series loss to the Los Angeles Dodgers. They had captured American League (AL) West titles in 1969 and 1970. They then slumped abysmally, save for a frustrated rush at the pennant in 1976, for the next decade.

The 1981 Twins, in fact, had little to celebrate. The strike-marred season—the last to be played in Metropolitan Stadium—found the team mired at the bottom of the AL West. The team did, however, have a promising new hitter named Hrbek, who would play his first full season in 1982. Also in that inaugural year of the Metrodome, the Twins' new indoor facility, Kirby Puckett became the first-round choice in the amateur draft.

Two years later, Griffith sold the franchise to a local banker named Carl Pohlad, and Puckett became a Twin for his first full season. The retirement of Griffith—long awaited by his detractors, who thought him needlessly stingy—marked the end of a 70-year dynasty, for Griffith's adoptive father, Hall-of-Famer Clark Griffith, had preceded him as manager and owner.

When the Twins captured the world championship in 1987, putting an end to a 63-year dry spell, the Griffith legacy could still be felt. The stars, the ballpark, and the management were new, but the magic was much the same as that which had lit the club during the sporadic glory days of seasons past.

"The Oldest Baseball Team"

In the summer of 1859 baseball, of a fashion, came to the nation's capital. The first amateur team was named the Potomacs and was largely comprised of government clerks. The Nationals were organized in the fall, on November 27, to provide the Potomacs with local competition. By 1862 these teams were complemented in the city by the Pythians, the Jeffersons, and the Washingtons.

Not until the mid-1880s, though, did Washington, D.C. really come on the scene as a baseball town worthy of serious attention by the National League. According to Morris Bealle, "Many of Washington's teams were a disgrace to any self-respecting public. From 1872 to 1891 the [Nationals] team was owned by the Hewitt family, 7th Street feed dealers with no baseball experience and little more than a shoestring for operating capital."

In 1884, the club was thwarted in its efforts to enter the American Association but found itself a member of the twelve-team Union Association, in which it finished fifth. The following year, the Nats finished at the top of the eight-team Eastern League after the league-leading Richmond team disbanded.

Buoyed by a pennant, financial solvency, and the election of Washingtonian Nick Young to the presidency of the National League, the Nats eagerly acquired big-league status in 1886 and changed their name to the Statesmen (they continued to be popularly known as the Nationals).

Unfortunately, the honeymoon was short-lived. The Statesmen finished last in '86, second to last in '87, last in '88, and last in '89. At the close of 1889, the National League awarded the destitute Hewitt franchise to Cincinnati. Highlights during these first four years were scarce. There was the unexpected blossoming of a lanky catcher named Cornelius McGillicuddy, who was brought up from Hartford with his battery mate, Walter Gilmore.

McGillicuddy, of course, was none other than Connie Mack, who went on to manage at Milwaukee and Pittsburgh before assuming ownership of the Philadelphia Athletics. There was, as well, the base-stealing of center fielder William E. Hoy. In 1887, he led the league with 82 stolen bases. Little else distinguished the fledgling team, which had lately come to be referred to in the newspapers as the Senators.

In 1890, owner Walter Hewitt obtained a franchise with the recently formed Atlantic Association, which in addition to Washington consisted of the Baltimore Orioles, the Hartford Yankees, the Jersey City Skeeters, the Wilmington Peach Blossoms, and Newark, New Haven, and Worcester. The Washington club survived until August 10 and then folded due to insufficient capital.

Harrison Bennett became the club's newest booster and secured a franchise in the American

Team Information at a Glance

Founding date: December 7, 1900 (as Washington Senators);
October, 1960 (as Minnesota Twins)

Home stadium: Hubert H. Humphrey Metrodome
501 Chicago Ave. S.
Minneapolis, MN 55415
Phone: (612) 375-1366
FAX: (612) 375-7480

Dimensions: Left-field line—343
Center field—408
Right-field line—327
Seating capacity: 55,883

Team colors: Navy blue and scarlet
Team nickname: Senators, 1901-61 (also known as the Nationals, 1901-56);
Twins, 1961—
Logo: Name Minnesota Twins superimposed on a baseball

Franchise record	Won	Lost	Pct.
(1961-1993)	2664	2611	.505

World Series wins (3): 1924, 1987, 1991
American League championships (6): 1924, 1925, 1933, 1965, 1987, 1991
American League West division first-place finishes (4): 1969, 1970, 1987, 1991
League/division last-place finishes (13): 1903, 1904, 1907, 1909, 1944,
1949, 1955, 1957, 1958, 1959, 1981, 1982, 1990

Association for 1891. Prior to the season start, the club purchased land at 7th and Boundary and erected a new, 4000-seat park; nearly twenty years later, the park was destroyed by fire and rebuilt as Griffith Stadium.

Washington finished last in 1891, but good news came in December. The National League had decided to expand to twelve ballclubs after purchasing—and in essence dismantling—the American Association clubs in Boston, Chicago, Columbus, Milwaukee, and Washington. The three remaining American clubs, St. Louis, Balti-more, and Louisville, were admitted intact to the league. Washington was resurrected through the entrepreneurship of Philadelphians George and Earl Wagner, whose seasoned Athletics helped to get the franchise started.

Wagner Greed

Virtually all sources agree that the Wagners invested in the Washington franchise for one reason only: money. During the eight years in which they controlled the team, Washington's best finish was seventh in 1897. The following year the club recorded its worst season ever, 51 wins and 101 losses. There were several fine rookie players during the Wagner period (Bill Hassamaer, Win Mercer, Gene DeMontreville, Buck Freeman) as well as the uniformly admired play of catcher Deacon McGuire.

However, in the words of Shirley Povich, "the era of the Wagners was frustration piled on frustration. The two Philadelphians piously professed to be rabid baseball fans, do-gooders for the great national game, but they revealed themselves as promoters who were trying to collect a huge return, and did."

When the league purchased the team from them in 1899, they departed Washington $230,000 richer than when they came. The team ended the century under the official title of the Senators; they also ended it defeated, demoralized, and defunct (the league decision actually came on January 15, 1900, at which time the clubs located in Baltimore, Cleveland, and Louisville were also dropped).

"First in War, First in Peace, and Last in the American League"

In September 1900 Charles Comiskey, Clark Calvin Griffith, and Byron Bancroft Johnson met secretly in Chicago to discuss the possibility of forming a new major league. Johnson, president of the Western League, was at the very least determined to fight the National League on the issue of drafting rights. As it stood, National League teams had the oppressive advantage of drafting Western players for $500 apiece, without limit or approval by minor league owners. Consequently, the minor league was continually thwarted in its attempts to obtain major league status.

Among Johnson's demands was the restriction of the draft to two players from each minor league team and the opening of Western teams in Cleveland, Louisville, and Washington. The National League refused to budge, let alone compromise. Thus challenged, Johnson and his right-hand man, Comiskey, enlisted the support of Griffith,

then a star pitcher for the Chicago Cubs and vice president of the Ball Players' Protective Association, a union with considerable negotiating power. After having their own demands denied, Griffith and the other officers of the Association waged a battle with the National League in the newspapers while reminding NL ballplayers not to sign new contracts unless recommended by the Association to do so.

On December 7, 1900, after the fallout had cleared, Washington was again in the major leagues, this time as part of the renegade eight-team American League that Johnson had succeeded in forming (in all, 111 National Leaguers were signed by the AL during its first year). Jimmy Manning, owner-manager of the minor league Kansas City club, was to be the Senators new skipper; he lasted just one season and continued a precedent of brief and largely ineffective management.

From 1901 through 1911, the Senators came close to fulfilling an uncomplimentary description: Washington—"first in war, first in peace, and last in the American League." The team finished in sixth twice, seventh five times, and last place four times. David Nemec listed the 1909 Senators as the worst of the early American League era. Under manager Joe Cantillon, the 1909 team finished 19 games behind the St. Louis Browns with a win-loss record of 42-110, a record low 380 runs, and a record 29 games in which it failed to score (the 1904 team, under Malachai Kittredge and Patsy Donovan, was worse overall at 38-113).

The Senators' debut decade was marked by two promising signings, however. The first was that of slugger Ed Delahanty in 1902. The sum of $4,000 was enough to persuade the hard-drinking, hard-hitting outfielder to abandon his eleven-year career with the Philadelphia Phillies, to the absolute shock of National League fans and owners. In his first year with Washington, Big Ed captured the AL batting title with a .376 average.

All was not well between Washington management and the hitter, though. Because of a $1,500 dispute over his salary for 1903, Delahanty signed a controversial three-year contract with the

Transcendental Graphics

"Big Ed" Delahanty

New York Giants, complete with a $4,000 bonus for leaving Washington. The two leagues settled the contract issue peaceably, with Delahanty forced to remain with the Senators due to a reserve clause in the original contract. Problems persisted during the 1903 season, including the ill-advised switch of Delahanty from left to right field.

On July 2, the hitter disappeared from the Detroit hotel where the team had been staying. Then on July 7, team manager Tom Loftus received a letter from a Pullman railroad superintendent. The letter reported that a passenger who had been brawling had been ejected from a train traveling near Niagara Falls. Belongings left on the train were those of Senator player No. 26. Two days later, Delahanty's mutilated body was found several miles below the International Bridge. It was never determined whether Delahanty fell, jumped, or was pushed from the bridge. The Delahanty tragedy remains one of the most compelling mysteries in baseball history.

A far different mystery—not so much mystery as marvel—involved the curious and unparalleled fast-ball delivery of a humble Kansas-born pitcher. On June 29, 1907, Cantillon announced the signing of Walter Johnson, then a Weiser, Idaho, player with a modest but well-earned reputation as "the strikeout king of the Snake River Valley League." A traveling salesman had tipped off Cantillon, who in turn recruited injured Senators catcher Cliff Blankenship to scout Johnson as well as sign Western Association outfielder Clyde Milan.

After Blankenship had witnessed Johnson's prowess on the mound, he clinched a mid-season deal and reported back to Cantillon that Johnson was indeed the "fastest pitcher since Amos Rusie." History would eventually record that Johnson, nicknamed "The Big Train," was the fastest-throwing, and possibly the greatest, pitcher of all time.

Cantillon kept Johnson out of the spotlight until August 2, when the Senators faced a double-header with Detroit, a notoriously hard-hitting club led by Ty Cobb. When Johnson took the mound, fans were unprepared for his almost leisurely-looking sidearm delivery. The results of his pitching, though, quickly took their toll on the Tiger hitters. Povich states that Cobb "twice found it expedient to try laying down bunts" rather than take a full cut at the blistering fast ball. Even Tigers manager Bill Donovan was thoroughly impressed with Johnson, declaring: "In two years he'll be greater than [Christy] Mathewson."

By all accounts, the signing of Johnson was the best thing ever to happen to the chronically inferior Senators. The second best thing was the eleventh-hour prevention of Johnson from joining the Federal League after the 1914 season. It was the good fortune of the Senators that Johnson devoted his entire career to the team. As early as September 1908 Johnson attained stardom when he pitched three shutouts against the Yankees (then the Highlanders) over a four-day period. The following season, he suffered along with his offensively weak club, losing ten games by shutout scores and going 13-25 for the season; nonetheless, he led the league in strikeouts (164). Johnson and George McBride, regarded as the best shortstop in the American League, were the two most outstanding Senators during the team's first decade in the AL.

The Griffith-Johnson Era

During the 1910s, Johnson dominated major league pitchers. In 1912 he won an AL record 16 straight games. In 1913, he logged a whopping 36 victories. These years, as well, marked the dawning of a new era for the Senators under new manager Clark Griffith. Griffith was hardly new to the job. He had spent the previous eleven seasons as a manager and held the distinction of carrying the White Sox to the American League's first pennant in 1901.

The "Old Fox of Baseball," as he was already being called, engineered a swift turnaround in 1912 for a club that had finished seventh a year earlier under Jimmy McAleer. By the middle of June, the Senators were in first place and had established a modern record of 17 consecutive wins.

Johnson, as might be expected, was in top form. In addition to posting his own record streak of 16 straight wins, he finished the year with a 1.39 ERA, easily the best in the majors. Although the Senators finished second, the Red Sox outpaced them by 14 games and went on to win a memorable 8-game (including one tie game) World Series.

In 1913 Griffith wanted the pennant desperately, so much so that he offered to buy Ty Cobb from Detroit for the unheard-of price of $100,000. The deal never materialized and Griffith was saved an administrative crisis, for none of the team's nine directors had been told about or given their approval of the costly bid. A strong offense (which Cobb personified) was, in fact, all that Griffith needed. There were glimmers of one in the hitting

(.318) of first baseman Chick Gandil and the stolen bases (74) of league-leader Clyde Milan, but the runs simply weren't there.

This was all the more unfortunate, given that Johnson had his best year ever and almost single-handedly carried his team to within 6½ games of pennant-winning Philadelphia. He led the league in wins, strikeouts, and fewest hits per game, finishing with the fifth-best ERA of all time (1.14). He also became the first and only pitcher to win the Chalmers Award (a short-lived precursor of the MVP award). Johnson's lofty place in pitching history was cemented early in the season. From April 10 to May 16, the Big Train threw a consecutive 55 scoreless innings, a record that lasted for 55 years, topped only by Don Drysdale in 1968 and Orel Hersheiser in 1989.

Although Washington had clearly erased its last-place stigma, the team weathered another ten years of mediocre finishes (its best was a four-games-out, third place wrapup in 1918). At the end of a dismal 1919 season, Griffith, who had complained that the team's stockholders were needlessly stingy when it came to the purchase of talent, decided to buy the franchise and thereby exert greater control over the team's direction.

The 1920 Senators, finally, became a respectable hitting club, with Sam Rice, Joe Judge, and Frank Brower all batting over .300. Ironically, this time power was not balanced with strong pitching, for Johnson had developed a sore arm and posted his worst season ever, 8 wins and 10 losses; as a team, the Senators posted the worst ERA in the league.

A Magical Year

Griffith stepped down as manager the following year in favor of veteran shortstop George McBride. Three years and three managers later the Senators found the perfect combination of hitting, fielding, pitching, and coaching to win the pennant and the World Series. In 1924 the newly installed Senators player-manager was 27-year-old second baseman Stanley (Bucky) Harris.

Although he had other nicknames (the Idaho Kid, the Kansas Cyclone, Barney), Big Train was the one that served Hall-of-Famer Walter Johnson best. The moniker was an unabashed tribute to his pitching power, a talent that remained with Johnson throughout a career that extended from 1907 to 1927. During that time, the Train garnered 416 AL victories, a career record that has yet to be surpassed (Cy Young's 511 game total includes career victories from both leagues).

Johnson rose to the ranks of pitching's elite because of his rocket fastball. As Honig writes: "He never had more than a fair curve, but right to the end of his career, the fastball was enough." If Johnson had a weak spot, it was that he was too much a gentleman; he was forever afraid that one of his high-velocity pitches might kill a batter (there were no batting helmets during his era).

According to Harvey Frommer, "Some players made a living out of this knowledge and dug in against him. `It was a disgrace the way I took advantage of him,' said Ty Cobb.... `Knowing he would not throw at me, I crowded the plate outrageously and hit the outside pitch more often than I was entitled to.'" Despite this hesitancy, and despite suffering regular defeats because he played for a chronically poor-hitting club, Johnson amassed a number of astounding records during his lifetime.

Photo: *Transcendental Graphics*

Walter Johnson

Season stats:

Consecutive shutout innings: 56
Lowest season ERA: 1.09 (1913)
Most wins in a single season: 36 (1913)
No hitters: 1 (July 1, 1920, against Boston)
Winning streak: 16 games in 1912
AL leader in wins: 1913-16, 1918, 1924
AL leader in ERA: 1912, 1913, 1918, 1924
AL leader in strikeouts: 1910, 1912-19, 1921, 1923, 1924

Career stats:

Wins: 416 (2nd to Cy Young's 511)
Shutouts: 110 (1st among all pitchers)
Strikeouts: 3,508
Games pitched: 801
Complete games: 531
Innings pitched: 5,923
Lifetime ERA: 2.17
Manager, Washington Senators, 1929-1932
Elected to Hall of Fame: 1936

MINNESOTA TWINS

The 1924 Senators

The 1924 World Series was an all-time classic for a number of reasons, not least of which was the seventh-game, extra-inning victory by Walter Johnson, pitching in relief. During this season, everything coalesced for the Senators. More than 60 years would pass before the franchise was again able to capture the world title. Among the lesser-known heroes of this club was Oswald Bluege, whom Bealle labeled "the greatest fielding third baseman who ever played the game." Listed below is the bulk of the team, along with season and series statistics.

	Series BA	Season BA
Bucky Harris, 2b	.333	.268
Goose Goslin, lf	.344	.344
Sam Rice, rf	.207	.334
Earl McNeely, cf	.222	.330
Joe Judge, 1b	.385	.324
Ossie Bluege, 3b	.192	.281
Muddy Ruel, c	.095	.283
Roger Peckinpaugh, ss	.417	.272

Pitchers

	Series ERA	Season ERA
Walter Johnson (23-7)	2.63	2.72
Tom Zachary (15-9)	2.04	2.75
George Mogridge (16-11)	2.25	3.76
Firpo Marberry (11-12)*	1.13	3.09

* with 15 saves

Johnson, at 36, was fully recovered from arm problems and still dazzling the fans; big-hitting Leon "Goose" Goslin was embarking on his third full season with the team; aging shortstop Roger Peckinpaugh had been snatched from the Yankees in 1922; young third baseman Oswald Bluege had been seasoned with the minor league Minneapolis Millers before coming to the club in 1923; and center fielder George Earl McNeely came on board late in the season to spur a race with the Yanks and flesh out the "Big Four" (which also included sluggers Goslin, Rice, and Judge).

Johnson led the team to the top of the AL, with 6 shutouts, 23 wins, and 158 strikeouts. Johnson was supported, this time, by the best pitching staff in the league, which included Tom Zachary, George Mogridge, and Firpo Marberry, the first relief ace in major league baseball. Leading the offense was Goslin, with a .344 average and a league-leading 129 RBIs.

The Senators-Giants series was hailed at the time as perhaps the greatest ever. As it got under-way, the big story was not that the Giants had won a fourth straight National League pennant, but that the great Walter Johnson had finally been favored with a world-class team. Games 1, 2, 6, and 7 were each decided by a single run. Astonishingly, the Senators entered game 7 with Johnson having lost both of his previous starts. Right-hander Curley Ogden was elected by Harris to take the mound.

Harris, it turned out, had something up his sleeve. Through the first six games of the series, the Giants biggest weapon had been Bill Terry, with his .429 series average. His only limitation was that Giants manager John McGraw didn't trust him that year against left-handed pitchers. After Ogden had pitched to just two batters, Harris pulled him in favor of lefty George Mogridge. By the sixth inning Terry, after having grounded out and struck out, was replaced by a pinch hitter.

The big hitter thus out of play, Harris completed his plan by bringing in Marberry, the right-handed reliever. In Glenn Dickey's words, "Harris, the rookie manager, outsmarted the legendary McGraw." Despite such maneuvering, the Senators were far from victory. At the bottom of the eighth, the Giants still led by 3-1. Then, a late rally that loaded the bases led to a freakish grounder by Harris, which hopped over the Giants' third baseman, Freddy Lindstrom, and brought two runs in.

Much to the delight of Washington fans, Johnson took the mound in the ninth inning with a reinvigorated fastball. The game turned into a tense pitching battle that wasn't decided until the bottom of the twelfth when, to the eternal chagrin

Transcendental Graphics

Bucky (Stanley) Harris

of Lindstrom, another errant grounder hopped past third base and brought in the winning run. Johnson, the sentimental favorite, had won the most important game of his career.

In 1925, Griffith again fielded a pennant-winning team. Finishing 8½ games in front of the Athletics, his Senators were a triple threat. They had a fierce running game (Rice and Goslin were tied for second in stolen bases), a deadly double-play combo (Peckinpaugh to Harris to Judge), and a fortified pitching staff that now featured veterans Stanley Coveleski, Walter ("Dutch") Reuther, and Vean Gregg.

The World Series against Pittsburgh went the full seven games. Johnson won games 1 and 4; Alex Ferguson, game 3. Facing a 3-1 deficit, the Pirates rallied and managed to subdue Johnson in the deciding game by a score of 9-7. They were helped by a fatal Peckinpaugh error, the eighth committed by the regular season MVP during the course of the series.

The ageing Senators faded after that season. Johnson pitched without distinction, except for earning his 110th shutout—an all-time career record—in 1927, his final year. The Big Train was among the first five players elected to the Baseball Hall of Fame when it was established in 1936. Johnson also managed woeful Senators teams from 1929 to 1932.

In 1933 the Senators, under player-manager Joe Cronin, returned to the limelight. Their rise to the top of the AL was credited to a number of astute trades, including those for pitchers Earl Whitehill and Jack Russell. In the end, they were no match for the Giants, now led by Bill Terry. New York—with the aid of the screwballs thrown by Carl Hubbell, who won two games and allowed no earned runs in 20 innings—took the series in five games.

The following year, the Senators dropped to seventh in the league. Not until a decade later did they again seriously vie for the AL title. Under neophyte manager Ossie Bluege, the club moved from seventh in 1942 to second the following year under the dark cloud of wartime. In 1944 the club receded to last, but then rebounded spectacularly the next year.

By September 1, the Senators were just a game and a half behind the Tigers. That month, they seesawed: up to a half game back, then down to two and a half back. A possibility for deadlock still existed until the Tigers closed the season by beating the Browns and finishing one and a half games ahead of the Senators. Thus did the topsy-turvy club nearly become the first team in the twentieth century to move from last to first during the course of a single season.

The Torch Passes

The 1950s were a hollow decade for the Senators. During this period, the club had the dreary distinction of attracting the lowest attendance in the major leagues. In 1952, the Senators finished slightly above .500 to take fifth place. They repeated in 1953 with a 76-76 season, their last .500

finish as a Washington-based team. Even in this dreariest of times, though, there were outstanding players.

These included first baseman Mickey Vernon, who won the AL batting crown in 1953; pitcher Bob Porterfield, a Yankee release who led the AL in wins and shutouts in the same season; hurlers Pete Ramos and Camilo Pascual, the latter of whom would shine brilliantly as a Twin; third baseman Eddie Yost, a masterful fielder and recurrent All-Star; two Rookies of the Year, Albie Pearson (1958) and Bob Allison (1959); and slugger Roy Sievers, who became the first Senator ever to lead the AL in home runs, racking up 42 in 1957 (he also led the league in RBI, 114, and total bases, 331). Two other sluggers, Jim Lemon and the emerging Harmon Killebrew, rounded out a feisty, heavy-hitting offense.

Just a year before Clark Griffith's death in 1955, Povich wrote that the Old Fox had fashioned one of the healthiest franchises in the American League. Despite a dearth of pennants, the Senators were financially stable; furthermore, only three times in some 40 years had they allowed themselves to slip to the bottom of the pile. Contained, savvy management, rather than highly evolved farm systems and big financing, had been the key to the club's durability as well as its prestige among other major league owners. It was this tradition and this franchise that Calvin Griffith inherited at mid-decade.

The younger Griffith first entered the world of professional baseball as a batboy for the Senators in 1922. Thus he shared, early on, in some of the finest years of the team's history. He would soon share again, after suffering through the dark years of the late 1950s and then completing one of the most stunning franchise moves in baseball history.

Major League Baseball Arrives in Minnesota

The Senators' final year in Washington proved to be auspicious. After three successive

Transcendental Graphics

Harmon Killebrew

years in the cellar, manager Cookie Lavagetto led his team to 73 wins and a 5th place finish in 1960. Full of young talent, the Senators were headed in the right direction. Nonetheless, they seemed perennially cursed by second division performances. It had long been Griffith's desire to move the franchise out of the nation's capital, where attendance had steadily dropped along with the team's fortunes. A new venue was needed to maintain the solvency of the team and, it was hoped, revive the team's fortunes.

Griffith's top choice was Minneapolis, a city long tantalized by the minor league play of the Millers and overripe for big league action. Ever since 1955, when the construction of Metropolitan Stadium in the populous suburb of Bloomington was completed, Minneapolis and St. Paul business leaders had proven their zeal for a major league sport franchise. In late October 1960, Griffith received approval for the deal from the

American League, which expanded to ten teams (a new Senators team as well as the Los Angeles Angels were installed) and a 162-game season.

The Minnesota Twins, dubbed after the Twin Cities that claimed them, commenced their inaugural season on April 11, 1961. Playing away against the defending AL champion Yankees, the Twins routed their opponents 6-0. The starting lineup was as follows: Killebrew, first base; Lenny Green, center field; Zoilo Versalles, shortstop; Allison, right field; Reno Bertoia, third base; Earl Battey, catcher; Lemon, left field; Billy Gardner, second base; and Ramos, pitcher.

Other players who comprised the core 1961 roster included second baseman Billy Martin (acquired at the beginning of June), third baseman Bill Tuttle, and left-handers Jack Kralick and Jim Kaat. Clearly the team possessed a number of strengths. Perhaps foremost was the hitting power of Killebrew.

Harmon's Hammer

Killebrew came to the majors directly from high school. From 1954 until 1958, his career was marked by occasional play as a utility infielder and a pinch hitter and by repeated returns to minor league clubs. Then came 1959, his first full year as a Senator. Killebrew's bat came alive as he proceeded to pace the league with 42 homers; only Cleveland's Rocky Colavito matched Killebrew's performance that season.

In 1960, Killebrew belted a respectable 31 home runs. The following year his rise to stardom was fully underway as he launched 46 and became one of the primary attractions at Met Stadium. Although Minnesota's seventh-place finish could not have pleased Griffith, the number of fans Killebrew and his teammates packed into the stands certainly did. Some 1.3 million entered the gates that year, placing the franchise in firm financial health once again.

Of course, 1961 was a notorious year for the longball. There was Maris's myth-shattering 61, Mantle's 54, and 46 by Orlando Cepeda and Jim Gentile to keep Killebrew company. Perhaps the Twins' modest finish served as inspiration, both for the club and their star slugger. In 1962 the Twins grabbed second, remaining in contention with the Yankees until late September.

Pascual was at the top of his game, with 20 wins and league-leading numbers in strikeouts (206), shutouts (5), and complete games (18). Kaat was also in fine form, with 18 wins and the lowest ERA on the club. Griffith's wisdom in moving the club was again validated this year by the attendance figures, the highest in the AL. As if to cap this highly successful year, Killebrew handily outshone Maris and Mantle in both homers (48) and RBIs (126). Despite his .243 batting average, Killebrew was a slugging sensation.

One of the foremost needs of the 1962 Twins was a dependable .300 hitter (they were also known at the time for their loose defense and lack of speed). Rich Rollins and Vic Power came closest at .298 and .290, respectively. On the Twins' roster, though, was a 21-year-old lefty with nine at bats and an average of .444. His name was Tony Oliva and he was just two years away from answering the Twins' need for consistent hitting.

In 1963, Pascual was again the league-leader in strikeouts, amassing a 21-9 record, while Killebrew showcased his specialty with 45 homers. Because of the additional contributions of Allison, Jimmie Hall, and Battey, the Twins garnered the second highest number of homers (225) in baseball history (the '87 Tigers later matched the feat). The Twins took third that year, though with the same number of wins (91) as the previous year.

Undoubtedly the best thing to happen to the Twins in 1964 was the full-time play of Oliva, though as Peter Bjarkman writes, the club "again bashed the longball with remarkable authority." In all, the team tallied 221 homers, with Killebrew (49), Oliva (32), and Allison (32) leading the crew. Despite a tie for 6th that year, the Twins were cheered by such slugging performances and, especially, Oliva's runaway Rookie of the Year season. Not only was he the team leader in runs (109), hits (217), and batting average (.323), he was the league leader in each of these categories.

Sam Mele had joined the Twins as manager when the first season was just 66 games old. Like everyone else involved with baseball, he was accustomed to the Yankees being at the top of the AL. He was also accustomed to strong year-in, year-out performances from the stars of his club and had already savored the thrill of the pennant race.

Mele's 1965 Twins

In 1965 he fielded a club worthy of toppling the Yanks, who were no longer near the top, for Yogi Berra had been fired and the long-dominant team was in disarray under the new ownership of CBS. Instead, Minnesota battled Chicago and Baltimore. Finishing first with a 7-game margin and a 102-60 record (still the best in the history of the franchise), the Twins were now faced with the monumental challenge of overcoming the Los Angeles Dodgers and the awesome pitching of Sandy Koufax (26-8) and Don Drys-dale (23-12) in the World Series.

The Twins had stellar pitchers of their own. Right-hander Mudcat Grant (21-7) had been acquired from Cleveland in 1964 and was expected to lead the threat from the mound. Pascual, who had lost six weeks during the season due to a torn muscle, was expected to be ready. In addition, Kaat (18-11), Jim Perry (12-7), and reliever Al Worthington (21 saves) could be expected to play major roles in complementing a Twins offense that included the league batting champ, Oliva; the league MVP, Versalles; and four 20-plus home-run hitters, Don Mincher, Hall, Allison, and Killebrew (his atypical 25 for the season reflected a sustained elbow injury).

Playing to the home crowd, the Twins easily took the first two games of the series, winning 8-2 and 5-1, respectively. The Dodgers took their turn in games three, four, and five as the series increasingly became a pitching duel (Claude Osteen fired a shutout in the third, as did Koufax in the fifth). In game six Grant went the distance for the second time, pitching a six-hitter and blast-

ing a three-run homer to even the tally at 3-3.

Game seven was all Koufax's. He pitched his second shutout, struck out ten batters, and ended up with an astonishing series ERA of 0.38 for 24 innings pitched. The dominance of Koufax was reflected in the Twins team batting average, just .195, despite a wealth of talent. The Twins, as good as they were, were simply no match for the great hurler.

AL West Leaders, AL West Losers

In 1967 the Twins, with Rookie of the Year Rod Carew, embarked on a return to the limelight, or so they thought. A World Series program featuring the Twins and the Cardinals had already been prepared when Boston bested the one-game-up club in the final two September meetings to finish one game ahead and claim the AL championship.

The Twins' next chance came in 1969, the club's first year under manager Billy Martin and the beginning of divisional play. Hampered by a

Transcendental Graphics

Rod Carew

groin injury in '68, Killebrew now returned with one of his best seasons ever, leading the league in both homers (49) and RBIs (140) and capturing the AL MVP award. Rich Reese, Carew, and Oliva all turned in .300-plus seasons (Carew took the league title with .332) and both Perry and Dave Boswell reached the 20-game mark.

The team finished nine games ahead of Oakland to secure the AL West, but in the East there loomed Baltimore, with 109 wins; an offense fired by Boog Powell, Brooks Robinson, and Frank Robinson; and the pitching trio of Mike Cuellar, Dave McNally, and Jim Palmer. The Orioles swept the Twins in three straight. According to local sportswriter Sid Hartman, the dismal outcome led to the immediate firing of manager Billy Martin, who ignored Griffith's advice to start Kaat in the third game; Bob Miller was started instead, leading to an 11-2 blowout.

The 1970s began solidly for the Twins, who repeated as AL West leaders, backed by Cy Young winner Perry (24-12), AL hit leader Oliva, and home-run master Killebrew. The Twins also, predictably, again fell to the dominant Orioles in the ALCS in three straight. For the remainder of the decade, the club never again finished better than third in its division. This was especially unfortunate for such talents as Rod Carew, who ruled the decade with a composite batting average of .343 and was 1977's AL MVP, and pitcher Bert Blyleven, who garnered an AL shutout title and secured the team record for strikeouts before being traded in '76.

The Twins closed the decade with a finish narrowly above .500. It was to be their last until 1987. The team's fortunes had turned and many placed the blame squarely on the shoulders of Griffith, who by the late 1970s had become known for selling his high-salaried veterans and replacing them with lesser, inexpensive talent. In due course, gate receipts began dropping.

The Twins became an indoor team in 1982. They also lost a club record 102 games, planting themselves firmly in last place in the AL West. There was perhaps one glimmer of hope that year for a rejuvenated team. It was not to be found

among the pitching staff, who compiled the worst ERA in the majors. Neither was it to be found in team speed, for the Twins also claimed bragging rights for the fewest bases stolen. The glimmer was to be found in the batting and fielding of Kent Hrbek.

The only Twin to bat above .300 that year, Hrbek cranked out 23 home runs and 92 RBIs. His '83 season was somewhat less impressive, but he, like the rest of the team, was beginning to blossom. In 1984 a renewed pitching assault, led by left-hander Frank Viola (18-12), as well as an offensive charge consisting of Hrbek, Puckett, Gary Gaetti, and Tom Brunansky, was beginning to take shape.

The club finished an even .500 that year, dropping four final games to Cleveland to allow Kansas City to clinch the division. Shortstop Greg Gagne entered the lineup the following year and Blyleven, hot as ever, rejoined the club to provide veteran leadership. 1985 and 1986 proved to be mediocre years due primarily to a lack of pitching depth. However, by 1987 a world-class team had been formed, though few would have guessed it at the start of the season.

The Metrodome Miracle

Rookie manager Tom Kelly's '87 team had plenty of talent, consisting of outfielders Puckett, Dan Gladden, and Brunansky; infielders Hrbek, Steve Lombardozzi, Gagne, and Gaetti; catcher Tim Laudner; and pitchers Viola, Blyleven, Juan Berenguer, Les Straker, and newly acquired ace reliever Jeff Reardon.

As David S. Neft and Richard M. Cohen recorded, that year "no one in the A.L. West took charge of the divisional race until late in the season. The Twins finally grabbed first place, primarily because their home record of 56-25 was the best in the major leagues." Thus it happened that the Twins, with a winning percentage of just .525, faced off against Sparky Anderson's Tigers for the AL pennant. To nearly everyone's astonishment—and the loudly-expressed delight of Metrodome

AP/Wide World Photos

Kent Hrbek

crowds—the Twins pulled off what seemed impossible in just five games. By vanquishing Detroit they had set a new AL record for the lowest winning percentage by a pennant winner. This was accomplished by picking up a crucial win on the road in game four, featuring solo homers by Gagne and Puckett. Now it was time to face the Cardinals, as well as the possibility of winning the first world title in over 60 years.

The Twins were still the clear underdogs in this landmark World Series, the first with games played indoors. However, they had one major element in their favor: if the battle were to go the full seven games, Minnesota would have the home field advantage. No one could have predicted, though, what an advantage that would turn out to be. By the end of the series, fans and the media had rechristened the parachute-topped edifice the Homerdome, a testament to the inexplicable magic it held for Twins hitters.

The series started with a bang, with the Twins

clobbering the Cardinals 10-1 thanks to a grand slam by Gladden and a two-run homer by Lombardozzi. With the thunderous cheers of Minnesota fans reverberating incessantly, the Dome was not only deadly to outsiders but deafening to all. Two more homers, by Gaetti and Laudner, came in game 2 and the Twins won 8-4. Then the Cardinals retaliated with three wins of their own at home.

Back came both teams to the Metrodome. In game 6 Tommy Herr blasted one of only two homers for the Cardinals during the series and the only Cardinal homer within the Dome. On the other side it was DH Don Baylor, with a two-run homer in the fifth, and Hrbek, with a grand slam in the sixth. Fittingly, the Twins two best pitchers, Viola and Reardon, combined forces in game 7 to seal the Cardinals fate with a 4-2 win.

Team of Destiny

In 1988, the Twins proved no match for Tony LaRussa's Oakland team, but they could nonetheless be proud of their ability to draw 3 million fans for the first time in American League history. The next year the team slipped quietly below .500. In 1990 they committed the unthinkable by sinking to last place in the AL West. Curiously, the season's fortunes turned full circle the following year, with the addition of a few names to the lineup—Chuck Knoblauch, Mike Pagliarulo, Chili Davis, and Jack Morris.

As early as June of '91, Minnesota fans had an inkling that they were witnessing a team of destiny. At that time, the Twins were in the midst of a club-record 16-game winning streak that played no small part in placing them 8 games ahead of Chicago in the AL West at the end of the season. This was a vastly different team than the '87 Twins in terms of performance.

Now the Twins had the best winning percentage in the league (.586), the best club batting average (.280), and the most hits (1557). They also had a superb pitching staff led by Scott Erickson (20-8), veteran Jack Morris (18-12), Kevin Tapani

AP/Wide World Photos

Kirby Puckett

(16-9), and expert closer Rick Aguilera (42 saves). Yet, as the post-season played out, it became apparent that there were as many similarities as differences.

Echoing the 1987 ALCS, the Twins dashed Toronto's hopes for the pennant in a 4-1 shootout. To complete the Cinderella matchup for the series, Atlanta (another cellar dweller in 1990) succeeded in besting Pittsburgh 4-3 in the NLCS. The Twins brought to the fray, among others, hot-hitting AL Rookie of the Year Knoblauch and the warrior-like Jack Morris, a standout pitcher in the 1980s and a stellar performer in big games.

The Homerdome, of course, could also be counted on for its own unique contributions. The Twins emerged victorious at the end of this nail-biting series—one destined to rank among the game's greatest—with five games decided by a single run, Puckett's 11th inning homer to win

game 6, and a thrilling 1-0, 10-inning final game. Tom Kelly received his due as American League Manager of the Year, as did executive vice-president Andy MacPhail, named Major League Executive of the Year. Such were the finest hours in one of the finest seasons of the franchise.

What's Next?

Morris, the hometown hero, shocked fans in December of '91 by announcing his plans to abandon Minnesota for Toronto. He would be missed, but the fans still had their beloved Kirby Puckett. The Twins kept the crowds coming to the Dome in '92 with a pennant race that persisted into the first weeks of September. They finished with 90 wins, six games behind the A's, and led the majors in hitting (.277).

Everything looked promising for '93, particularly after MacPhail brought home superstar Dave Winfield (born in St. Paul) and owner Carl Pohlad inked a huge deal with Puckett to keep him in Minnesota for the likely duration of his career. Zander Hollander's *1993 Complete Handbook of Baseball* predicted that the Twins would return to the top of the AL West and then overtake the Orioles for the championship.

This was assuming the presence of strong starter John Smiley and first-rate fielder Greg Gagne. Instead, by the end of August, if not sooner, the Twins were woefully out of contention. Little had gone the team's way, save for Puckett's individual achievements during the All-Star game, for which he was named MVP.

In a sign of the times, Puckett was switched from center to right field after the All-Star break, an expected move by Kelly, given the Puck's decreasing speed, but one that nevertheless signaled the end of an era.

One bright spot for the team occurred in September when Dave Winfield got his 3,000th career hit, becoming only the 19th player in league history to achieve that mark. The Twins finished in a tie for fifth place in the AL West with a 71-91 record.

Declining revenues make it next to impossible for Pohlad to seek help in the high-priced free agent market, so the Twins will approach 1994 with basically the same cast as in '93. A woefully inexperienced pitching staff will be counted on to improve its performance, and the once-solid Twins' batting order will need to regain its stroke if the club is to have any hope of contending.

SOURCES

BOOKS

Bjarkman, Peter C. "Washington Senators-Minnesota Twins: Expansion-Era Baseball Comes to the American League," *Encyclopedia of Major League Baseball Team Histories*, Westport, CT: Meckler, 1991, pp. 487-534.

Cox, Craig, "On Top of the World," *The 1992 Twins Yearbook,* Minneapolis: Minnesota Twins, 1992.

Dickey, Glenn, *The History of the World Series Since 1903*, New York: Stein and Day, 1984.

Hollander, Zander, ed., *The Complete Handbook of Baseball, 1993*, 23rd ed., New York: Penguin, 1993.

Kelly, Tom, and Ted Robinson, *Season of Dreams: The Minnesota Twins' Drive to the 1991 World Championship*, Stillwater, MN: Voyageur Press, 1992.

Kerr, Jon, *Calvin: Baseball's Last Dinosaur*, William C. Brown Publishers, 1990.

Mona, Dave, and Dave Jarzyna, *Twenty-Five Seasons: The First Quarter Century of the Minnesota Twins*, Minneapolis: Mona Publications, 1986.

Neft, David S., and Richard M. Cohen, *The Sports Encyclopedia: Baseball*, 12th ed., New York: St. Martin's Press, 1992.

Povich, Shirley, *The Washington Senators: An Informal History*, New York: G. P. Putnam's Sons, 1954.

PERIODICALS

Hartman, Sid, "Morris the Foremost of Many Twins Heroes," *Star Tribune,* October 28, 1991, p. 2C.

Lenihan, Jeff, "On Top of the World: Morris and Larkin Key Another Magic Carpet Ride," *Star Tribune,* October 28, 1991, pp. 1C, 4C.

Sinker, Howard, "A Game for the Ages: Larkin's Big Hit Turns Agonizing to Ecstasy," *Star Tribune,* October 28, 1991, pp. 1A, 12A.

—*Jay Pederson*

AMERICAN LEAGUE EAST

BALTIMORE ORIOLES

This is a tale of two cities and one franchise. The cities are St. Louis, Missouri, and Baltimore, Maryland. From 1902 to 1953, St. Louis had a franchise in the American League. For the St. Louis Browns it was nearly always the worst of times. From 1954 to the present, the same franchise has been in Baltimore. For the Baltimore Orioles it has often been the best of times.

The old St. Louis Browns had a few legitimate stars—George Sisler, Ken Williams, and Urban Shocker would have been standouts on any team—but by and large they fielded an aggregation of no-names, with predictably dismal results. It took a world war (and not the First World War at that) for the Browns to win a pennant.

In contrast, the Baltimore Orioles have produced a galaxy of stars: Brooks Robinson, Boog Powell, Frank Robinson, Jim Palmer, Dave McNally, Mike Cuellar, Ken Singleton, Cal Ripkin, Jr., Eddie Murray, and many others. The Orioles finished first in the American League East five out of six times from 1969 to 1974. Even though the magic ended, at least for a time, in the mid-1980s, the Baltimore franchise has been a remarkably successful one. This rags-to-riches saga of the Browns and Orioles began, oddly enough, in Milwaukee, Wisconsin.

Brewers to Browns

Baltimore had a franchise in 1901, the first season of the American League. The Orioles, managed by 28-year-old John McGraw, finished in fifth place, ahead of Washington, Cleveland, and Milwaukee. But after the 1902 season, this Oriole team pulled up stakes, creating an opening in the American League for a New York franchise. Baltimore became a minor league city, its team a fixture in the International League for more than half a century.

The American League franchise that Baltimore acquired in September 1953 had its origin in the last-place Milwaukee Brewers of 1901. The Brewers, managed by Hugh Duffy, became the St. Louis Browns in 1902, with Milwaukee, like Baltimore, dropping back into the minors. The 1902 St. Louis Browns debuted impressively under manager Jimmy McAleer, finishing second in the league, with skilled players like Bobby Wallace at shortstop and Jesse Burkett in left field, both future Hall of Famers. On the mound were Jack Powell (22-17) and Red Donahue (22-11). It looked like an auspicious start, but looks were deceiving.

In 1903 Wallace, Burkett, Powell, and Donahue all had off years, and the Browns faded to sixth. Things went from bad to worse. McAleer's Browns finished sixth again in 1904, then last in 1905. Pitching was unreliable, or unsupported, or both. Fred Glade, the ace of the staff in 1904—18

wins, 15 losses—plummeted to 6-25 in 1905. Harry Howell, despite some glittering ERAs, failed to break even in the won-lost column in his years with the Browns. Left fielder George Stone hit well, winning the batting title in 1906 with a .358 mark. But team hitting was weak.

The Browns finished in the second division until 1908, when McAleer, still at the helm, brought them in fourth. They were in contention for the pennant most of the way. A big help that year was aging Rube Waddell, an all-time great acquired from the Athletics. It was Waddell's last good season, 19-14 and an ERA of 1.89.

But when the Browns, playing in their brand-new Sportsman's Park in 1909, tumbled to seventh place, Jimmy McAleer gave way to a new manager, Jack O'Connor. The team responded in 1910 by sinking into the cellar, winning 47 and losing 107. The highest batting average among the

Trancendental Graphics

Bobby Wallace

Team Information at a Glance

Founding dates:
St. Louis Browns: December 3, 1901
Baltimore Orioles: September 29, 1953

Home stadium: Oriole Park at Camden Yards
333 W. Camden St.
Baltimore, MD 21201

Dimensions: Left-field line—335 feet
Centerfield—400 feet
Right-field line—318 feet
Seating capacity: 48,000

Team uniforms:
Home—base color white, with orange and black trim
Road—base color gray, with orange, black, and white trim

Team name: Browns, 1902-53; Orioles, 1954-present; other Baltimore baseball teams in the major
and minor leagues have been called Orioles since the 1880s

Logo: Stylized orange-and-black bird

Franchise record:	Won	Lost	Pct.
Browns (1902-1953)	3,414	4,465	.433
Orioles (1954-1992)	3,350	2,931	.533

World Series wins (3): 1966, 1970, 1983
American League championships (7): 1944, 1966, 1969, 1970, 1971, 1979, 1983
American League East division first-place finishes (7): 1969, 1970, 1971, 1973, 1974, 1979, 1983
League/division last-place finishes (12): 1905, 1910, 1911, 1913, 1933, 1937, 1939,
1947, 1951, 1953, 1986, 1988

regulars (.258) belonged to Bobby Wallace. Left-handed pitcher Bill Bailey, in his fourth year with the Browns, posted a 3-18 record.

With the team going nowhere, manager O'Connor apparently decided to help nice-guy Nap Lajoie of the Cleveland Indians nose out Detroit's detested Ty Cobb for the batting title. The race between the two hitters became the famous "touring car battle," because the leading hitter would get a classy new Chalmers automobile, courtesy of the manufacturer. In a doubleheader against the Browns on October 9, 1910, with the batting title hanging in the balance, Nap Lajoie went 8-for-8 against Brownie pitchers. Six of his hits were bunts toward third base, where rookie Red Corriden had been told by O'Connor to play deep for the hard-hitting Lajoie. The scheme came to naught; Cobb won the batting crown anyway.

PROFILE	George Sisler

If ever a single ballplayer were the franchise, that player was George Sisler, first baseman for the St. Louis Browns. A few of Sisler's teammates, notably outfielder Ken Williams and pitcher Urban Shocker, were very good, but Sisler was unmatched, nonpareil. He would have been a superstar for any ball club in any era, but for the always-struggling Browns, he was a wonder.

Sisler, like Babe Ruth, could have been a pitcher. In 1915, his first season in the majors, he divided his time among first base, the outfield, and the pitching mound. He was the starting pitcher in eight games that season and completed six. His won-lost record of 4-4 is somewhat misleading. One of his losses was a 1-0 game, and he posted a fine earned run average of 2.83. But Sisler, like Ruth, was just too good a hitter to keep out of the daily lineup.

In 1916 and thereafter through 1927 (minus the 1923 season, which he missed because of a serious sinus infection) he spent most of his time as the Browns' regular first baseman. Gorgeous George, 5-feet-11-inches tall, batted and threw lefthanded. In addition to being one of the great hitters of all time—his .407 batting average in 1920 and .420 in 1922 were eye-opening even in the lively-ball era—he was also a notable base stealer, leading the American League four times. As a defensive first baseman he had skill, range, and grace.

Hitting, however, was his forte. His 257 hits in 1920 remain the all-time major-league high for a single season. His .340 lifetime batting average matches Lou Gehrig's. Perhaps the most telling tribute to his abilities came from Ty Cobb, a man not noted for lavishing compliments on opposing players. He called George Sisler "the nearest thing to a perfect ballplayer."

Chalmers generously gave both men a touring car. But league President Ban Johnson insisted that Jack O'Connor be released, and he was.

His replacement as manager, veteran shortstop Bobby Wallace, had no better success than his predecessor, as the Browns once again finished last. Not until Branch Rickey took over as manager in 1914 did the team show signs of life. Even then the improvement was marginal, as they struggled to hold onto fifth place, 28½ games behind the pennant-winning Philadelphia Athletics of Connie Mack.

George Sisler and His Era

Without question, the greatest ballplayer who ever spent an extended period of time in a St. Louis Browns' uniform was first baseman George Sisler. Sisler joined the club as a rookie in 1915 and put in 12 of his 15 major league seasons as a Brown. These were among the club's best seasons, but—

except for 1922—they were seldom really good seasons. Sisler, however, was consistently brilliant, reaching his peak in 1922, when he batted an awesome .420, led the league in hits with 246, triples with 18, runs with 134, and stolen bases with 51.

The 1915 Browns finished sixth, with Sisler playing not only first base but also the outfield—and pitching, at which he compiled a 4-4 record with a 2.83 ERA. But Gorgeous George, as he came to be called, was just too potent a hitter to keep out of the regular lineup. Although he pitched a few innings after 1915, his real home was first base from 1916 until the end of his career. After the 1915 season, the Browns were acquired by Phil Ball, an entrepreneur who had made his fortune in ice plants.

For his $425,000 investment in St. Louis baseball, Ball acquired a team with potential, never, alas, to be fully realized. The 1916 Browns, managed by Fielder Jones, may have given him hope—they won more games than they lost, while finishing fifth—and they more than doubled their attendance over 1915 (when the Federal League's second place St. Louis Terriers, with Eddie Plank on the mound, had drawn fans away from Sportsman's Park).

The 1917 Browns faded to seventh. The high point of the season occurred in early May, when two Browns pitchers, Ernie Koob and Bob Groom, pitched no-hitters on successive days against the Chicago White Sox. George Sisler's .353 batting average stood in a class by itself. Second baseman Del Pratt, catcher Hank Severeid, and outfielder Burt Shotton all had subpar seasons.

In the war-shortened 1918 season the team finished fifth, repeating that performance in 1919, then moving up to fourth in 1920. The pitching staff was improving. In 1920, Urban Shocker, who came over from the Yankees in 1918, won 20 games while losing 10. Dixie Davis, new to the club in 1920, won 18 and lost 12. With George Sisler batting .407 and belting 19 home runs, and with the stellar play of an impressive outfield— Jack Tobin, Baby Doll Jacobson, and Ken Williams—the Browns looked better than their 76-77 won-lost record.

In 1921 they moved up to third place. Urban Shocker won 27 games to lead the league. The outfield of Tobin, Jacobson, and Williams batted a composite .351 for the season, an all-time major league record. This team had class. The stage was set for a pennant race in 1922, a heady experience for Browns' fans.

The 1922 Browns won 93 games, the most in the 52-year life of the ball club. Sisler had his dazzling .420 season, during which he hit in 41 straight games. Shocker won 24 games. Pitcher Elam Vangilder enjoyed his best season, 19-13. Ken Williams drove in 155 runs and hit 39 home runs, both league-leading totals. (Babe Ruth, out for a third of the season, finished with 35 homers.) Sisler and Williams placed first and second in the league in stolen bases. At the plate the Browns put together the league's highest batting average and slugging average, and on the mound they posted the league's lowest ERA. Four players topped 100 RBIs, the first time in major league history.

The Browns, under manager Lee Fohl, serving his second year at the helm, remained in contention all the way. But the 1922 Yankees were a great team, too, and at season's end the New Yorkers had nosed out St. Louis by a single game. The second-place Browns attracted 712,918 fans, a total never again achieved or even approached.

It was downhill for the rest of the 1920s, although by Browns' standards, a couple of the seasons were fairly good. The team finished third in 1925, with George Sisler as player-manager, and 1928, with an essentially new team under Dapper Dan Howley after Sisler was sold to the Washington Senators for $25,000 at the end of the 1927 season and left fielder Ken Williams went to the Boston Red Sox.

The Browns' new first baseman was Lu Blue, a solid ballplayer but no Gorgeous George. The new left fielder was Heinie Manush, who batted .378 and drove in 108 runs. Manush, a future Hall of Famer, played only one more full year for the Browns before being traded to the Senators for another Hall of Famer, outfielder Goose Goslin. In 1929 the Browns finished fourth—their second straight season in the first division. Such good fortune was not to last.

Hard Times at Sportsman's Park

The 1930s were grim years for the St. Louis Browns. (By contrast, it should be noted, they were glorious years—"Gas House Gang" years—for the National League Cardinals, who also played at Sportsman's Park.) The Browns finished in the second division every season between 1930 and 1941, including three times in the cellar. During the entire decade, fewer than a million fans in all turned out to watch the Browns play.

In 1934 ownership of the Browns passed from Phil Ball, the owner since 1915, to Donald Barnes, an investment banker whose financial judgment in this instance was none too shrewd. Dismal attendance meant financial problems, and financial problems meant that even the good players who came along soon got sold to help keep the club afloat.

Thus, pitcher Bobo Newsom, acquired in 1934, was sold in 1935, reacquired in 1938, then sold again in 1939. Outfielder Goose Goslin joined the club in 1930, performed brilliantly, but was traded to Washington after the 1932 season.

Outfielder Moose Solters put in one good season for the Browns, 1936, then departed for Cleveland. Outfielder Beau Bell had two outstanding seasons, 1936 and 1937, and one adequate season, 1938, before being dealt to Detroit. The 1936 Browns had a strong starting lineup but lost 95 games, finishing seventh. The problem was pitching.

Among the players who stayed with the Browns for a while during this period, the best was Harlond Clift, their third baseman from 1934 to 1943. Clift's best years were 1937 and 1938. He drove in 118 runs in both of those years, hit 29 and 34 homers, and batted .306 and .290.

Another solid player, outfielder Sammy West, put in five full seasons and part of a sixth for the Browns, 1933 to 1938, hitting .300 or better four times. Early in the decade the most consistent pitchers were veteran George Blaeholder and Walter (Lefty) Stewart. Late in the decade, with the team finishing seventh or eighth each year, there were no effective Brownie pitchers whatever, except the peripatetic Newsom.

In 1938 the ERA of the pitching staff was a dismal 6.01. Even Newsom's was 5.06, although he won 20 games while losing 16. Newsom won the opener that year, for which owner Donald Barnes had promised to buy him a new suit. After the game, Barnes tried to hand Bobo some money for the suit. Newsom reportedly responded, "Keep the sugar.... Bobo bought the suit before the game. The bill is on your desk."

Close observers of the last-place 1939 St. Louis Browns would have seen few signs to suggest a third-place finish in 1942 and a pennant in 1944. True, George McQuinn, a classy fielding, hard-hitting first baseman had arrived in 1938. Jack Kramer began pitching for the Browns in 1939, though with no special distinction. Outfielder Chet Laabs arrived via the Tigers that year.

Trancendental Graphics

Luke Sewell

But the other architects of the Browns' brief wartime success were either riding the bench or playing elsewhere.

War Brings a Pennant

The 1940 Browns captured sixth place—their highest finish since 1934—but they started poorly in 1941. Owner Don Barnes decided he needed a new manager. He had already tried and discarded Rogers Hornsby (three seasons), Jim Bottomley (part of a season), Gabby Street (one season), and Fred Haney (since 1939). Now he handed the managerial reins to Luke Sewell, a long-time catcher from Titus, Alabama—a man who knew how to work with pitchers. The Browns needed that.

Joining the staff in 1941 were Bob Muncrief, a veteran Texas League hurler, and Denny Galehouse, a right-hander who had lost but never won in double figures for the Indians and Red Sox. Muncrief went 13-9 in 1941 with a 3.65 ERA; Galehouse was 9-10 with a 3.64 ERA. These were excellent performances for Brownie pitchers. Right-handers Eldon Auker and Bob Harris did well, too, but their 5.00+ ERAs were reminiscent of days gone by.

In 1942 the Browns climbed into third place. Rookie shortstop Vern (Junior) Stephens broke in with a bang, batting .294 and driving in 92 runs. Future Hall of Famer Rick Ferrell, a catcher for the Browns from 1929 to 1933, was back behind the plate for them in this first year of U.S. involvement in World War II. Outfielder Walt Judnich departed for the military, stalling his promising career.

Another new pitcher, Al Hollingsworth, a left-hander cast off from various teams, turned in a 10-8 year with a 2.96 ERA. But if the Browns were thinking of a pennant in 1943, they were to be disappointed. They fell back to sixth place, even though their pitching staff improved with the addition of Steve Sundra (15-11, 3.25 ERA) and Nels Potter (10-5, 2.78 ERA). Few realized it—certainly not most sportswriters—but the stage was set for the Browns to win their first and only pennant.

Part of the success of the 1944 Browns must be attributed to their military draft status. Eighteen men on the 33-player roster, including George McQuinn and Vern Stephens, held 4-F classifications. Others were exempt from service for various reasons. Some had already served (catcher Frank Mancuso and pitchers Jack Kramer and Sig Jakucki). Others held defense plant jobs (outfielder Chet Laabs and third baseman Mark Christman).

Still others were too old to be early draft picks (pitcher Al Hollingsworth, outfielder Mike Kreevich, and second baseman Don Gutteridge). With both superstars and journeymen players from other teams in the military or in the process of being drafted, wartime baseball offered the Browns an opportunity that peacetime would have denied.

The Browns took full advantage. They won their first nine games and never fell out of contention afterwards. By the last week of the 1944 season, the Detroit Tigers were leading the Browns by half a game. The Browns faced the Yankees in a crucial four-game series (during which the last-place Washington Senators split their own four-game series with the Tigers, giving the Browns a chance).

Jack Kramer and Nels Potter combined for a doubleheader victory over the Yankees. Next Denny Galehouse shut out the Yanks, 2-0. In the final game of the season Sig Jakucki, who the year before had been pitching semipro ball, topped Mel Queen 5-2 before an overflow crowd of 34,625 at Sportsman's Park. The Browns, albeit with a far weaker team than in 1922, finally had their pennant.

Unhappily for Browns' fans, the World Series had a less satisfactory ending. The St. Louis Cardinals, with Stan Musial, Mort Cooper, Walker Cooper, Marty Marion, Max Lanier, and Harry (The Cat) Brecheen, had won 105 games during

Trancendental Graphics

Rick Ferrell

the regular season. They won four more games from the Browns in the Series. Luke Sewell's men put up a fight, though. The Browns won the first game, 2-1, on George McQuinn's two-run homer in the fourth inning. Denny Galehouse had a shutout for eight innings but yielded a run in the ninth.

The Browns won the third game on five straight singles, a walk, and a wild pitch, all coming after two were out in the third inning. The final score was 6-2. At this point the Browns led the series two games to one. But they lost the next three straight. McQuinn came through handsomely for the Browns, however, batting .438 and driving in five runs.

In 1945 the Browns fell to third place. This final war year saw the much-publicized debut of a one-armed outfielder, Pete Gray, in a St. Louis

Browns' uniform. Gray played in 77 games, 61 of them as a starting outfielder. He posted a .218 batting average. Some of Gray's teammates considered him mainly a gate attraction and felt that his weak hitting (more than his split-second delayed throwing from the outfield) might have cost them a pennant. In any case, Pete Gray's major league career ended when the war ended. So did the Browns' brief tenure in the first division.

Muckerman, DeWitt, Veeck, and Sayonara

After the war, Donald Barnes sold all his capital stock in the Browns and retired to the life of a country squire at his thousand-acre estate in

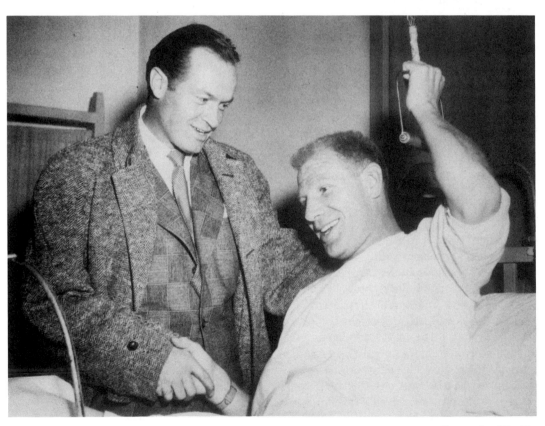

Transcendental Graphics

Bill Veeck (right) with celebrity and sports team owner Bob Hope

ODDITIES	Hypnotizing the Browns

The Browns always needed all the help they could get. Actually, they needed more help than they ever got. Even before owner Bill Veeck, master of gimmickry, brought his bag of tricks to St. Louis, the previous owners, Bill and Charley DeWitt, had been struck by an inspiration. Following a conversation with Dr. David F. Tracy, a psychologist and hypnotist, Bill and Charley announced that their ball club would use the services of Dr. Tracy in 1950 to shore up the confidence of the Brownie players by autosuggestion. Dr. Tracy took his duties seriously. "There are certain pitchers on the Browns," he told an interviewer, "who worry that they'll throw the ball in the wrong place when a fellow like Joe DiMaggio is up." (True enough. There were Red Sox pitchers like that, too.)

Anyway, Dr. Tracy promised to work on their mental state and presumably help them "think" the ball over the corners of the plate, thereby shutting down the Yankee Clipper and other tough hitters. The owners of the Browns seemed to regard Dr. Tracy's assignment mainly as one offering great opportunities for publicity, which they pursued vigorously. Hard-bitten field manager Zack Taylor considered the idea idiotic and Dr. Tracy a nuisance, who, in a worst-case scenario, might put Brownie players to sleep on the field. He banned the psychologist from the bench.

Sportswriters had a field day. Bob Cooke, hearing that Dr. Tracy would try to help Brownie pitchers "keep the ball away from DiMaggio," saw that as no problem. "Sometimes they keep it 400 feet away from him,"

Clarkson Valley. The purchaser was Richard Muckerman, owner of the Polar Wave Ice and Fuel Company. Determined to make the Browns a successful franchise, Muckerman spent freely, refusing to haggle over contract terms or training expenses. This made him popular with the players, but it counted for nothing in the standings.

The 1946 team finished seventh, despite the return of centerfielder Walt Judnich. (Far more illustrious stars were returning to the Yankees and Red Sox.) In 1947, the Browns—managed by the appropriately named Muddy Ruel—were back in the cellar. The next year they moved up to sixth, even though not a single pitcher broke even; Fred Sanford lost a league-leading 21 games. These were not memorable teams, although third baseman Bob Dillinger and a few others put up respectable numbers.

But iceman Muckerman's foray into baseball was proving too expensive and too time-consuming for him. In early 1949 he sold the franchise to Bill and Charley DeWitt for a million dollars. The DeWitts, who had worked their way up the baseball administrative ladder, knew the game but

lacked the cash to build a profitable ball club.

The Browns lost 101 games in 1949, not an auspicious start, and nearly matched that total in 1950. Attendance continued to skid. Of the pitchers, only Ned Garver seemed able to win in double figures. Left fielder Roy Sievers made a strong debut in 1949, batting .306 with 91 RBIs, but tailed off thereafter.

Two games against Boston on June 7 and 8, 1950, spotlighted the Browns' pitching problems. They lost the first game 20-4, the second one 29-4. The DeWitts began casting about for a new owner and found him in the person of the irrepressible Bill Veeck, who bought a controlling interest in the club just a week after those two merciless drubbings by the Red Sox.

Bill Veeck was a showman, a master of promotional gimmicks. He had already proved it in Cleveland when he "buried" the Indians' 1948 pennant in a mock funeral service on the day in 1949 when the team was eliminated from contention. He brought a couple of stunts to St. Louis, too.

The most famous one was signing Eddie

Transcendental Graphics

Satchel Paige

Gaedel, a three-foot seven-inch midget, to a Browns' contract and inserting him—with the number 1/8—on August 19, 1951, as a pinch hitter for rookie Frank Saucier. Detroit catcher Bob Swift tried lying prone to give pitcher Bob Cain a target for the midget's minuscule strike zone. It was no use. Cain walked Gaedel on four pitches.

The next day American League president Will Harridge ordered Gaedel's contract rescinded. Veeck charged discrimination against "short people," but to no avail. A few days later Veeck instituted "Grandstand Managers' Night," letting the fans hold up placards to make key decisions in the game. Manager Zack Taylor went along with it, and the fans managed well. The Browns won the game 5-3.

But only 3,925 fans were on hand, suggesting once again that the Browns were in enough trouble for the long-rumored franchise move to another city to be taken seriously.

The 1950 Browns finished in seventh place, as did the 1952 team. The 1951 and 1953 Browns

were cellar-dwellers. In the Browns' last three seasons, Satchel Paige, the legendary and apparently ageless African-American pitcher, compiled an 18-23 record. (Hank Thompson and Willard Brown had broken the color barrier for the Browns back in 1947.) Out of money, if not out of gimmicks, Veeck sold the team to a Baltimore syndicate on September 29, 1953.

Introducing the Orioles

The Baltimore Orioles had a long and honored history prior to 1954, but it was almost entirely a minor league history. When the St. Louis franchise came to Baltimore, it was the first time since 1902 (when New York replaced Baltimore in the American League) that a relocation had occurred. And even if the major league Orioles in their new ballpark, Memorial Stadium, played like the old Browns—18 of 38 of them, after all, *were* old Browns—that first year's attendance in Baltimore (1,060,910) made the prospect of franchise moving a very tempting one for other club owners.

The 1954 Orioles finished seventh under manager Jimmy Dykes, losing 100 games. Former Brownies Vern Stephens, Dick Kryhoski, Clint Countney, Bobby Young, Billy Hunter, Don Larsen, Bob Turley, and Duane Pillette joined newcomers Eddie Waitkus, Cal Abrams, Lew Kretlow, and Bob Chakales. None of them had much to write home about that season, and all would be gone within a year or two.

Paul Richards took over as both general manager and field manager in 1955, and while the team still finished next to last, no one could doubt that a major rebuilding effort was underway. In the winter of 1954, Richards completed a massive 17-player deal (some say 22 players were involved) that may have given up more talent, such as pitchers Bob Turley and Don Larsen, than it obtained. The only new player of note—and the only real Oriole star for some time—was Gus Triandos who, after a season at first base, became the Birds' regular catcher.

The trade also brought popular Willie Miranda, a classic good-field-no-hit shortstop, to Baltimore. Trades continued throughout the 1950s, but the team did not rise very high in the standings. The Orioles finished sixth in 1956, fifth in 1957, and sixth again in 1958 and 1959. Yet there was a sense of progress. The Baltimore farm system was being steadily strengthened.

After the 1958 season, Lee MacPhail, Jr., son of a former Yankee owner, was named general manager. In 1959 the Oriole pitching staff looked solid. Hoyt Wilhelm, a knuckleballer destined for the Hall of Fame, posted a 2.19 ERA to lead the league. Milt Pappas, a rookie the year before, compiled a 15-9 record. Outfielder Gene Woodling, in his second full season as an Oriole, batted an even .300 and drove in 77 runs. Third baseman Brooks Robinson spent part of the season at Vancouver, but that would be his last stint in the minors. For most of 1959 the team stood in third or fourth place, fading to sixth only in mid-September.

It had taken a while, but Paul Richards had built a pennant contender—maybe even a dynasty, since so many of the players were young. The Birds vaulted into second place in 1960, right behind the mighty Yankees of Mantle and Maris. Rookie Chuck Estrada won 18 games to tie Cleveland's Jim Perry for the league lead. Jack Fisher, a second-year man, pitched 29-1/3 consecutive scoreless innings. First baseman Jim Gentile, in his first full season in the majors, hit .292, cracked 21 homers, and drove in 98 runs. Brooks Robinson sparkled at third base and batted .284 with 175 hits. All in all, Baltimore's prospects looked bright.

Two Robinsons and Some New Pitchers

The Orioles won 95 games in 1961. Ordinarily that would be enough to win the pennant. But the Mantle-Maris Yankees won 109 games, and the Cash-Colavito-Kaline Tigers won 101. Lefthander Steve Barber, in his second season in the majors, won 18 games to lead the Orioles. But the Yankees' Whitey Ford won 25, and the Tigers' Frank Lary won 23.

The Orioles' Jim Gentile hit 46 home runs (and drove in 141 runs), but the Yankees' Roger Maris and Mickey Mantle hit 61 and 54 homers respectively, while the Tigers' Rocky Colavito belted 45. In other words, the Orioles were good, but the opposition was formidable. The Birds finished third—and then all but fell apart in 1962.

Some contender. Some dynasty. The Orioles, under new manager Billy Hitchcock, skidded to seventh place in 1962. Brooks Robinson played as capably as ever, fielding flawlessly and batting .303 with 23 homers and 88 RBIs. The rest of the team was another story.

There were, however, two high points. Outfielder John (Boog) Powell, a newcomer, showed more power than consistency—but what power! One of his home runs at Memorial Stadium measured 469 feet on the fly. And late in August the Orioles met the mighty Yankees in a five-game weekend series. Baltimore won all five games. Aside from these two events, 1962 was a distinct disappointment.

So were the next three seasons, though to a lesser extent. The Birds averaged 92 wins per season from 1963 to 1965 but could finish no higher than third. Luis Aparicio, acquired from the Indians, replaced Jerry Adair at shortstop in 1963, with Adair moving to second base.

General manager Lee MacPhail seemed to be making all the right moves. Hank Bauer took over as field manager in 1964 and did an exemplary job, converting Boog Powell to a first baseman in 1965 and installing rookies Paul Blair in centerfield and Dave McNally and Jim Palmer on the mound. Again the team had the look of a pennant contender.

And in 1966 it was—with one major addition. Frank Robinson, the Orioles' new right fielder, arrived from the Cincinnati Reds in a trade for Milt Pappas. Robinson responded to his new assignment by winning the triple crown, batting .316 with 49 home runs and 122 RBIs.

The Birds' young pitching staff, anchored by Dave McNally, Jim Palmer, Wally Bunker, and

Although third baseman Brooks Robinson spent many more seasons in an Oriole uniform than did outfielder Frank Robinson, both men made an indelible mark on Baltimore—and American—baseball.

Brooks Robinson (right) spent all or part of 23 seasons as a Baltimore Oriole. He first appeared on the scene in 1955; he took his final bow in 1977. At the height of the Orioles' success, 1969 to 1974, he was an established old pro at third base, one of the game's great defensive artists at the hot corner. His almost unbelievable stops and assists awed television viewers nationwide in postseason play.

In his outstanding career, Robinson won 16 straight Gold Gloves and led the American League in fielding average a record ten times. He was no slouch as a hitter either. In his best season offensively, 1964, he batted .317, hit 35 doubles and 28 home runs, drove in 118 runs, and was named American League MVP. With his friendly personality, long tenure, and sparkling exploits, Brooks Robinson was one of the most popular Orioles ever.

Photo: *Transcendental Graphics*

AP/Wide World Photos

Frank Robinson, a superstar for the Cincinnati Reds from 1956 to 1965, came to Baltimore in 1966 via a trade. He played a central role in helping what had been a good but not great Oriole team become a pennant winner. He captured the triple crown that year, hitting a career high 49 home runs and leading the league (but not surpassing his own Cincinnati season marks) with a .316 batting average and 122 RBIs. Robinson, reputed to be disruptive, proved to be the catalyst of the finest of all Oriole teams.

In 1966, the year of his Baltimore debut, he became the first player in baseball history to receive the MVP Award in both leagues, having won it five years earlier with the Reds. Robinson collected 586 home runs in his major league career to put him fourth on the all-time list. In 1975 while he was still an active player, the Cleveland Indians named him the first black manager in major league baseball.

Steve Barber, with Eddie Watt, Moe Drabowsky, and Stu Miller in relief, was effective without being sensational. Palmer, in his second year, won the most games, 15-10, while Steve Barber, 10-5, had the best ERA, 2.30.

Besides Frank Robinson, two other Orioles drove in a hundred or more runs: Boog Powell, 109, and Brooks Robinson, 100. Dave Johnson, up from the Rochester farm team, played well at second base. This balanced and impressive team won 92 games and lost 63 under manager Hank Bauer. It then swept the Los Angeles Dodgers in four straight games to win the World Series. Back-to-back homers in the first inning by Frank and Brooks Robinson, plus brilliant relief work by Moe Drabowsky, gave the Birds the first game, 5-2. The Dodgers did not score again in the Series.

Jim Palmer pitched a 6-0 shutout in game two. The last two games were 1-0 shutouts fashioned by Wally Bunker and Dave McNally. The needed runs came on a 430-foot homer by Paul Blair in game three and a less monumental homer by Frank Robinson in game four. (Robinson's longest home run had come way back on May 8 when he blasted a Luis Tiant pitch into Memorial Stadium's west parking lot, the only ball ever hit completely out of the park.)

The Orioles did not repeat in 1967. They did not even come close, finishing sixth, with exceptional performances from hardly anyone except the two Robinsons and Paul Blair. Pitcher Jim Palmer, 3-1, spent much of his time on the disabled list. Dave McNally dropped to 7-7, Wally Bunker to 3-7, and Steve Barber to 4-9. Other than reliever Moe Drabowsky, the brightest lights on the mound were Tom Phoebus, 14-9, and Jim Hardin, 8-3, both called up from Rochester. A new leadoff hitter, Don Buford, acquired from the White Sox, added strength to the lineup.

When the 1968 Birds started slowly, new owner Jerry Hofberger and his new general manager, Harry Dalton, fired Hank Bauer and replaced him with Earl Weaver. Managers come and go, but Earl Weaver, who had worked his way up through the managerial ranks of the Baltimore farm sys-

Transcendental Graphics

Jim Palmer

tem, came and stayed. He arrived at exactly the right moment.

Earl Weaver, Pennant Fever

Although he was unable to pull a pennant out of the hat in 1968 (the team played at a .585 clip under his direction), he brought it in second behind the Tigers. Over the winter Dalton and Weaver made a highly significant deal, obtaining left-handed pitcher Mike Cuellar from the Astros. The Oriole pitching staff was already strong; with Cuellar it was superb.

Everything clicked in 1969—right up until the World Series. By April 16 the Orioles were in first place to stay. By season's end they had racked up 109 victories, the third highest total in American League history. Mike Cuellar led the pitching staff at 23-11, with a 2.38 ERA. Dave McNally went 20-7, Jim Palmer 16-4, and Tom Phoebus 14-7. Eddie Watt, Pete Richert, and Dick Hall were outstanding in relief.

Boog Powell, Dave Johnson, Frank Robinson, Paul Blair, and Don Buford all hit above

Earl Weaver's Second Retirement

Not many major league managers retire to a standing ovation, but Earl Weaver did. Remarkably enough, it happened on the day the Orioles lost the Eastern Division championship to the Mil-waukee Brewers. On the last day of the 1982 season, the Orioles had tied the Brewers for the division lead in the first game of a doubleheader. One game would decide the outcome. Unhappily for O's fans, the verdict of the final game soon became evident, as the Brewers romped to a 10-2 win over Jim Palmer.

Even this bitter loss did not dampen the tribute to Weaver. A crowd of 51,642 gave the departing manager a succession of standing ovations that lasted 45 minutes. Later a number of fans gathered at the front of the deserted O's dugout, chanting, "We want Weaver! We want Weaver!" At last the diminutive manager reappeared and doffed his hat. In their book, *The Pitcher,* John Thorn and John B. Holway wrote, "It was a tribute we have never seen accorded to any other manager."

their lifetime averages. Smooth-fielding shortstop Mark Belanger, a career .228 hitter, batted .287. The Orioles led the league in fielding percentage and fewest errors. Brooks Robinson, whose batting average slid to .234, fielded brilliantly, committing only 14 errors at third base. Donald Honig in his *Baseball's 10 Greatest Teams* chose the 1969 Orioles as one of the ten.

The strong, admirably balanced team seemed a cinch to defeat the National League's "Amazin'" New York Mets in the World Series, even though the Mets topped Atlanta three games to none in the new divisional play-offs. The Mets proved even more "amazin'" than most of their fans probably expected. Baltimore, like New York, breezed through the play-offs, defeating Minnesota three games to none.

But the World Series was a different story. The Orioles took the first game, 4-1, behind Mike Cuellar, but then the roof fell in. The Mets won

the next four games, as the Baltimore bats fell silent—a .146 team batting average for the Series. In the final game, Baltimore blew a three-run lead, lost 5-3, and it was all over until the next year.

That next year, 1970, saw a fairly tight pennant race turn into an O's runaway in August. The Orioles clinched the pennant on September 16 and closed out the season with 11 straight wins, giving them a 15-game margin over the second-place Yankees. This team was virtually identical with the previous year's, and their won-lost total, 108-54, was just a game off the '69 pace.

The Birds had a trio of 20-game winners: Mike Cuellar, 24-8; Dave McNally, 24-9; and Jim Palmer, 20-10. Boog Powell, who batted .277, hit 35 home runs, and drove in 114 runs, was voted the American League's Most Valuable Player. Frank Robinson, who had earned the award in 1966, hit .305, while platooned outfielder Merv Rettenmund had his best year ever at .322.

Once again the Birds eliminated the Minnesota Twins three games to none in the championship series. They continued to win in the World Series, taking three games from the Cincinnati Reds before being edged in the fourth game, 6-5. The Orioles bounced back to win the fifth game and the Series.

Brooks Robinson, the World Series MVP, excelled in the field and at bat. He batted .429, drove in six runs, and made one brilliant play after another at third base. In three of the five games, the Reds jumped off to a 3-0 lead, only to see their lead evaporate each time as the result of one or more timely Oriole home runs.

Baltimore seemed unbeatable in the American League East as it rolled to another division championship under Earl Weaver in 1971. Again the team was almost unchanged, except for the presence of Pat Dobson, acquired from the San Diego Padres in exchange for Tom Phoebus. Dobson won 20 games for the Birds, joining a quartet of 20-game winners whose other members were Cuellar, Palmer, and McNally.

The team won 101 and lost 57, their third 100+ season in a row and their third consecutive division title. In the league play-offs they defeated a powerful Oakland A's team in three straight games. Against the Pittsburgh Pirates, featuring Roberto Clemente and Willie Stargell, they won the first two World Series games, but then lost three in a row.

The sixth game and with it the Series seemed lost when McNally loaded the bases in the top of the tenth inning of a 2-2 tie. However, he worked his way out of the jam, and in the bottom of the tenth Frank Robinson and Merv Rettenmund singled, and Brooks Robinson hit a sacrifice fly to bring home the winning run. It all came down to game seven, in which the Pirates' Steve Blass tossed a four-hitter to best Mike Cuellar 2-1.

Although it was not obvious at the time, the 1971 Orioles had reached an apex. It seemed the team would never be quite so good again. In 1972 Jim Palmer hung in there with a 21-10 season and Mike Cuellar with 18-12, but Dave Nally, at 13-17, and Pat Dobson, 16-18, signalled the end of the great days—as did the trading of 36-year-old Frank Robinson to the L.A. Dodgers.

Actually, the faltering offense was probably more responsible for the Orioles slide to third place (behind Detroit and Boston) than the pitching was. Not a single major starter or reliever had an ERA higher than McNally's 2.95. No complaint there. But newcomer Bobby Grich, a utility infielder in 1972, led all batters with an unspectacular .278. Paul Blair and Merv Rettenmund skidded to .233 each.

Still, 1972 could be written off as just one of those seasons, with the hope that 1973 would be better. And it was. Earl Weaver's men, now with Bobby Grich as their full-time second baseman, reclaimed the division title, winning 97, losing 65. But the magic was not quite what it had been. Moreover, the Oakland A's in the AL West—with Vida Blue, Catfish Hunter, and Reggie Jackson—were now a true powerhouse. In the 1973 play-offs the Orioles fell to the A's, three games to two, and sat out the World Series.

The O's were still a very good team, still being renewed with fresh talent (outfielder Don Baylor debuted in 1972 and put in five good seasons for the Birds), but Oakland dominated the majors in the mid-1970s. Baltimore won the division title again in 1974, with a slightly reduced number of wins (91-71), and once more lost to the potent A's in the AL championship series.

The Birds Fly Lower

For four seasons, 1975 through 1978, the Orioles were a competitive, well-balanced, first-division team. They averaged 91 wins per season, yet finished second three times and fourth once. Weaver, widely regarded as a managerial genius, was never in danger of losing his job.

The team even improved in some respects. Outfielder Ken Singleton and pitcher Mike Torrez arrived in 1975 in a trade with Montreal. First baseman and designated hitter Lee May came over from the Astros. Singleton turned out to be the Birds' only .300 hitter in 1975, and May drove in 99 runs. Torrez stayed just one season, but he won 20 games for the second-place Orioles. Doug DeCinces, the heir apparent to Brooks Robinson's third-base job, moved up from Rochester.

Changes continued in 1976, the biggest one being the acquisition of Oakland superstar Reggie Jackson, whose .502 slugging average for Baltimore led the league. But free agency and Yankee money lured Jackson away after one year. A long-term Oriole, catcher Rick Dempsey, arrived later that season.

The O's had no .300 hitters in 1976, but they did have two 20-game winners: Jim Palmer (22-13), at the top of his form, and Wayne Garland (20-7), who had blossomed from a two-game winner the previous year. Baltimore finished second in 1976 at 88-74.

By 1977 the core of the next pennant-winning Oriole team was in place. The only holdovers from the stellar 1971 club were careerists Mark Belanger and Jim Palmer. The new faces for a late-1970s pennant drive were Eddie Murray at first base, Rich Dauer at second, Doug DeCinces at third, Ken Singleton and Al Bumbry in the outfield, Rick Dempsey behind the plate, and Mike Flanagan, Dennis Martinez, and Scott McGregor on the mound. This was a remarkable transformation in key personnel for a team that continued to be competitive season after season even though not finishing first. They fell to fourth—but won 90 games—in 1978.

Then lightning struck again. With Earl Weaver still at the helm, the Orioles captured the pennant in 1979, winning 102 games, losing 57. Six pitchers won in double figures, but only Mike Flanagan turned in a 20-win season, 23-9. None of the regulars batted .300, but outfielder Gary Roenicke, in his first full year, connected for 25 home runs, as did Eddie Murray, while Ken Singleton batted .295, hit 35 homers, and drove in 111 runs. The 1979 Orioles defeated the California Angels in the AL championship series but lost to the Pittsburgh Pirates in the World Series after leading three games to one.

The Orioles won 100 games again in 1980, but the Yankees won 103. The surprising ace of the 1980 Baltimore pitching staff was Steve Stone, 25-7, who had been dealt from team to team, averaging about nine wins a season before being picked up by the Orioles the year before.

In the strike-shortened 1981 season, the O's had a 59-46 record but failed to make the play-offs in the split-season plan the leagues adopted. They came back strong in 1982, but not quite strong enough, losing out by a single game to the Milwaukee Brewers. The 1982 season is noteworthy for the arrival of a new shortstop, Cal Ripkin, Jr., to replace the veteran Mark Belanger. Earl Weaver had already announced his intention to retire at the end of the 1982 season, and he did.

Weaver's replacement, Joe Altobelli, a journeyman first baseman who had earlier managed the San Francisco Giants for three seasons, led the O's to a pennant in his first year at Baltimore. He headed basically the same team that had won the Series four years before, although third baseman Doug DeCinces had been dealt to California, John Shelby was now in the outfield, and pitchers Mike Boddicker (16-8) and Storm Davis (13-7) had become starters. Jim Palmer, at age 37, pitched infrequently, but left-hander Scott McGregor had a fine year, 18-7.

Cal Ripkin, in just his second full season in the majors, chalked up some impressive batting stats for a shortstop—or anyone else. He collected 211 hits, batted .318, led the league with 47 doubles, hit 27 home runs, and drove in 102 runs. Ripkin won the league's Most Valuable Player Award, edging out teammate Eddie Murray, who posted some good stats himself: a .306 batting average, 33 homers, and 111 RBIs.

In the league championship series, Baltimore eliminated the Chicago White Sox three games to one. Mike Boddicker struck out 14 batters in the second game, hurling a five-hit, 4-0 shutout. The last game went into the tenth inning tied 0-0, when Tito Landrum, a part-time outfielder, broke the deadlock with a solo home run; the Orioles went on to score two more runs to win the league title.

The World Series against the Philadelphia Phillies went swimmingly as well, the Orioles losing the first game but winning the next four. Boddicker and McGregor both pitched effectively. McGregor lost the first game, 2-1, but came back with a five-hit shutout in game five. Boddicker's ERA in the World Series was 0.00 on the basis of his superb three-hit shutout in the second game. Eddie Murray homered twice in the final game, and Rick Dempsey, the Series MVP, added a homer and a double.

Needed: A Comeback

The same team that had seemed so finely tuned in capturing the world championship in 1983 had to settle for fifth place the next year. This sounds like more of a fall than it was. The Tigers walked away with the division title, winning 104 games, but the next four teams were tightly bunched within a game or two of each other. The Orioles were considerably nearer to second place than to sixth. Nevertheless, a real slide in the standings had begun, and it would not end for several years.

In 1985 the O's finished fourth, led by Eddie Murray and Cal Ripkin. Joe Altobelli was fired early in the season and was replaced by none other

PROFILES	**Here a Ripkin, There a Ripkin ...**

Cal Ripkin, Sr., and his older brother, Bill, spent their playing careers in the minor leagues. Cal, Sr., who alternated between catching and pitching, broke in in 1957 with Phoenix of the Class C Arizona-Mexico League. In 1961 he became a playing manager with Leesburg of the then-Class D Florida State League. A cog in the Baltimore Oriole system, he moved up the managerial ladder, with stops at Aberdeen, Elmira, Rochester, and Asheville, finally becoming an Oriole coach in 1976. A decade later, Cal, Sr., replaced Earl Weaver (after Weaver's ill-fated return) as manager of the Orioles, a job Ripkin held for a year and a half.

Meanwhile, his son Cal Ripkin, Jr., had risen through the Baltimore farm system, taking over as the Orioles' regular shortstop in 1982. By the time of Cal, Sr.'s, managerial debut in 1987, there was no question that his son had become a star of the first magnitude. By 1992, in addition to his many honors and awards, Cal, Jr., was pursuing one of the thus-far impregnable records in major league baseball—Lou Gehrig's consecutive-game playing mark of 2,130 games.

Then there was brother Billy, four years younger than Cal, Jr. Billy Ripkin followed his brother's route to the top. He played shortstop (and other infield positions) at Bluefield, Charlotte, and Rochester before moving up to Baltimore as a second baseman. In his first year with the O's, Billy hit .308. In 1990 his .291 batting average led the team. Billy, unlike Cal, Jr., proved to be prone to injuries, but he quickly established himself as a capable, if not a superstar-quality, player at the major league level.

AP/Wide World Photos

Cal Ripkin Jr.

than the old retiree, Earl Weaver. But the team itself was the problem (especially the pitching), not the manager. Weaver's O's did no better than Altobelli's, and the legendary skipper should have taken the hint.

Instead, he returned in 1986 and presided over, of all things, a last-place finish. The starting pitchers were giving up too many runs for the batters to overcome. Mike Boddicker, the ace of staff, won 14 and lost 12 with a bloated 4.70 ERA. Scott McGregor, Mike Flanagan, and Storm Davis, once supremely effective, all had losing records. Eddie Murray and Cal Ripkin, joined by outfielder Fred Lynn in the twilight of his career, continued to do well, and rookie outfielder Larry Sheets showed promise. But changes were needed, and many came.

In 1987 Cal Ripkin, Sr., became the new manager. He found himself with two sons in the infield—a Hall-of-Fame-bound shortstop and a rookie second baseman, Billy, who appeared in 58 games, batted .308 and fielded with assurance. Except for Boddicker, the pitching staff was new, but new did not mean better. The pitchers, other than Dave Schmidt, performed worse than the ones they replaced. The Orioles came in a distant sixth with a 67-95 record. Cleveland obligingly lost 101 games, thus keeping Baltimore out of the cellar.

All the Ripkins were slated to stay on in 1988, but the team collapsed utterly, finishing last—far, far back—with 54 wins and 107 losses. (Shades of the old St. Louis Browns!) Clearly Ripkin the Elder could not survive such a season—in fact, he could not survive the opening weeks of it, as the O's lost their first 21 games, setting a new American League record.

In came Frank Robinson to manage. But after such a horrendous start, 1988 was a hopeless campaign for the Orioles. One bright note amid the gloom was the news that Baltimore would soon be getting a brand new ballpark to replace Memorial Stadium.

The new home of the Orioles, a $105 million facility to be called, officially, Oriole Park at Camden Yards, would be located in the city's Inner Harbor area. The 48,000-seat ballpark would be ready for the 1992 season.

But the immediate question was, would the Birds improve in 1989? The answer was yes. A host of trades brought an army of new faces, and new arms, including those of Jeff Ballard, Gregg Olson, and Pete Harnisch. The Orioles bid fair to climb from last place to first in one breathtaking leap, but in the end they had to settle for second place behind the Toronto Blue Jays.

This dazzling comeback proved misleading, however, as the 1990 Orioles sank back to fifth place, and the 1991 team skidded to seventh. The ups and downs still had not ended. In 1992 the Birds, now in their new but classic Camden Yards ballpark, made another quick ascent and remained in contention well into September, falling back finally to third place.

Changes abounded for the team in 1993. On August 2nd, the team was sold for $173 million. Then, in September, the team went on a winning streak to pull within 1½ games of American East-leading Toronto and also enjoyed the 43rd consecutive sellout at Camden Yards.

First baseman David Segui told *Sports Illustrated,* "Even early in the season, when we weren't playing well, this place was packed every night.... Now that we're playing with the season on the line, there's real electricity here. You can feel it. And it really does pick you up."

In *Sports Illustrated* Ben McDonald added, "You go to spirng training and work your butt off for six weeks. and this is what it's for: the last two weeks of the season, playing the two teams you've got to beat, with a crowd that's going to be into it."

Whether the Orioles of the future are poised for a pennant or headed for a fall was unclear in light of the rollercoaster ride of the previous few seasons. What was abundantly clear, though, was that over a period of four decades Baltimore had made an orange-and-black silk purse out of a Brown sow's ear.

SOURCES

BOOKS

Baseball Register: 1945, 1965, 1980, 1992 Editions, The Sporting News Publishing Co., 1945, 1965, 1980, 1992.

Beard, Gordon, *Birds on the Wing: The Story of the Baltimore Orioles,* Doubleday, 1967.

Borst, Bill, *Still Last in the American League: The St. Louis Browns Revisited,* Alwerger & Mandel Publishing Company, 1992.

Bready, James H., *The Home Team,* 1979.

Hawkins, John C., *This Date in Baltimore Orioles-St. Louis Browns History,* Stein & Day, 1982.

Honig, Donald, *Baseball's 10 Greatest Teams,* Macmillan, 1982.

Ivor-Campbell, Frederick, "Team Histories: Baltimore Orioles," *Total Baseball,* edited by John Thorn and Pete Palmer, Warner Books, 1989.

Lieb, Frederick G., *The Baltimore Orioles: The History of a Colorful Team in Baltimore and St. Louis,* G.P. Putnam's Sons, 1955.

Mead, Willliam B., *Even the Browns,* Contemporary Books, 1978.

Reichler, Joseph L., editor, *The Baseball Encyclopedia,* 7th edition, Macmillan, 1988.

Veeck, Bill, with Ed Linn, *Veeck, as in Wreck,* G.P. Putnam's Sons, 1962.

Voigt, David Quentin, *American Baseball: From the Commissioners to Continental Expansion,* Pennsylvania State University Press, 1983.

PERIODICALS

Baseball Magazine, September 1920.

Collier's, September 2, 1944.

New York Times, September 30, 1953.

New Yorker, May 1, 1954.

Sports Illustrated, August 13, 1979; September 20, 1993.

—Gerald Tomlinson for Book Builders, Inc.

BOSTON RED SOX

All of New England cheers for the Boston Red Sox, a team that has provided high drama, hope, and heartache to generations of fans. The Red Sox became charter members of the American League in 1901 and have played for most of their ninety-plus years in Boston's venerable Fenway Park. Few franchises in any sport can claim a more devoted following or more frenzied press coverage than the Sox—and no baseball team anywhere can boast a more bizarre history as the century nears an end.

Bostonians claim—very seriously—that the team labors under a curse. The Red Sox have not won a World Series since 1918. Between that year and 1986 they made four World Series appearances and lost all four in the seventh game. Other promising seasons have ended in sudden-death playoff losses or lackluster autumn performances. In his book *The Curse of the Bambino,* Dan Shaughnessy writes: "The Red Sox have almost always been competitive, and they have perfected

the Big Tease/Near-Miss seasons that have become as much a part of Boston as the Old North Church and the Union Oyster House. This is why Red Sox fans are different from [Chicago] Cubs fans. Both teams date back to the beginning of baseball time, both play in wonderful old ballparks, and both have legions of sophisticated followers starving for a World Championship. The difference is that the Cubs are usually bad while the Red Sox are usually good enough to tease their fans into thinking that this is the year. It's easy to sit in the Wrigley [Field] bleachers and drink beer and laugh at the Cubbies. It's tough to watch the Red Sox bring you to the point of satisfaction, then let you down. It's like *almost* sneezing."

So powerful is the image of the Red Sox as choke artists, or victims of a strange curse, that their plight has become the stuff of jokes throughout New England. Stories abound of couples exchanging wedding vows that include "till death

Transcendental Graphics

Jimmy Collins

do us part, or the Red Sox win the World Series." Boston sports talk show host Eddie Andelman— a man in the prime of life—has already had his tombstone carved to read: "HE NEVER LIVED LONG ENOUGH TO SEE THE RED SOX WIN IT ALL." The team's peculiar reputation even drew mention in the nation's *Congressional Record,* when Massachusetts representative Silvio Conte noted: "Red Sox fans have felt the ecstasy of victory in their grasps so many times, have had their fists clenched, waiting for that final out in heady anticipation, only to be put through the agony of another lost victory. It is a ritual that has been repeated many more times than a kinder and gentler God would ever allow."

Certainly the story of the Boston Red Sox can lead one to believe that larger forces are at work in major league baseball. The team's many spectacular losses confound all logical explanation. Fans and foes alike regard Boston's history as extraordinary, legendary, and ultimately frustrating— like *almost* sneezing.

From Pilgrims to Red Sox

Baseball has always been a popular sport in Boston. The city had a professional franchise as early as 1871, when a team known as the Red Stockings played within the National Association of Professional Base Ball Players. That Red Stockings team won four straight Association championships from 1872-75 and was even featured in exhibition games in England. When the National League (NL) formed in 1876, the Red Stockings joined and became known as the Beaneaters, and later the Braves. The team was popular and profitable, and Boston seemed a likely location for a second professional club.

That club arrived in 1901, the year Bancroft Johnson introduced the AL. Johnson formed his new league from teams that had been part of the defunct Western League, adding other franchises in major eastern cities. Boston's AL entry was financed by Charles Somers, a coal, lumber, and shipping magnate. A new ballpark was built on Huntington Avenue, and the team took the field in April of 1901.

The new franchise was called by a number of names—"The Somersets," presumably a reflection on the owner, "The Pilgrims," "The Puritans," and even "The Plymouth Rocks." The name shuffle ended in 1907, when the Braves stopped wearing red stockings. The AL franchise quickly adopted the red footwear and the name Red Sox, forging a link with the proud Red Stockings tradition from the previous century.

Somers wanted his team to be competitive, so from the outset he recruited able and popular players. The first Boston manager was Jimmy Collins, a third baseman formerly with the Braves. Other Braves stars who defected to the Pilgrims included Chick Stahl, Buck Freeman, and pitcher Ed "Parson" Lewis. The team's first superstar

TEAM INFORMATION AT A GLANCE

Founding date: April 25, 1901 (charter member of American League)

Home stadium: Fenway Park
Lansdowne and Jersey Streets
Boston, MA 02215

Dimensions: Left-field line—315 feet
Center field—420 feet
Right-field line—302 feet
Seating capacity: 33,925

Team uniforms: Home—base color white, red letters, navy trim
Road—base color gray, red letters, navy trim
Team nickname: Pilgrims, 1901-07; Red Sox, 1907—
Logo: Two red socks in front of a baseball

Franchise record:	Won	Lost	Pct.
(1901-1993)	7,321	7,043	.510

World Series wins (5): 1903, 1912, 1915, 1916, 1918
American League championships (10): 1903, 1904, 1912, 1915, 1916, 1918, 1946, 1967, 1975, 1986
American League East division first-place finishes (5): 1975, 1978, 1986, 1988, 1990

came to Boston from the St. Louis Cardinals. His name was Denton "Cy" Young. Young quickly established himself as the best pitcher in baseball on the way to a Hall-of-Fame career. He spent seven seasons in Boston and still holds franchise records for wins (193), losses (112), innings pitched (2,768.1), shutouts (38), and no-hitters (2).

In their very first season the Pilgrims finished a respectable second to the Chicago White Sox. Young won 33 games for Boston. The following season Young won 32 games and the team finished in third place. By 1903 a fine squad had assembled under new owner Henry J. Killilea. The Pilgrims boasted three 20-game winners in Young, Tom Hughes, and Bill Dineen, and the team cruised to first place in the AL.

It happened that Killilea knew Pittsburgh Pirates owner Barney Dreyfuss. The two men decided in August of 1903 that if their teams finished atop their respective leagues, they would meet in an informal "world championship" play-off. Thus the Boston team became the first AL entry in the first World Series, meeting the NL Pirates in a best-of-nine contest. A standing-room-only crowd of 16,242 packed into the Huntington Avenue park to see Boston begin the playoff with a 7-3 loss to Pittsburgh. The Pilgrims won five of the next seven games to claim the first-ever modern world championship of baseball.

At season's end in 1903 the team changed hands again. The new owner was John I. Taylor, whose father was publisher of the *Boston Globe*.

The team continued to win, topping the AL again in 1904. This time, a disgruntled New York Giants owner declined to allow his franchise to participate in a post-season playoff—he was angry because the upstart AL had established a team in New York City. Fans in both cities reacted strongly in favor of a world championship. Eventually the Giants owner backed down, but not in time for a 1904 Series. Boston had to settle for its second league championship, and it was years before the team reached post-season play again.

Boston slid to fourth place in 1905 and had a disastrous 49-105 campaign in 1906. Taylor fired Collins as manager and hired Stahl, who committed suicide during spring training in 1907. Between 1907 and 1909 the Sox employed four different managers as the team struggled to finish in the middle of the league. Fortunes began to turn in 1909. Taylor bought the services of pitcher Smokey Joe Wood and an outfielder named Tristram "Tris" Speaker. In 1910 the club added outfielders Duffy Lewis and Harry Hooper, players who were particularly strong on defense. This nucleus helped move the Sox from a fourth place team in 1910 to a contender in 1912.

The Glory Years

A new era for Red Sox baseball began in the spring of 1912. The team had outgrown its Huntington Avenue facility, so Taylor built a new ballpark in the quiet, residential Fenway section of town. Fenway Park opened for official business on April 20, 1912, when some 27,000 spectators watched the Sox defeat the New York Highlanders. The grand event was overshadowed by the sinking of the Titanic in the North Atlantic, which happened the same week. Some old-timers suggest that the eerie coincidence is the first hint of the notorious curse at work.

In their comfortable new ballpark the Red Sox—now under manager Jake Stahl—won the 1912 AL pennant. Speaker hit .383, and Smokey Joe Wood went 34-5 with a 1.91 earned run average (ERA). The Sox finished a full 14 games

ahead of the second-place Washington Senators. By that time the World Series was established in its current best-of-seven format. Boston met the New York Giants in the fall classic and won the championship in a tough seven-game battle. It was sweet revenge for the insult the Giants had delivered in 1904.

From 1912 until 1918 the Red Sox dominated professional baseball. The team won pennants in 1912, 1915, 1916, and 1918 under owners James R. McAleer (1912-13), Joseph J. Lannin (1913-16), and Harry Frazee. Remarkably, the Sox won every World Series they appeared in during this period.

After the Series win in 1912, Boston slumped to fourth place in 1913. Owner Lannin went shopping and found a prospect in Baltimore. The International League Baltimore Orioles had hired an unruly slugger named George Herman Ruth who had grown up in the city's St. Mary's Industrial School. Ruth was a left-handed pitcher who could also hit the ball, and his contract was sold to Boston for $2900. Lannin offered Ruth $2500 for one year.

Babe Ruth made his debut in 1914, when the Sox finished in second place with a 91-62 record. The Babe did not burst upon the scene as a fabulous rookie. He pitched well, but manager Bill Carrigan did not hesitate to pinch-hit for him in late innings. In fact, Ruth finished out the 1914 season in the minor leagues at Providence, Rhode Island. The next year was a different story. Ruth won 18 games on the mound in 1915 and hit .315 in 42 games. The Red Sox advanced into another World Series, this time against the Philadelphia Phillies, and won the championship in five games. Ruth did not see any World Series action—a vital indicator that Boston's team had remarkable depth.

Red Sox fans knew they had a superstar on their hands by 1916, when Ruth pitched to a 23-12 record with a league-leading 1.75 ERA and also batted a respectable .272. Once again Boston advanced to the league championship and the World Series, this time meeting the Brooklyn Dodgers. Ruth's first World Series outing was a phenomenal 13-inning duel that the Sox finally won, 2-1. Boston won the World Series in five games.

As Bruce Chadwick notes in *The Boston Red Sox,* "The Boston fans were in love with their team and in love with Ruth. As the Roaring Twenties approached, the Red Sox's glory was only beginning to unfold. Boston would have the best team in the country, that much was clear." The high expectations were about to be dashed in one of baseball's most memorable disasters.

Before the start of the 1917 season, the Red Sox changed hands again. The new owner was Harry H. Frazee, a New York-based entertainment mogul who had made his money on Broadway musicals. Frazee was doing well at the time with a hit play called *Nothing but the Truth,* and he seemed willing to spend substantial sums to lure good players to Boston. When the Red Sox finished in second place in 1917, Frazee recruited Stuffy McInnis, Amos Strunk, Wally Schang, and Joe Bush from the Philadelphia Athletics and promised to let Ruth play every day.

The Red Sox had one more glory year in 1918. Under new manager Edward Grant Barrow the team posted a 75-51 record for another AL pennant. The 1918 World Series offered a welcome relief from the serious business of World War I. The Sox met the Chicago Cubs and took the world championship in six games. It was not until the eighth inning of the fourth game that Ruth ended his Series record of 29 and two-thirds scoreless innings.

Boston fans were delighted. Their championship Red Sox were young and aggressive, show-

Transcendental Graphics

Cy Young

Transcendental Graphics

Herb Pennock

ing all the earmarks of a true baseball dynasty. No one could have foreseen the events that were about to unfold or the consequences they would have for the five-time world champions.

Financial Woes Doom Sox

Frazee had fallen upon hard times. He needed funds to support his Broadway plays, and creditors were calling in their notes on the Red Sox. First, in 1919, the baseball owner sold Ernie Shore, Dutch Leonard, and 21-game-winner Carl Mays to other teams. Then he feuded with Ruth over salary and bonuses. The Red Sox slid to sixth place despite Ruth's record-setting 29 home runs and 114 runs batted in (RBIs).

By the end of the 1919 season Frazee was near the bottom of his financial barrel. It happened that his New York office was two doors from the business establishment of Jacob Ruppert, owner of the New York Yankees. The two men were good friends. When Frazee became desperate for cash, Ruppert offered a solution. The Yankees acquired Babe Ruth for the vast sum of $125,000 cash. Ruppert also loaned Frazee $300,000 to be secured by a mortgage on Fenway Park. Outraged Boston fans called the sale of Ruth "the crime of the century." Worse was yet to come.

To this day they call it "the rape of the Red Sox." Frazee, still strapped for cash, sent a veritable army of Boston stars to the Yankees: pitchers Sam Jones, Herb Pennock, Waite Hoyt, and Joe Bush, catcher Wally Schang, and outfielder Mike McNally. In return the Red Sox got a handful of mediocre players and one talented catcher, Muddy Ruel. The exodus continued in 1922 when the Yanks bought shortstop Joe Dugan and outfielder Elmer Smith. Chadwick notes: "Boston had the best players in baseball—the problem was they were all playing for the Yankees." Indeed, 11 of the 24 players on the Yankees' first world championship team came from the Red Sox.

Needless to say, the Sox were decimated by the excessive trading. Boston finished dead last in the league nine times in the first 12 seasons without Ruth, who left in 1920. According to Shaughnessy, "Frazee's name was mud in Boston then, just as it is now." The legend of the curse stems from this rock-bottom period in the team's history when fans watched their favorite superstar—and all his best mates—travel south to bring championships to a rival franchise.

Ironically, Frazee invested his cash from the Yankees into a new production called *No, No, Nanette* that became a huge hit and restored his fortunes. The show's success did not come in time to save the Sox. Frazee sold the franchise on July 11, 1923. The day the sale was announced, the 1923 Red Sox did not have a single player left from the championship season of 1918.

The 1920s Red Sox suffered through year after year of dismal failure. Owners Bob Quinn and Winslow Palmer could not stem the tide of misfortune. Boston lost over 100 games in 1925,

1926, 1927, 1930, and 1932. In the latter year, the Sox finished 64 games behind the league-leading Yankees with a 43-111 record. Fenway Park's third-base bleachers burned down in 1926 and were not replaced. No one wanted to sit there. By the first years of the Great Depression, some of the city's amateur games were outdrawing the Red Sox. Chadwick writes of the team: "The Red Sox were the disgrace of the American League. They had no players, no promise, and no future."

The Yawkey Era

All hope seemed lost in 1933, but then another new owner arrived. Thomas Austin Yawkey had inherited millions from his businessman uncle, William Hoover Yawkey. William Yawkey had owned the Detroit Tigers, and young Tom had grown up fielding practice ground balls hit by Ty Cobb. Baseball was in Tom Yawkey's blood, and four days after he received his multimillion dollar inheritance he announced the purchase of the Red Sox. He was exactly what the team needed in its hour of despair.

Shaughnessy writes: "Two men emerged from the rubble of Frazee's ruins: Tom Yawkey and Ted Williams. Yawkey purchased the ball club from Quinn on February 25, 1933, and Williams came along six years later to lead the Red Sox into a new era: an era of high payrolls, home runs, and underachievement. With Yawkey writing the checks and Williams bashing the baseball, the Red Sox took on a new identity. No longer a laughing-stock, they struck fear into the opposition, yet still failed to get back to the holy land where Ruth had taken them."

Chadwick likewise notes that the owner "emptied his very deep pockets into the ballclub in 1933, and in 1943, and in 1953, and in 1963. He never held back in his love for the Red Sox or his willingness to spend money to acquire the talent he needed. In all the years he owned the team, nobody took more pride in the Red Sox than Tom Yawkey, and no one hurt as much that there was never a world championship. Whatever hap-

pened to the Red Sox from 1933 on, the ups and downs, triumphs and tragedies, it was all thanks to Yawkey."

Yawkey was thirty years old when he acquired the team. He was delighted with his new business. He socialized with the players and saw to it that they were well-paid. He spent $750,000 to reconstruct Fenway Park, creating essentially the quirky facility that now serves as the Sox home. He hired Hall-of-Famer Eddie Collins as his first general manager and shortstop Joe Cronin as player-manager. Yawkey's largesse and determination brought Boston out of the cellar and into contention for the penthouse. As Shaughnessy observes, "There would be varying degrees of success and failure in future decades, but the Boston Red Sox never again finished in last place."

Fans were encouraged. Attendance picked up at Fenway Park, and in 1935—Cronin's first year as skipper—the Sox beat the hated Yankees five straight in Boston. The team also acquired pitcher Lefty Grove in 1935. An aging veteran, Grove developed finesse pitches and won 20 games for Boston that year. He stayed with the team until 1941 and won his 300th game in his very last outing.

Yawkey also purchased Hall-of-Famer Jimmie Foxx, who arrived in 1935, smacked 41 home runs, and amassed 143 RBIs. Slowly Boston began to ascend in the league ranks. The team finished sixth in 1936 and fifth in 1937. In 1938, an 88-61 record was good enough for a second place finish. Chadwick writes: "Yawkey and Cronin had completely turned around the fortunes of the team and won back the hearts of the Boston fans."

"Teddy Ballgame"

The big story in 1939 was the arrival of a young rookie from San Diego, California. Ted Williams, just 21, announced his determination to be the greatest hitter who ever lived. The doubters smirked and then watched in awe as Williams batted .327, hit 31 homers, and led the league in

Transcendental Graphics

Ted Williams

RBIs during his rookie year. Suddenly the Red Sox had a star who could compete seriously with the Yankee power hitters to the south.

Although never particularly gracious with fans—and downright hostile to reporters—Williams blazed a marvelous trail through the American league. In 1941 he hit .406 on the season, with 37 home runs and 120 RBIs. That accomplishment was only eclipsed by the fabulous performance of Joe DiMaggio, with his 56-game hitting streak for the New York Yankees.

"Teddy Ballgame has become such a legend over the years that today we forget why he grew to such mythic proportions," writes Chadwick. "Here was a great power hitter who slammed 521 home runs and still hit .344 lifetime. Here was a man who had the second-highest slugging average in history and also rapped out 2,654 hits. Here was a man who was famous for his home run clouts each season ... and still won batting titles in six different years. He hit .304 in eighteen All Star games

against the best pitching in the world.... The man never batted below .318, he hit thirty or more homers in eight years, and he had a hundred or more walks eleven times. In addition, Williams was named MVP [Most Valuable Player] twice (and should have been twice more), won two Triple Crowns, hit .388 at age thirty-nine, and won his final batting crown at forty. And he did all of this despite fighting for his country for five years, first in World War II and then in the Korean War."

Despite the addition of Williams, right fielder Dom DiMaggio (Joe's brother), and shortstop Johnny Pesky, the Red Sox entered the World War II years as distant second-place challengers to the mighty Yankees. At season's end in 1942, all three sluggers left Boston for active military duty.

"The 1943, 1944, and 1945 seasons were lean for all of baseball, but typically, the Boston Red Sox were hit the hardest," notes Shaughnessy. "There are those who believe the Sox would have won the American League flag in all three war years, and based on what happened when the boys came home, a case can be made for a midforties Sox dynasty. But it's always something with the Red Sox, and this time it was something bigger than any baseball game."

Boston's roster had returned to strength by the beginning of the 1946 season. Williams, Pesky, Bobby Doerr, Tex Hughson, DiMaggio, and Joe Dobson all returned from the service ready to play. The Sox won 21 of their first 25 outings and finished with a remarkable 104-50 record, a full 12 games ahead of the second-place Tigers. Fans all over New England were thrilled. Many of them could not even remember the last time the team had been in a World Series.

The Jinx Begins

Honors were heaped upon the 1946 Red Sox. Eight members of the team were invited to the annual All Star game in July. Williams, who batted .342 with 38 homers and 123 RBIs, was named the AL's MVP. Tex Hughson won 20 games on the mound and Dave Ferriss won 25. Boston entered the 1946 World Series 20-7 favorites over the St. Louis Cardinals, who had fought to a slender victory in the NL pennant race.

Chadwick writes: "It was a fine year, 1946, but it was also the year the great Sox jinx began. The jinx, painfully familiar to Boston fans by now, crept into the team bats sometime in the summer of 1946 and took up permanent residence. What the legendary jinx entails is that no matter how well Boston plays, the team never quite makes it to the World Series, or if it does, Boston loses. That's exactly what happened in 1946."

Boston was expected to defeat St. Louis easily. Instead, the Cardinals won Games 2, 4, and 6. The seventh and final game showdown occurred in St. Louis. Williams and company took the field confident that they would bring the championship crown back to Boston. Instead, Tuesday, October 15, 1946 became the first in a string of heartbreaks for the New England faithful.

The deciding play broke a 3-3 tie in the bottom of the eighth inning. Sox reliever Bob Klinger gave up a leadoff hit to Enos Slaughter. Two outs later, Slaughter was still on first. Then Harry Walker hit a sinking shot to left center. Boston centerfielder Leon Culberson—who had replaced the injured DiMaggio—gave chase. Culberson relayed the ball back to Pesky in the infield. Pesky didn't realize that Slaughter was streaking for home until it was too late. The shortstop's throw to the plate did not arrive in time, and St. Louis scored the go-ahead run. At game's end the score remained 4-3, and the Cardinals were world champions.

Some call Walker's hit a single and credit Pesky with the run. Others see it as a double and doubt if Pesky—one of the game's best shortstops—could have thrown Slaughter out anyway. Dan Shaughnessy sees it yet another way: "Pesky was just another Series role player struggling to contribute when the Curse of the Bambino tapped him on the throwing shoulder." By Shaughnessy's reckoning, the dreaded Red Sox curse began on the day when Frazee sold Babe Ruth—the "Great Bambino"—to the Yankees and the Curse has marred every Sox season since.

"In New England, the betrayal of the Bambino remains a regional embarrassment, and it was clear that the Sox were still paying for the sins of Frazee when Boston's powerhouse teams of the late forties failed in the clutch," contends Shaughnessy. "Never was this more painful than in 1948 and 1949 when the Boston Red Sox won 192 baseball games, compiled an aggregate winning percentage of .621, drew 3,155,448 fans to Fenway Park, yet failed to win a pennant. Boston finished second both years, one game out of first place. These Red Sox were no longer a laughable lot. Instead, they were muscle-flexing silver medalists. They were the forefathers of a new device that would torture Boston fans into the 1990s. This is when the groundwork was laid for a macabre series of near misses."

In 1947, Yawkey hired former Yankee manager Joe McCarthy as Red Sox skipper. Cronin became general manager. McCarthy had led the Yankees through the team's glory years and now vowed to bring the same kind of success to Boston. It was not to be.

The Curse Continues

A fine 1948 Red Sox team—bolstered by the acquisition of pitchers Ellis Kinder and Jack Kramer—slugged it out for the pennant in a tight race with the Yankees and the Cleveland Indians. At season's end the Sox and the Indians had identical 96-58 records and tied for first place. The stage was set for a sudden-death playoff game, the first in AL history. The managers of both teams were secretive about their choices for starting pitcher. McCarthy in particular kept his Red Sox players guessing nearly until game time. Then he picked righthander Denny Galehouse, whose season record stood at a mediocre 8-7.

Several Boston starting pitchers fumed, and fans watched in horror as Galehouse was routed in the fourth inning. Cleveland won the game easily, 8-3. Shaughnessy records the fate of Denny Galehouse: "Galehouse barely made the team in 1949, pitched once, then was released and retired. He hasn't been in Boston in forty years and has little realization that he's still better remembered than the great molasses flood of 1919. The man entrusted with Boston's hopes in the first playoff game in American League history never won another game in the major leagues." If possible, a worse tragedy awaited Boston's fans in 1949.

Few baseball rivalries are more heated than that between the Red Sox and the Yankees. The hard feelings in Boston date to—what else?—the "rape of the Red Sox" by Frazee in the early 1920s. The competition intensified in the 1940s when Boston nearly always ran second place to New York. Fans at Fenway Park loved to see the Yankees lose, turning out in record numbers to urge the Sox to victory.

In 1949, one of the most powerful Red Sox teams ever engaged in a down-to-the-wire pennant race with the Yankees. Boston was down by 12 games at the All Star break but won 59 of their last 78 games, including a dramatic come-from-behind victory over the Yanks in the last week of the season.

With two games remaining to play, Boston travelled to New York needing to win only once to guarantee the pennant. The Red Sox jumped to an early 4-0 lead in the first game but lost it 5-4. Suddenly the Yankees were tied for first place, and the winner of the season finale would also go to the World Series.

For the decisive game McCarthy tapped pitcher Ellis Kinder, who had won 23 games for Boston in 1949. Despite having pitched in relief in four of the previous seven games, Kinder worked wonders on the mound for the Red Sox. The Yankees held a slender 1-0 lead going into the eighth inning. In the top of the eighth, McCarthy lifted Kinder for a pinch hitter who did not deliver. When the Yankees came up to bat in the bottom of the eighth, they peppered two relief pitchers for four runs. The Yankees held on to win it, 5-3.

The news hit Boston like a ton of bricks. The team had needed only one win in two outings to take the pennant but had lost twice. Fans who had stood in line for hours to buy World Series tickets went home with wallets full of money. A mock

Transcendental Graphics

George Kell

funeral procession was held in Lawrence, Massachusetts, featuring a casket with RED SOX emblazoned on its side.

Shaughnessy writes: "This is where it starts—the stuff the Red Sox of the 1980s and 1990s have come to hate. These were the forefather sins that the Red Sox of today are still paying for—until a championship is won. The Red Sox were punished with twenty-eight straight years of ineptitude after Ruth was sold, but in the 1940s a new form of denial took hold, and it has proven to be a far worse strain on the fragile psyche of the New England region.... The fact that the 1949 Sox folded in the face of the Yankees made the pain particularly unbearable and fortified the theory that larger forces were at work."

The stunning loss in 1949 seemed to drain the

strength from the Red Sox. As the Yankees blossomed again in the 1950s behind Mickey Mantle and Roger Maris, the Sox slid into the middle of the pack and stayed there. One by one the members of the fine 1940s Boston teams retired or were traded. Williams remained, but he spent part of the decade on active military duty.

Other stars had their own problems. First baseman Harry Agganis died suddenly of a blood clot at the age of 25. Outfielder Jimmy Piersall, beloved for his flamboyant and eccentric behavior, suffered a nervous breakdown and required hospitalization. Potential superstar Jackie Jensen—the 1958 AL MVP—had to retire prematurely because he hated to fly in airplanes.

Shaughnessy calls the Red Sox of the 1950s and early 1960s "lead-footed sluggers, rewarded by an indulgent owner and mocked by the baseball community." The writer adds: "Red Sox players were too comfortable and it showed. These were the years when New England fans rarely tasted the thrill of the race after Memorial Day. You followed the Sox to see if Ted Williams or Pete Runnels or Carl Yastrzemski could win another batting title, but there was little hope of a pennant race. The last gasp losses in the great races of 1948 and 1949 drained the team and the fandom and there was not much to cheer about for the next seventeen seasons."

Williams retired in 1960. In his last season with Boston he batted .316 and hit 29 home runs—including one on his very last at-bat. The next spring, a rookie named Carl Yastrzemski took Williams's place in left field. Teddy Ballgame had left big shoes to fill, but Yastrzemski seemed equal to the task. By 1963, "Yaz" had won the first of his three AL batting championships. His performance was the highlight of an otherwise unremarkable Red Sox team.

As the 1960s progressed, Boston began to fall in the standings, finishing in eighth place in 1962 and 1964 and in ninth place in both 1965 and 1966. The 1965 Red Sox, for instance, lost 100 games and drew only 652,201 fans for the season. In 1966 the team was only a half game out of last place at year's end.

1967 and the Impossible Dream

Late in the 1966 season, Boston manager Bill Herman was fired and replaced with Dick Williams, a former utility infielder. No one held high expectations for Williams's first full year as skipper, 1967, but the crusty manager performed a near miracle. The team had played sub-.500 baseball for eight straight seasons, but in 1967 everything turned around.

Behind the offensive production of Yastrzemski, who won the Triple Crown (44 home runs, 121 RBIs, .326 average), and the capable pitching of ace Jim Lonborg (22-9), the Sox engaged in one of the most thrilling pennant races of modern times. "There was little hint of the Curse during this magical tour," writes Shaughnessy. The season's only major disappointment was the loss of slugger/outfielder Tony Conigliaro, who was struck in the face by a fastball on August 18.

The 1967 pennant race was tightly contested by four teams—the Red Sox, the Detroit Tigers, the Minnesota Twins, and the Chicago White Sox. On the final weekend of the season, Boston hosted the Twins. The Red Sox needed to beat Minnesota twice to take the lead in the standings. The underdog Sox were victorious in both games, while Detroit lost the second game of a doubleheader to the California Angels. Boston won the pennant.

The 1967 World Series featured the Red Sox against the St. Louis Cardinals. The Sox were again underdogs, and they fell behind three games to one in the fall classic. Lonborg kept the team alive by pitching for a victory in Game Five, and a rookie hurler named Gary Waslewski had a good outing for a Sox win in Game Six. Williams asked Lonborg to start in Game Seven, and the able pitcher agreed. Unfortunately, Lonborg had not had enough rest, and the Cardinals won easily, 7-2. The world championship continued to elude the Boston Red Sox.

Shaughnessy writes: "The Red Sox have blown many pennant races, lost the only two playoff games in American League history, dropped an American League Championship Series in four straight, and lost the seventh game of

Transcendental Graphics

Carl Yastrzemski

the World Series four times since Ruth was sold to the Yankees.... In all these disappointments, only the 1967 team is spared the second-guessers and the harsh historians who have scrutinized and plagued all other Sox teams since 1918. Nobody held the ball, nobody tripped rounding third base, nobody threw an ill-timed wild pitch, nobody made a hideous and regrettable hunch, nobody let a ground ball slip through his legs and into history. It was okay for the 1967 Red Sox to lose the seventh game of the World Series because they'd already performed the great service of bringing a moribund franchise back to life and registering millions of new members to the party of the long-suffering."

More Heartbreak

In 1968 Boston dropped to fourth place after Lonborg was injured in a skiing accident and Conigliaro failed to return. The next year the team

finished in third place. Williams, once hailed as a genius, was fired near season's end after well-publicized quarrels with owner Yawkey. The 1970 Red Sox began the year under a new manager, Ed Kasko. These years were dominated by the mini-dynasty of the Baltimore Orioles, so Boston was only able to finish third in 1970 and 1971. Then the celebrated curse reared its head again.

The Red Sox returned to the pennant race in 1972 under Kasko. As in 1967, the race was very close. Boston eliminated the Orioles on September 30 but faced a tough final series in Detroit. The Sox needed to win two of their last three against the Tigers in order to take the pennant. Boston was thoroughly deflated after a fluke loss in the first game. A basepath blunder by shortstop Luis Aparicio killed a Red Sox rally and led to the Tiger win. It was a classic case of the curse at work.

The Tigers were leading 1-0 at the time, but Boston had put men at first and third with Yastrzemski up to bat. Yaz hit a shot that scored the runner from third easily. Aparicio took off from first and slipped not once but twice rounding third. When he tried to retreat to the third base bag he found Yastrzemski already there. Both men were thrown out in an unorthodox double play. The next night, ace Red Sox hurler Luis Tiant pitched well but could not hold the Tigers, who won on an Al Kaline single. Boston had needed to win two of three and had lost the first two.

More heartbreak awaited the Red Sox faithful in 1974. Boston leaped into first place during the early part of the season and held a comfortable lead until early September. Then the team slumped horribly, losing eight straight and going 14-24 after August 23. The slump enabled the streaking Orioles to pass Boston for the pennant, causing much glee in Baltimore.

According to Shaughnessy, the 1974 Red Sox—who finished third after leading most of the year—"toughened New England fans for what was to come. From 1972 through 1988, the Red Sox nine times led the American League East after the All-Star game yet won the division in only three of those years." Shaughnessy adds: "There are people in all walks of life who would rather do

| HOME FIELD | Fenway Park: Beantown's Glittering Jewel |

One of professional baseball's most beloved landmarks, Fenway Park has served as the home of the Red Sox since 1912. Its limited seating capacity of 34,000 virtually ensures that the Red Sox will play to many a packed house each year, no matter how well or how poorly the team is performing.

The stadium was constructed in the residential neighborhood of Fenway in 1912 and was refurbished in 1934 by longtime Red Sox owner Tom Yawkey. Yawkey wanted to expand the park, particularly on the left field perimeter, but was unable to do so because a street and a railroad ran close to the outfield walls. The inability to enlarge the facility gave birth to "The Wall," better known as "The Green Monster," in left field.

Constructed to prevent batted balls from falling on neighboring Lansdowne Street, and a mere 315 feet from home plate, the fabled Green Monster has served as a target for generations of hitters from the days of the Great Depression to the present era. It has literally shaped the personnel recruited by Boston and has long been a factor in the team's offensive strategy.

Newcomers to Fenway first notice that the park does not have an upper deck. Then they notice something else—a homey atmosphere where fans sit close to the field in seats that might, at one time, have held their great-grandparents. In his book *The Curse of the Bambino,* Boston area writer Dan Shaughnessy calls Fenway Park "a charming, priceless antique, steeped in history and beloved by the millions who pour through its portals from April to October, year after hopeful year."

Shaughnessy adds: "It is very old with odd, classic, asymmetrical lines, like a rambling Victorian house. You can almost hear the small children playing and smell the pies baking—even when it's empty. Antiques frame and retain the past, and our selective memories remind us that the past was very good. An old ballpark is very good."

the chasing than be chased. The Red Sox and their fans today are more relaxed when the team is behind than when the team is sitting on a first-place lead. Let the record show that the foundation for this inverted logic was poured during the summer of 1974."

The 1975 Red Sox were bolstered by the arrival of two rookies. Outfielders Fred Lynn and Jim Rice brought a new dimension to the team. Lynn, a Californian by birth, batted .331 with 21 homers and 105 RBIs. Not to be outdone, Rice hit .309 with 22 homers and 102 RBIs. Lynn finished first and Rice second in the Rookie of the Year voting, and Lynn also won the AL MVP award. The "Gold Dust Twins" were joined in the lineup by Yastrzemski, catcher Carlton Fisk, shortstop Rick Burleson, outfielder Dwight Evans, and slugger Cecil Cooper, while Luis Tiant turned in another stellar year on the mound. This talented

squad won 95 games and held onto first place from June till season's end.

Boston appeared in its first American League Championship Series (ALCS) in 1975, meeting the three-time World Champion Oakland Athletics. Oddsmakers gave the Red Sox little chance of defeating the mighty A's with their veteran stars such as Reggie Jackson, Vida Blue, and Sal Bando. Not only did Boston win the ALCS, they actually swept Oakland three games in the best-of-five series. "We were a strong club, but there's no doubt that it was the year of the Red Sox," Jackson told Shaughnessy. "They couldn't do anything wrong. Yaz was the perfect player at that time."

The 1975 World Series, pitting the Red Sox against the Cincinnati Reds, did more to revive national interest in baseball than any event of the 1970s. People all over the world watched the underdog Red Sox battle the Big Red Machine through seven tight games. Boston won the first game with a 6-0 Luis Tiant shutout and took a 2-1 lead into the ninth inning of the second game before losing 3-2. Game Three featured an extra inning contest that the Reds won 6-5. Tiant returned to the mound for Game Four and held on to win a close one, 5-4. The Reds won Game Five and led the Series three games to two when the teams returned to Fenway Park on October 21.

Rain delayed the start of Game Six for a full three days. When play resumed, Red Sox manager Darrell Johnson decided to start Tiant again. Shaughnessy writes: "It was clear from the outset that the layoff had done nothing to diminish the intensity or execution of play, and what unfolded was arguably the best World Series game of all time. Game Six has taken on a life of its own in the years since it was played, and it gets larger and more thrilling in each retelling. Some distance allows that there may be other contenders for the title of the Greatest Game Ever Played, but by any measure 1975's Game 6 will stand as one of the top ten games in World Series history, and one that came at a time when baseball needed it most."

In the game, Boston trailed 6-3 in the eighth inning. With two on and two out in the eighth, Sox pinch hitter Bernie Carbo crushed a three-run homer to center field. The contest went into extra

AP/Wide World Photos

Carlton Fisk (27) jumps on home plate after blasting the game-winning home run in the 12th inning of Game 6 of the 1975 World Series

innings and lasted well past midnight. In the bottom of the twelfth, Carlton Fisk came to bat for the Red Sox.

Fisk hit a shot that hugged the left field foul line and threatened at any moment to twist into foul territory. A television camera placed inside Fenway Park's left field wall caught Fisk as he waved, gyrated, and seemed to will the ball to stay fair. The ball hit the foul pole for a Boston home run, and the ecstatic Fisk rounded the bases joyously. According to Shaughnessy, "Fisk's pole shot and his tour-de-bases has become synonymous with the thrill of victory."

The moment of glory was short-lived. In Game Seven the jinx returned, and the Reds won 4-3 in the ninth inning to take the World Series crown. "It was a remarkable Series," Shaughnessy writes. "In six of the seven games the winning team came from behind. Five games were decided by one run, two games were settled in the ninth, and two others went into extra innings. There were thirteen lead changes and/or ties in the seven games.... The Sox allowed the Reds to keep coming back, and the Reds did keep coming back, and that is why they, not the Red Sox, deserved to be World Champions."

The 1975 World Series was the last chance Thomas Yawkey had to see his team win a championship. Yawkey died on July 9, 1976, after a year-long battle with cancer. His forty-year-plus ownership of the Red Sox never yielded a World Series victory, but it did provide New England with a stable franchise that sometimes contended for post-season play. No other professional baseball team has ever been owned as long by one individual as Boston's, and Yawkey's name is now enshrined in the Baseball Hall of Fame.

The Red Sox remained competitive through the rest of the decade, but each year brought new disappointments. Johnson was fired in 1976 after the team finished in third place. The new manager, Don Zimmer, had been the third base coach under Johnson. Zimmer's edition of the Red Sox won 97 games in 1977 and finished in second place. What happened the next year is still the stuff of legend in Boston.

"The Boston Massacre"

The 1978 Red Sox grabbed first place in the AL East on May 13 and won 26 of their first 30 games in Fenway Park. Boston led by nine games as late as July 20, but a combination of Sox losses and Yankees victories pulled the hated pinstripers into serious contention by September. On September 7, the Yankees arrived in Boston for a four game series. New York stood just four games behind in the standings. Call it the "Curse of the Bambino," plain bad luck, or a case of the jitters, but the Red Sox dropped all four games in front of the home town crowd. "Aptly dubbed 'The Boston Massacre,' this series scarred a new generation of Red Sox fans," Shaughnessy writes. "New York did it to Boston again."

The humiliation was not over. The Red Sox and Yankees both won at a record pace during the rest of the regular season and finished tied for first with 99-63 records. The stage was set for another sudden death playoff game to determine the winner of the AL East. The game was played in Fenway Park on October 2, 1978.

Boston held a 2-0 lead through six innings behind the sharp pitching of Mike Torrez, but the Yankees stayed competitive for their ace Ron Guidry. In the top of the seventh inning, Yankees Chris Chambliss and Roy White each stroked hits. They were both aboard with two outs when the number nine hitter, Bucky Dent, came to the plate. Dent noticed a problem with his bat, and the game was slightly delayed. Torrez did not continue to throw while Dent selected a new bat. When Dent returned to play, he stroked the first pitch toward deep left field.

Fenway Park's left-field wall is one of baseball's foremost landmarks. Known as "The Wall" or "The Green Monster," it towers over the field and provides a ready target for looping home runs or screeching doubles. Bucky Dent's shot was a looper that would have been a routine pop fly ball in any other major league ballpark. Instead, it caught the wind and landed in the net atop The Green Monster for a home run.

"Jesus Christ, I still can't believe it went in the

net," Yastrzemski told Shaughnessy in 1989. "I thought I had a chance at it at first. The wind was blowing from right to left, and he kind of pulled it down toward the corner and it just kept on carrying and carrying and the wind blew it a little more toward the line, and boom. It was just an empty feeling, but there again, typical of our team. We had the lead and blew it." Dent's three-run homer—his fifth in 124 games—sparked a Yankee comeback. After nine innings New York won the game, 5-4.

"Nineteen seventy-eight. Nothing compares," Shaughnessy states. "The New England baseball fan is paralyzed at the mere mention of the year. The mind calcifies. This was the apocalyptic, cataclysmic fold by which all others must be measured.... No Sox fan could have braced for the horror of losing the flag to the Yankees after leading the hated New Yorkers by fourteen games on July 20."

It took the Boston franchise eight years to recover from the fall of 1978. The early 1980s brought the trades of Fred Lynn and Rick Burleson to California for Jim Dorsey, Frank Tanana, and Joe Rudi. Carlton Fisk was declared a free agent and signed with the White Sox in 1981. Zimmer was fired after the 1980 season and replaced with Ralph Houk. Yastrzemski retired in 1983. Rice's production leveled off as his salary demands escalated. In 1983 the Red Sox dropped to 78-84, their first sub-.500 season since the 1960s.

To make matters worse, the front office was in turmoil. Tom Yawkey's steady ownership had given way to a three-way partnership between Mrs. Yawkey, Haywood Sullivan, and Edward G. LeRoux, Jr. The partners quarreled amongst themselves over club business, and their feud spilled into the newspapers when they held rival press conferences in the same room on the same night in June of 1983.

Eventually the battle found its way into a court of law, and LeRoux ended up selling his share of the team back to Mrs. Yawkey and Sullivan. When the dust cleared, Jean Yawkey had assumed the bulk of responsibility for the Red Sox, albeit through her associates John Harrington and general manager James "Lou" Gorman, who arrived from the New York Mets organization in 1984.

The Ralph Houk years were generally uneventful for the Red Sox, but several new arrivals showed potential. One of them was 1982 rookie Wade Boggs, who would pound more than 200 hits a season for seven straight years and win five batting championships between 1983 and 1988. Others included pitchers Dennis "Oil Can" Boyd, Al Nipper, and Roger Clemens. These new faces helped to keep fans in the Fenway seats through several moderately interesting seasons. At the end of the 1984 campaign, Houk was replaced by John McNamara.

1986: A Strike Away

In McNamara's first year as Red Sox skipper the team finished at an even .500, 81-81. The following year was altogether different. In the offseason between 1985 and 1986 the Sox acquired pitchers Calvin Schiraldi and Wes Gardner, as well as veteran slugger Don Baylor. Baylor provided leadership as the club got off to a good spring start and sneaked into first place on May 11.

Everything worked well for the Red Sox that year. Clemens pitched masterfully for a league-leading 24-4 year and a Cy Young Award. Boggs batted a sensational .357. Weak links in the lineup were strengthened with the arrival of outfielder Dave Henderson and shortstop Spike Owen. As the Red Sox entered the stretch with high hopes of winning the AL East, Gorman recruited veteran pitcher Tom Seaver from the White Sox.

Shaughnessy writes: "Unlike their 1946 or 1975 forefathers, the 1986 Red Sox were an overachieving lot, able to perform well beyond expectations while spitting at the cynics who predicted doom. They had an unusually deep pitching staff. They were good and they were lucky. They performed with the energy of the innocent and didn't fully understand what it was all about until the final hours." Some of the younger players could not understand why the

Boston press and fans were so skeptical. It took a devastating World Series event to initiate them into the workings of the infamous Red Sox curse.

The Red Sox won the AL East on September 28th, 1986. In their first best-of-seven AL playoff series they met the California Angels. The playoff provided drama aplenty, as the Angels took a 3-1 lead in the series. All seemed lost in the fifth game when California rode a 5-2 lead into the ninth inning, but this time Boston rallied. Baylor hit a two-run homer to narrow the lead to 5-4.

With two out, relief hurler Gary Lucas hit Sox catcher Rich Gedman with a pitch. The Angels pulled Lucas in favor of Don Moore, and Moore gave up another two-run homer, this time to Dave Henderson. The Sox pulled ahead 6-5, but California tied the game in the bottom of the ninth. The game went to Boston in extra innings, 7-6, on a Henderson sacrifice fly.

That hard-fought game turned the tide of the ALCS for the Red Sox. They trounced the Angels 10-4 in the sixth game and 8-1 in the seventh for the opportunity to meet the formidable New York Mets in the 1986 World Series.

Those not inclined to be superstitious might suggest that the whole grim history of the Boston Red Sox put an added pressure on the 1986 AL champions. The Red Sox reputation for choking in clutch situations was dragged out and examined, just days before the team's ultimate, nerve-shattering, all-time worst bout of bad luck and slipshod play. Once again the younger players were baffled by the legions of Boston skeptics until the moment when destiny called and the Red Sox crumbled.

The Mets were highly favored to win the 1986 World Series, but Boston won the Series opener behind a Bruce Hurst four-hitter, 1-0. Then the Red Sox completely sandbagged New York in Game Two with an easy 9-3 victory. The Mets came back to even the Series at two games apiece, but the Sox took Game Five, 4-2. Boston went back to the Big Apple needing to win only one game to clinch a World Series crown.

"Game 6 of the 1986 World Series was ... sinister and hideous even by the lofty standards of the Boston Red Sox," Shaughnessy writes. "Lug-

AP/Wide World Photos

Roger Clemens

ging sixty-eight years of failure into the bottom of the tenth inning at Shea Stadium, the Sox came within a single strike of winning the World Series, but failed. The Boston uniforms proved too heavy. The Curse of the Bambino was too strong." The game was tied 3-3 at the end of nine innings, but Henderson hit a home run in the tenth and the Sox added an insurance run to take a 5-3 lead. In the bottom of the tenth the Mets earned two quick outs on fly balls. Boston was one out away from the championship.

Shaughnessy claims that fans all over New England woke their children to let them see the much-anticipated event as it unfolded around the midnight hour. Thus the children were awake to cry with their parents as the Red Sox folded gracelessly. Relief pitcher Calvin Schiraldi gave up a single to the Mets' Gary Carter. The next batter, Kevin Mitchell, also singled. The next batter, Ray Knight, hit a broken-bat single on an 0-2 pitch. Carter scored to make the score 5-4,

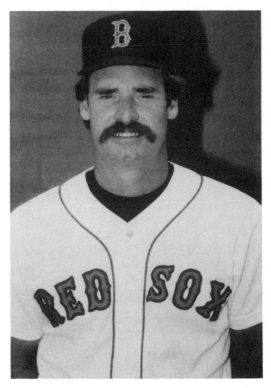

AP/Wide World Photos

Wade Boggs

Boston. Then Schiraldi was pulled in favor of reliever Bob Stanley. Stanley racked up two strikes on Mookie Wilson before throwing a wild pitch that scored a Met run.

With the score tied at 5-5, Stanley went back to work against Wilson. On Stanley's tenth pitch, Wilson knocked an easy chopper down the first base line. As Wilson streaked toward first and Stanley rushed to cover the base, first baseman Bill Buckner eased back to field the ball. The ball rolled between Buckner's legs, Wilson was safe, and the winning run scored.

The Mets went on to win Game Seven by a score of 8-5. Shaughnessy writes: "The Red Sox had blown pennants before and three other times had lost the seventh game of the World Series, but no team in the history of the game ever got this close to the threshold without actually winning.

Losing on a final play that involved a ball going through an infielder's legs provided the perfect lasting image for sixty-eight years of failure.... It is a Charlie Brown error that calls for the perpetrator to say, 'Rats!'" Shaughnessy adds: "Given the circumstances and the fact that it happened during this age of hype, replay, and videocassette recorders, [Bill] Buckner's gaffe stands as the most famous error in baseball history—celluloid proof that the Red Sox indeed are cursed, perhaps forever."

Forever the Bridesmaid?

A rebound was not long in coming. The 1988 Red Sox started slow under unpopular manager John McNamara but staged a remarkable midseason comeback after McNamara was fired and replaced by Joe Morgan. Morgan inherited a team that was plagued by bad publicity. Boggs, still a league-leading hitter, found himself the target of a palimony suit. His accuser, Margo Adams, revealed embarrassing details of Red Sox player behavior on road trips. Her stories caused friction in the Boston clubhouse, but Morgan was able to cool tempers and get the team back on track. He got off to the most successful start in managerial history as the Sox won 12 straight, 19 out of 20, and clinched the AL East with two days left in the season.

Morgan's honeymoon with Boston met its end in the 1988 ALCS, when the Oakland A's swept the Red Sox in four games. Still, he held onto the reins in 1989, when Boston finished third in the East, and 1990, when the Sox returned to the pennant race with a first place, 88-74 record. It is unfortunate that the affable Morgan found his fine teams in contention with the mighty Oakland A's in both of the AL championships during his tenure. He compiled a .542 winning percentage with his teams during the regular season but never won a playoff game. In 1990 the hapless Sox were once again swept by the Athletics in four games, costing Morgan his job. Former Red Sox infielder Butch Hobson became Boston's manager in 1991.

Led by Clemens' outstanding 18-10 record, 2.62 ERA, and league-leading 241 strikeouts, the Sox pitching staff was the team's strength in 1991, but weak hitting, poor team speed, and shaky defense spoiled any hopes of a title that year, or in 1992. After a slow start in 1993, the Red Sox caught fire at midseason and catapulted themselves into the thick of the AL East pennant race.

Though they eventually finished in fifth place with an 80-82 mark— star pitchers Clemens and Frank Viola combined for only 22 wins—the Sox were bolstered by the performances of several young players, including shortstop John Valentin and pitcher Aaron Sele.

The 1990s editions of the Boston Red Sox seem to be plagued by the same factors that have dogged the team for decades. They are always talented and always in the pennant race, just a heartbeat away from the World Series victory that has eluded them since 1918. Retirement and trades of such superstars as Rice and Boggs have done little to erode the team's rich potential.

The front office is once again stable after the rocky years in the 1980s, with Harrington serving as majority general partner and Sullivan at second in command. Chadwick concludes: "Whatever the decade brings, it's certain to be full of excitement. Statistics and standings show that the team has been consistent [during the early 1990s]. The hitting is there, the pitching is there, the depth is there. The fan support is certainly there. The wait for a world championship has been a long one and the fans of New England have been patient, but it has to come and it has to come soon."

Dan Shaughnessy is not as optimistic. In true Boston fashion, he contends that Red Sox fans "remain in a holding pattern in hardball purgatory, still waiting to get back to the promised land." All talk of a curse aside, the Boston franchise has provided its fans with some truly memorable moments—and a tradition of bizarre events stretching back through the mists of time. Winners or losers, New England's Sox are never plagued with the true curse of fielding a boring team.

SOURCES

Berry, Henry, *Boston Red Sox,* Macmillan, 1975.

Chadwick, Bruce, *The Boston Red Sox: Memories and Mementoes of New England's Team,* Abbeville Press, 1992.

Cole, Milton, *Baseball's Great Dynasties: The Red Sox,* Brompton Books, 1990.

Creamer, Robert, *Babe,* Simon & Schuster, 1974.

Gammons, Peter, *Beyond the Sixth Game,* Houghton, 1985.

Halberstam, David, *Summer of '49,* William Morrow, 1989.

Hirshberg, Al, *What's the Matter with the Red Sox?,* Dodd, 1973.

Shaughnessy, Dan, *The Curse of the Bambino,* Dutton, 1990.

Walton, Ed, *Red Sox Triumphs and Tragedies,* Stein & Day, 1980.

Williams, Ted, and John Underwood, *My Turn at Bat,* Simon & Schuster, 1969.

—Anne Janette Johnson

DETROIT TIGERS

One of the oldest and proudest franchises in the American League is the Detroit Tigers. The Tigers have been playing professional baseball at the corner of Michigan and Trumbull in downtown Detroit since the American League was founded in 1901. Few sports teams of any sort have shown greater stability or fan support through the 20th century. The changing economic circumstances in the Motor City have done little, if anything, to dampen the enthusiasm for a hometown team that has seen World Series action in five different decades.

In 1989's *The Detroit Tigers: An Illustrated History,* longtime Tiger manager Sparky Anderson wrote of Detroit: "I can't think of a better place to make your living if you happen to be in this game of baseball. You never get bored around here. Something is always going on.... Detroit has been a great baseball town all through this century."

While many historic franchises have moved to suburban stadiums, the Tigers continue to play in their traditional ballpark, a Michigan Registered Historical Site. While other teams experiment with new logos and redesigned uniforms, the Tigers remain in their time-honored white garb with the trademark Old English "D." The Tigers were an institution in Detroit before magnate Henry Ford built his first factory, and decades before the expanding automobile industry brought waves of laborers to the region.

"Our ball club has been with us through almost all of this century," remarked sportswriter Joe Falls in *The Detroit Tigers.* "It got us through those early years when Henry Ford was trying to convince us that it was better to sit down in a moving machine than to climb onto a horse in order to get around town. Our team has brought us happiness and sadness. It gave us a reason to cry and a reason to laugh. It gave us a reason to feel proud. It brought us diversion, and that's very important in this hardworking town."

The Tigers are well-represented at the Baseball Hall of Fame in Cooperstown, New York. Hitting legend Ty Cobb played for Detroit for 21 years. The stylistic and lethal Charlie Gehringer spent his entire 18-year career in the city, as did Al Kaline. The 1940s were dominated by slugger Hank Greenberg, the first great Jewish athlete in Detroit. Ask fans in the Motor City for their favorites, however, and other names pop up. In 1968 the nation was mesmerized by pitching phenomenon Denny McLain, the last hurler to win 31 games in a single season. Several years later, Mark "The Bird" Fidrych grabbed headlines for talking to the ball on his way to the 1976 Rookie-of-the-Year honors.

In more recent years the very image of Detroit baseball was captured by the grand World Series victory gestures of volatile Kirk Gibson, whose home runs helped the Tigers win the 1984 crown.

Even the stadium facility itself is the object of fan worship. In 1988, then-owner Tom Monaghan seriously pursued the option of constructing a new ballpark outside the city. Tiger fans found the idea so repulsive that they formed a human chain around aging Tiger Stadium and literally hugged the building. "If you walk around enough and talk to enough people, you can get a feeling they truly do love this ballpark," Falls wrote. "More than any other structure in the city, the people of Detroit relate to Tiger Stadium. They all know where it is, what it looks like, and what it feels like. Tiger Stadium—formerly Bennett Park, Navin Field, and Briggs Stadium—has become an enduring symbol of Detroit." The Tigers have made that "enduring symbol" a home of champions.

Baseball Arrived in Detroit

Professional baseball came to Detroit in 1881, when the population of the city was a mere 120,000. Back then the "Detroits," as they were called, played in the National League. The home field was Recreation Park, at the corner of Brush

and Brady, and the team owner was Detroit mayor W. G. Thompson. The team lasted eight years and won the National League pennant in 1887.

Despite its on-field success, the franchise suffered from shaky finances and folded in 1888. Its lasting contribution to the history of the Detroit Tigers came in the person of catcher Charlie Bennett.

Bennett played for the Detroits throughout the eight seasons the team spent in town. He was part of the 1887 championship team and made his home in Detroit after his playing career ended. In 1894 he slipped while boarding a train in Kansas City and lost both his left foot and his right leg under the train's wheels.

The unfortunate accident only increased his popularity in Detroit, and when a new baseball park was built in the city at the turn of the century, it was named Bennett Park in his honor. The ballpark was opened in 1896 at the site of the current Tiger Stadium, and Bennett hobbled onto the field on crutches to catch the ceremonial first pitch.

Two years before Bennett Park opened, major league baseball returned to Detroit thanks to the initiative of Cincinnati entrepreneur Ban Johnson. Johnson accepted Detroit's application to join the new Western League, a confederation of teams thought to be on a par with the popular National League. The owner of the new Detroit franchise was Wayne County sheriff James D. Burns. Play commenced with the 1894 season.

What's in a Name?

Oddly enough, the team did not really have a name at first. Sportswriters called it "Detroit," "the Detroits," or even "the Wolverines," thereby relating it to the nearby University of Michigan. The name "Tigers" is thought to have been first coined by an anonymous *Detroit Free Press* headline writer in 1895. The writer titled an April 16, 1895, story "Strouthers' Tigers Showed Up Very Nicely" and ran the accompanying box scores under the headline "Notes of the Detroit Tigers of 1895." This is the earliest print record of the

TEAM INFORMATION AT A GLANCE

Founding date: April 25, 1901 (first game by Detroit Tigers in
American League; charter member of American League)

Home stadium:
Tiger Stadium
2121 Trumbull
Detroit, MI 48216

Dimensions:
Left-field line—340 feet
Center field—440 feet
Right-field line—325 feet
Seating capacity: 52,416

Team uniforms: Home—base color white, navy blue trim
Road—base color gray, orange and navy blue collar
Team nickname: Tigers, 1901—
Logo: Old English "D"

Franchise record	Wins	Losses	Pct.
	7,371	6,861	.518

World Series wins (4): 1935, 1945, 1968, 1984
American League championships (9): 1907, 1908, 1909, 1934, 1935,
1940, 1945, 1968, 1984
American League East division first-place finishes (3): 1972, 1984, 1987

Tiger name. By the following year it was the accepted franchise name, and the players began wearing tiger-striped stockings.

Although Detroit never finished higher than third place in the Western League, fans supported it in enough numbers to assure a box office profit. The operation still had a shoestring budget, however. Players often wore the same unwashed uniforms for weeks at a time. Bennett Park had been built on top of cobblestones, and hard-hit balls often took weird bounces. The ballpark was small even by the standards of those days—it seated only 6,000 customers and did not provide a dressing room for the visiting team.

The lack of adequate seating—and the rather steep price of tickets—led to the construction of rickety "wildcat bleachers" beyond the outfield fence. For fifteen cents, fans could purchase room to stand and watch the game. "These outlaw seats attracted an unsavory element that constantly caused trouble in the neighborhood," Falls wrote. "Gambling and fistfights were rampant. The regular fans were subject to verbal abuse as they walked through the alley on their way inside the ballpark. The police tried to control these bullies, but could never quite do it. They would restrain them one day, but the wildcats would be back the next."

In 1901 the Western League changed its name to the American League and gained status equal to that of the established National League. Detroit was one of the Western League teams that profited from the inclusion in the new confederation. Suddenly the city had a baseball franchise of national consequence.

American League Debut

The Tigers had their American League home debut on April 25, 1901, at Bennett Park. More than 10,000 people showed up, filling the small stadium well beyond its capacity. The overflow crowd sat behind ropes in the outfield. Those who stayed faithfully through the entire nine innings were rewarded with a fabulous game. Milwaukee led 13-4 when the Tigers came to bat for the last time in the game. Remarkably, Detroit rallied to score ten runs in one inning, to win 14-13.

For purposes of record-keeping, the Detroit Tigers ball club considers 1901 its first official season. The club finished 74-61 under manager George Stallings, who left the organization that year.

Trancendentdental Graphics

Sam Crawford

Navin Took Over

At the end of the 1901 season, Burns sold the Tigers to Samuel F. Angus, an insurance man. Angus appointed a young bookkeeper named Frank J. Navin to manage the team's financial affairs. Navin was a quiet, stern-looking man who discovered quickly that he loved baseball. He was to become a guiding force for the Tigers through three-and-a-half decades, eventually becoming half-owner and president of the club. It is hard to say how the Detroit Tigers might have fared had Frank Navin not made them his life's work.

In 1902, for instance, the club plunged to seventh place in the league standings. Angus's bankroll was quickly depleted, and he announced a desire to sell the team. Quietly determined to keep the Tigers in Detroit, Navin scouted for a new owner. He courted millionaire lumber baron William Clyman Yawkey, who was the richest man in Michigan at the time.

Yawkey agreed to purchase the club but died before the transaction was completed. Undaunted, Navin turned to Yawkey's son, William Hoover Yawkey, who had inherited $10 million. The younger Yawkey bought the Tigers for $50,000 and gave Navin $5000 worth of stock in the team. From there Navin began to build a productive franchise.

The process took time. In 1903 manager Edward Grant Barrow took over the team, and two of the first notable Tiger players—pitcher "Wild Bill" Donovan and outfielder "Wahoo Sam" Crawford arrived. Barrow lifted the Tigers to fifth

Trancendental Graphics

Ty Cobb

place in 1903, but the team slipped back to seventh the following season.

Increasingly at odds with Navin and Yawkey, Barrow resigned late in 1904 and was replaced by Bobby Lowe. At the start of the 1905 campaign, Lowe was succeeded by Bill Armour. The new manager had a nucleus of talent, with the likes of Crawford, third baseman Bill Coughlin, and outfielder Matty McIntyre. He was therefore not terribly impressed when a young rookie arrived in Detroit in August of 1905.

The Cobb Era

That rookie was Tyrus Raymond Cobb. He was 18 years old, stood five-foot-eleven, and weighed just 160 pounds. He had just finished a season with the Augusta, Georgia, team in the South Atlantic League and had been optioned to the Tigers for $750. He came to Detroit on the train, with a suitcase of clothing in one hand and several of his favorite bats in the other. On August 30, 1905, he appeared at Bennett Park, signed a contract to play baseball for $1800 a year, and donned a Tiger uniform for the first time. He was a Tiger for 20 years.

"Some say Cobb was the greatest player of all time," Falls noted. "He certainly compiled one of the great records of all time. For twenty-three straight years he batted better than .300. He won twelve batting championships. At one time he held 90 major league records, including the highest career batting average—.367—a mark that stands to this day. But it was his personality, not his numbers, that made him such a fascinating figure. He was cold, calculating, cunning, crafty, and caustic.

"He was not a large man ... but he played with an intensity that frightened those around him. He was an all-out competitor who would stop at nothing to beat you. He would think nothing of sinking his spikes into your ankles if he thought you were going to tag him out. He was—in his way—a master showman. He was a man with a massive ego who had to keep inventing new ways to satisfy that ego."

The Detroit fans gave Cobb grudging admiration, at best. Not so his teammates and first manager. They responded to Cobb's aloofness with taunts and tricks, further alienating him. Falls quotes Cobb as saying: "When I came up to Detroit, I was just a mild-mannered Sunday School boy. Sam Crawford then was the big dog in the meat house and I was just a brash kid. But, as soon as they started to put my picture in the papers and give me some publicity, the old-timers began to work on me. They practically put a chip on my shoulder, hazed me unmercifully and every time I'd put down my hat I'd find it twisted into knots on my return.

"But now that I look back on it, I think that's a better system than the gentlemanly treatment the rookies get these days. If I became a snarling wildcat, they made me one." And in the world of professional sports, it is never a bad idea to have at least one snarling wildcat on your team. Manager Armour tried to instruct Cobb and got absolutely nowhere. So Cobb spent long stretches on the bench during 1906, and the Tigers finished a dismal sixth place. Navin fired Armour at the end of the 1906 season and hired Hugh A. Jennings, an ebullient, freckle-faced infielder from the Baltimore Orioles. Jennings was Detroit's first player-manager, and the crowds loved his boundless enthusiasm. Soon the fans were imitating his hearty cries of "Ee-Yah! Ee-Yah!" and "Atta-boy!" to encourage the players.

Jennings recognized immediately that Cobb was an exceptional player. The affable manager made allowances for Cobb's moods and didn't try to teach the mercurial hitter any techniques. Jennings was also quite lenient with Cobb, creating a double standard that was not lost on Cobb's teammates. That "star treatment" for Cobb worked wonders for the Tigers, however. In 1907 Cobb won the first of his twelve batting titles and hit .350 for the season. That performance, combined with Crawford's batting acumen and three pitchers who won more than 20 games, propelled Detroit to its first American League championship.

Trancendental Graphics

Hughie Jennings

World Series Debut

The 1907 World Series pitted the Tigers against the Chicago Cubs. The Cubs were cresting a wave of victory with their lethal infield combination of Joe Tinker, John Evers, and Frank Chance. The Series opened at Chicago with a rare 3-3 tie game. The contest went into the record books as a tie because it had to be called for darkness. Chicago then beat Detroit four straight to claim the Series crown. Discouraged by the Tigers' loss—and the lackluster season attendance—owner Yawkey sold Navin enough stock to make Navin half-owner of the club by 1908. Navin became president of the Tigers and held the post for almost 30 years.

Jennings returned with all his enthusiasm in 1908 and helped guide the Tigers to a first-place finish with a 90-63 record. The league championship was not decided until the final game of the season, when Detroit leaped one-half game past Cleveland. The Tigers went to another World Series, again meeting the Cubs.

Navin was so confident of a victory that he erected temporary bleachers in the Bennett Park outfield and hung yards of canvas to obstruct the view from the wildcat seats. Unfortunately, both the fan turnout and the Series outcome were disappointing to the Tigers. The Cubs won in five games, and no more than 12,000 Detroit spectators paid to see the Series during its brief appearance in the city.

Detroit topped the American League again in 1909 with a 98-54 record. Jennings and his Tigers had won a third straight pennant, and the team never looked in better form. In the World Series, the Tigers met the Pittsburgh Pirates with their own hitting marvel, Honus Wagner. The genial Wagner was the very antithesis of the snarling Cobb, who had won the American League home run title that year.

This time the Tigers were favored to win the Series, but Pittsburgh proved just as tough as Chicago. The Pirates won game one, the Tigers game two, the Pirates game three, the Tigers game four, the Pirates game five, the Tigers game six, and

Trancendental Graphics

Harry Heilmann

the Pirates game seven, by shutout. The Tigers had failed to win a World Series in three consecutive appearances. They would not appear in the fall classic again for a quarter of a century.

Navin proved himself a shrewd owner who could turn a profit even in lean years and a tough negotiator with his players and managers. If his stern and bookish demeanor did not please the crowd, his ambition to keep the Tigers strong—and in Detroit—did. The team finished in third place in 1910 and second place in 1911.

During the off-season after the 1911 campaign, Navin demolished Bennett Park and rebuilt the stadium. The diamond was turned around so home plate faced the way it does today, and concrete grandstands were erected. The new park, which seated 23,000 comfortably, was dedicated on April 20, 1912, and named Navin Field.

Their shining new ballpark notwithstanding, the Tigers continued to fall in the standings, finishing sixth in 1912 and 1913 and fourth in 1914. The 1915 campaign was particularly disappointing for Jennings. The Tigers turned in 100 victories for the first time in their history but still failed to take the pennant when Boston won 101. During the World War I years the Tigers slipped back into mediocrity or worse. In both 1918 and 1920 they finished seventh, and a fourth-place finish in 1919 was only assured by Cobb's .384 average and twelfth batting title.

Cobb the Manager

Once a jovial, carefree man, Jennings grew more and more grim as the years passed and his teams failed to contend. Finally, in 1920, he resigned as manager of the Tigers. His playing career had ended in 1918. As his replacement, Jennings heartily endorsed none other than Cobb, a man who had never earned much affection from his teammates.

Cobb did not want the job, and he said so. He did not want any distractions from his performance on the field. He agreed to take the post only after being coerced, and then growled to the press: "This is anything but a present. This thing has been forced on me." Nevertheless, once Cobb accepted the job, he tackled it with his usual bottomless determination. He helped groom his successor as batting leader, Harry Heilmann, and he pushed the Tigers back to third-place finishes in 1922 and 1924 and a second-place finish in 1923.

Falls quotes Cobb on his years as a player-manager: "In no way do I consider myself a failure as a manager. I took over a seventh-place club in 1921, and, with one exception, all my clubs won more games than they lost. We were in the first division four times. We played interesting and exciting ball. We drew well on the road. Next to the Yankees, we were the best draw in the league."

Many of those road spectators must have come to catch the last seasons of Cobb, whose 3,902 regular season hits stood as a record until 1985. Cobb lasted six seasons as manager of the Tigers and then wound up his career with a two-

Trancendental Graphics

Charlie Gehringer

year stint in Philadelphia. He retired from baseball a wealthy man, having wisely bought stock in such companies as Coca-Cola and General Motors. Forever surly and reclusive, Cobb moved home to Georgia and stayed there until his death in 1961 at the age of 74. He was selected to the Baseball Hall of Fame in 1936.

During Cobb's tenure as manager, Navin suffered a brief setback. Yawkey died prematurely in 1919. Faced with the loss of a partner, Navin persuaded auto industrialists Walter O. Briggs, Sr., and John Kelsey to purchase Yawkey's share of the Tigers. The deal was important in many respects. It kept Navin at the helm, but it also introduced Briggs, the next important mover-and-shaker in Tigers history. The stable—and aggressive—front office helped guide the team through some more lean years in the late 1920s under managers George Moriarty (1927-28) and Bucky Harris (1929-33).

Trancendental Graphics

Mickey Cochrane

Team Remodeling

The early Depression years were a "rebuilding" time for Detroit in more than one respect. The Navin Field grandstand was double-decked in 1924, and slowly the nucleus of another championship team began to arrive. First on the scene, in 1924, was Charley Gehringer, a Michigan native who played second base and hit better than .300 through most of his 19-year career. Gehringer had settled into place nicely by 1930, when first baseman and power hitter Hank Greenberg joined the team.

A pitcher with the unlikely name of School-boy Rowe made his debut in 1933, and batting phenomenon Leon "The Goose" Goslin came in a trade with Washington in 1934. These players—especially Gehringer and Greenberg—kept the game interesting for Detroit fans during years when the team did not contend for a pennant. Then, as they matured, they propelled the Tigers back into post-season play.

The Great Depression hit Detroit very hard. Factories closed or scaled back to skeleton crews. Unemployment was rampant, dissatisfaction visible everywhere. Curiously enough, the fans began flocking to Navin Field in 1934 as their Tigers moved into contention for the league championship. Attendance soared to 919,191 in 1934 and topped one million in 1935—an amazing total representing more than one-quarter of baseball's paying customers during the Depression years.

The reason for the surge in interest was plain to behold. The Tigers were back. In 1934 Navin bought Mickey Cochrane's services from the Philadelphia Athletics. Cochrane had been the Athletics' catcher and had compiled some commanding numbers on both offense and defense during his nine-year playing career.

Navin made Cochrane a player-manager, and the bandy-legged catcher quickly became known as "Black Mike" for his no-nonsense managing style. Cochrane, Goslin, Greenberg, and Gehringer formed a potent force, and Schoolboy Rowe added his talents with a 24-8 season on the mound. The 1934 Tigers won the pennant by a seven-game margin over the Yankees and brought the World Series back to Detroit.

"There should have been resentment toward these men, who were making a good living by playing a boy's game at such a difficult time," Falls wrote. "Just the opposite was true. The fans, needing an outlet from all the worries of the day, embraced them as heroes. At least they could go to the ballpark and know there was still some normality in the world.... The players were untouched by the Depression, and that was fine with everyone. They represented a symbol of hope for those down on their luck."

The 1934 World Series degenerated into a seven-game brawl. The Tigers met the St. Louis Cardinals, a brash team whose "Gashouse Gang" teased Greenberg with ethnic slurs and predicted they would return South with "Tiger skins."

Tempers ran so high by the seventh game that an incident on the basepath between Tiger fielder Marvin Owen and St. Louis runner Joe Medwick almost halted the game. Medwick had words with Owen after a slide into third base. At the time, St. Louis was ahead 9-0, and the Detroit fans were frustrated anyway.

When Medwick ran to his position in the outfield in the next inning, he was showered with vegetables, rolled-up newspapers, scorecards, and anything else the Detroit faithful could find to throw. The situation became so desperate that Medwick was removed from the game by decree from the baseball commissioner, Kenesaw Mountain Landis, who was on hand to watch the Series.

The World Series defeat stunned the Tigers. The early part of the 1935 season found them in last place during April and a dismal sixth on May 28. From there they rallied, and by the end of July they held first place firmly. They never relinquished the lead, winning the pennant by a three-game margin. Greenberg, who batted .328 with 36 home runs, 13 triples, 46 doubles, and 170 runs batted in, was named the league's most valuable player.

Trancendental Graphics

Goose Goslin

Championship Tigers

The 1935 World Series offered a welcome rematch with the Chicago Cubs, nemesis from the Tigers' early days. A victory looked doubtful after the second game, when Greenberg suffered a broken wrist that eliminated him from play. Cochrane was forced to shuffle players around the infield and insert Flea Clifton, the club's weakest batter, into the lineup.

Confounding the odds, the Tigers went on to take the Series with strong offensive performances by Gehringer and Pete Fox. On October 7, 1935, Detroit won its first fall classic. The fans celebrated all night and then treated their hometown heroes to a ticker tape parade through the streets of the Motor City.

No one was happier about the world championship than Navin. He had literally waited a lifetime for the achievement, and in his joy he dedicated the club's share of the victory money to another enlargement of Navin Field. Ironically, within a month of the World Series victory, Navin was dead. He suffered a heart attack while horseback riding on November 13, 1935. He was buried in Detroit, in a mausoleum guarded by two huge stone tigers.

Briggs quickly bought Navin's share of the Tigers and became sole owner of the franchise. Briggs, too, was a dedicated Detroiter who poured time, money, and energy into the team. His first years as owner-president were anything but easy. In 1936 Cochrane suffered a nervous breakdown requiring extended rest away from the club. Managing duties were turned over to coach Del Baker. Detroit finished the year in second place, but a dismal 19-and-a-half games out.

Cochrane returned to his job in 1937 but nearly lost his life in a tragic beaning on May 15, 1937. He was struck on the left temple by a pitch and spent four days in critical condition. After his recovery he tried to return as manager, but little went right for him. Briggs fired him early in the 1938 season.

"Cochrane's departure seemed to signal the end of the happy days in Detroit," wrote Falls, "but the Tigers showed surprising strength in the war years, which were just on the horizon. No team in baseball was more colorful than the Tigers in those turbulent times from 1939 to 1945."

In the late 1930s the Detroit ballpark was expanded again. This time Briggs double-decked all but the centerfield bleachers and put a roof over the plant. The park at Michigan and Trumbull could seat 53,000 comfortably, and it was renamed Briggs Stadium.

The Tigers finished 26-and-a-half games out of first place in 1939 and looked to be completely in the shadow of the powerful New York Yankees of the period. Then, in 1940, general manager Jack Zeller made some moves. Zeller persuaded Greenberg to try an outfield position, then hired Rudy York for first base. A colorful addition to the lineup came in the person of Louis Norman "Bobo" Newsom.

Newsom was an able pitcher, as he was to prove with the Tigers. He was also outspoken, testy, and at times downright eccentric. During the 1940 season, Newsom won 21 games for Detroit, and, according to Falls, "never stopped talking. He was bragging about himself from the beginning of the season to the end. What made his record so remarkable is that he broke his thumb and was out for three weeks."

Behind Newsom the Tigers fought hard for a first-place finish throughout the year. The pennant came down to a three-game series against second-place Cleveland during the last weekend of the season. The Tigers needed to win only one of the three games to clinch the pennant, so a rookie pitcher named Floyd Giebell was given a start against Cleveland's ace, Bob Feller.

Surprisingly enough, Giebell shut the Indi-

Tigers on the Air

The Baseball Hall of Fame in Cooperstown, New York, features several Tigers who left the field for careers in the broadcasting booth, as well as one announcer who never hefted a bat. These "Tigers on the Air" include:

Harry Heilmann • Nicknamed "Old Slug," Heilmann played 15 years for Detroit (1914-29) and then spent 17 years doing play-by-play on the local radio. Heilmann's career batting average was .342, and he was a star on the Tiger teams that made the World Series in 1934 and 1935. He was elected to the Hall of Fame in 1952.

Al Kaline • An outfielder, Kaline spent his entire 21-year playing career with the Tigers. In 1955, his second full season, he became the American League's youngest batting champion with a .340 average. He was 20 at the time. Kaline was elected to the Hall of Fame in 1980 after retiring from baseball in 1974. Today he is a play-by-play announcer for Tiger baseball on Detroit television.

George Kell • Kell brought his batting prowess to the Tigers for six years beginning in 1946. In 1949 Kell won the American League batting championship by a margin of .3429 to .3427 over Ted Williams. The difference between the two men's seasons was so slight that Kell won the championship literally in his last at-bat of the year. Kell was elected to the Hall of Fame in 1983. He works with Kaline broadcasting Tiger baseball games on television.

Ernie Harwell • A fixture on Tiger radio for decades, Harwell hypnotized generations of fans with his affable yet professional radio play-by-play. Harwell never played baseball. He began his broadcasting career in Atlanta, Georgia, in 1940. In the 1950s he announced games for the New York Giants and the Baltimore Orioles. Harwell moved to Detroit in 1960 and called the games continuously until 1991. He was dismissed by the local radio station and the Tiger front office that year, but the outcry was so great that he returned to the radio for one last season in 1993. Harwell was elected to the Hall of Fame in 1981.

Trancendental Graphics

Hank Greenberg

the seventh game and lost in a narrow 2-1 Reds' victory. The following year Newsom slumped to a 12-20 record and saw his salary slashed from $34,000 to $12,500. He was traded to the Washington Senators in 1942.

World War II Woes

A worse bit of news awaited Tiger fans. On May 17, 1941, Hank Greenberg became the first American Leaguer to be drafted into the U.S. Army. Greenberg left for active duty just as wartime production of engines, tanks, and other military equipment brought new prosperity to Detroit. The Tigers finished the 1941 season in fourth place.

No professional baseball team escaped the effects of compulsory military service during World War II. "Baseball had become something of a bad joke by the end of the war," Falls contended. "The game was being played by a ragtag collection of players." Detroit lost Gehringer, Barney McCoskey, Pat Mullin, Birdie Tebbets, Al Benton, Freddie Hutchinson, and Greenberg, as well as a promising rookie slugger named Dick Wakefield, who batted .355 in 1944 and helped the Tigers claim a second-place finish.

By 1945 some players were beginning to return to their teams, but the rosters were still depleted. The year is particularly memorable for the Tigers, however, especially in light of how they won the pennant.

The Washington Senators finished the 1945 season with an 87-67 record. Figuring that the team had no hope of a pennant, the owner let the players go home a week before the season ended so he could rent the stadium to the local football team. "All the Senators could do was sit and wait for the outcome of the Detroit games," wrote Falls. "The Tigers went into the last two days in St. Louis with an 87-65 record. If they won one game, the pennant would be theirs; if they lost both games, it would be a tie [with Washington], with a one-game playoff set in Detroit for the following Monday."

ans out, and the Tigers won 2-0 to clinch the pennant. In the 1940 World Series they met the Cincinnati Reds. The Series stretched to seven games, with Newsom winning two for Detroit with a predictable lack of modesty. Newsom got the start in

As the Browns edged ahead of the Tigers, the Washington players packed their suitcases and checked the train schedule. Then in the ninth inning of the first Detroit-St. Louis game, Greenberg smacked a line drive home run that firmly clinched the 1945 pennant for the Tigers. The first American Leaguer in the military—and among the first to be demobilized—Greenberg was hailed in Detroit as the hero of the age.

Falls noted: "The Tigers played the Cubs in the [1945] World Series and both teams were so weak—their rosters so depleted—that columnist Warren Brown of the *Chicago American* wrote: 'This is one World Series that neither team can win.'" No one showed much style or flair in the contest. Each team shuffled through 19 players trying to field a winning combination, and the Series stretched to seven games. The Cubs won the sixth game in 12 innings.

It was a close and controversial affair. Tiger Chuck Hostetler lost his balance and fell trying to run to home plate during regulation innings. He was tagged out. The moment seemed inconsequential at the time, but the Tigers went on to tie the game and force the extra innings. The Cubs scored the winning run on a base hit to left field that got past Greenberg.

When the official scorekeepers charged Greenberg with a two-base error, he protested vigorously. The official scoring was later changed, but not in time to make the sports page deadlines. In Game 7, the Tigers roared back with a vengeance. They pounded in five runs in the first inning and went on to capture the Series crown in a 9-3 win over the Cubs.

It would be more than 20 years before Detroit would go to the World Series again.

The 1950s were hardly a wasted decade for the Tigers, however. Their roster included such fine talents as third baseman George Kell, who won the 1949 batting championship on his very last at-bat of the season; Al Kaline, who in 1955 became the youngest hitter ever to win a batting championship; and Harvey Kuenn, who hit .353 in 1959 and added able defense both in the infield and outfield.

Trancendental Graphics

Hal Newhouser

Pitcher Hal Newhouser finished out his years with Detroit during this period, after having contributed during the 1940s pennant-winning seasons. The 1950s also saw the beginning of night games at Briggs Stadium. The park was slated to receive lights before World War II, but when the war broke out the project was shelved. The field was finally lit in 1948—Detroit was the last American League city to install stadium lights.

Management Mishaps and Angry Fans

If any one factor worked against the Tigers during the period, it was the club management. Cochrane (1934-38), Del Baker (1938-42), and Steve O'Neill (1943-48) had all managed clubs to at least one first-place finish. Their successors struggled. Red Rolfe (1949-52) tinkered with his talent and skippered a promising 1949 team that held first place as late as September 15 before

Transcendental Graphics

Al Kaline

falling to the Yankees.

When the team slumped to fifth place by 1951, Rolfe was released and replaced by Fred Hutchinson. Hutchinson lasted only two years and was denied a contract renewal in 1954. He was replaced by Bucky Harris, who lasted only two years.

Between 1957 and 1963 a veritable army of managers came and went: Jack Tighe, Bill Norman, Jimmy Dykes, Bill Hitchcock, Joe Gordon, and Bob Scheffling. The Tigers languished in fourth or fifth place throughout the period, with the exception of a second-place finish in 1961.

The 1950s also marked a milestone in Tiger ownership. The elder Walter Briggs died in 1952, and his son became president of the ball club. The younger Briggs sold the team in 1956 to an 11-man group for $5,500,000. The most notable member of the syndicate was John E. Fetzer, the next great leader of the Detroit organization.

Fetzer gained control of the Tigers in 1960 and held the club presidency until 1978, thus bringing to an end a period of relative instability following the Briggs sale.

The Fetzer takeover also gave the Tigers general manager Jim Campbell, who would develop a new generation of Tiger players into potential World Champions in both the 1960s and the 1980s. Falls claimed that from the beginning of his tenure, Fetzer "let Campbell run the show. Entirely. All Fetzer asked was a weekly report from Campbell and, please, run it like a business and keep the books in the black."

Problems with managers continued in the 1960s. Charley Dressen, in his second full season in 1965, suffered a heart attack during spring training and was temporarily replaced by coach Bob Swift. The following year Dressen suffered another spring heart attack. Swift again stepped in but soon discovered he had lung cancer. He was relieved by Frank Skaff midway through the 1966 season. By year's end both Dressen and Swift had died.

In 1967 Campbell hired Mayo Smith to manage the Tigers. The team was starting to show promise again. Kaline was still in the lineup and still productive. Norm Cash had been batting over .300 almost each year since arriving in Detroit in 1960, and the pitching staff boasted two interesting starters, Mickey Lolich and Denny McLain.

The 1967 pennant race was one of the tightest ever, but Detroiters were more concerned with the civil unrest that brought rioting and destruction to the inner city. When interest turned again to baseball in the fall, fans found the Tigers neck-and-neck with the Boston Red Sox and the Minnesota Twins. The Red Sox won the pennant on the final day of the season when Detroit lost its closing game at home.

Falls wrote: "The fans—mostly white—rioted in the ballpark. They stormed the field and battled with the stadium guards and city police. They even fought each other. They ripped up the pitcher's mound, tore out home plate, and flung chunks of grass into the air. Fights were breaking out everywhere among people who only moments earlier had bonded together in their affection for a baseball team. Now they were flailing out at everyone around them, throwing chairs on the field and tossing cushions into the dugouts in frustration and rage.... It was the lowest point in the history of baseball in Detroit."

1968: The Golden Year

The frustrated fans had only to wait until 1968 for a reason to cheer. The 1968 Tiger team was among the most popular and exciting in Tiger history. Detroit had suffered through 23 years without a pennant. The troubled citizens were desperately in need of something to believe in, some demonstration that their hometown had not been gutted by the ill will of 1967.

Just when fans needed it the most, the Tigers delivered. They jumped into first place on May 10, 1968, and never relinquished the lead again. At season's end they had won 103 games. "Maybe no team in history ever had a grander time reaching the top," Falls remembered. "They were a boisterous crew. They played hard on the field and they played hard off the field. They liked each other and hung out together and they had a manager who let them go.... The players were also careful not to overdo the parties. They held them only on days which ended in 'y.'"

The undisputed leader of this gang of good ol' boys was McLain. McLain flashed through the major leagues like a comet, dazzling fans by winning 31 regular season games (a feat not accomplished since 1934). Thoroughly stuck on himself, McLain provided lively controversy during the season by alternately complaining about the fans and bragging about his talent. As the Tigers cruised into the League Championship Series, McLain was featured on television talk shows and in a *Life* magazine spread.

McLain posted his 30th win of the season on September 14, 1968, and the Tigers clinched the pennant three days later. The entire city rallied around the team as the Tigers prepared to meet the St. Louis Cardinals in the World Series. In Game 1, the flamboyant McLain lasted only six innings, while Cardinal pitcher Bob Gibson shut out the Tigers 4-0.

Detroit evened the Series in Game 2 with an easy 8-1 victory behind pitcher Lolich. Then the Cardinals won back-to-back games for a 3-1 Series lead. The Tigers weren't through, though. Lolich returned to the mound for Game 5, and the Tigers won it 5-3 on a Kaline base hit. Game 6 also went to the Tigers, a 13-1 victory for McLain.

Game 7 featured the dreaded Bob Gibson again. His pitching opponent was Lolich, performing after only two days' rest. Gibson held the Tigers scoreless through six innings, but Detroit finally rallied and won the game 4-1. A team that liked excuses to party had found the ultimate one: a World Series crown.

Post-Championship Blues

Sadly, the Tigers were unable to parlay the Series crown into a lasting pattern of winning. In 1969 they finished second in the new Eastern Division of the American League. The following year McLain was suspended three times for fighting and various violations of league rules; he was traded to the Senators at year's end. "No player in history ever squandered more wealth and talent in a shorter period of time than this man," wrote Falls.

In 1971 Campbell brought Billy Martin to manage the Tigers. Martin did his best to coax another championship year out of the aging superstars, and in 1972 Detroit won the American League East. The League Championship Series went to the Oakland Athletics in five games, two of them extra inning affairs.

According to Falls, the 1972 Tiger showing was the last hurrah for the 1968 champions. "After that the Detroit ball club all but disintegrated," he wrote. "For the rest of the decade, the Tigers finished third, sixth, sixth, fifth, fourth, fifth, fifth, losing a record nineteen games in a row in 1975." Martin left mid-way through 1973 and was replaced by Ralph Houk.

AP/Wide World Photos

Sparky Anderson

Houk and Campbell initiated a wholesale overhaul of the Tigers, with emphasis on youth. In 1976 pitcher Mark Fidrych, nicknamed the Bird, made his major league debut. Fidrych was a curly-haired phenomenon who could be seen talking to the ball between pitches. He flailed his arms when he pitched, stomped the mound, and even patted the dirt to perfection. Fans loved him. According to Falls, "Where the Tigers normally drew 15,000, they would get 40,000 if Fidrych was pitching. Other teams asked weeks in advance for the Detroit pitching rotation so they could hype Fidrych's appearance in their own ballparks.

The Bird showed up in Detroit at exactly the right time. The city was down on its luck and looking for a lift." The peculiar ace was named Rookie of the Year in 1976 after compiling a 19–9 season with a league-leading 2.34 earned run average. Tragically, he injured his knee during spring training in 1977 and never pitched effectively in the majors again. His entire career in Detroit spanned some 48 games.

Other heroes began appearing out of the minors in the late 1970s. Pitcher Jack Morris arrived in 1977. Shortstop Alan Trammell, infielder Lou Whitaker, and catcher Lance Parrish all made the team in 1978. Slugger Kirk Gibson and pitcher Dan Petry joined in 1980. Campbell had succeeded in assembling a new group of young talents. Now all that remained to be done was to find a good manager to lead the team.

Sparky Began Reign

On June 12, 1979, that manager came to Detroit. His name: Sparky Anderson. George Lee Anderson was only in his mid-forties, but he already had a considerable reputation in the major leagues. Never a successful player himself, he had become nationally known as the skipper of the Cincinnati Reds, who appeared in four World Series matchups and had come away with victories in two of them. Anderson had been unexpectedly fired by the Reds ownership following a second-place finish in 1978. He came to Detroit vowing to prove the Reds wrong.

Detroit warmed to Anderson immediately. The prematurely white-haired manager became involved in the community and seemed endlessly willing to talk to reporters. He was neither stodgy nor excessively temperamental; in fact, he presented the picture of the ultimate working-class hero: just a nice guy doing his job. "I can't believe they pay us for this," he told Falls, "something we did for nothing as kids."

Signed to a contract running through 1984, Anderson took over the Tigers and ran what he called an "extensive spring training." He experimented with a multitude of players, allowed younger starters to find their way in game situations, and encouraged Campbell to extend multiyear deals to the likes of Trammell and Parrish. The Tigers finished the strike-shortened 1981 campaign in second place and seemed poised to challenge for the division championship the following year, until injuries slowed their pace.

In 1983 Detroit emerged as a bona fide pennant contender. Morris turned in his first 20-win season. Parrish finished the year with 27 home runs and 114 runs batted in. Three Tigers—Parrish, Whitaker, and Trammell—won Gold Glove awards in the same year. The season was also notable because the Tigers had changed hands again.

The new owner was Thomas S. Monaghan, another Michigan native who had made a vast fortune as founder of Domino's Pizza. Monaghan paid $53 million for the team and immediately signed Campbell to a five-year contract as Tiger president and chief executive officer. Monaghan also extended Anderson's contract through 1986

after the Tigers finished the year in second place with a 92-70 record.

The 1984 Joy Ride

The 1984 season was one long joy ride for the Detroit Tigers. The club jumped off to an incredible 35-5 start and simply dominated the A.L. East the entire season. They won 104 games in the regular season and broke attendance records by drawing 2,704,794 fans.

The rallying cry became "Bless You, Boys," as Sparky and company looked confidently toward the postseason. Falls wrote: "Everybody chipped in and the team blended perfectly. The Tigers became an irresistible force, clinching the divi-

AP/Wide World Photos

Lou Whitaker

AP/Wide World Photos

Alan Trammell

sion early and running over the overmatched Kansas City Royals in three quick games in the playoffs."

Detroit was favored to win the 1984 World Series. Everyone was in top form: Morris and Petry both looked unbeatable, and if they weren't, reliever Willie Hernandez—with 32 saves—was on hand to mop up. Whitaker, Parrish, and Trammell were joined on offense by Larry Herndon and the explosive Gibson.

It took only five games for the Tigers to defeat the San Diego Padres for the 1984 World Series crown, and the feat was accomplished at home in Detroit. Crowds both inside and outside the stadium celebrated with an intensity that threatened to become dangerous; indeed, several cars were burned and a number of people injured during the night. With Detroit's World Series victory, Anderson became the first major league manager to win the fall classic in both leagues.

Anderson kept the Tigers competitive through most of the 1980s, but it was not always easy. Injuries eroded the abilities of Gibson and Morris in 1985. Parrish suffered a season-ending back injury in 1986. Still the team could count on strong pitching from Hernandez, Petry, and Frank Tanana, and the Tigers finished in third place in both 1985 and 1986.

In 1987, with fewer injuries, the Tigers became locked in a see-saw battle for first place with the Toronto Blue Jays. The lead in the American League East changed four times over the final 50 games of the season. Then Detroit and Toronto went head-to-head in seven of the last 11 games of the year to determine the champion.

Rarely has baseball been more exciting during a regular season. All seven of the Detroit-Toronto games were decided by one run. The Blue Jays swept three of the first four in Toronto, but the Tigers rallied to win the fourth in 13 innings. Detroit trailed by one game when Toronto arrived in the Motor City for a final three-game series. In front of sellout crowds, the Tigers won all three games. The clincher came on a Sunday afternoon, when Tanana shut out the Jays 1-0, on a solo home run blast by Larry Herndon.

If anything, this nail-biting AL East championship was more satisfying than the 1984 campaign had been. Some of the credit rested with Trammell, who had turned in his best year on offense after being moved to the clean-up position. Pitching had been good throughout, with Morris winning 18, Walt Terrell a career-high 17, and Tanana 15. Remarkably, Detroit had won six of the last eight games of the season. The autumn surge notwithstanding, the Tigers lost to the Minnesota Twins in a best-of-seven League Championship Series.

Entering the 1989 season, the Tigers were the most successful team in the American League during the 1980s. Detroit had finished in third place or better every year between 1983 and 1988 and had won the American League East twice. Anderson was proud. He had been there the whole time.

The Sinking Tigers

Then everything began to collapse at once. Star players had been abandoning the Tigers for the free agent market, and by 1989 Morris, Gibson, Parrish, and Petry were gone. In just one season the proud franchise plunged from second place to dead last, with a dreadful 59-103 record. The pressure became too great even for Anderson. He was diagnosed with extreme exhaustion in May of 1989 and was sent home to California to rest for several weeks.

Upon his return to the team in June, Anderson told the *Providence Journal* that each loss of his long career had hit him like "a ton of bricks" and that he was particularly disheartened by the Tigers' dismal start in 1989. "I don't believe there has ever been an individual ... that would take losses harder and keep them inside longer than I do," Anderson said. "Inside I die a thousand deaths. People do not realize how hard that is on you and how hard that is on your nerves."

Anderson rebounded and scaled back the scope of his charity work and non-baseball activities. The Tigers began to rebound in the 1990s as well. Infielder Cecil Fielder joined the team in 1990 and immediately became productive on offense. His home run prowess helped Detroit to finish in third place in 1990 and tie for second place in 1991.

Fielder also topped the major leagues in RBI totals three years in a row—1990, 1991, and 1992—becoming the first player since Babe Ruth to lead the majors three straight times. Unfortu-

AP/Wide World Photos

Cecil Fielder

nately, the Tigers didn't fare as well in 1992. They slipped back under .500 with a 75-87 record and a sixth-place finish.

Campbell retired as president of the Tigers in 1990. His successor was another popular Michigan sports figure—Glenn E. "Bo" Schembechler, former coach of the University of Michigan football team. Schembechler had retired from coaching due to heart trouble. He was a close friend of Monaghan's and was eager to accept a job with the Tigers.

Beloved though he was in Detroit, Schembechler was unable to improve the Tigers' standing in the American League East. His association with the increasingly unpopular Monaghan also weighed against him: many fans deeply resented the owner's attempts to relocate the Tigers outside of Detroit. At any rate, Schembechler was fired when Monaghan sold the baseball club to Michael Ilitch on August 26, 1992.

Motor City Mogul

Ilitch made his fortune the same way Monaghan had—by selling pizza. In Ilitch's case, the company was Little Caesar's. He and his wife had founded the chain in 1959 in Garden City, Michigan, and had parlayed their success into a more than $2 billion-a-year national franchise. Ilitch is no stranger to Michigan's sports fans. In 1982 he bought the Detroit Red Wings hockey club. Later he purchased the management company that runs Detroit's Joe Louis Arena (home ice to the Red Wings), Cobo Arena, and the Fox Theater. In addition, he owns the Arena Football League's Detroit Drive.

Perhaps because he had made a commitment to the city with his hockey team, Ilitch could see the benefits of keeping the Tigers in Detroit. In 1993 he completed an $8 million renovation plan for aging Tiger Stadium. The facelift included a new color-action scoreboard, a "Tiger Plaza" for fans, and cosmetic improvements to the historic structure.

In addition, Ilitch has instituted other changes

designed to draw fans to the ballpark. Youngsters are invited to run the bases after Monday night games, hot dogs and peanuts are routinely distributed as promotional giveaways, and selected enthusiasts are designated as "couch potatoes" and invited to relax on a sofa in the lower deck in right field for the duration of the game.

And fans have responded to the changes. By August of 1993, attendance figures had topped the 1.6 million mark, bypassing 1992's season total of just over 1.4 million. Ilitch has also taken his commitment to the team one step further. He has stated that—if the Tigers do indeed move to a new stadium in the near future—he would pay for the construction of the facility.

Sparky Anderson won his 2,000th game as a professional baseball manager on April 15, 1993, when the Tigers beat the Oakland A's 3-2. Anderson's longevity in Detroit is almost unprecedented in today's baseball market. If he has not rewarded the Tigers ownership with multiple World Series appearances as he did in Cincinnati, he has at least kept the team competitive in an era of skyrocketing salaries and league expansions.

Nevertheless, Anderson is not one to rest on his laurels. He told Falls he expects to be out of a job some day—it's part of the game. "I know you can wear out your welcome, no matter how well you may do your job," he said. "They just get tired of you. They've heard all your stories and seen all your stuff—they know your whole act—and they want something different. They want something new. It's unavoidable. I'm flattered I've lasted this long."

In mid-1993, even as the Tigers slid out of first place, Ilitch extended Anderson's contract through 1995; it was a testament of the owner's faith in his team's manager. "I thought it was important to have [Sparky] out at the helm and in a position of total command," Ilitch told Jerry Green in an interview in the *Detroit News and Free Press.*

Anderson's 15-plus years in Detroit serve as a fine case study of what has gone right with the club. The Tigers and their city have benefitted from long periods of stability on every level of the organization. Without owners like Navin and Briggs the team might have faltered during Detroit's lean years. Without players like Cobb, Kaline, Greenberg, and Trammell, the franchise might not have seen so much World Series play.

And without a manager like Sparky Anderson, the Tigers would indeed be adrift in the American League East, baseball's toughest division. As Falls put it, a hardworking town like Detroit needs diversion and a reason to cheer. The Tigers have brought those cheers, longer than almost anyone can remember—and the fans on Michigan and Trumbull are cheering still.

SOURCES

BOOKS

Falls, Joe, *The Detroit Tigers: An Illustrated History,* Prentice-Hall, 1989.

PERIODICALS

Detroit Free Press, May 23, 1989; April 13, 1993; July 23, 1993; August 19, 1993.
Detroit News and Free Press, August 22, 1993.
Providence Journal, June 6, 1989.

—*Mark Kram*

NEW YORK YANKEES

No other sports franchise in history has been as consistently successful as the New York Yankees. Despite a two-decade dearth of pennants at the beginning of its history and a one-decade dearth after 1981, the Yankees were dominant for so long—indeed, for the better part of four and a half decades—that "Break up the Yankees" became a familiar cry of baseball fans throughout the nation.

The attention focused on the Yanks can be explained in part, but only in part, by New York City being the media capital of America, thus magnifying the exploits of its local heroes. But without exaggeration, the record of the Yankees from the 1920s through the 1970s is remarkable. The team won the American League pennant well over half the time and went on to victory in 22 World Series.

The legend took some time to develop. Indeed, New York City lacked a franchise in Ban Johnson's new American League, founded in 1901. Not surprisingly, Johnson wanted a team in New York, given the city's standing as the nation's largest metropolis, and in 1903, after some political maneuvering, the Baltimore Orioles became the New York Highlanders. The club moved to a ballpark in upper Manhattan. Despite having a few stars such as Jack Chesbro and Wee Willie Keeler, the Yankees (as they became known officially in 1913) finished no higher than second place in any of their first 18 seasons. Then came Babe Ruth.

Although baseball is quintessentially a team sport, superstars are not only household names, they are also convenient reference points in baseball history. The Ruth era, which is to say the 1920s and early 1930s, is regarded as the first Yankee dynasty. Babe Ruth joined the club in 1920. The Yanks won pennants in 1921, 1922, 1923, 1926, 1927, 1928, and 1932. Lou Gehrig came on board in 1925, and the latter part of this era (which merged gradually into the next) can be thought of as the Ruth-Gehrig era.

After three second-place finishes in the mid-1930s, the Yanks climbed back into first place in 1936. That was the year Joe DiMaggio broke into the lineup, and, with DiMaggio as heir apparent, 1936 marked the beginning of the second Yankee dynasty. For the next seven seasons—through the middle of World War II—the Yanks won the pennant every year except one.

They won the World Series as well in 1936, 1937, 1938, 1939, 1941, and 1943. The war disrupted major league baseball (DiMaggio and many other players did not return from military service until 1946): but once the league was stabilized, the Yanks took pennants in 1947, 1949, and 1950.

Could the pinstriped dominance continue? It could, and did. In 1951 a youngster from Commerce, Oklahoma, began roaming the Yankee outfield alongside the ailing Joe DiMaggio. He was Mickey Mantle, the muscular, switch-hitting superstar of the third Yankee dynasty.

As before, the older era faded almost imperceptibly into the new. Joltin' Joe retired after the '51 season. Mantle played through 1968. During the Mantle Era the Yanks won pennants from 1951 through 1953, from 1955 through 1958, and from 1960 through 1964—twelve in all, plus ten World Series.

There has been no fourth Yankee dynasty. Although the team did well in the late 1970s when Reggie Jackson was garnering headlines, the aura of invincibility was gone. Under controversial owner George Steinbrenner (since 1973), free agency, and a musical-chairs procession of managers, the team has been unable to finish first since the strike-shortened 1981 season. The nadir came in 1990 when the club lost more games than it had in any season since 1912.

The Highlanders Come to Manhattan

In 1901 there were eight teams in the new American League. All eight cities except Washington, D.C., are represented in the league today, but almost from the outset two of them, Baltimore and Milwaukee, were relegated to the minors. "Even before the 1902 season began," Ban Johnson wrote, "we were determined to invade New York by transferring the Baltimore franchise." Understandably, the long-established New York Giants of the National League had no desire to see a rival major league team in their city.

A conference between NL and AL spokesmen convened at the St. Nicholas Hotel in Cincinnati in January 1903 in an attempt to iron out this and other differences. At the meeting Johnson obtained the go-ahead to locate a club in New York City.

Finding a site for the stadium proved more difficult, but he did find two New York investors willing to buy the Baltimore franchise. One was Frank Farrell, the city's "poolroom king"; the other was William (Big Bill) Devery, a former police commissioner. These two put up $18,000, hired Joseph W. Gordon, a coal dealer and politician, as the team's first president, and, through Gordon, obtained a lease on property in Washington Heights (the "highlands," so to speak) on which to build a ballpark.

Construction began with only six weeks to go until opening day. Fortunately, the Highlanders spent their first two weeks on the road. By opening day, April 20, 1903, the wooden ballpark was ready. More than 16,000 fans turned out to hear the 69th Regiment Band play "Yankee Doodle" and to watch New York's right-handed pitcher Jack Chesbro win a 6-2 game against Washington.

This Highlander team, which finished in fourth place with a 72-62 record, had some real talent. Joining 21-game winner Chesbro on the mound were Jesse Tannehill and Clark Griffith (who was also the team's manager), and in the outfield was Wee Willie Keeler, a lifetime .345 hitter who stood five-feet-four-and-one-half inches tall. Chesbro, Griffith, and Keeler were all destined for the Baseball Hall of Fame. Nevertheless, in 1903 (as in every season through 1920) the Highlanders/Yankees struggled in vain to break through to the top.

TEAM INFORMATION AT A GLANCE

Founding date: January 9, 1903 (approval of New York as an
American League city; franchise transferred from Baltimore)

Home stadium: Yankee Stadium
E. 161st St. and River Ave.
Bronx, NY 10451

Dimensions:
Left-field line—318 feet
Center field—408 feet
Right-field line—314 feet
Seating capacity: 57,545

Team uniforms: Home—base color white, dark blue pinstripes
Road—base color gray, dark blue trim
Team nickname: Highlanders, 1903-12; Yankees, 1913—
Logo: Hat with stars and stripes perched on baseball bat within outlined baseball

Franchise record:	Won	Lost	Pct.
(1903-93)	8,061	6,287	.562

World Series wins (22): 1923, 1927, 1928, 1932, 1936, 1937, 1938, 1939, 1941,
1943, 1947, 1949, 1950, 1951, 1952, 1953, 1956, 1958, 1961, 1962, 1977, 1978
American League championships (33): 1921, 1922, 1923, 1926, 1927, 1928, 1932,
1936, 1937, 1938, 1939, 1941, 1942, 1943, 1947, 1949, 1950, 1951, 1952, 1953,
1955, 1956, 1957, 1958, 1960, 1961. 1962, 1963, 1964, 1976, 1977, 1978, 1981
American League East division first-place finishes (4): 1976, 1977, 1978, 1980
League/division last-place finishes (4): 1908, 1912, 1966, 1990

Lean Days for the New Franchise

From 1903 through 1912 the New York Highlanders played in their wooden stadium atop a rock pile in upper Manhattan where Columbia Presbyterian Hospital stands today. Prosaically named the New York American League Ballpark, its center-field fence was 542 feet away from home plate, effectively precluding straight-away home runs except the inside-the-park variety. The dis-

tances down the right-field and left-field lines were equally intimidating to hitters: 400 and 365 feet respectively. Fans soon began referring to the place as Hilltop Park or The Hilltop. Sports editors found the nickname Highlanders too long for easy headline-writing and, according to Marty Appel of the *New York Times,* started calling the team the Yankees in newspapers as early as 1904.

In that year, 1904, the team came within a whisker of winning the pennant. The Boston Pil-

Transcendental Graphics

Jack Chesbro

grims, having added New York's Tannehill to a pitching staff headed by Cy Young, finally won out, but it was a seesaw battle all the way into October. Jack Chesbro racked up 41 wins for the Highlanders, a total never since surpassed and never likely to be. He lost 12 games.

The Highlanders, still managed by pitcher Clark Griffith, lost the crucial final game of the 1904 season to the Pilgrims on a wild pitch by Chesbro, who once said of his spitball that "there was always in evidence the chance of a wild pitch." A crowd of 28,540 fans packed Hilltop Park for the decisive game.

In 1906 the Highlanders came close again, finishing second to the Chicago White Sox, the so-called "hitless wonders." Hal Chase was now at first base for the New Yorkers, having joined the team the year before. Chesbro pitched well, winning 24 games, but it was Al Orth, a veteran of the

Phillies and the Senators, who led the staff (and the league) with 27 victories. Wee Willie Keeler batted .302—the fifteenth consecutive season (and the last) in which he topped .300.

Clark Griffith resigned as manager during the 1908 season. Not only were his Highlanders off to a poor start, but the owners, Farrell and Devery, had taken to shouting suggestions at him from the bench. Kid Elberfeld, the Highlanders' shortstop from 1903 to 1907, took over as manager for the rest of the season. His record of 27 wins and 71 losses, resulting in a last-place finish for the New Yorkers, did not earn him a contract for 1909. George Stallings managed the 1909 team to a fifth-place finish, tried again in 1910 and had the team in second place when he resigned with just 11 games to go. Hal Chase filled in and was given the job for the 1911 season.

Although no one ever denied that Chase was a superb first baseman, the decision to make him a manager raised some eyebrows. Chase, after all, was a man who, to quote Eliot Asinof in *Eight Men Out,* "enjoyed the company of gamblers, if not for pleasure, then certainly for business." He was often hounded by jeers of "What are the odds?" Clearly, the odds against this sporting-life skipper doing a good job as manager were pretty long, and after a sixth-place finish in 1911 the Highlanders handed the reins to Harry Wolverton, a journeyman third baseman whose one-season managerial effort ended in a last-place finish for New York in 1912, a distant 55 games behind pennant-winning Boston.

In 1913 the Yankees—as they were now officially called—made two major moves. They abandoned Hilltop Park and became a tenant of the Polo Grounds, home of the National League's New York Giants. Trying to change their fortunes at their new ballpark, they persuaded Frank Chance, the Chicago Cubs' "Peerless Leader," to manage the club. Chance changed his plans for retirement and accepted the challenge. He probably regretted it, because the 1913 and 1914 Yankees had very little going for them.

In 1913 they had a fine right-handed pitcher named Russ Ford, but he put in only a so-so final year with the team. Ford had won 26 games for them in 1910 and 22 in 1911; his ERA as a Yankee (2.54) is the lowest in team history. Young Roger Peckinpaugh played shortstop for both seasons. A fine career lay ahead of him as both a player and a manager, but he was only a fair hitter. That matters little for a shortstop, except that no one else on the 1913 and 1914 teams (other than outfielder Birdie Cree) could hit much better than Peckinpaugh. The 1913 Yanks finished in seventh place; the 1914 team tied with the White Sox for sixth.

Ruppert and Huston Take Over

After 12 years the ownership team of Frank Farrell and Big Bill Devery was ready to opt out— at a suitably large profit. To their credit, they had brought an American League franchise to New York, although the teams they fielded never quite measured up. New blood was needed, not just on the diamond but in the front office as well.

It came at the top in the form of Colonel Jacob Ruppert, a 47-year-old beer baron and realtor, and Colonel Tillinghast L'Hommedieu Huston, 45, a construction magnate. The two, seeking to acquire a major league club in New York, were brought together by Ban Johnson, who wanted Gotham City to have a competitive team in the American League, not just an also-ran. The Giants, led by manager John McGraw and pitchers Christy Mathewson and Rube Marquard, were perennial contenders in the National League, a fact that galled the prickly president of the junior circuit.

Ruppert and Huston acquired the Yankee franchise on December 31, 1914, for $460,000— approximately 25 times what Farrell and Devery had paid for it. Still, it was a remarkable bargain, as time would show. The new owners moved quickly to acquire rookie first baseman Wally Pipp from the Tigers. They also signed Wild Bill Donovan, an aging Tiger pitcher, to manage the Yankees.

Yet the team did not change much immediately. Veteran pitchers Ray Caldwell and Ray

Transcendental Graphics

Willie Keeler

Fisher stayed on. The lineup showed no dramatic improvement except for the addition of Frank (Home Run) Baker in 1916; Donovan guided the club to fifth-, fourth-, and sixth-place finishes over the next three years.

Soon the two owners began to quarrel, and in 1917 when Huston went to war in France, his complaints arrived by cable. One of them had to do with Colonel Ruppert's hiring a new manager for the 1918 season. Ruppert's choice was scrappy little Miller Huggins, a long-time second baseman and five-year St. Louis Cardinal manager. Ban Johnson, ever solicitous for the New York franchise, had recommended Huggins for the position. Colonel Huston wired his disapproval, suggesting Wilbert Robinson of the Dodgers instead. The objection went for naught.

For three seasons there was improvement under Miller Huggins, noticeable but modest. The

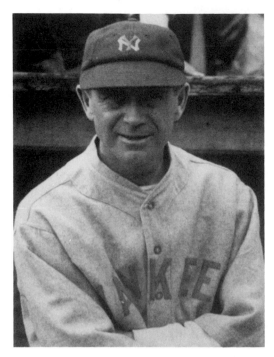

Transcendental Graphics

Miller Huggins

war-shortened 1918 season brought the Yanks a fourth-place finish. The next year they moved up a slot, but this slight gain was secondary to the important though controversial deal Ruppert made in July 1919 with Harry Frazee, owner of the Boston Red Sox—the first of many Frazee deals that would deplete the Red Sox and strengthen the Yankees.

The player in question was Boston pitcher Carl Mays, whom Ban Johnson had recently suspended, specifying that he not be traded. Ruppert had many reasons to be well-disposed toward Johnson, but business being business, the Yankee owner sought and obtained an injunction permitting Mays to play for New York. The incident was a stunning blow to Johnson's power as league president, one from which he never fully recovered.

Right-hander Mays had a 14-14 record for the Yanks in 1919, but the team as a whole went 80-

59, good for a third-place finish, a scant 7½ games behind the first-place Chicago "Black Sox"—for this was the year of the sensational World Series-fixing scandal. Inasmuch as Yankee teams had been posting records that put them, on average, about 28 games behind the league leaders for a dozen years, this was a welcome gain. A respectable finish was not the big off-season story, however. That occurred on January 5, 1920, when the Yankees announced the most significant player purchase in baseball history.

Enter the Bambino

The purchase of George Herman Ruth for about $125,000—more than double the amount of money previously paid for a ballplayer—marked a turning point not only in the saga of the Yankees but in the history of baseball. Unquestionably, Babe Ruth helped the Yankees win a succession of pennants.

But more than that, he helped America forget the tarnished image of baseball created by the "Black Sox" scandal of the previous year. The Babe was a new hero, a man of gargantuan appetites and achievements, a different kind of idol for a more explosive kind of baseball. He ushered in the era of the "big bang," the crowd-pleasing home run.

The Bambino had been a great pitcher for Boston, with an 89-46 record from 1914 through 1919. Playing the outfield regularly in 1919, he belted 29 home runs to break a record that had stood for 35 years. He was 25 years old and still had most of his career ahead of him. Harry Frazee knew that Ruth was exceptionally good, but thought that $125,000 was the asking price for a franchise, not an individual player (failing to foresee that for New York the Babe would virtually be the franchise).

Ruth demonstrated his prowess right away, although the Yanks finished third in 1920. His stats give a revealing glimpse of why the Yanks were about to ascend into the stratosphere. While batting .376, Ruth led the league in home runs with

Transcendental Graphics

Babe Ruth

54 (his nearest rival hit 19), in runs scored with 158, in RBIs with 137, in walks with 148, and in slugging percentage with .847, the highest in the history of baseball.

The Yankees won their first pennant in 1921, but lost the World Series to the Giants. Ruth enjoyed another spectacular season, upping his home run total to 59 and his RBIs to 171. Under manager Miller Huggins, a proven winner, changes in the lineup were nearly all for the better.

New York obtained future Hall-of-Fame pitcher Waite Hoyt from Boston (as Frazee continued to give away the store). Wally Schang, also from Boston, took over behind the plate, while outfielder Bob Meusel, a Yankee rookie in 1920, put in a fine sophomore year, banging out 24 homers to tie for second in the league behind Ruth.

Once again, Harry Frazee, who apparently could not do enough for the Yankees, recommended his Red Sox business manager, Ed Barrow, to Colonel Huston. The Yankees hired him, and Barrow, a hard-headed businessman and an astute judge of talent, helped to build the Yankee empire.

From the Polo Grounds to Yankee Stadium

The Yanks won the pennant again in 1922 and then lost the World Series—once again to the Giants. By this time the Yankees had worn out their welcome at the Polo Grounds. They had become so popular with the fans as to be something of an embarrassment to their hosts, and before the 1922 season Giants owner Charles Stoneham had asked the Yanks to leave. Anticipating something of the sort, Ruppert and Huston had taken an option in 1920 on a 10-acre piece of land in the Bronx, less than a mile from the Polo Grounds.

Construction of the new Yankee Stadium began on May 5, 1922 and was completed in time for opening day, April 18, 1923. In only 185 working days the White Construction Company of Cleveland had erected the three-deck, reinforced-concrete and steel grandstand and 40,000 square feet of wooden bleachers with the now-famous copper-frieze facade. White may have done the work, but it would forever be known as "The House That Ruth Built." Ruth had made the Yankee franchise a gold mine.

On a more mundane level, the dimensions of the park favored left-handed power hitters, which of course the Babe was. Deep left-center field was so far away, extending from 395 to 460 feet from home plate, that it came to be known as "Death Valley"—the deceased of the region being right-handed hitters.

On opening day of 1923 John Philip Sousa and the Seventh Regiment Band led a procession to center field to hoist the 1922 American League pennant. Governor Al Smith tossed out the first ball. Babe Ruth, fittingly, blasted the first home run in the new stadium, a third-inning shot off

Transcendental Graphics

Tony Lazzeri

Boston's Howard Ehmke, into the right-field bleachers. The Yanks won the game 4–1.

They also won the pennant that year and, at last, the World Series, defeating the Giants four games to two. In 1924 and 1925 they lost out, however, first by a little, then by a lot. They finished a close second to Washington in 1924, but dropped all the way to seventh place in 1925.

Their "Murderers' Row" was nearly assembled—Lou Gehrig had replaced Wally Pipp at first base at the end of the 1924 season, and slugging outfielder Earle Combs was playing his first full season for the Yankees. A fine pitching staff featured Herb Pennock, Urban Shocker, Waite Hoyt, Bob Shawkey, and Sad Sam Jones.

One reason for their failure in 1925 was the illness of Babe Ruth. Years of high living finally caught up with him on the Yankees' barnstorming trip north from spring training. He checked into a hospital, underwent an operation for an intesti-

nal abscess, and missed nearly a third of the season. His production at the plate dropped, the pitchers' ERAs inched up (except for Pennock's), and the Yanks had to settle for the rung above the dismal and depleted Red Sox.

Those Championship Seasons

The 1925 season was an aberration. The next year the Yankees rebounded strongly, taking the AL pennant in 1926 and then both the pennant and the World Series in 1927 and 1928. By this time shrewd trades and acquisitions had created a team for Miller Huggins that seemed to be all but invincible. "Break-up-the-Yankees" fever first began to rage during this period when it began to look as if the American League pennant race was essentially over on opening day.

In fact, the 1926 Yankees, while impressive, were far from unbeatable. Even though they now had Tony Lazzeri at second base, Mark Koenig at shortstop, and Joe Dugan at third base (not to mention Gehrig at first and Ruth, Combs, and Meusel in the outfield), they were closely pursued by Cleveland, Philadelphia, and Washington. In the 1926 World Series the Cardinals edged them four games to three.

Then came the year of years. In his book *Baseball's 10 Greatest Teams,* Donald Honig writes: "The '27 Yankees—it is a phrase that stands by itself in the lexicon of baseball, connoting mountaintop greatness—set records by scoring 975 runs and posting a .489 slugging average, which is still the major league record. They batted .307 and led the league in everything except doubles (they were second) and stolen bases. They had the individual leaders in every offensive department except stolen bases and batting average." The Yanks won 110 games, played .714 ball, and out-distanced a strong Philadelphia Athletics team by 19 games.

The 1928 Yanks did nearly as well, although the Philadelphia A's, winning 98 games and playing at a .641 clip, hung in there, cutting the Yanks' 13½ game lead down to 2½ by season's end. In

Lou Gehrig: In the Shadow of Ruth

PROFILE

Throughout much of his career Lou Gehrig, the Iron Horse, performed in the shadow of the greatest Yankee of them all, Babe Ruth. For only one season, 1935, did Gehrig, who played in 2,130 consecutive games, not share the spotlight with either the Bambino or, later, the Yankee Clipper, Joe DiMaggio, who joined the team in 1936. And for Gehrig and the Yanks alike 1935 was something of an off season.

Until he was struck by the disease that killed him, first baseman Gehrig had very few off seasons. His lifetime batting average was .340, his slugging average .632, and his RBI total 1,990, the latter two figures good for third in the all-time record book (although Ruth topped him in these three categories, with a .342 BA, .690 SA, and 2,056 RBIs).

Gehrig's power, like Ruth's, was legendary. Hall-of-Fame catcher Bill Dickey, Gehrig's friend and roommate said, "Lou could hit hard line drives past an outfielder the way I hit hard line drives past an infielder.... Lou drove in 150 runs five different times. You know, I never drove in 150 runs in my life." In fact, the Iron Horse, or Columbia Lou, as he was sometimes called, drove in more than 100 runs every year but one in his 14 full seasons with the Yankees.

Joe DiMaggio, recalling his days with Gehrig, said, "I never saw such power, but as Lazzeri had remarked that first day I joined the club, 'Kid, you should have seen him when!'" Sportswriters who did see him when never doubted his greatness—but they nearly always linked him with Ruth.

In 1928, after the Yanks had won their second straight series four games to none, a *New York Times* reporter wrote, "What the Yanks have done in their last two World Series has been incredible and superhuman. They can't be weighed and measured by ordinary standards as long as they have two fiends in human form like G. Herman Ruth and H. Louis Gehrig, by far the two greatest ball players ever on one team."

When Gehrig, with less than two years to live, stepped to the microphone before 61,808 fans on Lou Gehrig Appreciation Day, July 4, 1939, he said, "What young man wouldn't give anything to mingle with such men for a single day as I have for all these years?... I think I'm the luckiest man alive." The best-known photo of that day shows Babe Ruth with his arms around Gehrig, looking protective as the Iron Horse smiles modestly.

"I'm not a headline guy," Gehrig once said. "When Babe's turn at bat is over, whether he strikes out or belts a home run, the fans are still talking about him when I come up. If I stood on my head at the plate, nobody'd pay any attention." In that, he was being too modest. The fans noticed. So did the sportswriters, who voted him into Baseball's new Hall of Fame by acclamation in December 1939.

Photo: *Transcendental Graphics*

Legend has it that the 1927 Yankees were the game's greatest team. Legend is probably right. The basic lineup—which in the days before the designated hitter included the starting pitcher—gives a good picture of just how formidable this best of all Yankee teams was. (Batting averages are for the 1927 season.)

Leading off: **Earl Combs, cf, .356** • Combs, a lifetime .325 hitter, enjoyed his best season in 1927. The speedy center fielder rapped out 231 hits and 23 triples to lead the American League in those categories.

Batting second: **Mark Koenig, ss, .285** • Koenig once said, "Just putting on a Yankee uniform gave me a little confidence, I think. That club could carry you." Koenig, a switch-hitter, had a better-than-average season in 1927, except for his league-leading 47 errors.

Batting third: **Babe Ruth, rf, .356** • This was the year the Bambino hit his 60 homers. He also drove in 164 runs and had a slugging average of .772. These are towering figures, but they were fairly standard for Ruth—even the home runs. He had hit 54 and 59 in previous seasons.

Batting cleanup: **Lou Gehrig, 1b, .373** • The Iron Horse led the league (and set a new major league record) with 175 RBIs. He hit 47 home runs. Only the Babe himself had ever hit more homers in a season. Gehrig, like Ruth, had so many great seasons that 1927 was about par for him.

Batting fifth: **Bob Meusel, lf, .337** • Meusel, a .309 lifetime hitter, posted his highest average ever in 1927. He hit only 11 home runs, though, compared to his 33 (to lead the league) in 1925. His 103 RBI total is impressive considering that Ruth and Gehrig were regularly clearing the bases ahead of him.

Batting sixth: **Tony Lazzeri, 2b, .309** • This was Lazzeri's second year in the majors. He drove in 102 runs and cracked 18 home runs. While 18 homers may not seem like a large total, it was good for third in the league—the only time in baseball history that the three top home run hitters all played for the same team.

Batting seventh: **Joe Dugan, 3b, .269** • "Jumping Joe" Dugan was nearing the end of a major league career that began in 1917. A lifetime .280 hitter, his performance in 1927 was adequate, but his best years were behind him.

Batting eighth: **Pat Collins, c, .275** • Catching was not the Yankees' strongest suit in 1927. Thirty-year-old Pat Collins alternated behind the plate with Johnny Grabowski. Both were capable enough, but not until 1929 with the arrival of Bill Dickey did the Yanks really have a catcher to match the rest of the team.

Batting ninth: The pitchers:
Waite Hoyt, rh, 22-7, ERA 2.63
Wilcy Moore, rh, 19-7, ERA 2.28
Herb Pennock, lh, 19-8, ERA 3.00
Urban Shocker, rh, 18-6, ERA 2.84

Waite Hoyt and Herb Pennock are in the Baseball Hall of Fame. Urban Shocker, a four-time 20-game winner with the St. Louis Browns, died of a heart attack near the end of the 1928 season.

Wilcy Moore, used mostly in relief, was a one-season wonder in 1927. A 30-4 record in 1926 at Greenville in the South Atlantic League had prompted the Yanks to purchase him, paying very little and acquiring one of the anchors of baseball's greatest team.

Two other pitchers, Dutch Ruether (13-6, ERA 3.38) and George Pipgras (10-3, ERA 4.11) had fine seasons, too. Ruether was at the end of his career, while Pipgras was just getting started—he would win 24 games in 1928. These six pitchers deserve considerable credit for the success of the 1927 Yankees, as their ERAs suggest.

the 1928 World Series the Yanks trounced the St. Louis Cardinals just as decisively as the 1927 team had beaten the Pittsburgh Pirates—four games to none in both Series.

In 1929 Connie Mack's Philadelphia A's finally caught up with the Bronx Bombers, winning the league championship easily (and gaining a place on Honig's *10 Greatest* list). Sadder news than this for Yankee fans was the sudden death of Miller Huggins from blood poisoning. On September 20, 1929, feeling ill, he turned the team over to coach Art Fletcher, and five days later, at the age of 50, Huggins died.

Bob Shawkey managed the team to a third-place finish in 1930. For the revved-up Yankees that was no longer good enough, especially when, in addition to their other stars, they now had a top-notch catcher, Bill Dickey, on the roster. Not only

was Dickey outstanding behind the plate, but in his first two full seasons in the majors, 1929 and 1930, he batted .324 and .339 on his way to a 17-season lifetime average of .313—all in Yankee pinstripes. The team had talent aplenty. The question was, could Colonel Ruppert and general manager Ed Barrow find a new skipper to fill Miller Huggins's shoes?

Success Continues Under Joe McCarthy

The man they found was Joe McCarthy, an ex-minor league infielder who had managed the Chicago Cubs for five seasons, leading them to a pennant in 1929. Dubbed Marse Joe by a Chicago sportswriter, he was a strict disciplinarian who, as

Trancendental Graphics

Bill Dickey

Transcendental Graphics

Joe McCarthy (right)

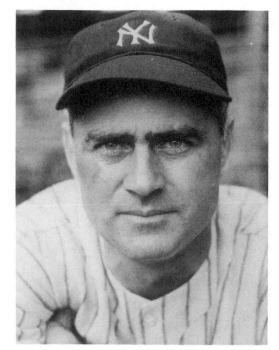

Transcendental Graphics

Earl Combs

a rookie manager, had fired Grover Cleveland Alexander for excessive drinking, and for five seasons had kept Hack Wilson, another devotee of the bottle, sober enough on the field to put up some highly impressive stats, including 190 RBIs in 1930, which no Yankee (or anyone else) ever topped. To the Yankee brass Marse Joe seemed like the right kind of boss to manage Babe Ruth and company.

Insisting that his players wear jackets and ties off the field, McCarthy ran the Yankees with such businesslike precision that White Sox manager Jimmy Dykes was moved to call him "a push-button manager," while legions of anti-Yankee fans decided that rooting for the coolly efficient Yankees was like rooting for U.S. Steel. Be that as it may, Joe McCarthy's Yanks, after finishing second in 1931, captured the pennant in 1932, winning 107 games and losing 47.

Although the lineup did not differ greatly

from that in the final years under Huggins, the pitching staff did. Herb Pennock and George Pipgras were still there, but the newer mainstays included Lefty Gomez, Red Ruffing, and Johnny Allen.

The 1932 World Series against the Cubs was Babe Ruth's last. In the third inning of the third game, with Charlie Root on the mound for the Cubs, the Bambino made the most of it. Gesturing prophetically toward the stands, he blasted a home run to the general area where he had pointed. So the story goes anyway; there have always been doubters. The Yanks swept the Series.

The Depression year of 1932 marked another milestone in Yankee history. It was the year in which Colonel Ruppert hired George M. Weiss, a minor league executive, to run the Newark Bears of the International League—and, as it turned out, to put together a farm system on the order of the one Branch Rickey was building for the Cardinals.

Weiss succeeded brilliantly at both tasks. In 1937 Newark fielded what is generally regarded as the best team ever in minor league baseball. By the end of the decade the extensive Yankee farm system was the envy of the majors.

From 1933 through 1935 the Yankees stayed near the top of the standings but never finished *at* the top. They came in second each year, first to Washington, then to St. Louis, then to Detroit. In 1932 Frank Crosetti inherited the Yankee shortstop job, which he would retain for 17 seasons. Red Rolfe took over at third base in 1934, holding down the position for nine years. In 1935 George (Twinkletoes) Selkirk drew the thankless task of replacing Babe Ruth in right field. Selkirk, a nine-year regular thereafter, did a workmanlike job for the Yanks, but no one ever mistook him for a superstar.

As the 1935 season came to a close, Gehrig, Dickey, Ruffing, and Gomez were among the veteran Yankee stars. They were about to be joined by a slender kid from San Francisco, who from the very beginning would put his own stamp of excellence on a team that seemed forever able to rejuvenate itself to stay competitive.

DiMaggio Heads the New Yankee Dynasty

It is easy to date the Yankee dynasty that followed Ruth's retirement. The year it began was 1936, with a team that nearly matched the exploits of the 1927 Yanks. Playing first base was Lou Gehrig, the "Iron Horse," having one of his typically great seasons, batting .354, belting 49 homers to lead the league, and driving in 152 runs. Then there was Bill Dickey, also putting in a stellar year at .362, with 107 RBIs. Indeed, the team as a whole hit for a .300 average, Red Ruffing won 20 games, newcomer Monte Pearson won 19, and the Yanks finished 19½ games ahead of Detroit.

In addition to those accomplishments, the Yankee front office boasted one more: in 1935, at the behest of scout Bill Essick, the Yanks had signed 21-year-old Joe DiMaggio. Hailing from

Transcendental Graphics

Joe DiMaggio

San Francisco's Fishermans' Wharf, DiMaggio had been starring in the outfield for the San Francisco Seals of the Pacific Coast League for three years. He finished the 1935 season on the Coast, batting .398 (two years earlier he had hit safely in 61 consecutive games for the Seals), then joined the Yanks for the 1936 season, replacing the retiring Earl Combs.

DiMaggio put in one of the finest rookie seasons any ballplayer ever had. He batted .323, with 44 doubles, 15 triples, and 29 home runs. He drove in 125 runs. But figures tell only part of the story. DiMaggio's grace and quiet intensity, both in the outfield and at bat, were apparent even to the casual fan. DiMaggio's dramatic debut was pro-

Transcendental Graphics

Lefty Gomez

logue; he followed it up with a dozen glittering seasons, during which the Yankees captured pennant after pennant.

As for 1936, having taken the flag, the Yanks went on to defeat the Giants four games to two in the World Series. Lefty Gomez won two of the games, while DiMaggio batted .346, Red Rolfe .400, and Jake Powell, a midseason acquisition from the Senators, hit .455 and scored eight runs.

Joe McCarthy's Yanks went on a rampage after their great 1936 season. They won pennants in 1937, 1938, and 1939, and proceeded to trounce their World Series opponents each year. In 1937 they beat the hometown Giants four games to one. In 1938 they pummeled the Chicago Cubs four games to none, and a year later the Reds likewise succumbed in four straight. These were heady times for the men in pinstripes, though not without sadness.

Colonel Jacob Ruppert died of phlebitis on January 13, 1939, and Ed Barrow, one of his trustees, was elected club president. Early in the 1939 season Lou Gehrig, having played in 2,130 games, asked to be benched in Detroit. Something was physically wrong with him. That something was amyotrophic lateral sclerosis, which came to be known as Lou Gehrig's disease. A deterioration of the central nervous system, it was irreversible and fatal. The Yankees held Lou Gehrig Appreciation Day at Yankee Stadium on July 4, 1939. Less than two years later Gehrig died at the age of 37.

Another event occurred in 1939 that would have far-reaching consequences for baseball. On September 1 Hitler invaded Poland, igniting World War II. This had no direct effect on the 1940 or 1941 seasons (third- and first-place finishes for the Yankees) since the U.S. had not yet entered the conflict. But beginning in 1942 major league clubs were faced with a unique challenge—fielding competitive teams while many of their stars and journeyman players were away.

That problem was still on the distant horizon as the Yankee juggernaut added to its strength in the prewar years: outfielder Tommy Henrich and right-handed pitcher Spud Chandler signed on in 1937, second baseman Joe Gordon in 1938, outfielder Charlie Keller 1939, and shortstop Phil Rizzuto in 1941. Of these five long-time Yankee regulars, three—Chandler, Gordon, and Keller—had recently played for Weiss's potent minor league Newark Bears.

War and Its Aftermath

The 1942 Yankee lineup showed few effects of the war that began for the U.S. on December 7, 1941. The Yanks won 103 games in the regular season to finish far ahead of second-place Boston. They ran into a revised World Series scenario, however, as the Cardinals defeated them four games to one. Except in the Series the Yankee pitching was outstanding. Righthander Ernie Bonham, who had joined the club in 1940, compiled a 21-5 record, while Hank Borowy, newly acquired, went 15-4 and Spud Chandler 16-5.

By 1943 many of the Yanks had gone to war, among them DiMaggio, Henrich, Rizzuto, and Ruffing. A few replacements, like outfielder Bud Metheny, were strictly wartime fill-ins. Others proved their worth over a longer period, among them second baseman Snuffy Stirnweiss, third baseman Billy Johnson, and outfielder Johnny Lindell, all of whom played into 1950. First baseman Nick Etten, a wartime star, stayed on through 1946. In the 1943 World Series the Yanks returned to their winning ways, beating the Cardinals four games to one.

A tight pennant race in 1944 went to the St. Louis Browns, as the Yanks had to settle for third. Between this season and the next, the ownership of the Yankees changed. The Ruppert estate sold the club on January 25, 1945, to a triumvirate consisting of Larry McPhail, Dan Topping, and Del Webb, for $2.8 million. No one expected immediate change or improvement, and none came. In the last and bleakest year of wartime baseball, the team dropped to fourth.

DiMaggio, Henrich, and Rizzuto returned for the 1946 season. So did manager Joe McCarthy, who expressed unhappiness with the new Yankee ownership. After just 40 games he resigned, and coach Johnny Neun took over for the rest of the season. The Yanks drew over two million fans in 1946, the first time ever, but this attendance figure had more to do with postwar euphoria than with the performance of the team. Boston walked away with the pennant, with New York a distant third.

Bucky Harris, a major league manager for five different teams since 1924, led the Yankees to an easy pennant in 1947 and a disappointing third-place finish in 1948. First baseman George McQuinn, who had knocked around the minors and the lowly St. Louis Browns for years, outhit everyone on the team except Joltin' Joe. But more important, three soon-to-be-familiar faces first appeared on the Yankee roster that year—catcher Yogi Berra and pitchers Allie Reynolds and Vic Raschi.

The Yanks edged the Brooklyn Dodgers four games to three in the 1947 Series, best remembered for Al Gionfriddo's spectacular catch of a 415-foot drive off the bat of Joe DiMaggio in the sixth inning of game 6 to keep the Dodgers' hopes alive.

In 1948 Eddie Lopat, a left-handed pitcher, came over from the White Sox and posted a 17-11 record to go along with Allie Reynolds' 16-7 and Vic Raschi's 19-8. DiMaggio led the league in home runs with 39 and RBIs with 155, but the Yanks still came in a shade behind Cleveland and Boston.

The second-place Red Sox, embarrassingly enough, were managed by Joe McCarthy. Two-year Yankee manager Bucky Harris's days were numbered. When Larry MacPhail sold his one-third interest in the club and departed in a huff, it fell to general manager George M. Weiss to hire a new skipper for the Bronx Bombers.

The Professor Works His Magic

The man Weiss chose to manage seemed hardly the Yankee type. He was Charles Dillon Stengel, known as Casey, a man of uncertain age, though probably then 60. Because of a brief coaching stint at Ole Miss as a young man, he was sometimes called the Professor, later the Old Professor, but his manner was anything but professorial. A rowdy, tough-as-nails, sometimes clownish outfielder, Casey was named manager of the hapless Brooklyn Dodgers in the mid-1930s and later of the equally futile Boston Braves. On the positive side, he led minor league Oakland to a pennant in 1948, and in 1949 he got his chance to duplicate the feat with the premier franchise in major league baseball.

Stengel inherited a first-rate ball club but by no means an invincible one. The Yankee pitching staff and outfield seemed to be set, but the infield, except for shortstop Rizzuto, was a question mark. George McQuinn had retired, Snuffy Stirnweiss was aging, and newcomers Jerry Coleman and Bobby Brown looked at least as capable as last year's regulars.

Stengel solved his problems in part by introducing the platoon system. Bobby Brown alternated with Billy Johnson at third base. Jerry Coleman and Snuffy Stirnweiss shared the chores at second base. Tommy Henrich spent half his time at first base, allowing recent arrivals Hank Bauer, Gene Woodling, and Cliff Mapes to patrol the outfield.

It all worked. The Yankees eked out a pennant in 1949 and humiliated Brooklyn in the World Series. After this triumph the general thread of the story (though not the details) gets somewhat monotonous. The Yanks finished first in all but two of their 11 seasons under Stengel—second in 1954 (with a 103-51 record), and third in 1959 (a genuinely poor year).

Many of the races were close. Take 1950. The lineup was about the same as the year before except that rookie Joe Collins now alternated at first base with Tommy Henrich and Johnny Mize. Mize, 36, had been acquired from the Giants at the end of the previous season. Over his four full years with the Yankees, he became one of the most consistent and devastating pinch hitters of all time. He was old, but as Dan Parker of the New York *Daily Mirror* wrote:

> *Your arm is gone; your legs likewise,*
> *But not your eyes, Mize, not your eyes.*

Transcendental Graphics

Casey Stengel (second from left)

DiMaggio's stats held up fairly well in 1950, but old injuries persisted and rumors of retirement continued to surface. Lefthander Whitey Ford, a towheaded 21-year-old product of the extensive Yankee farm system, came up from Kansas City in June to bolster the pitching staff. Ford posted a 9-1 record for the rest of the season. Billy Martin, a brash 22-year-old second baseman, also arrived in 1950 and quickly won favor with the hard-bitten Stengel.

Although this was an outstanding Yankee team, the Tigers, the Red Sox, and the Indians were tough, too. Any one of them could have won the pennant, but it was the Yanks who prevailed. The Bombers went on to sweep the Philadelphia Phillies' Whiz Kids in the World Series.

Mantle and the 1950s

In 1951 Mickey Mantle, a 19-year-old prospect from Class C Joplin of the Western Association, so impressed manager Stengel in spring training that Casey started the youngster in right field on opening day, flanking Joe DiMaggio (now in his last year) in center, and Jackie Jensen in left. As talented as Mantle was, he struggled that first year, was sent down to Triple-A Kansas City, and then recalled later in the season.

His .267 batting average was the lowest he would record in his first 15 years in the majors, but from the start he began smashing the kind of "tape measure" home runs that would earn that designation from a Yankee publicist a couple of years later, based on a 565-foot clout at Griffith Stadium in Washington.

Also new to the team in 1951 was pitcher Tom Morgan, a 21-year-old righthander, joining old pros Vic Raschi, Eddie Lopat, and Allie Reynolds. Whitey Ford was in military service, this being the first full year of the Korean conflict. By the end of the decade Tom Morgan would be at Los Angeles, the other 1951 pitchers retired, and Jackie Jensen with the Red Sox; but Mickey Mantle would just be hitting his stride. So, too, would Whitey Ford, who, like Mantle, played well

Transcendental Graphics

Mickey Mantle

into the 1960s. This was a decade in which the Yankees were virtually unstoppable. They won the pennant and the World Series in 1951, 1952, and 1953. They lost out in 1954 when the Cleveland Indians won an astonishing—and record-breaking—111 games (of a 154-game schedule for a .721 won-lost percentage), while the second-place Yanks won "only" 103.

But the Yanks bounced back in 1955, nosing out Cleveland, then losing the World Series for the first time ever to the arch rival Brooklyn Dodgers. It took the Dodgers seven games to do it, finally triumphing on Johnny Podres' shutout and Sandy Amoros's famous sixth-inning running catch of a Yogi Berra fly down the left-field line.

The Yanks won the pennant easily in 1956 and beat the Dodgers in another seven-game World Series, best remembered for the fifth-game Yankee victory in which Don Larsen, not a brilliant pitcher through most of his career, hurled a perfect game, 2-0. Not a batter reached base as the

Transcendental Graphics

Whitey Ford

rangy righthander, in his second season with the Yanks, threw just 97 pitches.

In 1957 and 1958 the Yankees again took pennants, losing the first Series to the Milwaukee Braves of Warren Spahn, Lew Burdette, Hank Aaron, and Eddie Mathews and winning the second against the same team, both in seven games.

Next season, 1959, brought trouble. Early on, the Yanks dropped into the cellar for the first time since 1940. In late May Casey Stengel, 68 years old, said, "We're having a bit of trouble with everything. You got nine guys not hitting, and the pitching isn't so hot either, and what are you going to do?" At season's end they were in third place, and Stengel, after orchestrating a decade of Yankee dominance, began to hear criticism.

George M. Weiss's last great trade brought Roger Maris to the Yankees in 1960 in a multi-player deal with the Kansas City Athletics (a consistent victim of the Yankees in such deals). Everyone knew that Maris had great potential—but

so did Norm Siebern, one of the Yanks that Weiss traded away. With the acquisition of Maris, a new Murderers' Row emerged in the early 1960s, consisting of Mantle, Maris, and Berra, along with first baseman Bill (Moose) Skowron, catcher-outfielder Elston Howard, and later, though briefly, Joe Pepitone and Tom Tresh.

For five more years, 1960 through 1964, the Yankees rode roughshod over the rest of the American League. Even the most fervent Yankee-haters could hardly have imagined what lay ahead. At the beginning of the 1960s, with the M & M Boys in the outfield and Whitey Ford, Bill Terry, and Jim Bouton on the mound, the Bronx Bombers looked about as tough as they ever had.

The M & M Boys

Mantle contributed 40 home runs in 1960 and Maris had 39 as the Yanks again won the pennant. In the World Series they suffered one of the more memorable upsets in Series history when in game seven they blew a 7-4 lead in the last of the eighth, tied the game at 9-9 in the top of the ninth, and then watched as Pittsburgh's second baseman Bill Mazeroski, not known as a power hitter, homered in the last of the ninth to give the Pirates a 10-9 victory and the World Championship. Five days after the season ended, the front office announced that Casey Stengel was retiring. In fact, after a triumphant decade at the helm of the Yankees he was being fired.

The big news in 1961 was not the league's expansion to ten teams, nor the performance of Ralph Houk as the Yanks' new manager, nor even the Yankees winning the pennant. Most people expected that. The big news in 1961 was the Mantle-Maris battle for the home run crown, ending in Maris's 61 homers, breaking Babe Ruth's season record, albeit with an asterisk since Ruth had done it in 154 games, Maris in 162 (although Maris accomplished the feat in fewer at-bats). Mantle ended the season with 54 homers, still good today for one of the top ten slots in that exclusive category.

The Yanks trounced Cincinnati in the World Series. When pitcher Whitey Ford extended his Series scoreless-inning streak to 32, he also broke a Babe Ruth Record. Back in 1918, as a Red Sox pitcher, Ruth had established the Series scoreless-inning mark at $29^2/_3$.

Maris dropped back to 33 home runs in 1962 and Mantle to 30, but the Yankees won the pennant. Ralph Terry led all American League pitchers with 23 wins, and second baseman Bobby Richardson led in hits with 209. For the last time in a long time the Yanks also won the Series, defeating San Francisco four games to three. It was a fine second season for manager Houk, and he repeated the performance in 1963, posting a 104–57 record, with Whitey Ford winning 24 games and Jim Bouton 21.

The World Series was another matter, as Los Angeles pitchers Sandy Koufax, Don Drysdale, and Johnny Podres tamed the Yankee sluggers, and the Dodgers swept the Series four games to none. At the end of the season, the Yankees announced that Ralph Houk would be moving up to the general manager's job and Yogi Berra would take over as field manager.

The Yankees struggled throughout 1964 but managed to prevail. They had Mantle, Maris, and Tresh in the outfield, Ellie Howard behind the plate, Joe Pepitone at first base, Bobby Richardson at second, Tony Kubek at short, and Clete Boyer at third. None of these players had a particularly good year—they all seemed to be getting old or injured at once.

When the Yanks lost the Series to St. Louis in seven games (despite Richardson's Series record 13 hits), Yogi Berra lost his job. Yankee

Transcendental Graphics

Yogi Berra

Roger Maris always knew that Yankee fans wanted Mickey Mantle, not him, to break Babe Ruth's single-season home run record—if indeed anyone was going to break it. He said as much, and he included the Yankee ball club among the rooters: "They were really rooting for Mantle to break the record, not me," he said. After all, Mantle had already led the league in homers four times, once, in 1956, with 52. Maris, a 27-year-old outfielder, was a newcomer to the Yanks, and while he had hit 39 home runs in 1960, no one would have predicted his 1961 home run explosion.

Sportswriter Jimmy Cannon, who was especially harsh on Maris, wrote: "The community of baseball feels Mantle is a great player. They consider Maris a thrilling freak who batted .269." Certainly, the 1961 home run race between the M & M Boys was thrilling. And although "freak" seems a bit strong, the truth is that Maris (a lifetime .260 hitter) had only one truly great season in his career.

In that respect he resembles such players as Jim Gentile of the 1961 Orioles, Zoilo Versalles of the 1965 Twins, and many others—the difference being that Maris broke a hallowed record set by baseball's greatest hero. Small wonder that Maris was later moved to say, "It would have been a helluva lot more fun if I'd never hit those 61 home runs.... All it brought me was headaches."

In 1961 it brought him persistent media attention, which he never cared for. When he hit his 61st homer off Tracy Stallard of the Red Sox on October 1, the last day of the season, the staid *New York Times* featured it in a three-column front-page story including the classic photo of Maris hitting it. As time went on, baseball fans have reluctantly begun to accept the fact that Maris's triumphant achievement was just that, a brilliant one-season feat, not a preposterous fluke. He broke the Babe's record, even if it took him 162 games. Since that October day more than 30 seasons have come and gone, and no one has topped Maris's total yet.

Photo: *Transcendental Graphics*

fans were outraged at the callousness of his firing, but Yogi was fortunate in a sense. The Yanks were about to fall apart, and it is unlikely that Berra or anyone else could have averted it.

Johnny Keane, whose Cardinals had edged Berra's team in the 1964 Series, piloted the 1965 and 1966 Yankees under the aegis of their new owner, the Columbia Broadcasting System. After the 1964 season CBS bought out Dan Topping and

Del Webb, fired long-time team announcer Mel Allen, and presided over what became general chaos. The team finished sixth in 1965 and last in 1966. When Keane got his walking papers at mid-season 1966, Houk returned to manage through 1973. After those three straight pennants, 1961-63, when the M & M Boys were at their peak, Houk never saw another one.

Retirements and trades devastated the Yankee powerhouse, and the free-agency draft (started in 1965) made rebuilding difficult and costly. Players like shortstop Horace Clarke, outfielder Hector Lopez, and catcher Jake Gibbs were adequate but not outstanding, while the pitching staff, with the exception of Mel Stottlemyre, who arrived in 1964, was ineffective.

In short, the once-mighty Yankees stumbled through the late 1960s and early 1970s, finishing ninth in 1967, fifth in 1968, fifth in 1969, a distant second in 1970, fourth in 1971, and fourth in 1972. Except for Stottlemyre's 20 or more wins in 1965, 1968, and 1969, few individual performances stood out. Beginning in 1969 outfielder Bobby Murcer connected for 20 or more homers for five consecutive seasons. Future All-Star catcher Thurman Munson joined the team in 1969.

Neither Murcer nor Munson made much immediate difference, however. These were obviously not the Yanks of old, and CBS began to have serious doubts about its $14 million investment. The prestige of the team, a main reason for the purchase, had been eroded by nearly a decade of lackluster play, and CBS faced the dismaying prospect of selling the franchise at a loss.

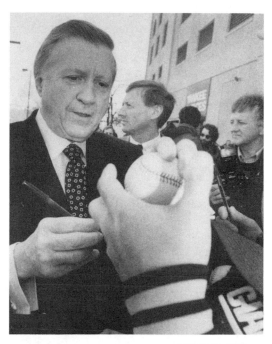

AP/Wide World Photos

George Steinbrenner

Steinbrenner to the Rescue

The management team that CBS fielded included Mike Burke, head of the division overseeing the Yankees, and general manager Lee MacPhail, son of Larry MacPhail. In 1973 Burke joined with George M. Steinbrenner III and others to buy the Yankees for $10 million. Steinbrenner, 42, a Cleveland shipbuilder, expressed satisfaction with the management team of Mike Burke and general manager Lee MacPhail, saying, "I'll stick to building ships," a statement that would come back to haunt him repeatedly.

In point of fact, Steinbrenner had Gabe Paul, Cleveland's GM, waiting in the wings to run the Yankees. When Burke learned of this, he resigned. Ralph Houk soon discovered that Steinbrenner had no intention of sticking to shipbuilding, and left after the 1973 season to manage the Tigers.

In 1974 Lee MacPhail moved on to head the American League.

Gabe Paul, upon becoming Yankee general manager, checked to see which players on the roster seemed worth saving. Among them were Mel Stottlemyre, Bobby Murcer, Thurman Munson, and Roy White. White, a good if unspectacular outfielder, would stay through 1979, spending his entire 15-year playing career with the Yankees.

Two other acquisitions added strength: relief ace Sparky Lyle from the Red Sox and third baseman Graig Nettles from the Indians. The most important addition, however, was a free agent who cost Steinbrenner big money—pitcher Catfish Hunter, coming off four straight 20+ winning seasons for the Oakland A's. Hunter's highly publicized five-year contract was worth $3.5 million.

Shrewd trades helped the Yankees, including the 1974 deal that brought first baseman Chris Chambliss and relief pitcher Dick Tidrow from

Cleveland. Another trade sent Murcer to the Giants in 1975 for Bobby Bonds, who in turn was dealt to the Angels for starting pitcher Ed Figueroa and outfielder Mickey Rivers. The team slowly bettered its position in the standings, finishing fourth in 1973, a close second in 1974, and third in 1975.

Rebuilding the Stadium and the Team

The Yankees were slowly rebuilding, obtaining less and less help from a fading farm system—with the notable exception of left-handed pitcher Ron Guidry, who arrived via Kingston, West Haven, and Syracuse. The House That Ruth Built needed major rebuilding, too. It was ultimately a $100 million dollar job, and it prompted the Yanks to play their 1974 and 1975 home games at Shea Stadium, the New York Mets' ballpark.

Pillars at Yankee Stadium were removed, elevators and escalators were installed, new and wider seats were put in, the outfield dimensions were changed, access roads to the ballpark were improved—but the famous facade remained.

In years past, starting in 1932 with a monument to Miller Huggins, the distant center field area had become a veritable Yankee Hall of Fame, with monuments honoring Ruth and Gehrig, plus a number of plaques. Though far from home plate, these memorials and the flagpole were all a part

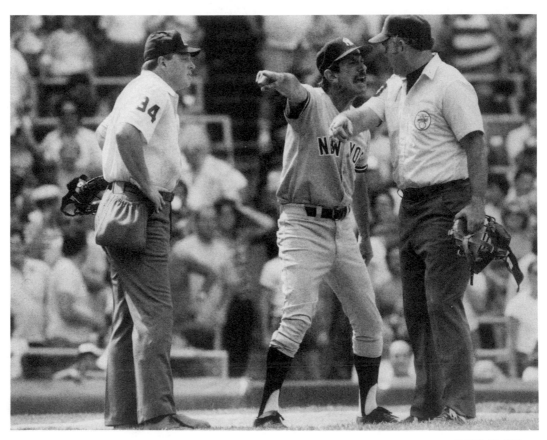

AP/Wide World Photos

Billy Martin (center) disagrees with an umpire's call

of the playing field. In 1937 Joe DiMaggio caught a homeric Hank Greenberg fly behind the flagpole, and manager Casey Stengel is reputed to have watched a long drive ricochet behind the monuments before shouting in exasperation, "Ruth, Gehrig, Huggins—someone throw the ball." In the rebuilt stadium these monuments and plaques were incorporated in the "Memorial Park" section, safely behind the outfield wall.

The new Yankee Stadium was ready for opening day 1976. Managing the team was 47-year-old ex-Yankee infielder Billy Martin, who had already managed the Twins, Tigers, and Rangers with some success and plenty of acrimony. Martin had finished up the 1975 season when Bill Virdon, a skipper perhaps too quiet for Steinbrenner, was released. Now Martin was on his own, a testy competitor but a skilled tactician, coordinating a solid lineup that included two recently acquired Yankees with bright futures: outfielder Lou Piniella and second baseman Willie Randolph.

Billy Martin always played to win, and the 1976 Yankees did win. They took the division title and the league championship. Then they ran into Cincinnati's "Big Red Machine" in the World Series and limped away after four straight losses.

Free Agents and Clubhouse Feuds

Free agency was made to order for free-spending George Steinbrenner, who seems to have viewed it as a quick way to obtain a new Murderers' Row. His first blockbuster purchase (after Catfish Hunter) brought heavy-hitting Oakland outfielder Reggie Jackson to the Yankees in 1976 after he had played out his option year in Baltimore.

Jackson, an exceedingly bright and gifted athlete, proved to be more skilled at self-promotion than at diplomacy. In spring training 1977 he referred to himself as "the straw that stirred the drink." [Thurman Munson was the team captain—the first since Lou Gehrig—and Reggie's remark did not help make him a clubhouse favorite.]

AP/Wide World Photos

Goose Gossage

Nevertheless, the Yankees, despite bitter internal dissention, went on to win the pennant that year. In the World Series against the Dodgers, Jackson pounded out nine hits, five of them home runs, and, unforgettably, three successive homers in the final game, each one on the first pitch, each one against a different pitcher, and each one farther than the previous blast. Thus he became "Mr. October."

The Yanks repeated as world champions in 1978, a year in which Ron Guidry went 25-3 with a 1.74 ERA and fireballing reliever Goose Gossage, signed as a free agent, joined Sparky Lyle, 1977's Cy Young winner, in the bullpen, giving the Yanks (unnecessarily) two of the best left-handed short relievers in baseball. Lyle departed the next year.

Reggie Jackson and Billy Martin continued to feud; Steinbrenner continued to interfere; and a frustrated Martin, angry at both his star and his boss, blurted out to reporters, "One's a born liar, the other's convicted." Steinbrenner had in fact been convicted of contributing illegally to President Nixon's reelection campaign, but it would have been wiser not to point it out.

Martin, anticipating his fate, resigned the next day, to be replaced by taciturn Bob Lemon, hired away from the Chicago White Sox. Under Lemon the Yanks won 48 of 68 games—including four lopsided victories over the Red Sox in September's "Boston Massacre." Even so, the Yankees and Red Sox tied for the division lead. A one-game playoff gave the Yanks the title when light-hitting shortstop Bucky Dent lofted a three-run homer in the seventh inning to erase a 2-0 Red Sox lead.

The Yanks went on to defeat Kansas City for the league title and then beat Los Angeles in the World Series. Mr. October banged out nine hits and drove in eight runs, matching his previous year's Series totals (except that he hit only two homers instead of five).

Manager Lemon started the 1979 season, but when the Yanks played barely .500 ball, a disappointed Steinbrenner decided to give Billy Martin a second chance. Under Martin the team did marginally better but could finish no higher than fourth, which led, predictably, to Billy's second dismissal.

Although the '79 Yanks had a disappointing season, they did produce a 20-game winner. He was veteran left-handed starter Tommy John, 21-9, another of Steinbrenner's assortment of free agents, who had toiled most recently for the Los Angeles Dodgers.

The 1979 season was marked by tragedy. In early August catcher Thurman Munson was landing his twin-engine Cessna Citation at the Akron-Canton airport. Something went wrong, the plane crashed, and Munson died in the flaming wreckage. The 32-year-old Yankee captain, the American League's Most Valuable Player in 1976, was eulogized by Bobby Murcer and Lou Piniella at the funeral in Canton, Ohio, and later mourned by thousands in a moving ceremony at Yankee Stadium.

Struggling Through the 1980s

No one could doubt that a persistent and costly attempt was being made to create a Yankee dynasty like those of old. In 1980 and again in the strike-shortened 1981 season the effort showed some signs of success. The Yanks took the division title in 1980 under new manager Dick Howser, winning 103 games, but then lost to Kansas City in the American League Championship Series. That three-game loss to K.C. cost Dick Howser his job as manager. Complaints began to mount that Steinbrenner's win-or-else policy was causing disaffection and would more likely lead to internal disarray than to a dynasty.

The Cassandras were right. Although the Yanks did not disintegrate—they had too much talent for that—neither did they live up to their owner's expectations. They lost the World Series to the Dodgers in 1981, four games to two. After that it was mostly downhill through the 1980s, but not all the way down.

By staying competitive (though not quite competitive enough) the Yankees won more games in the 1980s than any other major league team. They finished third in 1983 and 1984 and second in 1985 and 1986. Still, the days of consecutive .600+ winning seasons were over.

The Yankees had many fine individual players, including outfielder Dave Winfield. Acquired as a free agent in 1981 and signed with a no-trade clause, he played for the Yankees throughout the decade—despite a running feud with Steinbrenner, who contemptuously called him "Mr. May." The six-foot-six Winfield drove in more than 100 runs in six of nine seasons. His first year with the Yankees was Reggie Jackson's last, as Mr. October left via free agency for the California Angels.

In 1982 first baseman Don Mattingly, a homegrown product of the Yankee farm system, unusual in the 1980s, made his first major league appearance. From 1984 through 1987 Mattingly put up stats reminiscent of Lou Gehrig. The 1984 season was enlivened by a race for the batting title between Mattingly and Winfield. It went down to the final game before the new Yankee first base-

PROFILE — Don Mattingly

Just as the 1925 Yankees collapsed without the full-time services of Babe Ruth, so the 1990 Yankees plummeted when first baseman Don Mattingly went on the 90-day disabled list.

Mattingly, a six-time All-Star, won the American League batting title in 1984, his first full year in the majors. The next year he drove in 145 runs to lead the league.

The year after that, 1986, he collected 238 hits (an all-time Yankee record), while batting .352 and hitting 53 doubles. In 1987 he homered in eight straight games to tie a major league mark and connected for six grand slam home runs to set a new record.

These achievements are those of a superstar, and Mattingly was surely that for his first few seasons. But chronic back pains led to surgery, his batting average dropped, and his presumptive status as the game's best player had to be reassessed.

AP/Wide World Photos

man edged out his teammate, .343 to .340.

Yet even with all this talent, not to mention Dave Righetti, a left-handed pitcher who starred as both a starter and a reliever, the Yanks could not win consistently. Fans complained about a collection of squabbling prima donnas not functioning as a team.

And they wondered why the short-fused owner refused to back his managers through the least hint of adversity. Manager Gene Michael followed Howser, but soon gave way to Bob Lemon (again), who lost his job to Gene Michael (again), who lost his to Clyde King. Billy Martin returned for a third time, lost out to Yogi Berra, who in turn gave way to Billy Martin (again), who was replaced by Lou Piniella. Remarkably, Sweet Lou hung on for two seasons, 1986 and 1987, before Steinbrenner dismissed him in favor of Billy Martin (for the fifth and last time), then

Dallas Green, and finally Bucky Dent, to round out the 1980s.

The Yankees' best season of the decade was 1985 under Billy Martin (succeeding Yogi Berra who lasted only 16 games). Speedy Rickey Henderson, one of the best leadoff hitters in baseball and the best base-stealer ever, joined the club via free agency, having previously starred for the Oakland A's. Aging knuckleballer Phil Niekro had come over the year before, after 18 seasons with the Atlanta Braves.

Given these additions, plus Don Mattingly driving in 145 runs and Dave Winfield 114, the Yanks were in contention all the way. Both Henderson (.314) and Niekro (16-12) had excellent years. Ron Guidry won 22 games while losing only six. Nonetheless, the Toronto Blue Jays finished first, winning the pennant by two games.

As in the previous decade, the 1980s ended

on a note of tragedy when, on Christmas Day 1989, Billy Martin, 61, was killed in a motor vehicle accident in upstate New York.

Fall of Steinbrenner, Decline of the Yankees

On July 30, 1990, Commissioner Fay Vincent handed down a ruling that Yankee fans, fairly or unfairly, cheered. George Steinbrenner, the commissioner said, must remove himself from the day-to-day operations of the New York Yankees. Vincent based his decision on evidence gathered during a long investigation, showing that Steinbrenner had paid a known gambler, Howard Spira, $40,000, presumably to try to uncover information that would damage the reputation of Dave Winfield and the Dave Winfield Foundation. Winfield and Steinbrenner had been at odds for a long time, but this particular act, Vincent declared, was not in the best interests of baseball.

Steinbrenner stepped down on August 20, as ordered, naming Robert Nederlander, one of the Yankees' limited partners, to run the organization. Rumors of Steinbrenner's eventual return circulated almost from the day he left.

The Yanks finished last in 1990, losing 95 games, with few bright spots to pierce the gloom. One glimmer was the emergence of outfielder Roberto Kelly. He led the team with a .285 batting average and stole 42 bases. Another ray of hope was rookie first baseman Kevin Maas, who replaced the injured Don Mattingly during the season. Maas set a major league record by hitting 15 home runs in the shortest span of time ever recorded in a major league career.

A slight but definite improvement in 1991 raised the Yankees from last place to fifth, but there was still little to cheer about. Second baseman Steve Sax, traded to the White Sox at the end of the season, led the team with a .304 batting average, while outfielder Mel Hall drove in the most runs, 80. The only pitcher to win in double figures was righthander Scott Sanderson, 16-10. The 1992 season was slightly better, but 1993 proved to be a breakthrough year. With a good blend of experience and youth, the Yankees played inspired ball for much of the season.

Tied for the division lead on August 29, the Yankees could not keep pace with the surging Toronto Blue Jays and finished in second place, seven games back, with an 88-74 record. A revived Mattingly batted .291 with 17 homers and 86 RBIs, while Danny Tartabull added 31 homers and 102 RBIs, and Mike Stanley hit .305 with 26 homers and 84 RBIs. Pitcher Jimmy Key went 18-6 with a 3.00 ERA, and Jim Abbott, despite a sub-par year overall, threw a no-hitter on September 4 against Cleveland.

Whether the Yankees will produce a fourth dynasty remains to be seen. George Steinbrenner's goal when he took over the team in 1973 was to restore it to what he considered its rightful place in baseball. He seemed to be doing that in the late 1970s, but things never quite came together again after Munson's death, the 1981 players' strike, and the departure of Reggie Jackson.

The recent Yankee teams have had some powerful hitters but have too frequently lacked enough reliable starting pitchers, a prerequisite (despite all the media emphasis on Ruth, Gehrig, DiMaggio, Mantle, and Maris) that made the first three dynasties possible.

Although Steinbrenner's own future remains uncertain, the franchise is one with a proud past, a profitable present, and a promising future. Almost certainly there are some great Yankee teams on (or just beyond) the horizon. A new baseball dynasty, on the other hand, whether of the Yankees or of some other team, is perhaps as iridescent a vision as the one that saw George Steinbrenner sticking to shipbuilding.

SOURCES

BOOKS

Allen, Maury, *Damn Yankee,* Times Books, 1980.

Anderson, Dave, Murray Chass, Robert Creamer, and Harold Rosenthal, *The Yankees: The Four Fabulous Eras of Baseball's Most Famous Team,* Random House, 1979.

Appel, Marty, "New York Yankees: Pride, Tradition, and a Bit of Controversy."

Encyclopedia of Major League Baseball Team Histories: American League, edited by Peter J. Bjarkman, Meckler, 1991.

Baseball Guide: 1992 Edition, The Sporting News Publishing Co., 1992.

Baseball Register: 1992 Edition, The Sporting News Publishing Co., 1992.

Forker, Dom, *The Men of Autumn: An Oral History of the 1949-53 World Champion New York Yankees,* Taylor Publishing Company, 1989.

Gallagher, Mark, *The Yankee Encyclopedia,* Leisure Press, 1982.

Golenbock, Peter, *Dynasty: The New York Yankees, 1949-1964,* Prentice Hall, 1975.

Graham, Frank, *The New York Yankees,* G.P. Putnam's Sons, 1943.

Honig, Donald, *Baseball's 10 Greatest Teams,* Macmillan, 1982.

Honig, Donald, *The New York Yankees: An Illustrated History,* Crown Publishers, 1981.

Ivor-Campbell, Frederick, "Team Histories: New York Yankees," *Total Baseball,* edited by John Thorn and Pete Palmer, Warner Books, 1989.

Lally, Dick, *Pinstriped Summers: Memories of Yankee Seasons Past,* Arbor House, 1985.

Lowry, Philip J., *Green Cathedrals,* Society for American Baseball Research, 1986.

Lyle, Sparky, and Peter Golenbock, *The Bronx Zoo,* Crown Publishers, 1979.

Mayer, Ronald A., *The 1937 Newark Bears: A Baseball Legend,* Wm. H. Wise & Company, 1980.

Murdock, Eugene C., *Ban Johnson: Czar of Baseball,* Greenwood Press, 1982.

Reichler, Joseph L., editor, *The Baseball Encyclopedia,* 7th edition, Macmillan, 1988.

Reidenbaugh, Lowell, *Take Me Out to the Ball Park,* The Sporting News Publishing Co., 1983.

Thorn, John, and John Holway, *The Pitcher,* Prentice Hall, 1987.

Tullius, John, *I'd Rather Be a Yankee: An Oral History of America's Most Loved and Hated Baseball Team,* Macmillan, 1986.

Vogt, David Quentin, *American Baseball: From the Commissioners to Continental Expansion,* University Park: The Pennsylvania State University Press, 1983.

PERIODICALS

New York Daily News, June 13, 1992.

New York Times, April 22, 1903; July 12, 1927; July 17, 1927; October 10, 1928; July 5, 1939; October 2, 1961; September 22, 1986.

New York Times Magazine, March 9, 1952.

Sporting News, January 17, 1903; June 22, 1992.

—*Gerald Tomlinson* for Book Builders, Inc.

TORONTO BLUE JAYS

At this point in major league history, only the New York Mets have risen as far and as fast after expansion as the Toronto Blue Jays. Every expansion team has had to make do with a combination of untried rookies and over-the-hill veterans. The Blue Jays were no exception. In 1977, the first year of major league baseball in Toronto, the team lost 107 games. A year later they lost 102. The year after that they lost 109—the same number as the Mets in their third year. In Toronto, as in New York, the team attracted plenty of dedicated fans from the start, however. And in Toronto, as in New York, the organization had a well-thought-out plan for improvement.

The Blue Jays, under manager Bobby Mattick, remained mired in last place in 1980 and in both halves of the strike-interrupted 1981 season. Bobby Cox took over as manager in 1982, and that year for the first time the Blue Jays left the cellar—almost. They finished in a tie with Cleveland for sixth place. But that ended their misery. In 1983 they went from losers to winners, 89-73, to finish in fourth place, nine games back. After an identical won-lost record and a second-place finish the next year, the Blue Jays vaulted into first place in 1985, winning 99 games in their ninth season in the majors. (The Mets had won 100 in their eighth year.)

Toronto had assembled one of the best outfields in baseball by this time—Jesse Barfield, Lloyd Moseby, and George Bell—along with a solid pitching staff that included Dave Stieb, Jimmy Key, and Tom Henke. Nevertheless, the Blue Jays lost the American League Championship Series to the Kansas City Royals. It was a close, hard-fought battle in which Toronto jumped off to a lead of three games to one only to blow the final three games.

After three seasons out of the money (though very close in two of those seasons, including a 96-66 second-place finish in 1986), the Blue Jays, under manager Clarence (Cito) Gaston, returned to first place in the American League East in 1989. They could not prevail against Tony LaRussa's Oakland A's in the ALCS, however, and still had to wait for their chance to compete in a World Series.

The Red Sox edged out the Blue Jays for first place in 1990. But in 1991 the magic was back, though the personnel had changed considerably, and Toronto won the division championship, only to lose once more in the ALCS, this time to the Minnesota Twins.

Finally, Cito Gaston's Blue Jays took the division championship in 1992, knocked off the AL West champion Oakland A's in the league playoffs, and went on to defeat the Atlanta Braves in the World Series. Pitcher Jack Morris, acquired from the Twins, posted a 21-6 record in the regular season and won two World Series games. Catcher Pat Borders collected nine hits in 20 at-bats in the fall classic and was named Series MVP.

Opening Day!

Toronto had to wait a long time for major league baseball. Although A. G. Spalding is said to have suggested in 1886 that the Canadian metropolis would made a good site for a National League franchise, the city instead became one of the mainstays of the International League in the high minors.

For 72 consecutive years, from 1895 to 1967, the Toronto Maple Leafs fielded teams in the International League, often featuring former or future major leaguers. In the 1960s, as major league fever swept Toronto, attendance at Maple Leaf games declined precipitously, and the franchise went to Louisville for 1968.

In January 1976 a group of Toronto investors, headed by Donald J. McDougall, president of Labatts Breweries, almost latched onto the National League franchise of the financially strapped San Francisco Giants. The deal fell through, but that same year the American League voted to expand to 14 teams and announced that franchises would be offered to Toronto and Seattle. The entry fee of $7 million was only about half of what the Toronto consortium, which also included Robert Howard Webster, chairman of *The Globe and Mail* newspaper, had been prepared to pay for the Giants. The nickname Blue Jays, chosen in a "Name That Team" contest, was suggested in 154 of more than 30,000 separate entries.

One of the key appointments to the new Blue Jay staff was Pat Gillick as vice-president for player personnel. Gillick, until then the farm director of the Yankees, had a tough job. Time and events—a pennant within a decade—would prove how expertly he performed it.

Work soon began on modifying and improving Exhibition Stadium, which had been built in 1959 for football. Opening day at the Toronto ballpark, April 7, 1977, was a better day for skiing than for baseball. The temperature stood right at the freezing mark, and snow showers greeted the 44,649 hardy fans who showed up in parkas, overcoats, and snow suits, stomping their approval (and keeping their feet warm) in lumberjack boots and galoshes.

The visiting Chicago White Sox, no strangers to cold weather, jumped off to a 2-0 lead when Richie Zisk clouted a two-run homer in the top of the first inning. In the bottom half of the same inning, a rookie first baseman for the Blue Jays, Doug Ault, lined a Ken Brett pitch over the wall in left center field.

Two historians of the early Blue Jays, Phillippe van Rjndt and Pat Blednick, wrote that "the reaction rivaled the pandemonium generated by Moses's parting of the Red Sea. The bitter cold, the cached booze [the sale of alcohol was not allowed in the stadium at that time], the wailing kids, everything went out the window as 44,000 rose to their feet in an ovation that would have gone over well in Rome's Coliseum. It was TRIUMPH!...HEROISM!...TOTAL EUPHORIA!"

And that was only the beginning. Ault, a tall Texan, homered again in the third inning.

TEAM INFORMATION AT A GLANCE

Founding date: 1977

Home stadium: The SkyDome
300 Bremner Boulevard
Toronto, Ontario, Canada M5V 3B3
Dimensions: Left-field line—328 feet
Center field—400 feet
Right-field line—328 feet
Power alleys—375 feet

Seating capacity: 50,516

Team uniforms: Home—base color white, with blue-and-red club logo over left chest; word "Blue
Jays" in dark blue split lettering with white center arched over chest above logo.
Road—base color gray, with blue-and-red club logo over left chest; word "Blue Jays"
in dark blue split lettering with white center arched over chest above logo
Team nickname: Blue Jays.
Logo: Stylized blue jay imposed over red outline of a baseball, with a solid
red maple leaf behind the bird's crest; words "Toronto Blue Jays"
in medium blue split lettering around outline of baseball

Franchise record	Won	Lost	Pct.
(1977-1993)	1,351	1,344	.501

World Series wins (2): 1992, 1993
American League championships (2): 1992, 1993
American League East first-place finishes (5): 1985, 1989, 1991, 1992, 1993
League/division last-place finishes (5): 1977, 1978, 1979, 1980, 1981

The world of major league baseball might soon forget Doug Ault, but not that crowd at wind-blown, snow-swept Exhibition Stadium on April 7, 1977. He was the first Blue Jay hero.

"We Want Beer!"

The opening day throng chanted, "We want beer!," happily oblivious to the fact that hot coffee might have been more appropriate. It took five years for the stadium to begin serving beer, and even when it did (in 1981) the Blue Jays were still flailing about in the cellar. The Jays won their opening day game, 9-5, but lost 107 games during that first season.

Nonetheless, they had a .310 hitter, Bob Bailor, and an American League Player of the Month, Otto Velez (in April, no less). Pitcher Dave Lemanczyk's 13-16 won-lost record was noteworthy for a last-place expansion team. Another pitcher, Jim Clancy, up from Jersey

When the Toronto Blue Jays played their inaugural game on April 7, 1977, it was in a stadium—the Canadian National Exhibition facility—that had been built for football. Exhibition Stadium was an elongated structure open at one end with plenty of seats along what, in football games, were the sidelines. Major reconstruction was needed to make the stadium serve for baseball. More seats had to be installed, and an outfield fence had to be built. When the fence was in place, a sizable open expanse of grass remained beyond the right-field barrier—the rest of the football field, actually.

The expansion Blue Jays made Exhibition Stadium their home for the first 12½ years. They went from a 107-loss, last-place finish in their first season to a 99-win, first-place finish in their ninth season. In a memorable game on June 26, 1978, the Blue Jays pummelled the Baltimore Orioles 24-10, scoring nine runs in the second inning. In that blow-out inning the Jays' second baseman Dave McKay and outfielder Otto Velez each hit two doubles. It was one of many big days at Exhibition Stadium.

Nevertheless, from the beginning it was assumed that the CNE grounds were only a temporary home for the Blue Jays. Sooner or later Toronto fans would have a true baseball stadium to call their own. It was later rather than sooner. Groundbreaking ceremonies for Toronto's futuristic SkyDome took place in October 1986. The stadium was to have a retractable roof that could be opened or closed in less than half an hour. At the north end of the stadium would stand a 364-room hotel with 70 rooms overlooking the playing field. Not everyone was pleased with the venture. Amid controversies over financing, construction delays, cost overruns, and worries about traffic jams, the new architectural and technological wonder took shape. It was to open for the 1989 season, but work on it was not yet completed.

Finally, with the job still not wholly done, the Blue Jays met the Milwaukee Brewers in the first American League game in the SkyDome. The Jays' Jimmy Key pitched and lost, and the Brewers' Paul Molitor got the first hit in the new ballpark. Fred McGriff of Toronto provided some solace for the hometown fans, however, blasting the first SkyDome homer.

The Blue Jays always drew well at Exhibition Stadium, which had a seating capacity of 43,737; but in the SkyDome, seating 50,516, attendance went right through the retractable roof. In 1991 the Blue Jays chalked up 4,001,526 paid admissions. No other major league baseball team came anywhere near that number.

City in the Eastern League, did less well (4-9) but was destined to spend 13 seasons with the Blue Jays.

Toronto's manager, Roy Hartsfield, a former second baseman for the Boston Braves, had no reason to be disappointed. No one expected a winning season; many of the lost games were close ones; and 1,701,052 fans kept the turnstiles clicking from April to October.

Bailor, Velez, Lemanczyk, and Clancy returned for the 1978 campaign, but there were also many new faces. Among them were two old veterans, both bona fide home run hitters—outfielder Rico Carty, recently of the Cleveland Indians, and first baseman John Mayberry, from the Kansas City Royals. They lived up to their prior stats, Carty slamming 20 homers before being traded to Oakland (where he hit 11 more), and Mayberry connecting for 22. Pitcher Jim Clancy won 10 games while losing 12, but Dave Lamanczyk dropped to 4-14 with a 6.26 ERA. The Blue Jays lost 102 games to finish in seventh place again, 40 games back.

Things had to get better for the Blue Jays, but not in 1979. Whatever building was going on—and much was—it had yet to become evident in the standings. Roy Hartsfield's last year at the helm saw the team lose 109 games and finish the season all but out of sight, 50½ behind first-place Baltimore.

The Blue Jays were last in the AL East in hitting, last in pitching, and last in fielding, but there was one bright spot amid the gloom. A young pitcher from Santa Ana, California, started the season at Class A Dunedin, moved up quickly to Triple-A Syracuse, and in early June reported to the Blue Jays. He was Dave Stieb; and his 8-8 record for hapless Toronto in 1979 was an encouraging portent. Shortstop Alfredo Griffin's .287 batting average led the team, and Mayberry repeated as home run leader with 21.

Still Seventh, but....

Bobby Mattick, a pre-World War II shortstop for the Cubs and the Reds, took over as manager of the Blue Jays in 1980. Toronto was still going nowhere in the standings, although at last, in the fourth year of the franchise, the team succeeded in losing fewer than 100 games. In fact, some quite positive things happened in 1980. Jim Clancy won 13 games, and Dave Stieb won 12. On the other hand, they lost 16 and 15 respectively, but these were two solid starting pitchers, in need of some support at the plate.

Despite the fact that first baseman John Mayberry belted 30 home runs and DH Otto Velez hit 20, the team's combined batting average was 16 points below that of the next weakest-hitting team in the division—which, curiously enough, was the pennant-winning Yankees. But help was on the way for the Blue Jays.

During the 1980 season the arrival of outfielder Lloyd Moseby, a product of the Blue Jays' farm system, put a rising star on the Toronto roster. Later in the season, Willie Upshaw, the first baseman in Toronto's future, moved up from the minors as well. Cautious optimism seemed in order for 1981.

The lengthy players' union strike of 1981 created a muddle in the standings, resulted in a split season with an odd playoff arrangement, and left many individual and team totals looking puny. For example, Dave Stieb won 11 games in the strike-shortened season (losing 10—the first winning season for a Toronto starter). That record is more impressive than it sounds, for no pitcher in the majors won more than 14 games in a year that saw the teams play fewer than 110 games.

Bobby Mattick, still managing the Blue Jays, could not have been happy about the first half of the split season. His ball club got off to a wretched start, 16 wins against 42 losses, for a won-lost percentage of .276. On May 15 an unheralded fast-ball pitcher for the Cleveland Indians, Len Barker, who would go 6-6 that year, hurled the twelfth perfect game in the history of the major leagues, defeating the Blue Jays, 3-0.

In retrospect, Toronto shortstop Alfredo Griffin almost ruined Barker's perfect game on the first pitch. He sent a slow roller toward the shortstop, and Cleveland's Tom Veryzer, on a nice play, threw the speedy Griffin out by an eyelash.

The second half of 1981 was considerably better than the first for the Blue Jays. In fact, they played .500 ball until the very end of the season, when they began to lose, falling to a 21-27 mark. George Bell briefly joined Lloyd Moseby in the outfield, but while Moseby had come to Toronto to stay, Bell still needed more seasoning at Syracuse. Jesse Barfield also appeared briefly in the Blue Jays' outfield, coming up from Double-A Knoxville near the end of the season.

Ernie Whitt spent his second of 10 full seasons behind the plate for the Blue Jays. Danny Ainge, in his third year as a part-time infielder, batted .187 and decided to pursue a career with the Boston Celtics, shooting baskets rather than scooping up grounders. Overall, the 1981 Blue Jays showed marginal improvement, if that, over the previous year's team, and few were surprised when Bobby Mattick got his walking papers.

Dave Stieb: Never a 20-Game Winner

Dave Stieb was the all-time ace of Toronto Blue Jay moundsmen. A native of Santa Ana, California, he was chosen by the Jays in the fifth round of the free-agent draft on June 6, 1978, in the second year of the ball club's existence. Stieb was assigned to Dunedin of the Florida State League, where during that year and the next he won seven games without a loss, earning a promotion to Triple-A Syracuse. He did so well at the higher level (5-2 with a 2.12 ERA) that Toronto called him up.

In his second year as a pro he was pitching in the majors—and holding his own, doing very well, in fact, for a last-place team. A six-foot-one-inch righthander, Stieb broke even in 1979, going 8-8, then 12-15 in 1980, and in strike-shortened 1981 (still a last-place finish for the Jays) he posted a winning record, 11-10. In 1980 and 1981 Stieb made the American League All-Star team.

Over the next four seasons he won consistently—17 games in 1982 and 1983, 16 in 1984, and 14 in 1985. He was the class of the Toronto pitching staff as the Jays made their way from worst to first. In 1986 Stieb, like the team itself, suffered a setback, he won only seven games and lost 12. But he came right back, winning 13, 16, 17, and 18 games over the next four years.

He never won 20 games in a season, though. One reason was that the Blue Jays, weak on offense, often lost the close games, the pitcher's duels, the very games Stieb was likely to be in. Then, too, Stieb's contract had a clause calling for bonus payments based on the number of innings pitched, a clause rewarding the organization for using him sparingly. He did finally pitch a no-hitter—but only after three brilliant one-hitters, each of which went down to the last out before a batter spoiled his effort.

On September 11, 1988, it was Julio Franco of the Cleveland Indians whose bad-hop, two-out, ninth inning single erased Stieb's no-hitter. Six days later, at Baltimore, a two-out, ninth-inning pinch hitter for the Orioles, Jim Traber, singled to right field to nix what could have been Stieb's second straight no-hitter. Less than a year later, on August 4, 1989, Stieb lost not merely a no-hitter but a perfect game when, with two down in the ninth inning, the Yankees' Roberto Kelly doubled to left field, leaving the Blue Jay ace (and the Toronto franchise) still without a no-hit game on the books. The year after that, however, Dave Stieb got what he had been denied for so long. On September 2, 1990, he pitched a 3-0 no-hit victory over the Indians.

What Stieb did not get in 1990 was 20 wins. After racking up 11 victories in the first half of the season, he could win only seven games thereafter. His 18-6 record that year was his best ever, but he lost his last three starts.

Blue Jays Rising

After five consecutive seasons in the American League East basement, it was clearly time for the Blue Jays to move up. Their farm system was starting to produce real major leaguers. Pitcher Dave Stieb was showing clear improvement from year to year. Jim Clancy and Luis Leal had the potential to break out of the doldrums. Lloyd Moseby, George Bell, and Jesse Barfield had the potential to become an all-star outfield.

But so far this was nearly all promise, not performance. The man who took over as skipper for 1982 would be expected to deliver on the promise. That man was Bobby Cox, an ex-Yankee infielder and, more recently, manager of the struggling but improving Atlanta Braves. In his first year at Toronto, 1982, Cox led the Blue Jays to a sixth-place tie with Cleveland.

Willie Upshaw, replacing John Mayberry at first base, paced the team in homers (21) and RBIs (75). Second baseman Damaso Garcia, in his third year with the Blue Jays, hit .310. At shortstop was the veteran Alfredo Griffin, while a steady new third baseman, Rance Mulliniks, arrived from Kansas City via a trade for Phil Huffman, an undistinguished pitcher (6-18 for the Blue Jays in 1979).

On the mound for Toronto were Dave Stieb (17-14), Jim Clancy (16-14), and Luis Leal (12-15). These Blue Jay players, on a team that barely escaped the cellar in 1982, would with the exception of Griffin be on hand to celebrate a division title three years later. So would long-time catcher Ernie Whitt and outfielders Lloyd Moseby and Jesse Barfield. Pat Gillick and the rest of the Toronto organization had handled the expansion franchise well. Their efforts were about to pay off.

In 1983 the numbers in the win column finally surpassed those in the loss column. The Blue Jays finished only nine games behind division-champion Baltimore, although two other teams, Detroit and New York, also came in ahead of them. Stieb, Clancy, and Leal all improved their records. Stieb (17-12) ranked third in the league in ERA (3.04), strikeouts (187), and complete games (14). Veteran pitcher Doyle Alexander was acquired from the Yankees late in the season, an addition that proved valuable then and later.

Moseby, in his best major league season so far, hit .315, while Garcia batted .307 and Upshaw .306. The team's home run production jumped from 106 in 1982 to 167 in 1983, with Upshaw (27), Barfield (27), and newly acquired designated hitter Cliff Johnson (22) leading the way. The Blue Jays, who had been AL East patsies for six seasons, were victims no longer. They were contenders.

Toronto's high hopes for the 1984 season were quickly shattered, however—as were those of other AL East contenders—when the Detroit Tigers came out of the gate like a racehorse, winning all but four of their first 39 games and leaving the rest of the field in the dust. Bobby Cox's Blue Jays won 89 games, good for second place, but Sparky Anderson's Tigers won 104, outdistancing Toronto by 15 games.

The season's surprise batting champ of the Blue Jays was much-travelled outfielder Dave Collins, who had been platooned with Jesse Barfield. Collins came to the Blue Jays from the Yankees in 1983 and put in a career year, hitting .308, stealing 60 bases (just six fewer than the A's Rickey Henderson), and sharing with teammate Lloyd Moseby the league lead in triples with 15.

The 1984 season also marked George Bell's debut as a full-time Blue Jay outfielder. He responded by belting 39 doubles, 26 homers, driving in 87 runs, and batting .292. Stieb (16-8), Alexander (17-6), and Leal (13-8) anchored a strong pitching staff. This Toronto team, once so laughable, appeared to have everything—hitting, pitching, fielding, base running, and esprit de corps. Barring a miraculous repeat performance by the Detroit Tigers at the start of the next season, the Blue Jays stood a good chance of finishing atop the AL East in 1985.

Payoff '85

The Toronto bullpen had not matched the effectiveness of the starting rotation even after the free-agency acquisition of Dennis Lamp in 1984. For the 1985 season, Tom Henke came up from Triple-A Syracuse, after having seen limited action previously with the Texas Rangers. Bobby Cox hoped that the combination of Lamp and Henke, along with Blue Jay veteran Jim Acker and free-agent Bill Caudill, would solidify the bullpen in 1985. It did.

Exhibition Stadium saw a record outpouring of fans that year—2,468,928 of them—as the Blue Jays battled for the top spot in the American League East. Detroit faltered, the Yankees improved, and the high-flying Jays took over first place in mid-May, leaving no doubt throughout the summer that they were the team to beat. It all came down in the end to a weekend series with the Yankees. On October 5, ex-Yankee Doyle Alexander, now a Blue Jay stalwart working on a 17-10 season, pitched Toronto to a 5-1 victory over the Yanks. The Blue Jays had done it. After just nine seasons, five of them in the cellar, they were champions of their division.

Who were the heroes? The whole team. Or, to look at it another way, Pat Gillick and the front office were the heroes. Their trades had been mostly good, and their farm system had quickly developed into an impressive producer of quality players.

Still, in order to win, a team needs nine men on the field. The 1985 Blue Jays had a formidable outfield in Barfield, Moseby, and Bell, who collectively banged 73 homers and drove in 250 runs. The infield had been improved by the full-time use of Tony Ferdandez at shortstop. Ferdandez, one of the gifted corps of ballplayers (including George Bell) who have come from San Pedro de Macoris in the Dominican Republic, hit .289 in his first full season as a major leaguer. The rest of the infield, the now familiar trio of Upshaw, Garcia, and Mulliniks, had good years. Behind the plate, the reliable Ernie Whitt served his sixth consecutive full season.

Among the pitchers the most startling record belonged to Dennis Lamp—11 wins, 0 losses, every win coming in relief. Dave Stieb's 14-13 mark was subpar for him, but his 2.48 ERA led the league. Left-hander Jimmy Key, coming off a 4-5 rookie season, went 14-6 with a 3.00 ERA. If there were no superstar-level statistics among the youthful 1985 Blue Jays, there was a high degree of competence and consistency that made continued success likely.

That success did not come in the American League Championship Series, though. The Blue Jays came close, winning three games and losing three, before Kansas City's Jim Sundberg broke open the hard-fought seventh game with a three-run triple in the sixth inning to give the Royals the AL pennant. There was disappointment in Toronto, but there was also the feeling that next year would be at least as good, and maybe better.

From Jimy to Cito

Manager Bobby Cox took off for Atlanta, where he became vice-president and general manager of the Braves, a ball club clearly in need of help. To fill his shoes in 1986, the Blue Jays chose Jimy Williams, a retired shortstop from the Cardinals' organization. (In their first decade the Blue Jays seemed to have a special liking for ex-infielders as managers.) Williams's Blue Jays learned to their dismay how hard it is to repeat as division champions.

Although they made a determined drive for the title in August, getting to within 3½ games of the pacesetting Boston Red Sox, they faltered in September, finishing in fourth place. It was the year their pitching deserted them. Dave Stieb and Jimmy Key both failed to win in their first six tries, and Stieb ended the season at a disappointing 7-12. Key bounced back to record a 14-11 season. Doyle Alexander, who had won 17 games in 1984 and again in 1985, faltered and asked to be traded. The Jays dealt him to Atlanta.

An unexpected pitching bonus appeared in the person of Mark Eichhorn, a rookie sidearm reliever who blossomed overnight into a dazzling hurler with a tough sinker and a bewildering changeup. (Said Dusty Baker of the Oakland A's, "I've never seen anybody throw that slow.") Eichhorn posted a 14-6 record, and his 1.76 ERA would have led the league easily, but he fell five innings short of qualifying.

The Blue Jay offense showed some punch. Jesse Barfield belted 40 homers, scored 107 runs, and drove in 108 runs—all team records at the time. He hit .289, had a slugging average of .559 (second in the AL), and his rifle arm put him at the top of the league in outfield assists for the second straight year. George Bell hit .309, slugged .532 (good for fourth in the league), and tied Barfield for the team record in RBIs

That Championship Outfield
PROFILES

When the Blue Jays won their first division title in 1985, their regular outfielders were Jesse Barfield in right, Lloyd Moseby in center, and George Bell in left. This outfield was hailed at the time as something special, although none of the three players had a career year in 1985. If Barfield, Moseby, and Bell had put their best years together in one sunlit season, the results would have looked like this:

• **Jesse Barfield** (1986), rf, .289 In 1986 Jesse Barfield led the league in home runs with 40. He scored 107 runs and drove in 108. His slugging average of .559 was second in the league to Don Mattingly's. Barfield's strong, accurate arm made him a terror to baserunners, and in 1986, as in a few other years, he led the league in assists.

• **Lloyd Moseby** (1987), cf, .282 Although Moseby was an All-Star pick in 1983, batting .315 and hitting 15 triples to tie for the league lead, his best season was 1987. He belted 26 homers that year, scored 106 runs, and drove in 96. Moseby received less media attention than Barfield and Bell, but he was a solid Blue Jay asset for ten seasons.

• **George Bell** (1987), lf, .308 George Bell's most productive year was, like Moseby's, 1987, when the Blue Jays finished second. His 47 homers eclipsed Barfield's prior team record but fell two short of matching Oakland's Mark McGwire's total for the year. Bell's 134 RBIs and 369 total bases led the league. His slugging percentage, .605, like his home run total, was second to McGwire's.

This was a very good outfield indeed, though scarcely in a class with the 1927 Yankees' trio of bombardiers—Babe Ruth, Earl Combs, and Bob Meusel. Still, it is almost impossible for an organization to put three star-quality players in the outfield in any given year. The Blue Jays met the challenge in 1985 with Barfield, Moseby, and Bell.

with 108. Another stellar performer was shortstop Tony Fernandez, who paced the team in hitting at .310 and led all AL shortstops in fielding at .983.

This team had the look of contenders, and in 1987, once again, they challenged all the way, although as Blue Jays' historian Peter J. Bjarkman points out, the season could fittingly be labeled "The Year of the Ultimate Collapse." The dramatic end-of-season choke, in which the Jays could not win a single needed game out of three with the title-winning Tigers, landed them in second place, two games out.

Even George Bell, enjoying a memorable MVP season, slumped in the crucial final week. Bell, batting .308 for the season, convincingly erased the previous year's team-high home run and RBI records. He unloaded 47 homers in 1987 and drove in 134 runs, to lead fellow outfielders Barfield and Moseby, who had fine seasons themselves.

Despite this impressive outfield, however, and despite the noteworthy debut of rookie first baseman Fred McGriff—not to mention the fine 96-66 record—Williams's talent-laden Blue Jays were themselves also-rans for a second time.

Williams got another chance in 1988, and again the team came up short. They finished in a tie for third place, two games back. Bell feuded and sulked over his designated-hitter role, coming, as it did, on the heels of a superb season (though not so superb on defense, where Bell was sometimes a bit shaky).

Then there were injuries to Tony Fernandez, Jimmy Key, and others. The most remarkable story of the season involved Dave Stieb's two consecutive missed no-hitters, each lost on what was potentially the last pitch of the ballgame.

A strong finish could not obscure the fact that the Blue Jays, a team with undeniable pennant potential, had failed again to win its division title. A bit surprisingly, Williams got a contract to manage for a fourth season. He lasted only 36 games, however, when a 12-24 record and sixth place in the standings convinced the front office it was time for a change. Into the breach stepped Clarence (Cito) Gaston, the 45-year-old Toronto batting coach, who was viewed as a stop-gap skipper.

But while the executives looked for a permanent replacement (ex-Yankee manager Lou Piniella was said to be favored) the Blue Jays started to fly high under Gaston. Consequently, the former National League outfielder (breaking the infielder rut) got the managerial job for keeps, becoming the third black skipper in major league history.

Triumph at the SkyDome

Cito Gaston had his work cut out for him. The Blue Jays' organization believed it had a winning team, a first-place team, and expected to be proven right. But when Gaston took over the club, it had already racked up two dozen losses against only a dozen wins. Quite a reversal would be needed—and quite a reversal is what occurred. Under Gaston the 1989 Jays played at a .611 clip, versus .333 under Williams.

The Blue Jays were supposed to open the 1989 season in their spectacular new SkyDome stadium, an architectural marvel with an immense retractable roof—just the thing for the kind of weather that had marked the Blue Jays' frigid, windswept inaugural game back in 1977. No more games in a football stadium where bold Lake Ontario seagulls swooped down to claim dropped peanuts, popcorn, and Crackerjacks in the late innings, as fainthearted spectators began to leave.

Fans called the oblong bowl the "Big Bird Feeder" and referred to the circling gulls as "S— Hawks." There would be little nostalgia for the old ball park.

As it turned out, however, the Toronto faithful had to put up with Exhibition Stadium for a couple of extra months, well into the 1989 season, because of construction delays on the Sky-Dome. The extra time gave third baseman Kelly Gruber a chance to hit for the cycle on April 16 at Exhibition Stadium, the first Blue Jay to accomplish that feat.

And then on May 4, still in the old ballpark, rookie outfielder Junior Felix came to bat for the first time in the majors—and swatted a home run on his first pitch. He was only the eleventh rookie in big league history to homer on the first pitch thrown to him.

Meanwhile, Jesse Barfield was traded to the Yankees, signaling the breakup of the Blue Jays' celebrated Barfield-Moseby-Bell outfield. Bell continued to complain about his DH role.

In mid-May the Blue Jays embraced Cito Gaston; in early June they moved into the Sky-Dome; and in late September they won the pennant. In a close and exciting conclusion to the season, Toronto, one game in the lead, fought it out with Baltimore in a weekend series at the Sky-Dome. In two thrill-packed games the Blue Jays wrapped up the AL East championship, winning the first game 2-1 in extra innings and the second one 4-3.

George Bell, sulking no longer, finished strong, batting .297 for the season and driving in 104 runs. Fred McGriff cracked 36 homers and contributed 92 RBIs. On the mound Dave Stieb went 17-8. Tom Henke was near-perfect in relief, registering 20 saves, a 1.92 ERA, and striking out 116 batters while giving up only 25 walks.

This was a solid team, but could they beat the AL West champion Oakland A's? Most people thought not. Most people were right. The A's of Jose Canseco, Rickey Henderson, Dave Stewart, and Dennis Eckersley took the first three games, lost the next one 6-5, then won the final contest. The Blue Jays could point with some pride to their second division title, but they still had no American League pennant and no World Series rings.

Winning It All

The Boston Red Sox foiled the Blue Jays' bid to repeat as AL East champions in 1990, but the battle went down to the last day of the season, when a Boston win and a Toronto loss dropped the Jays to second place, two games behind. Two of the newer players, first baseman John Olerud and catcher Pat Borders, made their presence felt, while old pros George Bell and Tony Fernandez had good but not great seasons.

Dave Stieb, as usual, proved vital to the team's success, notching 18 wins against six losses. Tom (The Terminator) Henke did yeoman relief work, with 32 saves and a 2.17 ERA. Yet the ball club choked in the final few games, something they were becoming noted for. Rath-er than finishing a hopeless last, the Blue Jays were being consigned to a frustrating, near-miss second or third.

Still, it was hard to fault Cito Gaston or anyone else in the organization. The Jays were playing consistently fine baseball and outdrawing everybody. In 1990 a total of 3,885,284 fans jammed the SkyDome, a bulge of more than 1,300,000 paid admissions over first-place Boston—a greater bulge than Cleveland's entire season's attendance. (Even the most jaundiced baseball historian might find it hard to believe that the old Triple-A Toronto Maple Leafs in their final 1967 season had drawn just 67,216 diehard fans.)

On to 1991. Were the Blue Jays a choke-prone baseball powerhouse—or were they perhaps world champions in the process of putting

AP/Wide World Photos

Jack Morris

AP/Wide World Photos

Paul Molitor

it all together? They certainly had no great difficulty in sweeping to a third AL East title in 1991, over-matching the Red Sox and Tigers by seven games each. And yet they once more ran aground in postseason play, losing the ALCS in five games to the Minnesota Twins.

The Toronto cast of stars kept changing—outfielders Joe Carter and Devon White, second baseman Roberto Alomar, starting pitcher Juan Guzman—all contributed greatly in 1991. But the outcome from year to year did not seem to vary a great deal. The Toronto team, ever in flux yet paradoxically stable, had begun to look like a renewable source of baseball energy.

That impression was strengthened in 1992. The Blue Jays were simply not to be denied during the regular season. They added 40-year-old Dave Winfield to their roster, inserted him in the cleanup spot, and he responded with a

.290 batting average, 26 home runs, and 108 RBIs. Joe Carter bombarded opposing pitchers with 34 homers and drove in 119 runs. Young Roberto Alomar led all Blue Jay batters with 177 hits and a .310 average.

Pitching dominance shifted from Dave Stieb (4-6) to free-agent newcomer and long-time superstar Jack Morris (21-6) and second-year sensation Juan Guzman (16-5). Reliable Jimmy Key posted a 13-13 mark, and Todd Stottlemyre went 12-11. Duane Ward, with an ERA of 1.95 and 12 saves, was effective in relief.

Toronto's toughest competitors in 1992 were the Milwaukee Brewers and Baltimore Orioles, neither team a real threat the year before. When the season ended, though, Phil Garner's Brewers were four games behind the high-flying Jays, and John Oates's Orioles trailed by seven.

The Blue Jays had won the division championship again. Their postseason opponents from the AL West, the next hurdle on the way to the World Series, were the Oakland A's, whose 99-66 regular season record exactly matched Toronto's.

This time, for the first time, the Blue Jays made it past their ALCS rivals, defeating the still dangerous but less than invincible A's four games to two. Cito Gaston's men prepared for their first World Series, where they would face the newly risen Atlanta Braves.

Managing the Braves—indeed, a key member of the Atlanta organization after being lured away from Toronto—was the ex-skipper of the division-champion 1985 Blue Jays, Bobby Cox. The Atlanta Braves were making a repeat appearance in the World Series, having played the Minnesota Twins in the 1991 fall classic, losing it in a squeaker, four games to three.

The 1992 Braves featured the same top performers: pitchers Tom Glavine, John Smoltz, Steve Avery, and Charlie Leibrandt; and hitters Terry Pendleton, Ron Gant, Dave Justice, and Sid Bream. The Blue Jays had comparable talent, given the arrival of Jack Morris and Dave

Winfield, plus the rise of Juan Guzman and Roberto Alomar. It promised to be a well-matched and probably a well-pitched World Series.

Few fans were disappointed, although some were mortified and many were annoyed when a U.S. Marine color guard raised the Canadian flag upside down. The Marines apologized and got it right the next time. On the field the Blue Jays lost the first game, wasting a Joe Carter homer, as Tom Glavine outhurled Jack Morris, 3-1. The Jays won game two, an exciting come-from-behind 5-4 victory powered by a pinch-hit home run in the top of the ninth inning off the bat of Ed Sprague.

Game three also was decided in the ninth, in Toronto's favor again, as Alomar singled, stole second, and scored on a base hit by Candy Mal-donado. Enjoying a two-games-to-one margin, Cito Gaston started Jimmy Key, and a Pat Borders home run followed four innings later by a Devon White RBI single gave Key all the runs he needed for a 2-1 win.

With the Blue Jays needing only one more victory to clinch the World Championship, it looked as if fans in the United States would have to resign themselves to the first-ever Canadian triumph in what for 90 years had been (its name notwithstanding) a U.S. Series rather than a World Series.

Atlanta gave one last gasp, winning game five, 7-2, behind John Smoltz. Pat Borders drove in both of the Jays' runs in the losing effort. The sixth game went into extra innings, tied 2-2, the Braves having evened it up in the ninth inning on a single, a walk, and a single. In the top of the 11th inning the Jays' Devon White was hit by a pitch, and Alomar singled. Forty-something Dave Winfield stepped to the plate and delivered a two-run double to put Toronto ahead 4-2.

That almost did it, but not quite. The Braves made a stand in the bottom of the inning, scoring one run before reliever Mike Timlin, the seventh Blue Jays' moundsman of the day, retired the final batter. The Toronto Blue Jays, an expansion team that suffered the inevitable

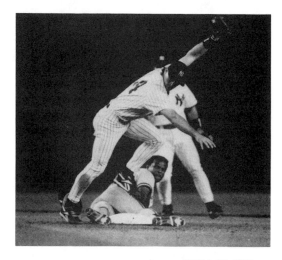

AP/Wide World Photos

Rickey Henderson

humiliations in their early days but persisted, doing virtually everything right, had made it to the pinnacle of the baseball world.

The Blue Jays didn't rest on their laurels for the 1993 season. During the offseason, they overhauled their lineup, losing such players as Henke, Winfield, and Key to free agency while adding a dozen new players, including veterans Paul Molitor and Dave Stewart, to the club, among other moves. Because of the number of roster changes, Toronto was not a clear-cut favorite to repeat as champions, but after trailing the red-hot Detroit Tigers early in the year, the Jays moved back into first by midseason.

Though boasting one of the most potent offenses in baseball, led by John Olerud, who flirted with a .400 average through August, Roberto Alomar, and Molitor, the Blue Jays could not pull away from the likes of New York, Baltimore, and Detroit, primarily due to their inconsistent starting pitching.

Even the late-season acquisition of perhaps the game's best leadoff hitter, Rickey Henderson, didn't provide the expected spark to ignite Toronto. It took a strong September stretch drive to clinch the pennant with a 95-67 record, seven games ahead of New York.

In the ALCS, the Jays ousted the Chicago White Sox in six games and prepared to defend their title against the National League champion Philadelphia Phillies. The 1993 World Series matched up two explosive, high-scoring teams: The Blue Jays featured Olerud, Molitor, and Alomar, who finished one-two-three in the AL batting race, as well as Carter, who belted 33 home runs with 121 RBIs, while the Phillies showcased hard-nosed Lenny Dykstra, powerful John Kruk, and slugger Darren Daulton.

The Series opened in Toronto. Game One went to the Blue Jays, 8-5, but the Phillies battled back, taking Game Two, 6-4. After capturing Game Three in Philadelphia for a two games to one lead, Toronto appeared be on a roll, but not even a confident Jays squad could have been prepared for the riotous goings-on in Game Four.

On a rainy night in Philadelphia, fans were treated to one of the most entertaining games in World Series history. Six batters walked in the first inning, which ended 4-3 in favor of Philly. Jays starter Todd Stottlemyre scraped up his chin trying a head-first slide into third base.

The Toronto bullpen phone wasn't working, which caused the wrong Jays reliever to show up during one of the game's nine pitching changes. And to make matters worse for the Blue Jays, the Phillies seemed to score at will and led 12-7 after a five-run fifth inning, expanding their lead to 14-9 heading into the eighth.

But an incredible six-run rally off Phillie relief pitchers Larry Andersen and Mitch Williams pushed the Jays in front, and their own relievers, Mike Timlin and Duane Ward, combined to shut down the Phillies over the last two innings to secure the win. In the highest-scoring World Series game in history, the Jays prevailed over the Phillies by a score of 15-14.

With the Jays seemingly in control of the Series, Philadelphia bounced back, taking Game Five, 2-0, and coming back from a 5-1 deficit in Game Six in Toronto to take a 6-5 lead into the bottom of the ninth inning. Williams again took the mound for Philadelphia and promptly walked Henderson on four ptiches.

Devon White then flied out, and Molitor singled, moving Henderson into scoring position. Carter stepped to the plate. With a two-and-two count on the Jays slugger, Williams threw a fastball down and in, which Carter drove over the leftfield wall for a three-run homer, propelling the Jays to an 8-6 victory and their second consecutive World Championship.

The soft-spoken Molitor, a team leader both on and off the field who at age 37 had perhaps his finest season as a pro, was named World Series MVP for his 12 hits, .500 average, 10 runs scored, and 24 total bases. The first Series title captured on Canadian soil was history.

Are there other titles in the Blue Jays' future? With a front-office that aggressively pursues top-quality players. A nucleus of exceptional talent, and a huge following of devoted fans, the chances certainly look good.

SOURCES

BOOKS

Baseball Guide, The Sporting News Publishing Co., 1980, 1982, 1983, 1985, 1987, 1991, 1992.

Baseball Register, The Sporting News Publishing Co., 1980, 1983, 1985, 1987, 1991, 1992.

Bjarkman, Peter C., "Toronto Blue Jays: Okay, Blue Jays! From Worst to First in a Decade," in Encyclopedia of Major League Baseball Team Histories, edited by Peter C. Bjarkman, Meckler, 1991.

Hollander, Zander, editor, The Complete Handbook of Baseball 1992, 22nd edition, Signet, 1992.

Ivor-Campbell, Frederick, "Team Histories: Toronto Blue Jays," in Total Baseball, edited by John Thorn and Pete Palmer, Warner Books, 1989.

O'Neal, Bill, *The International League: A Baseball History, 1884-1991,* Eakin Press, 1992.

Owens, Tom, et al, *Baseball 1991 Almanac,* Publications International, 1991.

Reichler, Joseph L., editor, *The Baseball Encyclopedia,* 7th edition, Macmillan, 1988.

Reidenbaugh, Lowell, *Take Me Out to the Ball Park,* The Sporting News Publishing Co., 1983.

Stieb, Dave, and Kevin Boland, *Tomorrow I'll Be Perfect,* Doubleday, 1986.

Van Rjndt, Phillippe, and Patrick Blednick, *Fungo Blues—An Uncontrolled Look at the Toronto Blue Jays,* McClelland & Stewart, 1985.

The World Almanac and Book of Facts 1993, Pharos Books, 1992.

PERIODICALS

Baseball America, September 10-24, 1992; December 25, 1992; January 9, 1993; February 21, 1993.

Maclean's, May 12, 1980.

Sports Illustrated, July 18, 1983.

—*Gerald Tomlinson* for Book Builders, Inc.

American League West

CALIFORNIA ANGELS

The California Angels (then called the Los Angeles Angels) finished third in the American League in 1962—their second year of existence—but plunged all the way to ninth place the next year. This became a recurring pattern for the Angels: a strong finish followed by a collapse the following season. The Angels won no pennants prior to the start of division play in 1969, and after that they took another 11 years to win a division title.

The 1979 club, managed by Jim Fregosi, had plenty of talent, virtually all of it signed and developed by other ball clubs. On the mound was baseball's all-time strikeout king, Nolan Ryan (with 223 Ks that year), and in the outfield, driving in more than 100 runs apiece, were Don Baylor and Dan Ford. Also topping 100 RBIs was second baseman Bobby Grich.

After winning the division title by three games over Kansas City, the Angels lost the 1979 American League Championship Series to the Baltimore Orioles, three games to one. The next year the team followed its triumph-and-collapse pattern by dropping to sixth place in the AL West, finishing ahead of only the pitiable Seattle Mariners.

The Angels rose to the top of the AL West again in 1982, posting their best won-lost record ever, 93-69. They were thought to have a good shot at winning the pennant, too, especially after taking the first two games of a best-of-five American League Championship Series from the Milwaukee Brewers. But the Brewers rebounded to win the next three games, and once more the Angels went home to watch the World Series on TV.

Despite having a strong ball club in 1983, at least on paper, California dipped in the standings, this time to fifth place. For a team with such classy pitchers as Tommy John, Ken Forsch, Mike Witt, and Bruce Kison—not to mention hitters like Rod Carew, Reggie Jackson, and Fred Lynn—the Angels had their owner and ex-cowboy movie star Gene Autry wondering why the only Champion he had been able to buy was his horse.

Following second-place finishes in 1984 and 1985, the Angels of 1986, managed by Gene Mauch, won the division championship by their widest margin ever, five games, and jumped off to a three-games-to-one lead in the ALCS against the Boston Red Sox. A mere one strike away from elimination, Boston fought back, winning game five on a Dave Henderson home run. The Bosox went on to win games six and seven and capture the pennant.

The Angels, as if in frustration—and in keeping with their tradition—skidded to sixth place the next year. They recovered partially in 1989, coming in third with a solid 91-71 record. But an American League pennant, and a trip to the World Series, continued to elude them.

The Los Angeles Angels

Before the 1961 season the American League expanded to ten teams. One of the two new franchises went to Los Angeles, the other to Washington, D.C. (the Senators' old franchise moved to Minnesota). The Los Angeles expansion team was named the Angels, the same as L.A.'s defunct minor league team in the Pacific Coast League.

For their first year, the Los Angeles Angels played at old Wrigley Field, a ballpark with very short power alleys. American League teams, including the Angels, hit home runs with drumbeat regularity there: a total of 248 homers, far more than in any other major league ballpark. Five L.A. players connected for 20 or more round-trippers—outfielder Leon Wagner, 28; outfielder Ken Hunt, 25; outfielder Lee Thomas, 24; catcher Earl Averill, 21; and first baseman Steve Bilko, 20.

Nevertheless, only 603,510 fans showed up to watch the team play, about a third as many as the National League's Los Angeles franchise, the Dodgers, drew. The Angels, managed by veteran skipper Bill Rigney, finished eighth in the 10-team American League.

To placate Dodger owner Walter O'Malley, who hated to see his monopoly in L.A. disturbed, the Angels had to agree to play at the new Dodger Stadium when it opened in 1962. Upon moving there, the Los Angeles Angels did stunningly well in their sophomore year, winning 86, losing 76, and finishing third behind New York and Minnesota. Leon Wagner, "Daddy Wags," blasted 37 homers and drove in 107 runs.

The year 1962 marked the debut of screwball pitcher and highly-publicized rookie-about-town Bo Belinsky who won five straight games at the outset—including the Angels first no-hitter—before settling into mediocrity. Rookie Dean Chance was the ace of the staff, going 14-10 with a 2.96 ERA. Bill Rigney was named American League Manager of the Year.

Then came the season after, 1963, and the Angels, with basically the same roster, finished ninth, superior only to their cohorts in expansion, the Washington Senators. Chance slipped to 11-18, although with a fine 3.19 ERA, while the partying Belinsky went 2-9, ERA 5.75. "Daddy Wags" continued to perform well at the plate, batting .291, with 26 homers and 90 RBIs.

Owner Autry retained manager Rigney, and the Angels fought back in 1964 to finish fifth with an 82-80 record. The headliner that year was Chance, who enjoyed the best season of his career, leading the league in wins (20), shutouts (11), and ERA (1.65). The Angel pitching staff as a whole was formidable, racking up 28 shutouts—the most in the majors since 1909—and posting a team ERA of 2.91. The hitters were another matter.

In an inexplicable trade, Leon Wagner, the Angels' most popular player and best hitter, was dealt over the winter to the Cleveland Indians for aging first baseman Joe Adcock. Although Adcock led the 1964 Angels with 21 home runs and drove in 64 runs, "Daddy Wags" belted 31 homers and knocked in 100 runs for the Tribe.

Two Angel players who would later become noted major league managers were teammates on these pre-"California" Angels. One was shortstop Jim Fregosi, chosen in the expansion draft from the Boston Red Sox roster. He played 11 seasons for the Angels. The other was catcher Bob (later Buck) Rodgers, who was plucked from the Detroit

TEAM INFORMATION AT A GLANCE

Founding date: April 11, 1961

Home stadium: Anaheim Stadium
2000 Gene Autry Way
Anaheim, CA 92806
Phone: (714) 937-7200

Dimensions: left-field line—333 feet
Center field—404 feet
Right-field line—333 feet
Seating capacity: 64,593

Team colors: Navy blue and scarlet.
Team nickname: Angels, 1961-present (team was called Los Angeles Angels, 1961-65; California Angels, 1966-present)
Team logo: Capital "A" with wings and a halo

Franchise record	Won	Lost	Pct.
(1961-1993)	2,553	2,729	.483

American League West division first-place finishes (3): 1979, 1982, 1986
League/division last-place finishes (3): 1974, 1975, 1991

Tigers roster in the same draft. He spent his entire nine-year playing career with L.A./California. In the brief era of the Los Angeles Angels, 1961 through 1965—and, indeed, until 1969—Bill Rigney remained at the helm of the Angels.

By this time, Gene Autry wanted out of Dodger Stadium. He received an attractive package deal from the city of Anaheim, home of Disneyland, and began building Anaheim Stadium near the Santa Ana Freeway in 1965. The prospective tenants continued to struggle through a seventh-place season at Dodgerland. Dean Chance had a pretty good year, 15-10, with a 3.15 ERA, but the Angels as a whole were uninspiring. On September 2, 1965, the Autry organization embraced the entire Golden State as its domain, renaming the ball club the California Angels.

Stars, But No Flag

The Angels' farm system seldom produced quality players who stayed with the ball club. The result was frequent trading, signing bonuses, and, with the advent of free agency, outbidding other teams for the services of established stars. One highly-publicized bonus baby, signed in 1964, was Rick Reichardt from the University of Wisconsin. Snared for the then-sizable sum of $200,000, Reichardt proved to be an adequate but unsensational outfielder, whom the Angels finally traded away in 1970.

PROFILE

Nolan Ryan

By the end of the 1993 season Nolan Ryan, a right-handed fireball pitcher, had put in 27 seasons in the major leagues. He played for four different teams, beginning with the New York Mets from 1966 through 1971. Pitching in the shadow of Tom Seaver and Jerry Koosman, he had a mediocre record and was considered expendable.

In December of 1971 the Mets traded him, along with three other players, to the California Angels for infielder Jim Fregosi. Ryan improved immediately and immensely, winning 19 games for the fifth-place Angels in 1972 and striking out a league-leading 329 batters. The following season he fanned 383 hitters, a twentieth-century record, and pitched two no-hit games: a 3-0 victory against the Kansas City Royals on May 15 and a 6-0, 17-strikeout win against the Detroit Tigers on July 15. These were the first of his seven career no-hitters—three more than the runner-up, Sandy Koufax.

Ryan's career strikeout total, 5,668, is so far ahead of anyone else's that it appears to be unreachable. For years he and lefty Steve Carlton were neck-and-neck in career strikeouts, but Carlton, a durable pitcher, retired in 1988 with a total of 4,136 strikeouts. Ryan just kept going.

According to his autobiography, *Throwing Heat,* Ryan wanted to stay with the Angels and did not intend to file for free agency. But Gene Autry's new general manager, Buzzy Bavasi, refused throughout 1979 to negotiate a renewal of Ryan's contract, and in the end the flame-throwing superstar signed with the Houston Astros, for whom he pitched through 1988. He then moved on to the Texas Rangers. At the age of 46 his yearly strikeout total dropped somewhat, but he continued to add numbers to a host of all-time major league pitching records.

Ryan announced plans to retire following the 1993 campaign, but an injury to his throwing arm caused him to hang up his spikes before the season's end.

California finished sixth, fifth, and eighth from 1966 through 1968, after which the American League was split into two divisions of six teams each (seven starting in 1977). The 1967 season was considerably more exciting for Angels' fans than a fifth-place finish suggests. The team stayed in contention until the last week. Newly-acquired first baseman Don Mincher supplied the power (25 homers, 76 RBIs) and relief pitcher Minnie Rojas (12-9, ERA 2.52) won the American League's Fireman of the Year award. After contending in 1967, the Angels, in typical fashion, floundered the next year.

The 1969 Angels finished third in the American League West, despite a none-too-robust 71-91 won-lost record. Rigney was gone at last, fired after 10 straight losses early in the season and replaced by Harold (Lefty) Phillips, the Angels' pitching coach. The Angels put together an 86-76

season in 1970, good for third place, then reversed the figures, 76-86, in 1971, putting the team fourth in the AL West. After that season, Phillips got the ax, and Del Rice, an ex-catcher for the Cardinals and Braves, took over.

During these years pitcher Clyde Wright, a product of the Angels' farm system, began winning in double figures, posting a 22-12 record in 1970. So did Andy Messersmith, probably the best pitcher to come out of the Angels' farm system, who posted a 20-13 mark in 1971.

The California front office continued its trading, and in December of 1971 hit the jackpot, trading their veteran shortstop Jim Fregosi to the New York Mets for, among others, pitcher Nolan Ryan. For some reason Ryan had never done well in New York, but in Anaheim he blossomed. While the Angels were finishing fifth, fourth, and last in 1972, 1973, and 1974, Nolan Ryan was mowing down batters at a league-leading (and record-setting) clip. In 1972 he struck out 329 batters. In 1973 he upped that total to 383 (a modren record) and followed with 367 whiffs in 1974. Ryan was the Angels' first superstar.

The club was acquiring other big-name players, most of them in their declining years. For the 1972 season they obtained one-time Cardinal star outfielder Vada Pinson. They added Hall-of-Fame-bound slugger Frank Robinson as a designated hitter in 1973. But none of this dealing in the early 1970s raised the performance of the ball club above .500.

Building Toward Success

Hard-nosed Dick Williams took over as manager in mid-season 1974, succeeding Bobby Winkles, an ex-college coach. Williams' no-nonsense style was not the answer, and the Angels finished last in 1974 and 1975. With the team's won-lost record at a dismal 39-57 in 1976, Williams was handed his walking papers. Coach Norm Sherry took over, and the Angels played at a 37-29 pace the rest of the way, finishing in a tie for fourth place.

Pitcher Frank Tanana, a first-round draft choice of the Angels in 1971, was developing into California's ace starter, going 16-9 with a 2.62 ERA in 1975 and 19-10 with a 2.49 ERA in 1976. Meanwhile, Nolan Ryan continued to strike out batters at a prodigious rate—327 in 1976, and 341 in 1977.

The advent of free-agency in major league baseball gave big-spending owner Gene Autry a golden chance, or so it seemed, to buy his team's way to victory. Prior to the 1977 season The Angels signed star second baseman Bobby Grich of the Baltimore Orioles and two quality outfielders, Don Baylor and Joe Rudi of the Oakland Athletics.

These were big-name ballplayers, and attendance at Anaheim Stadium rose substantially. But the real impact of these new acquisitions, and others, was not felt until 1978, mainly because of

injuries. There was even one death. Young Mike Miley, who was thought to be the Angels' shortstop of the future, was killed in an auto accident in January of 1977.

The Angels finished fourth in 1977, even with Grich, Baylor, and Rudi, and veteran outfielder Bobby Bonds in the lineup. Bonds was dealt to the Chicago White Sox at the end of the season in exchange for, among others, pitcher Dave Frost and catcher Brian Downing.

In 1978 Lyman Bostock, a young but established star for the Minnesota Twins, joined the Angel ranks via free-agency. Bostock was an accomplished outfielder and a .300+ hitter. Although designated hitter Don Baylor led the Angels at the plate that year with 34 home runs and 99 runs batted in, Bostock and rookie third baseman Carney Lansford, up from El Paso of the Double-A Texas League, also contributed to the strong offense. The pitching staff was led by Frank Tanana, who turned in an 18-12 record, and reliever Dave LaRoche, who registered 25 saves. The Angels and the Texas Rangers tied for second place in the AL West.

Over the winter California added two new, costly, and significant players to their roster. The first was Dan Ford, acquired in a December of 1978 trade. Ford, an outfielder from the Twins, was needed to replace Lyman Bostock in left field. Bostock, nearing the end of another fine season in late September of 1978, was shot and killed in Gary, Indiana—an innocent bystander at a lovers' quarrel.

The second major acquisition was Rod Carew, one of the great hitters in modern baseball. Carew came from the Twins in February of 1979 in a one-for-four-player deal. A lifetime .328 hitter, he had enjoyed his greatest year in 1977, batting .388 for the Twins and leading the league with 239 hits.

Three Firsts

Over the next seven years the Angels won the AL West division championship three times. Sev-

AP/Wide World Photos

Don Sutton

eral players had career years in 1979 as the Angels moved far out in front by midseason and took over the AL West lead for good at the end of August. Don Baylor, with 36 homers and a .296 batting average, drove in 139 runs to lead the league. Brian Downing hit .326, his only .300+ season in a 15-year career. Downing outhit Rod Carew, who, slowing down with age, moved to first base from his usual second-base position and dropped to .318 at the plate. Dan Ford, Carney Lansford, Bobby Grich, outfielder Rick Miller, and DH Willie Aikens all checked in with batting averages of .280 and up. Ford and Grich each drove in 101 runs.

If the Angels' pitching in 1979 had matched their hitting, the team would have won the division title by a wide margin. But the pitching, while adequate, showed only sporadic flashes of brilliance. Nolan Ryan led the league with 223 strikeouts and five shutouts, posting a 16-14 record.

Frank Tanana spent nearly two months on the disabled list, pitched only 90 innings, and compiled a 7-5 record.

The one Angel pitcher who had a career year was Dave Frost, 16-10. Rookie reliever Mark Clear did reasonably well in relief, 11-5 with a 3.63 ERA, but veteran Dave LaRoche had problems. The 1979 Angels, under second-year manager Jim Fregosi, finished three games ahead of the Kansas City Royals.

In the AL East the Baltimore Orioles, managed by Earl Weaver, won the division championship convincingly, and few doubted that the Birds would make short work of California in the ALCS. Baltimore won the best-of-five series in four games. Only a ninth-inning bloop double by Larry Harlow (traded from Baltimore to California that year) prevented a three-game sweep by the O's. With Harlow's last-minute hit the Angels won the third game of the Series, 4-3. The next day Baltimore pitcher Scott McGregor shut down the Angels' attack, allowing only six hits in the O's 8-0 win.

The 1980 Angels, far from repeating as division champs, straggled home in sixth place. No starting pitcher on the Angels' staff had a winning record—and the Angels' superstar pitcher was gone. After the 1979 season, Nolan Ryan opted for free agency, and the Houston Astros signed him. Without Ryan, the Angels went nowhere in 1980.

Help was on the way, however. Pitchers Ken Forsch, Geoff Zahn, and Steve Renko arrived from other ball clubs for the strike-shortened 1981 season, but did not make a difference that year. Another pitcher of the future made his appearance in 1981. He was Mike Witt, a 1978 California draft choice and a future All-Star. In January 1982 the Angels snared their free-agent catch of the decade in 36-year-old outfielder Reggie Jackson, best known for his stints with the Oakland A's and New York Yankees.

In 1982 Reggie Jackson hit a league-leading 39 home runs for the Angels and drove in 101 runs. Third baseman Doug DeCinces, acquired from the Orioles in January of 1982 in a trade for Dan Ford,

In Memorium

The California Angels have experienced an inordinate amount of tragedy. Dick Wantz, a right-handed pitcher and native Californian, debuted with the Angels on April 13, 1965, and died of a brain tumor a month later. Jim McGlothin, an Angels' pitcher for five seasons, was traded to Cincinnati after the 1969 season. He died of cancer at the age of 33. Reliever Minnie Rojas, whose 27 saves made him the American League Fireman of the Year in 1967, lost two children in an automobile accident in 1968 and was himself paralyzed from the neck down. Two promising young shortstops, Chico Ruiz and Mike Miley died in auto accidents in the 1970s.

The most widely publicized fatal accident on the Angels' team was that of Lyman Bostock, an outfielder whose four-year major league batting average of .311 suggests what an exceptional ballplayer he was and might have become. He was accidently killed on September 23, 1978, the victim of a bullet intended for someone else. A more recent tragedy was the July 18, 1989, suicide of relief pitcher Donnie Moore, Moore's agent said the Angels' hurler never got over the home run ball he threw Dave Henderson of the Boston Red Sox on October 12, 1986. The pitch, a fork ball, cost the Angels the fifth game of the American League Championship Series. Had they won the game, which they led 5-2 going into the ninth inning, they would have gone on to play in the World Series.

blasted 30 homers and drove in 97 runs. Catcher Brian Downing connected for 28 round-trippers, his highest total ever, and drove in 84 runs. This season was another one in which the proven stars lived up to their potential on offense, and the pitching was more than adequate. Geoff Zahn paced the hurlers with an 18-8 mark, a career year for him.

The Angels, now under skipper Gene Mauch, once again nosed out the Kansas City Royals to take the AL West title. In the ALCS the Angels began on a high note, taking the first two games from the AL East champion Milwaukee Brewers.

The first game was won on DH Don Baylor's slugging (five RBIs), the second on Bruce Kison's five-hit pitching. No team had ever come back from a two-games-to-none deficit in a league championship series, but the Brewers accomplished it on the hitting of Paul Molitor, Mark Brouhard, and Cecil Cooper. The Angels were once again denied a trip to the World Series.

California faded to fifth in 1983 as injuries hit hard and the Angels (with the exception of Rod Carew) didn't. At the All-Star break Carew was batting an eye-popping .402, but then he too was injured, tailed off, and finished at .339, second in the league to Boston's Wade Boggs—but still the

highest average ever for an Angel hitter. The starting pitchers faltered, with only Bruce Kison, 11-5, posting a winning record. In 1984 the Angels finished second, but with an unimpressive 81-81 won-lost record.

The next year, though, manager Gene Mauch, returning after a couple of seasons away, guided the team to a solid 90-72 record and came within a whisker of winning the division title, losing out finally to Kansas City.

Hopes were high for 1986, given the 1985 stretch-drive performances of veteran pitchers Don Sutton and John Candelaria and the arrival, via the farm system, of a new first baseman, Wally Joyner. All performed well, with rookie Joyner belting 22 homers and driving in 100 runs while batting .290. He cooled off in the second half of the season (after having 74 RBIs by the All-Star break) and ceded Rookie of the Year honors to Oakland's Jose Canseco.

For the first time in their history the Angels had three 15-game winners on the mound. Mike Witt posted an 18-10 record; sophomore Kirk McCaskill went 17-10; and Don Sutton, 15-11. John Candelaria had a glittering 10-2 mark after missing much of the first half of the season with

For a team like the New York Yankees, this date would be a minor footnote. But it looms large in the history of the California Angels, because this was the date on which the Angels blew their best chance to play in a World Series.

After winning the American League West title, the Angels took three of the first four games in the 1986 AL Championship Series against the Boston Red Sox. Mike Witt won the opener at Fenway Park, 8-1. The Red Sox evened the Series the next day, 9-2, but the Angels came back to win the third and fourth games at Anaheim Stadium. The stage was set for California to march off with the flag in the fifth game, on October 12 in Anaheim. It didn't happen.

The Red Sox took a 2-0 lead on catcher Rich Gedman's two-run homer off Mike Witt in the second inning. The Angels came back to take a 3-2 lead, the big blow being Bobby Grich's two-run homer in the sixth inning, a drive that bounced off Dave Henderson's glove over the fence. After adding two insurance runs in the seventh, the hopes of Angel fans soared. Their team carried a 5-2 lead into the top of the ninth inning. Bill Buckner singled for the Red Sox, and, after Jim Rice struck out, Don Baylor blasted a home run to cut the Angels' lead to 5-4. Dwight Evans then popped up for the second out. The next batter was Rich Gedman, who already had collected three hits off starter Mike Witt. Gene Mauch, master strategist, decided to change pitchers. He brought in left-handed reliever Gary Lucas to pitch to left-handed batter Gedman.

In the bullpen was righthander Donnie Moore, getting ready to pitch to right-handed hitting Dave Henderson. Lucas hit Gedman with his first pitch, the first batter he had nicked all year. Gedman trotted down to first base, and Moore trotted in from the bullpen. Tired and just getting over shoulder and back injuries, Moore got ahead of Henderson, one ball and two strikes. He then missed with a pitch and Henderson fouled off two more. Finally, Moore threw a fork ball that stayed up. The ball came to rest on the far side of the left-field fence, and Boston was ahead, 6-5.

Still, it wasn't over. The Angels tied the score in the bottom of the ninth, and the game went into extra innings. Moore stayed on the mound for the Angels. In the top of the 11th Dave Henderson's sacrifice fly brought in a run to give the Red Sox a 7-6 lead. The Angels failed to score in the bottom on the 11th, and the Series moved back to Boston, where the Red Sox took the final two games with ease. The only sour-grapes satisfaction Angel fans could take from postseason play was that a few days later Boston blew the series to the New York Mets on first baseman Bill Buckner's famous 10th-inning error in the sixth game.

injuries. The Angels won the AL West title by their greatest margin ever, five games, and went into the ALCS fully expecting to defeat the AL East's Boston Red Sox.

The American League Championship Series, having become a best-of-seven contest, went the full seven games. The Angels jumped out to a lead of three games to one. Then in game five, on October 12, 1986, they came very close to clinching a World Series appearance at last. The game was tied 6-6 at the end of nine innings. But in the top of the 11th the Red Sox scored a run, and the Angels went down to defeat, 7-6. The hapless Californians proceeded to lose the next two games, and Boston advanced to the World Series.

Still Trying

In time-honored fashion the Angels fell apart the next year, sinking to sixth place. And this time there was no early indication that they would bounce back. Two bright spots in the 1987 lineup were Wally Joyner (34 homers, 117 RBIs) and rookie outfielder Devon White (24 homers, 87 RBIs, 32 stolen bases). But the team batting average was the lowest in the league, and the pitching was shaky. Mike Witt compiled a 13-6 record through July, but won just three games the rest of the way and finished at 16-14. John Candelaria, 8-6, spent two months on the disabled list and was dealt to the New York Mets in September. Don Sutton and rookie Willie Fraser both finished at an even .500. Only rookie reliever DeWayne Buice, with 17 saves, had a first-rate season.

Over the winter the Angels picked up free-agent outfielder Chili Davis and traded outfielder Gary Pettis to Detroit for pitcher Dan Petry. Nine days before the 1988 season began, Gene Mauch resigned as manager and was replaced by Cookie Rojas, the Angels' advance scout. Neither Rojas, Davis, nor Petry made much difference, as the Angels finished with the same won-lost record as the previous year. This time it was good for fourth place.

The Angels hired Doug Rader, formerly the skipper of the Texas Rangers, to take over from Cookie Rojas in 1989. They also acquired a veteran pitcher who, along with a suddenly intimidating Chuck Finley and an uninjured (for a change) Kirk McCaskill, almost carried the Angels to a pennant. The pitcher was Bert Blyleven, born in The Netherlands but raised a stone's throw from Anaheim Stadium. Ineffective for Minnesota in 1988, he went 17-5 for the Angels in 1989, with a 2.73 ERA, on his way to winning the AL Comeback Player of the Year award.

With Finley at 16-9 and a 2.57 ERA and McCaskill at 15-10 with an ERA of 2.93, it was the pitchers, for a change, who sparked the Angels' success. (Mike Witt, however, who had once seemed so promising, dropped to 9-15 with a 4.54 ERA and was traded away early in the 1990 season.) California won 91 games while losing 71 in 1989, finishing third behind Oakland and Kansas City.

The next three seasons were disappointing. The Angels never rose higher in the final stand-ings than 14 games back, and in the year they did that, 1991, they placed last in their division with an 81-81 record. Wally Joyner, after a couple of disappointing seasons, came back in 1991 with a .301 batting average, 22 home runs, and 96 runs batted in. But free agency put him in a Kansas City Royals' uniform in 1992. Pitcher Jim Abbott had an impressive 18-11 season in 1991 with a 2.89 ERA. But the next year he fell to 7-15 (albeit with a 2.77 ERA), and the Angels traded him to the Yankees.

Outfielder Luis Polonia, acquired from the Yankees during the 1990 season, became the Angels' most consistent hitter, batting .296 in 1991 and a team-leading .286, in 1992. But Polonia lacked power at the plate. So did everyone else. Third baseman Gary Gaetti led the team in homers in 1992 with an anemic total of 12. Pitching, too, remained a problem, especially with Abbott gone.

Manager Buck Rodgers, who took over the Angels late in 1991, looked as if he might need the disintegrator gun of his comic-book namesake to fend off disaster in the immediate future. The 1993 season, however, proved to be a pleasant surprise. Though the Angels finished 71-91, the strong showing of several young players, including infielders Gary DiSarcina, Damion Easley (.313), and J. T. Snow (16 homers, 57 RBIs), and outfielders Chad Curtis (.285, 48 stolen bases) and AL Rookie of the Year Tim Salmon (.283, 31 homers, 95 RBIs), bodes well for the future.

SOURCES

BOOKS

Baseball America's 1992 Directory, Baseball America, 1992.

Baseball Guide, 1983, 1987, 1991, 1993 editions, The Sporting News Publishing Co., 1983, 1987, 1991, 1993.

Baseball Register, 1980, 1987, 1993 editions, The Sporting News Publishing Co., 1980, 1987, 1993.

Baseball Record Book, 1993 edition, The Sporting News Publishing Co., 1993.

Beverage, Richard E., *The Angels: Los Angeles in the Pacific Coast League, 1919-1957,* The Deacon Press, 1981.

Beverage, Richard E., "Los Angeles Angels-California Angels: A Cowboy's Search for Another Champion," *Encyclopedia of Major League Baseball Team Histories: American League,* edited by Peter C. Bjarkman, Meckler, 1991.

Ivor-Campbell, Frederick, "Team Histories: California Angels," *Total Baseball,* edited by John Thorn and Pete Palmer, Warner Books, 1989.

Newhan, Ross, *The California Angels,* Simon and Schuster, 1982.

Reichler, Joseph L., editor, *The Baseball Encyclopedia,* 7th ed., Macmillan Publishing Company, 1988.

Ryan, Nolan, and Harvey Frommer, *Throwing Heat,* Doubleday and Company, 1988.

Siwoff, Seymour, editor, *Who's Who in Baseball,* 55th, 60th eds., Who's Who in Baseball Magazine Co., 1970, 1975.

PERIODICALS

Baseball America, February 7, 1993; March 7, 1993; April 4, 1993.

Sports Illustrated, August 13, 1984.

—*Gerald Tomlinson* for Book Builders, Inc.

OAKLAND ATHLETICS

The history of the Athletics franchise is almost as colorful as the team's green and gold uniforms. The Athletics have played on both American coasts and in the heartland—in Philadelphia, Kansas City, and Oakland, to be exact. With nine World Series crowns, 14 first-place league finishes, and ten American League West divisional flags, the A's can point proudly to a job well done in their first century of performance. Since moving to Oakland, California, in 1968, the scrappy A's have established themselves as the only team in recent history to win three consecutive World Series championships. Only the New York Yankees have won the World Series more often than the Athletics, a franchise that single-handedly changed the title "American League West" to "American League Best."

The Athletics have flourished—and floundered—under the guidance of two extraordinary men. For its first 50 years of existence, the club was managed and partly owned by Connie Mack, a baseball giant known in his day as the "Tall Tactician." Mack's sharp eye for young talent and gentlemanly managerial tactics brought the A's nine American League championships and five World Series crowns before 1950. All told, Mack managed the Athletics 50 years, through boom periods and long, last-place droughts. Records come and go in professional baseball, but it is not likely that history will ever see another manager who works with a team continuously for half a century. In their book *Baseball's Great Dynasties: The Athletics,* James Duplacey and Joséph Romain called Mack "one of the most respected and dignified figures ever to stroll between the white lines."

The other dominant figure in Athletics history inspired almost everything but respect. Charles O. Finley bought the franchise in 1960 and ran it his way for 20 years. Flamboyant and controversial in the extreme, Finley feuded with his players, his managers, league officials, and even his fellow team owners. At every turn he challenged hide-bound baseball tradition, striving to fill the stadium seats while leaving his own indelible mark on the team. Finley had few fans on the diamond or in the stands, but he managed to forge a franchise that won three straight World Series titles in the early 1970s.

In the 1979 book *The Great Teams: Why They Win All the Time,* author Robert A. Liston wrote: "The Oakland A's *are* Charlie Finley. He made the ball club and he turned around and destroyed it. The club in its championship years reflected his personality. If there was an ingredient other than talent that made the team click, it came from Finley." Liston concluded: "Like him or not, Finley has been a fresh breeze, or maybe a tornado, in the staid halls of baseball."

Superstars of every era have donned Athletics uniforms. In Connie Mack's heyday the team boasted Jimmie Foxx, Nap Lajoie, Lefty Grove, Rube Waddell, and Mickey Cochrane, to name just a few. In the Finley era, such talents as Reggie Jackson, Vida Blue, Jim "Catfish" Hunter, and Bert Campaneris terrorized American League opponents.

More recently the Athletics have continued their winning ways behind the likes of José Canseco, Rickey Henderson, Mark McGwire, and Dennis Eckersley. And the future looks bright for a club with a solid farm system, a commitment to its city, and hefty revenues from increasing home attendance. As Duplacey and Romain put it, "The machine is well-oiled, there's money in the bank, and some of the best men in the game are on the Oakland staff."

The American League was the brainchild of Byron Bancroft Johnson, an entrepreneur from Norwalk, Ohio. Johnson became president of the Western League in 1893, and almost immediately launched plans to challenge the long dominance of the National League. By the turn of the century he had achieved his goal. The American League officially began play in 1901.

In some cities—Detroit, Cleveland, and Washington, D.C., for example—Johnson had no competition from the established National League and

Transcendental Graphics

Connie Mack

thus could expect good attendance. Nevertheless, he acted on a hunch and introduced American League teams in several cities that also hosted a National League franchise. One of those cities was Philadelphia.

Philadelphia was a proven major league town, the home of the Phillies in the National League. The Phillies' fans and management must have been horrified when the rival club arrived in town and proceeded to lure top players from the Phillies and elsewhere onto its roster. Even the name "Athletics" harked back to a Philadelphia team from the previous century in an attempt to link the new franchise with hometown tradition.

The pilot of the fledgling ballclub was an ex-ballplayer by the name of Cornelius Alexander McGilicuddy. From his earliest days as a player, the stringy catcher had been known as Connie Mack—a nickname that stuck because it fit in the

TEAM INFORMATION AT A GLANCE

Founding date: April 25, 1901 (charter member of American League)

Home stadium: Oakland/Alameda County Coliseum
Oakland, CA 94621
Phone: (415) 638-4900

Dimensions: Left-field line—330 feet
Center field—400 feet
Right-field line—330 feet
Seating capacity: 46,942

Team uniforms: Home—base color white, forest green letters, gold trim
Road—base color forest gray, forest green letters, gold trim
Team nickname: Athletics, 1901—
Logo: Elephant holding two baseball bats in its trunk

Franchise record:	Won	Lost	Pct.
(1901-1993)	6,877	7,459	.480

World Series wins (9): 1910, 1911, 1913, 1929, 1930, 1972, 1973, 1974, 1989
American League championships (15): 1902, 1905, 1910, 1911, 1913,
1914, 1929, 1930, 1931, 1972, 1973, 1974, 1988, 1989, 1990
American League West division first-place finishes (10): 1971,
1972, 1973, 1974, 1975, 1981, 1988, 1989, 1990, 1992
Last place finishes (24): 1915, 1916, 1917, 1918, 1919, 1920, 1921, 1935, 1936, 1938, 1940,
1941, 1942, 1943, 1945, 1946, 1950, 1954, 1956, 1960, 1964, 1965, 1967, 1979, 1993

box scores. Mack began his professional baseball career in 1884 as a catcher in the Connecticut League. He joined the National League in 1886, playing for the Washington Statesmen and later for the Pittsburgh Pirates. His first managerial stint came in 1894 with the Pirates, when he was 32.

Mack lost his job with the Pirates in 1896 and was thus available and eager to fit into Ban Johnson's plans. With financial backing from Philadelphia businessman Benjamin Shibe, Mack moved to Philadelphia in 1900 and proceeded to build a team. His first move confirmed everyone's worst

fears: he lured two hot prospects, Napoleon "Nap" Lajoie and Lave Cross, from the Phillies. Mack also signed an unknown pitcher from Gettysburg College, Eddie Plank, and courted pitcher Edward "Rube" Waddell, then with the Pirates.

In 1901, their first year of existence, the Athletics finished a respectable fourth in the standings. Lajoie batted .422 and won the Triple Crown, leading the league that year in batting average, homeruns, and runs batted in. By the following season Mack had assembled a talented young squad. Six regulars—led by Cross—hit better than

Transcendental Graphics

Eddie Plank

.300, Plank won 20 games, and Waddell led the league in strikeouts. The Philadelphia Athletics won the 1902 American League pennant with 83 victories. The World Series had yet to be established on an official level, so the A's had to be content with being the best in their league.

The "White Elephants" in Philadelphia

Money was tight for the Athletics in those days, but Mack turned even this to his advantage. *Pioneers of Baseball* author Robert Smith wrote: "Connie had to struggle hard in Philadelphia. With money from Ben Shibe ... Connie was able to get a ball park next door to a brewery and to lure a number of National League stars his way. He also used Charles Comiskey's trick of giving his club

a name that still lived in baseball fame around Philadelphia—the Athletics. But his operation was so meagerly financed that it had trouble staying afloat and John McGraw, owner at that time of the Baltimore franchise in the new league, allowed that Philadelphia was a 'white elephant' to the league operation. The Athletics flaunted white elephants on their pennants and uniforms for many years thereafter."

Over the next three seasons, Mack carefully built his "white elephant" team into a contender. Plank and Waddell continued to pitch superbly, and hurlers Albert "Chief" Bender, Andy Coakley, and John "Schoolboy" Knight also performed well for the club. Attendance picked up at the new Shibe Park, and the crowds seemed particularly fond of the gentlemanly Mack, who managed in street clothes and never called his players by their colorful nicknames.

The 1905 Athletics climbed into first place again and took the pennant with 92 wins. This time they got their World Series opportunity, meeting the New York Giants in a best-of-seven set. To Giants' manager John McGraw's delight, the young team from Philadelphia lost the Series in five games.

The A's slipped off the pace in the ensuing years, as Mack tinkered with the lineup and exercised his talents for recruiting hot young prospects. By 1910 the wily owner-manager had stars aplenty and was ready to contend again. The roster included future Hall of Famers Eddie Collins, Frank "Home Run" Baker, and Stan Coveleski.

Mack's "$100,000 infield," made up of "Stuffy" McInnis at first, Collins at second, Jack Barry at shortstop, and Baker at third, became the nucleus of the first great A's dynasty.

Pitching, too, provided an embarrassment of riches, with Bender and Jack Coombs combining for a won-lost total of 54-14 in 1910 as the team cruised to first place with 104 victories. This time the Athletics would not be denied a World Series crown. They defeated the Chicago Cubs in five games.

Duplacey and Romain noted: "This accumulation of pure talent and sound supporting players won four pennants and three World Series titles over the next five years, averaging 98 wins a season, and establishing itself as the first 'dynasty' in American League history."

Mack and his "white elephants" rode high with a first place finish and a World Series victory over the Giants in 1911, a pennant and another Series stomping of the Giants in 1913, and a pennant with a World Series loss to the Boston Braves in 1914. In *The American League: An Illustrated History,* Donald Honig called this incarnation of the Athletics "up to that point the greatest team in American League history."

Fate intervened and broke up Mack's dynastic ballclub. In 1914 yet another upstart league was initiated, the Federal League. Taking a page from the American League's book, the Federal League owners bid high for the services of established major league players, especially the well-known

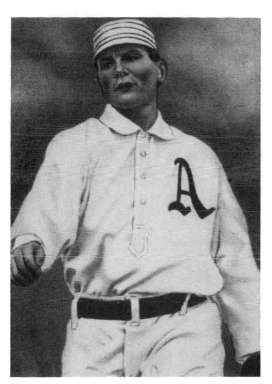

Transcendental Graphics

Chief Bender

Athletics. Ray Robinson noted in *Baseball's Most Colorful Managers:* "As the A's won again in 1914 and entered the World Series against the Boston Braves, there were new rumblings in the baseball world.

"Another major league known as the Federals was trying to assert itself, by waving healthy bundles of dollars under the noses of stars of both leagues. Mack's players were as vulnerable as any others. How much that lure of cash and the internal wrangling that was going on among the Athletics contributed to the team's incredible failure in the 1914 Series against George Stallings's 'miracle' Braves can never really be accurately assessed. But Mack always blamed his club's abysmal showing—four straight losses for the first time in Series history—to the intervention of the Federal League's moneybags."

By 1915 Mack had sold, traded, or lost nine players, including Collins, Coombs, Herb Pennock, McInnis, Plank, and Bender. The effect was devastating. The A's won only 43 games in 1915 and finished 1916 with a .235 "winning" percentage, 40 games behind the first-place Washington Senators.

Between 1915 and 1921 the club finished in last place each season. Robinson wrote: "However, if the benevolent leader in the dugout was disheartened, he didn't show it. He was convinced he could rebuild his team. He knew that all the king's horses and all the king's men couldn't put Humpty-Dumpty together again. But he still thought the anemic old elephant in Philly could be resuscitated with an influx of talent."

Fortunes began to reverse in 1922, when the Athletics left the cellar for the first time in seven years. One of the catalysts for the slow rebirth was catcher Mickey Cochrane, who joined the club in 1925. Cochrane had made the team as an infielder, but Mack moved the youngster behind the plate, setting the stage for Mickey's Hall of Fame career. In 1926 another promising rookie arrived. James Emory Foxx was an unknown from the sparsely-populated eastern shore of Maryland. Ironically, he had been a catcher, but Mack moved him to first base.

Yet another superstar lured to Philadelphia during the mid-1920s was pitcher Lefty Grove. Grove, purchased from Baltimore for the staggering sum of $100,600, quickly established himself as the AL's premier fastball artist, leading the league in strikeouts his first seven years. Outfielder Al Simmons rounded out the new nucleus of talent, hitting better than .350 from 1924 through 1931 and driving in more than 100 runs each of those years.

Athletics Crumble Yankee Dynasty

The A's faced a daunting task: they had to dethrone the New York Yankees, a team that included the likes of Babe Ruth and Lou Gehrig.

Transcendental Graphics

Frank Baker

Honig noted: "It took a remarkable team to make that Yankee squad sweat, and that was exactly what Connie Mack had put together."

Still, Mack continued to tinker. Prior to the 1928 season he decided to drop the elephant logo from the team uniforms. Although it is doubtful that this move had any real effect on club morale, Duplacey and Romain nevertheless contended that "the A's did begin to fly up the American League standings like the weight of an elephant had been lifted from their shoulders."

Mack's Athletics brought Yankee domination to a screeching halt in 1929, winning 104 games behind strong pitching from George Earnshaw and Lefty Grove. Cochrane, Simmons, and Foxx—all lethal hitters—were abetted by outfielders Bing Miller and Mule Haas. The 1929 A's cruised to a first-place finish—a full 18 games ahead of the Yankees—and advanced to the World Series to meet the Chicago Cubs. If Connie Mack was not a legend before this memorable fall classic, he certainly achieved that status during the ensuing five games.

At the outset of the 1929 World Series, Mack had Earnshaw (a 24-game winner) and Grove (a 20-game winner) on the bench. In a move that startled everyone, he tapped right-hander Howard Ehmke to start game one. Ehmke had not pitched for weeks; in fact, he had only worked 55 innings all season.

What most people didn't know was that Mack had sent Ehmke to scout the Cubs for the last weeks of the regular season. Ehmke had done his homework well.

According to Robinson, "Ehmke was so good in that first Series game, so well rested, so well versed in the respective weaknesses of Cub batters like Hack Wilson, Charlie Grimm, Gabby Hartnett, Riggs Stephenson, and Rajah [Rogers] Hornsby, that he breezed through to a 3-1 victory, as 50,000 Cub fans watched in bewilderment. In addition, just to rub it in, Ehmke struck out 13 Cubs, a World Series record at that time. It was probably the most perplexing pitching choice in World Series history. But nobody had reckoned with Mr. Mack's wizardry in the care and fondling of pitchers." The Athletics won the 1929 World Series in five games.

Mack was determined to repeat in 1930. His team met his expectations superbly, copping another pennant with 102 season victories. Grove led the league with a 28-5 record. Foxx and Simmons combined to drive in 321 runs, second in the league to the still potent Ruth-Gehrig tandem.

In the postseason Philadelphia took another World Series crown, this time defeating the St. Louis Cardinals in six hard-fought games. The highlight—and some say the decisive blow—in the 1930 Series was a Jimmie Foxx 2-run homer in the ninth inning of game five.

The A's juggernaut rolled on in 1931, seeming to grow stronger all the time. Grove won 31 games and lost only four, at one point stringing together 16 victories in a row. Simmons led the offense with a .390 average. Philadelphia cruised to another pennant with 107 wins, a franchise record that endures to this day. In the World Series the A's were to face the same Cardinal team they had defeated soundly the previous year, so the team went into the post-season as heavy favorites.

St. Louis was looking for revenge, and in the 1931 World Series they got it. Cardinal star Pepper Martin stole bases—and the show—as St. Louis pounded out a seven-game Series victory. Duplacey and Romain concluded: "The final pitch of that Series ended the glory years of the Philadelphia team. Although Jimmie Foxx was to slug 58 homers and drive home 169 runs in 1932 and become the second and last Athletic to win the Triple Crown in 1933, the Philadelphia Athletics' days as a force in the American League were over."

Part of the problem was money. Mack and his cohorts had spent liberally to recruit and maintain such top talent as Grove and Foxx. As the Great Depression deepened, and attendance fell off in Philadelphia, Mack was forced to break up his fine team. It was a gradual process. The Athletics finished in second place in 1932 and in third place in 1933, but the best players departed in trades or sales. Simmons, Haas, and Earnshaw went to Chicago; Foxx and Grove joined the Boston Red

Transcendental Graphics

Lefty Grove

Sox; and Cochrane journeyed west to Detroit for a fine stint as player-manager of the Tigers.

The results were predictable. Between 1935 and 1950 the A's finished dead last ten times and failed to reach .500 on 12 occasions. Some years were downright dreadful: in 1940 the team went 54-100, in 1943, 49-105. Mack was well into his eighties by the mid-1940s, but he stayed at the helm. His last decent season came in 1948, when a team boosted by returning veterans of World War II racked up 84 victories for a fourth-place finish. That season was followed by two more years below .500, and Mack finally decided to retire.

A's Lose Mack

Robinson wrote: "In 1950, as Mr. Mack took his perch in the Philadelphia dugout for his fiftieth and final year, hopes were high that the A's might produce a miracle and give the revered manager one last flag. Instead, as the pitching staff fell completely apart, the A's sank to last, winning only 52 games.... Their manager was a sad, bewildered, disappointed man, edging close to his ninetieth year." Mack lived six more years, still maintaining close ties to the team through his replacement manager, Jimmy Dykes.

Connie Mack died at the age of 94. Duplacey and Roman noted that the Tall Tactician "would long be remembered as much for his innovative baseball technique as he would for the civilian clothes he wore in the dugout." Under Mack's guidance the A's had won nine pennants and five World Series titles—but they had also finished in last place 17 times.

Few major league teams in any sport were more closely linked with a single dynamic individual than were the Athletics and Connie Mack. Even the home ballpark in Philadelphia, where the team played for much of its history, was named Connie Mack Stadium. Robinson simply remembered Mack as a man whose name "was synonymous with baseball for more than a half century."

During Mack's last illness, his family sold the Athletics franchise to businessman Arnold Johnson. Johnson found himself in possession of a withering franchise. The 1954 Philadelphia Athletics compiled a 51-103 record, finishing in last place, 60 games out. Fan support had dwindled to a mere trickle by then—the team drew only 304,000 customers during its last year in the City of Brotherly Love.

Even before he bought the team, Johnson had decided to move it. When play resumed in the spring of 1955, the A's had a new home, in Kansas City, Missouri. It had taken 54 years, but the National League finally won the battle for Philadelphia's baseball fans.

Johnson's decision to relocate seemed sound. Housed in Kansas City's spacious new Municipal Stadium, the Athletics drew over a million fans during their first year in town—despite finishing in sixth place with a 63-91 record. Kansas City had previously been the site of an important farm team for the New York Yankees. Municipal Stadium was contracted by one of the Yankees' owners, and Johnson tapped Parke Carroll, the former general manager of the Yankee farm team, as the new Athletics GM.

According to Duplacey and Romain, "the new K.C. team was a classic example of the more things change, the more they stay the same.... To say Carroll worked in concert with his former employers would be a decided understatement. Most of the talented players the A's nurtured soon found their way into Yankee pinstripes." Promising A's players sent to New York included Ryne Duren, Clete Boyer, Hector Lopez, and Roger Maris. In return for this talent drain, the Yankees sent past-their-prime players like Billy Martin, Hank Bauer, Bill Renna, and Don Larsen to the A's. Duplacey and Romain concluded: "For many marginal players with the Yankees, Kansas City was known as ... Siberia."

The Kansas City A's were not without merit, however. Lou Boudreau and Harry Craft, both fine managers, each spent three years leading the team. Vic Power batted .319 in 1955, and Harry Simpson drove in 105 runs in 1956, before leaving for the Yankees. Fans flocked through the turnstiles during the "honeymoon" years of 1955 and 1956, but after that interest waned rapidly. As Duplacey and Romain put it, "It was hard to take pride in a franchise that reached the triple figures in the loss department four times." Into this disappointing state of affairs jumped Charles O. Finley.

A native of Ensley, Alabama, Finley had grown up on a hog farm and had literally worked his way from rags to riches. As a young man he nearly worked himself to death, putting in time on an assembly line during the day and selling insurance at night. Stricken with pneumonic tuberculosis in 1946—widely attributed to overwork—he lay near death in a sanitarium for months and months. When he began to recover, he devised plans for a group disability insurance company aimed particularly at the medical profession. After his recovery he implemented his plan, earning a million dollars profit in the first two years of work.

Finley loved baseball. What little spare time he had as a youngster and young adult had been spent playing the game. He realized he lacked the talent to become a professional ballplayer, so he began to dream of greater things, like owning his own team. By 1954 he had saved enough to buy a franchise, and he went shopping. The Kansas City A's became an attractive prospect, and Finley pursued the team aggressively.

"Charles O. Finley was not exactly welcomed with open arms when he attempted to purchase the Kansas City A's," wrote Duplacey and Romain. "Most baseball men were wary of the vociferous self-promoter but nevertheless they allowed him to buy into the suffering squad." In December of 1960 Finley acquired a 52 percent interest in the Athletics for $1,975,000. Just two months later he bought the remaining stock for roughly the same price. Major league baseball would never be the same again.

The Finley Era

Years later, Finley told the *New York Times:* "When I came into baseball in Kansas City ... they told me I'd have to have this and I'd have to have that. I went out and hired Frank Lane, who was supposed to be the best general manager available. I found out one thing about baseball people right away. They like to make the game sound so complex that nobody but them can run it. It doesn't take a genius to run a ball club.... I fired Lane and became my own general manager."

Finley took control of the Athletics, from the front office to the dugout. From his base in Chicago, he would listen to games on the radio and telephone his instructions straight to the A's manager. This did not endear him to the men he hired to skipper the team. In Finley's first eight years as owner of the A's, seven different managers worked for him and either quit or were fired.

Nor did Finley confine his interference to the field of play. He became nationally known for the outlandish promotional stunts he devised to boost attendance. Among his innovations were a mechanical rabbit in an A's uniform that popped out of the stadium turf with fresh baseballs as needed;

a flock of sheep—with shepherd—cropping grass behind right field; pink fluorescent lights to mark the foul lines; and a new mascot—Charlie O. the mule. Finley also retired the staid white and blue Athletics uniforms in favor of new garb in forest green and shocking gold. The uniforms were deemed in bad taste when they debuted in 1963, but since then many other franchises have adopted colorful uniforms as well.

Some of Finley's innovations made their way into major league history. It was Finley who first suggested, in 1964, that World Series games be played at night, under the lights, so working people could see them. He was also the first to propose extracting the pitcher from the batting order in favor of a "designated hitter." Other Finley ideas—such as giving batters three balls for a walk rather than four, and using bright orange baseballs for easier visibility—met with thinly veiled scorn.

Under the tempestuous Finley, the A's continued to flounder. "This team was just plain awful," Duplacey and Romain admitted. Even the introduction of two expansion teams in 1961 did little to improve the Athletics' hopeless lot. The team finished in last place in 1964, 1965, and 1967. Its best showing was a seventh-place, 74-86 season under manager Alvin Dark, in 1966. During those years, Finley both wooed the Kansas City fans by offering outlandish promotions and alienated them by attempting to move the franchise to Dallas or Louisville, Kentucky.

One glimmer of hope appeared as the Kansas City A's continued to suffer. Finley put his scouts to work locating youngsters with potential, then he signed them, often right out of high school. One by one, players such as Reggie Jackson, Sal Bando, Jim "Catfish" Hunter, Bert Campaneris, John "Blue Moon" Odom, and Vida Blue signed with the Athletics and reported to various farm teams. These players were too young to help the A's while the team was in Kansas City, but they would become the driving force for a number of championships once the club left town.

In 1967—another last-place year for the A's, this one with 99 losses—Finley applied to have his franchise moved to California. The American League gave him permission, and the Athletics departed for Oakland.

A New Home in Oakland

The 1968 Oakland A's featured a number of talented but relatively unknown players. On May 8, 1968, a young right-hander named "Catfish" Hunter pitched a perfect game—a feat that had not been accomplished since 1922—against the Minnesota Twins. The Oakland infield boasted shortstop Bert "Campy" Campaneris, probably the best-known Athletic at the time. In the outfield, youngsters Joe Rudi and Reggie Jackson caught

the national eye. The A's won 82 games in 1968, the highest total for the team in twenty years. A period of rebuilding had begun that would climax in dramatic fashion.

Reggie Jackson was the big Oakland newsmaker in 1969. Jackson, who had grown up in Pennsylvania and attended Arizona State University, signed with the Athletics in the free agent draft of 1966. He made his debut with the team in Kansas City and moved west with it to California. In 1968 he belted 29 home runs, and by 1969 Jackson had hit the stride that would take him to the Hall of Fame.

As Honig described it, he became "a bona fide big ripper," smashing 47 home runs, second highest in the league. An intelligent man with a

Transcendental Graphics

Jim "Catfish" Hunter

healthy ego, Jackson met his match in Charlie Finley—and vice versa. As the 1969 season wound to a close, the two men became embroiled in highly-publicized contract negotiations which were settled to neither's satisfaction. Duplacey and Romain wrote: "When the new decade began, Jackson was totally drained emotionally, and his on-field performance suffered as a result. He dropped to 23 homers and 66 RBIs, finishing with a lowly average of .237."

The problems Jackson had with Finley would be encountered repeatedly by other team stars, almost always with the same results. Morale was never high among the Oakland A's. Teammates bickered between themselves, managers came and went all too quickly, and almost everyone detested Finley. Nevertheless, talent prevailed, and this feuding, discontented bunch took the field and played baseball with an intensity rarely matched in recent history.

The A's began the 1971 season with yet another new manager. Finley hired Dick Williams, who had recently lost his job with the Red Sox. Williams was tough, straight-talking, and aggressive—just the man the angry A's needed to channel their energies. Duplacey and Romain suggested that the players hated Williams and Finley so much "they won just to spite them."

Whatever their motivation might have been, the 1971 Oakland A's were ready to win. Williams had two excellent starting pitchers in Vida Blue (1971 American League Most Valuable Player and Cy Young Award winner) and Catfish Hunter, and a lethal reliever named Rollie Fingers, who turned in 17 saves. The 1971 A's won 101 games and finished first in the American League West.

The Athletics, who had not made a post-season appearance since the Great Depression, faced the Baltimore Orioles in the American League Championship Series. The veteran Orioles featured a starting staff with four 20-game winners and a recent history of American League domination—they dispatched the A's in three straight games. Duplacey and Romain noted: "Despite the disappointment of missing the fall classic, the team had built a solid nucleus and it was clear they

were only a player or two away from winning it all."

The missing link arrived during the winter of 1971-72. Oakland traded Rick Monday to the Cubs for pitcher Ken Holtzman. Holtzman, a left-hander, was a steady performer who had an off-year in 1971. His play picked up immediately when he joined the A's, and he averaged 19 wins per season during his three years with the team.

The Angry A's

All was not smooth sailing for the tempestuous A's as the 1972 campaign got under way. Another contract dispute—this time with Vida Blue—threatened to rob the team of one of its most valuable assets. Blue wanted more money, based on his award-winning 1971 campaign. Finley countered that 1971 was just Blue's first year as a starter and that he would have to prove himself over several seasons. Enraged, Blue threatened to sit out the entire season. Finley did not back down. The stalemate was finally broken by baseball's commissioner, Bowie Kuhn, but Blue managed only six wins in 1972.

Honig called the 1972 A's "a team of personalities, enlivened occasionally by clubhouse punch-outs among themselves" who were "united by two things: a spirited zest to win, and their dislike for owner Charles O. Finley." Earning the nickname the "angry A's," the team won 93 games. Hunter, Holtzman, "Blue Moon" Odom, and Fingers led the pitching staff, while Jackson, Bando, Mike Epstein, and Joe Rudi made up the offense.

Finley promised bonuses to anyone who grew a mustache, so many of the players sported facial hair, especially the flamboyant reliever Fingers. His handlebar mustache soon became his trademark, and he wore it for the rest of his career.

A second consecutive American League West championship brought the A's to the League Championship Series against a resurgent Detroit Tigers team. The Tigers, managed by Billy Martin, bowed to Oakland in a tightly-contested series, three games to two. True to their "angry A's" reputation, the Oakland players initiated a bench-clearing brouhaha in the second game, after Bert Campaneris took exception to a bean ball from Detroit pitcher Lerrin LaGrow. Campaneris was benched for the rest of the series, but the A's surged on without him to earn their first visit to the World Series since 1930.

Ironically, the man who would come to be known as "Mr. October"—Reggie Jackson—was forced to sit out his very first World Series appearance. Jackson tore a hamstring muscle stealing home in the last game of the League Championship Series. He watched from the bench while his replacement, Gene Tenace, joined the lineup. The A's met the Cincinnati Reds in the 1972 World Series, and—as fate would have it—Tenace turned the tides for Oakland. He hit home runs in his first two series at-bats—a World Series first—and his three runs batted in were all the offense the A's needed to win game one.

As the series stretched to seven games, Tenace was the star once again, driving in two runs in Oakland's 3-2 seventh-game victory. Tenace, who had hit only five home runs during the 1972 season, was named Series Most Valuable Player for his four home runs, nine RBIs, and .348 batting average. Catfish Hunter earned two World Series wins, holding the Reds to five runs in 16 innings.

It was more of the same in 1973. Off the field the players quarreled, Finley flexed his muscles, and Williams grumbled. On the field Oakland looked tougher than ever. Pitching was still the team's strong suit: Holtzman (21-13), Hunter (21-5), and Blue (20-9) were all 20-game winners, and Fingers chipped in with 22 saves. During one stretch, Hunter won 13 straight starts, and his final winning percentage of .808 led the major leagues.

Remarkably, only one Athletics hitter, Joe Rudi, had better than a .300 batting average. With 94 wins, Oakland took the American League West by six games to set up another League Championship showdown with the Baltimore Orioles.

The A's were eager to avenge their 1971 ALCS loss to the Orioles. The 1973 Championship Series went the maximum five games, including an extra-innings Oakland win in the third game

and a dramatic come-from-behind Baltimore victory in game four. Hunter drew the starting assignment in the series tie-breaker, then shut down the Baltimore offense, allowing only five hits in the 3-0 Oakland win. The A's advanced to the World Series once again, this time against the New York Mets.

Charlie Finley had always exercised free reign over his team, even during games. In the 1973 fall classic, he did it in front of a national audience. The A's quickly lost game one of the series, but the controversy began with game two. The A's trailed by two runs going into the bottom of the ninth, but were able to tie the score and send the contest into extra innings.

The score remained tied until the 12th, when the Mets scored four runs on a pair of errors by Oakland second baseman Mike Andrews. The Mets won the game 10-7, and Finley was incensed. Determined to punish Andrews, Finley tried to have the player suspended. After that failed, the owner tried to put Andrews on the disabled list. When Commissioner Bowie Kuhn intervened, Finley backed down—but he ordered Dick Williams not to use Andrews again during the Series. Andrews, an eight-year veteran, sat on the bench while the Athletics came from behind to win their second straight World Series.

Williams Leaves a Winner

The Andrews affair—played out as it was on national television—was the last straw for Dick Williams. It is rare for a manager to resign after having just won a World Series; rarer still, to quit after winning two consecutive world titles. Williams did just that, announcing his intentions immediately following Oakland's seventh-game victory. *New York Times* columnist Red Smith observed: "Williams ... has done Good Time Charlie's bidding for three years and managed to keep a civil tongue behind his mustache, but the Andrews caper was too much for his stomach." As usual Finley asserted himself. Williams had signed a contract midway through the 1973 season, and the irascible owner would not release him from it.

Duplacey and Romain noted: "Williams spent half of the 1974 season collecting his salary for watching the major league managerial jobs he wanted get filled by other candidates." One of those jobs was with the New York Yankees. Finally, when the lowly California Angels fired their skipper, Williams was released from his contract and allowed to depart.

Williams's successor was Alvin Dark, returning for a second stint as Oakland's manager. Now it was Dark's turn to lead the surly band of malcontents who eased their frustration by winning baseball games. Hunter won 25 games and the Cy Young Award in 1974, while Jackson belted 29 homers, and the A's racked up 90 wins and their fourth division championship in as many years.

The Athletics once again topped the Orioles in the League Championship Series, limiting Baltimore to just one run in the last 27 innings of series play. Holtzman pitched a five-hitter in the second game, Blue turned in a masterpiece shutout in the third game, and Hunter and Fingers combined for a one-hitter in the fourth and decisive contest.

The Oakland victory set the stage for the first-ever all-California World Series, pitting the A's against the Los Angeles Dodgers. Behind the strong pitching of Holtzman, Hunter, and Fingers, the "angry A's" made history with their third consecutive World Series title, defeating the Dodgers four games to one. According to Duplacey and Romain: "Oakland had established themselves as one of baseball's greatest teams, becoming the only squad other than the New York Yankees to string together three straight World Series victories."

These championships, along with four straight division titles, prompted observers to grudgingly admit that Finley must have done something right. The A's were often underdogs in their various post-season matchups. Even Honig conceded that the club "was not the measure of the recent Baltimore contingents or of earlier Yankee teams." Yet Oakland achieved success, for a shining moment, on a par with the best days of the vaunted New

AP/Wide World Photos

Vida Blue (left) and Reggie Jackson

York Yanks. Finley certainly had luck on his side, but the wily owner also showed skill in signing young talents and grooming them in the farm system. Everyone from Vida Blue to Catfish Hunter, from Sal Bando to Reggie Jackson to Joe Rudi, had come straight through the Oakland system. Finley's stroke of luck was that they all matured at the same moment.

Now his luck was about to run out. The first rumblings came from Catfish Hunter. Hunter's contract had stipulated that half his salary be paid to an insurance company in the form of deferred payments to an annuity. This method of compensation put Finley at a tax disadvantage, so the owner neglected to make the payments.

When Hunter found out, he took the matter before an arbitration panel. The panel ruled in Hunter's favor and declared the pitcher a free agent. In a flash, the talented ace signed with the Yankees for a seven-figure salary. When the 1975 season began, the A's found themselves without their number one starter—and the free agent bug had been planted in a number of the other top stars.

The changes were slight at first. Despite the loss of Hunter, the Athletics went 98-64 in 1975, winning their fifth straight divisional crown. Vida Blue won 22 games and Rollie Fingers saved 24, while Jackson, Rudi, Billy Williams, and Gene Tenace all hit more than 20 home runs. The A's 98-64 record in 1975 was the team's best since 1931.

The 1975 Boston Red Sox featured a lineup of canny sluggers and a crafty pitcher, Luis Tiant. It was the Sox who finally broke Oakland's string of post-season successes with a three-game sweep of the A's in the American League Championship Series. Then the mighty Oakland dynasty began to crumble in earnest.

Finley was quite well known for keeping a strict rein on salaries and other costs. Even through its championship years the Oakland team did not draw vast crowds. Finley nevertheless earned a profit on the franchise each year, principally because he kept his front office staff to a bare minimum and his player salaries relatively low. Over the years he was helped immensely by baseball's reserve clause, which bound an individual to a team even if that individual did not have a signed contract.

In 1975 the reserve clause was declared invalid in court, opening the door to the inflated salaries and bidding wars so common in baseball today. Finley was not about to play that game, so he decided to trade or sell his best players before they could waltz away on their own. He sent Jackson and Holtzman to Baltimore in 1975 and tried to sell Blue, Rudi, and Fingers as well.

Baseball Commissioner Kuhn intervened "in the best interests of baseball" and forced Finley to keep Blue, Rudi, and Fingers in Oakland. Finley bided his time and then shopped his stars around again.

Duplacey and Romain wrote: "Rarely has the baseball world seen a group of athletes like the Oakland A's of this era. With ultimate confidence in each other and their abilities, they became one of the finest clutch teams of all time. The team won 21 post-season games during its reign as champions, 14 of those games by one run.... Yet, in one brief three-month period, it all came unraveled. When the team took the field in 1977, the only remaining player from the glory days was Vida Blue." To nobody's particular surprise, the likes of Bando, Tenace, Campaneris, and Fingers all had declared free-agency and left Oakland. Just as in the days of Connie Mack, the team could not recover from such a vast talent drain.

After a second-place finish in 1976, the A's tumbled to the basement in 1977 with only 63 wins. The finish was even more embarrassing because the Seattle Mariners had joined the AL West as an expansion team that year and were thus expected to turn up at the bottom. Managers Jack McKeon and Bobby Winkles played musical chairs, and the only highlight was rookie Mitchell Page's 75 RBIs.

As dismal as the 1977 season was, it hardly set the stage for 1979, when the Athletics lost 108 games. Manager Jim Marshall had only joined the club in time for spring training that year, and he viewed the season as an opportunity to give a new crop of younger players a chance to learn by doing. Matt Keough, Dwayne Murphy, Rickey Henderson, and Mike Norris were just a few of the new faces who took the field for Oakland in 1979.

Duplacey and Romain wrote: "The fans in the Oakland area revolted in the only way they knew how, by staying away from the ballpark. Only 304,000 dared go to the Coliseum in 1979, and it was evident that Charlie Finley's grip on the team was slipping."

Finley tried to sell the team to businessmen in Denver, but he could not extricate himself from a long-term lease with the Oakland Coliseum. To save money while the team floundered, Finley stripped the front office of personnel, pared down his farm system, and sold fringe players wherever he could. Baseball had always been a business to him, and he did not like to lose money.

Finley had not abandoned the team entirely, however. In 1980 he hired the Athletics' 22nd manager, Billy Martin. The volatile Martin had already served as skipper in Minnesota, Detroit, and New York, but his ability was still in doubt. That would change once he established himself in Oakland. "Martin took control of the A's with such force, even Finley could only sit back and watch the proceedings," observed Duplacey and Romain. "The A's aggressive style of hit and run, run and hit, and steal-steal-steal became known as 'Billy Ball' and it attracted baseball fans all around the nation."

"Billy Ball" found its quintessential practitioner in Rickey Henderson. Henderson grew up in Oakland and had signed with the A's right out of high school in 1976. After a few years in the minors, he joined the parent club on June 23, 1979, and quickly established himself as a starter. It did not take Martin long to assess Henderson's potential, both as a hitter and a threat to steal bases. The manager gave Henderson *carte blanche* to steal at will, and with his fearless, head-first dive, Rickey stole 100 bases in 1980, breaking the American League record for most steals in a year.

Martin's influence on the Athletics was felt most strongly on the pitching staff. Essentially the same hurlers who had compiled a team earned run average of 4.75 in 1979 re-grouped for a 3.46 ERA in 1980, while pitching a remarkable 94 complete games. The rotation was anchored by 22-game-winner Mike Norris as well as Rick Langford and Matt Keough. With fine performances from his starters, and a good outfield consisting of Henderson, Murphy, and Tony Armas, Martin was able to reverse the Athletics' fortunes in a single season. The team that had won only 54 games in 1979 finished 83-79 in 1980, good for second place in the American League West.

Finley's Reign Ends

On November 3, 1980, an era came to an end in Oakland. Charlie Finley finalized the sale of the Athletics to California businessman Walter Haas. According to Duplacey and Romain, Haas "inherited a team that was, simply put, in critical shape. Finley had reduced the front office operation to six people, without a promotion or advertising depart-

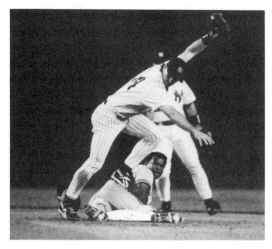

AP/Wide World Photos

Rickey Henderson

ment. The Oakland farm system, which had developed almost all the stars that made the team one of the greatest ever to perform on the diamond was nearly bone dry.... Most of the minor league system's best resources had already been called up to the big league and they were the last drop of oil from the well. Haas had acquired a team whose buds were in blossom, but whose roots were dying."

Those "buds" had some spunk to them, however. In the strike-shortened season of 1981, the Athletics were in first place when play was suspended on June 12th. When the strike was settled and games resumed in late July, the baseball commissioner declared that division winners of the first half and the second half would meet in a best-of-five divisional playoff. Thus Oakland was guaranteed post-season play as early as the first week of August, 1981.

In the first-ever American League West playoff series, Oakland met and swept the Kansas City Royals, three games to none. The A's pitching staff dominated the series, allowing only two runs in three games. The regular 1981 A.L. Championship Series pitted the A's against the Yankees, an interesting matchup given Martin's previous association with the New York team. As Duplacey and

Romain noted, however, "The series was tangy, but Martin would never savor ... sweet revenge." The Athletics scored a total of four runs as the Yankees swept them in three games to advance to the World Series. Duplacey and Romain concluded that after the third and decisive game, "amid the subdued patrons in the A's clubhouse was a distraught Billy Martin. He had brought the team out of the deepest of cellars to climb the pinnacle of success, and while the mood in the dressing room was optimistic, Billy Martin knew his future lay elsewhere."

Martin remained with the Athletics for one more year, a disappointing season that saw the A's finish in fifth place with a 68-94 record. The highlight of 1982 was provided by Rickey Henderson, now coming into his own as a superb leadoff hitter and one of the premier base stealers of all time. On September 11, 1982, Henderson set a major league record for most stolen bases in a season, surpassing the record of 118 set by Lou Brock. Henderson ended the year with 130 steals, a record that will likely last for some time to come. This milestone, coming in an otherwise lackluster season, gave Oakland fans a reason to come to the Coliseum.

In the mid-1980s owner Haas set about rebuilding the struggling Athletics. Haas took steps to strengthen a farm system that had been tapped dry during Finley's last years. The new owner also hired a number of free-agent superstars on short contracts, hoping for an added punch here and there in the lineup. Many fine players in the twilight of their careers came to the coast for a final season or two, including Joe Morgan, Reggie Jackson, and Davey Lopes. On the other hand, Haas traded Henderson to the Yankees for pitcher Jay Howell and four minor league prospects.

The biggest problem facing the Athletics in mid-decade was pitching. Duplacey and Romain noted that the staff of strong starters in 1981 may have been aged prematurely for want of a good reliever. Subsequent trades for promising hurlers never quite worked out for the team. By 1985, the authors stated, the Athletics were "staffed by the two extremes of aging or unproven arms."

AP/Wide World Photos

José Canseco

Rookies Improve Club's Fortunes

The tide began to turn in 1985 with the arrival of outfielder José Canseco. Canseco joined the Athletics on September 2nd and batted .302 with five home runs in 19 games. One of his home runs—a mammoth shot that reached the roof of Chicago's Comiskey Park—was a sign of things to come. According to Duplacey and Romain, "the rebirth of one of baseball's greatest franchises was underway."

Brash, handsome, and powerfully built, Canseco made outrageous predictions about his ability and then set about backing them up. Once considered too slight to make the majors, he matured into a six-foot-three-inch, 240-pound player with power *and* speed. The A's front office quickly tagged Canseco as the harbinger of a new era of greatness, emblazoning his picture on the cover of the 1986 media guide under the title "The

Natural." (Ironically, Canseco "the Natural" later had to deny allegations that he had built his muscles with the aid of anabolic steroids.)

Canseco made his first All-Star appearance as a rookie, ended the 1986 season with 33 home runs and 117 RBIs, and was named American League Rookie of the Year.

Canseco's rookie year also marked the arrival of yet another new manager. Tony LaRussa became the Athletics' manager on July 7, 1986. He assumed responsibility for a team that was 31-52 and almost immediately turned the franchise around. The rest of the season the A's went 45-34, with help from the bats of Carney Lansford, Dave Kingman, and Canseco. The pieces of the puzzle were beginning to fit together, and more help was on the way.

As brilliant as Canseco's rookie year had been, it would be eclipsed in 1987 by another youngster, Mark McGwire. McGwire smacked 49 home runs—a club record—in his first full year with the A's. He combined with Canseco to form the "Bash Brothers," a nickname based on their slugging ability and on their habit of bashing forearms as a victory salute. McGwire was named Rookie of the Year in 1987, while the Athletics finished right at .500, 81-81, their best showing since 1981.

Prior to the 1988 season, Walter Haas decided to bring back the elephant as the team logo. It was a minor point, but it was a rather touching reminder of the long and storied history of the Athletics franchise. Some have suggested that Haas made the move out of superstition, but whatever his motives, the Oakland A's began 1988 poised on the brink of greatness again. Pitchers Bob Welch, Dave Stewart, Storm Davis, and Todd Burns took the mound for Oakland, and they were backed up by reliever Dennis Eckersley. Eckersley had not expected to become a relief pitcher when he arrived in Oakland in 1987, but he blossomed in the role and proved a pivotal element on a new championship team. Another newcomer in 1987, shortstop Walt Weiss, would bring Oakland its third consecutive Rookie of the Year award.

Duplacey and Romain observed: "The Oak-

AP/Wide World Photos

Mark McGwire

land Athletics of 1988 put on an awesome display, taking the lead in the AL West on April 20 and never looking back. Every aspect of the A's game fell into place during the regular season schedule, and when the leaves took on their autumn colors, the A's had racked up 104 wins and a 13-game lead in the division." Stewart turned in 21 victories, Welch 17, and Davis 16, while Eckersley earned 45 saves.

The big news from Oakland in 1988 was once again José Canseco. At the outset of the season he boasted that he would hit 40 home runs and steal 40 bases that year. Canseco may not have made the prediction had he known that no major leaguer had ever accomplished that feat. Having spoken, however, he proceeded to make good on his promise, finishing the year with 42 home runs, 124 RBIs, and 40 steals, not to mention a .307 batting average. It's no wonder the Athletics began to refer to Canseco as "the franchise."

In the 1988 American League Championship Series, the Athletics faced the Boston Red Sox, the same team that had dealt them defeat in 1975. Few men on either team were old enough to remember the 1975 ALCS clearly, but the fans did, and they wanted revenge. This time they got it. The A's won

AP/Wide World Photos

Tony LaRussa

the first outing 2-1; came from behind to win the second game 4-3; cruised to a 10-6 victory in game three; and swept the series with a 4-1 win in the fourth game. Canseco tied an American League Championship Series record for home runs, and Eckersley earned a save in each of the four games.

This set the stage for another all-California World Series, with the A's meeting the Dodgers on the coast. The underdog Dodgers, with their limping slugger Kirk Gibson and their quiet pitching ace Orel Hershiser, pulled off an upset of LaRussa's Athletics, beating Oakland four games to one.

Duplacey and Romain wrote: "Explaining Oakland's demise in the World Series begins by looking at the following statistics: Canseco and McGwire had one hit apiece, the team batted .177 and scored just 11 runs. They were outscored in almost every inning by the Dodgers and they were out-homered by the supposedly anemic Dodger bats 5 to 2. The simple mathematics of those figures put the Dodgers in the winner's circle and the A's back in the drawing room to prepare for the next season."

The Series loss notwithstanding, optimism ran high in Oakland as 1989 began. No team had repeated as American League champions since the Yankees did it in 1977-78, but LaRussa was confident. Pitching continued to be excellent, as Dave Stewart won 20 games for the third consecutive year, and Davis and Welch both won more than 16. With Eckersley on the disabled list part of the season, Gene Nelson and Rick Honeycutt combined for 20 saves.

A healed Eckersley contributed 33 more. LaRussa acquired needed offensive punch in mid-season by securing the return of Rickey Henderson. Glad to be back home, Henderson batted .378 the remainder of the season, scored 41 runs, and stole 23 bases. His contributions would continue as Oakland clinched the American League West and advanced to the AL Championship Series against the Toronto Blue Jays.

The Jays and the A's were pretty well matched in the 1989 ALCS, except for the presence of Rickey Henderson. Oakland clinched the playoff

AP/Wide World Photos

Dennis Eckersley

in five games, while Henderson led both teams in steals (eight), total bases (fifteen), runs (eight), RBIs (five), walks (seven), on-base percentage (.609), and slugging percentage (1.000). He reached base 14 times, and his stolen base total set a new record for a post-season series. At series end, he was named Most Valuable Player.

Earth-shaking World Series

The 1989 World Series will long be remembered as the first-ever all-Northern California World Series *and* the first World Series to be postponed by an earthquake. The Oakland Athletics and the San Francisco Giants prepared to play a Series in two ballparks that were linked by mass transportation, separated only by the crisp waters of San Francisco Bay. Oakland won the first two

matchups in the Series, including a complete-game shutout pitched by Stewart.

As the two teams prepared for game three in San Francisco's Candlestick Park, the ground began to shake beneath them. A major earthquake, measuring 7.1 on the Richter Scale, buffeted the entire region, causing massive damage and serious loss of life in both Oakland and San Francisco.

The World Series was postponed for 11 days while the two bay-side cities tried to regroup. When it resumed, the Athletics won another two games straight, sweeping the Giants and winning the 1989 World Series crown. Stewart, who became the first pitcher to win two American League Championship Series games and two World Series games in the same year, was named World Series MVP.

According to Duplacey and Romain, "The Oakland Athletics had come full circle, restoring the pride and winning attitude that had been lost during the middle years of the decade. They faced the 1990s with the opportunity to once again be a dynasty team of destiny."

Unbowed, the "dynasty team" strode into 1990 with another division-winning 103-59 season. Stewart won 20 games for a fourth consecutive year, and Welch contributed 27 wins of his own. The A's grabbed their third pennant in a row with a stunning four-game sweep of the Red Sox, and the team prepared for their third consecutive World Series, this time against the Cincinnati Reds.

The Reds had upset a strong Pittsburgh Pirates team to advance to the World Series, and they were on a roll. Cincinnati defeated Oakland in four straight games, including a game one shutout by Reds' pitcher José Rijo. Duplacey and Romain called the 1990 World Series "one of the greatest upsets in Series history," adding: "The A's may have had the best talent but, on this occasion at least, the Reds had the best team."

The 1990 World Series loss stunned the A's, who finished 1991 in fourth place, with an 84-78 record. A resurgence began in 1992, however. The Athletics fought a tight race with the Minnesota Twins through the summer, finally taking the division lead for good on August 5th. A late-season trade astounded the Bay-area faithful: José Canseco was traded to the Texas Rangers for outfielder Ruben Sierra and pitchers Jeff Russell and Bobby Witt.

Once Sierra recovered from a bout with chicken pox, he helped his new team sweep a three game series against Minnesota in mid-September to secure the Western Division title. Eckersley continued to be the A's pitcher of note, leading the American League with 51 saves.

The 1992 American League West championship was the tenth for the Athletics, the most of any major league team since divisional play began in 1969. It was a fitting way to celebrate the 25th anniversary of the team's move from Kansas City to Oakland and the 90th anniversary of their first American League championship.

The elephant logo remained on the A's shirt sleeves as the team journeyed north to meet the Toronto Blue Jays in the League Championship Series. Oakland's season came to an end in a sixth game at Toronto's vast SkyDome, as the Jays took the American League flag and advanced to the World Series.

Injuries ruined the A's repeat chances in 1993; McGwire, outfielders Dave Henderson and Lance Blankenship, and catcher Terry Steinbach missed significant portions of the season. Welch, Ron Darling, Storm Davis, and Shawn Hillegas—the veterans of the pitching staff—all struggled, and Eckersley (4.16 ERA) had his worst year as an Athletic.

The A's became only the second team in major league history to go from first place to last in a single season, finishing 68-94. The spate of injuries forced the team to use its young talent, and the emergence of rookies like pitchers Todd Van Poppel and Steve Karsay, second baseman Brent

Gates, and designated hitter Troy Neel was encouraging.

More than any other team, the Athletics put to rest the notion that the American League West was somehow inferior to the entrenched teams in the East. As parity settles over the major leagues and expansion dilutes the talent pool, teams with intelligent management, committed ownership, and experienced players will be the stuff from which dynasties are made. The Oakland Athletics are one such team, and the elephant on their jerseys—now in a fiercer, more belligerent incarnation—will serve as a reminder of the many dramatic championships the franchise has put together through a century of play.

SOURCES

BOOKS

Duplacey, James, and Joséph Romain, *Baseball's Great Dynasties: The Athletics,* New York: Gallery Books, 1991.

Honig, Donald, *The American League: An Illustrated History,* New York: Crown, 1987.

Liston, Robert A., *The Great Teams: Why They Win All the Time,* New York: Doubleday & Co., 1979.

Robinson, Ray, *Baseball's Most Colorful Managers,* New York: Putnam, 1969.

Smith, Robert, *Pioneers of Baseball,* New York: Little, Brown & Co., 1978.

PERIODICALS

New York Times, October 19, 1973.
New York Times Magazine, July 15, 1973.

—*Mark Kram*

SEATTLE MARINERS

An American League expansion team that made its debut in 1977, the Seattle Mariners never completed a season above .500 until 1991—15 years later. Even then, they earned only a fifth-place finish in the seven-team American League West. Through 1992 the Mariners finished as high as fourth only twice, in 1982 and 1987.

Prior to 1969, baseball in Seattle meant the minor league Rainiers of the Pacific Coast League. Major league baseball arrived with the Seattle Pilots, an American League expansion franchise. The Pilots of 1969 played to meager crowds in Sick's Stadium, the hastily refurbished home of the Rainiers.

In 1970 the franchise moved to Milwaukee, where the Pilots became the Brewers. Eight years later, in 1977, with a newly built domed stadium called the Kingdome awaiting them, a second Seattle expansion team arrived in town. Their nickname, the Mariners, was chosen from among 15,000 contest entries.

Although the neophyte 1977 Mariners did not end up last in the AL West, they came close, with Oakland claiming the cellar. Among the first-year favorites of Seattle fans were pitcher Glenn Abbott and outfielder Ruppert Jones, neither of whom lived up to expectations in later years. Between 1978 and 1981 the Mariners shuttled between sixth and seventh place, trying through trades and farm-system development to improve their lot. In 1982, under manager Rene Lachemann, the Mariners climbed to fourth place, led by the hitting of Bruce Bochte and Richie Zisk and the pitching of Floyd Bannister, Gaylord Perry, and relief ace Bill Caudill.

In 1983 they were back in last place, suffering the third 100+ loss season in their brief history. Manager Lachemann gave way to Del Crandall, who was replaced by Chuck Cottier, who left in favor of Dick Williams. Old pro Williams, a pennant-winner at Boston, Oakland, and San Diego, whipped the 1987 Mariners into shape for a fourth-place finish, but lost his job the next June with a 23-33 record.

Bill Plummer, an ex-backup catcher for the Cincinnati Reds, took the helm and led the Mariners to their first winning season in 1991, with 83 victories and 79 defeats. Though this record earned Seattle only a fifth-place finish in the AL West, the Mariners won only four fewer games than the second-place Chicago Cubs, and Seattle fans hoped the team was on its way at last.

"Rupe! Rupe! Rupe!"

On September 29, 1976, pitcher Dave Johnson of the Baltimore Orioles was the first player purchased by the new Seattle Mariners, one of whose six owners was comedian Danny Kaye. But Johnson never threw a pitch for the Mariners before he was picked up on a waiver claim by the Minnesota Twins in May of 1977. The first player drafted by the Mariners was Ruppert Jones, a talented 22-year-old outfielder with Kansas City. Jones was a favorite with the fans whose chants of "Rupe! Rupe! Rupe!" thundered through the cavernous domed stadium.

The Mariners played their first game at the Kingdome on April 6, 1977, under skipper Darrell Johnson, an ex-catcher who had led the Red Sox to a pennant in 1975. Journeyman pitcher, Diego Segui, the only Pilot to become a Mariner, took the hill for the home team and was inevitably dubbed "The Ancient Mariner." Segui lost the opener, 7-0, to California and he did not improve as the season progressed, in the end winning no games at all and losing seven.

Ruppert Jones, on the other hand, did well in 1977, fielding well and batting .263 with 24 homers and 76 RBIs. Outfielder Lee Stanton, nearing the end of his career in the majors, did even better, hitting .275 wtih 29 homers and 90 RBIs. But the Mariners' pitching left a lot to be desired.

The ace of the staff, Glenn Abbott, posted a 12-13 record with a 4.46 ERA. John Montague had a modest 8-12 record, but in late July he tied Steve Busby's American League record by retir-

ing 33 batters in a row—the last 13 he faced in one game, the first 20 he faced in the next.

Fans who were hoping 1978 would be a better year were sorely disappointed. It was the worst in the short history of the franchise, as the Mariners lost 104 games and finished 35 games back. Leon Roberts, an outfielder acquired from Houston, provided most of the offense, batting .301 with 22 homers and 92 RBIs.

Second baseman Julio Cruz, a superb fielder but a weak hitter, became a favorite of the remaining Seattle fans (considerably diminished in numbers) who came to the Kingdome that year. In 1979 Cruz improved at the plate (to .271, his best season ever), and the Mariners improved to 67-95, good for sixth place.

Over the winter the team had acquired Floyd Bannister, a coveted young pitcher. Bannister's record in 1979, 10-15 with a 4.05 ERA, was disappointing, but the club anticipated better things from him in days to come. Mike Parrott was the Mariner pitcher with the best record, 14-12 and a 3.77 ERA. Two other promising pitchers on the staff were southpaw Rick Honeycutt (11-12) and reliever Shane Rawley (5-9).

Bruce Bochte, shifted from the outfield to first base, came through with a .316 batting average, 16 homers, and 100 runs batted in. Designated hitter Willie Horton, a long-time Detroit outfielder nearing the end of his playing days, still showed his old power, belting 29 round-trippers and driving in 106 runs.

Trading and Drafting

The 1979 Mariners had some strength to work with. Their outfield of Ruppert Jones, Leon Roberts, and Tom Paciorek (a veteran of the Dodgers and Braves), while hardly sensational, seemed adequate. However, for the 1980 season they traded Jones, used Paciorek in a utility role, and saw Roberts suffer through a mediocre year. Seattle had a first-rate outfielder, Dave Henderson, who was coming up through the farm system, but he was not yet ready for the majors.

Team Information at a Glance

Founding date: April 6, 1977

Home stadium: The Kingdome
411 First Avenue South
Seattle, WA 98104

Dimensions: Left-field line—331 feet
Center field—405 feet
Right-field line—312 feet
Seating capacity: 59,702

Team uniforms: Home—base color white with blue trim;
Road—base color gray with blue trim
Team nickname: Mariners, 1977-present
Team logo: A stylized mariners' compass

Franchise record	Won	Lost	Pct.
(1977-1993)	1,166	1,532	.432

Bruce Bochte performed well at first base, batting .300 and driving in a team-high 78 runs. But second baseman Julio Cruz dropped to .209, catcher Larry Cox hit .202, and outfielder Joe Simpson, .249, had little power or consistency at the plate. The pitching ace of 1979, Mike Parrott, beat the Blue Jays before an opening night crowd of a mere 22,588 at the Kingdome. That was his last win of the season, as he proceeded to lose 16 games in a row, finishing with a 1-16 mark and a 7.28 ERA.

The whole 1980 season was like that for the Mariners, who fell into the cellar again, 59-103. Manager Darrell Johnson got the ax at midseason. His replacement, Maury Wills, had no better success and lasted only 24 games into 1981 before being replaced by Rene Lachemann.

Split-season 1981 found the Mariners still struggling on the field and at the gate. In January of that year George Argyros, a California real estate developer, purchased a majority interest in the club. He promised a turnaround, and the 1981 team did show some improvement.

Their overall record, with Tom Paciorek hitting a career-high .326, put them slightly ahead of the Minnesota Twins in the AL West. Paciorek provided a burst of heroics at the Kingdome early in the season when he belted ninth-inning homers in two successive games as the Mariners came from behind both times to defeat the New York Yankees.

Two days before Paciorek's blasts, Rene Lachemann, who had been managing Seattle's Triple-A Spokane ball club, was named to replace the sulky Maury Wills. ("I had Dave Henderson ... on that team," Wills recalled later. "I didn't like

| HOME FIELD | "A Home Run ... No ... Off the Speaker" |

In 1976 and 1977 when the Mariners' expansion roster was being created, the front office assumed that the ball would not carry well in the Kingdome. They bassed their reasoning on their knowledge of the situation at Houston's Astrodome, and they were wrong. Their faulty logic resulted in a search to obtain good pitchers rather than trying to acquire power hitters.

To their surprise, the ball carried very well indeed in the Kingdome, with hard-hit fly balls bouncing off distant roof-mounted speakers with alarming frequency. A fair ball bouncing off a speaker remained in play, which meant that a sure home run could become a single or a double, as one did for the Mariners' Willie Horton on June 5, 1979—a blow that would have been his 300th career home run.

During the winter of 1980-81 the height of the speakers was raised from 110 feet to 133½ feet above the playing field. Management's intent was to make it harder for hitters to launch towering shots against the speakers, and the move worked. (Willie Horton's lost homer, by the way, was soon avenged. The very next night, June 6, 1979, he blasted the 300th round-tripper of his career, its trajectory unimpeded by a speaker.)

him and I didn't play him.") Under Lachemann the team's competitiveness increased. The Mariners' 1981 draft picks—pitchers Mike Moore, Mark Langston, and outfielder Phil Bradley—promised a better team in the future.

The 1982 ball club was marginally better, winning 76 games, losing 86, and taking fourth place. Mike Moore, after only a year at Lynn in the Double-A Eastern League, came up to Seattle. He was not quite ready, going 7-14 with a 5.36 ERA. But Floyd Bannister had his best season so far (12-13, ERA 3.43), and 43-year-old Gaylord Perry, signed as a free agent, won 10 and lost 12—his win on May 6 was a milestone, the 300th of his career. He beat the Yankees, 7-3 that day, going the distance. Reliever Bill Caudill, 12-9, all of his decisions in relief, registered 26 saves with a 2.35 ERA. Designated hitter Richie Zisk led the Mariners with 21 homers, while Bruce Bochte, for the third time, posted the team's best batting average, .297.

By 1983 the Mariners should have been ready (as the Toronto Blue Jays were) to hold their own in divisional competition. Toronto by then had a solid, competitive ball club. But Seattle's first-round draft picks, except for 1981, had not worked out. This left the team little choice but to make trades and other acquisitions in trying to build a winning team.

It was not working, as the 1983 season demonstrated. Seattle had another celler-dweller, a 102-game loser, no .300 hitters, no winning pitchers, and no clear prospects for improvement. Owner George Argyros, far from sparking a turnaround, appeared intent on keeping salaries down and building equity for an eventual sale of the ball club.

Mark Langston and Alvin Davis

Still, a major league club cannot function without a few quality players. One such, a right-handed pitcher named Mark Langston, had been working his way up through the Seattle farm system. Another, a left-handed first baseman named Alvin Davis, had been doing the same. By 1984 both were ready for their debut as Mariners. The two, who had been teammates at Chattanooga in the Double-A Southern League the year before, broke in with a bang.

Langston compiled a 17-10 record with a 3.40 ERA, led the league in strikeouts with 204, and was named American League Rookie Pitcher of the Year by *The Sporting News*. Davis batted .284 with 27 homers, 116 runs batted in, and was named American League Rookie of the Year.

In addition to Langston and Davis, the 1984 Mariners had a pretty fair outfield, though without great power, in Al Cowens, Dave Henderson, and newcomers Steve Henderson (a veteran acquired from the Cubs) and Phil Bradley (a rookie from the farm system). The other infielders besides Alvin Davis were second baseman Jack Perconte (from the Indians), shortstop Spike Owen (homegrown, in his second year), and third baseman Jim Presley (a rookie and also a farm product).

Perconte paced the team with a batting average of .294. Owen, a capable defensive shortstop, hit .245, about par for him, and Presley, chosen in the free-agent draft of 1979, spent about half his time in 1984 at Salt Lake City in the PCL, hitting .317 for the Triple-A Gulls but only .227 for the Mariners. Despite a losing season (74-88) and only a fifth-place finish, Seattle fans began to have expectations. So did the team's management, coining the slogan "See It Happen" for 1985.

It failed to happen in 1985—that is, if "It" meant moving up in the standings. The Mariners ended with the same won-lost record as the year before (74-88) but dropped one rung in the AL West, elbowing out only the Texas Rangers. Moreover, Seattle finished 17 games back, as opposed to 10 games back in 1984. Still, this youthful Mariner team supplied plenty of fireworks in the Kingdome, led by designated hitter Gorman Thomas's 32 home runs, the most ever for a Seattle player.

Thomas, who sat out the 1984 season with an injury, was named the American League's Comeback Player of the Year. In home run production Jim Presley (28) and Phil Bradley (26) were not far behind Stormin' Gorman. Mark Langston suffered injuries and a sophomore jinx, falling to 7-14 with a 5.47 ERA, but Mike Moore in his fourth season took up the slack, going 17-10 with a 3.46 ERA, almost duplicating Langston's performance of the previous year. Manager Chuck Cottier, a mild-mannered ex-second baseman, had taken over the reins late in the 1984 season. His relative success in 1985 earned him a new contract for the next season.

The next season, 1986, was one of those recurring disappointments for Mariner fans. A 9-19 start quickly cost Chuck Cottier his job, and the new man in charge, Dick Williams, who had in his time led Boston, Oakland, and San Diego to the World Series, made some changes but could not lead the 1986 Mariners out of the depths. Third baseman Jim Presley, the team's only All-Star pick, delivered 27 homers and 107 RBIs. Danny Tartabull arrived from Triple-A Calgary and made himself welcome with 25 homers and 96 runs batted in. Phil Bradley had a slow start but ended up with a team-leading .310 batting average. Other hitters fell below expectations.

The pitching turned shaky. Mike Moore, the previous year's ace, dropped to 11-13. Mark Langston led the league in strikeouts with 245 but posted only a 12-14 record. Meanwhile, the Mariner hitters presented opposing pitchers with plenty of strikeouts, setting an all-time American League team record by whiffing 1,148 times. On April 29 at Fenway Park, Red Sox hurler Roger Clemens struck out 20 Seattle batters to set a new major league mark of his own.

Still Building

Late-season and winter trades made significant changes in the Mariner roster for 1987. One trade sent Spike Owen and Dave Henderson to the Red Sox for shortstop Rey Quinones and others. Rising star Danny Tartabull, along with minor league pitcher Rick Luecken, was dealt to Kansas City in exchange for pitchers Scott Bankhead, Steve Shields, and outfielder Mike Kingery.

These trades were not especially helpful, but the Mariners nonetheless got off to a better-than-average start. Second-baseman Harold Reynolds, a farm-system product, proved his value with fine hitting (.275) and even better base-running (60 steals to lead the league).

Alvin Davis and Mark Langston were back at the top of their form, Davis batting .295 with 29 homers and 100 RBIs, Langston chalking up 19 wins against 13 losses and striking out 262

Dick Williams and "The Best Year"

In his autobiography, *No More Mr. Nice Guy,* Dick Williams explains the changes he made after taking over the Mariners in mid-1986 trying to make them a winning team. He names the players on his "hit list," the ones he thought were no longer contributing and were beyond his discipline: Barry Bonnell, Gorman Thomas, Al Cowens, Steve Yeager, and Milt Wilcox.

Once rid of these flawed "veteran influences," he brought up second baseman Harold Reynolds from Triple-A (praising Reynolds' "great mix of foot speed and bat speed") and moved Danny Tartabull to the outfield. ("If nothing else, didn't they see what a bad second baseman Danny Tartabull was?")

Williams' baseball philosophy was, "I hate to lose—period," and he tried his best not to lose at Seattle. After reviewing his preseason efforts in his book, he asks, "So why wasn't 1987 the best year in Mariners history?" and answers, "Hey, it was. We finished just seven games out of first place."

Photo: *AP/Wide World Photos*

True enough, based on how close the Mariners came to first place (rather than on the number of victories). Dick Williams in his only full year at the helm did better than any other Seattle manager. He departed in disgust, but his stay in Seattle did not diminish his reputation as one of the best managers in recent decades.

batters to lead the league once more. Designated hitter Ken Phelps connected for 27 home runs and Jim Presley hit 24 with 88 RBIs. Phil Bradley's .297 batting average was the team high.

The Mariners finished in fourth place, tying their highest previous standing and stood a mere seven games back of pennant-winning Minnesota. Dick Williams had almost done it.

The next year, as usual, brought disillusionment. The Mariners were not in contention in 1988. Far from it. Over the winter they had traded away Phil Bradley and pitcher Lee Guetterman. Guetterman, signed by Seattle in the free-agent draft in 1981, progressed slowly through the farm system, finally making it to the Mariners in 1987.

His 11-4 record that year gave him the league's best winning percentage, but his success was thought to be a fluke.

The main fruits of these two trades were outfielders Glenn Wilson (traded to Pittsburgh in August), Henry Cotto (.259 for the Mariners), and pitchers Mike Jackson (6-5) and Steve Trout (4-7). Mark Langston and Alvin Davis had good but not exceptional years, and the team as a whole never got started. Manager Dick Williams, fired in June, was replaced by Jimmy Snyder, who oversaw the rest of another last-place effort on the part of the Mariners.

The 1989 season ushered in the two-year managerial tenure of Jim Lefebvre, a former L.A.

second baseman, minor league manager, and Oakland A's coach. More important than that, 1989 also brought to the Mariners' outfield a 19-year-old player who looked very much like the future of the franchise—Ken Griffey, Jr.

After only two years in the minors, Griffey at age 19 so dominated spring training that he opened in the Mariners' outfield against Oakland on April 3, 1989. In his first trip to the plate, Griffey doubled. When the team opened at the Kingdome, he homered in his first game, then homered again in his second. A broken finger kept him on the disabled list for a month, probably costing him Rookie-of-the-Year honors.

The Mariners finished sixth, 73-89, with Alvin Davis, now a DH, pacing the hitters at .305 with 21 home runs and 95 RBIs. Aging outfielder Jeff Leonard, acquired via free agency, cracked 24 homers and drove in 93 runs. The pitching ace was Scott Bankhead, off the disabled list at last, with a 14-6 record and a 3.34 ERA. In August 1989 George Argyrose sold the ball club to a group headed by two Indianapolis businessmen.

Seattle fans' hopes soared for 1990. In spring training, Oakland A's manager Tony LaRussa said, "Five teams in our division are capable of winning 90 games this season, and the Mariners are one of them." Maybe, but the Mariners won only 77 and finished only fifth, despite some exciting events and some great performances.

The biggest Mariners' news story of 1990 was the appearance of a father and son playing on the same major league team at the same time: Ken Griffey, Sr., and Ken Griffey, Jr. It was a first, and

AP/Wide World Photos

Ken Griffey, Jr. (left) and Ken Griffey, Sr.

Ken Griffey, Jr.

Few teenage ballplayers attract the kind of media attention Ken Griffey, Jr., did. The Mariners' first draft choice in June 1987, Griffey, then age 17, was assigned to Bellingham in the short-season Northwest League. In 53 games he hit .320, with 14 homers and 40 RBIs. After 1988 stints in San Bernardino (Class A) and Vermont (Double-A) Griffey made the big jump to the majors when he was 19.

Immediate comparisons arose, with Hall-of-Famer Al Kaline (a Tiger at 18), and with Jose Canseco (an Athletic at 22). Once sportswriters saw him play the outfield, they added the name of Willie Mays to their glowing analogies. E. M. Swift, writing in *Sports Illustrated*, added to the list of "inescapable comparisons" young Griffey's "throws from the outfield that are of the same general caliber as the cannon shots of Roberto Clemente."

Predictions of future performance are always chancy, but after four years in the majors, Ken Griffey, Jr., certainly appeared to be the real thing. In those first four seasons he batted .301, hit 80 home runs, and collected 344 RBIs. These, of course, were just his basic four-year batting stats, the bare bones of his achievement.

He quickly proved to be a natural in all facets of the game, a marquee attraction, a superstar at an age when most ballplayers, even very good ones, are still in the minor leagues. No one has yet said (as a flack once said of rookie Clint Hartung, the forgotten Hondo Hurricane), "He should go straight to Cooperstown." But the burgeoning praise has come close.

both the elder and the younger Griffey came through—Griffey, Sr., batting .377 in 77 plate appearances, and Griffey, Jr., batting .300 with 22 homers and 80 RBIs for the full season.

Hitting .302, young third baseman Edgar Martinez shaded Griffey, Jr., for the team lead in batting. Pitchers Erik Hanson (18-9) and Randy Johnson (14-11) led the Mariners' youthful and promising mound staff. Seattle finished fifth, after which manager Jim Lefevbre departed for Wrigley Field to take over the Chicago Cubs, and Bill Plummer, once Johnny Bench's backup catcher with the Cincinnati Reds, inherited the manager's job for 1991.

A Winning Season at Last

Forget pennant fever. Just a season above .500 would help to reward the faithful at the Kingdome. The 1991 Mariners, under Bill Plummer, finally delivered it. Their 83-79 finish, a .512 percentage, sounds less impressive than it was.

Seattle had a realistic shot at second place in 1991, since the second-place Chicago White Sox came in at 87-75, a .537 percentage. The Twins stood alone atop the AL West, eight games up. The other six teams were bunched. At the very bottom of the division the California Angels played .500 ball, 81-81.

Ken Griffey, Jr., continued to improve—batting .327 in 1991, with 22 home runs and 100 RBIs, making spectacular plays in center field, and attracting more media attention than any Mariner in the team's brief history. Third baseman Edgar Martinez hit for a .307 average, his second straight .300 season. The top starting pitchers, Randy Johnson and Brian Holman, won 13 games each, while relievers Bill Swift and Mike Jackson recorded 17 and 14 saves respectively.

The Mariners' first winning season, plus the emergence of Ken Griffey, Jr., as one of the game's youngest-ever superstars (along with the consistently fine hitting of Edgar Martinez) seemed to augur greater progress in the 1990s than the Mariners had enjoyed in the eighties. But 1992 offered no proof of this.

Despite the continuing success of Griffey (.308) and Martinez (.343) and the emergence of left-handed pitcher Dave Fleming (17-10), the team still lacked depth, experience, and stability.

The Mariners finished the 1992 season in last place—the sixth time in 16 years—and, although the luster of a few individual players grew, the team as a whole remained adrift on a trackless sea.

SOURCES

BOOKS

Baseball Guide: 1980, 1983, 1985, 1987, 1991, 1992 Editions, The Sporting News Publishing Co., 1980, 1983, 1985, 1987, 1991, 1992.

Baseball Register: 1980, 1983, 1987, 1991, 1992 Editions, The Sporting News Publishing Co., 1980, 1983, 1987, 1991, 1992.

The Complete Handbook of Baseball, 1992, 23rd edition, edited by Zander Hollander, Signet, 1992.

Ivor-Campbell, Frederick, "Team Histories: Seattle Mariners," *Total Baseball,* edited by John Thorn and Pete Palmer, Warner Books, 1989.

Lowry, Philip J., *Green Cathedrals,* Cooperstown, NY: Society for American Baseball Research, 1986.

O'Donnell, James, "Seattle Mariners: Waiting for a Winner in Baseball's Forgotten City," *Encyclopedia of Major League Baseball Team Histories: American League,* edited by Peter C. Bjarkman, Meckler, 1991.

The Baseball Encyclopedia, 7th edition, edited by Joseph L. Reichler, Macmillan, 1988.

Reidenbaugh, Lowell, *Take Me Out to the Ball Park,* The Sporting News Publishing Co., 1983.

Who's Who in Baseball 1978, 1979, 63rd, 64th editions, edited by Seymour Siwoff, Who's Who in Baseball Magazine Co., 1978, 1979.

Williams, Dick, and Bill Plaschke, *No More Mr. Nice Guy: A Life of Hardball,* Harcourt Brace Jovanovich, 1990.

Wills, Maury, and Mike Celizic, *On the Run: The Never Dull and Often Shocking Life of Maury Wills,* Carroll & Graf Publishers, 1991.

PERIODICALS

Baseball America, February 7, 1993; March 7, 1993.

Sports Illustrated, May 7, 1990.

—*Gerald Tomlinson* for Book Builders, Inc.

TEXAS RANGERS

The history of the Texas Rangers to date has not been a very happy one. Four times the team has finished five games back in the American League West, but it has never finished first. Pennant fever has been absent from Dallas and Fort Worth since the days when both cities sponsored teams in the Double-A Texas League. More than three decades into the history of the major league franchise, there are no tales of post-season play, no recollections of league championships decided on memorable hits or errors, no box scores of World Series games won and lost.

This is a team that got its start not in Arlington, Texas—a fast-growing city of more than 250,000 people between Dallas and Fort Worth—but rather in Washington, D.C., as the Washington Senators. The first season of the franchise was 1961. These second-chance Senators, an expansion ball club, were not the team that once boasted Walter Johnson, Goose Gos-

lin, and Joe Judge. That original Washington team moved west in 1961 as the Minnesota Twins. The new Senators, who abandoned decrepit Griffith Stadium after one season, are best remembered for their skyscraping slugger Frank Howard.

The team played 11 futile seasons in the nation's capital, never finishing better than 15½ games back, then moved to their present home in the Lone Star State. From the outset their ballpark has been Arlington Stadium (originally called Turnpike Stadium), located just west of the Six Flags Over Texas amusement park.

Between 1961 and 1971 the Washington Senators had four big-name managers—Mickey Vernon, Gil Hodges, Jim Lemon, and Ted Williams—but little success. They lost 100 or more games in each of their first four years. Their only winning season came in 1969, under manager Ted Williams, when they finished fourth in the American League West, with an

86-76 record.

The team has fared considerably better in Texas, although at the very beginning the Rangers reverted to their old Washington ways, losing 100 games in 1972, their first season, and 105 the next.

In the late 1970s, under a succession of managers, the Rangers did quite well, finishing second in 1977 and 1978 and third in 1979. The dominant team in the AL West in those days was Kansas City, although the California Angels edged past both K.C. and the Rangers in 1979. After a fairly good showing in split-season 1981 with Don Zimmer at the helm, the Rangers again fell on hard times but then enjoyed a modest revival in the late 1980s under manager Bobby Valentine, a revival enhanced by the December 1988 signing of ageless fire-baller Nolan Ryan.

"... and Last in the American League"

Long before 1961, baseball fans across American knew that Washington was "first in war, first in peace, and last in the American League." In the 1950s the hapless Senators had occupied the cellar four times, and not once in the decade had they finished in the first division.

Moreover, their home ballpark, downtown Griffith Stadium, was deteriorating, and owner Calvin Griffin vigorously pursued his plan of moving the Senators to Bloomington, Minnesota. He succeeded—but with the understanding that a new expansion franchise would be granted to Washington, D.C., thus keeping major-league baseball in the nation's capital.

The 1961 season opened with ten teams in the American League. The two newcomers were the Minnesota Twins (featuring ex-Senators Harmon Killebrew, Bob Allison, Camilo Pascual, and Jim Kaat) and the hastily assembled new Washington Senators (with draftees Gene Woodling, Dale Long, Willie Tasby, and Dick Donovan).

On paper, both teams looked respectable. In action, neither fared well. The Twins finished sixth; the Senators finished in a tie with K.C. for last place (or ninth, to put a better face on it). Mickey Vernon, a recently retired first baseman and a veteran of the Senators, managed the club that season. Pitcher Dick Dononvan had the best ERA in the league but only a 10-10 won-lost record. The Senators traded him away, along with Gene Green (the team's home run leader) and Jim Mahoney, for unpredictable outfielder Jimmy Piersall, who had hit .322 for Cleveland in 1961 but fell to .244 for Washington.

The Senators moved into their new home, D.C. Stadium (later RFK Stadium) for the 1962 season. The new surroundings helped not at all. The team dropped to undisputed tenth place in 1962 and showed no signs of revival in 1963. Not only did the Senators finish last in the standings, with 106 losses, they were the weakest American League ball club by far in hitting, fielding, and pitching—a clean sweep.

Forty games into the 1963 season Gil Hodges replaced Mickey Vernon as manager. Only marginal improvement, if any, was evident. The 1964 Senators, despite losing 100 games, edged out the K.C. Royals for ninth place. Pitchers Claude Osteen (15-13) and Ron Kline (10-7) had winning records, unusual for Senator hurlers. But the new Washington entry, after four seasons of play, had a combined .370 won-lost percentage and seemed to be a hopeless cause.

The Frank Howard Era

For those first four seasons the Senators quite literally had no stars. Outfielder Chuck Hinton batted .310 in 1962, third best in the league, but he was a journeyman, not a hero. The first, and really the only, shining light for the new Washington Senators came on board via a multi-player trade with the L.A. Dodgers in December of 1964. He was outfielder Frank

TEAM INFORMATION AT A GLANCE

Founding date: April 10, 1961 (Washington Senators, expansion);
April 21, 1972 (Texas Rangers)

Home stadium (1972-93): Arlington Stadium
1250 Copeland Rd.
Arlington, TX 76004
Dimensions: left-field line—330 feet
Center field—400 feet
Right-field line—330 feet
Seating capacity: 43,508

(1994—)The Ball Park in Arlington
Arlington, TX 76011

Team uniforms: Home—base color white, with blue and red trim
Road—base color gray, with blue and white trim
Team nickname: Senators (Washington)—same name as that of D.C. ball club
that became Minnesota Twins, 1961-1971; Rangers (Texas)—1972-present
Logo: Word "Rangers" in red script across white baseball with red stitches,
imposed on blue outline map of Texas with white-and-red border

Franchise record	Won	Lost	Pct.
Washington (1961-1971)	740	1,032	.418
Texas (1972-1993)	1,665	1,826	.477

(Hondo) Howard, commonly called Big Frank Howard inasmuch as he stood 6'7" and weighed 255 pounds.

Howard was a tower of power. In his first year with the Senators he belted only 21 homers, but by the time he hit his stride, from 1969 to 1971, his home run totals read 44, 48, 44. Howard was a box office attraction, and he added not only strength but also maturity to the lineup.

The Senators moved up to eighth place in 1965, stayed there in 1966, and then got all the way to sixth (ahead of the Indians, Yankees, and Kansas City A's) in 1967. Yet except for Frank Howard and third baseman Ken McMullen, the roster offered few rays of hope for the future. The managerial hope, Gil Hodges, left after the 1967 season to take charge of the comparably wretched New York Mets. Jim Lemon, a former slugger for the original Senators, served one rocky, tenth-place season as skipper of the talent-starved Washington club.

Divisional play began in 1969, which meant that sixth place became last place in either segment of the American League. But the headline news in Washington that season was, first, the managerial debut of legendary hitter and Hall-of-Fame luminary Ted Williams, and, second, the remarkably improved play of the Senators. They finished fourth in the AL East, 23 games back, but won more games than they lost.

Pitcher Dick Bosman turned in a 14-5 record

PROFILE　　　　Frank Howard: The Franchise

For their entire 11-year history, the expansion Washington Senators were a study in futility. They finished in the first division only once, in 1969. It was Ted Williams's first year as manager and, not surprisingly, it was one of Frank Howard's best seasons. The 6'7" ex-basketball and baseball star from Ohio State had been an L.A. Dodger for five seasons, after signing for a $108,000 bonus and playing a season at Green Bay in the Three-I League and another season in Double- and Triple-A ball.

In 1960, as a platooned Dodger outfielder, he belted 23 homers and won Rookie of the Year honors. His greatest moment with the Dodgers came in the 1963 World Series when his fifth-inning home run off Whitey Ford, a tape-measure shot into the upper deck of left field at Dodger Stadium, put L.A. ahead of the Yankees in game four. The Dodgers swept the Yankees in four games.

Traded to the Washington Senators in December of 1964, Howard became not just a superstar for the expansion Senators but their *only* superstar—ever. He was the franchise. An awesome home run hitter, he was unpretentious, good-natured, and popular with both his teammates and the public. Ted Williams once said to him, "Mantle and Jimmy Foxx hit it hard, but you're the strongest guy I've ever seen play this game. I'd have hit a thousand home runs if I'd been as strong as you." As it was, Howard hit 382 career homers. He bunched 10 of them in just 20 at-bats during six games in 1968, the "year of the pitcher" in which Carl Yastrzemski was the only .300 hitter in the American League.

Yet Howard was more than a home run hitter for Washington; although he led the Senators in homers for seven seasons in a row, he also had the highest batting average on the team for six of those seasons. In 1969, when the Ted Williams-led team made its astonishing bid for the title, Frank Howard (variously called "Hondo," "The Horse," and "The Capital Punisher") batted .296, slammed 48 home runs, scored 111 runs, drove in another 111, and registered a slugging average of .574.

At RFK Stadium they began to record with white paint some of the distant seats where Hondo's homers had landed. Before long the far reaches of the ballpark were dotted with white seats.

with a league-leading 2.19 ERA. Reliever Darold Knowles went 9-2 with a 2.24 ERA. Big Frank Howard launched 48 home runs, while first baseman Mike Epstein pounded out a career-high 30 round-trippers. Attendance rose to 918,106 at RFK Stadium—the second-highest turnout in 71 years of major-league baseball in Washington.

The Senators' surprising 86-76 record earned Ted Williams AL Manager of the Year honors and raised hopes for an even better 1970 season. But the Thumper's magic apparently faded over the winter. The Senators skidded to the cellar in 1970, winning 70 games, losing 92. Dick Bosman did well again, though, going 16-12; Frank Howard connected for 44 home runs and 126 RBIs (both league-leading totals); and

Mike Epstein socked 20 homers. Reliever Darold Knowles chalked up 27 saves with a fine 2.04 ERA, but his won-lost mark of 2-14 detracted a bit from the whole.

The Senators gave their superstar manager another chance, and while the Senators improved to fifth place in the standings, topping the inept Indians, their won-lost record declined to 63-96. A trade had sent first baseman Mike Epstein to the Oakland A's in exchange for Don Mincher, a veteran first sacker nearing the end of his career. Mincher hit for a somewhat higher average but with less power than Epstein.

A cynic might say the team was going nowhere. But owner Bob Short, a millionaire trucker who had bought the franchise for $9.4 million in December of 1968, had other ideas.

The team might be going nowhere in the standings, but Short was determined to move it geographically—to the Dallas-Fort Worth area. The owner had been talking players out of buying homes in the D. C. area, and now his reason became clear.

Short, who no longer bothered to pay the rent at RFK Stadium, offered to sell the ball club, but at an inflated price. No one bought. Finally, on September 21, 1971, the owners voted 10-2 to allow Short to take the Senators to Texas. President Richard M. Nixon averred that it was "heartbreaking" news. Senator Sam Ervin of North Carolina grumbled, "Professional sports club owners treat clubs like private playthings."

Bob Short donned a ten-gallon hat and introduced himself to the folks of the Dallas-Fort Worth area. The Texas Rangers would play in minor-league Arlington Stadium, which was hastily renovated and its seating capacity increased to 35,694.

Hello Texas, Goodbye Thumper

Bob Short, the owner of the Texas Rangers, approved the printing of bumper stickers that read: "World Series, '72, Arlington, Texas." In fact, the first-year Rangers won 54 games, lost 100, and finished 38½ games behind first-place Oakland. Even worse, they finished 20½ games behind fifth-place California. A World Series would demand some rebuilding, which began with the resignation of Ted Williams. Thumper said he felt that "this club has reached bottom. There is no way to go but up."

His replacement was Whitey Herzog, an ex-outfielder for various ball clubs. There were some capable players on the Texas team, such as hard-hitting outfielder Jeff Burroughs and smooth-fielding first baseman Jim Spencer, but the pitching was a disaster. Only young, newly acquired Jim Bibby, at 9-10—no Texas pitcher reached double figures in the win column that year—with a 3.24 ERA, looked promising. Her-

Transcendental Graphics

Gaylord Perry

zog's Rangers were stumbling along at 47-91 when the White Rat, as they called him, got the axe. Williams was correct when he said there was no way to go but up. But the Rangers failed to go anywhere, finishing a distant last.

Into the managerial hot seat came fiery Billy Martin, a turnaround specialist, who in only four years of managing had already led the Twins and the Tigers to division championships. Martin did it again—almost. He took a team that had lost 105 games the year before, 37 games out, and brought them home in second place, 84-76, a mere five games back.

How did he do it? For starters, he got some pitching by acquiring old pro Ferguson Jenkins (in exchange for Bill Madlock and another player) from the Chicago Cubs. Jenkins won 25 games for the 1974 Texas Rangers, losing 12 and posting a 2.83 ERA. Jim Bibby won 19 games (although he also lost 19).

Jeff Burroughs hit .301, belted 25 homers, and drove in 118 runs on his way to being named the American League MVP. Shortstop Toby Harrah was second on the team in home runs with 21 and in RBIs with 74. First baseman

Dallas and Fort Worth were archrivals in the Double-A Texas League for decades. When television and major-league expansion brought hard times to the minors, the two cities joined to create a single franchise. In 1965, after a one-year flirtation by Dallas with the Pacific Coast League, the Dallas-Fort Worth Spurs opened in their newly constructed ballpark, Turnpike Stadium in Arlington, north of the former Arlington Downs racetrack and near the Six Flags Over Texas amusement park.

The ballpark was in a natural bowl, the playing field 40 feet below the surrounding ground. No excavation was required. The original seating capacity of the stadium was 10,000, but the architects designed it for expansion. In 1970 its capacity was doubled to 20,000. Then, when Bob Short got the green light from other baseball owners to move his new Washington Senators franchise to Texas (the old one having gone to Minnesota), a further enlargement of Turnpike Stadium took place, creating a seating capacity of 35,694. A name change accompanied the enlargement; the park home of the new major-league Texas Rangers would be called Arlington Stadium. In 1978 the ballpark was expanded again, to hold 41,384 fans.

The first Texas Rangers game in Arlington Stadium, on April 21, 1972, created a major traffic jam. Many fans bound for the ballpark were still fuming in their cars when, in the first inning, Big Frank Howard drove a pitch on a line over the fence in dead center field, 400 feet away, for the first major-league home run in Arlington Stadium. By then it was a seven-year-old, ever-expanding facility, an undomed, natural-grass ballpark in which the gigantic scoreboard bore the shape of the State of Texas.

The Rangers played their 1,750th and last game in Arlington Stadium on October 3, 1993, opting for a new, $176-million stadium constructed just beyond the old right-field bleachers. After the game—the season finale—home plate was dug up and taken to the new park for duty beginning with the 1994 season. The new park will host the 1995 All-Star Game.

Mike Hargrove, making the big jump from Gastonia of the Class A Western Carolina League, hit .323 with 62 RBIs on his way to being named AL Rookie of the Year.

Another .300 hitter was utility infielder Lenny Randle, who batted .302 and drove in 49 runs. Veteran outfielder Cesar Tovar just missed the .300 mark, batting .292 and driving in 59 runs. This, for the previously downtrodden Rangers, was quite a ball club, and once again hope for the future began to glimmer at Arlington Stadium.

Billy Martin, like Ted Williams, suffered a sophomore jinx. The Rangers fell below .500, Martin fell out of favor, and halfway through the season Frank Lucchesi, a former manager of the Phillies, took over. The team finished third in 1975 and in a tie for fourth in 1976. Although these were losing years, they were not especially bad years, certainly not by Washington-Texas standards. Mike Hargrove, Jeff Burroughs, and Toby Harrah had fine seasons. The pitching improved. Although Ferguson Jenkins left for Boston after the 1975 season, his place was taken by Gaylord Perry, Nellie Briles, and Bert Blyleven. The stage was set for 1977, the best season in the history of the franchise.

The most striking thing about the 1977 season is how unsettled it was. Ordinarily, a winning team has stable management, one or more outstanding stars, and a player or two having a career year. The Rangers, winning 94, losing 68, had none of these. New owner Brad Corbett gave Frank Lucchesi his walking papers after 62 games, with the team at 31-31. Eddie Stankey and then Connie Ryan filled in briefly. Finally, Billy Hunter, an ex-shortstop, was named to manage the club. Under Hunter the Rangers won 60 games and lost 33 over the last two thirds of the season.

From 94-68 to 62-99

Hunter returned to manage in 1978, and a number of new players appeared in Ranger uniforms that year. Pitcher Jon Matlack was acquired in a winter trade. Ferguson Jenkins returned after two seasons with the Red Sox. Outfielder Al Oliver, a lifetime .303 hitter, arrived from Pittsburgh in exchange for Bert Blyleven. And early in the season Bobby Bonds came over from the Chicago White Sox.

Although this appeared to be a distinctly improved ball club, the 1978 Rangers finished third rather than second, compiling an 87-75 won-lost record. Al Oliver finished second in the AL batting race at .324, and Bobby Bonds smashed a team-leading 29 homers. The RBI leader was designated hitter Richie Zisk with 85. Just before the close of the 1978 season, Billy Hunter was inexplicably fired, and Pat Corrales, an ex-catcher, was named to manage the Rangers in the coming season.

With Bump Wills (son of Maury Wills) at second base and Buddy Bell (son of Gus Bell) newly installed at third, the 1979 Rangers had two second-generation major leaguers in the lineup. Bell drove in 101 runs and hit 18 homers. Wills had a fairly typical .273 year. In the outfield, Al Oliver, hitting .323, was joined in mid-season by Mickey Rivers, who was acquired from the Yankees and batting .300. The team finished third, five games back. The next year, however, the Rangers, still under Pat Corrales, fell below .500 and ended up in fourth place.

Don Zimmer was named to manage in 1981, the year of the strike and the split season. The Rangers finished second in the first half, third in the second half, and were not involved in the complex round of play-offs. Altogether the team played at a .543 clip, as Al Oliver, at .309, again led the club in hitting. Pitcher Doc Medich, a

AP/Wide World Photos

Nolan Ryan

Ranger since 1978, enjoyed his fourth straight winning season, 10-6, ERA 3.08. Newly acquired left-hander Rick Honeycutt got off to a good start, going 11-6 for the Rangers with a 3.30 ERA. Zimmer was invited to return.

The 1982 Rangers started slow and never picked up. By late July the front office had seen enough. Zimmer was ousted, and coach Darrell Johnson assumed the task of seeing the team through to a dismal sixth-place finish, 64-98.

There were bright spots, however. One was outfielder Larry Parrish, picked up from the Montreal Expos, along with first baseman Dave Hostetler, in exchange for the popular Oliver. It was a good trade.

Oliver was past his prime, while Parrish

Bobby Valentine was a hot prospect for the L.A. Dodgers back in 1968. He was assigned to Ogden of the Pioneer League, a Rookie-classification outfit then managed by Tommy Lasorda. It was some team of kids at Ogden, with Bill Buckner at first base, Steve Garvey at third, and Tom Paciorek in the outfield. Valentine's major-league playing career hardly matched that of those other three; he drifted from the Dodgers to the Angels to the Padres to the Mets to the Mariners, playing any position that needed filling at the time. Generally, he appeared in fewer than a hundred games a season.

When he was named manager of the struggling Texas Rangers in 1985, few observers expected the 35-year-old skipper to stop drifting as a consequence. But when the 1986 Rangers performed well beyond expectations, finishing a strong second, Valentine, a brash native of Stamford, Connecticut, settled in for a long stay in Texas.

His teams, unlike the '86 contenders, began to inhabit positions in the middle of the standings, however, despite an influx of quality players—Scott Fletcher, Julio Franco, Rafael Palmeiro, Ruben Sierra, José Canseco, Bobby Witt, Nolan Ryan, and Kevin Brown. Nothing seemed to work for Valentine, at least not well enough, and he was let go in 1992. Some felt that he (and indeed the whole organization) had ignored fundamentals and the need for teamwork, much as manager Ted Williams was often accused of doing.

The acquisition of Canseco, in particular, reminded sportswriters of the day back in 1972, at the Rangers' first training camp, when a discussion started on how to handle a rundown play. "The heck with it," snorted an impatient Williams. "Let's hit."

had half a dozen productive seasons ahead of him and would become the Rangers' career home run leader with 156. Over the next three seasons the ball club, under manager Doug Rader, a long-time third baseman for the Houston Astros, finished third, seventh, and seventh.

Rader's Rangers started fast in 1983 with what appeared to be a pretty good team. On the mound were knuckleballer Charlie Hough, Rick Honeycutt, Frank Tanana (after an unhappy 7-18 season), Mike Smithson, and Danny Darwin. Jim Sundberg was putting in the last of his 10 seasons behind the plate for the Rangers.

The team did not end the 1983 season with a winning record, nor did any Ranger player appear among the league leaders in major categories. Still, they seemed better than a last-place team, which they promptly became in 1984 and 1985 (even with a not-quite-ready-for-prime-time Dave Stewart joining the mound staff).

Certain players did well enough—first baseman Pete O'Brien and outfielder Gary Ward, in particular—but the team remained mired in the nether regions. Rader departed after just 22 games of the 1985 season, and Bobby Valentine, cocky but charismatic, inherited the unhappy job of seeing the Texas Rangers through to the end of a 62-99 season. The best that could be said was that the team staved off, just barely, the disgrace of a 100-loss campaign.

A Valentine But No Pennant

"Greener than a mint julep and rawer than a Montana blizzard" is how sportswriter Jim Reeves described the 1986 Texas Rangers. Bobby Witt, pitching for Tulsa of the Texas League in 1985, posted an 0-6 record with a 6.43 ERA. Nevertheless, he vaulted straight to the Rangers the next year, having not yet won a professional game. Witt won 11 of them in 1986, all at the major-league level, while losing nine.

Outfielder Pete Incaviglia came straight off the Oklahoma State campus, one of those rare aves never to play in the minors. The rookie blasted 30 homers for the Rangers to tie the all-time team high and drove in 88 runs. Unfortunately, he also set an AL record for strikeouts, whiffing 185 times.

Then there was reliever Mitch Williams, who appeared in 80 games for the Rangers in 1986, setting a major-league record. Prior to that he had won two games at the Double-A level and a few more at Class A. Outfielder Ruben Sierra got the call at mid-season to say goodbye to Oklahoma City and pack his bags for Arlington. In just 113 games for the Rangers he collected 13 doubles, 10 triples, and 16 homers. Shortstop Scott Fletcher, acquired from the White Sox, fielded smoothly and batted an unexpected .300.

Attendance at Arlington Stadium hit a new high, 1.7 million. This was an exciting ball club. For a full month, from late May to late June, they led their division, but in the end they had to settle for second place, five games back of the California Angels.

What happened thereafter was probably predictable. In 1987 the Rangers tumbled into a tie for sixth place and then in 1988 claimed sole possession of sixth. Not so predictably, Texas management stayed with manager Bobby Valentine, and in 1989 the arrival of Hall-of-Fame shoo-in pitcher Nolan Ryan, outstanding second baseman Julio Franco, and star first baseman-apparent Rafael Palmeiro helped lift

AP/Wide World Photos

And he pitches, too: Texas slugger José Canseco pitched an inning in relief during a 15-1 Boston blowout of the Rangers in May 1993.

the Rangers to fourth place, then to third in 1990 and 1991.

In 1991 Julio Franco became, at .341, the first Ranger to win the AL batting crown. Palmeiro was close behind at .322, and Ruben Sierra followed at .307. In 1992 the team—after three straight .500-plus seasons—dipped to .475 and finished fourth. The pitching outshone the hitting, as Kevin Brown posted a 22-11 mark and José Guzman, after coming back strongly in 1991 following serious shoulder injuries, performed even better in 1992, with a 16-11 record.

On August 31 a trade sent outfielder Sierra and pitchers Bobby Witt and Jeff Russell to Oakland for power-hitting outfielder José Canseco. General Manager Tom Grieve and rookie manager Kevin Kennedy made other massive changes in personnel during the off-season. Kennedy had been named to replace Toby Harrah, who was tapped earlier in the 1992 season to supplant Bobby Valentine, who had finally been dismissed after 1,186 games without a title.

Before the 1993 season, Ryan announced that he would retire at the end of the year. With an explosive lineup behind him, the major-league's all-time strikeout leader hoped to go out with a bang, but instead he suffered through a disappointing, injury-plagued final season.

Kennedy demonstrated exceptional managerial skills in his first year at the helm, guiding the Rangers to a second place finish in the AL West with an 86-76 record. Juan Gonzalez achieved superstar status, slugging 46 homers for his second consecutive home run crown, and Palmeiro, with 37 homers, proved himself one of the league's best power hitters.

Closer Tom Henke set a career-high in saves with 40, and solid pitching performances from starters Kenny Rogers and Roger Pavlik kept the Rangers in title contention for a good part of the season, helping to soften the blow of losing Ryan.

Canseco, who was expected to contribute mightily to the team's pennant hopes, injured his elbow during an ill-fated pitching attempt

and, like Ryan, sat out much of the year. Big changes could be in store for the Rangers in 1994; Palmeiro and Franco are both free agents, Canseco may again miss the season, and several pitchers may be dealt or let go. Kennedy will count on the continued development of young sluggers Gonzalez and Dean Palmer, as well as pitchers Rogers, Pavlik, and Henke, to help the club.

SOURCES

BOOKS

The Baseball Encyclopedia, 7th edition, edited by Joseph Reichler, Macmillan, 1988.

Baseball Guide: 1980, 1983, 1985, 1987, 1992 Editions, The Sporting News Publishing Co., 1980, 1983, 1985, 1987, 1992.

Baseball Register: 1980, 1983, 1987, 1992 Editions, The Sporting News Publishing Co., 1980, 1983, 1987, 1992.

Bjarkman, Peter C., "Washington Senators-Texas Rangers: There Are No Dragons in Baseball, Only Shortstops," *Encyclopedia of Major League Baseball Team Histories: American League,* edited by Peter J. Bjarkman, Meckler, 1991.

The Complete Handbook of Baseball, 1992, 23rd ed., edited by Zander Hollander, Signet, 1992.

Ivor-Campbell, Frederick, "Team Histories: Texas Rangers," *Total Baseball,* edited by John Thorn and Pete Palmer, Warner Books, 1989.

O'Neal, Bill, The Texas League, 1888-1987: *A Century of Baseball,* Eakin Press, 1987.

Reidenbaugh, Lowell, *Take Me Out to the Ball Park,* The Sporting News Publishing Co., 1983.

Voigt, David Quentin, *American Baseball: From Postwar Expansion to the Electronic Age,* Pennsylvania University Press, 1983.

Whitfield, Shelby, *Kiss It Goodbye,* Abelard-Schuman, 1973.

PERIODICALS

Baseball America, February 7, 1993.
Detroit News, October 4, 1993.
Sports Illustrated, May 1, 1972.

—*Gerald Tomlinson* for Book Builders, Inc.

NATIONAL LEAGUE CENTRAL

CHICAGO CUBS

The Chicago Cubs are older than the National League (NL). They go all the way back to 1870 when the National Association of Professional Baseball Players was established, with the Chicago White Stockings as a founding member. When the NL was formed in 1876, the White Stockings, under manager A. G. "Al" Spalding, were already a team well known to American sports fans. After the White Stockings became the Cubs in 1902, the new American League (AL) team in Chicago adopted the honored but abandoned name, shortening it to White Sox.

The White Stockings wasted no time in making themselves a force in the NL. They won the pennant in 1876, 1880, 1881, 1882, 1885, and 1886—six first-place finishes in the NL's first 11 seasons. The star of these years was Adrian "Cap" Anson, who acted as player-manager from 1879 through 1897. Although the Cubs fell on hard times for a number of seasons at the turn of the century, they came back strong in 1906 under

player-manager Frank "The Peerless Leader" Chance, who, like Anson before him, was primarily a first baseman. The Cubs won pennants in 1906, 1907, 1908, and 1910, capturing World Series titles in 1907 and 1908.

It was during this period that columnist Franklin P. Adams immortalized the double play combination of "Tinker to Evers to Chance," but he ignored the stellar pitching staff, which included the hard-to-beat Mordecai "Three Fingers" Brown, Ed Reulbach, and Jack Pfiester. After 1910 another decline in the team's fortunes set in, and not until near the end of World War I, in the war-shortened 1918 season, did the Cubs again finish first, led by pitcher Hippo Vaughn.

After the war William Wrigley, Jr., a wealthy chewing gum magnate, acquired a controlling interest in the team. Wrigley did not turn the Cubs into an immediate success. They languished until the year of the stock market crash, 1929, when, with a trio of slugging outfielders—Kiki Cuyler,

Hack Wilson, and Riggs Stephenson—as well as second baseman Rogers Hornsby, they captured the pennant. But, as would become their standard procedure, the Cubs lost the World Series, this time to the Philadelphia Athletics.

In the next decade the Cubs finished first three more times, in 1932, 1935, and 1938, and were never lower than third. They lost all three World Series: twice to the New York Yankees, once to the Detroit Tigers. Nevertheless, these were heady years for fans at Wrigley Field: the years of Billy Herman at second base, Bill Jurges at shortstop, Gabby Hartnett behind the plate, and Lon Warneke, Charlie Root, and, after 1934, Bill Lee on the mound.

The good times would not last long, however. The Cubs won the pennant in wartime 1945 under manager Charlie Grimm, getting fine performances from first baseman Phil Cavaretta, outfielder Andy Pafko, and a quintet of veteran pitchers, including Hank Wyse and Claude Passeau.

After that the team went belly up, finishing last in 1948, 1949, 1951, and 1956. Even Leo Durocher, brought in to manage in 1966, could not bring the Cubs a pennant, although he did jolt them out of the doldrums and into the first division. The stars of this "almost-but-not-quite" era were outfielder Billy Williams, third baseman Ron Santo, aging Hall-of-Fame shortstop/first baseman Ernie Banks, and, preeminently, pitcher Ferguson Jenkins.

After Durocher left in 1972, the Cubs went into another decade-long swoon, showing few signs of life until 1984, when they vaulted unexpectedly into first place in the NL's East Division. They failed to get past San Diego in the league championship series, however, and for the next few seasons fell back into their old losing habits.

Then in 1989 they struck again, taking the NL East crown. This time they fell victim to the San Francisco Giants in the league playoffs. By then a few elderly Cubs' fans could still remember the team's last pennant in 1945, but only the oldest greybeards among them could recall the Cubs' last World Series triumph in 1908. Some Cub fans found solace in contemplating their splendid old

Transcendental Graphics

Adrian C. "Cap" Anson

ballpark, Wrigley Field, a handsome stadium with green vines covering its brick outfield wall. Still, a winning team would have been a nice bonus.

Cap Anson's White Stockings

As old as Wrigley Field is—it has been in continuous NL use since 1916—the Cubs are nearly half a century older. They originated in the post-Civil War period, when baseball changed from a gentlemen's sport to a potential career for gifted athletes. Large crowds brought in money and, with it, professionalism.

Some ballplayers were apparently paid even before the Civil War, but after the war the practice escalated. In 1869 Henry Chadwick, the English-born "Dean of Baseball Writers," listed the Chicago White Stockings as one of a number of commercialized ball clubs. By 1871 there was a professional league, the National Association, operated by the ballplayers themselves.

The White Stockings were leading all other teams in the league when, near the end of the season, the great Chicago fire destroyed, among much else, the White Stockings' Lake Street ball-

TEAM INFORMATION AT A GLANCE

Founding date: April 25, 1876 (first game in National League)
Same team played in National Association, 1871-75

Home stadium: Wrigley Field
1060 West Addison Street
Chicago, IL 60613

Dimensions: Left-field line—355 feet
Center field—400 feet
Right-field line—353 feet
Seating capacity: 38,710

Team uniforms: home—base white with royal blue pinstripes
Road—base gray with blue, red, and white trim;
Team nickname: White Stockings, 1876-1889; Anson's Colts, 1890-1897;
Orphans, 1898-1900; Cubs 1901-present (nickname officially adopted in 1907)
Team logo: large letter "C" followed by "ubs" in red within blue outer circle

Franchise record	Won	Lost	Pct.
(1876-1993)	8,936	8,307	.518

World Series wins (2): 1907, 1908
National League championships (16): 1876, 1880, 1881, 1882, 1885,
1886, 1906, 1907, 1908, 1910, 1918, 1929, 1932, 1935, 1938, 1945
National League East division first-place finishes (2): 1984, 1989

park. The team played the remaining games on the road, lost many of them, and finished second.

The fire kept Chicago out of the National Association for a couple of seasons, but the real story of the Cubs begins, in any case, with the formation of the NL in 1876. William A. Hulbert, a Chicago coal dealer, gained the presidency of the White Stockings and quickly began to build a winning team.

During 1875 he lured a number of star players from other teams, including pitcher Al Spalding of the Boston Red Stockings and infielder "Cap" Anson of the Philadelphia Athletics. Raiding other teams' rosters violated Association rules, but it was a common practice. Hulbert then moved to organize a new league, the National League of Professional Baseball Clubs, to be controlled by owners, not players. His team-building, like his league-building, paid off. The National Association, caught off guard, folded. And the Chicago White Stockings, with pitcher-manager Spalding winning 47 games and third baseman Anson batting .356, easily beat out St. Louis and Hartford for the NL championship.

The White Stockings did not repeat as champions for the rest of the decade. Spalding retired as a player in order to concentrate on his sporting goods business. Anson stayed on, becoming the teams' manager in 1879 and leading the White Stockings to five pennants between 1880 and 1886. As manager he was a harsh taskmaster. He marched his men onto the field in military formation and enforced a strict and unpopular no-drinking rule.

As a player he ranks as the greatest of the nineteenth-century stars. In 22 years in the NL his batting average dipped below .300 just twice. He was a power hitter in the dead-ball era, connecting for 21 home runs in 1884, a year in which Chicago—although finishing fourth—let fly an astonishing barrage of round-trippers. Ned Williamson, the White Stockings' third baseman, led the league with 27 homers. Second baseman Fred Pfeffer followed close on his heels with 25, and outfielder Abner Dalrymple hit 22.

The next year, 1885, they all dropped off considerably, but the team nonetheless won the pennant, as ace pitcher John Clarkson turned in a 53-16 record. His battery mate that year and the next was the popular Michael "King" Kelly, who, in 1886, batted .388 to lead the league, while the White Stockings were winning their second pennant in a row.

But Hulbert, ever the businessman, found the Red Stockings' $10,000 offer for Kelly irresistible, and in 1887 the "King" went off to Boston. In 1888 Clarkson attracted the same offer and joined Kelly in Beantown.

The loss of these two stars did not give Boston a pennant, but it did weaken the Cubs, who lost out to Jim Mutrie's New York Giants in 1888 and to both New York and Boston in 1889. The Players League of 1890 threw major league baseball into a tizzy.

Many of Anson's Cubs, including outfielders Hugh Duffy and Jimmy Ryan, veteran shortstop Williamson, and pitcher Ad Gumbert, departed for teams in the new league. The Cubs signed a number of young replacements, prompting a new nickname for the ball club, "Anson's Colts."

The Colts, Orphans, and Cubs

After finishing second in 1890 and 1891 behind the dazzling pitching of Bill Hutchinson, who won 42 games in 1890 and 43 in 1891, the Colts fell apart, dropping to seventh place in 1892. Hutchinson still led the league in victories, with 37, but only Ryan (back from his Players League defection) and second-year infielder Bill Dahlen hit well. Anson himself slipped to .272, the lowest season batting average of his career.

Anson improved his average to .314 in 1893, but his floundering Colts finished ninth in the 12-team league. Hutchinson, unable to adjust to the increased pitching distance (to the current sixty feet six inches, as a matter of fact), went 13-16, and his strikeouts dropped from 316 the previous year to 80.

When Anson's Colts improved only marginally over the next three seasons—never climbing higher than fourth—and then slid back to ninth place in 1897, it signaled an end to the career of the greatest star and one of the premier managers of the nineteenth century. The embittered Anson tried to buy the ball club, failed, and turned down Spalding's suggestion for a testimonial dinner. "The public owes me nothing," he said stiffly.

Anson's Colts, minus Anson, became the "Orphans." Not that they lacked a manager, however; Tom Burns, a former third baseman, took over for the next two years, gaining a fourth-place finish in 1898, then tailing off to eighth.

But that inept team of 1898 had on its roster the means of its own revival. The player was Frank Chance, who began his career as the Cubs' catcher, later moving to first base and eventually taking over as manager. The Orphans began to improve at the turn of the century, just in time to be raided by Ban Johnson's upstart AL. Just as defections to the Players League had produced the nickname "Colts," now defections to the AL brought about the nickname "Cubs," courtesy of a Chicago sportswriter. Over in the AL the new Chicago White Sox (with their borrowed name) won the pennant.

Frank Selee, who had led Boston to five NL pennants in the 1890s, was hired to manage the

HISTORY | **The Winningest Team Ever**

The 1906 Chicago Cubs won 116 games, the all-time major-league record for victories in one season. They lost 36. No other ball club—even after the season was lengthened from 154 to 162 games—ever won that many or lost that few again. The Cubs of 1906 (and 1907 and 1908) had many strengths, but the one that stands out most vividly is their superb pitching staff.

Mordecai "Three Fingers" Brown (pictured at left), Ed Reulbach, Jack Pfiester, and Carl Lundgren were close to impossible to hit that season, as were newcomers Jack Taylor and Orval Overall. The entire Cub pitching staff's earned run average was 1.76.

Did the Cubs have the hitting to support this brilliant pitching? They had enough. Third baseman Harry Steinfeldt, a veteran of the Cincinnati Reds playing his first year for the Cubs, put in a career year, batting .327 and driving in a league-leading 83 runs. First baseman Frank Chance hit .319, led the league in stolen bases with 57, and tied for the league lead in runs scored with 103.

The Cubs' only other .300 hitter, Johnny Kling at .312, shared catching duties with light-hitting Pat Moran. "Wildfire" Schulte's team-leading seven circuit clouts, accompanying a .281 batting average, may not sound like many homers, but Brooklyn's Tim Jordan led the league with a mere 12. Schulte, an outfielder for the Cubs, also collected 13 triples to share the league lead.

Some of the other Cub regulars had less impressive seasons at the plate. Shortstop Joe Tinker batted .233, well below his career average of .263. Second baseman Johnny Evers, at .255, was slightly off his usual pace. Among the outfielders, Johnny Slagle had an unproductive year, batting .239 and driving in only 33 runs. Jimmy Sheckard, acquired from Brooklyn, did slightly better, hitting .262 with 45 RBIs. Still, the team's combined batting average of .262 led the league, as did its .339 slugging average.

It seems fair to say, however, that the pitchers more than the hitters carried the 1906 Cubs to their 116 regular-season victories. Both failed in the World Series though, as "The Hitless Wonders" of the crosstown White Sox outhit the Cubs .198 to .196, while the Sox pitchers, especially Big Ed Walsh and Nick Altrock, were outdueling the Cubs' star hurlers.

Photo: *Transcendental Graphics*

Transcendental Graphics

Joe Tinker

Cubs in 1902. He installed Chance at first base, acquired infielders Joe Tinker and Johnny Evers, added Jimmy Slagle to the outfield, and directed the club to a third-place finish in 1903 and a second-place finish in 1904.

Tinker to Evers to Chance

The Cubs stood on the verge of greatness, but they lacked the pitching to compete with the Giants' Christy Mathewson and Joe "Iron Man" McGinnity. Selee corrected that, too. He obtained Mordecai "Three Fingers" Brown in a shrewd trade with the Cardinals following the 1903 season. He signed rookie pitcher Ed Reulbach in 1905.

During the 1905 season, Selee, ill with tuberculosis, took a leave of absence. He never returned. The new manager was first baseman Chance, heading a team with enormous potential. The Cubs finished third in 1905, behind John

McGraw's formidable Giants and Fred Clarke's tough, competitive Pittsburgh Pirates. But three Cub pitchers won 18 games apiece, and two more won 13 each—a portent of what might happen, and did, in 1906.

The 1906 Chicago Cubs, under manager Chance, rank as one of the best teams in baseball history. They won 116 games, a major league record, finishing 20 games ahead of the Mathewson-McGinnity Giants. Harry Steinfeldt, acquired from the Cincinnati Reds, held down third base for the Cubs in 1906 and contributed greatly to their success. Outfielder Jimmy Sheckard came over from Brooklyn.

But the real story of 1906 was the pitching staff. "Three Fingers" Brown, at 26-6, had the league's best earned run average (ERA), 1.04, good for second place among all-time one-season

Transcendental Graphics

Johnny Evers

ERA leaders (behind Dutch Leonard with 1.01). The other Cub pitchers—Reulbach, 19-4, veteran Carl Lundgren, 17-6, newcomer Jack Pfiester, 20-8, and midseason arrivals Jack Taylor, 12-3, and Orval Overall, 12-3—all had lower ERAs, amazing as it seems, than did the Giants' McGinnity, 2.25, or Mathewson, 2.97.

In the World Series of 1906 the rampaging Cubs faced "The Hitless Wonders," the Chicago White Sox. Who could doubt the outcome? The best hitters in the White Sox lineup carried averages in the .270s against Steinfeldt's .327, Chance's .319, and catcher Johnny Kling's .312, and the Cubs' pitching appeared dominant. But a Cubs' victory looked easier on paper than it proved to be on the field.

The White Sox won the first game, 2-1, despite a four-hitter by Brown. The Cubs took Game Two on a dazzling one-hitter by Reulbach. But the White Sox came back, behind the two-hit, 12-strikeout pitching of Ed Walsh, to best Pfiester, who, like Brown, lost a four-hitter. In Game Four Brown's two-hitter was good enough (barely) to gain a 1-0 victory, as Evers singled in Chance with the game's only run in the seventh inning. Then the sky fell. The White Sox bombed Reulbach and reliever Pfiester 8-6 in the fifth game and did the same to Brown, 8-3, in Game Six. "The Hitless

Transcendental Graphics

Frank Chance

Wonders," batting .198 for the Series, reigned as World Champions. The Cubs, chastened, hoped to redeem themselves the next year.

They did just that. The Cubs of 1907, although winning fewer games than in 1906—a league-best 107—were nearly as intimidating. The pitching remained awesome, with Pfiester at 1.15 leading the ERA parade, and Overall, 23-8, and Brown, 20-6, chalking up the most wins.

The team batting average of .250 was a shortcoming, but the team's fielding average of .967 and team ERA of 1.73 were most impressive. The Cubs waltzed to a four-games-to-none triumph over the Detroit Tigers in the World Series, with Overall, Reulbach, Brown, and Pfiester each winning a game.

The 1908 season was not as easy for the Cubs. In fact, if the New York Giants' Fred Merkle had touched second base on September 23 in a game against the Cubs, the Giants might have won the pennant. The Giants had runners on first and third with two outs in the bottom of the ninth inning. After Al Bridwell lined a clean single to center field, driving in the runner on third, Merkle, the runner at first base, turned to go the clubhouse.

But Cub second baseman Evers was sure the umpire would call Merkle out for failing to go to second base, with the force-out negating the run. Evers grabbed a ball (though perhaps not the game ball), stepped on second, and watched the umpire make the "out" call. Because of the chaos caused by fans swarming onto the field, the game was declared a tie.

The season eventually ended in a dead heat between the Giants and the Cubs, and a replay of the September game was scheduled. This time the Cubs defeated Mathewson and the Giants, 4-2, to advance to the World Series.

As in the previous year, their opponents were the Tigers, and again the Tigers succumbed, this time four games to one. Overall won two games for the Cubs and Brown the other two, one of them in relief. Ty Cobb collected four hits in the only game the Tigers won, with Pfiester taking the loss.

The Cubs finished second in 1909—with 104 wins—as the fired-up Pirates won 110. In 1910 the

When serious fans talk baseball and the talk turns to the romance of ballparks, the name Wrigley Field is sure to come up. Wrigley Field goes back to 1914 when it was called Weeghman Park, pride of the long-defunct Federal League. In 1916, with the Federal League gone, the ballpark became the home of the Cubs. Today it is a traditionalist's dream, a baseball-only facility with natural grass, no dome, and, until 1988, no lights.

It is steeped in history, the place where Babe Ruth supposedly called his home run in the 1932 World Series, the place where Mike Schmidt of the Phillies blasted four homers in an April game in 1976, and where, three days earlier, the Mets' Dave Kingman had hoisted a homer 550 feet to carom off the side of a house on the east side of Kenmore Avenue.

When the Cubs moved into Wrigley Field, their manager was Joe Tinker. Hippo Vaughan was the ace of the pitching staff. The great Cub stars of the Depression years—Kiki Cuyler, Hack Wilson, Riggs Stephenson, Charlie Root, Lon Warneke—were still kids. Cub catcher and manager Gabby Hartnett, who hit his famous "homer in the gloamin" in 1938, had by then played at Wrigley Field for 17 seasons.

When Grover Cleveland Alexander thrilled fans at Wrigley, "Mr. Cub," Ernie Banks, had not yet been born, nor had Ferguson Jenkins, Rick Sutcliffe, Ryne Sandberg, and many others who would later bring Cub fans to their feet in the timeless ballpark. None of these players would ever own a World Series ring (at least not for their efforts with the Cubs), and no pennant would fly at Wrigley Field after the one the team captured in wartime 1945.

Yet Wrigley field, with its vine-covered brick walls in the outfield, is, says Cub aficionado Jim Langford, "more than a park with a charm all its own; it is more than a functional antique. Wrigley Field is a shrine to the endurance and resilience of hope. It is a witness to the fact that teams do not have to win pennants to inspire and keep allegiance.... There is something uniquely familial, American, traditional about Wrigley Field, something shared by no other ballpark in the country, save perhaps by Fenway Park in Boston and Comiskey Park on the south side of Chicago."

Cubs came back to win 104 games again, and this time it was enough for the pennant. But against the Philadelphia Athletics in the World Series it was painfully evident that the great days were over. The A's hit the Cub pitchers hard, and Chicago avoided being swept in the Series only by a ninth-inning run-scoring triple by Chance in Game Four, which tied the score, followed by Sheckard's RBI single.

The 1911 Cubs were no pushovers, finishing second. There were a few new faces in the lineup and on the mound. In 1912 third baseman Heinie Zimmerman took baseball's Triple Crown, batting .372, hitting 10 homers, and driving in 103 runs to lead the league in all three categories.

Zimmerman had been with the club since 1907, but found it tough to break into an infield consisting of Steinfeldt, Tinker, Evers, and Chance. Cub pitcher Larry Cheney, in his first full year in the majors, won 26 games to lead the league, losing 10. Still, these performances were not enough. The Cubs slipped to third place, and owner Charles Murphy fired Chance, who responded by calling Murphy a cheapskate who would not spend enough money to get top ballplayers.

A Pennant for Wrigley Field

The "Peerless Leader" had a point about Murphy's failings, and in 1914 the owner himself was eased out by his partner, Charles P. Taft. The Federal League, with its Chicago Whales team, created further havoc, but the eventual outcome was a happy one for the Cubs. Charles Weeghman, the owner of the Whales' franchise, built a new ballpark at the corner of North Clark and West Addison Streets.

When the Federal League folded after the 1915 season, Weeghman formed a group to buy the Cubs from Taft and moved them from West Side Park on Polk and Lincoln (now Wolcott) Streets to the former Whales' home. For a time they called it Cubs' Park, but after William Wrigley, Jr. gained control of the team, the ballpark became Wrigley Field.

The Cubs did not fare very well in the wake of Chance's departure, finishing fourth or fifth from 1914 through 1917. Then something surprising happened. In 1918, with war raging in Europe, the season came to a premature end after Labor Day. Had any team won the pennant? Not really, but the Cubs were in first place, had a terrific won-lost record, 84-45, and were awarded the flag.

Astonishingly, there was a World Series, which the Boston Red Sox won in six games. Cub pitcher Hippo Vaughn, who had had an outstanding 22-10 season with a 1.74 ERA, won the fifth game of the Series after being charged with disheartening losses in Games One and Three.

The Cubs had seen their last World Series for quite a while. They took third place in 1919, as Vaughn, 21-14, continued at the top of his form and Grover Cleveland Alexander, 16-11, acquired from the Philadelphia Phillies after the 1917 season, added strength to the mound staff.

But the Cubs' position in the standings did not improve. The team finished in the second division from 1920 through 1922, then rose to fourth in 1923, fell to fifth in 1924, and slumped to eighth in 1925. This was their first descent to the cellar in 53 years.

Three managers—Bill Killefer, Rabbit Maranville, and George Gibson—all tried to stave off the Cub disaster that year, as did Alexander, who finished 15-11, and new first baseman Charlie "Jolly Cholly" Grimm, who hit .306, but to no avail. The club hired a new skipper for 1926, Joe McCarthy, a former minor league second base-

Transcendental Graphics

Hack Wilson

man who had managed pennant-winning Louisville in the American Association the previous year.

McCarthy, Hornsby, and Grimm

Over the winter of 1925-26 the Cubs not only hired McCarthy to manage, they also picked up squat, powerful Hack Wilson, a future Hall-of-Fame outfielder. In early June of 1926 they acquired another outfielder, Riggs "Old Hoss" Stephenson, from Indianapolis of the American Association. Wilson hit .321 for the Cubs in McCarthy's first year and belted 21 homers to lead the league. Stephenson checked in with a .338 average. The Cubs rose from last place to fourth.

They remained in fourth place in 1927, then climbed to third in 1928, having added outfielder Kiki Cuyler to the clearly improving team. Although Freddie Maguire had performed competently at second base in 1928, the Boston Braves had a veteran second baseman who could probably do better. His name was Rogers Hornsby. The Cubs gave up five players (including Maguire) plus the unheard-of sum of $120,000 to bring Hornsby, the "Rajah," to Chicago.

Wilson's greatest year was yet to come, but 1929 was a pretty good one. The five-foot-six-inch, 190-pound center fielder hit .345 with 39 home runs and a league-leading 159 runs batted in (RBIs). Hornsby, not to be outdone, hit .380 with 39 homers and 149 RBIs. Nor were these the only Cub sluggers in 1929. Stephenson hit .362 and drove in 110 runs, and Cuyler went .360 with 102 RBIs.

The best pitching marks for McCarthy's talented crew were turned in by Charlie Root, 19-6, Guy Bush, 18-6, and Pat Malone, 22-10. The Cubs drew 1,485,166 fans, many of whom began to regard their team as unbeatable. In the World Series the Philadelphia A's under Connie Mack proved otherwise, taking four out of five games from the outgunned Chicagoans. Jimmy Foxx's timely hitting helped the A's win the first two games.

The Cubs came back with a 3-1 win behind Bush, with Cuyler delivering the key hit, a two-run single. But Game Four was a disaster, as the Cubs blew an 8-0 lead in the seventh inning, the A's scoring 10 times to pull it out and take a three-games-to-one lead in the Series. Wilson's costly error in that game made him the goat of Series, despite his team-leading eight hits.

The 1930 Cubs made a strong run for the pennant but lost out to the St. Louis Cardinals. As if to atone for his error in the fall classic, Wilson went on a tear. His .356 batting average was nowhere near good enough to lead the league—the Giants Bill Terry hit .401, and the Cubs' Stephenson hit .367—but in two other departments his stats were stunning. He blasted 56 home runs, still an NL record. And he drove in 190 runs, still a major league record.

Near the end of the 1930 season McCarthy, knowing that his Cubs would not overtake the Cardinals, resigned. Hornsby took over as manager for the last four games and was named to head the club in 1931.

The Cubs finished third under the hard-nosed Hornsby. Wilson, about whom it was said, "He was a lowball hitter and a highball drinker," had a disappointing year, batting .261 and hitting only 13 homers. The Cubs traded him to the Cardinals for spitball pitcher Burleigh Grimes. Both players, superb a few years earlier, were over the hill. The Cubs needed new blood.

They got it on the pitching mound from Lon Warneke, who in his first full season went 22-6 with a 2.37 ERA. In the infield they got it from Billy Herman, taking over at second base from Hornsby. Bill Jurges shifted over to shortstop and Woody English moved to third, while reliable Charlie Grimm remained at first base. In the outfield Wilson's replacement, Joe Moore, hit .305 and matched Wilson's 1931 home run total of 13.

In August, 1932, with the Cubs locked in a pennant race with the Pirates and Brooklyn Dodgers, Hornsby was dismissed. Grimm replaced him as manager, and the Cubs took the flag. In the World Series the New York Yankees of Babe Ruth and Lou Gehrig rolled to victory in four straight games, outscoring the Cubs 37 runs to 19.

One of baseball's most famous World Series moments—Ruth's legendary "called" home run—occurred in Game Three, when the Babe stepped to the plate to face the Cubs' Root. After waving his bat toward the outfield, Ruth smacked a home run into the center field bleachers.

Although the Cubs dropped to third place in 1933 and 1934, they played exciting baseball. Frank Demaree was now the full-time center fielder. Outfielder Chuck Klein arrived in 1934 via a trade with the Philadelphia Phillies, and in 1935 the Cubs transformed Augie Galan from a utility infielder to a regular outfielder.

Stan Hack became the full-time third baseman in 1934, and in that year, too, a 17-year-old first baseman—a native of Chicago—made his first appearance in Grimm's lineup. That player, Phil Cavarretta, would enjoy a long stay with the team. The pitching staff was strengthened by the arrival in 1934 of rookie Bill Lee and in 1935 by the acquisition of left-hander Larry French from the Pirates. This strong, well-balanced Cubs' team, with Hartnett still behind the plate (since 1922, in fact), won 18 games in a row in a rousing stretch drive that ended in a face-off with the second-place Cardinals in St. Louis.

The Cubs won three straight from the Cardinals—increasing their consecutive game streak to 21—to clinch the pennant. The World Series, as usual, was another story. Facing the AL champion Tigers, the Cubs got off to a good start, as Warneke tossed a four-hitter, winning 3-0. But Detroit bounced back with three straight victories, lost a second game to Warneke (who was relieved by Lee after six innings), and then took the Series with a ninth-inning 4-3 win over the Cubs.

Other fine Cubs' teams finished a close second to Bill Terry's New York Giants in 1936 and 1937. In 1938 a few new names appeared on the roster, most notably that of former Cardinal great Dizzy Dean, whose fastball was a thing of the past but who cost the Cubs $185,000 and three ballplayers anyway. Diz, through canny use of his "nuffin' ball," pitched his way to a 7-1 record as the Cubs won the pennant. Warneke was gone (to the Cardinals), and the ace of the staff was now Lee, who compiled a 22-8 record with a 2.66 ERA.

Part way through the season, with the Cubs in third place, manager Grimm stepped down in favor of catcher Hartnett. The Cubs climbed slowly toward the top, and by September 28 were just a half game behind the Pirates, whom they met that day at Wrigley Field.

The two teams battled back and forth, and in the bottom of the eighth inning, Chicago scored twice to tie the game, 5-5. Root held Pittsburgh scoreless in the top of the ninth, and in the home half of the ninth, Cavarretta flied out to right, and Carl Reynolds grounded out. The Cubs were down to their last out.

With night falling, manager Hartnett stepped to the plate and swung at two curves, missing the first pitch and fouling off the second. Reliever Mace Brown tried another curve, but this time

Transcendental Graphics

Gabby Hartnett

Hartnett connected. He drove it deep to left center field, way back, clearing the wall. Hartnett's hit became known as the famous "homer in the gloamin'," and while it did not ensure the pennant, it did buoy up the Cubs and dishearten the Pirates. In the end the Cubs took the pennant by three games, winning 21 of their final 25 games.

But this spectacular finish, as in the past, did not carry over to the World Series, particularly since the opponents were the Yankees. The mighty Yanks romped home with four straight wins and the championship.

Patience During Adversity

After 1938 the Cubs fell on hard times. A revamped lineup did not help. The ball club, still under Hartnett, fell to fourth in 1939, fifth in 1940, sixth in 1941, and—where would it end? In 1941, the United States entered the second World War.

World War II changed the shape of American baseball and brought wrenching changes to all major league ball clubs, with many established stars leaving the game to serve in the armed forces.

It had little effect at first on the Cubs' place in the standings. They finished sixth in 1942, fifth in 1943, and fourth in 1944. Hartnett was fired after the 1940 season, to be replaced by Jimmy Wilson, who for five years prior to that had managed the Phillies to seventh- and eighth-place finishes. Wilson did slightly better for the Cubs, but not well enough to keep his job. He surrendered the helm to Grimm after a 1-9 start in 1944.

Under "Jolly Cholly" the ball club played at a 74-69 clip and finished fourth. "Big Bill" Nicholson, a veteran outfielder, led the league in homers with 33 and RBIs with 122, while first baseman Cavarretta hit .321 and drove in 82 runs. Pitchers Hank Wyse and Claude Passeau enjoyed winning records. Rookie second baseman Don Johnson looked promising, as did young outfielder Andy Pafko. Cub fans were modestly optimistic about 1945.

Considering that 1945 was the fourth year of war, and that many players were still in the service, the Cubs' lineup was fairly strong. Most of the players had respectable major league careers either before or after the war. In the infield were Cavarretta at first base, Johnson at second, Lenny Merullo at short, and Hack at third. Behind the plate were Mickey Livingston and Paul Gillespie (both wartime-only major leaguers). In the outfield were Nicholson in right, Pafko in center, and Peanuts Lowrey in left.

The starting pitchers were Wyse, Passeau, Paul Derringer, and Ray Prim. To this solid rotation the Cubs added Hank Borowy, purchased in midseason from the Yankees. Borowy's 11-2 record proved vital as the Cardinals hung close to the pennant-winning Cubs. The big guns on offense for Chicago were Cavarretta, who led the league in batting at .355, and Pafko, who added 110 RBIs. Three other Cubs topped 80 RBIs—Cavarretta, Nicholson, and Lowrey. The Cubs' only 20-game winner was Wyse, 22-10, but Passeau was 17-9, Derringer 16-11, and Prim 13-8.

Over in the AL the Detroit Tigers won the flag in 1945. The Tigers, like the Cubs, were a team that had some nonwartime players of note, among them Hank Greenberg, Rudy York, Hal Newhouser, and Virgil Trucks. The World Series went to seven games, with the Tigers winning the last game 9-3. Cub pitchers threw shutouts in Games One and Three, the first by Borowy, 9-0, the second a one-hitter, 3-0, by Passeau. Hack and Cavarretta collected 11 hits each for the Cubs, and Nicholson drove in eight runs. But the Tiger attack, led by Greenberg's three doubles and two homers, proved decisive.

The pennant-winning Cubs of 1945 welcomed a few returning combat veterans in 1946—Eddie Waitkus at first base, Clyde McCullough behind the plate, and Johnny Schmitz on the mound—but many of the wartime players remained in the lineup. The Cubs finished third in 1946, slipped to sixth in 1947, and by 1948 were in the cellar. Grimm survived the 1948 season, but when the Cubs started poorly in 1949, Frankie Frisch was hired to manage. He fared no better than Grimm.

The team, finishing last again, had a few good men. Outfielder Hank Sauer, a 1949 arrival from the Cubs, was a quality player. So were wartime holdovers Pafko and Cavarretta. But most of the newcomers added little to the ball club.

The Cubs rose to seventh place in 1950, but dropped to eighth again in 1951. Cavarretta tried his hand at the helm, and for one atypical year, 1952, the team broke even, 77-77, and finished fifth. It was one of Sauer's better seasons. He belted 37 homers and drove in 121 runs to lead the league in both departments. Pitcher Bob Rush had his best year, 17-13, as did Paul Minner, 14-9.

After that it was downhill. The Cubs finished no higher than sixth through 1957. Hack managed the team for three of those forgettable years—forgettable, that is, except for the arrival of a new shortstop in 1953, Ernie Banks. Purchased from the Kansas City Monarchs, a Negro League team, the 22-year-old Banks appeared only briefly in 1953, but in 1954 he became the Cubs regular shortstop.

Ernie Banks: "Mr. Cub"

Shortstop Ernie Banks played his first game as a Chicago Cub on September 17, 1953, having just arrived (in exchange for $35,000) from the Kansas City Monarchs. On May 12, 1970, a hardy 5,264 fans showed up in the rain at Wrigley Field to watch—they hoped—the Cubs play the Atlanta Braves. The weather improved, Pat Jarvis took the hill for the Braves, and Ernie Banks, by then a first baseman and a year from retirement, deposited a Jarvis curve ball in the left-field seats. It was home run number 500 for the great and cheerful player everyone called "Mr. Cub." It was also his 1,600th run batted in.

Cub fans had seen many glittering stars in the lineup—Cap Anson, Gabby Hartnett, Frank Chance, Hack Wilson, Riggs Stephenson, Phil Cavarretta—but Ernie Banks played in more games than any of them, and he collected more hits, more doubles, more homers, more total bases, more runs batted in, and more extra-base hits than any other Cub. His 512 career homers tie him with Eddie Matthews (between Willie McCovey and Mel Ott) on the all-time list. From 1955 to 1960 he hit more than 40 home runs every year but one.

Banks was not a great fielder or an adept base runner, and his .274 lifetime batting average hardly challenges Ty Cobb's. Yet Ernie Banks was a superstar all the way. He captured the imagination of Cubs' fans during the long drought that followed World War II and has yet to be convincingly broken. His infectious enthusiasm, coupled with his explosive power at the plate, made him the most popular Cub of his time—and perhaps the most popular since Cap Anson inspired a new nickname for the White Stockings. There is some irony in the fact that Banks, a black, would have been snubbed by Anson, who refused to take the field against a team with nonwhite players. Times change. Anson is in the Hall of Fame, and so is Banks.

Photo: *Transcendental Graphics*

He stayed with the club through 1971, shifting to first base in 1961 because of an ailing knee. Banks accumulated 512 career home runs, and by the time he retired as a player he was universally known as "Mr. Cub." Elected to the Hall of Fame in 1977, he was the first Cub to have his uniform

(No. 14) retired, in 1982. Banks never played in a World Series game. Only rarely, near the end of his career, did he play on a first-division team.

The Cubs, having gone nowhere in 1954, 1955, and 1956 under Hack, got a new manager, Bob Scheffing, in 1957. Scheffing had been a

Transcendental Graphics

Billy Williams

catcher for the Cubs as recently as 1950. He found greater success behind the plate than he did at the helm.

Banks played well—brilliantly, in fact, under Hack and Scheffing—but few other Cubs were producing, especially the pitchers. Scheffing lasted three seasons, during which Bank clubbed 135 home runs and drove in 374 runs—an average of 45 homers and 125 RBIs per year. A few more Ernie Bankses and Scheffing would have been a managerial genius. As it was, the old-time catcher got the ax, and for 1960 the Cubs opted for nostalgia, naming Charlie Grimm to manage the team once again.

Twenty-four Years in Limbo

Third baseman Ron Santo joined the Cubs in 1960, having spent one season in the minors, at San Antonio of the Texas League. Santo, like Banks, was a superb ballplayer—and there was another on the Cubs' roster: outfielder Billy Williams. While Santo was coasting through a single minor league season, Williams was fighting his way from Ponca City to Pueblo to Burlington to San Antonio to Fort Worth ... and only then to the Cubs. Even after arriving, he dropped back to Houston for a season, but by 1961 he was ready ... or more than ready. He hit 25 homers as a rookie, drove in 86 runs, and quickly added his name to that of Banks and Santo as a Cub of distinction.

The Cubs went through a series of managers as the team fought to regain respectability. Occasionally, a Cub pitcher would have a good season. Left-hander Dick Ellsworth won 22 and lost 10 with a 2.11 ERA in 1963. Larry Jackson led the league with 24 victories in 1964, losing only 11. But a few personal breakthroughs were not enough. The Cubs were perennial losers.

Then in 1966 came a turnaround specialist, that brash and demanding managerial veteran of the Dodgers and Giants, the success-driven Leo Durocher. He inherited a ball club in trouble, and in 1966, after the expansion of the NL to ten teams, but before divisional play, the Cubs finished in last place. (Durocher's preseason prediction that the Cubs were not an eighth-place team had proved all too accurate; they were a tenth-place team.)

Durocher's Cubs would not remain in the cellar. There was a turnaround, and in 1967 the Cubs rose to third place. Said Williams, "We used to ... be waiting for something to happen. Now we're making things happen." One of the Cubs making things happen was pitcher Ferguson Jenkins.

In 1967 he won 20 games and lost 13. This was the first of six seasons in a row that the future Hall-of-Famer recorded 20 or more victories. For all six of these seasons Leo Durocher was the Cubs' manager, and in all six the team played better than .500 ball. They never won a pennant under "Leo the Lip," but they finished second twice—1969 and 1970—and never sank below a tie for third place.

Only once between 1967 and 1971 did the Cubs have a 20-game winner on the staff to keep

Jenkins company. That was in 1969, when Bill Hands went 20-14. Other pitchers of note during the Durocher years were Ken Holtzman, who had a couple of 17-win seasons, and Milt Pappas, who won 17 in 1971 and again in 1972.

In 1970 first baseman Jim Hickman enjoyed a career year, batting .315, hitting 32 homers, and driving in 115 runs. That same year Williams hit .322, clubbed 44 homers, and drove in 129 runs, while Santo contributed 26 homers and 114 RBIs to the second-place cause.

The Durocher era came to an end in 1972 when, at midseason, "The Lip" said he was "stepping aside" in favor of Whitey Lockman, who became the twenty-third manager of the Cubs. Under Lockman the team finished second to the Pirates of Willie Stargell and Roberto Clemente.

But Lockman was not the answer. The Cubs, after six straight winning seasons, fell to 77-84 in 1973, finishing in fifth place.

For the next ten years, from 1974 through 1983, they would end up anywhere between 11 and 27 games out of first place and from third place at best to sixth at worst. Of course, after 1969, and the start of divisional play, sixth place became the cellar, which the Cubs occupied three times, counting the split-season of 1981. Managers and players alike changed frequently over these years.

Rick Reuschel became the mound ace, winning 20 games while losing 10 in 1977. Outfielder Dave Kingman brought oohs and aahs from the fans for his batting power, leading the league in homers with 48 in 1979. Bill Buckner performed well at first base, taking the NL batting title in 1980

Transcendental Graphics

Fergie Jenkins

with a .324 average. Infielder Ryne Sandberg arrived in 1982 and showed signs of future stardom. Nevertheless, the Cubs had been out of contention for a long time, and at the end of the 1983 season, they seemed likely to remain so.

You Can't Lose 'Em All

In 1981 the Wrigley family sold the Cubs to the Chicago Tribune Company. The new management wrought a number of changes as the club tried to find a winning combination for the 1980s. They seemed to have discovered it in 1984 when the Cubs vaulted from fifth place to first in the NL East. Key newcomers were pitchers Rick Sutcliffe from the Cleveland Indians and Dennis Eckersley from the Boston Red Sox, both acquired early in the season. Sutcliffe went 16-1 for the Cubs, winning the NL Cy Young Award, while Eckersley posted a more modest 10-8 mark.

Back in 1982 the Cubs' front office had relieved the Phillies of shortstop Larry Bowa and catcher-outfielder Keith Moreland. For the 1984 season they raided the Phillies again, this time for outfielders Bob Dernier and Gary Matthews. The front office also added pitcher Scott Sanderson from the Montreal Expos. A year earlier they had picked up third baseman Ron Cey from the Los Angeles Dodgers.

This cobbled-together team, playing for ex-Kansas City Royals' manager Jimmy Frey, had real talent and did well, leaving the favored New York Mets six and a half games back at the finish. They lost their first shot at a World Series in nearly four decades, however, when the San Diego Padres defeated them three games to two in the NL Championship Series. The Cubs beat the Padres handily in the first game of the Series, 13-0, on two home runs by Matthews and solo shots by Dernier, Sutcliffe, and Cey. Chicago also won the second game, 4-2, but after that it was all San Diego. The Padres slammed the door on the Cubs in each of the next three games, sending them back to Chicago, still without a pennant since the last year of World War II.

AP/Wide World Photos

Ryne Sandberg

The hastily assembled Cubs' team that had hung together in 1984 fell apart in 1985. There were some good individual performances such as Sandberg's .305 batting average, 26 home runs, and 88 RBIs, and Moreland's career best .307 average and 106 RBIs. But the pitching, despite the superstar names on the staff, was ineffective, posting the highest earned run average in the division and the second highest in the league.

The 1985 Cubs finished fourth, 23½ games back. They showed no signs of improvement in 1986. Far from it. They skidded to fifth place, 37 games out. Their hitting was about average, and they led the league in home runs, but their pitching was flat-out terrible. Eckersley, Sutcliffe, and Sanderson won 20 games among them but lost 36, a .357 percentage.

Managerial musical chairs ensued to no avail, for in 1987 the Cubs finished last in the NL East.

This occurred despite outfielder Andre Dawson's spectacular season (immediately after he departed the Expos, with whom he had played for a decade). Dawson blasted 49 homers and drove in 137 runs for the Cubs, both league-leading totals. Sutcliffe, too, did well in '87, winning 18 games (tops in the NL) while losing 10. No one else matched these two players' performances, and there seemed little hope for the 1988 Cubs without a major overhaul.

Under a new manager, Don Zimmer, who once was once a utility infielder for the Cubs, the team improved somewhat in 1988, finishing fourth, 24 games out. They featured a few players who were either new or newly impressive. One was first baseman Mark Grace, batting a solid .296 as a rookie. Another was pitcher Greg Maddux, who, after starting the season at Iowa, came up and compiled an 18-8 won-lost record for the Cubs.

The 1989 Cubs repeated the startling ascent of the 1984 team, winning 93 games, losing 69, and taking first place in the NL East, six games ahead of the Mets. Two rookie outfielders, Dwight Smith and Jerome Walton, turned in batting averages of .324 and .293 respectively, and Walton walked off with NL Rookie of the Year honors. Grace, shrugging off a sophomore jinx, raised his batting mark to .314. Sandberg collected the most hits of any Cub, 176, and the most home runs, 30, while hitting .290.

Complementing this sturdy offense was some remarkably fine pitching. Maddux, 19-12, Sutcliffe, 16-11, and Sanderson, 11-9, all had above-average seasons, while Mike Bielecki, who had been struggling for a decade, mostly in the minors, suddenly came up with an 18-7 year.

Put all these performances together and a pennant might seem, at long last, like a real possibility. Forget it. Since 1908 the Cubs had been nothing if not consistent in their postseason efforts, and 1989 was no exception. They fell docilely to the San Francisco Giants, four games to one.

There was no encore. Injuries wreaked havoc on the 1990 Cubs, at one point costing them all five starting pitchers. Walton broke his right hand and hurt his left wrist, which kept him out of the lineup for 81 games. The Cubs faded to 77-85 and finished in a tie for fourth place, 18 games behind Pittsburgh.

They did no better in 1991 or 1992. Indeed, they did precisely the same—fourth place both years. The major triumph of 1992 was the one the club gained over Major League Baseball Commissioner Fay Vincent's plan, tied to the admission of the expansion Colorado Rockies and Florida Marlins, to shift the Cubs from the NL East to the NL West. (The White Sox had been in the AL West from the outset of divisional play.)

This plan outraged the Cubs' owners, who maintained that geography ought not to take precedence over tradition. Tradition won, Fay Vincent lost (resigning his office over this and other contretemps), and the Cubs stayed in the NL East.

The 1993 season brought some pleasant surprises; though the Cubs again finished in fourth place, their record improved to 84-78, only the third winning season for the club since 1972. Relief pitcher Randy Myers set an NL record with 53 saves, and center fielder Sammy Sosa became the first Cubs player to hit 30 HRs and steal 30 bases in a season.

None of this, however, was enough to save the job of manager Jim Lefebvre, who was fired and replaced by bench coach Tom Trebelhorn, who becomes the Cubs' eleventh manager in the last eleven years. Trebelhorn inherits a team that could be strong enough to contend for a division crown in baseball's realigned divisions. The Cubs have been assigned to the National League's new Central Division, there to continue their timeless search for a pennant and, perhaps someday, somehow, after a barren eight decades and counting, a World Championship as well.

SOURCES

BOOKS

Banks, Ernie, and Jim Enright, *Mr. Cub,* Follett, 1971.

Baseball Guide: 1985 Edition, Sporting News Publishing, 1985.

Baseball Guide: 1992 Edition, Sporting News Publishing, 1992.

Baseball Register: 1980 Edition, Sporting News Publishing, 1980.

Baseball Register: 1992 Edition, Sporting News Publishing, 1992.

Brown, Warren, *The Chicago Cubs,* Putnam, 1946.

Enright, Jim, *The Chicago Cubs,* Macmillan, 1975.

Goldstein, Richard, *Spartan Seasons: How Baseball Survived the Second World War,* Macmillan, 1980.

Thorn, John, and Pete Palmer, editors, *Total Baseball,* Warner Books, 1989.

Langford, Jim, *The Game Is Never Over: An Appreciative History of the Chicago Cubs, 1948-1980,* Icarus Press, 1980.

Reichler, Joseph L., editor, *The Baseball Encyclopedia, 7th edition,* Macmillan, 1988.

Reidenbaugh, Lowell, *Take Me Out to the Ball Park,* Sporting News Publishing, 1983.

Tiemann, Robert L., and Mark Rucker, editors, *Nineteenth Century Stars,* Society for American Baseball Research, 1989.

Voigt, David Quentin, *American Baseball: From the Gentleman's Sport to the Commissioner System,* University of Pennsylvania Press, 1983.

Voigt, David Quentin, *American Baseball: From the Commissioners to Continental Expansion,* University of Pennsylvania Press, 1983.

Wheeler, Lonnie, *Bleachers: A Summer in Wrigley Field,* Contemporary Books, 1988.

PERIODICALS

Baseball America, February 7, 1993.

Baseball Digest, July, 1978.

Baseball Research Journal, 1978, 1979.

Chicago Cubs Program/Magazine, 1986.

Sports Illustrated, May 6, 1975.

—*Gerald Tomlinson* for Book Builders, Inc.

CINCINNATI REDS

In 1869 the Cincinnati Red Stockings became the first acknowledged professional baseball club in the United States. But only after the founding of the National League (NL) in 1876, with its regular schedules and relative stability, did the history of modern baseball really begin. The Red Stockings of Cincinnati became a charter member of the new league.

After just five seasons, however, the club dropped out of the league, remained unaffiliated for a year, and then in 1882 joined the new American Association, a rival major league. With pitcher Will (Whoop-La) White winning 40 games for them, the Reds took the American Association pennant in their first year. Their .688 winning percentage (55-25) is still a club record.

The Reds stayed in the American Association for eight seasons before returning to the National League. Despite being baseball pioneers, they were far from consistent winners in the pro ranks. Seldom finishing higher than fourth place, the

Cincinnati Reds struggled for decades before winning their first National League pennant in 1919. They won it handily that year, but their victory in the World Series was tainted by the fact that key players on the Chicago White Sox took a dive.

Two decades later, in 1939 and 1940, Cincinnati put together back-to-back pennant winning seasons. This was the era of pitchers Bucky Walters and Paul Derringer, of first baseman Frank McCormick, and of manager Bill McKechnie. The Reds faded after World War II, finishing in the second division for 11 consecutive seasons. In 1956, with Birdie Tebbetts managing and half the team hitting at least 28 home runs, Cincinnati was in the race all the way, winning 91 games but coming in third, two games back.

After four more seasons of trying, the Reds under manager Fred Hutchinson took the flag in 1961. Routed by the Mantle-Maris Yankees in the World Series, the team did not rise to the top again in the nineteen sixties, although they played above

.500 in every season but one. Then in the 1970s the franchise really took off. The team left storied old Crosley Stadium for Riverfront Stadium in 1970, and they left those near-misses behind them.

A galaxy of stars appeared in Cincinnati uniforms during the decade—Pete Rose, Johnny Bench, Tony Perez, Dave Conception, George Foster, Joe Morgan, Ken Griffey. This "Big Red Machine" was an aggressive, power-hitting, smooth-fielding ball club with good, but never outstanding, pitching.

Among the mainstays on the Big Red mound staff were Gary Nolan and Ray Billlingham. Late in the seventies Tom Seaver arrived, but by then the Reds' glory days were mostly over. During the decade Cincinnati won the division title six times: 1970, 1972, 1973, 1975, 1976, and 1979. They won the NL pennant four times and the World Series twice.

The 1980s started poorly after the strike-shortened 1981 season. The Reds occupied the cellar twice before scrambling up to fifth place. Then from 1985 through 1988 they finished second each year—losing out to Los Angeles in 1985, Houston in 1986, San Francisco in 1987, and Los Angeles again in 1988. In 1989 all three of those teams, along with San Diego, topped the Reds, who beat out only Atlanta in the NL West.

A year later Cincinnati's new manager, Lou Piniella, led them to the NL West championship, a National League Championship Series (NLCS) victory over Pittsburgh, and a surprising sweep of the Oakland A's in the World Series. They were back on top—but not for long. Next year they fell back to fifth, and in 1992 they claimed their familiar 1980s slot, second place.

Early Red Stockings

The Cincinnati Reds are the oldest professional baseball team in the United States. Some ballplayers, to be sure, were being paid long before any fully professional team existed. As the sport became increasingly popular around the time of the Civil War, the practice of charging admissions

caught on, and players shared in the gate receipts. But, starting in 1869, only the touring Red Stockings, organized by Cincinnati businessman Aaron Champion, paid every player a salary.

English-born Hall-of-Famer Harry Wright recruited the team, one of whose members was shortstop George Wright, his brother. Only one player on the ten-man roster was a Cincinnatian. This was a pro team pure and simple, and they proved it by compiling a 57-0-1 record on a cross-country tour. (The tie was a disputed 17-17 contest with the Troy Haymakers.)

In 1870 the Red Stockings got off to a fast start, too, winning their first 27 games before being stopped on June 14 by the Brooklyn Atlantics, 8-7, in a rousing 11-inning game. Another defeat later in the season took some of the luster off the Red Stockings, and they reverted to amateur status in 1871.

When the National League was founded in 1876, Cincinnati joined as a charter member. The Red Stockings were back in the pro ranks, but they were hardly the ball club they had been in 1869-70 with the Wright brothers and star pitcher Asa Brainard. In fact, they were terrible. The 1876 Cincinnati Red Stockings, under playing-manager Charlie Gould won only nine games while losing 56—a .138 mark. They improved very little in 1877, finishing at 15-42.

But the next year, under manager and third baseman Cal McVey, they astonished everyone by nearly upending powerhouse Boston, a team that featured the ex-Cincinnati Wright brothers, Irish-born pitcher Tommy Bond, and future Hall-of-Famer Orator Jim O'Rourke. For their part, the Red Stockings could now boast bespectacled pitcher Will White (the first major leaguer to wear glasses), catcher Deacon White (Will's older brother), and rookie outfielder King Kelly (bound for the Hall of Fame).

The 1878 Red Stockings finished second on a 37-23 record. After dropping back to fifth in 1879, they plunged to the cellar in 1880. Minus McVey and Kelly, ace hurler Will White struggled through an 18-42 season and, suffering from a sore arm, was shipped to Detroit.

TEAM INFORMATION AT A GLANCE

Founding date: April 25, 1876. [National League]

Home stadium: Riverfront Stadium
100 Riverfront Stadium
Cincinnati, OH 45202

Dimensions: Left-field line—330 feet
Center field—404 feet
Right-field line—330 feet
Seating capacity: 52,952

Team uniforms: Home—base color white with scarlet
Road—base color gray with scarlet block letters
Team nickname: Red Stockings, 1876-80; Reds, 1882-present
(briefly called Redlegs during the 1950s)
Logo: Red wishbone "C" with word "Cincinnati" in white block letters
within top of "C" and word "Reds" in larger white block letters at bottom;
carricature of ballplayer (with baseball for a head) running within the "C."

Franchise record*	Won	Lost	Pct.
(1876-1993)	8,717	8,472	.507

* Includes 1882-89 American Association totals.

World Series wins (5): 1919, 1940, 1975, 1976, 1990.
American Association championship (1): 1882.
National League championships (9): 1919, 1939, 1940, 1961, 1970, 1972, 1975, 1976, 1990.
National League West division first-place finishes (7): 1970, 1972, 1973, 1975, 1976, 1979, 1990.
League/division last-place finishes (12): 1876, 1877, 1880,
1901, 1914, 1931, 1932, 1933, 1934, 1937, 1982, 1983.

In the American Association

Will White had to be sent somewhere, because Cincinnati was expelled from the National League in 1880 for selling beer in the ballpark and playing games on Sunday. The Cincinnati owners joined with others to form a new league, the American Association (AA), placing teams for the 1882 season in Cincinnati, Louisville, St. Louis, Pittsburgh, Baltimore, and Philadelphia. The AA charged only 25 cents admission, compared to the NL's 50 cents. Moreover, it allowed Sunday games, and, not surprisingly given the number of brewmaster owners, it permitted the sale of beer and even whiskey in the stands.

In this six-team circuit the Cincinnati team, now the Reds, won the pennant in the league's first year, as pitcher Will White, after appearing in only two games for Detroit, returned to Cincinnati and went 40-12. The leading player on offense was third baseman Hick Carpenter, having the best year of his career at .342. Playing-manager Pop Snyder, a catcher, hit .291. After the season ended, the Reds played a couple of exhibition games against Pop Anson's NL pennant-winning Chicago White Stockings, the Cincinnatians taking one game and losing one.

The remaining seven of the Reds' seasons in the American Association were less happy. The team finished third in 1883 despite a 61-37 won-lost record and a fine year for Will White, 43-22. Charlie Jones, Cincinnati's center fielder, cracked 11 home runs, an unusually high total in that deadball era, although first-place Philadelphia's Harry Stovey, baseball's leading power hitter of the time, led the league with 14.

In 1884 Cincinnati faded to fifth place and was again in serious contention for an AA pennant. Even in 1887, when Cincinnati, under new manager Gus Schmelz, finished second to St. Louis, the Reds were 14 games back.

Transcendental Graphics

Heinie Groh

A number of factors combined to kill the American Association. One was the appearance of a third major league, the Players League, founded in 1890. Another was that the National League was simply more prestigious. It attracted the better ballplayers. Finally, the AA became polarized between strong and weak franchises, lessening fan interest and putting the weaker franchises under growing financial pressure. When the American Association called it quits after the 1891 season Cincinnati had already transferred to the National League.

Back home in the National League in 1890, the Reds came in fourth, 10½ games behind Brooklyn. They had a new manager in Tom Loftus, a good pitcher in Billy Rhines (28-17 with a league-leading 1.95 ERA), and a second baseman who deserves special attention. John (Bid) McPhee played second base for Cincinnati for 18 years, mostly without a glove. He had signed on in 1882, the first AA season, and he stayed with Cincinnati through 1899.

Considered the best second baseman in the game, he suffered an ankle injury in 1897 that threatened to end his career. Cincinnati sportswriters and fans staged a special benefit for him, raising $3,500 (real money in those days) to help tide him over and perhaps bring him back. Bid McPhee, an idol in the Queen City, did return to play for two more seasons. He was a gentleman in a rowdy era, and a stellar player on an uninspiring team.

From 1891 through 1900 their best showing was third place in 1898 under manager Buck Ewing, a native Cincinnatian and a Hall of Famer for his playing career, mainly with the New York Giants. Outfielder Elmer Smith had one of his better years in 1898, batting .342, as did pitcher Pink Hawley, acquired from Pittsburgh, who finished the season 27-11.

In 1901 Cincinnati sank to the cellar for the first time. The next year John T. Brush, the Reds' controversial and puritanical owner, sold the franchise to a local group who named August (Garry) Herrmann, an ex-water commissioner, to run the ball club. Herrmann never produced a pennant winner for Cincinnati, but he did play a major role in American baseball.

He was one of the four architects of the National Agreement of 1903, the landmark truce reached in Cincinnati between the warring National and American Leagues that restored the primacy of the reserve clause and stopped player raids by guaranteeing the status and territory of the 16 franchises. According to baseball historian David Q. Voigt, "Time would show that this Cincinnati peace gave major-league baseball fifty years of rock-ribbed stability, with not one franchise shift taking place in either league."

Garry Herrmann was named chair of the National Commission, the three-person group established to make the National Agreement work. Since the other two members were the presidents of the National and American Leagues, it would appear that the NL got the best of things by having the Cincinnati owner as the chair. But, in fact, Herrmann, although an NL owner, was a close friend of AL president Ban Johnson, and the arrangement worked well. What did not work so well was the Cincinnati ball club on the field. From the turn of the century until World War I the Cincinnati Reds never came close to a first-place finish.

Transcendental Graphics

Joe Kelley

A Lonely, Tainted Triumph

During these years of futility, Cincinnati had a number of fine players. In the early years, 1898-1905, Harry Steinfeldt, later of the Tinker-to-Evers-to-Chance Cubs' infield, held down third base for the Reds. Hall-of-Fame outfielder Joe Kelley put in four seasons with the Reds, 1903-06, near the end of his playing days. On the mound, Bob Ewing, 1902-09, was a reliable starter, posting a winning record for a so-so team, with a lifetime ERA of 2.49.

In 1915 the Reds had Buck Herzog at shortstop and Red Killefer in the outfield. The New York Giants decided they wanted both players, and to get them they gave up their aging but brilliant hurler Christy Mathewson and future

Hall-of-Fame outfielder Edd Roush. It was a good trade for Cincinnati, although Mathewson, his pitching days nearly over, would for the most part be managing the Reds rather than taking the mound for them.

The 1916 Reds, with Mathewson at the helm in the last half of the season, finished in a tie for seventh place. They had a few good ballplayers, among them first baseman Hal Chase, who led the league in hitting with a .339 average, and third baseman Heinie Groh, in his fourth year with the Reds.

In the war years, 1917-18, Cincinnati moved up in the standings to fourth, then to third. Near the end of the 1918 season, with the Reds out of the pennant race, Mathewson joined the army. The

Transcendental Graphics

Edd Rousch

war was almost over, but Matty ran into poison gas in France, which brought on pulmonary tuberculosis. He died in 1925 at Saranac Lake, New York, at the age of 41.

Pat Moran, who had guided the Phillies to a pennant in his first try in 1915, took over for the 1919 Reds. Hal Chase, a good first baseman but a notorious gambler, was gone, having ambled over to the mound one day in 1918 and suggested to Reds' reliever Jimmy Ring that he lose the ball game and thereby earn a few extra dollars from Chase. Ring reported the incident to Mathewson, who insisted that Chase be let go. He was, and the Reds acquired another and better first baseman, veteran Jake Daubert, from Brooklyn.

During the off-season the Reds also purchased a couple of needed pitchers—Ray Fisher from the Yankees and lefty Slim Sallee from the

Giants. With Heinie Groh at third base and Edd Roush in the outfield, the 1919 Reds were a team to reckon with. They got off to a fast start. After faltering a bit in May and June, they passed the Giants for good in late July.

The pitching could hardly have been better. Their new pitchers, Fisher and Sallee, went 14-5 and 21-7 respectively. Two other Reds' hurlers enjoyed career years—Hod Eller, 20-9, and Dutch Ruether, 19-6 with a 1.82 ERA. By the end of the season Pat Moran's Reds led the second-place Giants by nine games. Their World Series opponents would be the Chicago White Sox.

Whole books have been written about the 1919 World Series. It is generally assumed that the underdog Cincinnati Reds would have lost to the Chicago White Sox except for the misdeeds of eight "Black Sox" nogoodniks, recruited by Chick Gandel, who did what they had to do in order to ensure a Reds' victory and a tidy payoff for themselves. No one will ever know what the outcome would have been had not Lefty Williams grooved pitches and Happy Felsch bumbled about in the outfield. What it was, for the record books, was a Cincinnati triumph, five games to three.

The 1920 team, with basically the same roster, led the league going into September but slumped at the end to finish third. The stars were Roush (.329), Daubert (.304), Groh (.304), and outfielder Pat Duncan (.295). The RBI leaders were Roush (90) and Duncan (83). Although the Reds dipped to fifth place in 1921, they came back to challenge in 1922 and 1923.

On the mound for Cincinnati from 1921 though 1933 was future Hall-of-Fame southpaw Eppa Rixey, formerly a Phillies' star. In 1921 Rixey hurled 301 innings and yielded only one home run, the stingiest single-season mark from then until now. In 1922, one of his best seasons, he won 25 games and lost 13 for the Reds.

Rixey was the winningest left-handed pitcher in the National League (266 lifetime) until Warren Spahn came along and broke his record. Eppa Rixey used to say ruefully that no one would ever have heard of him except for Warren Spahn's career totals. But good as he was, Rixey could not

The Tainted 1919 World Series

No World Series has received more attention than the one in 1919 that involved the Black Sox scandal. The Series pitted Kid Gleason's Chicago White Sox against Pat Moran's Cincinnati Reds. The Reds won it, five games to three, at least in part because eight players on the Chicago team—pitchers Lefty Williams and Eddie Cicotte in particular—were bribed by gamblers to throw the Series. When the scandal came to light in late 1920, it tainted forever the Cincinnati Reds' only World Series victory before 1940.

Yet whether Chicago would have won easily, or, indeed, have won at all, without the Black Sox's paid-for mistakes, is a moot question. Historian George W. Hilton, writing in the *Baseball Research Journal* of 1975, argues that the White Sox ball club was not the shoo-in many assume. "It was a fading version of the 1917 World's Champions.... The 1919 club was assigned third place in the *Chicago Tribune*'s pre-season prediction for the American League.... The team won 88 games [against the Reds' 96] and took the pennant by a margin of 3½ games [against the Reds' nine], hardly a performance to make its triumph in the World Series the assured outcome that most later writers have assumed."

bring the Reds a pennant by himself; and the team, although playing well through most of the 1920s, could not reclaim the flag.

In 1924 Jack Hendricks replaced Pat Moran as manager and saw the team through a close but unsuccessful pennant race in 1926. The first baseman that year was Wally Pipp, who came over from the Yankees after losing his job to Lou Gehrig. Chuck Dressen, later to manage the Reds (and, more notably, to head the Dodger "Boys of Summer"), played third base for the 1926 Reds. The catcher, Bubbles Hargrave, is less well known, but he led the league in batting that year with .353, while a teammate, outfielder Cuckoo Christenson, pressed him for second place at .350. The Reds contended for the pennant all the way, but late-season losses dropped them back of the Cardinals by two games at the finish.

The 1930s began grimly for the nation and for the Reds. The Depression-era team suffered a depression all its own, locked in the cellar, starving for wins in 1931, 1932, 1933, and 1934. The managers changed, the players changed, but the fortunes of the team remained those of the apple-sellers on the street. There were two bright notes. Ernie Lombardi, one of the great, slow-footed catchers of all time, arrived in 1932 and would be on hand to see better days. Likewise pitcher Paul Derringer came on board, a 1933 acquisition from

the Cardinals. Two future Hall of Famers, outfielder Chick Hafey and first baseman Sunny Jim Bottomley, put in several seasons for the Reds in the early thirties but had retired by the time the Reds made a significant run for the title. After

Transcendental Graphics

Eppa Rixey

Transcendental Graphics

Bill McKechnie

rising to sixth and fifth in 1935 and 1936, the Reds tumbled back into the cellar in 1937. It was Hafey's last season. He shared the outfield with another Hall of Famer, Kiki Cuyler, also nearing the end of a long career. Clearly, the Reds were going to need something more than over-the-hill superstars to get them out of the horse latitudes.

Two in a Row, Then Limbo

Cincinnati industrialist Powel Crosley, Jr., bought into the ball club early in the Depression. Redland Field, home of the Reds since 1912, became Crosley Field in 1934, and on May 14, 1935, in a game against the Phillies, night baseball—already well established in the minors—first came to the majors. Attendance improved, but the team still lacked the ingredients required for success on the field.

The breakthrough came in 1938 with the hiring of Bill McKechnie as the Reds' manager. McKechnie inherited some talent, most of it obtained under Crosley's aegis. First baseman Frank McCormick had been up and down with the Reds since 1934. In 1938 he came into his own, batting .327 and driving in 106 runs. Second baseman Lonnie Frey and shortstop Billy Myers had been with the club since 1935. Outfielder Harry Craft and pitcher Johnny Vander Meer were 1937 additions.

Vander Meer, a left-hander, wrote himself into the record books on June 15, 1938, when he pitched his second consecutive no-hitter, a feat never accomplished before or since in the majors. It was a rather ragged 6-0 victory over the Brooklyn Dodgers (the first one had been against the Boston Bees four days earlier), one that Leo Durocher almost ruined for Vander Meer, when, with two out in the ninth, he slashed a pitch down the right-field line that went foul at the last instant. Lippy Leo then drove another liner to center that Harry Craft caught at his shoe tops for the final out. Vander Meer's pitching career was nothing out of the ordinary—he suffered from wildness—but those two games of June 11 and 15, 1938, gave him a sure paragraph, or at least a footnote, in subsequent histories of the game.

The 1938 Reds fashioned a fourth-place finish, their highest standing in more than a decade. But it was only prologue, because in 1939, having added a key player during the previous season, pitcher Bucky Walters from the Phillies, the Reds put it all together in 1939. They led the pack most of the way, outdistancing a fast-closing Cardinal team by four and a half games, as they won 97 games and lost 57.

First baseman Frank McCormick had the season of his life, batting .332 with 18 home runs and 128 runs batted in. Outfielder Ival Goodman also outdid himself, batting .323 and driving in 84 runs. Always reliable Ernie Lombardi, a fixture behind the plate, hit .287, banged 20 homers, and drove in 85 runs.

On the mound Bucky Walters topped all NL pitchers with 27 wins (11 losses) and a 2.29 ERA. Paul Derringer was equally effective, winning 25,

Transcendental Graphics

Ernie Lombardi

losing only seven, and posting a 2.93 ERA. A third pitcher of note was Junior Thompson, a rookie, who turned in a 13-5 record with a 2.54 ERA.

This was a first-rate team having a very hot season, but when they went up against the intimidating New York Yankees in the World Series, they folded, losing four straight games. Their consolation was that there would be a next year. There was, and 1940 was the best year Cincinnati ever had between the birth of the Red Stockings and emergence of the Big Red Machine in the 1970s. The basic lineup was unchanged. The star pitchers of 1939 were back. The Reds won 100 games for the first time in their history and swept to a second consecutive pennant without much difficulty.

Once again Frank McCormick and Ernie Lombardi powered the offense. For the third straight year McCormick, batting .309, led the league in hits, with 191 in 1940. He also led in doubles with 44 and paced the team in homers with 19 and RBIs with 127. Another McCormick, rookie outfielder Mike, batted an even .300. Ernie Lombardi's .319 batting average was the highest on the club, and his 74 RBIs, while far short of Frank McCormick's total, was good for second place.

The Big Three of the pitching staff—Bucky Walters, Paul Derringer, and Junior Thompson—maintained their mastery. Walters won 22, lost 12, and posted a 2.48 ERA. Derringer won 20 while losing 12, and Thompson went 16-9. A newcomer to the staff, Jim Turner, acquired from the Boston Bees, did all right, too, winning 14 and losing seven.

When the curtain fell on the regular season, Cincinnati led the strong but outclassed Brooklyn Dodgers by 10 games. Would they fold again in the World Series? Perhaps not. For one thing they would not be facing the Yankees. In 1940 the Detroit Tigers, with Hank Greenberg, Charlie Gehringer, Schoolboy Rowe, and the much-traveled Bobo Newsom stood atop the American League. The Tigers were a superb team, but they found the Reds considerably harder to beat than the Yanks had.

In fact, the Tigers fell to Bill McKechnie's team, four games to three. Bobo Newsom won two games for the Tigers, one of them a three-hit shutout, but Bucky Walters and Paul Derringer each won a pair for the Reds. One of the batting stars for Cincinnati was an outfielder named Jimmy Ripple, acquired from Brooklyn near the end of the season. Ripple's homer in game two and his double in game seven were crucial to the Reds' victory.

There seemed to be every reason to think the Reds would repeat their success in 1941. But the booming bats fell silent, and the team faded to third place behind Brooklyn and St. Louis. The Reds' pitching ace was a rookie, Elmer Riddle, rather than Walters or Derringer. Riddle won 19 games (three of them in relief) and lost only four. His .826 won-lost percentage and 2.24 ERA took league honors. But Riddle was not to be the savior of the ball club, although he won a league-leading 21 games in wartime 1943.

Indeed, salvation was a long way off. The Reds finished in the first division from 1938 through 1944, but starting in 1945—the final year of World War II—Cincinnati fell into a malaise. The team failed to play .500 ball for 11 seasons in a row. Their best finishes were fifth place in 1947, 1954, and 1955.

Then in 1956, under third-year manager Birdie Tebbetts, they came alive. One reason for their revival was a rookie outfielder named Frank Robinson, up from the minors. Robinson made his presence felt immediately. He batted .290, hit 38 home runs (topped only by Brooklyn's Duke Snider), and drove in 83 runs. The '56 Reds' outfield combined for 250 RBIs as Gus Bell contributed 84 and Wally Post 83.

Veteran first baseman Ted Kluszewski set the RBI pace for the team with 102. Catcher Ed Bailey was a tiger on offense, too, batting .300, slamming 28 homers, and driving in 75 runs. The Reds' team slugging average of .441 left the other NL teams far behind. Yet Cincinnati, with a 91-63 record, finished only third—a very close third—to the Brooklyn Dodgers and the Milwaukee Braves.

This looked like a team with a future, but its immediate future proved to be mostly downhill. The Reds went from third place in 1956 to fourth in 1957, fourth again in 1958, a tie for fifth in 1959, then to sixth in 1960. Few saw this as the road to a pennant, but it was, as the Reds came through in 1961 under second-year manager Fred Hutchinson.

The Hutchinson Years

The Reds' team that won the pennant in 1961 bore only a slight resemblance to the team that had finished such a strong third in 1956. Outfielders Frank Robinson, Gus Bell, and Wally Post were still on hand, but Vada Pinson had won the full-time center-field job. The infield was all new, as was the pitching staff.

Of the holdovers, only Frank Robinson put up the kind of numbers he had in the past. In fact, he put up better numbers, batting .323, hitting 37 homers, and driving in 124 runs. Those are superstar stats in anybody's league, yet Robinson would improve on every one of them in 1962.

Among the other Reds of 1961, Vada Pinson hit .343, part-time outfielder Jerry Lynch, .315, and part-time shortstop Leo Cardenas, .308. Two newcomers, first baseman Gordy Coleman and third baseman Gene Freese, each smacked 26 homers and collected 87 RBIs. Four Cincinnati pitchers had outstanding years—Joey Jay (21-10), Jim O'Toole (19-9), Bob Purkey (16-12), and Jim Brosnan (10-4). Purkey, like Robinson, would reach Olympian heights in 1962, winning 25 games and losing only five.

Individual performances aside, however, 1961 was the year of the Reds. They trailed the L.A. Dodgers briefly in August but then pulled ahead to win by a four-game margin. "Never taken seriously as pennant contenders," writes Jim Brosnan in *Pennant Race*, his player's diary of the season, "the Reds found ways and means to win often enough in the season of '61." He quotes manager Fred Hutchinson on those apparently simple ways and means: "We've got pitching and hitting. That's all baseball is—pitching and hitting." It sounds

Transcendental Graphics

Frank Robinson

easy, but in 1961 the Reds won just their fifth pennant (one of them in the American Association) since the founding of the National League in 1876.

They did not win their third World Series. The New York Yankees, in the year that Roger Maris hit 61 homers and Mickey Mantle hit 54, were just too tough—even with Maris batting .105 in the Series and the injured Mantle .167 (in six plate appearances). Yankee pitcher Whitey Ford was unhittable, almost literally, as he extended his Series scoreless inning streak to a record 32, winning two games, and posting a 0.00 ERA.

The Reds took game two, 6-2, behind Joey Jay, but that was all. The Series star for the Reds was rookie catcher Johnny Edwards, up from Indianapolis. In game two the Yankees intention-ally walked batters twice to get at Edwards. Each time the young catcher came through with an RBI hit.

After 1961 the Reds played well—winning 98 games in 1962 and 92 in 1964, for instance—but never repeated as league champions. They dropped below .500 only once in the 1960s. That was in 1966, the year after they traded superstar Frank Robinson to the Baltimore Orioles. Robinson won the Triple Crown and the American League MVP for the Birds. Although his loss, in a poor trade for Milt Pappas and two others, was a blow to Cincinnati in the short run, the team had already begun to acquire the core of their power-house team of the 1970s.

Pete Rose took over at second base in 1963, the first of his 24 years in the majors. In 1964 he was joined by first baseman Tony Perez. The two had met as teenage infielders At Geneva, New York, in their first year of pro ball. One of the pitchers who would last through the Reds' glory days arrived in 1967. He was Gary Nolan, also a product of the Reds' farm system. Another player who made a brief appearance in Cincinnati that year was a youthful catcher, Johnny Bench. He returned in 1968 to stay, spending his entire Hall-of-Fame career behind the plate for the Reds.

In 1969, the first year of division play, the Reds were in the thick of a remarkable five-way race in the new six-team NL West. Only San Diego's expansion Padres were not a threat, finishing 41 games out. As the season wound down, the teams to beat were Atlanta and San Francisco.

Cincinnati, led by Dave Bristol in his third and last year as manager, was edged out by both of them and came in third, four games behind. The Reds had some very hot hitters in 1969. Pete Rose led the league with a .348 average and tied his career-long season-high home run total with 16. Tony Perez, now at third base, hit .294 with 37 homers and 122 RBIs. First baseman Lee May nearly matched Perez's power totals, with 38 homers and 110 RBIs.

Second-year catcher Johnny Bench showed no signs of a sophomore jinx as he hit .293, slammed 26 round-trippers, and drove in 90 runs.

Outfielder Bobby Tolan, ordinarily a middling hitter, had his first of two fine seasons, batting .305 with 21 homers and 93 RBIs. The 1969 team's league-leading 177 homers and .422 slugging average foreshadowed the arrival of the Big Red Machine.

A Riverfront Decade

The Reds played their last game at Crosley Field on June 24, 1970, before 28,027 fans. Six days later they played their first game at new Riverfront Stadium with 51,050 in attendance. Cincinnati won the Crosley Field game, 5-4, over the San Francisco Giants on home runs by Johnny Bench and Lee May. They lost their Riverfront opener, 8-2, to the Atlanta Braves. It was not an omen.

The Reds would do very well indeed in their first decade at the new ballpark, starting in 1970 with the division championship. Johnny Bench paced all NL hitters with 45 homers and 148 RBIs. Four Reds' regulars batted over .300—Tony Perez (.317), Pete Rose (.316), Bobby Tolan (.316), and rookie outfielder Bernie Carbo (.305) having the best season of his career. Pitcher Gary Nolan benefited from all that hitting, going 18-7, and Jim Merritt, in his last good year, went 20-12.

The Reds won 102 games for rookie manager Sparky Anderson. No other team in the division posed a serious threat, as Cincinnati left second-place L.A. 14½ games behind. In addition to their other stars, the Reds had a new shortstop whose name would soon become familiar to baseball fans across America—Dave Concepcion. A native of Venezuela who had risen rapidly through the Reds' farm system, Concepcion batted .260 as a rookie, a few points behind his lifetime average. A superb shortstop, he was also something of a clown, once jumping into a clothes dryer shouting, "I've gotta get hot!"

The Reds rolled to victory in the 1970 NLCS, winning three straight games. Their World Series opponents were Earl Weaver's Baltimore Orioles, now fortified with ex-Red Frank Robinson. They had won 108 games in the regular season. In the first two games of the World Series the Reds took 3-0 leads only to lose them, and the game, each time. Baltimore's Boog Powell and Ellie Hendricks had key extra-base hits in both games. Birds' pitcher Dave McNally helped his own cause in game three with a grand-slam home run.

McNally's 9-2 victory, the third straight Oriole win, made a Baltimore sweep of the Reds look like a real possibility. But in the fourth game it was the Reds who came from behind, eking out a 6-5 victory on Lee May's three-run homer in the eighth inning. In game five Cincinnati took a 3-0 lead in the top of the first, but it quickly evaporated as the Birds scored two runs each in the first, second, and third innings, going on to win the game 9-3 and the Series four games to one. It was a disappointing conclusion for Reds' fans, but the team was beginning to realize its potential.

1971 was a year in which no one on the Reds except pitchers Don Gullett and Clay Carroll could seem to get going. Gullett, a pitcher in his sophomore season, did well, 16-6 with a 2.64 ERA. Carroll posted a 10-4 record in relief with a 2.49 ERA. Otherwise, 1971 was a season to forget, a fourth-place finish and the Reds' only losing record of the decade (79-83). A young outfielder, George Foster, obtained early in the season from the Giants, gave few hints of the great seasons he had ahead of him.

A trade with Houston in November 1971 brought second baseman Joe Morgan, outfielder Cesar Geronimo, and pitcher Jack Billingham to Cincinnati. The Reds had to give up slugging first baseman Lee May, but with Tony Perez moving over to first base, nothing was lost. In 1972 the Reds put their 1971 failings behind them and coasted to the NL West title.

The NLCS proved a bit tougher than in 1970, going to a full five games before, in the ninth inning of the deciding contest, the pitcher for the Pittsburgh Pirates, Bob Moose, uncorked a wild pitch. George Foster scored from third base, and the Reds went to the World Series. It was a moment of high drama at Riverfront Stadium as Foster charged home with the winning run.

At Findlay and Western Avenues | HOME FIELD

When the 1884 Cincinnati Reds were forced out of their home ballpark on Bank Street by an upstart ball club in the Union Association, management had to find a new site fast. They picked a brickyard at the corner of Findlay and Western Avenues and quickly put up wooden stands. Unfortunately, on opening day, 1884, the stands at the new facility, called League Park, collapsed, killing one person and injuring many others. When the Reds (who were in the American Association at the time) were readmitted to the National League in 1890, they played at the renovated Findlay Avenue park. In 1894 they rebuilt it, turning the playing field around so that batters would not have to peer into the late afternoon sun.

League Park burned in the fall of 1901 and was replaced on the same site by a new wooden facility, grandly called Palace of the Fans. In the fall of 1911 that, too, burned. The replacement, still at the same location, was was built with concrete and steel and was called Redland Field. Unlike the earlier Cincinnati ballparks, Redland Field contained clubhouses, so the players did not have to suit up before coming there. The first game as Redland Field (renamed Crosley Field in 1934) was played on April 11, 1912. The last game was played there on June 24, 1970. Between those two dates the ballpark was altered many times. One of the major alterations came in 1935 when lights were installed for night baseball. President Franklin D. Roosevelt pushed a button in the White House and more than 600 lamps went on at Crosley Field.

In January of 1937 nearby Mill Creek overflowed, covering the field with 21 feet of water. Pitchers Lee Grissom and Gene Schott rowed a boat over the center-field fence for the benefit of wire service photographers. On June 11, 1938, the Reds' Johnny Vander Meer pitched a no-hitter at Crosley Field against the Boston Bees. That was of passing interest, but four days later, facing the Brooklyn Dodgers at Ebbets Field, Johnny Vander Meer did it again. He pitched a second straight no-hitter. It had never been done in the majors before, and has it has never been done since.

On June 30, 1970, Riverfront Stadium, a superstructure with a bouncy carpet for a playing field, opened as the new home of the Reds. Home plate became Crosley Field's only physical link with Riverfront when it was moved from the old ballpark to the new. Many of the Reds' great players appeared in both parks, among them Pete Rose and Johnny Bench.

The Oakland A's, without their injured superstar Reggie Jackson, defeated the Reds four games to three in the 1972 World Series. Every game except game six, an 8-1 Reds' victory, was decided by a single run. The A's won the first two games, 3-2 and 2-1. Then in game three Jack Billingham took the mound for the Reds and tossed a three-hit shutout. Anything less would have been too little, for Oakland's Blue Moon Odom threw a four-hitter, losing it 1-0 on a Perez single, a sacrifice bunt, and a Geronimo single.

After losing game four, 3-2, Cincinnati bounced back. Pete Rose, with a homer and an RBI single, was the hero in the Reds' 5-4 win in the fifth game. Game six was easy, an 8-1 Reds' win,

and it all came down to game seven.

In game seven the A's led all the way, winning a close 3-2 victory. Oakland catcher Gene Tenace, a .225 hitter in the regular season, got two hits and two RBIs in the deciding game. That gave him a total of nine runs batted in for the Series, along with four homers. Pete Rose said about Tenace that "for a week against us, he was Ruth and Cobb. What I liked about him was that he played so hard...." Tony Perez collected 10 hits for the Reds, and Bobby Tolan knocked in six runs in a losing cause.

In 1973 Cincinnati won their division title on a 99-63 record but ceded the playoff series to the semi-amazin' New York Mets, three games to

Pete Rose: Charlie Hustle

An author writing a history of the National League early in the 1970s tried to predict the player of the decade. His guess was Cesar Cedeno, which says something about the hazards of predicting, because when the seventies ended, there was only one possible choice for the honor, and *The Sporting News* confirmed it: The Player of the Decade was Pete Rose.

When 19-year-old Pete Rose reported to his manager at Geneva, New York, in the Class D New York-Penn League, he said, "I'm your new second baseman." It was early in the 1960 season, and the second baseman already there was Tony Perez, an 18-year-old Cuban destined to play beside Rose on and off for three decades.

AP/Wide World Photos

Perez moved over to third, neither of them fielded or hit very well, and the Geneva Red Legs finished in last place. But Pete Rose hustled. He ran out walks, emulating one of his baseball heroes, Enos Slaughter of the St. Louis Cardinals. "The idea of running out the walks," Rose told biographer Roger Kahn, "came from Slaughter.... If that makes me a hot dog, pass the mustard."

After two more years in the minors—at Tampa, Florida, and Macon, Georgia—Rose took over at second base for the Cincinnati Reds. In an exhibition game with the Yankees he ran out a walk as usual. "Charlie Hustle," they sneered. And "Charlie Hustle" he became. He also became the National League Rookie of the Year in 1963.

By the time he retired as an active player in 1986—after 19 years with the Reds, five with the Phillies, and part of the 1984 season with the Expos—Pete Rose held a host of records. He had played in more games than any other major leaguer in history: 3,562. He had come to bat more often than any other player: 14,053 times. He had made 4,256 hits, more than the previous record-holder, Ty Cobb. He had collected more than 200 hits in each of ten seasons. He stood second in two-base hits to Tris Speaker on the all-time list, with 746. He was not especially fast, but his aggressive head-first slides were legendary. He lacked long-ball power, but on April 29, 1978, he hit three homers in one game.

Rose readily admitted that many players in the majors had more talent than he did. But Rose, who neither drank nor smoke, kept himself fit and played every inning of every game with determination. He was a sparkplug on four pennant-winning Cincinnati teams. Moving on to Philadelphia, he helped the Phillies capture two pennants. A team player and an intense competitor, Pete Rose on the ball field, though not off it, always had the bearing of a surefire winner.

two. In 1974 the Reds won 98 games and lost 64, but the L.A. Dodgers had one of those years, winning 102, leading the NL West most of the way, and relegating Sparky Anderson's men to second place.

The Big Red Machine

The Cincinnati Reds of 1975 and 1976 rank among the finest teams of all time. Sportswriters and fans called them the Big Red Machine. In 1975 the Reds won 108 games, their highest total ever, and in 1976 they won 102. In the NLCS they breezed past the Pirates in 1975 and the Phillies in 1976, winning six games, losing none. In 1975 they squeaked past the Boston Red Sox to win the World Series, four games to three. A year later they humiliated the New York Yankees, four games to none.

Who were these guys? In general, they were the old, familiar players all reaching the top of their form at the same time. Tony Perez was at first base, Joe Morgan at second, Dave Concepcion at shortstop, and Pete Rose—a standout at any position he played, at third. Johnny Bench was behind the plate. The outfield consisted of Ken Giffey, Cesar Geronimo, and George Foster. This was a powerful, smooth-functioning outfit.

In 1975 the RBI leaders were Johnny Bench (110) and Tony Perez (109). A year later the leaders were George Foster (121) and Joe Morgan (111). In addition to their power on offense—a .280 team batting average in 1976—the Reds led the league in fielding both years. They had speed on the basepaths, too, although only Joe Morgan was among the league leaders in stolen bases.

The pitching of the Big Red Machine is harder to assess. The remarkable number of capable hurlers gave six pitchers double-digit win totals in 1975 and seven in 1976. Nobody won more than 15 games in either of the Reds' two great seasons.

Gary Nolan won 15 games each year, and both Jack Billingham and Don Gullett won 15 in 1975. Gullett's 15-4 total with a 2.42 ERA paced the staff in 1975. Rollie Eastwick was superb in relief both years, posting an 11-5 mark in 1976, all in relief, with a 2.08 ERA. He led the league in saves both years.

Despite their dominance in the NL West, the Reds had no easy time with the AL pennant-winning Boston Red Sox in the 1975 World Series. It was a dramatic, hard-fought affair that went down to the seventh game. In game six Red Sox catcher Carlton Fisk homered in the 12th inning at Fenway Park to keep Boston alive. This game, in which pinch-hitter Bernie Carbo tied the game for the Sox with a three-run homer in the eighth inning, is regarded as one of the most thrilling ever played in the fall classic.

In game seven the Reds fought back from a 3-0 deficit to win, 4-3, on Joe Morgan's single with two out in the ninth inning. Pete Rose collected 10 hits in the Series, and Rollie Eastwick won two games in relief.

The 1976 World Series against the Yankees was rather cut-and-dried, as the psyched-up Reds won in four straight games. Johnny Bench was the big gun for Cincinnati, batting .538 for the Series and driving in five runs with two homers in the final game. Don Gullett, Gary Nolan, Jack Billingham, and Pat Zachry each won a game.

The Reds, somewhat surprisingly, did not repeat as NL West champs in 1977 or 1978, finishing second to Tommy Lasorda's L.A. Dodgers both times. Dan Driessen replaced Tony Perez at first base, Perez having been traded to Montreal. Future Hall-of-Fame pitcher Tom Seaver came over in midseason from the New York Mets. He went 14-3 for Cincinnati (to add to his 7-3 record for the Mets that year). He would put in five full seasons for the Reds.

But perhaps the biggest news concerning the Reds in 1977 was George Foster. He had belted 29 homers in 1976, a career high to that point, so no one was quite prepared for his 1977 output, as Foster powered his way onto the list of all-time season leaders by blasting 52 home runs. Additionally, he drove in a league-leading 149 runs and batted a career-high .320. In 1978 Foster dropped off to 40 home runs and 120 RBIs; both totals were still good for the league lead.

Pete Rose took the free-option route to Philadelphia after the 1978 season and was replaced at third base by Ray Knight. Although the Reds were no longer the scourge of the NL West, they did squeeze past Houston to take the division title. Manager Sparky Anderson, who lost his job after two second-place finishes, was replaced by John McNamara for the 1979 season. In the NLCS that year the Reds succumbed to the Pirates in three straight games. The decade of the 1970s was over, and with it the era of the Big Red Machine.

Little Red, Someone Said

The Reds did not immediately collapse. They did well in 1980 and in strike-shortened 1981—although not quite well enough. Their third place finish in 1980 was close, and their combined 66-42 won-lost record in 1981 was the best in either league. However, the strange and complex playoff system devised for that unique season left Cincinnati out of the running. The Reds were officially credited with finishing second twice.

Between 1982 and 1984 they fell on hard times, ending up in the cellar the first two years and in fifth place the next. The inevitable managerial changes occurred. Near the end of the 1984 season the reins were passed to hometown hero Pete Rose. Rose was nearing retirement as a player (though not, it turned out, as a gambler), and he proved to be a pretty fair skipper, his Reds taking second place in 1985, 1986, 1987, and 1988.

AP/Wide World Photos

Johnny Bench

Then the gambling scandal broke, and on August 24, 1989, Pete Rose was permanently suspended from baseball by A. Bartlett Giamatti, the new baseball commissioner. Rose admitted to betting heavily on football and basketball through bookmakers plus associating with felons. He did not admit betting on baseball, but Giamatti concluded he had done so, including games in which his team was involved. The remarkable player who had collected more hits than Ty Cobb was out of the game, banished, his brief managerial career over.

The beleaguered Reds fell to fifth place in 1989, but with Lou Piniella at the helm for the 1990 season, Cincinnati's fortunes improved dramatically. The Reds swept to victory in 18 of their first 23 games, grabbing an early lead in the NL West and never relinquishing it. They became the first start-to-finish leaders in the National League since the advent of the 162-game season. It was a true team effort.

The players were young, and few of the standouts were household names—infielders Mariano Duncan (.306), Barry Larkin (.301), Chris Sabo (25 homers), pitcher Jose Rijo (14-8), along with a bullpen trio of "Nasty Boys": Rob Dibble, Norm Charlton, and Randy Myers. The Reds beat the Pirates in a close NLCS and went on to surprise nearly everyone by sweeping the Oakland A's in the World Series. The A's never scored after the third inning in any of the four games.

But the youthful world champions did not repeat. After falling to fifth place in 1991, with a bleak 74-88 record, they recovered to finish second in 1992, eight games behind the Atlanta Braves. A tumultuous offseason followed; owner Marge Schott was exiled from the team for making racial comments about several players.

On the field, injuries ruined any hopes the Reds may have had of capturing the 1993 NL West title; the team used 51 different players during the year and ended with a 73-89 record, their worst in eleven seasons. Although Rijo (14-9, 227 strikeouts), Hal Morris (.315), and Kevin Mitchell (.341, 19 homers, 64 RBIs) performed well, the Reds' pitching was ineffective. However, the team

AP/Wide World Photos

Marge Schott

hopes that the young players who filled in for the injured starters gained some valuable major-league experience that will pay off in the future.

SOURCES

BOOKS

Allen, Lee, *The Cincinnati Reds,* G. P. Putnam's Sons, 1948.

Baseball Guide, The Sporting News Publishing Co., 1980, 1987, 1991, 1992 editions.

Baseball Register, The Sporting News Publishing Co., 1965, 1980, 1987, 1992 editions.

Borst, Bill, *The October Classic: A World Series Compendium,* Krank Press, 1989.

Brosnan, Jim, *Pennant Race,* Harper & Row, 1962.

Carter, Craig, editor, *Daguerreotypes,* 8th Edition, The Sporting News Publishing Co., 1990.

Dickey, Glenn, *The History of National League Baseball,* Stein and Day, 1979.

Holway, John B., and Bob Carroll, "Lives of the Players," *Total Baseball,* edited by John Thorn and Pete Palmer, Warner Books, 1989.

Ivor-Campbell, Frederick, "Team Histories: Cincinnati Reds," *Total Baseball,* edited by John Thorn and Pete Palmer, Warner Books, 1989.

Lowry, Philip J., *Green Cathedrals,* Society for American Baseball Research, 1986.

Reichler, Joseph L., editor, *The Baseball Encyclopedia,* 7th edition, Macmillan, 1988.

Reidenbaugh, Lowell, *Take Me out to the Ball Park,* The Sporting News Publishing Co., 1983.

Rose, Pete, and Roger Kahn, *Pete Rose: My Story,* Macmillan, 1989.

Selzer, Jack, *Baseball in the Nineteenth Century: An Overview,* Society for American Baseball Research, 1986.

Tiemann, Robert L., and Mark Rucker, editors, *Nineteenth Century Stars,* Society for American Baseball Research, 1989.

Voigt, David Quentin, *American Baseball: From the Gentleman's Sport to the Commissioner System,* Pennsylvania University Press, 1983.

PERIODICALS

Baseball America, February 21, 1993.
Baseball Research Journal, 1975.

—*Gerald Tomlinson* for Book Builders, Inc.

HOUSTON ASTROS

The Houston Astros may be better known for their stadium than they are for all but a few of their star players. But when they started out in 1962, as the Colt .45s, the Harris County Domed Stadium, now called the Astrodome, had not yet been built. The Houston team, one of the first two expansion franchises in the National League (the other being the New York Mets), played their first three seasons in a temporary ballpark, Colt Stadium, a traditional 32,601-seat facility adjacent to the present Astrodome. The Colt .45s won their opener on April 12, 1962, defeating the Chicago Cubs, 11-2.

But the first few years of the Houston ball club were successful only in that the Colt .45s, who became the Astros in 1965 (the year they moved into the Astrodome), stayed out of the cellar. In their first and fifth seasons they beat out the Cubs and the Mets, finishing eighth in the 10-team league. In their second, third, fourth, and sixth seasons, they outdid only the forlorn Mets.

Then in 1967 they upstaged nobody, being nudged into the basement by the Mets, who featured young Tom Seaver and Jerry Koosman on the mound. The Astros had nowhere to go but up. The upward climb was long and arduous. When the Mets took the National League pennant in 1969, the Astros were next-to-last in the NL West division, although they did have their first 20-game winner in Larry Dierker.

The Astros finished second in 1972, their first winning season ever, but trailed the powerful Cincinnati Reds by 10½ games. A couple of third-place finishes in 1976 and 1977 resulted from barely break-even won-lost records, 80-82 and 81-81.

Not until 1979, under manager Bill Virdon, did the Astros have a genuinely good season. They won 89 games that year, lost 73, and finished second, just a game and a half behind the Cincinnati Reds. Two Houston pitchers, J. R. Richard and Joe Niekro, led a strong staff, made even stronger in 1980 with the acquisition of free-agent Nolan Ryan. Sadly, though, part way through the 1980 season, Richard—with a 10-4 record and a 1.89 ERA—suffered a stroke that ended his baseball career.

After losing to Los Angeles in the NL West playoff following the strike-shortened, split 1981 season, the Astros posted so-so records through the early 1980s, then enjoyed their best season ever in 1986. Once again pitching was the key. Mike Scott and Bob Knepper turned in banner years, and the Astros, under first-year manager Hal Lanier, won the NL West title by ten games over the Reds.

In an exciting NL Championship Series the Mets prevailed in six games. After that the Astros faded. The best they could achieve was a third-place finish in 1989. That season Mike Scott became a 20-game winner and first baseman Glenn Davis, displaying more power than usual for an Astro hitter, blasted 34 homers, and drove in 89 runs.

Colt .45s and Astros

Not many fans showed up to watch the new Houston Colt .45s in their temporary outdoor stadium. Yet, for an expansion team, they weren't bad. General manager Paul Richards, a shrewd judge of baseball talent, picked up a few good ballplayers in the expansion draft. Outfielder Roman Mejias, acquired from Pittsburgh, came through with a .286 batting average, 24 home runs, and 76 RBIs.

On the mound Dick Farrell, most recently with Los Angeles, had a losing record, 10-20, but a respectable 3.02 ERA. He also struck out 203 batters (fourth-highest in the NL) while walking only 55. Perhaps the best pick of all was a 17-year-old first baseman (later an outfielder) they signed in September of 1961 and assigned to Durham, North Carolina, of the Carolina League for the 1962 season. He was Rusty Staub.

For three years loyal fans of the Colt .45s had to contend with the sweltering Houston heat and the Texas-size mosquitoes. Spraying the mosquitoes between innings was a Colt Stadium ritual. It took dedication to accept such discomfort to watch an eighth- or ninth-place team, and fewer than a million fans a year paid their way into the temporary ballpark. Still, there were dramatic moments. On April 23, 1964, Houston pitcher Ken Johnson hurled a nine-inning no-hit game against Cincinnati—and lost. Errors by Johnson and second baseman Nellie Fox cost the home team the game, 1-0.

For the 1965 season the Colt .45s were renamed the Astros. A dispute with the Colt Firearms Company over the sale of trademarked novelty items led the ball club to look to Houston's NASA Space Center as an inspiration for their new nickname. That same year the team moved into what was dubbed "The Eighth Wonder of the World," and a "modern Xanadu," the air-conditioned Harris County Domed Stadium.

Neither the elegant ambiance nor the "Astro-Turf," installed out of necessity when the grass died after the clear glass panes of the dome were painted, brought success to the team. Those sparkling clear panes *had* to be painted. Fly balls could not be tracked in the daytime because of the glare caused by the glass. Thus was born artificial turf, the "rug" or "carpet," which immediately aroused the disdain of baseball purists.

The Astros played their first league game in the new domed stadium on April 12, 1965, before 42,652 fans, including 24 of America's astronauts. The Astros lost to the Phillies' Chris Short, 2-0, on a four-hitter when Richie Allen belted a two-run homer.

The Astros finished in ninth place in 1965, well ahead of the Mets. Only Dick Farrell won in double figures for Houston that year (11-11). Outfielder Jimmy Wynn's .275 batting average, 22 homers, and 76 RBIs carried off team honors in each of those categories. Wynn, like Rusty Staub, was a youthful draft choice who played a single season in the minors before debuting with Houston. Both players were mainstays of the Astros in their formative years, and both were stars but not superstars.

TEAM INFORMATION AT A GLANCE

Founding date: April 12, 1962

Home stadium: The Astrodome
8400 Kirby Drive
Houston, TX 77054
Phone: (713) 799-9500
FAX: (713) 799-9562

Dimensions: Left-field line—330 feet
Center field—400 feet
Right-field line—330 feet
Seating capacity: 53,821

Team colors: Orange and blue
Team nickname: Colt .45s, 1962-1964; Astros, 1965—
Team logo: orange circle with miniature blue picture of Astrodome
in top half and large letters spelling "Astros" in blue in bottom
half, with orbiting baseballs superimposed over both

Franchise record:	Won	Lost	Pct.
(1962-1993)	2,473	2,648	.483

National League West first-place finishes (2): 1980, 1986
League/division last-place finishes (3): 1968, 1975, 1991

A Couple of Winning Seasons

When division play began in 1969, the Astros had never won more than 72 games in a season—and had never lost fewer than 90. The new East-West arrangement seemed to suit them. Under manager Harry (The Hat) Walker the team broke even, 81-81, finishing in fifth place, 12 games behind division-leading Atlanta. Rusty Staub, who had batted .333 for the Astros in 1967 to put him among the league leaders, was traded to Montreal after the 1968 season.

No one on the 1969 Astros could top Jimmy Wynn's or shortstop Denis Menke's .269 batting averages. Both of these players were run producers, though. Menke garnered 90 RBIs, while Wynn drove in 87 runs and hit 33 homers. Pitcher Larry Dierker posted a 20-13 record, his best in 13 seasons with the Astros.

After fourth- and fifth-place finishes in 1970 and 1971, Houston, which had been improving on the field more than in the standings, finally put together a winning season. The Astros finished second in 1972, edging out the L.A. Dodgers by a

.001 margin. Their outfield, consisting of Jimmy Wynn, Cesar Cedeno, and Bob Watson, had real class. This trio averaged above .300 at the plate, hit between 16 and 24 homers apiece, and drove in 90, 82, and 86 runs respectively.

First baseman Lee May paced the team with 29 homers and 98 RBIs, and third baseman Doug Rader, despite a low batting average, drove in 90 runs. The top starting pitchers for the Astros, Don Wilson and Larry Dierker, won 15 games each.

The next two years were disappointing, as the Astros, under manager Leo Durocher, fell to fourth place in 1973 and then, under Preston Gomez, stayed there in 1974. Still, they were an improving ball club, playing at just about the .500 level. Lee May drove in 105 runs for them in 1973, and Cesar Cedeno drove in 102 the next year. Left-handed pitcher Dave Roberts had a career year for the Astros in 1973, going 17-11 with a 2.85 ERA. In 1974 right-hander Tom Griffin had his career year, 14-10. But the team as a whole could not put it together.

J. R. Richard at Apogee

In 1975 things fell apart. The Astros' 64-97 record that year was their worst ever, the only time their won-lost percentage fell below .400 (it was .398). Even so, there was reason to take heart. Manager Preston Gomez surrendered the reins to Bill Virdon near the end of the 1975 season, and a six-foot-eight right-handed pitcher, who had been shuttling back and forth between the Astros and their farm teams, finally arrived in Houston to stay.

He was J. R. Richard, 12-10 in 1975, but about to go on a tear. The success of Richard brought new excitement to the Astrodome but did not equal a division title until the 1980 season, during which the tall right-hander suffered a career-ending stroke. J. R. won 20 games in 1976 and then 18 games in each of the next three seasons. He continued to increase his yearly strikeout totals, reaching 303 in 1978 and 313 in 1979. His 2.71 ERA in 1979 led the league.

While Richard was hanging the K on all those batters, the Astros as a team were doing moderately well. But they were no threat to the division leaders, the Cincinnati Reds and L.A. Dodgers, until 1979. That year, with J. R. Richard (18-13) and Joe Niekro (21-11) leading the way, they stood atop the NL West for most of the summer, fading at the end to finish a game-and-a-half behind the Reds.

Bill Virdon's 1980 Astros won the NL West championship, but not without a long struggle and a sudden-death conclusion. The Astros and Dodgers sparred for the lead throughout the season. Houston's strong, well-balanced pitching staff, led by Joe Niekro, carried the burden—a burden made doubly heavy when ace hurler Richard (off to the best start of his career, 10-4, ERA 1.89) suffered a stroke and was unable to continue.

Joining the impressive pitching staff in 1980—and making it even more impressive—was California Angels' strikeout artist Nolan Ryan, obtained via free agency. The Astros seemed to have the division title won but then lost three games in a row to the Dodgers. The two teams finished the regular season with identical 90-72 records and a one-game playoff decided the matter. Joe Niekro pitched and won for the Astros, 7-1.

The Phillies of Mike Schmidt, Pete Rose, and Steve Carlton took the field against Houston in the NLCS. Carlton won the first game for the Phils, 3-1, on a two-run homer by Greg Luzinski. The second game was tied, 3-3, at the end of nine innings. In the 10th inning the Astros erupted for four runs, sparked by outfielder Jose Cruz's single and first baseman Dave Bergman's two-run triple. Houston won the game, 7-4, as a 10th-inning Phils' rally fell short.

In game three Joe Niekro pitched 10 scoreless innings and needed every one of them. It took an 11th-inning triple by Astro second baseman Joe Morgan and a sacrifice fly to push across the only run of the game. The Phillies took the next game, 5-3, in the third straight extra-inning contest, tying the series at two games apiece.

A fourth straight extra-inning game decided it. In a wild affair, with most of the scoring coming in the late innings, the Phillies pushed across a run

| HOME FIELD | "The Eighth Wonder of the World" |

When Pepper Martin played for the Houston Buffs of the Texas League in the late 1920s, all the games were played in the daytime. Lights did not arrive at Buff Stadium until 1930, which meant that players and fans alike braved the blistering heat of day. Lights probably helped the pitchers, but the comparative cool of the evening definitely helped attendance and made everyone on hand more comfortable, at least until home air conditioning arrived in the 1950s. Soon afterwards came the wild dream of air-conditioning an entire ballpark.

The fully enclosed and air-conditioned Harris County Domed Stadium was supposed to be ready to welcome Houston's National League expansion franchise in 1962, but construction delays held off the opening for three more years. When the stadium was ready, the Colt .45s had been renamed the Astros and the new palace of baseball was christened the Astrodome.

It was like no other ballpark in the world, covering nine and a half acres, with enough plumbing for 40,000 people to wash their hands at the same time. The center of the dome reached skyward to the height of a 26-story building. More than 4,500 seven-by-three-foot panes of glass formed the vast dome. The grass was real—at first. It was Tifway 419 Bermuda grass, a hardy strain but not hardy enough to survive what ensued.

Judge Roy Hofheinz, the Astros' owner, fearing that fly balls lost in the glare of the daytime glare of the clear glass panels would turn the game into a farce, regretfully ordered the glass painted. The painted panels eliminated the glare, but the grass died, and AstroTurf was born, a brainchild of the Monsanto Chemical Company.

The first game played at the Astrodome, on April 9, 1965, was an exhibition contest between the Astros and the New York Yankees. The home team won it, 2-1, in 11 innings on a Nellie Fox base hit. The one Yankee run came on a Mickey Mantle homer, the first home run in the new ballpark. On April 28, less than three weeks after the stadium opened, New York Mets' announcer Lindsey Nelson broadcast a game from the gondola suspended from the very top of the dome, over second base.

The stadium was supposed to be spacious enough to prevent balls hit in fair territory from caroming off any part of it. But on June 10, 1974, the Phillies' Mike Schmidt blasted one that hit the public address speaker 329 feet from home plate and 117 feet up. It would have been a 500-foot-plus home run, but the ball rocketed down to the playing field, and Schmidt was held to a single. No one can hit a ball out of the the the Astrodome, of course, but three players—Jimmy Wynn, Doug Rader, and Andre Dawson—have come as close as possible, hitting balls into the fifth and highest level of seats.

Common sense suggests that a game at the Astrodome would never have to be postponed because of rain. However, on June 15, 1976, the players were already at the ballpark when a cloudburst struck Houston, flooding the streets and highways. The umpires, stadium workers, and fans could not reach the park. The game was postponed because of wet grounds outside, rather than inside, the Astrodome.

in the top of the 10th to emerge on top, 8-7. Disappointing as this outcome was, the Astros clearly had become a force to be reckoned with in the National League.

In 1981, the year of the players' strike, Houston finished third in the first half of the split season, with a 28-29 record. In the second half the Astros came in first, with a 32-20 mark. Long-time L.A. Dodger pitcher Don Sutton, signed as a free agent, played a role in the Astros' success, going 11-9 with a 2.60 ERA. With Joe Niekro, Bob Knepper, and Nolan Ryan as the other starters, the Astros compiled a team ERA of 2.68 to lead the league by a wide margin.

In postseason play Houston faced the L.A. Dodgers, first-half division winners, in a best-of-five playoff series to determine the NL West champion. Nolan Ryan won the opening game for the Astros, 3-1, on catcher Alan Ashby's two-run homer in the ninth inning. Houston also won the second game, 1-0, in 11 innings when pinch-hitter Dennis Walling singled with the bases loaded. Joe Niekro pitched eight strong innings, and Joe Sambito won the game in relief.

Needing just one more victory to clinch the division title, the Astros failed in their next three attempts. The Los Angeles Dodgers won all three games, 6-1, 2-1, and 4-0, to become champions of the NL West.

By 1982 Bill Virdon was in his ninth season at the helm of the Astros. He had overseen their first successes, but in 1982, when the team faltered, Virdon was fired, and Bob Lillis took over. Nicknamed "Flea," Lillis was familiar to Houston fans as a weak-hitting utility infielder for the Astros between 1962 and 1967. Under his direction the 1982 team improved a bit but finished fifth, 12 games behind the Atlanta Braves.

In 1983 they continued to improve, helped by the acquisition of yet another fine pitcher—Mike Scott, master of the split-finger fastball. A former Met with unimposing stats, Scott came to life as an Astro, posting a 10-6 record in 1983, with better years to come. Niekro and Ryan won in double figures, as usual, and outfielder Jose Cruz put in one of his best seasons, batting .318, hitting 14 homers, driving in 92 runs, and stealing 30 bases. Shortstop Dickie Thon helped out with his .286 average, 20 homers, 79 RBIs, and 34 stolen bases. Houston finished fourth in 1983, third in 1984, and tied for second in 1985.

This improvement in the standings was not mirrored in the won-lost totals, which never moved much off the .500 mark. At the end of the 1985 campaign Hal Lanier replaced Bob Lillis as the Astros' manager. Lanier, like Lillis, had been a weak-hitting infielder in his playing days. He inherited a team with more talent than the record suggested.

The Astros' pitching was rock solid, with Scott, Ryan, and Knepper as starters, joined by rookie left-hander Jim Deshaies, steady reliever Charlie Kerfeld, and deft closer Dave Smith. First baseman Glenn Davis, along with outfielder Kevin Bass, brought more power to the lineup than the Astros had seen since the days of Jimmy Wynn and Rusty Staub.

The 1986 Astros waltzed home with the division championship, putting a 10-game spread between themselves and the second-place Cincinnati Reds. Mike Scott was at the top of his form, posting an 18-10 record, including five shutouts. His 2.22 ERA led the league, as did his 306 strikeouts. Bob Knepper won 17 games, and Nolan Ryan and Jim Deshaies won 12 apiece. Charlie Kerfeld went 11-2, all in relief, and Dave Smith chalked up 33 saves.

Glenn Davis batted .265, belted 31 homers and drove in 101 runs. Kevin Bass hit .311 with 20 home runs and 79 RBIs. Dennis Walling (.312) and Jose Cruz (72 RBIs) also had productive years.

The 1986 NLCS was a series to remember. The New York Mets won it, four games to two. The sixth game, a 16-inning thriller, so inspired sportswriter Jerry Izenberg that he wrote a book about it: *The Greatest Game Ever Played.* Unfortunately for the Astros, this great game gave the division title to the Mets and kept Houston out of the World Series once again.

Up and Down ... and Maybe Up

Hal Lanier's impressive debut won him the manager's job for the next couple of seasons. But since third place in 1987 and fifth place in 1988 were not what the organization had in mind, Lanier gave way to Art Howe in 1989. Howe had the usual Astro managerial credentials. He was an ex-infielder, who had played for Houston between 1976 and 1982. He differed from Lillis and Lanier, though, in having been a somewhat better hitter, with a .260 career batting average.

The team he took over in 1989 still featured excellent pitching, although Nolan Ryan had signed

The Houston Astros' 96-66 record in 1986 was less impressive than the New York Mets' gaudy 108-54. Not a single pitcher on the Mets' staff had lost in double figures, while Mike Scott and Bob Knepper, the aces of a superb Houston staff, had lost 10 and 12 games respectively. Still, it was no sure thing that the Mets would breeze past the Astros in the National League Championship Series. Anything could happen.

Most of what happened pleased the Mets more than the Astros—except when Mike Scott pitched. Scott started and finished two games, the first and the fourth, and they were masterpieces. In game one he struck out 14 batters to tie an NLCS record, while allowing just five hits. Glenn Davis's second-inning solo home run held up the rest of the way, and the Astros won, 1-0. Houston lost the next two games, 5-1 and 6-5, as Nolan Ryan and Bob Knepper failed to shut down the Mets' attack. For that, the Astros needed Mike Scott. In game four Scott pitched a three-hitter, Alan Ashby and Dickie Thon homered, and the Astros won, 3-1, to even the series at two games each.

In the fifth game Nolan Ryan pitched brilliantly, holding the Mets to just two hits and striking out 12 batters over the first nine innings. With the game tied 1-1 after nine, Charlie Kerfeld came in to pitch for the Astros. (Dwight Gooden, the Met starter, stayed on the hill through the 10th inning.) Neither team scored in the 10th or 11th, and it was still 1-1 going into the bottom of the 12th. Mets' catcher Gary Carter, who hit an abysmal .148 overall in the NLCS, stroked a run-scoring single to give the Mets a 2-1 victory.

Game six lasted 16 innings, and if it was not quite "the greatest game ever played," as sportswriter Jerry Izenberg suggested, it was certainly memorable. Houston starter Bob Knepper held a 3-0 lead going into the top of the ninth inning at the Astrodome. When the Mets rallied, Knepper surrendered the ball to reliever Dave Smith. The Mets tied it up, however, and the game went into extra innings—a lot of them. New York scored a run in the top of the 14th, but Houston outfielder Billy Hatcher evened the score with a long home run in the bottom of the 14th. Neither team scored in the 15th. Then in the top of the 16th the Mets appeared to put the game out of reach, scoring three times off Houston relievers Aurelio Lopez and Jeff Calhoun.

The score was now 7-4. In the bottom of the 16th inning the Astros were facing Met reliever Jesse Orosco, already credited with two wins in the series. Orosco struck out the leadoff hitter, shortstop Craig Reynolds, but walked pinch-hitter Davey Lopes. Astro second baseman Bill Doran then slapped a single to center, sending Lopes to second. Into the batters' box stepped Billy Hatcher, the memory of his 14th-inning homer fresh in his mind—and in Orosco's. Hatcher didn't hit one into the seats, but he did single, scoring Lopes and sending Doran to second. The score: 7-5. Next up for Houston was third baseman Denny Walling, who grounded the ball toward Keith Hernandez at first. Hernandez threw to second for one out, but the relay to first was too late. Doran moved over to third. There were two outs.

First baseman Glenn Davis came to the plate. He had hit 31 home runs during the regular season. The Mets' Keith Hernandez called time, walked to the mound, and reportedly told Orosco, "If you throw so much as one fastball, I'll kill you." Like Hatcher, Davis didn't slam one out, but he did hit a soft liner to center field that fell for a single. Doran scored, and it was a 7-6 game. Outfielder Kevin Bass stepped in. Bass had collected seven hits so far in the series, but now in the 16th inning he saw nothing but sliders from Jesse Orosco. The first five put the count at three balls and two strikes. The sixth slider sent Bass down swinging—and the Astros went home defeated.

with the Texas Rangers, and Bob Knepper had been released in midseason. Scott was outstanding in 1989—20-10 with a 3.11 ERA—and Deshaies was very good, 15-10, ERA 2.91. Danny Darwin, sometimes pitching out of the bullpen, had the first of two fine seasons, 11-4 with a 2.36 ERA.

Glenn Davis slugged 34 homers and drove in 89 runs, but the Astro offense as whole was only fair. Kevin Bass led the team with an even .300 batting average, but the next highest mark was outfielder Terry Puhl's .271. The Astros finished third with an 86-76 record.

1990 was a disappointing year for the Astros on all fronts. The usually reliable Mike Scott fell to 9-13, and Jim Deshaies dropped to 7-12. Houston was last in the league in club batting, eight points below the next lowest team. Glenn Davis, who was on the disabled list in July and most of August, saw his totals drop to 22 homers and 64 RBIs, while his .251 batting average matched his career low. The Astros tied the San Diego Padres for fourth place in the NL West, and looked forward to greater prosperity in 1991.

In the off-season they traded Glenn Davis to Baltimore for pitchers Pete Harnisch and Curt Schilling and outfielder Steve Finley. This was a good trade for the future, but the youthful Astros were out of their depth in 1991, losing as many games, 97, as they had in the early expansion year of 1965.

There were several bright young prospects in Astro uniforms, among the best and brightest of them was Jeff Bagwell, who became the first Astro to win NL Rookie of the Year honors. Bagwell hit .294 with 15 homers and 82 RBIs. Among the other promising young players were outfielder Steve Finley at .285, second baseman (formerly catcher) Craig Biggio at .295, and slick-fielding third baseman Ken Caminiti, .253 with 13 home runs and 80 RBIs. On the mound Pete Harnisch had a 12-9 year with a 2.70 ERA. This team was so young that when the Astros had a Family Day, there were not enough players' children to field a team against their parents.

In 1992 the team broke even, 81-81, as the young ballplayers continued to develop. Jeff Bag-well had a fine sophomore year, upping his homer total to 18 and his RBIs to 96. Steve Finley raised his batting average to .295, and Ken Caminiti lifted his by more than 40 points to .294.

Pitcher Pete Harnisch dropped off a bit, and veteran Mark Portugal had a disappointing year in which he lost two months to elbow surgery. To strengthen the mound staff, the Astros picked up free-agent relief pitcher Doug Jones, formerly with the Cleveland Indians. Jones recorded 36 saves, won 11 games, lost eight, and posted a 1.85 ERA. He became the first Astro reliever to lead the team in victories. With the signing of two free-agent pitchers, Doug Drabek and Greg Swindell, in December of 1992, the Astros moved a step closer to making their team a strong contender in the NL West.

The 1993 season proved disappointing, however, as Drabek and Swindell combined for a 21-31 record, and Jones was inconsistent. The Astros still managed a third place finish, 85-77, four games better than 1992, due mainly to a productive offense. The Astros set team records in batting average (.267), home runs (138), doubles (284), and extra-base hits (457). Pitchers Portugal, Harnisch, and Darryl Kile, who threw a no-hitter against the New York Mets, all had strong seasons.

At year's end, owner Drayton McLane, Jr. opted for new leadership, firing general manager Bill Wood and manager Art Howe and naming former Astros player Bob Watson to replace Wood and Pittsburgh bullpen coach Terry Collins to replace Howe.

SOURCES

BOOKS

Baseball Guide, 1980, 1983, 1987, 1991, and 1993 editions, *The Sporting News* Publishing Co., 1980, 1983, 1987, 1991, and 1993.

Baseball Register, 1980, 1987, and 1993 editions, *The Sporting News* Publishing Co., 1980, 1987, and 1993.

Complete Baseball Record Book, 1993 edition, *The Sporting News* Publishing Co., 1993.

The Complete Book of Baseball, 23rd and 24th editions, edited by Zander Hollander, Signet, 1992 and 1993.

Ivor-Campbell, Frederick, "Team Histories: Houston Astros," *Total Baseball,* edited by John Thorn and Pete Palmer, Warner Books, 1989.

Izenberg, Jerry, *The Greatest Game Ever Played,* Henry Holt and Company, 1987.

Reichler, Joseph L., editor, *The Baseball Encyclopedia,* 7th edition, Macmillan, 1988.

Reidenbaugh, Lowell, *Take Me out to the Ball Park, Sporting News* Publishing Co., 1983.

Who's Who in Baseball, 55th and 60th editions, Who's Who in Baseball Magazine Co., 1970 and 1975.

PERIODICALS

Baseball America, February 21, 1993; March 7, 1993; March 21, 1993; April 4, 1993.
New Yorker, May 14, 1966.

—*Gerald Tomlinson* for Book Builders, Inc.

St. Louis Cardinals

Few teams in all of professional baseball have had as eventful or successful a history as have the St. Louis Cardinals. And few have had a beginning that is more difficult to chart.

How many wins have the Cardinals piled up since their inception? You'll get different answers from different texts. The Cardinals' own media guide, for example, notes that the team's record in the National League from 1892 through the 1992 season, a period of 101 consecutive years, totals 7,805 games won, 7,659 games lost. Those figures are correct; the problem is that St. Louis had a team in the National League in 1876, the year that the league itself was formed. That St. Louis team, which was called the Browns, competed in the league for two years before disbanding.

A second entry into the league, also called the Browns, resurfaced in 1885, and again lasted for only two seasons before folding. The record of the team in its first two-year stint was 73-51; in the second it was 79-151. If you add the totals of those

two years to the totals of the team from 1892 to 1992, the overall becomes 7,957 games won, 7,861 games lost.

To cloud the issue, some historians, including Fred Lieb, who wrote *The St. Louis Cardinals* in 1944, maintain that the St. Louis team that played in the old American Association from 1882 through 1891, a team called the St. Louis Maroons, was actually the forerunner of today's St. Louis Cardinals. In the 1880s and 1890s the American Association was considered as a major league; the American League would not come into being until 1901.

The Maroons won four consecutive league championships and were the most popular team in America in those days. The Maroons' win-loss total was 782-428. If those numbers are tacked on to the 1892-1992 figures, the overall mark becomes 8,587 wins, 8,087 losses. In that scenario, only one other major league team, the Chicago Cubs, with 8,852 wins, has more regular season victories than the St. Louis Cardinals. The Pittsburgh Pirates win total in the National League from 1890 through 1992 is 8,351; Pittsburgh also had a team in the old American Association that won 538 games, which would bring their total to 8,889.

When St. Louis rejoined the National League in 1892, it was again called the Browns. The name "Cardinals" did not come into being until 1899, when a St. Louis sports writer, Willie McHale, suggested the name in his column in the old *St. Louis Republic* newspaper.

Of all the 28 teams in the major leagues today, only six can trace their roots all the way back to that charter year of 1876—the St. Louis Cardinals, the Chicago Cubs, the Cincinnati Reds, the Philadelphia Phillies, the San Francisco-New York Giants and the Boston-Milwaukee-Atlanta Braves. There were eight teams in that first National League, the other two were the Louisville Colonels and the Hartford Blues.

Through the decades the Cardinals have been blessed with some of the game's greatest players—Rogers Hornsby, Stan Musial, Frankie Frisch, Dizzy Dean, Johnny Mize, Grover Cleveland Alexander, Ducky Medwick and Bob Gibson, to name but a few. Even the immortal Cy Young, who won more games than any pitcher in the history of the game, and Kid Nichols, who won 30 or more games for seven years in a row, spent a portion of their great careers in a Cardinal uniform.

When the National League was formed in 1876, the nation's Centennial Year, it was a St. Louis jurist, Judge Orrick Bishop, who drew up the league's first Constitution and wrote the first player contract.

During more than a century of existence for the St. Louis Cardinals, the city has had other teams in baseball. In 1884 St. Louis was one of 12 teams in the Union Association. They won the league title in the only year of the loop's existence. The city also had a team in another short-lived undertaking, the Federal League, in 1914 and 1915. And of course the St. Louis Browns competed in the American League from 1902 until they moved to Baltimore in 1954.

According to statistics compiled by the Baseball Hall of Fame, through the 1992 season only three teams have put more players, managers, coaches and executives into the Baseball Hall of Fame: The New York-San Francisco Giants lead with 48; the Boston-Milwaukee-Atlanta Braves are second with 40; the Brooklyn/Los Angeles Dodgers follow with 38. The Cardinals and the Chicago Cubs are tied for fourth with 34. Of that total of 34, however, three played for the St. Louis Maroons of the American Association, giving further credence that that team was the forerunner of the present day St. Louis Cardinals.

Humble Beginnings

Ever heard of George Bradley? Probably not; not too many people have. For the record, he was the first man ever to pitch for a St. Louis professional baseball team. In 1876, in fact, he, was more than just the first St. Louis pitcher ... he was the whole pitching staff!

The Browns played 64 games that first year; Bradley started in all of them and completed 63 for a whopping 573 innings pitched (up until 1883 pitchers threw underhanded), winning 45 and losing 19 games. No St. Louis player since has come close to those wins and innings pitched totals. He hurled 16 shutouts that year and compiled a league leading 1.23 earned run average.

The records don't indicate who finished that single game that was not credited to Bradley; perhaps he and his catcher switched positions in the last inning. Bradley was no slouch at the plate either, hitting a respectable .249, the fifth highest average on the team, And finally, for this reason alone Bradley long ago should have been considered for inclusion in the Baseball Hall of Fame. He hurled the first no-hitter in major league baseball history, beating the Hartford Blues 2-0 on July 15, 1876.

The 1876 St. Louis Browns finished second in the National League, six games behind a powerful Chicago White Sox team. In addition to St.

TEAM INFORMATION AT A GLANCE

Founding date: 1892

Home stadium: Busch Stadium
St. Louis, MO 63102
Phone: (314) 421-3060

Dimensions: Left-field line—330 feet
Center field—414 feet
Right-field line—330 feet
Seating capacity: 56,227

Team colors: Cardinal red, white, and black
Team nickname: Originally Browns; later became Perfectos, 1892-1899; Cardinals, 1899—.
Logo: Cardinal wearing a baseball cap perched on a baseball bat, superimposed over a baseball; all
surrounded by red ring with St. Louis Cardinals printed in white lettering.

Franchise record	Won	Lost	Pct.
(1892-1993)	7,492	7,027	.516

World Series wins (9): 1926, 1931, 1934, 1942, 1944, 1946, 1964, 1967, 1982
National League championships (15): 1926, 1928, 1930, 1931, 1934, 1942,
1943, 1944, 1946, 1964, 1967, 1968, 1982, 1985, 1987
National League East division first-place finishes (3): 1982, 1985, 1987

Louis and Chicago, the other teams were the Boston Red Caps (which eventually became the Braves, not the Red Sox); the New York Mutuals, which became the New York Giants years later; the Philadelphia Athletics, which became the Phillies (the Athletics of the American League were an entirely different team); the Cincinnati Reds, the Louisville Colonels and the Hartford Blues. And those 1876 Chicago White Sox were the forerunners of the Chicago Cubs, not the American League Chicago White Sox. As L'il Abner used to say, "confusin' but amusin'."

That the 1876 St. Louis club was able to stay as close as six games behind the Chicagoans was somewhat amazing in itself. Led by future Hall of Famer and sporting goods manufacturer Al Spal-

ding, who doubled as manager and pitcher, the Sox had a *team* batting average of .337; they had five of the top six hitters in the league in their lineup and scored a total of 624 runs. By way of comparison, St. Louis scored only 386. Spalding led the league in wins with 47.

That first-ever St. Louis team was managed by Harmon Dehlman, who also played first base. Others on the team were Mike McGeary on second, Joe Battin on third; Dick Pearce and Denny Mack shared the duties at short, Joe Blong, Lip Pike and Ned Cuthbert were in the outfield, and John Clapp was the catcher. Pike was the team's top hitter, with a .323 average and 50 runs batted in; Clapp, at .305 and Battin, at an even .300, followed. Battin was also a great fielder and led the league third basemen in fielding average.

Team President John Lucas removed Harmon Dehlman as the club's manager, taking over the duties himself. After compiling a 14-12 record, he turned the duties over to George McManus, who had even less luck with the club, winning only 14 of 34 games as the Browns sunk to a 28-32 record and 4th place in the league. Gone were both Pike, the team's top hitter, and Bradley, its great pitcher, who had signed on with the rival Chicago White Sox.

In 1877 John Clapp paced the club offensively, hitting .318, and had 34 runs batted in. It was to be the last year for the team in the league, and the exit was marked by scandal. According to newspaper accounts of the day, team President Lucas attempted to close the gap between his club and the Chicago White Sox by signing several members of the Louisville team as well as the White Sox starting shortstop. During the season, however, four of the players picked up from Louisville were accused of throwing games the year before for gambling reasons.

They were subsequently barred from baseball for life in the first of the two great scandals to rock the game—the second the more infamous Black Sox scandal of 1919. There was talk that Lucas and his partners in the St. Louis organization knew of what the players had done, but signed them on anyway. This part was never proved, but Lucas resigned from the league in a huff, and disbanded the team.

King of the Hill

The city of St. Louis was without baseball for five years until 1882, when the American Association, then considered a major league, put a team into the city. The team was owned by Chris Von Der Ahe and Al Spink. (The latter, along with his brother, Al Spink, founded the *Sporting News,* the baseball world's bible, in 1866.) Von Der Ahe and Spink later hired Charles Comiskey as their manager-first baseman. Several years down the pike Comiskey would organize and own his own

St. Louis in the American Association			
Year	W-L	Pos.	Manager(s)
1882	37-43	5th	Ned Cuthbert, Ed Bran
1883	65-33	2nd	Ted Sullivan, Charlie Comiskey
1884	67-40	4th	Jimmy Williams
1885	79-33	1st	Charlie Comiskey
1886	93-46	1st	Charlie Comiskey
1887	95-40	1st	Charlie Comiskey
1888	92-43	1st	Charlie Comiskey
1889	90-45	2nd	Charlie Comiskey
1890	78-53	3rd	Tommy McCarty, Chief Roseman, Count Campeau
1891	86-52	2nd	Charlie Comiskey

team in the new American League, the Chicago White Sox.

The St. Louis team was again called the Browns, and within three years would become the most popular team in the country, winning four consecutive league titles. Those four champion Browns team had playoffs against the National League champs—the name "World Series" had not as yet been coined—winning one and tying another against the Chicago club, and losing to Detroit and New York in the other two.

The pitching stars for the team's first championship club in 1884 were "Parisian Bob" Caruthers, who compiled a 40-13 record and a 2.07 earned run average, the latter tops in the league; and "Scissors" Dave Foutz, who was at 33-14. In the second title year in 1885 Foutz came out on top with a 41-16 mark and a 2.11 era, while Caruthers followed with 30-14.

In 1887 Charlie "Silver" King paced the mound crew with a 34-11 record, while Caruthers dropped to 29-9 and Foutz 25-12. Caruthers and Foutz also played in the outfield during the season, with Caruthers pounding out a .357 average, and Foutz .375. The hitting star of the team, however, was outfielder Tip O'Neill, whose .435 average was the highest in the league.

In 1888, the last of the four championship years, King led the league in both wins and earned run average with a 45-21 record and a 1.64 era. O'Niel's average dropped to .335, but it was still good enough to lead the league.

The team finished second in 1889, but had two 30-game winners in King, at 33-17, and Elton "Icebox" Chamberlain, at 32-15. Comiskey left in 1890 and the Browns dropped to third. He returned a year later, leading the team to a second place performance and an 86-52 record.

Rookie Ted Breitenstein hurled a no-hitter in his first major league start, one of only three pitchers in the history of major league play ever to do so. After the 1891 season the league disbanded.

Of the 34 Hall of Famers that played in St. Louis, three were from that American Association club: Comiskey; Clark Griffith, who had a 14-6 pitching record for the 1891 team; and outfielder Tommy McCarthy. The latter was a speedy outfielder who hit .350 for the 1890 team and led the league with 83 stolen bases. For those 10 years in the American Association, the St. Louis entry had four first place finishes, three seconds and one third, compiling a 782-428 record.

In 1884 St. Louis played in the Union Association. The league lasted only one year, but in that brief stay the St. Louis entry won the championhip with a phenomenal 94-19 record and a .832 winning percentage. Fred Dunlop led the team and the league with a .412 batting average and 13 home runs.

A Waste of Talent

While the American Association Browns were flourishing, the city of St. Louis had another brief stint as a National League club, fielding teams in 1885 and 1886. The club was owned and managed by Henry Lucas, a prominent St. Louis businessman, who called the team the Maroons. The two years that the team managed to stay afloat were far from successful, on the field or at the box office.

In 1885 the Maroons won only 36 games and lost 72, finishing in the cellar; the next year they improved slightly, to 43 wins and a sixth place finish. But these two years were the same that the St. Louis Browns in the rival American Association were winning championships, and for St. Louis baseball fans, THE team was the Browns, not the Maroons.

The Browns lost money in both years, and a discouraged Lucas sold the franchise at the end of the 1886 season to John Brush, an Indianapolis department store owner. Brush moved the team to Indianapolis, where it later folded. He also had other teams in the National League in coming years, the Cincinnati Reds and the New York Giants.

The 1885 team and its 36-72 record finished a whopping 47 games behind the league leading Chicago Cubs. Nevertheless it had a few promising players on its roster; first baseman Alex McKinnon and second-sacker Fred "Sure Shot" Dunlop and shortstop Jack "Pebbly" Glasscock led the league in fielding for their positions, and had .294, .270 and .280 batting averages, respectively. Glasscock later (in 1890) would lead the league in hitting, but by that time he would be the property of the New York Giants. Pitcher Henry Boyle had only a 16-24 record but put together a commendable 2.75 earned run average.

In the second year of play Lucas turned the managerial duties over to Gus Schmelz, who improved the team's record somewhat, to 43-70, and a sixth place finish. Glasscock, at .325, and McKinnon, at .301, led the team offensively.

Return to the National League

With the demise of the American Association after the 1891 season, the National League opened up its arms again to embrace an entry from St. Louis. This time the welcome stuck, and St. Louis has been in the league every year since, more than 100 years. At a meeting between repre-

Cardinals MVP Winners

1925	Rogers Hornsby
1926	Bob O'Farrell
1928	Jim Bottomley
1931	Frankie Frisch
1934	Dizzy Dean
1937	Joe Medwick
1942	Mort Cooper
1943	Stan Musial
1944	Marty Marion
1946	Stan Musial
1948	Stan Musial
1964	Ken Boyer
1967	Orlando Cepeda
1968	Bob Gibson
1971	Joe Torre
1979	Keith Hernandez *
1985	Willie McGee

* Tied with Pittsburgh's Willie Stargel

sentatives of the two leagues in Indianapolis in December of 1891, the National League agreed to absorb three of the AA teams, Louisville, Baltimore and St. Louis.

The new St. Louis entry, again called the Browns, was owned by Chris Von Der Ahe, the big, blustery German who had owned and operated the St. Louis team in the American Association. The first seven years that the team was in the league, however, were the saddest in its history, with Von Der Ahe running the club like a circus sideshow. In those seven seasons, playing in a 12-team league, the Browns finished last twice, 11th three times, 10th once and rose as high as 9th once. Over the seven years Von Der Ahe used a total of 13 managers, even taking the helm on four separate occasions himself.

That 1892 team had a number of better than average ballplayers, including two pitchers, Ted Breitenstein and Heinie Peitz, who were particularly popular with the city's large German population.

Others on the squad included Bill "Kid" Gleason, who would go on to win 20 games (and lose 24) and hurl a team-leading 400 innings; first baseman Perry Werden, who paced the offense with eight home runs and 84 runs batted in; second baseman Jack Crooks, who led the league in walks with 136 despite hitting only .213; third baseman George Pinkney; shortstop Jack Glasscock; and outfielders Bob Caruthers, whose .277 average was tops on the team, Cliff Carroll and Dick Buckley.

Also on the team was 37-year-old Jim "Pud" Galvin, in the last year of his long career in which he totalled 361 wins, topping the 40 mark twice and winning 20 or more ten times. Galvin was named to the Hall of Fame in 1965.

Watkins Takes Over

With Von Der Ahe at the controls, all of this talent went to waste as the team won only 56 and lost 94 to finish 46 games out of first place behind the Boston Beaneaters. Von Der Ahe replaced himself as the team's manager after the 1892 season, naming Bill Watkins to the position. The club responded with a slight improvement to 57-75 and moved up a notch in the standings to 10th place.

Kid Gleason again led the team in pitching, but again lost more than he won, with a 21-29 record. Ted Breitenstein was close behind with a 19-20 performance, and led the league in earned run average with a 3.18 mark.

First baseman Perry Werden banged out 29 triples to lead the league; that total is still the highest ever for a St. Louis player, and the fourth highest in major league history to this date. Werden also led the team in runs batted in, with 94. Centerfielder Steve Brodie's .318 average was the highest on the team. Third sacker Jack Crooks upped his batting average to .279 and again led the league in base on balls, with 121. For the year the St. Louis club finished 30½ games behind the champion Boston Beaneaters.

A new manager, George Miller, the team's

third in three years, had about the same results. The St. Louis win-loss mark of 56-75 just about matched their 1893 effort, but the team did manage to move up to 9th place, this time 35 games behind the top club, the Baltimore Orioles.

Ace pitcher Ted Breitenstein had his best year in a St. Louis uniform, putting together a 27-25 record and leading the league in games, with 46, and in innings pitched, with 447. Third baseman George "Doggie" Miller led the Browns in hitting with a .339 average, while future Hall of Fame first baseman Roger Connor was at .321 and shortstop Fred "Bones" Ely chipped in with a .306 mark, and also led the club in home runs with 12 and in RBIs with 89.

Dismal Descent

Owner Chris Von Der Ahe was not too happy with his club during the year, using four different managers, including himself, to try to put a winner on the field. The year, however, became the worst for the team since it had re-entered the league, and they sank to a 39-92 mark and 11th place in the standings. Ted Breitenstein managed another 20-win season, finishing at 20-29; left fielder Duff Cooley led the Cardinals hitters with a .339 average and 191 hits; right fielder Tommy Dowd was also over .300, at .323.

Von Der Ahe outdid himself during the 1896 season, topping his four-manager performance of 1895 with five, and again took the reins himself, during a short stint in the middle of the year. The team was again one of the worst in the league, finishing at 40-90 for another dismal 11th place performance. First baseman Roger Connor, who was one of those five managers and who turned in a 9-37 record, led the team in hitting, with a .284 mark, in homers, with 11, and in runs batted in, with 72.

In 1897 the Browns sunk to the depths, winning only 29 games during the entire season and dropping 102 for a woeful .221 winning percentage. The win total and the winning percentage are the lowest in team history. A bright spot was

catcher Bill "Klondike" Douglas, who led the team with a .329 average. Francis "Red" Donahue had the best pitching stats, winning 11 and dropping 33, but leading the league in complete games, with 38.

If the 1897 season is to be regarded as the worst in St. Louis baseball history, the 1898 campaign wasn't far behind. The team again finished dead last in the league, this time losing a grand total of 111 games, still the most losses the team has ever endured. For the first time in four years, however, owner Von Der Ahe stuck with one manager, Tim Hurst, for the whole season.

Third baseman Lave Cross paced the Browns with a .317 average and 79 runs batted in, while "Brewery Jack" Taylor won the mound crown with a 15-29 record. At the end of the season, and with the urging of the league itself, the controversial Von Der Ahe sold his interest in the team and left baseball for good.

Under New Management

In a complicated move designed to bring a contending team to the city of St. Louis, the National League hierarchy in 1899 approved of what was in effect a switch of franchises, moving nearly all of the top players from the strong Cleveland Spiders to St. Louis. Frank Robinson, who owned the Spiders, had also become one of the new owners of the Browns, a situation which would not be permitted under today's rules.

Moving from Cleveland to St. Louis were the Spiders' manager, Patsy Tebeau and three future Hall of Famers—the immortal Cy Young, who would go on to win more games than any pitcher in the history of the game, hard-hitting outfielder Jessie Burkett and shortstop Bobby Wallace. Also moving to the St. Louis club were outfielder John Hendrick, who would steal 55 bases during the year, a mark that stood for 66 years until broken by Lou Brock in 1965, and pitcher Jack Powell.

Young won 26 and Powell 23 for the St. Louis team, and Burkett hit a rousing .402, missing the batting crown, however, when Philadelphia's Ed Delahanty topped out at .410. Burkett's 228 hits set a new St. Louis record. Wallace hit only .302 but led the team in homers, with 12, and RBIs, with 108, the first time a St. Louis player had ever topped 100. In addition to managing, Tebeau also played first base and hit a creditable .246.

Cleveland, on the other hand, received Lave Cross, Tommy Dowd, Joe Quinn and Joe Sugden, and the team sunk to a horrible 20-134 mark, the worst record ever in major league baseball to this day.

On opening day a crowd of 18,000 welcomed the "new" St. Louis Cardinals team, the largest crowd in the city's history up to that time. The club got off to a good start and led the league through the first month of play before fading and eventually finishing in fifth place with an 84-67 record.

A Colorful New Name

During the season Robinson decided to add more color to his team's uniforms with red stockings and trim. The new look caught the eye of a St. Louis sports writer, Willie McHale, who described the team in one of his stories as "the Cardinals." The name stuck, and became one of the best known in the world of sport. Another nickname, "the Perfectos," never really caught on and was forgotten by the end of the year. At the conclusion of the season the league shrank to eight teams, dropping Baltimore, Cleveland, Louisville and Washington.

Hoping to improve on his 1899 finish, St. Louis owner Frank Robinson wheeled and dealed for three more additions to the club, hard-hitting first baseman Frank McCraw, second sacker Billy Keister and catcher Wilbert Robinson (no relation to Frank), all from the defunct Baltimore team.

McCraw and Robinson would eventually be named to the Hall of Fame, but primarily for their careers as managers, McCraw with the Giants and Robinson with the cross-town Dodgers. McCraw

Transcendental Graphics

Jessie Burkett

did finish his playing career with an overall .334 average, however.

The trio didn't disappoint, with McCraw belting out a .344 average, Keister at an even .300 and Robinson .248 in a reserve role behind the plate. It was the team that was the disappointment. Despite having seven .300 hitters in the lineup—Jessie Burkett at .363, McCraw at .344, Mike Donlin at .326, Patsy Donovan at .316, Dan McGavin at .302, John Heidrick at .301 and Keister at .300, the team never got untracked and finished in 6th place, 19 games behind the leading Brooklyn Dodgers. Donovan tied for the league lead in stolen bases, with 45, and Cy Young turned in his 10th consecutive 20-win season with a 20–18 record.

McCraw, Keister, Robinson, and Young were all gone by the end of the year. Manager Tebeau didn't even make it that far, calling it quits about two-thirds of the way through the season. Owner

Robinson couldn't come up with what he thought was a suitable replacement, so he named his concessions manager, little Louie Heilbronner, as the club's new skipper. The players had great fun with the little Heilbronner, but somehow he managed to stick it through for the remaider of the campaign.

A New Century and a New League

While the brand new American League was playing its first major league season in 1901, the established National League was completing its 25th. The older league's eight teams were Boston, Brooklyn, Chicago, Cincinnati, New York, Philadelphia, Pittsburgh and St. Louis, a lineup that would remain intact until 1953.

The century was new, the two-league setup was new, but it was still a dead ball era. The value of the home run as an offensive weapon was exemplified by the St. Louis performance; fourth in the National League although leading both leagues in round trippers with 39.

Cardinal hitting star Jessie Burkett hit .382 to win his third batting crown—the first two were while he was still a Cleveland Spider—and also led the league in hits, with 228, and runs, with 139. The latter two were also highs for the Cards up to that point. The fourth place finish was also the highest the St. Louis club had climbed since coming back into the league ten years earlier.

On the mound Jack Harper led the way with a 23-13 mark. Shortstop Bobby Wallace had another good season, leading the team in runs batted in with 91 and doubles with 34, and also hit .322. Outfielder Patsy Donovan took over the managerial duties for the team, and it didn't affect his on the field performance as he hit a commendable .339 for the year.

The American League, which broke ground the year before, entered into a full-scale war with the older National League in 1902, raiding the National League's teams for whatever talent they could lure away, and placing rival teams in two National League cities, Chicago and St. Louis.

Retired Cardinal Numbers		
No.	**Player**	**Year**
6	Stan Musial	1963
13	Ken Boyer	1984
17	Dizzy Dean	1974
20	Lou Brock	1979
45	Bob Gibson	1975
85	August Busch, Jr.	1984

American League Commissioner Ban Johnson switched the Milwaukee franchise to St. Louis and resurrected the old name, Browns, for the team.

The Browns proceded to steal away some of the top players on the Cardinal roster, including pitchers Jack Powell (19-19), Jack Harper (23-12) and Willie Sudhoff (17-11), infielders Bob Wallace (.322) and Dick Padden (.256), and outfielders Jesse Burkett (.382) and Emmett Heidrick (.322). First baseman Dan McGann (.289) also left the Redbird club to join John McGraw in Baltimore.

The loss of their three top pitchers and five regulars, especially the hard-hitting Burkett, assured the team that their visit to the first division the year before would be a short one. With a makeshift lineup Manager Patsy Donovan's club sank to a 56-78 record and 6th place in the 8-team race. Donovan could find little offense other than his own, as he led the team in hitting with a .315 mark, as well as in stolen bases, with 34.

The Dead Ball Era

The Cardinals continued to plummet in 1903, falling all the way to the National League cellar. One of the rookies on the club, Mordecai "Three Finger" Brown, was with the team for only a single season, but went on to the Hall of Fame after a sparkling career with the Chicago Cubs. The reason Brown was with the Cards for only that one year was that St. Louis owner Frank Robinson traded him and two other players to the

Cubs for veteran pitcher Jack Taylor. After one good year, however, Taylor proved to be over the hill and was let go. The trade has been called one of the worst in Cardinal history.

Owners seldom take the blame for a team's misfortunes on the field; they assign that dubious honor to the manager. So after the season Robinson gave Manager Patsy Donovan his walking papers.

1903 also marked the first year of the playoff series between the two leagues, later to be called the World Series. In that first classic, Boston of the upstart American League outfought the Pittsburgh Pirates in an eight-game set, 5-3.

A Pitiful Offense

With future Hall of Famer Kid Nichols doubling as the team's manager and ace of the pitching staff, the Cardinals bounced back to post a 75-79 record, an improvement of 32 games in the win column over their 1903 performance, and a move up the standings from 8th to 5th place. Nichols, at 34, with his best years behind him, still hurled well enough to post a 21-13 record and a 2.02 earned run average. Only three other pitchers in the entire league won more games over the season.

Nichols's victory total was matched on his own team by the recently acquired Jack Taylor, who had a 21-19 record. With nearly all of its top hitters gone, however, the Redbirds had trouble putting any runs on the board. First baseman Jake Beckley, at .325, and catcher Mike Grady, at .313, were the exceptions, with the third and fourth highest averages in the league.

Manager Kid Nichols wasn't able to follow through on his first year at the helm, and in 1905 the club slipped back to 6th place with 96 losses. Third baseman Jimmy Burke was named to replace him after only 48 games, but could do no better and was also fired. Stan Robinson, owner Frank's brother, took over for the balance of the season. The one offensive star of the club was outfielder Homer Smoot, who led the team in

hitting with a .311 average and 16 triples.

1905 saw the renewal of the World Series rivalry between the two leagues after a one-year layoff. The New York Giants, under John McGraw, topped old Connie Mack's Philadelphia Athletics, 4-1.

In one of his last official acts for the team, owner Frank Robinson named John McCloskey as the club's new manager. Shortly after, Robinson announced his retirement as president of the franchise, citing poor health as his reason. Brother Stan Robinson was named to replace him. On the field, the team sank to a 52-98 record and seventh place in the standings.

In 1906 the Cards did not have a single hitter that averaged .300 or more for the year or knocked in as many as 50 runs, or a pitcher that won as many as 10 games. They did have a pitcher-catcher combo that probably gave the announcers of the day fits—on the mound, rookie hurler Irv Higgen-botham, and behind the plate, another first-year man, Art Hoelskoetter.

The 1906 club also had the distinction of finishing the year a whopping 63 games behind the league-leading Chicago Cubs, the most number of games off the top in the team's history. Although the team fell into the cellar, they did manage to narrow the gap between themselves and the champion Chicago Cubs the next year to "only" 55 games, an improvement on their 1906 finish.

Again the team's offense was pitiful, with no one hitting .300 or knocking in 50 runs. Stoney McGlynn strug-gled on the mound to a 14-25 mark, with the most complete games in the league, 33. Teammate Ed Karger turned in a 14-18 record and had a .203 earned run average. After three years, a seventh and two last place finishes, manager John McCloskey called it quits. A popular and energetic man, McCloskey later was credited with originating 10 minor leagues and managing or owning 47 different teams. But in 1908 his Cardinals finished dead last, 50 games behind the Cubs, again the league leader.

On the field, right fielder Red Murray's .282 average, seven homers and 62 RBIs paced the team. Those seven round trippers were good for third place in the league but it was still a dead ball era. On the mound, a 14-25 record again was the best on the team, this time by Bugs Raymond.

Moments in the Sun

With new manager (and future Hall-of-Famer) Roger Bresnahan at the controls, the Cardinals moved out of the cellar and up to seventh place with a 54-98 record. The win total was nothing to brag about, but it was the most for a St. Louis team in four years. Bresnahan, dubbed "The Duke of Tralee" because of his Irish beginnings, also served as the club's backup catcher, hitting .244. First baseman Ed Konetchy led the offense with a .286 average and 86 runs batted in.

With 98 losses, the hill corps didn't boast any winners, with Fred Beebe's 15-21 record tops. Three Finger Brown, the one who got away to the Chicago Cubs six years earlier, led the National League in wins with 27; over the four years 1906 through 1909 he won a total of 102.

A significant addition to the team prior to the 1910 season was diminutive second baseman Miller "The Mighty Mite" Huggins, picked up from the Cincinnati Reds. Despite being only a .265 hitter, Huggins managed to lead the league in base on balls with 116 and was second in runs scored, with 101. Another newcomer, Vic Willis, had won 23 games the year before with the Pittsburgh Pirates. But in 1910 with the St. Louis Cardinals, he was a disappointment at 9-12. Manager Roger Bresnahan again doubled as the team's backup catcher.

The highlight of the year was first baseman Ed Konetchy's .302 average, the first Redbird to top .300 in five years. He also banged in 78 runs to lead in that category. Defensively he was equally as outstanding, leading the National League in putouts with 1,499, in assists with 98 and in fielding average, with .991. Johnny Lush led the pitching squad with a 14-13 mark; it was his last year in the major leagues, however.

In 1911 St. Louis fans were treated to their

Trancendental Graphics

Roger Bresnahan

most entertaining year in some time as the Cards moved over the .500 mark for the first time since 1901. They also climbed into fifth place, their highest finish in seven seasons. Attendance moved up correspondingly, to a new record, 447,768, the first time the club had ever had more than 400,000 in a single year.

First baseman Ed Konetchy was again the hitting star, leading the league in doubles with 38, and pacing his team in hitting with a .289 average and in RBIs with 88. Right fielder Steve Evans had the highest bat mark with a .294 output. Miller didn't scare anyone with his bat, but did manage to score 106 runs, the second highest in the league. Although they eventually dropped to fifth place, the Cards were in the thick of the race for most of the year, only three games out of first at the halfway point.

Club President Stan Robinson didn't live to see the resurgence, dying unexpectedly on March

24 at age 54. He was replaced as the team's president by his niece, Helene Britton, called "Lady Bee" by the players. One of Lady Bee's major objections was foul language, and as such she had little use for the earthy Roger Bresnahan, and eventually fired her future Hall of Fame manager for that reason. On the mound, Bob Harmon led the team with a 23-15 mark, the first Cardinal to top 20 in seven years.

After an apparent upswing the year before, the Cards fell back into their losing ways in 1912—they lost 90 of them as a matter of fact, dropping them back to sixth place. The few high points of the year were first sacker Ed Konetchy's .314 average, 8 homers and 82 runs batted in, and Miller Huggins's .304 mark, his top year at the plate in his entire playing career.

Bob Harmon topped the hill crew with an 18-18 mark. Following the season the Cardinals' lady owner named Huggins as the team's new manager. A new face at the helm may have been what owner Lady Bee wanted, but it didn't do much to help the team, which fell all the way into the cellar again in 1913, with a 51-99 mark. Bob Harmon, after 21 and 18 wins in the previous two years, fell to an 8-21 record. Pitcher Slim Sallee was one of the few improved players on the squad, posting a 17-15 mark.

The Arrival of the "Rajah"

During World War I, in 1914, second-year manager Miller Huggins put it all together for the St. Louis Cardinals, driving his squad up to third place and an 81-72 record. It was the highest finish in Cardinal history, and represented an improvement of 30 wins over the 1913 finish. Attendance, which had dropped off after the record year in 1911, bounced back to 346,025.

During the year another league also began play, the Federal League, which put a third team into St. Louis. The club was under the managership of former Card hurler Three Finger Brown. The team's subsequent last-place finish caused great glee among the Cardinal players.

A primary reason for the Card's upswing in 1914 was the remarkable performance of their pitching staff, which led the entire National League with a team 2.38 earned run average. Pacing this stingy hill crew were Bill Doak, with a 20-6 record and a league leading 1.72 ERA, Slim Sallee at 18-17 and 2.73, and Pol Perritt at 16-13 and 2.36. Doak's individual crown was the first ERA championship ever for a Cardinal hurler.

In addition to his managerial duties, Huggins found time to lead the league in walks again, this time with 105. First baseman Johnny "Dots" Miller's .290 average and 88 RBIs led the team. Miller was in his first year with the team, acquired in a trade with the Pittsburgh Pirates for Ed Konetchy.

If, for nothing else, the Card's 1915 season was memorable for the debut of one of the greatest hitters of all time, the immortal Rogers Hornsby. The "Rajah's" rookie year was inauspicious; he played in only 18 games and hit a modest .246; but it was the beginning of 12 superlative, tumultuous years by the incomparable second baseman, the likes of which have never been achieved again.

For the year itself, however, Manager Miller Huggins's squad slipped back to sixth place and a 72-81 record, despite leading the league in hitting average, with a .254 mark, and in runs scored, with 590. The Redleg pitching crew, which had led the league in ERA the previous year, dropped to sixth in that category. Rookie hurler Lee Meadows was the only one of the staff to post a winning record, with 13-11. Tom Long's 25 triples led the league.

1916 was young Rogers Hornsby's first full year as the Card's second sacker, and Manager Miller Huggins last as a player. During the year the club sold its colorful lefthanded pitcher Slim Sallee to the New York Giants, for much needed working capital.

It was a most disappointing year for the team, which dropped to 60 wins and a tie for last place in the league. The 20-year-old Hornsby asserted himself as the Cards' top hitter, leading in average, at .313, in hits, with 155, homers with six, and runs batted in, with 65. Cardinal hurlers Bill Doak, Lee Meadows and Red Ames all had commendable earned run averages, at 2.63, 2.58 and 2.64, but their win-loss marks didn't fare as well, at 12-8, 12-23 and 11-16.

Late in the season, tired of running the ball club, owner Britton announced that she wanted to sell the club. A sale was eventually made to a group of St. Louis investors. The latter then named Branch Rickey to take over as the team's General Manager. In Miller Huggins's swan song as the Cards' skipper, the club climbed back to a third-place finish with 82 wins, the second highest victory total in the team's history.

Rogers Hornsby, at age 21 and in his second full year in the league, was now considered the top hitter of the senior circuit. His .327 average was second, but the young infielder led in total bases with 253, slugging average at .484 and in triples, with 17, and was third in homers, with eight. On the field he was no slouch, either, leading the league in double plays as a second baseman, with 82. The Cardinals' climb was reflected in the hill crews stats, led by Bill Doak with a 16-20 mark, Lee Meadows at 15-9, and journeyman Red Ames, at 15-10.

In 1918 World War I was in its final, violent stages, and the Cardinals were without their fiery little manager, Miller Huggins, who was now the skipper for the American League's New York Yankees. Under Jack Hendricks the Cards fell all the way to last in the league, with even Hornsby having an off year, hitting only .281. It was to be the only time in his long career that Hornsby would fail to top the .300 mark. It was still the dead ball era for the National League, where the 27 home runs hit by the entire Cardinal team was high for the loop.

General Manager Branch Rickey took over field duties as manager in 1919. Although the Cards won only three more games than they had managed the previous year, they did climb up two spots in the standings, to sixth. Hornsby, now playing third base to make room for newcomer Milt Stock, moved back into the league leaders in hitting, with his .318 average and 71 runs batted in, both second in the loop stats. Stock, who was acquired from the Phillies, hit .307 for the year.

Transcendental Graphics

Rogers Hornsby during his years as a player–manager with the Chicago Cubs in the 1930s

The Right Stuff

St. Louis entered the new decade with a move into a new stadium, Sportsman's Park, which was to be their home for the next 46 years. They also moved back up the ladder into a fifth place tie, a move that agreed with the fans, and attendance moved up accordingly to 325,845, the highest in six years.

Hornsby continued his phenomenal hitting, winning the league batting crown with a .370 mark, as well as taking titles in slugging, at .559, total bases, 329, doubles, 44, hits, 218 and runs batted in, with 94. Had there been a league MVP he would have been a virtual lock for the honor.

With Hornsby leading the way, and Milt Stock (now playing third, with Hornsby back at second) hitting .319, and first baseman Jack Fournier at .306, the Cards team average was .289, also tops in the league. Hornsby's batting title was the first

Transcendental Graphics

Sunny Jim Bottomley

for the Cards since 1901. Pitcher Bill Doak became the Redbirds' first 20-game winner in six years, posting a 20-12 record.

With the tremendous hitting of Roger Hornsby pacing the club, the Cardinals put together the finest season in their brief history in 1921, winning 87 games, their most ever, and finishing third in the league, matching their highest finish. Attendance moved up as well, to 384,790, the second highest in club annals.

Hornsby won his second National League batting title, hitting .397, just missing the magic .400 barrier. He also led again in slugging, with a .639 mark, the highest in league history; in total bases, with 378, also a new mark, in runs batted in, with 126, in hits, with 235, in doubles, 44, and triples, 18, and just missing out in home runs, slugging 21 to finish two behind the leader. Even so, that 21 home run total was the first time a

Cardinal hitter had ever reached 20. He also scored 131 runs, another team record.

For the first time the amazing Hornsby was given better than average support by his teammates. Left fielder Austin McHenry had his finest season at .350, third high for the league; first baseman Jack Fournier was fifth in the league with a .343 average; outfielders Jack Smith and Les Mann were both at .328; catcher Vern Clemons hit .320; swingman Joe Schultz was at .309; and the reliable Milt Stock chipped in at .307.

The club's team batting average of .308 was the tops in the league for the year and the highest for a St. Louis team up to that time. In any other year, McHenry's .350 average, 17 homers, 102 RBIs and 305 total bases would have made him the star of the team. Unfortunately for him, Hornsby was on the same squad. Pitcher Bill Doak enjoyed his finest season as well, posting only a 15-6 record but leading the league in earned run average with a 2.59 mark as well as in winning percentage, at .714.

By this time the Cardinals also had a new President, Sam Breadon, an administrator who is credited with starting the tradition of double headers on weekends. Breadon gradually acquired more and more of the stock in the club, and would eventually become its major stockholder and owner.

Rogers Hornsby in 1922 became the first National League player to win the triple crown, walloping out 42 home runs and 150 runs batted in, not only new Cardinal highs but the most ever up to that point for the entire league, as well as a .401 batting average. He was 26 years old, and at the height of his game. In one of the most outstanding hitting years ever put together by any major leaguer, Horsby also amassed 450 total bases, 250 hits and 141 runs, still Cardinal records, a .722 slugging percentage, the highest ever recorded in the league up until that time, and again led in doubles, with 46.

The team totalled 85 wins for the year. Those wins, coupled with their 87 in 1921, gave them the best two-year mark ever. At the turnstiles, they topped a half million for the first time, totalling 536,343. The year also saw the appearance of another future Hall of Famer, Sunny Jim Bottomley, who made an appearance late in the season, playing in 37 games and hitting .325. Brooklyn castoff Jeff Pfeffer led the hill brigade with a 19-12 mark, while offensively, in addition to Hornsby's heroics, Specs Topercer hit .324, outfielders Joe Schultz and Jack Smith .314 and .310, respectively, and infielder Milt Stock, .305.

The season was also marred by two untimely deaths, the first to catcher Pickles Dillhoefer, who died of pneumonia; the second to hard-hitting outfielder Austin McHenry, from a brain tumor.

In these early years of the 1920s the Cardinals perfected the first farm system operation in major league history, an innovation of their general manager and field manager, Branch Rickey.

Hornsby's value to the club was proven in the 1923 season, when the superstar second baseman missed 47 games due to assorted illnesses and the team dropped from a third place tie into fifth place.

Transcendental Graphics

Jesse Haines

A Star and His Supporting Cast

Hornsby teamed with newcomer Jim Bottomley to form the best one-two punch in the league—when the former was in the lineup, that is. Thanks to a ruling by the league office, Hornsby qualified for enough plate appearances to win his fourth straight hitting title with a .384 mark, while Bottomley was the league runnerup with a fine .371 average in his first full year of play.

Hornsby also led the loop in slugging again, this time with a .627 average. Bottomley, in addition to his high average, led the Cards in hits with 194 and in runs batted in, with 94. Offensive support was offered by outfielders Jack Smith, at .310, and Hy Myers, at an even .300. On the hill, the top performer was the veteran Jesse Haines, with a 20-13 record.

The highest batting average of the 20th Century in the major leagues, Rogers Hornsby's .424, didn't help the Cardinal fortunes in 1924 as the club dropped 15 more games in the loss column and slipped from fifth to sixth place. The team's overall performance was the reason that one sports writer, voting for the newly created Most Valuable Player Award, did not name Hornsby on any of 10 ballot places.

That lack of one writer's votes cost Hornsby the MVP title, which went to Brooklyn pitcher Dazzy Vance, who had a 28-6 record. But consider Hornsby's stats: that incredible .424 batting average, and league leading marks in total bases, with 375, in slugging, with a .696 average, in hits, with 227, and in doubles, with 43. He also pounded out 25 home runs, only two behind the league leader. Sunny Jim Bottomley had another solid year, hitting .316 and leading the Cardinals with 111 RBIs. During the year he was responsible for the most productive single day as a hitter in baseball history, banging home a record 12 runs with six straight hits. Ray Blades was the only other Redbird over .300, with a .311 mark. Although no Card hurlers won more than 10 games, steady Jesse Haines hurled the second no-hitter in Cardinal annals, beating Boston 5-0 on July 17.

Hornsby Named Manager

Manager Branch Rickey and star second baseman Hornsby had been at odds with one another for some time, a dislike that culminated in an all-out fistfight between the two during the 1925 season. That battle may have been the deciding factor that led to Rickey's dismissal as the team's skipper by President Sam Breadon. The latter then offered the job to Hornsby, who took the team when it was at a 13-25 mark and brought it back up over .500 to a 77-76 finish and fourth place in the standings.

Hornsby, who took his second triple crown in three years, hit .403, the third time over that .400 plateau in four years, an unprecedented hitting achievement. He also walloped 39 home runs and amassed 143 runs batted in, and led the league in slugging with a record .756 mark and in runs with 133. This time the MVP voters could not keep him from the title, and he was named as the National League's Most Valuable Player for 1925.

Teammate Jim Bottomley had an MVP quality year of his own, hitting .367, second only to Hornsby in the league, banging 128 RBIs, third high, 358 total bases, also third high, and leading the league in hits, with 227, and doubles, with 44. Sunny Jim also hit three grand-slam homers during the year. Outfielder Ray Blades had his best season ever, hitting .342, while future Hall-of-Famer Chick Hafey managed a .302 clip in his first full year. On the mound, Wee Willie Sherdel led the league in winning percentage, with a .714 mark, and a 15-6 record.

1926: The Road To Glory

At long last a National League pennant flew over St. Louis. The last championship for the city was provided by the St. Louis Browns of the old American Association, way back in 1888. It was only natural that the city went quite berserk, first upon capturing the National League title, then, several days later, with the dramatic winning of the World Series.

Transcendental Graphics

Grover Cleveland Alexander

Early in the season, owner Sam Breadon had made two key moves; first, he traded Heinie Mueller to the New York Giants for outfielder Billy Southworth, then he picked up on waivers the veteran Grover Cleveland Alexander. South-worth hit a solid .320 for the Cards, and although Alexander won only nine games for the club during the year, his heroics during the World Series has become a legend.

After the 39-year-old Alexander pitched the Redbirds to wins in the second and sixth games, the classic went down to the seventh game with the popular Jesse Haines on the mound for St. Louis. Haines nursed a 3-2 lead into the seventh inning, when their opponent, the powerful New York Yankees, loaded the bases with two out. Card Manager Rogers Hornsby then pulled Haines, and brought Alexander back to the hill with only a single night's rest. The old war horse came through for his new club, striking out the dangerous Tony Lazzeri to preserve the win and the championship.

During the 1926 season, which saw a record attendance of 681,575, Cardinal catcher Bob O'Farrell became the second St. Louis player to receive the league's Most Valuable Player Award.

O'Farrell's offensive statistics were only average, but he was selected primarily for his team leadership.

Hornsby, who was a big winner in his first full year as the team's manager, had, what was for him, a poor year as a hitter, with only a .317 average and 93 runs batted in. Jim Bottomley also had an off-year on average, dropping to .299, but led the team in homers, with 40, runs batted in, with 120, and total bases, with 305. Third baseman Les Bell had his best year with a .325 average, 100 RBIs and 189 hits. Cardinal hurlers were led by Flint Rhem's 20-7 mark.

The year was the start of the first of the Cardinal winning eras, this one from 1926 through 1934 in which they would go on to five NL Championships.

Hornsby Departs

An odd postscript to the tremendous championship year came about soon after the conclusion of the season. Hornsby, not the easiest person in the world to get along with, and St. Louis owner Sam Breadon got into a number of heated arguments over salary and whether the team should play in exhibition games. Breadon, finally fed up with his super but swell-headed star, traded him to the New York Giants for another second baseman, Frankie Frisch. He later named O'Farrell as the team's new manager.

It is most difficult to replace a legend, but the Fordham Flash, Frankie Frisch, did a pretty good job of it, taking Hornsby's place at second and hitting a team high .337 in 1927. He also led the club in hits, with 208, runs, with 112, tying teammate Jim Bottomley in doubles, with 31, and leading the entire league in stolen bases, with 48.

With crowd favorite Hornsby gone and catcher O'Farrell at the controls, the 1927 Cardinals came close to repeating as champions, but fell a game and a half short at 92-61, behind the Pittsburgh Pirates.

Bottomley paced the team in runs batted in with 124, homers with 19 and triples with 15. Young Chick Hafey swatted out a .329 average

Transcendental Graphics

Chick Hafey

and led the league in slugging with a .590 average. The club also came up with two 20-game winners in Jesse Haines, at 24-10, and the 40-year-old Grover Cleveland Alexander, at 21-10. With new manager Bill McKechnie at the helm, and Sunny Jim Bottomley having his greatest year, the 1928 Cardinals rose back to the championship of the National League.

Future Hall-of-Famer McKechnie accepted the Cardinal managership after a long tenure as the Pittsburgh Pirates' skipper. Bottomley was voted the league's Most Valuable Player after leading the Redbirds in home runs, with 31; runs batted in, with 136, and total bases, with 360 and leading the league in triples, with 20. His MVP award was the third for the Cardinals in the past four years.

On the hill, veteran Jesse Haines had another solid season with a 20-8 mark; Bill Sherdell was at 21-10, the only time in his major league career that he won as many as 20 games, and Grover

Cleveland Alexander, in the twilight of his career, came up with a 10-9 effort.

In the 1928 World Series, Babe Ruth and his Bronx Bomber teammates took the Cards apart, winning 4-1.

Almost Made It

Owner Sam Breadon, disgruntled because his National League Champion Cardinals were blown out in the '28 World Series, fired manager McKechnie and brought up Billy Southworth to handle the job. Former Card outfielder Southworth had been manager of the Cards' minor league team in Rochester, New York.

After half a season, however, Breadon concluded that he had made a mistake and called McKechnie back. Southworth's record at the time was 43-45. In the two days before McKechnie took over again, Gabby Street guided the team to two wins without a loss. McKechnie was not much more successful with the club, guiding them to a 33-29 record, but not enough to pull them out of fourth place in the standings.

Through the three managers the squad enjoyed a good year at the plate, paced by veteran Jim Bottomley, who had a .314 average to go along with a team leading 29 home runs and 137 runs batted in. The Card outfield all hit over .300; Chick Hafey at .338, Taylor Douthit at .336 and the colorful Ernie Orsatti at .332.

Hafey set a new club mark in doubles, with 47, and tied Bottomley in homers with 29, while Douthit led the team in hits with 206, rookie catcher Jimmie Wilson averaged a surprising .325, and star second sacker Frankie Frisch had another top season with a .334 average. Veteran hurler Grover Cleveland Alexander concluded his great career with a total of 373 wins, tying him for the most wins in National League history with the immortal Christy Mathewson.

McKechnie, tired of the managerial musical chairs in St. Louis, in 1930 agreed to a five-year pact as manager of the Boston Braves. Cards owner Sam Breadon then turned control of the club over to Gabby Street, his fifth opening day manager in five years. The move paid off as the Cards bounced back to the National League championship.

The Cardinal hitting attack was remarkable. For the first time in their history, before or since, every member of the starting lineup hit over .300. All-League second baseman Frankie Frisch was at .346, but the big news was rookie outfielder George Watkins, whose .373 average led the team, and is still the highest average for a Cardinal First year man. His .621 slugging average is also a Redbird rookie record.

Of the other two outfielders, Taylor Douthit banged out 201 hits, his second consecutive year over 200, and hit .303, while Chick Hafey was at .336. Catcher Jimmy Wilson hit .318; first baseman Jim Bottomley had a modest .304; shortstop Charlie Gelbert was also at .304; and third baseman Sparky Anderson (*not* the current Tigers manager) rounded out the starting crew with a .314 mark.

Even the reserves tore the cover off the ball: Showboat Fisher hit 374; Ray Blades was at .396, catcher Gus Mancuso hit .366 and Ernie Orsatti added a .321 effort. It was a hitter's year, with the whole Card lineup averaging .314, one that would easily lead the league in just about any other year. In 1930, however, the New York Giants were the top hitting team at .319, and the entire league averaged .303. Old standby Jesse Haines had a 13-8 record to lead the hill staff, and newcomer Burleigh Grimes was at 13-6.

To win the National League title the Cards had to pull off one of the most stirring stretch runs in league history. They were 10 games behind the Chicago Cubs as late as August 17. In the World Series all of the Cardinal hitting prowess seemed to evaporate. The team hit a meek .200 and lost in six games to the Philadelphia Athletics.

Getting Even

Manager Gabby Street's Cardinals repeated as National League kingpins, winning a club record 101 games, the first time in the team's history that they had topped the century mark.

Future Hall-of-Famer Frankie Frisch was named the league's Most Valuable Player, hitting a solid .311 and leading the league in stolen bases with 28 and doubles with 46. Hard-hitting outfielder Chick Hafey won the league batting title in the closest race the league has ever witnessed, hitting .3489 to edge out Bill Terry of the Giants, at .3486, and his own teammate, Sunny Jim Bottomley, who was right there too at .3482. Frish's MVP was the fourth for a St. Louis Cardinal in the past seven years.

Two rookies came through for the club; pitcher Paul Derringer compiled an 18-8 record in his first year in the big leagues, and outfielder Pepper Martin hit an even .300. Bill Hallahan's 19-9 record tied for the league lead in wins, and veteran Burleigh Grimes had his last good year at 17-9. On July 12, 1931, at Sportsman's Park, the club drew a new one-day attendance record, 45,715—about 13,000 over capacity.

In the World Series, Martin, now dubbed "The Wild Horse of the Osage," hit .500 and stole five bases as the Cards got even with the Philadelphia Athletics, winning in seven games. Hallahan and Grimes each won two.

After the World Championship 1931 season, owner Sam Breadon peddled off two of his stars, future Hall-of-Famers Chick Hafey and pitcher Burleigh Grimes. Those moves, plus an unprecedented string of injuries, plummeted the club all the way from first to sixth place in 1932.

The team's prime power hitter, Jim Bottomley, was able to play less than half the season, and Pepper Martin managed only 85 games and an anemic .235 average. Frankie Frisch followed his MVP year with a poor .292 average in 115 games. Only two Cards were able to play in as many as 127 games for the season, and only three had as many as 400 at bats.

Outfielder Ernie Orsatti was healthy and hit a team-leading .336, and George Watkins was at .312. The team came up with two more exciting rookies, however—Dizzy Dean, who was soon to become baseball's second biggest gate attraction (after Babe Ruth), and Joe "Ducky" Medwick.

Transcendental Graphics

Dizzy Dean

Dean pitched his way to an 18-15 record in his rookie year, while Medwick hit a robust .349 in the 36 games he appeared in.

In Chicago, Rogers Hornsby, playing, managing and arguing with another club, was fired by Cubs owner Bill Veech with his team in first place and two-thirds of the season gone. The Cubs' new skipper, Charlie Grimm, led the team to the championship. Hornsby had a hard time getting along with anyone.

The Gas House Gang

The Cardinals improved on their 1932 finish by 10 games but moved up only one slot in the standings, from 6th to 5th, and it cost Manager Gabby Street his job. After 91 games and a 46-45 record, team owner Sam Breadon replaced Street with his star second baseman, Frankie Frisch. The latter rallied the team to a 36-26 finish, raising hopes for the future.

Offensively the Cards were led by newcomer Ducky Medwick, who hit .306 and led the team in round trippers with 18, runs batted in with 98 and total bases with 296. Pepper Martin's .316 average was high for the club, and his 122 runs were high for the league. Departed superstar Rogers Hornsby returned at age 37 and hit a respectable .325, while Rip Collins, at .310, and Frisch, at .303, also had good years.

Second-year hurler Dizzy Dean won 20 against 18 losses and led the league in strikeouts with 199. Tex Carleton had a 17-11 year, and Wild Bill Hallahan was close behind with 16-13. Forty-two-year old Dazzy Vance was picked up from Brooklyn and turned in a 6-2 mark.

Team Manager Frisch made few changes in the club over the winter, but the ones he did make paid off. The most significant was bringing up Dizzy Dean's younger brother, Paul. Between them, "Me and Paul" won 49 games for the season; Dizzy, turning in a superlative 30-7 mark, and Paul 19-11. It was the first 30-win season in the National League since Grover Cleveland Alexander did it in 1919 with the Phillies. Dizzy led the league in strikeouts for the third straight year, this time with 195, and Paul was third with 150. The team swept to its fifth championship in nine years, along the way becoming known as "The Gas House Gang," one of the most popular teams in major league baseball history.

Rip Collins, the team's new first baseman, tied Mel Ott for the league lead in homers with 35, and led the loop in total bases with 369 and in slugging with a .615 mark. He was also fourth in hitting with a .330 average and second in RBIs with 128. In any other year he would have had a good chance at the MVP selection; but in 1934 the honor could only go to Dizzy Dean.

Ducky Medwick also had a banner year, hitting .319 with 40 doubles, 18 triples (high for the league) and 18 homers. First year catcher Bill Delancy chipped in with a .316 average, and player manager Frisch hit .305. Pepper Martin hit .289 and led the league in stolen bases, with 23. As a team the Cards led the loop in hitting with a .288 average, and in runs with 799. During the year Paul Dean hurled a no-hitter, topping Brooklyn 2-0 on September 21.

In the World Series the Redbirds outfought the Detroit Tigers in seven games, with Dizzy and Paul each winning two games. Dizzy's MVP award was the fifth for a St. Louis player in 10 years.

Close, but....

The Gas House Gang's 96 wins and their one-two pitching combo of the Dean brothers almost won it again in the 1935 campaign, but a 21-game winning streak by the Chicago Cubs at the end of the season was more than even they could overcome. Dizzy, with a 28-12 record, and Paul, at 19-12, paced the Cards on the mound, while outfielder Joe Medwick and first baseman

Transcendental Graphics

Johnny Mize

Rip Collins formed a double header headache of their own at the plate. Ducky led the league in total bases with 365, was second in batting average at .353, in runs batted in with 126, and in hits, with 224 and also had 23 homers and 46 doubles.

Collins hit .312, also had 23 home runs and knocked in 122 runs. Playing manager Frankie Frisch was at .294 and Pepper Martin at .299. Martin and Dean were named league All-Stars, and seven Cardinals, Dean, Frisch, Collins, Martin, and Medwick, as well as pitcher Bill Walker and second baseman Burgess Whitehead, were named to the All-Star game squad.

The Gas House gang started out the 1936 season as if they were going to recapture the National League crown, but when Paul Dean came down with arm troubles the club faltered and finished in a tie for second, five games behind the New York Giants.

Outfielder Ducky Medwick was practically unstoppable, adding to a .351 average with league-leading totals in hits, with 223, total bases, with 369, runs batted in, with 138, and doubles, with a grand total of 64. That doubles total is still the most ever for any National Leaguer and of course is also still a Cardinal high. Third sacker Pepper Martin hit .309, scored 121 runs and led the loop in stolen bases with 23.

Rookie Johnny Mize gave an indication of future stardom by hitting .329 and banging out 19 homers, Dizzy Dean had a 24-12 record for the year, not up to his previous standards but enough to garner All-League honors along with Medwick. Five Redbirds were named to the All-Star game, Dean, Medwick, Stu Martin (not Pepper), Rip Collins and shortstop Leo Durocher.

A Most Valuable Team

Despite Medwick's banner triple crown year in 1937, the Cardinals dropped down to 81 wins and fifth place in the league. Medwick, who was the unanimous choice for the loop's Most Valuable Player award (the Cards' sixth since 1925), led the league in hitting with a .374 average, in homers with 31 and in runs batted in with 154, the three components of the triple crown title. He also led the league in runs, with 111, hits, with 237, slugging average, .641, total bases, 406, and doubles, with 56. It was the most dominant performance in the history of the league.

Almost forgotten was second-year first baseman Johnny Mize's .364 average—second in the league—25 home runs, and 113 RBIs. Dizzy Dean, who suffered a broken toe in the All-Star game, fell to a 13-10 mark, while the veteran Lon Warneke paced the staff with an 18-11 record. Trying to pitch while his toe was still giving him pain caused the arm problems that would eventually end Dean's great career. Medwick, Mize, Dean, and Pepper Martin made the All-Star squad.

When a club doesn't win as many games as it is supposed to win, the owner's first recourse is to fire the manager, and that's what took place in the summer of 1938 in St. Louis, when Sam Breadon gave Frankie Frisch his walking papers. Coach Mike Gonzalez was named as the interim skipper for the remainder of the season.

Joe Medwick didn't repeat his phenomenal statistics of the previous year, but still led the Cardinals in runs batted in, with 122 and doubles, with 47, along with a .322 average. He also led the team in hits for the fourth straight year, this time with 190.

First baseman Johnny Mize continued to climb toward stardom, hitting .337 and leading the league in total bases, with 326, slugging, with a .614 average, triples, with 16, and banged out 27 homers. Joe Medwick was the Card's only representative at the annual All-Star game.

Prior to the season, Cards General Manager Branch Rickey peddled the now sore-armed Dizzy Dean to the Chicago Cubs for $200,000 in cash and two second-line pitchers.

Ray Blades, who 14 years earlier had hit a robust .347 as the Cardinal left fielder, in 1939 took over the remnants of the old Gas House Gang that had finished sixth the year before and drove them up the standings to a respectable second-place finish, four and a half games behind the champion Cincinnati Reds. The Cards won 27 games more than they had in 1938 and again paced the entire league in hitting, with a .294 team batting average.

Two prime reasons for the club's upsurge were the hard hitting duo of Ducky Joe Medwick and Johnny Mize. Medwick was second in the league with a .322 average, and also the runner-up in runs batted in, with 117, and hits, with 201. His 307 total bases were good for third in the loop. Mize led the NL in hitting with a .353 mark, in home runs, with 28, in slugging, with a .626 average, and in total bases, with 353. He was also third in RBIs, with 108. Had the Cardinals been first instead of second, his stats surely would have won him the league's MVP award.

Second-year man Enos "Country" Slaughter hit .320 and led the league in doubles, with 52. At third base, Pepper Martin still had enough left to hit .306. Five Cards were named to the All-Star team; pitcher Curt Davis, who posted a 22-16 record, Medwick, Mize, Terry Moore and Lon Warneke. Medwick was also named All-League.

Sitting On Top Of The World

Most writers picked the Cards to win it all in 1940 on the basis of their strong 1939 finish, but the Redbirds got off to a poor start and Sam Breadon fired his manager, Ray Blades, in the second month of the season. On June 14th Breadon turned the reins of the club over to Billy Southworth, back for a second try at the job.

As it turned out, Breadon's choice was a good one, and Southworth would go on to compile the best winning record in Cardinal history. For the five years, 1941 through 1945, his teams would average 102 wins a season and win three consecutive National League crowns.

For the 1940 season the big gun at the plate was Johnny Mize, who hit .314 and led the league in homers, with 43, runs batted in, with 137, slugging, at .636, and total bases, with 368. The 43 homers are still the most ever hit by a Cardinal, and topped the old record of 42 set by Rogers

Hornsby in 1922. During the year the Cards played their first night game at home, but were walloped by the Brooklyn Dodgers, 10-1.

Joe Medwick, a long-time Cardinal favorite, was hitting .304 when he was peddled to the Dodgers in the season's 37th game. The Gas House era was over. At the All-Star classic, the Cards were represented by Mize and outfielder Terry Moore.

The injury bug bit the Cardinals with a vengeance in 1941, putting just about everyone in the lineup out for lengthy periods with major ailments. Johnny Mize broke his hand, and catcher Walker Cooper and outfielder Enos Slaughter had broken collarbones. Terry Moore was beaned and almost killed. With a patchwork offense for nearly the whole season, Manager Billy Southworth was voted as the league's Manager of the Year for bringing the team as high as second in the standings.

Before his injury Mize was leading the club in hitting, at .317, in homers, with 16, and in runs batted in, with an even l00. Mize, Slaughter and pitcher Lon Warneke were named to the midseason All-Star game. On August 30 Warneke threw a no-hitter against the Cincinnati Reds, winning 2-0. Attendance for the year was 642,496, the second highest in team history.

Late in the year a promising rookie made his first appearance in a Cardinal uniform. In 12 games, that young man, Stan Musial, banged out 20 hits for a .426 average. It was the start of one of the greatest careers in major league history.

The Cardinals farm system, developed by Branch Rickey, began to pay dividends in 1942. In his first full year with the club was future Hall-of-Famer Stan Musial. With him in the Redbird outfield were Enos "Country" Slaughter and Terry Moore, and in reserve, Harry "The Hat" Walker; at third base Whitey Kurowski held the fort; at short, the fielding whiz Marty Marion; behind the plate Walker Cooper; and on the mound Johnny Beazly and Walker's brother Mort Cooper. All were products of the finest farm system in all of major league baseball.

During the year the Card offense was paced

by Slaughter's .318 and Musial's .315 averages; in the field Marion gobbled up everything in sight; and on the mound the National League MVP Mort Cooper, with 27 wins and only 7 losses, and Beazly's 21-6 formed the best one-two pitching punch in baseball. Mort Cooper and Slaughter were named All-League, while Mort and Walker as well as Moore, Slaughter and Jim Brown made the All-Star squad.

In the series, after dropping the first game to the Yankees, the Cardinals reeled off four straight wins to become Champions of the World again. After the season Rickey left the St. Louis organization to take on the duties of General Manager for the Brooklyn Dodgers, a move that would have major repercussions in baseball in the years ahead.

And Then There Was Musial

In 1943, as World War II raged, the Cardinals' new superstar Stan Musial became the club's eighth MVP. Along with that largess, the Cards swept to their second straight National League pennant. It was also their second consecutive 100-plus win year.

Musial led the league in hitting with a .357 average, banging out league leading marks also in slugging, .562, hits, 220, doubles, 48, and triples, 20. Other offense highpoints included Harry Walker's 29-game hitting streak, a new team high for the year; and Mort Cooper's 21-8 and Max Lanier's 15-7 win-loss marks and Howie Pollet's league-leading 1.75 earned run average.

Transcendental Graphics

Enos Slaughter (sliding)

Seven Cardinals, in addition to Manager Billy Southworth, made the All-Star squad; Mort and Walker Cooper, Lanier, Musial, Red Munger, Whitey Kurowski and Marty Marion. In the Series, the Redbirds were overpowered by the New York Yankees, 4-1.

1944 saw the first and only all-St.Louis World Series, in which the Cardinals outfought the American League Browns four games to two and recaptured the World Championship. During the season the Cards had reeled off their third straight National League pennant, winning over 100 also for the third consecutive year. The Cardinals also led the league in home runs with 100; it would be the last time they would do so.

For the first time since the MVP award was initiated two decades earlier, a fielding whiz rather than a slugging star got the nod as the honor went to Card shortstop Marty Marion. The award could easily have gone to Stan Musial however, as Stan the Man was second in hitting with a .347 average and led the league in hits, with 197 and doubles with 51, and was the most feared hitter in the league. Mort Cooper's 22-7 record led the hurlers, with Harry The Cat Brecheen at 16-5.

All-Star game selections included Red Munger, Walker Cooper, Whitey Kurowski, Marion, Musial, and Manager Billy Southworth. Ray Sanders, who led the league in RBIs, as well as Mort and Walker Cooper and Marion were named.

In the last year of World War II the Cardinals played their final campaign under Southworth, finishing second, three games behind the Chicago Cubs. Third baseman Whitey Kurowski was the club hitting star, leading the 1945 team in hitting with a .323 mark, in homers with 27 and in RBIs with 102. Second baseman Red Schoendienst paced the league in steals with 26.

Red Barrett, picked up early in the season from the Boston Braves, led the league in wins, finishing at 23-12 (21-9 with the Cards). He was backed up by Ken Burkhart, at 19-8, and Harry Brecheen, at 14-4. No All-Star game was played in 1945. Over the winter the Cardinals named Eddie Dyer as their new manager.

St. Louis and Brooklyn fought an exciting pennant race in 1946, finishing in a dead heat at 96-58. With a best-of-three playoff scheduled for the championship, the Dodgers journeyed to St. Louis for the first game, where Card hurler Howie Pollet came out a winner, 4-2. The second game was in Brooklyn, and the Redbirds won again, 8-4, and the crown was theirs.

Underdogs in the World Series to the powerful Boston Red Sox and their star slugger Ted Williams, the Cards fought back from a 2-3 deficit, winning the last two games. In the finale, Enos Slaughter's scoring dash from first on a single by Harry Walker was the key to the win. Harry The Cat Brecheen, who had only a 15-15 regular season record, won three games for the Cardinals.

During the season Stan Musial captured MVP honors with a magnificent performance—a .368 average, as well as league-leading figures in hits, 228, runs, 124, doubles, 56, triples, 20, slugging, .587, and total bases, 366. Country Slaughter had a .300 average and led the loop in RBIs with 130, and Whitey Kurowski added a .30-1 mark. Pollet led the league in wins with a 21-10 record and also led in ERA with 2.10, while Murray Dickson had a 15-6 effort.

Musial and Slaughter were both named All-League; those two, as well as Kurowski, Marty Marion, Red Schoendienst and Pollet were named as All-Star game reps. At the turnstiles the Cardinals had their greatest season ever, topping the million mark at 1,062,553.

The St. Louis Cardinals of 1947 were a solid team, quite capable of repeating as champions; unfortunately the Brooklyn Dodgers of 1947, with the likes of Pee Wee Reese, Duke Snider, Gil Hodges, and the first black ball-player in the league's history, Jackie Robinson, were one of the greatest teams of the century. As it was, the Redbirds finished only four games back with an 89-65 record.

Suffering a prolonged slump for the first time in his career, Stan Musial rallied during the last month of the season to bring his average up to .312. It was not up to par for him, but still led the team. Whitey Kurowski turned in another top performance with a .310 average and team leading figures in homers, with 27, and runs batted in, with a total of l04. Red Munger at 16-5, and Harry Brecheen, at 16-11, led the pitching crew.

At the annual All-Star game, St. Louis had seven representatives, Manager Eddie Dyer, Musial, Kurowski, Munger, Brecheen, Enos Slaughter and Marty Marion.

The Artful Dodgers

Stan Musial won his third Most Valuable Player award and led the league in virtually every hitting category in 1948: batting average, .376; runs batted in, 131; runs, 135; total bases, 429; slugging, .702; doubles, 46; and triples, 18. His home run total of 39 was only one under those of Ralph Kiner and Johnny Mize, who tied for the lead at 40. It was a most dominating performance.

Brecheen also had a banner year, winning 20 and losing only 7, leading the league in winning percentage, .741; strikeouts, 149; and ERA, 2.24. Musial and Brecheen were named All-League, and they—as well as Slaughter (.321), Schoendienst, and Marion were All-Star game picks.

Transcendental Graphics

Stan Musial

Transcendental Graphics

Red Schoendienst

By the closest of margins, the Cards failed to win the 1949 National League crown, finishing second for the third straight year, this time by only one game. The veteran Cardinal squad, led by the hitting of Stan Musial and Enos Slaughter, the fielding of Marty Marion and Red Schoendienst, and the pitching of Pollet and Brecheen, battled the Dodgers all season long. But in the last week of the season the Cardinals dropped four straight and Brooklyn took over.

Musial hit .338 with 36 homers and 123 runs batted in and led the league in hits, with 207, total bases, with 382, doubles, with 41, and tied teammate Slaughter for the team lead in triples with 13. Slaughter was close behind in average with a .336 mark. Pollet's 20-9 record led the hill squad. A new attendance mark was set at 1,430, 676.

During the 1940s the Cardinals had a regular season won-lost record of 960 wins, 580 losses for a .623 winning percentage, the best 10-year record to this date. During the decade they also won four pennants and three World Championships.

The 1950s

St. Louis sank to fifth place in 1950, winning only 78 games, their lowest finish in 12 years. The performance, as might be expected, cost manager Eddie Dyer his job. In Philadelphia, Eddie Sawyer's Whiz Kids won the National League title, with the Brooklyn Dodgers second.

Musial and Slaughter again led the Redbird hitting attack; Musial again paced the league in hitting with a .346 average, his fourth title, and also led the loop in hits, with 192, and in slugging, with a .596 average. During the year he put together a 30-game hitting streak, the second longest in Cardinal history. Rogers Hornsby had 33 in 1922. He also hit 28 homers and had 109 RBIs. Slaughter's average dropped to .290, but he banged home 101 runs. Red Schoendienst led the league in doubles with 43. To open the season the Cards played their first night opener.

Under the Cardinal's new manager, Marty Marion, the team improved by only three in the win column in 1951, but moved up two places in the standings from fifth to third.

Stan Musial continued as the top hitter in the league, leading the NL in average at .351, in runs with 124 and triples with 12, and also banged out 205 hits, 108 RBIs and 32 homers. He was the only Cardinal named All-League, and he, Red Schoendienst, Enos Slaughter and Wally Westlake, the latter picked up from Pittsburgh, were named to the annual All-Star squad.

Marion's tenure as the Cards' skipper lasted only one season. In 1952, "The Brat," Eddie Stanky, took over the reins. The Cards continued to improve, increasing their win total to 88, but remained in third place, this time eight games behind the leading Brooklyn Dodgers.

Musial won his sixth batting title over the past 10 years, at .336, and also led the loop in hits, with 194; runs, with 105, and doubles, with 42. He was named All-League and also to the annual All-Star game along with Schoendienst, who hit .303, Slaughter, who had 101 RBIs, and pitcher Gerry Staley.

Hitting A New Low

The St. Louis Club continued to languish in third place in 1953, this time tied with the Philadelphia Phillies at 83-71, and for the first time in seven years attendance dropped under one million.

Red Schoendienst was named All-League along with Stan Musial, and had the top offensive year of his career with a .342 mark, topping even Musial, who batted .337. The latter's 113 RBIs topped the team, as did his 30 homers and 127 runs; his 53 doubles were high for the entire league.

Despite their third-place finish, the 1953 Cardinals had six players on the All-Star squad: Schoendienst, Musial, catcher Del Rice, outfielder Slaughter, and pitchers Harvey Haddix and Gerry Staley. Haddix had a 20-9 record, Staley 18-9.

In 1954, for the first time in 16 years, the Cardinals lost more games than they won, finishing at 72-82 and in sixth place. It was the club's lowest finish since 1938. The team's poor performance was not matched by their great star Stan Musial, who led the team in hitting, at .330, in home runs, with 35, and in RBIs, with l26, and led the league in doubles with 41 and runs with 120. He was named All-League for a record eighth time. In a doubleheader on May 2 he walloped five home runs, a major league high.

Other Redbirds with great years included Schoendienst, with a .315 average, and outfielder Wally Moon, at .304. Pitcher Harvey Haddix added an 18-13 performance. Musial, Schoendienst, Haddix and Ray Jablonski were named to the All-Star classic.

Cardinal fans, hoping that their club's poor performance in 1954 was over and done with, were further disappointed in 1955 when the Cards victory total dropped to 68, their lowest since 1924, and a seventh-place finish, the furthest down the ladder they had been since 1919.

The showing doomed Eddie Stanky's job, and he was dismissed after 36 games and a 17-19 record. His replacement, former Card outfielder Harry Walker, fared even worse, with the Cards falling 51-67 under his guidance.

Veteran Stan Musial's average dropped off as well, to .319, but it was the only average over .300 on the team. Musial also led the team in round trippers, with 33, and RBIs, with 108. Cardinals at the All-Star game were Musial, Red Schoendienst, Harvey Haddix and Luis Arroyo.

Former Detroit Tiger hurler and manager Fred Hutchinson took over as the new Cardinal skipper in 1956. Although the club won only eight more games than it had in 1955, it moved up three places in the standings.

Musial, at 35 beginning to feel the effects of age, still led the team in hitting in 1957 with a .310 average, 27 home runs and 109 runs batted in. Second-year third baseman Ken Boyer was close behind with a .306 average and 26 round trippers. Both Musial and Boyer and outfielder Rip Repulski were named to the All-Star game.

Manager Fred Hutchinson drove his squad to 87 wins for the year, their first winning season in four years, but the Cardinals still finished second, eight games back of the Milwaukee Braves. The key to the Milwaukee club's success was the addition of second baseman Red Schoendienst, the former Cardinal star, who had been traded to the New York Giants and then to the Braves.

At age 36 Stan Musial found the fountain of youth, hitting a robust .351 to win his seventh National League batting title. Musial also belted out 29 homers and drove home 102 runs. Musial, Wally Moon, catcher Hal Smith and pitcher Larry Jackson were the St. Louis reps at the annual All-Star game. On the mound, Jackson and Lindy McDaniel had identical 15-9 records.

The Cards improvement in 1957 was short lived as the club fell back into a fifth place tie and a 72-82 record in 1958. With ten games left in the season, Hutchinson was given his walking papers and was replaced by coach Stan Hack. During the year Stan Musial collected his 3,000th base hit, and finished the season with a .337 average. Ken Boyer, who hit .307, led the club with 90 RBIs and 23 home runs. Sam Jones won only l4 games

Transcendental Graphics

Bob Gibson

but led the league in strikeouts, with 225. Musial, Don Blasingame and Larry Jackson were named to the All-Star game.

Solly Hemus's debut as the new Card manager in 1959 was far from auspicious, as the team fell back into 7th place in the NL standings with a 71-83 mark. Aging superstar Musial had his share of ailments and his worst season as a major leaguer, hitting only .255 with 44 RBIs. Joe Cunningham did his best to pick up the slack with a .345 average, his best ever.

Musial Calls It Quits

A 15-game improvement in the win column moved the 1960 Redbirds back into the first division; their 86-68 record was good for a third-place finish. The club was led by pitcher Ernie Broglio's 21-9 mark, his win total tying him with Warren Spahn of the Milwaukee Braves for the most in the league for the year. Larry Jackson added an 18-13 performance. Broglio's record earned him an All-League spot.

Musial improved his stats somewhat, but was still at .275, far below par for him. Ken Boyer had a .304 average and led the team with 32 homers and 98 runs batted in.

In 1961 Ken Boyer continued to shoulder the Card's offensive load, with 95 runs batted in, 24 homers and a .329 average, and earning All-League honors. After a 33-41 start, Hemus was replaced by Johnny Keane. Curt Flood had his best year to date with a .322 average, and Musial, in his 20th year, hit .288.

Both American and National leagues moved from a 154 to a 162 game schedule in 1962, and both leagues now had 10 teams. In the senior circuit, the two new clubs were the New York Mets and the Houston Astros. The Cardinals had virtually the same record as they'd had in 1961, they won four more and lost four more, but slipped a notch to sixth place.

First baseman Bill White led the offense, hitting .324 with 20 homers and 102 RBIs. Ken Boyer, named All-League, was close behind at .291 with 24 home runs and 98 RBIs. To the delight of his fans, Musial still had enough left at nearly 42 to hit .330 with 19 home runs, and was third on the team with 82 RBIs. In his third year, Bob Gibson won 15 against 13 losses, was fifth in the league in earned run average at 2.85 and third in strikeouts, with 208.

The 1963 Cardinals won more games (93), than they had in 14 years. But the big news was the retirement of Stan Musial, one of the game's all-time greats. Over a star-studded 22-year career, "The Man" amassed a total of 3,630 hits, 725 doubles, 475 home runs, played in 3,626 games, belted home 1,951 runs and compiled a .331 lifetime average.

At the time of his retirement, Musial's total number of hits and games played had been exceeded by only two other players in the history of both leagues; his doubles total by only one other before him; and his runs batted in by only five others. He had seven batting championships, topping the record of six held previously by Rogers Hornsby; he had three MVP awards; and was voted to the annual All-Star game a record 20 straight times. His familiar number 6 became the first ever retired by the Cardinals, and he was elected to the Hall of Fame in 1969.

During the year, shortstop Dick Groat's .319 average was the best on the club and third in the league; his 43 doubles were the best in the loop. Ken Boyer, with 24 homers and 114 RBIs, and Bill White, with 27 and 109, supplied the power.

Bob Gibson and Ernie Broglio each won 18 to lead the pitching staff, and Curt Simmons, at 15-9, was among the league leaders in earned run average with a 2.48 mark. The All-Star game, now back to a once-a-summer basis, had Cardinals Boyer, White, Musial, Groat and Julian Javier on the squad.

A Series Of Wins

Musial should have waited one more year to retire. In 1964 the Cardinals won their 10th National League pennant and 7th World Championship. The title was won with the identical record, 93-69, that they had in finishing second in 1963. Ken Boyer was named as the league's MPV after leading the league in runs batted in, with 119, and hitting 24 homers. It was the 12th MPV award to be won by a Cardinal.

Both Curt Flood and newcomer Lou Brock reached the 200-hit mark; Flood with 211 to lead the league, and Brock with an even 200. Flood hit .311 for the year, while Brock's .348 average would have been the tops for the league, but he did not get in enough plate appearances to qualify. Pittsburgh's Roberto Clemente won at .339. Acquired from the Cubs in a trade for pitcher Ernie Broglio, Brock stole 33 bases, the highest total for the team since Frankie Frisch stole 48 in 1927. Bill White added a .303 average to the offense.

On August 17, with the club in fifth place,

Card owner Gussie Busch fired his General Manager, Bing Devine. He was about to fire Manager Johnny Keane as well, but the club started to win, and within a short time moved into the league lead.

Cardinals who were All-League were Boyer at third, White at first and Dick Groat at short. All-Star game selections were Boyer, White, Flood, Groat and pitcher Ray Sadecki, who won 20 games. Bob Gibson was close behind with a 19-12 mark, and the veteran Curt Simmons had his last good year with 18 wins.

In the Series the Cards defeated the New York Yankees four games to three. Gibson won two games and catcher Tim McCarver led all hitters with a .478 average. After the Series, Manager Keane announced his resignation, and later signed on to manage the New York Yankees, the club he had just beaten.

St. Louis' win total dropped by only 13 in 1965, but that amount was enough to plummet the Cardinals all the way from Champions of the World to seventh place in the National League. Despite the performance on the field, attendance was up to 1,241,195, the most since 1949. The club's new skipper was former star second baseman Albert "Red" Schoendienst, in his first year as manager of a ball club.

On the field, Card outfielder Lou Brock stole 63 bases, more than any other St. Louis player in history. Curt Flood had the top average on the team, .310, and led in RBIs as well with 82. Bob Gibson, who won 20 and lost 12, fanned a total of 270 and was the team's only representative at the annual All-Star game.

Though still stuck in the second division in 1966, the Cardinals drew 1,712,980 fans, a new franchise record. The team's 83-79 mark and 6th place finish were slight improvements over their 1965 figures of 80-81 and 7th.

Lou Brock continued to run wild on the bases; his 74 steals led the league and represented a new high for the Cardinals. Orlando Cepeda, picked up in a trade with the San Francisco Giants, hit .303 for his new team; and Tim McCarver pulled off a rarity for a catcher, leading the league in triples with 13. On the mound, Bob Gibson won 21 and led the league in strikeouts with 268. Gibson, McCarver and Flood were All-Star game selections.

A decade earlier, several years after he had persuaded the board of directors of Anheuser Busch to purchase the Cardinals, August Busch Jr. made it known that if the team was going to continue to prosper in St. Louis, a new stadium would be needed. He took his idea to civic leaders and city officials, and subsequently his plan was carried out.

On May 12, 1966, Busch Stadium, the new home of the St. Louis Cardinals, officially opened. The Cards had closed old Busch Stadium on May 8 with a 10-5 loss to the San Francisco Giants. They opened the new facility in downtown St. Louis by defeating the Atlanta Braves, 4-3, in 12 innings. Later in the year the Cardinals hosted the annual All-Star game.

The 1967 Cardinals climbed all the way from sixth place to first in the National League and capped off a most successful season by topping the Boston Red Sox in the World Series for their eighth World Championship. Orlando Cepeda earned MVP honors after leading the league in runs batted in with 111, slugging 25 homers and hitting .325. Lou Brock also had a great year, again leading the league in stolen bases with 52 and in runs with 113, getting 206 hits and 21 homers.

Curt Flood hit a solid .335. Bob Gibson was having a fine year and had a 13-7 record before breaking his leg; young Steve Carlton was at 14-9, and 29-year-old rookie Dick Hughes had a 16-6 mark to top the league in winning percentage. Hughes would be out of baseball the next year, with a total of only 20 wins for his career. Cepeda, McCarver, Gibson and Brock were selected for the annual All-Star clash, and Cepeda and McCarver made All-League.

In the World Series, a recovered Bob Gibson pitched three complete-game victories and Lou Brock was the offensive star as the Cardinals outfought the Red Sox in seven games. Brock topped all series hitters with a .414 batting average, and also set a Series record by stealing seven bases. Roger Maris hit .385 and drove in seven runs, also a Card high for the Series. The club's attendance figure climbed over the two million mark for the first time.

Pitchers Have Big Years

Bob Gibson, the Cardinals' pitching ace, accumulated a 22-9 record for 1968, including 13 shutouts and 268 strikeouts as well as a 15-game winning streak and an almost unbelievable 1.12 earned run average in 304 innings pitched. The latter mark was a new major league record for a pitcher with at least 300 innings of work. His remarkable performance earned him the Cy Young as well as the league's MVP awards. In the first game of the Series against the Detroit Tigers he set a new Series high with 17 whiffs. A new single-day admission mark was set on June 23 in a double header against Atlanta, with 49,743 in attendance.

It was called "The year of the pitcher," as, in addition to Gibson's fantastic season, Denny McLain won 31 for the Detroit Tigers; Don Drysdale of the Los Angeles Dodgers hurled 58 $^2/_3$ innings of shutout ball; and Carl Yastrzemski of the Boston Red Sox won the batting championship in the American League with the lowest (.301) average ever to win the title in the history of the league.

Curt Flood's average was also .301, the Cardinals team high. Lou Brock hit .279 and led the league in doubles, with 46, triples, 14, and again in stolen bases, with 62. Flood and Gibson were named All-League; Gibson and Steve Carlton were All-Star game selections. Nelson Briles backed up Gibson's great year with a fine one of his own, at 19-11. Ray Washburne hurled the first no-hitter for the Cards in 27 years, beating San Francisco 2-0. In the World Series, Gibson had two wins and went into the finale against the Tiger's lefthander, Mickey Lolich, who also had two. Lolich out-dueled Gibson to claim the Championship.

The year 1969 began with the expansion of both leagues to 12 teams. In the National League, the lowly New York Mets rose from the depths of the second division to win the pennant, while the Cardinals fell from the top to fourth place.

Bob Gibson continued to be one of the dominant pitchers in baseball, winning 20 against 13 losses, with 269 strikeouts and a nifty 2.18 ERA. All-League selection Steve Carlton posted a 17-11 record, 210 strikeouts and a 2.17 ERA. No Cardinal hitter reached .300, but Lou Brock, who again led the loop in thefts, with 53, was close at .289. Joe Torre added a .289 mark with 101 RBIs, and Curt Flood was at .285.

For the second year in a row, Cardinal Manager Red Schoendienst was the All-Star game skipper. He was joined at the classic by his two pitching stars, Gibson and Carlton.

St. Louis dropped under the .500 mark to 76-86 in 1970 but tread water in the standings, remaining in fourth place, this time all by themselves. Both Joe Torre, who hit .325, and Lou Brock, who was at .304, topped 200 hits; Torre at 203, Brock right behind at 202. Dick Allen (who later became Richie) banged out 34 home runs, the most for a St. Louis player in 16 years. He also led the club with 101 RBIs. Bob Gibson, who won his second Cy Young award— the only St. Louis Cardinal pitcher ever to win the honor—had a sparkling 23-7 record and 274 strikeouts and was named All-League. He went to the All-Star squad along with Allen and Torre.

Prior to the season's start the Cardinals traded Curt Flood to Philadelphia. Flood refused to report, and subsequently sat out the entire season. His case eventually caused the death of baseball's reserve clause, binding a player to a team, and opened the door to the era of multimillion dollar salaries.

In 1971 the St. Louis team batting average of .275 led the National League, and the attack propelled the club up to second in the league's Eastern Division, seven games behind the Pittsburgh Pirates. The big gun in that attack was wielded by Joe Torre, now playing third base. Torre, who was named as the league's MVP, led the loop in hit-

Transcendental Graphics

Lou Brock

ting with a .363 average as well as in hits, with 230, RBIs, with 137, and total bases, with 352. He also pounded out 24 home runs. Matty Alou hit .315, Lou Brock hit .313 and catcher Ted Simmons was at .304. Brock also stole 64 bases and scored 126 runs to pace the league in both categories. He also had 200 hits.

On the hill, Steve Carlton took over as the Redbird ace, with a 20-9 record, while Bob Gibson slipped to 16-13 but hurled the first and only no-hitter of his career, beating Pittsburgh on August 14 by a 11-0 count. Both Carlton and Torre earned All-League honors; the two and Brock were voted to the All-Star squad. Manager Red Schoendienst completed his seventh straight season as the Cardinals mentor, a new team record. Brock also became the first player in league history to steal 50 or more bases for seven consecutive years.

Cardinals Top Ten in Hitting

(Through 1992 season)

Batting Average			Games		
1.	Rogers Hornsby	.359	1.	Stan Musial	3,026
2.	Johnny Mize	.336	2.	Lou Brock	2,289
3.	Joe Medwick	.335	3.	Enos Slaughter	1,820
4.	Stan Musial	.331	4.	Red Schoendienst	1,795
5.	Chick Hafey	.326	5.	Curt Flood	1,738
6.	Jim Bottomley	.325	6.	Ken Boyer	1,667
7.	Frankie Frisch	.312	7.	Ozzie Smith	1,625
8.	George Watkins	.309	8.	Rogers Hornsby	1,580
9.	Joe Torre	.308	9.	Julian Javier	1,578
10.	Rip Collins	.307	10.	Ted Simmons	1,564

The Downward Spiral

The Cardinals dropped 15 in the win column and more than 400,000 at the gate during the 1972 campaign. Bob Gibson improved his record to 19-11 and struck out 208, topping the 200 mark for the ninth straight year. He also reached a lifetime total of 2,786 strikeouts, a National League record for a righthander.

At the plate, Matty Alou led the club with a .314 average, followed by Lou Brock at .311 and Ted Simmons at .303. Brock again led the league in stolen bases, with 63. Despite the drop in fan turnout, the Cardinals' overall attendance figure reached fifty million. At the All-Star game, St. Louis representatives were Gibson, Brock, Joe Torre and Simmons.

Playing only .500 ball was enough to lift the Cardinals from fourth to second in the National League East during the 1973 season. Offensively, St. Louis was led by catcher Ted Simmons, who at .310 was the only Cardinal over .300. Simmons and Torre each had 13 homers to lead the team, but it was the lowest amount to lead the club in 30 years.

Lou Brock stole 70 bases to lead the league for the seventh time. His nine straight years with more than 50 thefts was a new major league mark, and his lifetime total reached 600. On the hill,

Rick Wise was 16-10 and Bob Gibson 12-10. Gibson struck out 142 and moved into second place on the all-time strikeout list. In the midsummer classic, Wise, Torre, and Simmons were the St. Louis representatives on the All-Star squad.

In 1974, for the second year in a row, St. Louis finished in second place in the National League East, but upped their win total to 86. The season marked the 10th consecutive year for Red Schoendienst as the team's manager. No other manager had ever led the club for as many as seven full years.

Lou Brock led the team again in stolen bases, this time with a new major league record 118, breaking Maury Wills's one-year mark. Bake McBride hit .309 and was named NL Rookie of the Year. Catcher Ted Simmons led the team in RBIs with 113, and Reggie Smith also hit .309. Bob Gibson struck out his 3,000th batter, only the second man in major league history to do so.

St. Louis and the New York Mets played a 25-inning battle before the Cards came out on top; it was the longest night game in history. Cardinals at the All-Star game were Simmons, Brock, Smith and pitcher Lynn McGlothen, who won 16 games, high on the team.

Bob Gibson retired after 17 years on the team, finishing with 251 wins. The future Hall-of-Famer was honored by a standing room only crowd of

50,548 on Bob Gibson Day, the largest regular season crowd in St. Louis history.

The Cards finished in a tie with the New York Mets for third place, 10 games behind the Pittsburgh Pirates. A quartet of Redbirds hit .300; Ted Simmons was second in the league with a .332 average; Lou Brock hit .309 and had 5-6 stolen bases; Reggie Smith was at .302 and Bake McBride at an even .300. Al Hrobosky had 13-3 as a reliever and tied for the league lead in saves with 22. Brock, Simmons and Smith were All-Star game picks.

Stumbling Along

The Cardinals won only 76 games in 1976, their lowest win total in 17 years, dropping to 5th place. That performance, plus a drop in attendance of nearly a half million, caused the retirement of manager Schoendienst. The redhead had been the Cardinals skipper for a record 12 years, compiling a win-loss mark of 1,010-925. (He would serve as an interim manager on two occasions in the future, in 1980 and 1990, bringing his win total to 1,042.) By way of comparison, the two leading managers in win totals before him, Branch Rickey and Frankie Frisch, won 458 and 457 respectively; Schoendienst had more than both of them combined.

During the season pitcher John Denny won the league's ERA title with a 2.52 mark, Lou Brock led the club in steals again, with 56, and hit .301, one of only two Redbirds over the .300 mark. Willie Crawford was the other, at .304, in his last year with the team.

Bake McBride was the only St. Louis player picked for the annual All-star game squad. Injuries limited him to only 272 at bats, and his .335 average did not count in the batting race.

Coach Vern Rapp took over as the Card's manager for the 1977 season, and the first-year skipper brought the club back up over .500 and into third place. Lou Brock broke Ty Cobb's lifetime record for stolen bases with number 893 on April 29. His theft total for the year, 35, was his lowest effort since he became a Cardinal, but it was still enough to lead the team for the 14th consecutive year.

Gary Templeton collected 200 hits for the 1978 team and led the league in triples with 18. He also hit a team high .322 and, along with teammate Ted Simmons, earned All-League and All-Star game honors. Third baseman Ken Reitz set a new fielding record for his position, commiting only 9 errors all season long. On the mound, Bob Forsch led the team with a 20-7 record.

The team sank to their worst record in 23 years in 1978 and Rapp was replaced after only 15 games and a 5-10 start. Coach Gary Krol took over for three games, winning two of them, before former star third baseman Ken Boyer was given the job.

One of the few highlights of the year took place on April 16 when Cardinals hurler Bob Forsch tossed a no hitter, beating the Philadelphia Phillies in Busch Stadium 5-0. Gary Templeton led the league again in triples, this time with 13. Ted Simmons, with All-League and All-Star game honors in his pocket, hit 22 home runs, the most ever for a Cardinal catcher.

In 1979 first baseman Keith Hernandez had his greatest year in the majors. He won the batting championship with a .344 mark, knocked in 105 runs, scored a league high 116 runs and hit a league high 48 doubles, got 210 hits and tied for the league's Most Valuable Player award with Pittsburgh's Willie Stargell. In his first full year at the helm, Manager Ken Boyer led the club to 86 wins, their best effort in five years.

For the third consecutive year Gary Templeton led the league in triples; his 19 were the highest total since 1946, when Stan Musial had 20. He also led the team in hits with 211. Ted Simmons broke his own homer mark for a catcher, hitting 26.

During the year Lou Brock collected his 3,000th hit, and later stole his 938th base, making him baseball's all-time stolen base king. All-League honors went to Hernandez, Simmons and Templeton; those three and Brock were All-Star game selections.

AP/Wide World Photos

Whitey Herzog

St. Louis had a total of four managers during the 1980 season, with Gary Krol and Red Schoendienst each filling in for the second time, and Whitey Herzog taking over for good at the end of the season along with the duties of general manager.

George Hendrick led the club in home runs, with 25, and runs batted in, with 109. 1979 MVP Keith Hernandez didn't repeat his 1979 figures, but he did lead the league in runs with 111 and the Cardinals in hitting with a .321 average.

Hendrick, Hernandez and Gary Templeton were named All-League; the first two and third baseman Ken Reitz were All-Star game selections. Reitz set another fielding mark at third, committing only 8 errors for the entire season.

Bringing The Trophy Back Home

The Cardinals had the best overall winning percentage for 1981; but because of the player strike and a season that was split into two halves, did not qualify for the playoffs. The seemingly impossible setup occurred when the Cards finished second in the first half of the season, before the strike, and second again in the second half, and yet their overall average was better than the teams that finished ahead of them in each half.

Dane Iorg was the Redbirds' top average hitter with a .327 mark. Bruce Sutter, obtained in a trade over the winter, won the Reliever of the Year award, and was the Cardinals only All-Star game participant.

Whitey Herzog stepped down as General Manager on Opening Day 1982, turning the job over to Joe McDonald. The Cards responded to the move, winning their first ever National League East Championship.

The team was characterized by an aggressive style of play, with seven players stealing bases in double figures, led by Lonnie Smith, who swiped 68. The team hit only 67 home runs, the fewest in the majors. At the turnstiles, the team climbed back up over two million for the first time in 14 years.

George Hendrick led the club in RBIs with 104, while Lonnie Smith led the league in runs with 120 and posted a .307 batting average. Reliever Bruce Sutter earned his second Relief Man of the Year award. The Smith Brothers, Ozzie at short and Lonnie in the outfield, earned All-League and All-Star game honors.

In the Series, the Cards came back from a 3-2 deficit in games to defeat the Milwaukee Brewers and bring the Championship trophy back to St. Louis for the first time in 15 years. Joaquin Andujar won two games and Sutter added another and a save. John Stuper became only the 14th rookie in baseball history to start two World Series games. Dane Iorg hit .529 and tied a Series record for hits by a designated hitter, and catcher Darrell Porter was named Series MVP.

Despite the fact that the Cardinals dropped all the way to fourth place in 1983, a new attendance record was set at 2,317,914. As a team, the Redbirds set a new club record with 207 stolen bases. George Hendrick, who moved from the outfield to first base after Keith Hernandez was traded, led the team for the fourth straight year in runs batted in, this time with 97, and also led the club in batting average with a .321 mark.

On the hill the big news was Bob Forsch's second no hitter, a 3-0 win over Montreal on September 26. Hendrick was the only Card All-League selection, and was joined on the All-Star game squad by Ozzie Smith and Willie McGee.

Fighting For Survival

The following year, the team showed a slight improvement over their 1983 performance, winning five more games and moving up a notch in the standings to third. Although no Cardinal hit as high as .300 or was among the leaders in any offensive category, shortstop Ozzie Smith was again recognized for his defensive ability and was voted All-League. On the hill, relief ace Bruce Sutter was again voted Reliever of the Year, and Joaquin Andujar posted a 20-14 record as a starter.

Outfielder Willie McGee was the catalyst leading the St. Louis Cardinals to the National League pennant in 1985. The team won 101 games, the sixth time they had topped the century mark in their long history. McGee was voted the National League's Most Valuable Player after leading the league in hitting at .353, in hits with 216 and in triples, with 18. Tommy Herr led the club in RBIs with 110. All of this success generated a great

AP/Wide World Photos

Displaying his acrobatic abilities, Ozzie Smith throws to first to complete a double play while jumping to avoid Andy Van Slyke's hard slide into second base.

AP/Wide World Photos

Lee Smith

gate, with a new attendance record of of 2,637,563 set.

First-year man Vince Coleman led the loop in steals with 110, the most ever for a rookie in either league, and was chosen Rookie of the Year. McGee, Herr and Ozzie Smith were named All-League; pitcher Joaquin Andujar, Jack Clark, Herr, McGee and Ozzie Smith made it to the All-Star game, Andujar posted a 21-12 record; John Tudor was at 21-8.

The Cards took the National League Championship Series from the Dodgers 4-2. Against Kansas City in the World Series they won the first two games on the road in Kansas City, but then dropped four of the next five when their hitting deserted them. In the sixth game the Cards took a 1-0 lead into the ninth, but a disputed call was enough to open the door for the Royals, who scored twice to take the win. Game seven was no

contest—11-0 Kansas City.

The defending National League Champs stumbled out of the gate in 1986. After the first two months of the season they had the worst record in the league. But the team righted itself and posted winning records during each of the next four months to finish third in the East.

Vince Coleman stole 107 bases to become the first player to ever steal 100 bases twice. Ozzie Smith won his seventh straight Gold Glove and Todd Worrell was named 1986 Rookie of the Year. He had a rookie record 36 saves and became the first player to lead the league in saves and to win rookie of the year honors.

The club topped the two-million mark for the fifth consecutive year and drew their 75 millionth fan since 1900. Smith was named All-League; he and Tommy Herr were the St. Louis players on the annual All-Star game squad.

The Injury Curse

Plagued by a rash of injuries to key players all through 1987, the Cardinals still managed to battle their way to another National League pennant. Whitey Herzog made use of a mixture of veterans and rookies. Several Cardinals enjoyed banner years.

Vince Coleman had his third straight year over 100 stolen bases. Jack Clark banged out 35 home runs and 106 runs batted in and led the league in slugging with a .597 mark. His homer total was the most for a Cardinal since Stan Musial hit the same number in 1954. He also set Cardinal records in striking out 139 times, and in drawing walks, 136.

Lonnie Smith led the team in doubles with 40 and hit .303. John Tudor posted an 11-2 record on the hill, good for a .833 winning percentage, the best in the league for the year and the highest in Cardinal history. For the first time the team passed three million at the gate, totalling 3,072,121 for the year. Ozzie Smith and Jack Clark won All-Star game and All-League honors; Willie McGee was also an All-Star game pick.

After coming back from a 3-2 deficit to win the National League Championship Series against San Francisco, the Cards got off to a bad start by dropping the first two games of the World Series at Minnesota. Returning to Busch Stadium, the Cards won three in a row. In game six the Redbirds took a 5-2 lead into the 5th inning, but were snowed under by the Twins and lost, 11-5. In the finale, Series MVP Frank Viola allowed only two second inning runs and Minnesota won, 4-2, for its first World Championship.

The defending National League champs struggled with injuries and a lack of offense in the early part of the 1988 season and never recovered. After picking up slugging outfielder Tom Brunansky in an April trade with Minnesota, St. Louis climbed back to within six games of the lead on June 12. Injuries to Bob Horner and Terry Pendelton crippled the team's attack and they dropped 19 games off the pace by the end of July.

Several pitchers had fine seasons, including newcomer Jose DeLion, who became the first Redbird pitcher since 1972 to strike out 200. Joe Magrane won the league ERA title with a 2.18 mark and won 15 games. Todd Worrell posted his third straight 30-save season, and Vince Coleman won the stolen base title for the fourth consecutive year. Another rookie, Jose Oquendo, became the first National League player since 1918 to play all nine positions in a season.

The Cardinals drew nearly 2.9 million fans, despite their fifth place finish. The largest crowd in St. Louis history, 51,647, saw the Cardinals-Pittsburgh game on April 8. All-Star game selections were Coleman, Worrell, Ozzie Smith and Willie McGee.

The same injury bug that crippled the team in 1988 struck again in 1989, but the team fought it off, winning 10 more games and moving up to third. The team was in the race right up until the final week of the season and in fact pulled to within a half game of the lead at one point. The improvement was reflected at the gate and a new attendance mark of 3,080,980 was set.

Pedro Guerrero led the team in RBIs with 117, led the league in doubles and hit .311. Jose Oquedo played in 163 games, the most ever for a Cardinal, and had a 23-game hitting streak. Vince Coleman swiped 63 bases to lead the league for the fifth time. On the hill, Joe Magrane won 18 and Jose DeLeon had 201 strikcouts. Coleman, Guer-rero and catcher Tony Pena were All-Star game picks. The season ended on a sad note when team owner August Busch died at age 90.

Herzog called it quits in 1990 after more than a decade at the helm. Coach Red Schoendienst took over again on an interim basis until Joe Torre was named as the new skipper. The team's last-place finish was their first in the basement since 1918.

Willie McGee led the league in hitting with a .335 average but was traded in August. Rookie catcher Todd Sell led the team in homers with 15. John Tudor made a comeback from arm woes and won 12 games, but retired at the end of the season.

Vince Coleman led the league in steals again, his seventh straight, this time with 77, and had a career high .292 batting average. Reliever Lee Smith, picked up in May, led the team in saves with 27. Jose Oquendo set a major league mark in fielding at second. Ozzie Smith was the only Cardinal on the All-Star squad.

The Cardinals were one of 1991's biggest surprises, shooting all the way up to second place in the National League East after finishing dead last the year before. Joe Torre, in his first full year at the helm, opened the season with a number of unproved players in key roles. Two of them were Ray Lankford and Felix Jose.

Lankford led the league in triples and had a team high 44 stolen bases. Emphasizing the running game, St. Louis had nine players with 10 or more thefts, the first time since 1917 that such a feat had been accomplished. Jose led the team in average at .305 and had 40 doubles. Todd Zeile moved from catcher to third base and led the team in home runs with 11 and RBIs with 81.

On the pitching staff, Lee Smith set a loop record with 47 saves, but injuries hit just about everyone else, and 12 wins by Bryn Smith topped the team. Lee Smith was also the team's only All-League pick; he, Jose and Ozzie Smith were named to the All-Star squad.

Although the team lost a number of players to various ailments in the first part of the 1992 season, they held a slim half-game lead after the first two months. Then chicken pox, of all things, side-lined team leader Ozzie Smith and the team began to slide.

Ray Lankford became the first Cardinal since 1967 to hit 20 home runs and steal 20 bases in the same year. Ozzie Smith earned his 12th All-Star game berth and his 13th Gold Glove award. He also chalked up his 2,000th base hit and 500th stolen base. Bob Tewksbury won 16 and was second in the league in ERA with a 2.18 mark. Lee Smith again led the league in saves, with 43. He, Ozzie Smith, Tewksbury, and Tom Pagnozzi were All-Star game selections.

—Jack Pearson

NATIONAL LEAGUE EAST

FLORIDA MARLINS

On April 5, 1993, a full house at Miami's Joe Robbie Stadium welcomed the Florida Marlins, the Sunshine State's first year-round major league baseball club. One of two expansion franchises awarded in 1991, the Marlins play in a densely populated region of southern Florida that includes large cities like Fort Lauderdale and Miami as well as vast suburban districts and smaller coastal towns. The citizens of the area are thrilled with their ball club, but the decision to locate a franchise in Florida was based not on mere enthusiasm but rather on firm business principles. As the only major league team in the state, the Marlins can hope to draw customers from a fan pool of more than four million Americans—with another 100,000 arriving every year.

The Marlins and their Denver counterpart, the Colorado Rockies, are the first expansion teams to enter the major leagues since 1977. Many American cities vied for the opportunity to win these coveted franchises. South Florida's winning proposal was largely the effort of H. Wayne Huizenga, a canny businessman who has made several fortunes in the course of a busy life. Huizenga, founder of the successful Blockbuster Video stores, beat stiff competition for the new National League ball club when he essentially offered to bankroll the team himself—a phenomenal accomplishment considering the fact that the franchise fee alone was $95 million. Huizenga did not solicit the team out of nostalgia or sentimentality. A pragmatic executive, he felt that South Florida will offer the ideal location for an extremely profitable baseball enterprise.

With his eye fixed firmly on profits, Huizenga could be expected to mount an aggressive campaign for a winning team. Expansion franchises as a rule take years to establish themselves as contenders. Huizenga hoped to speed up the process, thus assuring that he would continue to pack Joe Robbie Stadium after the novelty of having a team has worn off.

Residents of Florida are no strangers to major league baseball. Virtually since the turn of the century, teams have taken advantage of the state's climate for the important annual ritual of spring training. Cities like Miami and Fort Lauderdale have played springtime host to major league clubs that prepare for the regular season by mounting practice contests and lengthy conditioning sessions.

At best, however, spring training is only a tease; its low-key matchups don't count on season records. Veterans and superstars often pace themselves to avoid injuries, leaving the more dramatic action to hopeful prospects and threatened rookies. These characteristics notwithstanding, spring training baseball has always proven popular in Florida. It is both a tourist attraction and an essential rite of spring for Floridians. Its lasting popularity was one factor Huizenga could cite to prove that summer baseball would find fans in the state.

Minor league baseball has also been a Florida staple. Miami, for instance, has been represented in various minor leagues by teams such as the Tourists, the Whaoos, the Flamingos, the Sun Sox, and the Amigos. In 1956 legendary baseball promoter Bill Veeck introduced the Miami Marlins, a triple-A franchise from Syracuse, New York.

This Marlins team lasted four years at Miami Stadium. One of its stars was Satchel Paige, the famous Negro League pitcher who was still playing ball in his fifties. Paige was the starting pitcher on a night when the Marlins drew 51,713 fans to the Orange Bowl for a charity benefit game.

By the 1980s the various triple-A franchises had left South Florida, and the region's professional baseball consisted of a Class-A Florida State League. Miami's entry in that league was the Orioles. This later proved particularly appropriate because the Baltimore Orioles would come to use Miami as a spring training base. Prior to the arrival of the Marlins, in fact, the Orioles served as Miami's unofficial major league team, with nightly local radio coverage and frequent television coverage of games from Baltimore.

At first glance Florida seems an unlikely locale for a game played outside during the hottest months of the year. No one would have considered placing a major league team near Miami in, say, the 1920s, when much of the nation's population was in the northeastern states and California. Times have changed, however; retirees have moved to Florida in droves, and with them have moved legions of opportunists ready to serve them. Today Florida ranks fourth in population among America's 50 states, passed only by California, Texas, and New York. The dense concentration of people along both of Florida's coasts offers an attractive lure to those who want to invest in major league sports.

One such investor was Wayne Huizenga. Huizenga (pronounced "*high*-zinga") grew up in Chicago but spent his teenage years in Fort Lauderdale. The son of a Dutch immigrant carpenter, Huizenga finished high school in Florida and then drifted through a stint in the Army and several jobs in Chicago before returning to the South to seek his fortune. In 1962, at the age of 25, he bought a trash hauling truck and a client list from a garbage collector near Fort Lauderdale.

Huizenga drove the truck and collected the trash himself at first, but as the population of South Florida boomed, so did his business. His one-truck enterprise soon blossomed into Southern Sanitation, one of Florida's largest trash-disposal companies. In 1971 Huizenga joined forces with a Chicago relative to found Waste Management, Inc., an international conglomerate specializing in the disposal of household waste, chemical waste, asbestos, and radioactive waste. A $7.5 billion enterprise, Waste Management also contracts to clean up hazardous-waste sites all over the world.

Huizenga retired from the presidency of Waste Management in 1984 and moved from Chicago to Fort Lauderdale. Not satisfied in retirement, he founded Huizenga Holdings and bought more than 100 companies in a three-year span. One of those companies was a small Texas retailer of videotapes, Blockbuster Video.

When Huizenga bought into Blockbuster, it consisted of 19 stores, all in Texas. He expanded nationwide, buying other video chains and opening new stores, and within three years Blockbuster

TEAM INFORMATION AT A GLANCE

Founding date: July 5, 1991

Home stadium: Joe Robbie Stadium
2269 NW 199th St.
Miami, FL 33056
Phone (305) 623-6100
Seating capacity: 42,334

Team colors: Teal and white
Team nickname: Marlins
Logo: Leaping fish

Franchise record	Won	Lost	Pct.
(1993)	64	98	.395

became the dominant name in the videotape rental and sales industry. The success of Blockbuster catapulted Huizenga into the highest ranks of American wealth, landing him in the 151st spot on the *Forbes* 400 list for individuals.

In Fort Lauderdale Huizenga socialized with another prominent Floridian, Joe Robbie, who owned the Miami Dolphins football team and the stadium in which they played. Joe Robbie Stadium is that rare facility that was built entirely with private funds (Dade County leases the land for $1 a year). The park was completed in 1987 at a cost of $115 million.

Ever the optimist, Robbie saw to it that his stadium could accommodate a big-league baseball field comfortably, even though he signed an agreement to stage no more than 18 events per year in the facility. He hoped someday to lure a major league baseball team to the arena.

Joe Robbie died in January of 1990 with his finances in relative disarray. Huizenga began negotiations with the Robbie family to buy the stadium. Finally, in June of 1990, Huizenga acquired a 50 percent share of Joe Robbie Stadium plus 15 percent of the Dolphins. Shortly thereafter he announced his commitment to bringing major league baseball to South Florida.

Just months after Huizenga bought into Joe Robbie Stadium, a consortium of National League owners announced that the league would add two expansion teams in time to begin play in 1993. The owners formed an Expansion Committee and solicited expansion applications from interested parties.

The price tag was steep: $95 million just to buy the franchise. Potential owners would also have to pay all start-up costs for the team salaries for players, executives, scouts, and minor league personnel; purchase of equipment and office space; and other expenses. These could add at least another $30 million to the tab. Furthermore, the would-be owners were asked to provide a new stadium facility expressly for baseball as well as a convincing argument for solid fan support in their chosen location.

Huizenga faced competition not only from

such cities as Washington, D.C., Buffalo, and Denver, but also from right in his own back yard. Most observers agreed that Florida would get a franchise—the population numbers alone made a clear case for baseball in the Sunshine State.

Where that franchise would play was another matter. Orlando was one possibility. Another was St. Petersburg on the Gulf Coast. St. Petersburg seemed to have a distinct advantage: at taxpayer expense, the city had constructed a state-of-the-art, domed stadium just in hopes of luring a major league baseball team. On several occasions ownership groups in the city had come close to buying an existing major league franchise.

On September 18, 1990, the National League Expansion Committee heard presentations from all of the applicants for the two new franchises. All told, three potential investment groups from South Florida gave presentations. First the Miami Beacon Council gave a neutral report on the basic strengths of South Florida for baseball—its population, weather, and average income, among other things. Then each potential ownership group was given a chance to present its case. When Huizenga's turn came, he went to work with all the energy he had shown throughout his career.

In *Playing Hardball: The High-Stakes Battle for Baseball's New Franchises,* David Whitford wrote of that pivotal presentation: "By all accounts, Wayne was charming, forceful, a one-man show.... He said he would be happy to find a partner, or partners, if that's what baseball wanted, but at the same time he assured them that no such partner was needed, that even at $95 million he was prepared to do this deal alone. With cash, that was the key; he promised to sell stock, rather than borrow, in order to meet his obligations. And toward the end of the allotted half hour, as he was handing over a copy of the presentation book ... he jokingly offered to write a check for the full amount then and there." Whitford concluded: "The owners were impressed as hell."

On December 18, 1990, the Expansion Committee released its short list of contenders for the new franchises. Huizenga's group in South Florida made the cut, but so did groups in St. Petersburg and Orlando.

The next hurdle was an official visit by the Expansion Committee, whose purpose was to examine stadium facilities and other amenities in each potential major league site. The Committee arrived in South Florida on February 25, 1991, toured Joe Robbie Stadium, and took a helicopter ride across the four-county region that would be served by the ball club. Committee concerns about the open-air stadium in Miami were allayed by Huizenga, who asserted that he would be willing to build a dome over the facility if the local weather proved too inclement for summer baseball.

Further proof of regional support for the team was provided the following month, when the Baltimore Orioles and New York Yankees played two spring training games at Joe Robbie Stadium. The two-day event drew 125,013 fans, including a 67,654 sellout the first night (a spring training record).

Summer approached, and fans all over Florida waited impatiently for news from the National League Expansion Committee. Finally, on June 10, 1991, the word arrived that the Committee would recommend South Florida as the site of one of the new franchises. The National League owners voted unanimously to support the recommendation, and on July 5, 1991, the Florida Marlins were born.

Headlines in the next day's *Miami Herald* proclaimed: "GREAT CATCH! The Marlins Are Florida's Team." Accompanying pictures showed Huizenga celebrating with the area's business and political leaders. They had reason to smile. Apart from those in St. Petersburg and Orlando who were passed over—and a contingent in Miami that resented the name "*Florida* Marlins"—everyone in the state was enthusiastic.

The lack of a baseball-only stadium facility did not hamper Huizenga's cause. The ordinance limiting the usage of Joe Robbie Stadium had been repealed by the Dade County government. The facility would be upgraded with new dugouts, a new pitcher's mound, new clubhouses, and a new warning track. Still, Huizenga negotiated only a short-term lease with the arena, keeping his options open to construct a new ballpark as needed.

The enthusiasm deepened when the team's founder realized he had almost two years in which to recruit personnel and lay the foundations for the club. Previous expansion teams sometimes had to take the field within months after winning franchise rights. The extra time would give Huizenga's staff ample opportunity to scout talent throughout the major and minor leagues before making draft decisions.

Huizenga still acted quickly. Within days he had hired Carl Barger, president of the Pittsburgh Pirates, to be president of the Marlins. Barger and Huizenga were old friends, but the decision was a sound one from a business standpoint. The amiable Barger had spearheaded a drive to keep the Pirates in Pittsburgh in 1984 and then had led the club back to prominence in the National League East. He was the first of numerous executives who spoke enthusiastically about the opportunity to build a ball club completely from scratch.

Other executive positions were filled in the autumn of 1991. General manager Dave Dombrowski was recruited from the Montreal Expo organization, where he had been named UPI Major League Executive of the Year in 1990. Dombrowski then literally raided the Expo front offices, hiring Gary Hughes as scouting director, John Boles as farm director, Frank Wren as assistant general manager, and Angel Vasquez as director of Latin American Operations, to name just a few.

From the Pirates organization came Richard Andersen, vice-president of business operations, and Dean Jordan, vice-president of communications. Local interests were represented by Jonathan Mariner, who became vice-president of finance after years with the Greater Miami Chamber of Commerce, and Donald A. Smiley from South Florida Big League Baseball—the committee charged with coordinating franchise application activities.

As first-ever manager, the Marlins chose Rene Lachemann. Lachemann came to Florida from Oakland, where he had served as a first-base and third-base coach. Most of Lachemann's playing career had been spent in the minor leagues,

with the exception of a season at Kansas City in 1965. After retiring as a player in 1972, he managed a succession of minor league teams culminating in a stint as skipper of the Seattle Mariners from 1981 until 1984. In 1985-86 he had coached with the Red Sox organization. One of Lachemann's first moves as Marlins manager was to name his brother Marcel pitching coach.

Marlins minor league play began in 1992 with teams in the Class-A New York-Penn League and the Gulf Coast rookie league. The Marlins' first contract offer went to 16-year-old Clemente Nunez of the Dominican Republic, a right-handed pitcher who reported to the Gulf Coast League. The amateur draft in June of 1992 brought Charles Johnson, a catcher from the University of Miami who subsequently earned a spot on the Marlins' big-league roster.

As the Erie (Pennsylvania) Sailors farm team played the first professional baseball under the Marlins umbrella in the summer of 1992, Dombrowski and his staff prepared for the all-important Expansion Draft. This was the draft that would allow both the Marlins and the Colorado Rockies to select unprotected players from each of the existing major league franchises.

For the first time in history, the expansion teams were allowed to draw talent from both leagues. The established clubs protected 15 players for the first round of the draft, then 18 players (National League) and 19 players (American League) in the second round. The Expansion Draft was held on November 17, 1992. The Rockies and Marlins chose alternately. A total of 72 players were drafted in this manner.

Top Marlins draft selections included outfielder Nigel Wilson from the Toronto Blue Jays, right-handed pitcher Jose Martinez from the Mets, infielder Bret Barberi from the Expos, right-handed pitcher Trevor Hoffman from the Reds, right-handed pitcher Patrick Rapp from the Giants, and left-handed pitcher Greg Hibbard from the White Sox. Hibbard was later traded to the Cubs for infielders Gary Scott and Alex Arias.

Other notable Marlins expansion draft picks include Jeff Conine from the Royals, Carl Everett from the Yankees, Jim Corsi from the Oakland Athletics, and Danny Jackson from the Pirates. Jackson was subsequently traded to the Phillies for left-handed pitchers Joel Adamson and Matt Whisenant.

The Marlins received further strength from the addition of several seasoned major league veterans. Infielder Dave Magaden, formerly with the Mets, signed as a free agent in December of 1992. Infielder Walt Weiss arrived in a trade with the Oakland Athletics, and renowned knuckleball pitcher Charlie Hough signed a one-year contract. For Hough, who began pitching in the big leagues in 1970, the Marlins deal allowed him to play at the major league level just miles from his birthplace in Hialeah, Florida.

Just as all seemed ready for the first Marlin season, tragedy struck. On December 9, 1992, Carl Barger was stricken with a fatal heart attack at the baseball winter meetings in Louisville, Kentucky. A stunned Huizenga decided not to replace Barger during the 1993 season, so the Marlins began their playing history without a president.

That playing history began gloriously on April 5, 1993. Clad in their teal green pinstriped home uniforms with the leaping fish logo, the Marlins took the field before a roaring capacity crowd at Joe Robbie Stadium. Hough was the starting pitcher, and his first pitch was—no surprise—a knuckleball. The Marlins went on to win the contest 6-3 over the Los Angeles Dodgers. The Marlin victory raised the team record to 1-0. The Dodgers fell to 7,506-6,849. Opening Day souvenirs sold out an hour before the game began.

Despite a late-season swoon, the Marlins proved surprisingly competitive for an expansion club, finishing 64-98, good for sixth place in the seven-team National League East Division. Closer Brian Harvey had 45 saves, third best in the National League, and set a major-league record by recording a win or a save in 71.9 percent of the Mariners' wins.

Shortstop Walt Weiss was a defensive stalwart, and two rookies, Jeff Conine and Chuck Carr, had impressive seasons. Conine batted .292 with 12 home runs and 79 runs batted in, while Carr had a National League-leading 58 stolen bases and thrilled fans with his acrobatic catches in centerfield. During the season, the Marlins acquired all-star third baseman Gary Sheffield, who added a strong bat to the lineup.

As with any expansion team, the Marlins face a tough task. Virtually starting from scratch, they must compete with clubs that have been in existence since the nineteenth century, clubs laden with mystique, clubs basking in the largesse of bullish owners, and clubs with tried-and-true farm programs.

Sports Illustrated reporter Tim Kurkjian concluded that the Marlins "are not blessed with an abundance of talented players." On the other hand, Huizenga should prove to be an aggressive owner, and Dombrowski has firsthand experience of what it takes to strengthen a team.

In the meantime, the Marlins' novelty is sure to attract plenty of customers, at least through the mid-1990s. Wayne Huizenga's team name reflects the trend toward regional, rather than city-based, emphasis for major league baseball franchises—testament to the hopes that an entire state of sports fans will come to love that leaping fish.

SOURCES

BOOKS

Whitford, David, *Playing Hardball: The High-Stakes Battle for Baseball's New Franchises,* Doubleday, 1993.

PERIODICALS

Sports Illustrated, April 12, 1993.

—*Anne Janette Johnson*

MONTREAL EXPOS

For decades Montreal was one of the two Canadian cities, Toronto being the other, that made the International League international. The Montreal Royals, as they were called, gained prominence in the late 1940s as the top farm team of Branch Rickey's Brooklyn Dodgers.

Jackie Robinson broke professional baseball's color barrier playing for the Montreal Royals in 1946. Robinson won the batting title that year and moved on to star for Brooklyn. Other black players followed: Roy Campanella, Don Newcombe, Sam Jethroe.

In the early 1950s the Royals' star pitcher was Tommy Lasorda. But when Los Angeles acquired the Dodger franchise, the team's Triple-A farm club was moved to Spokane, and after the 1960 season the Montreal Royals faded from the scene.

Attendance had always been good in Montreal, one of the largest cities in North America, and it surprised no one when the city, the home of the Expo 67 world's fair, was awarded an expansion franchise in the National League for the 1969 season. This was the first year of divisional play, and predictably, the new Montreal Expos finished last. They played in Jarry Park, a temporary stadium built to accommodate the new ball club.

The Expos moved out of the cellar quite quickly, finishing fifth, ahead of Philadelphia, in 1971 and 1972. Then in 1973, still under their original manager, Gene Mauch, the Expos found themselves in contention for the pennant. They ultimately finished fourth, but they seemed to have enough talent, especially in outfielder Ken Singleton and pitcher Steve Rogers, to suggest that the usual expansion blues might already be behind them.

Such optimism proved premature, however, as the Expos sank from fourth place in 1974 to a tie for fifth in 1975 and then to last place, with 107 losses, in 1976. The team hired hard-nosed Dick Williams as manager, and things began looking up. In the strike-shortened, split season of 1981, the Expos finished first in the second half, won a playoff against the Phillies, and were crowned division champions—their only title to date. They lost the National League Championship Series to Los Angeles.

After that the Expos went into a decline, but recovered in 1987 under third-year manager Buck Rodgers to finish at 91-71, good for third place, just four games behind the Pennant-winning Cardinals. The 1987 team was sparked by third baseman Tim Wallach, outfielder Tim Raines, and first baseman Andres Galarraga. On the mound, veteran Oriole pitcher Dennis Martinez proved a valuable acquisition.

The team finished at exactly .500 in 1988 and 1989, rose a bit in 1990, then skidded to the cellar, 26 and a half games out, in 1991. Just as optimism had been premature in the 1970s, now pessimism seemed unwarranted. The 1992 Expos finished at 87-75, in second place, and looked as good as they ever had in their history.

Better Than the 1962 Mets

Jarry Park, built as a makeshift home for the Expos, had a seating capacity of only 28,000. It was still unfinished for the opening game on April 14, 1969, when an overflow crowd poured in to greet Montreal's new major league team. The fans were not disappointed, witnessing a wild 8-7 Expo victory over the defending NL champion St. Louis Cardinals. It was one of only 52 wins for the Expos that year under manager Gene Mauch, as the team fin ished in last place, losing 110 games, and trailing the league-leading New York Mets—themselves a recent product of expansion—by 48 games.

The Expos could take heart from the Mets' success, because only seven years earlier the hapless New Yorkers had suffered though a 40-120 season, the worst in modern baseball history, considerably below the '69 Expos' 51-110. Still, last place was last place, and while the 1970 Expos showed clear improvement by winning 73 games,

they remained in the cellar. A young Montreal pitcher, Carl Morton, turned in an impressive 18-11 won-lost record, but his success proved much more transitory than Jarry Park (which served the Expos for eight years). Morton spent only two more seasons at Montreal, both dismal, before being dealt to the Atlanta Braves.

Outfielder Rusty Staub, acquired from Houston in a January 1969 trade, had a pretty fair year at the plate in 1970, banging out 23 doubles, seven triples, 30 homers, and driving in 94 runs. After another good year in 1971, in which he batted .311 with 19 homers and 97 RBIs, the Expos traded him to the Mets for outfielder Ken Singleton, first baseman Mike Jorgensen, and infielder Tim Foli.

Montreal finished fifth in 1971, one rung up from the basement. In 1972 their three acquisitions for Rusty Staub all played regularly, but they made no difference in the standings, as the Expos again came in fifth, well ahead of the floundering Phillies.

Pursuing the Pennant

Expansion teams in their fifth year are not expected to make a run for the flag, but the Montreal Expos did, mainly because the 1973 National League East race was such a curious one. None of the teams played much above .500. The New York Mets, who eventually finished first, had an 82-79 record, .509. Merely breaking even put a team in contention, and the Expos almost broke even, finishing in fourth place at 79-83.

Outfielder Ken Singleton had a fine year, batting .302, hitting 23 homers, and driving in 103 runs—the first Expo to top 100 RBIs, although Staub had come close. Veteran third baseman Bob Bailey, an Expo from the beginning, having originally been purchased from the LA Dodgers, had a career-high 88 RBIs, along with 26 homers to lead the team in that category. Pitcher Steve Renko, a rookie in the Class of '69, enjoyed his best season, 15-11 with a 2.81 ERA. Reliever Mike Marshall appeared in 92 games, a major

TEAM INFORMATION AT A GLANCE

Founding date: April 14, 1969

Home stadium: Olympic Stadium
4549 Pierre-de-Coubertin Avenue
Montreal, Quebec H1V 3N7 Canada
Phone: (514) 253-3434

Dimensions: Left-field line—325 feet
Center field—404 feet
Right-field line—325 feet
Seating capacity: 60,011

Team uniforms: home—base color white, with blue pinstripes
Road—base color gray, with red, white, and blue trim
Team nickname: Expos, 1969—
Team logo: Stylized script letter "M" with left half in
red-and-white, right half in blue

Franchise record	Won	Lost	Pct.
(1969-1993)	1,948	2,034	.489

National League East first-place finishes (1): 1981
League/division last-place finishes (4): 1969, 1970, 1976, 1991

league record, won 14, lost 11, saved 31, and posted a 2.66 ERA. Rookie Steve Rogers attracted notice with a 10-5 record and a 1.54 ERA.

The 1973 Expos were a competitive ball club, and attendance at little Jarry Park continued to reflect the enthusiasm of Montreal's fans. Over the first five years (through 1973), paid admissions at Jarry Park averaged better than 1,250,000 per season—in a facility seating 28,000.

After finishing the 1973 season only three and a half games back, the Expos were guardedly hopeful about 1974. The acquisition of outfielder Willie Davis from Los Angeles added strength in the outfield, but the player they traded for him, reliever Mike Marshall, subtracted from their mound staff.

Once again the Expos finished in fourth place with a won-lost record virtually identical to that of 1973. Mike Torrez paced the pitchers with a 15-8 mark, while Steve Rogers suffered a sophomore jinx and ended at 15-22. Gene Mauch, one of the most respected non-winning managers in baseball history, still held his job as he had from the outset, but the next season would end that.

The Expos' 1975 outfield no longer featured Ken Singleton (sent to Baltimore in an ill-advised trade) or Willie Davis (off to Texas in an equally bad swap). They did have a promising young

Olympic Stadium, built for the 1976 Olympics, was supposed to have a retractable roof. It was designed with that in mind, and a gigantic roof umbrella tower—unfinished—rises in the deep reaches of center field. The retractable roof, an excellent idea in often-frigid Montreal, proved too costly for the city to afford. Officials talked about installing a permanent roof, like that on Houston's Astrodome, but discovered that the stadium itself was not strong enough to hold the weight of Montreal's heavy winter snows on a fixed roof. Consequently, when the stadium opened for the first Expos' game on April 15, 1977, it lacked a roof, and presumably always will.

On April 20, 1977, in the sixth game at Olympic Stadium, catcher Gary Carter belted three homers in a game against the Pittsburgh Pirates, the first Expo to do so. It was in a losing cause, as Pittsburgh scored eight times to win the game, 8-6. On September 10, 1980, rookie right-hander Bill Gullickson struck out 18 Chicago Cub batters at the Stadium, an Expo record. Next year, on May 6, 1981, the Expos tied a National League record when three batters—Mike Gates, Tim Raines, and Tim Wallach—hit successive triples. It happened in the ninth inning of a losing cause, as San Diego won the game, 13-5. Just four days later, on May 10, 1981, Expo pitcher Charlie Lea tossed the first no-hitter in Olympic Stadium, shutting down the San Francisco Giants, 4-0.

One of the most memorable events in the early days of Olympic Stadium was not a happy one. In 1981 the Expos made it into the National League Championship Series—their only time—by defeating the Phillies in a split-season playoff. The Los Angeles Dodgers, their opponents in the five-game NLCS, arrived in Montreal with the series tied one game to one. After four games it was tied two to two. Then on October 19, in the crucial fifth game, the Expos and Dodgers were tied 1-1 going into the ninth inning. Manager Jim Fanning pulled his starting pitcher Ray Burris and sent in his ace, Steve Rogers, to hold the line. Instead, with two men out Rogers served up a fat pitch to Rick Monday, and the oh-so-near Montreal Pennant disappeared into the seats; the Dodgers won, 2-1, thwarting the first real chance for a World Series to come to Canada.

---

catcher, Gary Carter, up from Memphis of the International League. In 1975 Carter, dividing his time between catching and playing the outfield, batted .270 with 17 homers and a team-leading 68 RBIs. Only two Expo pitchers won in double figures: Steve Rogers (11-12) and reliever Dale Murray (15-8). The 1975 Expos tied the Chicago Cubs for last place, and Gene Mauch departed to take over the Minnesota Twins.

Karl Kuehl took the helm in 1976, to be replaced by Charlie Cox late in the season, when it became glaringly apparent that the Expos were on their way to a season reminiscent of their first-year expansion-team effort. None of the regulars batted even .280; the Expos' leading hitter was young outfielder Ellis Valentine at .279.

The power, such as it was, came from third baseman Larry Parrish, whose 11 homers led the team. Parrish's 61 RBIs were also a team high. Gary Carter slid to .219 with six homers and 38 RBIs. The Expos finished last with a 55-107 record, 46 games behind division-leading Philadelphia. Attendance reached it lowest ebb.

Winning With Williams

A new approach seemed necessary. Dick Williams, fired the previous season from the California Angels after a shouting match with .208-hitter Bill Melton—applied for the manager's job with the Expos. He noticed "a farm system stocked with good players thanks to recent top draft picks" and decided that "Montreal seemed like a great place to call."

Williams took over the team in 1977. He inherited not only some promising young ball-players but also a sparkling new cookie-cutter stadium. Jarry Park, which had served "tempo-rarily" for almost a decade, lost its tenants to Olympic Stadium. Built for the 1976 Olympics, the new stadium cost $770 million but, even so, lacked the retractable roof that had been planned and promised. A crowd of 57,592 turned out on April 15, 1977, for the first game on the park's bright green artificial turf. The Phillies won, 7-2.

Manager Williams had a lineup with both power and potential, but the Expo pitching staff still needed attention. In the off-season the Expos had acquired slugging first baseman Tony Perez from the Cincinnati Reds, and he responded with

a solid output, batting .283 with 19 homers and 91 RBIs. Outfielder Andre Dawson, in his first full season in the majors, hit .282 with 19 homers and 65 RBIs. Ellis Valentine and Warren Cromartie joined Dawson in the outfield, Valentine slam-ming 25 homers and driving in 76 runs. Catcher Gary Carter led the club in home runs with 31 and knocked in 84 runs. The infield of Tony Perez at first, Dave Cash at second, Chris Speier at short, and Larry Parrish at third could stand comparison with most others in the league.

Williams's Expos posted a 75-87 record in 1977, placing them fifth, 26 games back. They had come a long way from the previous year but still had a long way to go.

The Expos signed free agent Ross Grimsley, a Baltimore Oriole pitcher, in December 1977.

AP/Wide World Photos

Red Sox slugger Andre Dawson broke into the majors with the Expos

Grimsley came through for Montreal in 1978—a 20-game winner, his first (and only) 20-win season and the first one for the Expos as well. He went 20-11 with a 3.05 ERA. Steve Rogers won 13 and lost ten, posting a 2.47 ERA. But even with respectable pitching, Montreal pushed up only as high as fourth place, still with a losing record, 76-86. The Expo lineup, basically unchanged from the previous year, looked better than its stats, and in 1979 it proved that to be the case.

Rodney Scott took over at second base, with Dave Cash hitting .321 off the bench. Third baseman Larry Parrish had a banner year, batting .307 with 30 homers and 82 RBIs. Outfielders Andre Dawson and Ellis Valentine powered 25 and 21 home runs respectively; catcher Gary Carter slammed 22.

Left-handed pitcher Bill ("Spaceman") Lee, acquired from the Red Sox, went 16-10 with a 3.04 ERA. Steve Rogers chipped in with 13 victories, while four Expo hurlers chalked up 10 wins each: David Palmer (10-2), Rudy May (10-3), Dan Schat-zeder (10-5), and Ross Grimsley (10-9). The Expos came very close to taking the division title in 1979, winning 95 games (the most ever for an Expo team), and challenging the Pittsburgh Pirates to the very end before falling off to second place, two games back. Dick Williams, combative and tactless, was cordially disliked by many of his players, but they did perform for him.

The 1980 team did nearly as well as the previous year's, winning 90 games, finishing second again, and, as before, coming within a whisker of the division title. This time it was the Phillies who won the crucial final games, leaving the Expos a single game back. Warren Cromartie, Larry Parrish, and Andre Dawson each drove in 70 or more runs—while Gary Carter was fourth in the league with 101 RBIs. Carter also placed fourth in the league in home runs (tied with LA's Dusty Baker) with 29.

Outfielder Ron LeFlore, acquired from Detroit in exchange for pitcher Dan Schatzeder, stole 97 bases to lead the league, and second baseman Rodney Scott swiped 63 to come in fourth. The Expos had first-rate pitching to go with their hitting and base running.

Steve Rogers, 16-11, had a 2.98 ERA; Scott Sanderson, in his third year as an Expo, also went 16-11, with a 3.11 ERA; and rookie pitcher Bill Gullickson, up from Memphis, broke in with a 10-5 record, and 3.00 ERA. Although either the 1979 or the 1980 Expos could, with a bit more luck, have advanced to postseason play, it took the 1981 season, with its players' strike and its split season, to elevate Montreal at last into the National League Championship Series.

The Expos' Only Playoff

In 1981 the players went on strike on June 11 and stayed out until mid-August. The two major leagues decided to count the first half of the season as one campaign and the second half as another. This worked to the advantage of the Expos, who occupied third place at the time of the strike (the Phillies stood first), but just barely won the second half, edging past the St. Louis Cardinals.

This pitted the Expos against the Cards for the NL East title. The Expos prevailed, three games to two. The heroes of this miniseries were Gary Carter with six RBIs, Chris Speier with run-scoring singles in the first two games, and Steve Rogers, who twice bested the Phillies' ace pitcher, Steve Carlton. The Expos weren't going to the World Series yet, but they *had* won the NL East championship, and now they had a shot at the NL West champions, the Los Angeles Dodgers.

The 1981 Dodgers were not a great ball club. As a team they led the league in nothing, and only the individual performance of 21-year-old Fernando Valenzuela, a chubby pitcher from Mexico who had quickly won the hearts of LA fans, attracted much notice. Valenzuela, whose 13 wins included eight shutouts, won both the NL Rookie Pitcher of the Year and Cy Young awards.

In the NLCS, however, it was Burt Hooten who baffled the Expo hitters most effectively. Hooten won the first and fourth games, allowing no earned runs. Valenzuela, after losing game two 3-0, came back in the fifth and final game to

PROFILE

The Two Tims

Tim Raines and Tim Wallach were teammates for the Memphis Chicks of the Double-A Southern League in 1979. Raines played second base that year, while Wallach, just out of college, put in time at both first base and third base. They both did well and in 1980 moved in tandem to the Denver Bears of the Triple-A American Association, where Raines, a five-foot-eight-inch 185-pounder, tore up the league, batting .345, stealing 77 bases, driving in 64 runs, and being named Minor League Player of the Year by *The Sporting News*. Wallach did all right, too, clouting 36 homers and driving in 134 runs. There seemed little doubt that these two players were Major League material, and they advanced together to Montreal in 1981.

The strike-riven 1981 season was not the best possible introduction to major league baseball, but Raines, now playing the outfield, batted .304, stole 71 bases, and won Rookie of the Year honors. Wallach, by contrast, struggled that year as the Expos tried playing him in the outfield and at first base as well as at third. He hit his stride a few years later. In 1984, 1985, and 1987 both Raines and Wallach were named to the National League All-Star team. Those were the best years for both players.

In this four-year span Raines, a switch-hitter, batted .309, .320, .334, and .330. Blessed with blazing speed on the base paths, he stole an average of 66 bases per year. Wallach could not match those particular stats, but he had stengths of his own. One of the best third basemen in the league, he typically hit in the .260s and with good power. He led the NL in doubles in 1987 and 1989, with 42 each year. Both players were bright and constant stars for the Expos through most of the 1980s, and Raines has a legitimate claim on the title of National League player of the decade.

handcuff the Expos on three hits as the Dodgers prevailed, 2-1. Bill Gullickson was charged with two of the Expos' three losses. The Dodgers went to the World Series. It would take another time (and another city's team) to bring the World Series to Canada.

Two Expo rookies of 1981 would make their mark on Montreal's baseball fortunes over the next few years. One was Tim Raines, the National League Rookie of the Year in that strike-shortened season. Raines, a speedy switch-hitter who stole 77 bases in 88 games in 1981, was the NL batting champ five years later and appeared on every All-Star roster from 1981 through 1987. He may well have been the top NL player of the 1980s.

The other important rookie of 1981 was third baseman Tim Wallach. Although less renowned, Wallach was a bona fide star too, hitting a career peak in 1987, when he batted .298, led the league with 42 doubles, slammed 26 homers, and drove in 123 runs.

Late in the 1981 season Dick Williams was

fired; he assumed it was, in his words, "for lack of communication and poor clubhouse skills and all that other stuff I'm always getting fired for." Jim Fanning, the Expos' farm director, took over the team, did well, and returned to manage in 1982.

The team slipped to third despite new first baseman Al Oliver's league-leading 204 hits, 43 doubles, 109 RBIs, and .331 batting average. Oliver, a lifetime .303 hitter, played most of his career for the Pirates and Rangers, but he put in two good years with the Expos before being traded to the Phillies in mid-1984.

Steve Rogers's 2.40 ERA led all NL hurlers in 1982, and his 19-8 won-lost mark gave him the league's second-highest winning percentage.

In 1983 Bill Virdon, once an outfielder for the Pittsburgh Pirates, became the Expos' new field manager. He brought them in third, but when they slipped to below .500 in 1984, Jim Fanning once more stepped in and finished out the season. Pete Rose, in the twilight of his playing days, spent much of the season with the Expos before being dealt to Cincinnati to finish out his career where it had begun. In 1984 Gary Carter led the league in RBIs with 106, but the team, showing little spark, faded to fifth. Charlie Lea (15-10) and Bill Gullickson (12-9) were the top pitchers for the Expos.

Enter Buck Rodgers

Dick Williams had managed the team for nearly five years. Buck Rodgers, an ex-catcher for the Dodgers and Angels with some managerial experience with the Brewers, led the Expos even longer, more than seven years, from 1985 into 1991—longer than Gene Mauch. As with Mauch and Williams, a Pennant-winning team eluded Rodgers, although his Expos of 1987 came nearly as close to the top as Williams' came in 1979, 1980, and 1981.

The 1985 Expos still had Dawson, Raines, and Wallach, but the middle infield now consisted of Vance Law at second base and Hubie Brooks at shortstop. Brooks drove in 100 runs to pace the team. The situation at first base was unsettled, but rookie Andres Galarraga looked like the heir apparent.

Behind the plate, replacing Gary Carter, was Mike Fitzgerald, batting only .207 for the year. Pitcher Bryn Smith, in his fourth year with the Expos, turned in an 18-5 won-lost record with a 2.91 ERA. The Expos finished third, dropped off to fourth in injury-plagued 1986, and then rebounded impressively in 1987.

The Expos third-place finish in 1987 came on 91 wins (their second most ever) and 71 losses, putting them just four games behind the first-place St. Louis Cards and one behind the second-place New York Mets.

Andres Galarraga had the kind of year Expo-watchers were hoping for from him—a .305 batting average, 40 doubles, and 90 runs batted in. A smooth-fielding first baseman with power at the plate, Galarraga showed a tendency—one that would worsen rather than improve in years to come—to strike out far too often.

Over the next two seasons the Expos com-piled identical 81-81 records, good for third place in 1988 and fourth place in 1989. Galarraga put in another fine year in 1988, leading the NL in hits (184), doubles (42), and total bases (329); placing second with a slugging average of .540; and earning a tie for third in home runs with 29. His stats paled considerably in 1989 and thereafter. Pitcher Dennis Martinez, whose major league career (mostly with Baltimore) dated back to 1976, put in two good years, 15-13 and 16-7. As always, the two Tims, Raines and Wallach, contributed effectively to the Expos' efforts, though neither was at his peak.

Some sportswriters predicted a last-place finish for Montreal in 1990, but the Expos surprised the doubters by finishing third, mostly on better-than-expected pitching. There were other positive signs as well; rookie shortstop Delino DeShields batted .289 and stole 42 bases, while rookie outfielder Larry Walker checked in with 19 home runs.

It thus came as something of a second shock when the Expos collapsed in 1991, at first under Buck Rodgers, who was replaced in June, and then the rest of the way under their new manager, Tom Runnells. A last-place team all the way, the 1991 Expos had youth and promise, but very little else.

That changed abruptly in 1992, as the re-charged Expos won 87, lost 75, and finished in second place, nine games back. Expo coach Felipe Alou replaced Tom Runnells in May. One of the players he managed that year was his son Moises, an outfielder on his way to a .282 rookie season. Another outfielder, Larry Walker, paced the hitters at .301 with 23 homers and 93 RBIs. Old reliable Dennis Martinez anchored the mound staff at 16-11 with a 2.47 ERA. Young Ken Hill, obtained from the Cardinals in exchange for Andres Galarraga, also posted a 16-11 mark with a fine 2.68 ERA.

The Expos continued their climb to the top in 1993, finishing 94-68, just three games back of first-place Philadelphia. Starting pitchers Jeff Fassero and Kirk Reuter and reliever Larry Wettel-and anchored the staff, and Marquis Grissom,

Darrin Fletcher, Moises Alou, and Delino De-Shields enjoyed good years at the plate.

SOURCES

BOOKS

Baseball Guide, 1980, 1983, 1985, 1987, 1991, and 1992 editions, *The Sporting News* Publishing Co., 1980, 1983, 1985, 1987, 1991, and 1992.

Baseball Register, 1980, 1983, 1987, and 1992 editions, *The Sporting News* Publishing Co., 1980, 1983, 1987, and 1992.

Hollander, Zander, editor, *The Complete Book of Baseball,* 23rd edition, Signet, 1992.

Holway, John B., and Bob Carroll, "Lives of the Players," *Total Baseball,* edited by John Thorn and Pete Palmer, Warner Books, 1989.

Ivor-Campbell, Frederick, "Team Histories: Montreal Expos," *Total Baseball,* edited by John Thorn and Pete Palmer, Warner Books, 1989.

O'Neal, Bill, *The International League: A Baseball History, 1884-1991,* Eakin Press, 1992.

Reichler, Joseph L. editor, *The Baseball Encyclopedia,* 7th edition, Macmillan, 1988.

Reidenbaugh, Lowell, *Take Me out to the Ball Park, The Sporting News* Publishing Co., 1983.

Shannon, Bill, and George Kalinsky, *The Ballparks,* Hawthorn Books, 1975.

Siwoff, Seymour, *Who's Who in Baseball 1975,* 60th edition, Who's Who in Baseball Magazine Co., 1975.

Williams, Dick, and Bill Plaschke, *No More Mr. Nice Guy: A Life of Hardball,* Harcourt Brace Jovanovich, 1990.

PERIODICALS

Baseball America, September 25-October 9, 1992, March 21, 1993.

Baseball Digest, February 1979.

Sports Illustrated, June 25, 1984.

—*Gerald Tomlinson* for Book Builders, Inc.

NEW YORK METS

No one expects an expansion team to do well at the very beginning, but in 1962 there were those who thought the fledgling New York Mets just might be competitive. Casey Stengel, the first manager of the Mets, remarked during a parade to a reception at City Hall, "The public thinks we can beat anybody. It's amazin'."

As it turned out, the Mets were better at beating themselves than at beating anybody else in the ten-team National League. They finished the 1962 season with 40 wins and 120 losses—the worst won-lost record in major league baseball in the twentieth century—and they did not improve much over the next few years. The Mets were a last-place ball club in 1967 and a ninth-place finisher in 1968.

Then came the 1969 "Miracle Mets" under manager Gil Hodges. In that first year of National League divisional play, the team won the NL East title, polished off the Atlanta Braves in the Championship Series, and proceeded, astonishingly, to

defeat the mighty Baltimore Orioles four games to one in the World Series. This was the stuff of legend, a ball club's meteoric rise from hapless to peerless.

For a while, the Mets made their transformation look real. They finished in third place in each of the next three seasons, then bounced back in 1973, under second-year manager Yogi Berra, to finish first again in the NL East. They edged out the favored Cincinnati Reds in the League Championship Series, but lost to the Oakland A's in the World Series.

After that, the euphoria ended for a while. The Mets were out of the running for the next decade, falling into last place in 1977, remaining there through 1979, then dropping back to the cellar again in 1982 and 1983. A succession of managers—Roy McMillan, Joe Frazier, Joe Torre (six seasons), George Bamberger, and Frank Howard—failed to rouse them from their stupor. In 1980 Frank Cashen was named general manager, with orders to rebuild, and in 1984 Davey Johnson was signed as field manager.

The steady improvement under Cashen (despite those early poor showings in the standings) became an eye-opening turnaround under Johnson. The Mets jumped to second place in the standings in 1984 and 1985, then walked away with NL East honors in 1986, leaving the second-place Phillies 21½ games back. They went on to win the NLCS from Houston and snatch an exciting World Series victory from the jaws of defeat, besting the Boston Red Sox four games to three.

After fading to second place in 1987, the Mets roared back in 1988 to win the NL East title by 15 games, but lost the National League Championship Series to the Los Angeles Dodgers in seven games. They then dropped off to a respectable, competitive second in 1989 and 1990. But instead of reviving once more, the Mets collapsed, finishing in fifth place in 1991 and 1992, far out of the National League race.

Casey Stengel and 120 Losses

The New York Mets, like so many other things in modern baseball, owe something to Branch Rickey. The 81-year-old "Mahatma," as he was called, had joined in 1951 with William A. Shea, a New York attorney, to create a third major league, the Continental League. Its franchises were to go to Atlanta, Buffalo, Dallas-Fort Worth, Denver, Houston, Minneapolis-St. Paul, New York, and Toronto.

The idea never came to fruition, but owners in the American and National Leagues were worried enough about it that they agreed to expand their own leagues by two teams each. In 1962 the National League added the New York Mets and the Houston Astros.

When Rickey decided against personally moving to New York, the Mets were left without their expected leadership. The principal backer of the club was Mrs. John Whitney Payson, who was assisted by M. Donald Grant, a Wall Street broker. Together they hired recently retired baseball exec-

utive George Weiss, who in turn hired Casey Stengel. Later Stengel would say, "Weiss kept calling me up on the phone ... interruptin' my bankin'." The Old Professor agreed to take over as manager of the so-far nonexistent team.

A player draft was arranged with the other clubs, and the Mets obtained what on paper looked like a group of reasonably good players. They chose first baseman Gil Hodges from the Dodgers; infielders Elio Chacon from the Reds, Don Zimmer from the Cubs, and Felix Mantilla from the Braves; and outfielder Joe Christopher from the Pirates. They picked pitchers Roger Craig from the Dodgers and Jay Hook from the Reds, along with Al Jackson, Bob Miller, and Craig Anderson, all from the Cardinals.

Trading some of their other draft choices, or paying cash, the Mets obtained infielder Charlie Neal, outfielders Richie Ashburn and Frank Thomas, and catcher "Choo Choo" Coleman. To the inexperienced eye this seemed like a fairly solid ball club, but the old Mahatma, viewing the Mets' scene from afar, suggested that Mrs. Payson had been had. There were too many ballplayers, whether bygone stars or journeymen, who were "about to go down the other side of the hill."

The Mets opened at St. Louis on April 12, 1962, after their scheduled opener had been rained out the previous day. They lost their first game, 11-4, and also lost their home opener at the Polo Grounds—prophetically, on Friday the 13th. The score was Pittsburgh 4, Mets 3.

The old pros on the ball club wasted no time in fulfilling Rickey's prophecy. As for the younger players, especially the pitchers, they were clearly unready for prime time (and, in general, never would be). Ex-Dodger pitcher Roger Craig, who had boasted an 11-5 record with a 2.06 ERA as recently as 1959, lost 24 games for the Mets in 1962.

Young Al Jackson joined him as a 20-game loser, while Jay Hook, a veteran but not an oldster, lost 19. (Hook had lost 18 games for the Reds in 1960, an intimation of what was to come.) The two most dismal records belonged to young pitchers Bob Miller and Craig Anderson, whose 1-12 and

TEAM INFORMATION AT A GLANCE

Founding date: April 11, 1962

Home stadium: Shea Stadium
126th Street and Roosevelt Avenue
Flushing, NY 11368
Phone: (718) 507-6387

Dimensions: Left-field line—338 feet
Center field—410 feet
Right-field line—338 feet
Seating capacity: 55,601

Team colors: blue, orange, and white
Team nickname: Mets, 1962—
Team logo: Word "Mets" in orange script on blue background
showing New York skyline superimposed on white baseball

Franchise record	Won	Lost	Pct.
(1962-1993)	2,372	2,740	.464

World Series wins (2): 1969, 1986
National League championships (3): 1969, 1973, 1986
National League East Division first-place finishes (4): 1969, 1973, 1986, 1988
League/division last-place finishes (10): 1962, 1963, 1964, 1965, 1967,
1977, 1978, 1979, 1982, 1983, 1993

3-17 marks were matched by equally poor ERAs of 4.89 and 5.35. How bad was the Mets' pitching? The staff's 5.04 ERA was one indicator. Another was the hitting of opposing stars, such as 41-year-old Stan Musial of the Cardinals. Stan "the Man" batted a sizzling .468 against the offerings of Stengel's pitchers.

The Mets' hitting, on the other hand, though the least potent in the league, was not hopeless. In fact, the team had one actual batting star—Frank Thomas, an aging ex-Pirate, who slammed 34 homers and drove in 94 runs while batting .266. Richie Ashburn, a long-time idol of Phillies' fans,

hit .306 for the Mets in this, his final season in the majors.

Other players who had good, if not brilliant, seasons at bat were Felix Mantilla, Charlie Neal, and Gene Woodling, a 40-year-old outfielder acquired from Washington, who, like Ashburn, would call it quits at the end of the 1962 season.

In fielding, as in batting and pitching, the Mets trailed the rest of the league. "Marvelous Marv" Throneberry, a first baseman obtained early in the season from Baltimore, committed 17 errors to lead the league. Poor Throneberry. He had been a fearsome power hitter in the high minors, but he is remembered today mostly as the butt of jokes about his fielding. ("We were going to give you a cake," Richie Ashburn told Marv on his birthday, "but we thought you'd drop it.")

All in all, the 1962 Mets were simply terrible. It has been said that a team with less than a .400 won-lost percentage is in the wrong league. The Mets played at an even .250 clip.

Manager Casey Stengel not only weathered this horrendous season, he became a darling of the fans and the press. They loved his barbed wit and scrambled syntax. When asked where the Mets would finish, he replied, "We'll finish in Chicago." Commenting on Don Zimmer, who was 0-for-34 at the time, he said, "He's the perdotious quotient of the qualificatilus. He's the lower intestine." When the pitcher he was yanking indicated he wasn't tired, the Old Professor shot back, "Well, I'm tired of you."

"Losing Gets You Down"

There were a number of new faces in the lineup for the Mets in 1963. The biggest name among them was Duke Snider, by then in the twilight of his career, having played 16 seasons for the Brooklyn and L.A. Dodgers.

The best young prospect was Ed Kranepool, an 18-year-old first baseman who had graduated a year earlier from James Monroe High School in the Bronx. He was destined to become the grand old man of the Mets, putting in more seasons with them (18) than Duke Snider served with the Dodgers.

But the regular first baseman for the Mets in 1963 was Tim Harkness, acquired from the Dodgers, a lifetime .235 hitter who for the last-place Mets—51 wins, 111 losses—batted a feeble .211. Even at that, he stood higher on the list than the Mets' new shortstop, Al Moran, who hit .193, and returning catcher Choo Choo Coleman who came in at .178.

Roger Craig repeated as the biggest loser in the league, posting a 5-22 record. Eighteen of his losses were consecutive, one short of the National

League record. His stats notwithstanding, Craig was a competent big-league pitcher. His 3.78 ERA in 1963 was no disgrace. "Losing gets you down, sure," he said, but he took it philosophically. "It taught me how to cope with adversity."

All the Mets pitchers had to cope with adversity that year, some more than others. Al Jackson's 13-17 was not too bad, but Jay Hook's 4-14 and 5.48 ERA pretty much spelled the end of his major league career. Three new acquisitions—Carl Willey, Galen Cisco, and Tracy Stallard—all had losing records, although Willey's 3.10 ERA was surprisingly good for a Met.

Once again the Mets finished last in batting, fielding, and pitching. Obviously, they would have to make a lot of changes if 1964 were to be any better. They made only a few, however, and 1964 was just as bad: 53 wins, 109 losses.

The best news of the year was their move into a brand-new ballpark, Shea Stadium, in Flushing Meadows, Queens, where they played before an opening-day crowd of 50,132. They ended up in last place for the third straight season. Roger Craig was gone, traded to the Cardinals, but sophomore Tracy Stallard contrived to lose 20 games and Galen Cisco 19. Newcomer Jack Fisher lost 17, and veteran Al Jackson (the top winner with 11) lost 16. Not much was expected of the Mets in 1965, and not much was forthcoming. They posted another horrendous won-lost record, 50-112—and even the beloved Old Professor finally got his walking papers.

Wes Westrum, a former catcher for the Giants, finished the 1965 season at the helm. He managed to deliver some Stengel-like lines—"Boy, that was a real cliffdweller!"—but few victories. Although his 19-48 record might not have gained him a contract renewal with some teams, it did with the Mets.

Then, in 1966, he led them to a ninth-place finish. The Chicago Cubs finished last, making this the first time the Mets had outshone any other team in the National League. Pitcher Bob Shaw, acquired from the Giants, actually had a winning record, 11-10, as did Dennis Ribant, 11-9. Manager Westrum was invited to return in 1967, but, perhaps predictably, the Mets reverted to their losing ways and finished last once more. Still, the 1967 Mets are worth looking at, if for no other reason than the arrival of rookie pitcher Tom Seaver.

After one year of seasoning at Jacksonville in the International League, the righthander—nicknamed Tom Terrific—became an immediate success in a Mets' uniform. He won 16 games, lost 13, posted a 2.76 ERA, and pitched 18 complete games, tying Juan Marichal and Gaylord Perry for the league lead in that category. Seaver seemed to be, and was, the Mets' first rising (rather than fading) superstar.

Also important to the Mets' future were catcher Jerry Grote, who had a rather unhappy year at the plate in 1967, and shortstop Bud Harrelson, who was playing regularly for the first time that year. Harrelson would remain the Mets' shortstop through 1977. Outfielder Ron Swoboda, in his third year with the Mets, enjoyed his best season ever, batting .281. (Swoboda had once muttered in the clubhouse, "Why am I wasting so much effort on a mediocre career?")

The Amazin's

No miracle occurred in 1968, but there was an important managerial change. Gil Hodges, who had ended his playing career with the Mets, now took over as the team's manager. He proved to be the right man, in the right place, at the right time. The Mets' front office—particularly Johnny Murphy—had shrewdly, if slowly, assembled a pitching staff that demanded respect.

Tom Seaver was back, of course, winning 16 games, losing 12, and lowering his ERA to 2.20. Joining him on the staff was left-hander Jerry Koosman, up from Jacksonville. Koosman won 19 games in 1968, lost 12, and posted an even lower ERA than Seaver (2.08).

Another of the staff's young pitchers, but one who would never quite hit his stride with the Mets, was a Texan with a blazing fastball, Nolan Ryan. In 1968 Ryan spent a month on the disabled list,

nursing blisters on his pitching hand, and ended the season with a 6-9 record.

The Mets' 1969 season proved to be cause for much celebration. A spate of books on the Mets' remarkable performance came out almost as soon as the World Series ended, and books and articles are still being written. In 1988 sportswriter Maury Allen published *After the Miracle,* a look at the Mets 20 years after that "historic, joyful summer." Art Shamsky, an outfielder for the '69 Mets, summed up the team's appeal in a conversation with Allen: "The 1969 Mets will be remembered forever," Shamsky said. "It was coming from behind, being so bad the year before, having so many great games, and the combination of personalities."

The 1969 lineup did not look especially awesome. Even the pitching staff, although excellent, had only three winners in double figures—Tom Seaver (25-7), Jerry Koosman (17-9), and Gary Gentry (13-12). By contrast, second-place Chicago and third-place Pittsburgh each had five winners in double figures, and the Cubs had two 20-game winners.

The Mets did not get off to a good start, but by the end of May the team began to win with some consistency, putting together an attention-getting 11-game winning steak. By late June the Mets were clearly in contention, but still trailing the Cubs. The Cubs began to fade in September, Gil Hodges's fired-up team won ten games in a row, and the "Miracle Mets" went on to take the NL East division title with ease, recording an even 100 victories.

Tom Seaver led the way, winning his last ten starts, while such unexpected heroes as Ron Swoboda came through in the clutch. On September 15, Steve Carlton, a left-hander for the Cardinals, struck out 19 Mets, a major league record. But Swoboda, who hit only nine home runs during the season, unloaded two of them off Carlton that day, and the Mets won the game.

The Mets had no trouble capturing the National League pennant, defeating the Atlanta Braves three games to none. Tom Seaver, Nolan Ryan, and Ron Taylor (in relief of Jerry Koosman) each

Lineup of the 1969 Mets

Since the heroics of 1969 were a true team effort, any given lineup is a bit misleading. Nevertheless, the Mets' lineup for the pennant-clinching game of September 24, 1969 (with annotations), gives a fairly accurate picture of the Amazin's.

Leading off: **Bud Harrelson**, ss, .248—Harrelson put in 13 seasons for the Mets and was their regular shortstop for ten of those seasons; he managed the ball club in 1990-91.

Batting second: **Tommie Agee**, cf, .271—Acquired from the White Sox, Agee, in his second season with the Mets, led the team in homers with 26 and RBIs with 76.

Batting third: **Cleon Jones**, lf, .340—This was Cleon Jones's career year. His next best season was 1971 when he hit .319. Jones, a 12-season Met, led the team in hits (164), doubles (25) and stolen bases (16).

Batting cleanup: **Donn Clendenon**, 1b, .252—Clendenon started the season at Montreal. He had his best year for the Mets in 1970, batting .288 with 97 RBIs.

Batting fifth: **Ron Swoboda**, rf, .235—"This boy can hit balls over buildings," Casey Stengel said when he first saw Swoboda. He could, but not very often. His rookie home run total, 19, was his highest ever.

Batting sixth: **Ed Charles**, 3b, .207—Charles put in eight years in the majors, mostly for Kansas City. This year was his last and least productive. He hit .263 lifetime.

Batting seventh: **Jerry Grote**, c, .252—Grote, like Harrelson, was a long-time Met, arriving in 1966 and leaving in 1977. Tough and aggressive, with a strong throwing arm, he was a very good catcher.

Batting eighth: **Al Weis**, 2b, .215—**Ken Boswell**, who batted .279, alternated with Weis at second base.

Batting ninth: **Gary Gentry**, rhp, 13-12, ERA 3.43—To complete the batting picture, Gentry collected six hits in 74 times at bat in 1969 for an .081 average.

won a game. Among the Mets' hitting stars in the three high-scoring games were outfielders Tommie Agee, Cleon Jones, and Art Shamsky, along with rookie third baseman Wayne Garrett. Cleon Jones, a solid .281 hitter in his 13 seasons in the majors, had a career year in 1969, batting .340, to finish third in the league, just behind Pete Rose and Roberto Clemente. Jones drove in 75 runs to lead the team. The only other Met to hit .300 for the season was Art Shamsky, with an even .300.

To cap a perfect season, the Mets would have to beat the powerful Baltimore Orioles in the World Series. The Birds boasted three pitchers with 20 wins—Mike Cuellar, Dave McNally, and Jim Palmer. They also had three hitters who had driven in more runs than Cleon Jones—Boog Powell, Brooks Robinson, and Frank Robinson. Most sportswriters expected the Orioles, laden with future Hall of Famers—to win the series. But the Amazin's were on a roll. After losing the first game to Mike Cuellar, the Mets edged the Orioles in game two, 2-1, as Ed Charles, Jerry Grote, and Al Weis hit successive two-out singles to push over the winning run.

Tommie Agee starred in the third game with a first-inning home run and two spectacular catches, while Gary Gentry and Nolan Ryan combined to pitch a shutout, 5-0. Game four was a squeaker, but the Mets won 2-1 in ten innings to give Tom Seaver the only World Series win of his career.

Gil Hodges's men concluded their miracle season with a 5-3 victory over the Birds. Late-inning homers by Donn Clendenon and Al Weis wiped out a Baltimore lead, and doubles by Cleon Jones and Ron Swoboda gave Jerry Koosman his second series win. Ed Kranepool, looking back on the season, said, "We weren't expected to win ... but we kept winning, winning, winning. One day we were the laughing stock of baseball, and the next day we were champions." On October 20, 1969, a host of fans and a blizzard of ticker tape greeted the triumphant Mets as they made their way up lower Broadway in New York City. The parade honoring the Mets drew more people than the one given for Neil Armstrong and the Apollo XI astronauts earlier in the year.

Staying Competitive

The Mets decided they needed a better third baseman than Ed Charles for the 1970 season. They released Charles in October and acquired Joe Foy from Kansas City, giving up a youthful outfielder, Amos Otis, in the deal. It was Johnny Murphy's last major deal—he died of a heart attack soon after—and his worst. Foy was a flop.

The Mets in general were less than miraculous in 1970, with Tom Seaver losing seven of his last eight decisions, Cleon Jones dropping from .340 to .277 at the plate, and Ed Kranepool being assigned to Triple-A after a .118 start (he finished at .170). Even so, the Mets were not without their strengths.

Donn Clendenon, Kranepool's replacement at first base, had a fine year, batting .288, driving in 97 runs, and hitting 22 homers. Tommie Agee did well, too, with a .286 batting average, 75 RBIs, and 24 home runs. The pitching trailed off, though. Koosman's 12-7, Gentry's 9-9, and Ryan's 7-11 records did not bespeak a pennant winner. Yet the Mets were tied for first as late as mid-September. They finished third, behind Pittsburgh and Chicago.

The next season, 1971, brought no improvement in the standings. The Mets finished in a tie for third place, despite the successful return of Ed Kranepool, the .319 batting average of Cleon Jones, and the return of Tom Seaver to the ranks of the 20-game winners (20-10, with a league-leading 1.76 ERA). In August Seaver pitched 31 consecutive scoreless innings. Left-handed reliever Tug McGraw, with the club since 1965 and a participant in the 1969 miracle, posted an ERA

even lower than Seaver's 1.70 and won 11 games (one more than Nolan Ryan) while losing only four (10 fewer than Ryan).

The Mets' main weakness was hitting. Cleon Jones led the team in RBIs with a mere 69. No Met hit more than 14 home runs. And Donn Clendenon, who had been so impressive the year before, skidded badly, his RBI total dropping from 97 to an anemic 37. Bob Aspromonte, the Mets' latest hope to fill the third-base slot, proved no better than his predecessors. Aspromonte's failure at third led to a chain of events that brought Jim Fregosi to the Mets from the California Angels—and cost the Mets Nolan Ryan.

Fregosi had been a steady performer for the Angels, while Ryan, his later brilliance notwithstanding, had been less than sensational in his five seasons with the Mets. Ryan and his wife disliked New York City, and he asked to be traded. At the time it seemed like a good idea. Who could know that Nolan Ryan would become an instant superstar at California, striking out 329 batters in 1972 to lead the American League and hurling nine shutouts along the way? Meanwhile Fregosi, formerly a shortstop, struggled through a .232 season as the Mets' third baseman.

Tragedy struck during spring training in 1972. On April 2nd, Easter Sunday, manager Gil Hodges suffered a massive heart attack and died after playing a round of golf with his coaches at West Palm Beach, Florida. On the very day of Hodges's funeral in Brooklyn, the Mets' front office announced that the manager of their 1972 team would be ex-Yankee star and manager Yogi Berra. The timing of this announcement was callous, but the choice was generally applauded.

A 13-day players' strike delayed the start of the season, but when the Mets got going they looked good. Tom Seaver breezed along as usual in 1972, winning 21 games, losing 12, and striking out 289 batters to lead the National League. Appearing on the mound almost as often as Seaver was Jon Matlack, a young left-hander up from Triple-A Tidewater (the Met's new top farm team in Norfolk, Virginia), who won 15 games, lost 10, and took NL Rookie of the Year honors. Another

Sportswriter Jack Lang tells an amusing story about M. Donald Grant, the stuffy, opinionated boss of the Mets. Lang was asking Grant about the seriousness of an injury Tom Seaver had just suffered, and Grant gave him the runaround. Lang tried to prod him, reminding him that they weren't talking about just another pitcher--this was "Tom Terrific." After all, said Lang, "He's 'The Franchise.'" Grant exploded. "Don't you call Seaver the franchise," he yelled. "Mrs. Payson and I are the franchise."

Lang tried to explain that calling Seaver "The Franchise" meant simply that the young superstar had been the prime mover in transforming the Mets from losers into winners, that Seaver was the best pitcher in the National League. Grant was having none of it. "Mrs. Payson and I are the franchise," he insisted. But Tom Seaver *was* "The Franchise" in a very real sense. No one bought tickets to watch M. Donald Grant make executive decisions, whereas from the moment Tom Seaver arrived in 1967, the Mets had a man on the mound who could consistently win ballgames for them.

Rookie of the Year in 1967, Cy Young Award winner in 1969, 1973, and 1975, Tom Seaver won in double figures 16 seasons in a row, although the last 4 seasons were for Cincinnati. He struck out more than 200 batters for ten consecutive seasons. He was chosen as the opening day pitcher a record 16 times. A shoo-in for the Baseball Hall of Fame, he won 311 games, lost 205, and posted a lifetime ERA of 2.86. Seaver, sometimes compared to Christy Mathewson, was able to win with both good teams and bad. Unquestionably *the* Met of the first quarter century, he was "The Franchise."

new arrival, but no rookie, was outfielder Rusty Staub. Staub, who had played for Houston and Montreal, batted .293 for the third-place Mets, missing nearly seven weeks of action because of a bone fracture in his right hand.

One of the much-heralded arrivals in 1972 was Willie Mays who came from the San Francisco Giants. The aging superstar appeared in 69 games for the Mets, hitting a home run in his May 14 debut to give his new team a 5-4 win over his former team. The 41-year-old "Say Hey Kid" batted .267 for the Mets, well below his lifetime average.

Another addition to the roster was left-handed power hitter John Milner, who alternated between first base and the outfield. Milner hit 17 home runs as a rookie, more than twice as many as Mays, but his .238 batting average and 38 RBIs were unimpressive. In fact, the Mets had the lowest team batting average in the National League, a paltry .225.

The modest success they enjoyed in 1972 was due mainly to their pitching staff, especially Tom Seaver, Jon Matlack, Jim McAndrew (11-8, his best of six seasons with the club), and relief ace Tug McGraw. For the fourth year in a row the Mets won more games than they lost and the team looked forward to 1973 with guarded optimism.

Another Season, Another Flag

Their optimism seemed to be misplaced. Despite their acquisition of a fine second baseman, Felix Millan, and a talented left-handed starting pitcher, George Stone, from Atlanta, the Mets soon ran into trouble. Injuries took a heavy toll. By mid-season the Mets were in last place, and Berra's job seemed to be on the line. As the Mets struggled through an unpromising August, Yogi kept telling his team what has since become a catch phrase, "It ain't over till it's over."

In September the Mets came to life. The race had been fairly close all along, and when Tug McGraw started saving games instead of blowing leads, as he had been doing earlier, the team took heart, winning 19 of 27 games in September. McGraw's rallying cry that season, "You gotta believe!," became as famous as Berra's. Felix Millan helped, batting .290 and playing second base flawlessly. George Stone helped, winning 12 games and losing only three.

The Mets had no 20-game winners—Seaver had to settle for 19, Koosman and Matlack for 14 each. It was a competent, balanced ball club, but not a dazzling one. John Milner led the team in homers with 23. Rusty Staub led in RBIs with 76.

Any one of five teams might have taken the division title in 1973, but in the end the Mets nosed out the Cardinals by 1½ games. The Pirates were 2½ back, the Expos 3½ out, and the next-to-last-place Cubs were only five games behind. The Mets' celebration was less raucous than in 1969. Shortstop Bud Harrelson said, "We knew we had a good ball club, and we kept fighting back through a lot of disappointment."

In the NL Championship Series the Mets edged Cincinnati's heavily favored "Big Red Machine" behind the brilliant pitching of Seaver, Koosman, Matlack, Stone, and McGraw. Rusty

Staub connected for three home runs, while Cleon Jones and Felix Millan chipped in with six hits apiece.

The World Series pitted the Mets against the Oakland As of Ken Holtzman, Vida Blue, and "Catfish" Hunter (20-game winners all), reliever Rollie Fingers, and "Mr. October," Reggie Jackson. The series went to seven games. For the Mets, Rusty Staub once again proved to be the big gun, banging out 11 hits and driving in six runs. But in game seven it was the A's hitting standouts, Reggie Jackson and Bert Campaneris, who made the difference. Each blasted a two-run homer in the third inning to provide Oakland with its margin of victory.

In the Depths of Despair

After almost winning the World Championship in 1973, the Mets went into a decline. They finished with respectable but unremarkable records from 1974 through 1976. In 1977, however, the team hit bottom. Though things were not as bad as they had been in the early 1960s, with a 64-98 record, there was definitely room for improvement.

The Mets traded Seaver to Cincinnati in 1977, without question the most unpopular trade in their history. Koosman lost 20 games that year to lead the league, and Matlack lost 15. Three Mets tied for the team's home run lead with 12 each, as if this were a new dead-ball era. A few notable players arrived during this grim period, but the team as a whole just would not gel.

Dave Kingman, a towering six-foot-six slugger, arrived from the Giants in 1975. The outfielder had home run power but struck out with alarming regularity, and his batting average usually hovered in the low .200s. He was traded to San Diego in mid-1977, but eventually returned to the Mets in 1981, via a trade with the Chicago Cubs.

Outfielder Lee Mazzilli, handsome and popular with the fans, came up through the Mets farm system. A native of Brooklyn, Mazzilli was an adequate major leaguer, but never the superstar the

Mets had hoped for when they chose him as their first-round draft pick in 1973. Craig Swan, a right-handed pitcher, played for the Mets throughout the entire period of their decline. He was not a bad pitcher—his 2.43 ERA led the league in 1978—but he received little offensive support.

Outfielder Steve Henderson put in some excellent years for the Mets in the late 1970s before being traded to the Cubs in 1981 for Dave Kingman. Catcher John Stearns did a capable job behind the plate during these gloomy years.

From 1977 through 1981 the Mets manager was Joe Torre, an active player at the time he took the assignment. He had been the NL's Most Valuable Player in 1971 as the Cardinals' third baseman. His woes as a manager had more to do with the front office than with any lack of competence on his part.

M. Donald Grant refused to enter into the free-agent market in a significant way. Consequently, the best available players went to other ball clubs, often to the Mets' cross-town rivals, the New York Yankees. One exception to Grant's free-agency abstinence was the signing of ex-Yankee and Oriole outfielder Elliott Maddox for the 1978 season. Maddox's good years were behind him, however, and he retired three years later.

The big news for the Mets in 1980 was not their fifth-place finish, ahead of the last-place Cubs, or even Lee Mazzilli's third (and last) truly productive season. Certainly, it was not the pitching staff, whose only 10-game winner (never mind 20 games) was the forgettable Mark Bomback. No, the big news that year was the arrival of J. Frank Cashen, the Mets' new general manager.

Mrs. Joan Whitney Payson, the owner of the Mets, had died in September 1975, to be replaced on the board of directors by her daughter, Mrs. Lorinda de Roulet. Grant continued to make most of the decisions. In late 1979 Mrs. de Roulet announced that the ball club was for sale. Fred Wilpon, a real estate operator, and Nelson Doubleday, Jr., of the publishing family, purchased the team, and within three months Frank Cashen was on board trying to rescue the faltering franchise.

Cashen, who had built a winning team in Baltimore in the late 1960s, did not promise instantaneous success, but he did start to improve the farm system and obtain players elsewhere, eventually leading to the Mets' revival. The strike-shortened 1981 season saw a few improvements. Hubie Brooks, up from Triple-A Tidewater, became the latest, and best, in a seemingly endless succession of "regular" third basemen as well as hitting a .307 that year. Dave Kingman returned to the Mets from his Chicago exile and responded with 22 home runs.

In 1982 George Bamberger replaced Joe

Ed Kranepool

No one ever mistook Ed Kranepool for one of the all-time greats. Yet he holds a place of distinction in Mets' history. For one thing, he was the youngest Met ever. When he played his first game for the team in 1962, he was 17 years old, a high school prospect who Casey Stengel thought would be a star. When he played his last game for the Mets in 1979, the tall, left-handed first baseman was 34 years old, an 18-season veteran (all with the Mets), and an old pro, but still not a star. In the only season he led the team in batting, his average was a mundane .253. As a brash youngster in 1963, Kranepool rebuffed a hitting tip from future Hall of Famer Duke Snider, snapping, "You ain't going so hot yourself." He was sent down to Buffalo that year, but soon came back to stay.

"Krane" was not an especially powerful hitter--his highest season total for home runs was 16, and his highest RBI total was 58. He was not known for being fleet-footed, either--he stole only 15 bases in his whole career. A capable fielder, he led all National League first basemen in 1971 with a .998 percentage. However, Krane's main claim to fame--and it is a considerable one--is that he was present at the beginning (five years before Tom "The Franchise" Seaver arrived) and was still there, still playing part-time, two years after Seaver was dealt to Cincinnati. The brash teenager had become the grand old man of the Mets.

Torre as manager, and a number of new and important faces appeared in the regular lineup. Wally Backman arrived from Tidewater to play second base. Mookie Wilson (the posters said "Mookie of the Year!") began to play center field on a full-time basis. Left fielder George Foster was obtained from Cincinnati, spurring memories of his 52-homer season for the Reds five years earlier.

The new Mets, still very much in the rebuilding stage, finished last under Bamberger in 1982 and last again in 1983. Although pitching remained a disaster, a number of farm-club hurlers looked distinctly promising. All-Star, Gold-Glove first baseman Keith Hernandez arrived from the Cardinals in exchange for pitcher Neil Allen and minor leaguer Rick Ownbey—probably the best trade in Mets' history.

Darryl Strawberry, Frank Cashen's first draft choice back in 1980, took over in right field. And, warming the hearts of many Mets fans, Tom Seaver returned to New York (though it was only for one year) after five seasons with Cincinnati. George Bamberger, fearing for his health, resigned in June of 1983 and was replaced on an interim basis by Mets' coach Frank Howard, a former manager of the San Diego Padres.

Davey Johnson to the Rescue

"A baseball team is like a vampire," Davey Johnson wrote in his 1986 book, *Bats*. "You always have to feed it new blood." Quite a bit of the new blood already existed when Johnson took over as manager of the Mets for 1984. He inherited an outfield of George Foster, Mookie Wilson, and Darryl Strawberry, and an infield of Keith Hernandez at first base, Wally Backman at second, and Hubie Brooks at third. The Mets' major weaknesses were at shortstop, behind the plate, and on the mound.

And the pitching was likely to be much better in 1984 than it had been in recent years. Ron Darling, who had come up briefly from Tidewater in 1983, would be pitching regularly in 1984.

Dwight Gooden, who had overwhelmed hitters at Class A Lynchburg the previous season, might be able to make the big jump to the majors. (He was more than able. Gooden won 17 games, lost 9, and earned Rookie of the Year honors.)

And over the winter, Frank Cashen had acquired young left-hander Sid Fernandez from the L.A. Dodgers. Darling and Fernandez were in their early 20s; Gooden was 19. In addition to these three newcomers, Davey Johnson inherited Walt Terrell as a starting pitcher and Jesse Orosco as a reliever. Johnson boasted, "I was sure that if anybody could turn the Mets around, I could." He was right in one sense—the Mets finished a strong second in 1984. But the idea that a magical turnaround occurred only because he was at the helm is misleading. The front office, mainly Frank Cashen, had been feeding the team new blood since 1980. The Mets were about to be impressively energized.

After the Mets' second-place finish in 1984, it seemed to Cashen and Johnson that just a little improvement might lead to a first-place finish in 1985. Instead, they got a lot of improvement. It came in the form of Gary Carter, an All-Star, Gold-Glove catcher who had spent more than a decade with the Montreal Expos. Carter was acquired in a trade that sent Hubie Brooks and three other players to Montreal.

Two new quality pitchers also arrived in 1985, via the Mets' farm system—Rick Aguilera and Roger McDowell. The high hopes of early spring were dealt a blow when Darryl Strawberry tore the ligaments in his right thumb in early May and had to go on the disabled list. Danny Heep, a utility outfielder, filled in and did well, but the Mets' 20-23 record while Strawberry was out stalled their momentum.

On June 11th the team suffered a single-game humiliation more embarrassing than any dealt to the early, awful Mets. Playing in Philadelphia, Davey Johnson's men ran into a 27-hit attack by the Phillies and lost the game 26-7, the worst shellacking in club history.

However, the Mets' real problem in 1985 was the St. Louis Cardinals. Led by Willie McGee and

Tommy Herr (both having career years), along with Jack Clark and some fine pitching help, the Cards 101-61 record was just a shade better than the Mets' 98-64.

The Mets, for their part, were doing well. Dwight Gooden went 24-4 with a 1.63 ERA to lead the league. Ron Darling was 16-6 with a 2.90 ERA. Gary Carter drove in 100 runs, Keith Hernandez 91, Darryl Strawberry 79, and George Foster 77. Young Howard Johnson, acquired from the Tigers, had a so-so year, alternating with Ray Knight at third base. But Davey Johnson thought third baseman Howard Johnson had a promising future, and he was right. The team had a bright future, too.

The 1986 Mets were the fruition of Cashen's careful rebuilding and Davey Johnson's able managing. They fulfilled their fans' most extravagant dreams, winning 108 games, losing only 54, and leaving the second-place Phillies 21 and a half games in the dust. "We don't just want to win," Johnson said at the start of spring training, "We want to dominate." And they did.

As in 1969, it was a team effort, but in 1986 the team was substantially stronger. The Mets' pitching was about as good as pitching can get. Although there were no 20-game winners, there were five starters (and one reliever) who won in double figures: Dwight Gooden (17-6); Ron Darling (15-6); Bob Ojeda, who was picked up from the Red Sox (18-5); Sid Fernandez (16-6); and Rick Aguilera (10-7). Roger McDowell (14-9) and Jesse Orosco (8-6) performed brilliantly in relief.

The regular lineup did equally well. There were few disappointments in 1986, except for shortstop Rafael Santana, who batted a weak .218, and aging George Foster, who was released in early August. Howard Johnson, still a part-timer, and Kevin Mitchell, up from Tidewater, filled in at shortstop from time to time. In the outfield, along with Darryl Strawberry, Mookie Wilson, and (occasionally) Danny Heep and Kevin Mitchell, the Mets now had an exciting, left-handed dynamo, Lenny Dykstra, also a farm-system product.

Second baseman Wally Backman, platoon-ing with newcomer Tim Teufel, formerly of the Twins, batted .320, while first baseman Keith Hernandez hit .310. Darryl Strawberry led the team in homers with 27, catcher Gary Carter in RBIs with 105, and center fielder Lenny Dykstra in stolen bases with 31. The Mets' .263 team batting average was the highest in the National League.

In the Championship Series the Mets defeated the Houston Astros four games to two. Jesse Orosco picked up three of the four victories in relief. Houston's right-hander Mike Scott handcuffed New York in both the games he pitched. The hitting standouts for the Mets were Hernandez, Dykstra, and Strawberry. Up against the Boston Red Sox in the World Series, the Mets staged one of the most dramatic comebacks ever, coming from behind in the 10th inning to win game 6. They went on to defeat Boston in the seventh and deciding game.

From Second Place to the Wilderness

Injuries plagued the Mets in 1987. The pitching staff was especially hard hit. Bob Ojeda, an 18-game winner in 1986, spent much of the season on the disabled list. Dwight Gooden, Rick Aguilera, Sid Fernandez, and Terry Leach also spent time on the disabled list, with Gooden and Aguilera being sent briefly to the minors for rehabilitation. Despite their handicaps, the Mets stayed close.

The ailing pitchers came through (Aguilera and Leach combined for a 22-4 record and Gooden went 15-9), Darryl Strawberry belted 39 homers and drove in 104 runs, and the Mets finished a strong second, three games behind the Cardinals. Outfielder Kevin McReynolds, acquired from San Diego after the 1986 season, had a fine year for the Mets, contributing 29 homers and 95 RBIs. Great things were expected of the ball club in the coming year.

The 1988 Mets almost repeated the blowout of 1986, winning the NL East by 15 games. Joining what was commonly called "the finest

AP/Wide World Photos

Gary Carter homers against Boston in the World Series

pitching staff in baseball" was David Cone, brought over from Kansas City in a trade. Cone proceeded to lead the staff with a dazzling 20-3 record and a 2.22 ERA.

Strawberry had another fine year at the plate, hitting another 39 home runs (this time to lead the league) and driving in 101 runs. Kevin McReynolds also put in a good year. Kevin Elster, up from Tidewater, was hailed as the Mets' shortstop of the future, but his weak hitting (.214) raised doubts.

The big news at the end of the season was the arrival of infielder Gregg Jefferies, who hit like a demon, finishing the year with a .321 batting average in 29 games. Of his 35 hits, 16 were for extra bases. Jefferies went on to collect seven more hits in the National League Championship Series against the Los Angeles Dodgers. Although the Mets had beaten the Dodgers in all but one of their regular-season games, the NLCS was a different story. The Mets' pitching turned suddenly shaky,

and the underdog Dodgers took the National League pennant four games to three.

After the 1988 season, the Mets' star began to fall. Not that they were a weaker team than they had been, or even that they were weaker than the other teams in the NL East. The problem was that, whatever their talents, they could finish no higher than second.

The Chicago Cubs, certainly less potent on paper than the Mets, won the title in 1989, and the Pittsburgh Pirates, led by Barry Bonds and Doug Drabek, captured it in 1990. The Mets finished six games back of the Cubs and four games behind the Pirates. Not too bad, but a slow start in 1990 cost manager Davey Johnson his job. The Mets replaced him with their old shortstop, Bud Harrelson. The club began winning, but soon reverted back to its losing ways.

The pitching staff showed some individual excellence—Sid Fernandez posted a 14-5 record in 1989; Frank Viola, a veteran acquired from the Twins, went 20-12 in 1990; and Dwight Gooden had a 19-7 record that year. But the team as a whole failed to deliver. The Mets' hitting tended to look better in the stats than in the clutch, although again there were exceptions. Howard Johnson had an outstanding year in 1989, batting .287 with 36 homers and 101 RBIs.

Strawberry and McReynolds continued to hit with power. Dave Magadan, whom Keith Hernandez had kept from playing regularly at first base, appeared at both first and third base in 1990 and batted .328, third highest in the league. These were the exceptions. Said manager Harrelson when the Mets were eliminated from contention, "I think we underachieved for most of the season. We were all guilty of it."

If the Mets were guilty of underachieving in 1990, what is to be said of their performances in 1991 and 1992, when they finished just one step up from the cellar? The departure of free agent Darryl Strawberry for Los Angeles at the end of the 1990 season took its toll on the team. So did injuries to key players. The only really productive hitter in 1991 was Howard Johnson—and he was very productive indeed, with 38 homers and 117 runs-batted-in, the most RBIs ever for a Met. The rest of the offense was subpar. Utility infielder Keith Miller had the highest Mets' batting average at .280. The club stood 11th in the National League in fielding with a .977 percentage.

Among the pitchers, only Gooden had an impressive won-lost record, 13-7, and he spent the last six weeks of the season on the disabled list, undergoing arthroscopic surgery in September. David Cone led the league in strikeouts with 241, but posted only a 14-14 mark. Sid Fernandez spent most of the season recuperating from injuries and, like Gooden, underwent arthroscopic surgery in September. All in all, 1991 was a season to forget.

AP/Wide World Photos

Dwight Gooden

The 1992 season proved to be the same. Despite the arrival of such big-gun reinforcements as outfielder Bobby Bonilla (from the Pirates), first baseman Eddie Murray (from the Dodgers), second baseman Willie Randolph (from the Brewers), right-handed pitcher Bret Saberhagen (from the Royals), and manager Jeff Torborg (the American League Manager of the Year in 1990 with the White Sox), the 1992 Mets fared poorly, winning just 72 games, losing 90, and barely eking out a fifth-place finish over the Phillies.

Outfielder Vince Coleman, the former Cardinal of whom much was expected, was sidelined with injuries in both 1991 and 1992. Near the end of the '92 season the Mets traded pitcher David Cone to the Toronto Blue Jays, and in October they acquired shortstop Tony Fernandez from San Diego. The changes didn't help; the Mets finished the 1993 season as the worst team in baseball at 59-103, 38 games out of first place.

Symbolic of the team's frustration, pitcher Anthony Young set a major-league record by losing 27 straight decisions. There was turmoil off the field as well; Coleman accidentally hit Gooden while swinging a golf club in the team's clubhouse and was later suspended after throwing a firecracker at a fan in Los Angeles. In another unfortunate clubhouse incident, Saberhagen threw bleach on a group of reporters and then tried to cover up his actions.

During the year, Torborg and general manager Al Harazin were replaced by Dallas Green and Joe McIlvaine, respectively. The team's future, unpredictable as always, might be summed up in Casey Stengel's wise observation about a baseball game: "You can win, or you can lose, or it can rain."

SOURCES

BOOKS

Allen, Maury, *After the Miracle: The 1969 Mets Twenty Years Later,* New York: Franklin Watts, 1989.

Baseball America's 1992 Directory, Durham, NC: Baseball America, 1992.

Baseball Guide: 1983, 1987, 1992 Editions, St. Louis: The Sporting News Publishing Co., 1983, 1987, 1992.

Baseball Register: 1983, 1987, 1992 Editions, St. Louis: The Sporting News Publishing Co., 1983, 1987, 1992.

Berkow, Ira, and Jim Kaplan, *The Gospel According to Casey,* New York: St. Martin's Press, 1992.

Breslin, Jimmy, *"Can't Anybody Here Play This Game?"* New York: Viking Press, 1963.

Cohen, Stanley, *A Magic Summer: The '69 Mets,* San Diego: Harcourt Brace Jovanovich, 1988.

Ivor-Campbell, Frederick, "Team Histories: New York Mets." *Total Baseball,* New York: Warner Books, 1989.

Johnson, Davey, and Peter Golenbock, *Bats,* New York: G. P. Putnam's Sons, 1986.

Lang, Jack, and Peter Simon, *The New York Mets: Twenty-five Years of Baseball Magic,* New York: Henry Holt and Company, 1986.

Mitchell, Jerry, *The Amazing Mets,* New York: Grosset & Dunlap, 1970.

Nelson, Lindsey, with Al Hirshberg, *Backstage at the Mets,* New York: Viking Press, 1966.

Reichler, Joseph L., ed, *The Baseball Encyclopedia,* 7th ed., New York: Macmillan Publishing Company, 1988.

Joy in Mudville, New York: McCall, 1970.

Vogt, David Quentin, *American Baseball: From Postwar Expansion to the Electronic Age,* University Park: The Pennsylvania State University Press, 1983.

PERIODICALS

Baseball Digest, April 1970.

New York Mets Yearbook, 1992.

New York Times Magazine, April 3, 1983.

The SABR Review of Books, 1988.

Sports Illustrated, August 13, 1962.

—*Gerald Tomlinson* for Book Builders, Inc.

PHILADELPHIA PHILLIES

The Philadelphia Phillies toiled in the National League for nearly a hundred years before they won their first World Series. For more than half of that time, from 1887 to 1938, they played in Baker Bowl, a "cigar box" ballpark known for its Lifebuoy soap advertisement on the right field wall—and for the scrawled message on it that read, "The Phillies use Lifebuoy and they still stink."

Even though Baker Bowl was the home park for some great ballplayers, including Ed Delahanty, Grover Cleveland Alexander, and Chuck Klein, the dismal assessment of the team was often accurate enough. The twentieth-century Phillies, in particular, were seldom contenders. Not until long after 1938 when Baker Bowl was razed and replaced by a gas station and car wash did they win with any regularity.

Philadelphia's first entry in the National League went by the name of the "Athletics," not the Phillies. On April 22, 1876, the team opened against Boston in the first game ever played in the National League. Prophetically perhaps, Philadelphia lost to Boston, 6-5, before about 3,000 fans. Near the end of a futile season, the Athletics, having won 14 games and lost 45, refused to go on their last western road trip. The league expelled them, and the Philadelphia franchise eventually went to Worcester, Massachusetts, where it remained from 1880 through 1882.

Philadelphia, however, was too large a city not to have a major league baseball team. The franchise returned. The new owners were Alfred J. Reach, a sporting-goods manufacturer, and Col. John I. Rogers, a lawyer and businessman.

On May 1, 1883, the Philadelphia Phillies played their first game. The site was Recreation Park, 24th Street and Columbia Avenue, and the opposing pitcher was Old Hoss Radbourn, on the mound for the Providence Grays. Although Providence prevailed, 4-3, and only about 1,200 spectators were on hand, fans were optimistic about the Phillies.

But hope soon turned to gloom. John Coleman, who lost that first game to Radbourn, went on to lose 48 games in 1883 (an all-time major league record), while winning 12. The Phils finished with 17 wins and 81 losses, a .173 percentage. Not surprisingly, the front office decided a new manager would be a good idea. William Henry (Harry) Wright agreed to take the job. The bewhiskered Wright, born in Sheffield, England, the son of a professional cricket player, was already famous as the man sportswriter Henry Chadwick called "the father of professional baseball."

Harry Wright's Ball Club

Harry Wright is in the National Baseball Hall of Fame, but not so much because of the performance of the Phillies under his direction as for his prior work in organizing the Cincinnati Red Stockings, the first all-professional baseball team. Still, Wright improved the Phils considerably, fielding a virtually new team in his first year and moving them two notches out of the cellar.

The biggest improvement came in the person of Charlie Ferguson, the team's best pitcher, best hitter, and best base runner. Ferguson quickly established himself as Philadelphia's favorite athlete and its first superstar. His best season was 1886, when he won 30 games, lost 9, and posted an ERA of 1.98.

That same year, 1886, saw left-hander Dan Casey join the pitching staff, and it began to look as if Harry Wright might be building a pennant contender. The team finished second in 1887, sparked by Ferguson (in his fourth 20-win season), Dan Casey (28-13), and newcomer Charlie Buffinton (21-17).

The Phillies might well have won their first pennant in 1888, but tragedy struck. In spring training Charlie Ferguson came down with typhoid fever. His teammates, although concerned, expected him to beat the disease. But complications set in, his health worsened, and on April 29, less than two weeks after his 25th birthday, he died. The team performed fairly well even without

Transcendental Graphics

Hoss Radbourne pitched against the Phillies in their first game (against the Providence Grays) on May 1, 1888. The Grays won 4–3.

their great star, but finished third behind New York and Chicago.

Harry Wright proved to be something of a hard-luck manager, foreshadowing Gene Mauch decades later. The Phils were always a first-division team under Wright, but never a pennant winner, though they had some fine players. Right

TEAM INFORMATION AT A GLANCE

Founding date: May 1, 1883

Home stadium: Veterans Stadium
Broad St. and Pattison Ave.
Philadelphia, PA 19148
Phone: (215) 463-6000
FAX: (215) 389-3050

Dimensions: Left-field line—330 feet
Center field—408 feet
Right-field line—330 feet
Seating capacity: 62,382

Team uniforms: Home—base color white, with maroon pinstripes and trim
Road—base color light blue, maroon trim with white edging
Team nickname: Phillies, 1883-present; Phils, 1942 (officially);
Blue Jays, 1944-1949 (but seldom used)
Team logo: Word "Phillies" in maroon script superimposed on white Liberty Bell
within blue field shaped like baseball diamond

Franchise record	Won	Lost	Pct.
(1883-1993)	7,777	8,793	.469

World Series won (1): 1980
National League championships (4): 1915, 1950, 1980, 1983, 1993
National League East division first-place finishes (5): 1976, 1977, 1978, 1980, 1983*, 1993
League/division last-place finishes (23): 1883, 1904, 1919, 1920, 1921, 1923, 1926, 1927, 1928,
1930, 1936, 1938, 1939, 1940, 1941, 1942, 1944, 1945, 1959, 1960, 1961, 1988, 1989

*Phillies won first half of shortened 1981 season but lost to Montreal in playoff

fielder Sam Thompson joined the club in 1889 and belted 20 home runs that year, the first National Leaguer to do so. Four years later Big Sam cracked out 222 hits. No player before him had topped 200.

And then there was center fielder Billy Hamilton, who arrived in 1890. Hamilton stole 102 bases that year and upped his total to 115 in 1891. And who patrolled left field in company with these two titans? After 1891 it was none other than Big Ed Delahanty, probably better known today than either Thompson or Hamilton, and, like them, a Hall of Famer. Until 1891 Delahanty had played various positions and put up average stats, but starting in 1892, he came into his own. In 1893 Big Ed batted .368 and drove in 146 runs. Yet this great outfield could not generate a pennant. The Phils

Transcendental Graphics

Sam Thompson

finished fourth in 1889, third in 1890, and fourth in 1891, 1892, and 1893. Their record was good but not good enough, and the owners, not without considerable regret, fired Harry Wright.

Twenty Years of Trying

From 1894 to 1914 the Phillies finished second twice and third four times. Their first third-place finish came in 1895 under manager Arthur Irwin, who replaced Harry Wright. The 1895 Phils had awesome power at the plate—Delahanty hit .399 and Thompson .392, and catcher Jack Clements chipped in at a .394 clip. Thompson's 18 homers and 165 RBIs led the league. Billy Hamilton hit .389 and topped the league in stolen bases with 95.

However, pitching was the problem. Jack Taylor won 26 games and Kid Carsey 24, both career highs, but their ERAs were 4.49 and 4.92. Moreover, the club had no reliable third starter, and even a .330 team batting average left the Phillies trailing the first-place Baltimore Orioles by 9½ games.

In the next three seasons, under three different managers, the Phils finished no higher than sixth. Then in 1899 they rebounded with a team that some still consider the best in the club's history. Nap Lajoie, yet another Hall of Famer, had come to the Phillies from Fall River of the New England League in 1896. Injuries plagued him throughout the 1899 season, but when he played, this star second baseman shone brightly, batting .380.

Elmer Flick (a future Hall of Famer) and Roy Thomas joined Ed Delahanty in the outfield—Billy Hamilton had been traded to Boston in 1896 following a salary dispute and Big Sam Thompson had retired. Flick and Thomas put in fine seasons, while Big Ed had his best year ever, banging out 234 hits, driving in 137 runs, and batting .408 to lead the league in those categories.

But what really made the difference was the pitching staff. The Phils had four dependable starters, including three 20-game winners, Wiley

Transcendental Graphics

Billy Hamilton

and into the mud while celebrating a spring-training victory over a college team in North Carolina.

Shettsline's managerial record was excellent and would have been even better except for the growing depredations of the new American League; Big Ed Delahanty was among those who switched leagues. In 1902, with a badly weakened lineup, the Phils finished in seventh place, 46 games out, and Shettsline got the ax.

Chief Zimmer, a veteran catcher, took over as skipper in 1903. He served just one season, a disastrous one in several ways. On August 6, the left-field bleachers collapsed, killing 12 people. The team itself had collapsed much earlier, and finished seventh once again. Chief Zimmer departed to become an umpire.

His replacement, Hugh Duffy, a Hall-of-Fame outfielder whose .438 batting average in 1894 has never been equaled, lasted three years at the helm, even though his first year saw the Phillies drop into the cellar for the first time since 1883, finishing 53½ games off the pace.

A slow recovery began after 1904 and accelerated in 1907 under manager Billy Murray, an Irishman with legendary wit. In one game a base runner took a huge lead off Phils' pitcher Harry Coveleski, who paid no attention. The runner stole second. When the inning ended, Murray asked his pitcher about it, Coveleski replied, "I didn't know he was there." After the game Murray solemnly asked each infielder in turn if he had told Coveleski of the presence of a base runner. All of them, puzzled, said no. Murray slammed his fist down. "From now on," he yelled, "we'll have no further secrets on this club." He went on, tongue-in-cheek, to demand that in the future they all inform Coveleski about base runners.

The Phillies finished third in 1907 but slipped to fourth in 1908. The highlight of the 1908 season came when Harry Coveleski single-handedly cost the Giants a sure pennant by winning three games from them in the last six days of the season. Following the end of the 1909 season and a disappointing fifth-place finish, a new owner, Horace Fogel, fired manager Billy Murray and

Piatt, Red Donahue, and Chick Fraser. The fourth man on the mound, Al Orth, was sometimes called "The Curveless Wonder." He won 13 and lost 3, with a league-leading 2.49 ERA. This solid, well-balanced team finished nine games behind the pennant-winning Brooklyn Dodgers.

The Phils finished third with a poor-fielding team in 1900 and second in 1901 with a club riddled by defections to Connie Mack's new American League team, the Philadelphia Athletics. From 1899 to 1902 the Phillies were managed by former ticket-taker and handyman Bill Shettsline, a portly chap who once fell out of his carriage replaced him with Red Dooin, a veteran catcher.

Not until 1911 did the Phillies have a man on the mound who would match in distinction all of those Hall of Fame outfielders, now gone. That was the rookie year of Grover Cleveland Alexander, whose 373 lifetime wins tie him with Christy Mathewson, behind Cy Young (511) and Walter Johnson (416), on the all-time list.

In 1911, with the Phillies finishing fourth, Alexander—affectionately known as Ol' Pete—won 28 games, lost 13, and struck out 227 batters. Beginning on September 7 of that year he pitched four consecutive shutouts. Two years later he had a 22-8 record as the Phils made an unsuccessful run for the pennant, finishing second to John McGraw's powerful New York Giants.

The batting star that season was jug-eared outfielder Gavvy Cravath, who hit .341 and led the lead in homers with 19 and RBIs with 128. The ace of the 1913 Phillies' pitching staff, surprisingly, was not Ol' Pete but a fellow Nebraskan, Tom Seaton, 27-12.

The 1914 season, Dooin's last as manager, saw the Phillies sink to sixth place in the standings. The new Federal League had lured away several Philadelphia players, just as the American League had done at the turn of the century.

Grover Cleveland Alexander stayed on, however, leading the National League with 27 wins, and Erskine Mayer added 21 more. But Tom Seaton jumped to Brooklyn's Federal League team in 1914. So did young left-hander Ad Brennan along with the Phils' longtime keystone combination, Mickey Doolan and Otto Knabe. The future did not look promising.

And Suddenly a Pennant

The importance of managers is often debated, but Pat Moran had a marked talent for winning in his first year with a ball club. Moran won a pennant with the Phils in 1915 and repeated with the Cincinnati Reds in 1919. Like Dooin, he had been a catcher, and he put his skills to work in honing the Phillies' pitching staff.

Transcendental Graphics

Elmer Flick

Ol' Pete posted a 31-10 record in 1915 with a dazzling 1.22 ERA. The steady Erskine Mayer finished at 21-15, while newcomer Al Demaree and future Hall of Famer Eppa Rixey also won in double figures. At the plate Gavvy Cravath was once again the big gun, blasting 24 homers and driving in 115 runs.

First baseman Fred Luderus had one of his best seasons, batting .315 and committed only 11 errors, practically a Golden Glove effort for Luderus, a notoriously ragged fielder. The team drew 449,898 fans, more than three times as many as it had the previous season.

Luderus had an outstanding World Series in 1915, batting .438 and driving in six runs. Alexander won the opening game, 3-1, but the Phillies then dropped the next four straight, each by one run. The pitching held up, but except for Luderus and rookie shortstop Dave Bancroft, the offense stalled completely. Still, the team had finally won a pennant and one World Series game. (The next

Phillie pitcher after Ol' Pete to win a game in the fall classic would be Steve Carlton in 1980.)

Pat Moran's Phillies came close to a pennant again in 1916, losing out to Brooklyn by 2½ games. This strong finish, remarkable considering the collapse of the offense, was due in large part to Grover Cleveland Alexander and two other moundsmen. Alexander won 33 games while losing 12, posting a 1.55 ERA, and hurling a record (perhaps an unbeatable record) 16 shutouts.

While Erskine Mayer had an off year, Al Demaree went 22-10 and Eppa Rixey 19-14. The Phils came in second in 1917, too, but this time they were ten games back of McGraw's Giants. Alexander won 30 games—his third year in a row with 30 or more. But the team as a whole was coming apart. Pitcher Al Demaree had been dealt to the Cubs, and Eppa Rixey struggled through a losing season.

These departures faded into insignificance, however, at the National League winter meetings. The big news—for Phillies' fans the calamitous news—was that Grover Cleveland Alexander had been traded to the Cubs for pitcher Mike Pendergast, catcher Pickles Dilhoefer, and $60,000 cash.

That trade subtracted 30 or so wins per season from the Phillies and left the fans in a foul mood. "I needed the money," explained Phils' president, William F. Baker. Manager Pat Moran later protested the trade, but Baker would not listen. If he could do without Ol' Pete, he surely could do without Moran. At the end of the 1918 season Pat was gone.

Back to the Cellar

From 1919 to 1931 the Phillies finished in last place eight times, in seventh place twice, in sixth place twice, and in fifth place once. Never out of the second division during these dozen years and usually far down in it—they nonetheless could point with pride to a few great individual ballplayers.

One of the better holdovers, Gavvy Cravath, who became the club's manager in 1920, made a

classic comment on the fortunes of the team. In response to a question about a game having possibly been fixed, Gavvy lamented, "I don't know why they gotta bring a thing like this up just because we win one. Gee, we're likely to win a game most anytime."

True enough. Irish Meusel, a lifetime .310 hitter, joined the club in 1918 after burning up the minors for five seasons. Cy Williams, a lifetime .292 hitter, came over from the Cubs the same year. And scrappy Casey Stengel signed on with the Phils in 1920. With Meusel in left field, Williams in center, and Stengel in right, manager Cravath figured the 1920 team would climb out of its 1919 home in the basement. "We're not a last-place club," he announced.

But they were, finishing half a game behind the seventh-place Boston Braves. That ended Cravath's managerial duties, but it had no effect on the Phillies' last-place finishes. The 1921 club ended the season 43½ games out, and William F. Baker traded Casey Stengel and Irish Meusel to the Giants. A year earlier he had unloaded shortstop Dave (Beauty) Bancroft, a future Hall of Famer, for cash.

The Phillies climbed into seventh place in 1922, with center fielder Cy Williams belting 26 home runs and ace hurlers Jimmy Ring and Lee Meadows winning 12 games each (but losing 18 each as well). Next season, under their new manager Art Fletcher, the Phils were back in the cellar, 45½ games out. Precedent would suggest another new skipper, but for some reason Baker had confidence in Art Fletcher, who led the team to a seventh-place finish in 1924 and a sixth-place finish in 1925. But the team faded to eighth in 1926.

These were forgettable seasons as far as pitching was concerned, although in 1925 the team had an array of hitters that caused fans to flock to Baker Bowl. These Phillies' sluggers are dim memories today: first baseman Chicken Hawkes, batting .322 and thereafter flying the coop; outfielder George Harper, batting .349 but continuing to bounce from team to team like one of those players known as "suitcase"; utility player Russ Wrightstone, batting .346 but used sparingly because of his fielding foibles.

When the Phillies dropped to last place in 1926, Art Fletcher gave way to one-season manager Stuffy McInnis, whose 1927 team also finished last, with a considerably worse record than Fletcher's.

At that point Burt Shotton was brought in to manage. Shotton spent most of his life in baseball, first as a fleet-footed outfielder for the St. Louis Browns and finally—long after his Phillies' days—as manager of the Brooklyn Dodgers, winning two pennants in three years. He won no pennants for Philadelphia.

The Phils came in last again in 1928, but 1929 produced, if not a winner, at least an exciting team. The outfield, as in seasons past, boasted some awesome hitters. Chuck Klein, brought up in 1928 from Ft. Wayne, connected for 43 homers to lead the league, while pounding the ball at a .356 clip. Lefty O'Doul, a veteran of the Pacific Coast League and the New York Giants, led the league with a .398 batting average. He also contributed 32 home runs.

The Phillies' infield had plenty of clout, too. First baseman Don Hurst, second baseman Fresco Thompson, third baseman Pinky Whitney, and catcher Spud Davis all hit well over .300. The problem was pitching. As Frank Bilovsky and Rich Westcott put it in their *Phillies Encyclopedia,* "This was a team that lived by the bat and died by the arm." A respectable showing without good pitching was impossible, and the Phils' brawny array of hitters had to settle for last place in the National League once more in 1930.

President William F. Baker died in December 1930, just after trading Lefty O'Doul and Fresco Thompson to Brooklyn. If he had dealt the two of them for pitching, it might have been a constructive move. But he dealt them mainly for cash. Still, anyone who supposed that Baker's departure and the advent of new blood signaled new hope for the Phillies was soon disappointed. The team finished last in 1930 and sixth in 1931.

In 1932 Gerald P. Nugent, an ex-purchasing agent who had married the boss's secretary, was

Transcendental Graphics

Casey Stengel

elected president of the Phillies. Nugent's ten years in office were among the team's bleakest. Always in financial straits, the new president proved to be a shrewd seller of talent rather than an innovative builder of a ball club.

Doormat of the National League

Nugent's tenure began on a positive note. The 1932 season ended with the Phillies in fourth place. The nation may have been in a deep depression, but the Phils had reached a pinnacle of sorts. They had made the first division for the only time between 1917 and 1949. Looking at the lineup, one might wonder why the team failed to win the pennant. (Looking at the pitching staff, though, one would quickly see why.)

Every regular in the lineup topped .300 at the plate except third baseman Pinky Whitney, whose .298 batting produced 124 RBIs, and Les Mallon, who shared second base with Barney Friberg.

Outfielders Kiddo Davis and Hal Lee had premier seasons. Chuck Klein's season, not surprisingly, was even better, as he led the league in hits (226), home runs (38), runs scored (152), and stolen bases (20).

After 1932 *deja vu* set in with a vengeance. From 1933 through the end of World War II the Phillies never finished higher than seventh. They finished in the cellar eight times, including five years in a row (1938-1942). They finished seventh five times. President Gerry Nugent began trading away his talent right away.

During the 1933 season he got rid of pitcher Ray Benge, outfielder Kiddo Davis, and third baseman Pinky Whitney. After the season he traded away catcher Spud Davis and his one true superstar, future Hall-of-Fame outfielder Chuck Klein. Nugent also fired manager Burt Shotton.

Hard times are synonymous with the 1930s, and the Phillies were hardly the strongest franchise in the league. Gerry Nugent kept the club afloat financially—some considered him quite a whiz at business—but only at the expense of the ball club on the field.

His trading and selling of players put cash in the Phillies' till but made it impossible for the Phils to compete against the teams that were acquiring his discarded talent. Then, too, as the ball club floundered on the field, attendance plummeted, and with it gate receipts. In 1933 attendance fell to 156,421—about half what it had been in most of the preceding years.

Jimmy Wilson, an ex-catcher, replaced Burt Shotton as manager in 1934. He led the club to its second straight seventh-place finish. The one bright spot in the revamped lineup was rookie pitcher Curt Davis, who won 19 games, lost 17, and posted a 2.95 ERA. In 1935 the Phillies claimed seventh place again. Staying out of the cellar that year was no problem at all, since the Boston Braves were incomparably worse, compiling a 38-115 record against the Phils' somewhat respectable 64-89.

HISTORY	Baker Bowl

When Baker Bowl opened in 1887, it was a state-of-the-art facility. Rebuilt after a fire in 1894, it was again the most modern park in baseball at the time. When it closed in 1938, it was an antiquated wreck. Nevertheless, it was a storied wreck.

In 1898 (two years after a swimming pool had been installed in the clubhouse) Tommy Corcoran of the Cincinnati Reds was coaching third base. Kicking at the ground, he uncovered a wire. The wire, he discovered as he continued to uproot it, led all the way to center field, up the brick wall, and into the Phillies' clubhouse. No, the wire had nothing to do with the swimming pool. What Corcoran found upon his arrival was reserve catcher Morgan Murphy with a pair of opera glasses and a telegraph machine. The Phils, it seemed, had been stealing signals from the opposing catcher and relaying them by concealed buzzer to their third-base coach.

More obvious and less devious were the three sheep that for years grazed on the outfield grass between games. The owners were always thinking of ways to save money or make money. For the 1915 World Series they added extra seats in front of the fence in center field. Unfortunately for the hometown rooters, Boston Red Sox hitters drove three ground-rule home runs into the extra seats to defeat the Phils 5-4 in the final game of the Series.

One of the Phillies' hitters who often benefited from Baker Bowl's short right-field wall was left-handed power hitter Chuck Klein. Klein once lined a pitch right *through* the rusting fence. Center field was tougher. No batter ever cleared the clubhouse wall in straightaway center, although in 1929 Rogers Hornsby, playing for the Cubs, came close. He smashed a ball through one of the clubhouse windows.

Transcendental Graphics

Chuck Klein

The Phillies had a number of ballplayers who did well in 1935. One was Dolf Camilli, a power-hitting first baseman acquired from the Cubs, who banged out 25 homers. Another, right fielder Johnny Moore (obtained from the Cincinnati Reds), batted .323 for the Phils. A third was Ethan Allen, a veteran outfielder who had come over from the Cardinals in 1934, batting .320 that year and leading the league in doubles with 42.

The Phillies lost 100 games in 1936 and finished last, even though they had a pretty fair lineup. Gerry Nugent's dictum that "you have to have some luck" seemed to fit. The Phils had no luck at all in 1936. They had reacquired Chuck Klein and Pinky Whitney. They got fine performances from Dolf Camilli and Johnny Moore.

And they had two pitchers with exceptional promise—Bucky Walters and Claude Passeau. Walters, converted from a third baseman, would

later pitch brilliantly for the Reds. Passeau, acquired from Pittsburgh, would have his best seasons with the Cubs. In 1936, hurling for the Phillies, Bucky Walters won 11 games but lost 21. Claude Passeau won 11 but lost 15.

In 1937 the Phils had their last opportunity until the end of World War II to look down on a lesser team—the Cincinnati Reds finished at the bottom, the Phillies seventh. Chuck Klein, whose best seasons were now behind him, came through with a .325 batting average and 15 homers. Dolf Camilli hit .339 and connected for 27 homers. Outfielder Morrie Arnovich, in his first full season for the Phillies, hit a solid .290.

But pitching, as usual, spelled trouble. Nobody had a winning record on the mound; no one's ERA was better than Passeau's 4.34. Hugh ("Losing Pitcher") Mulcahy, in his first full season, compiled an 8-18 record. (Mulcahy would have even more dismal stats, doing full justice to his nickname, in seasons to come.)

Baker Bowl, built in 1887 as the Philadelphia Base Ball Park, had been given its name in honor of William F. Baker. In 1938 the Phillies abandoned it and moved to Shibe Park, the 29-year-old home of the American League's Athletics. Said Connie Mack: "I'm sure the Phillies will play better at Shibe Park." He was too optimistic. They played worse, dropping to the National League cellar in 1938 and staying there until 1943.

The 1938 Phillies were just plain bad. Their hitting tailed off, and their pitching and fielding were the worst in the league. Manager Jimmy Wilson departed. The new skipper was Doc Prothro, a dentist in the off-season, who managed, if not to win, at least to keep his reputation as a knowledgeable baseball man despite three straight last-place finishes and a .301 won-lost percentage. Although Morrie Arnovich had his best season in 1939, and rookie third baseman Pinky May showed promise, the team as a whole showed nothing, losing 106 games and ending up 50½ games out.

No improvement appeared in 1940, but in 1941 there were a few hopeful signs. That seems odd in view of the fact that the 1941 Phillies lost 111 games, the most in team history, and finished

57 games back—true doormats in the season that saw Brooklyn win the pennant, while, over in the American League, the Yankees' Joe DiMaggio was hitting safely in 56 straight games and the Red Sox's Ted Williams was batting .406.

It was quite a season, but not for the Phils. Still, they had three genuine prospects on the roster: Outfielder Danny Litwhiler batted .305; first baseman Nick Etten batted .311; and second baseman Danny Murtaugh stole 18 bases to lead the league.

From the War to the Whiz Kids

It is generally conceded that the quality of baseball declined during World War II, reaching its nadir in 1945. This made not an iota of difference to the Phillies—officially called the Phils for the 1942 season at the request of their new manager, Hans Lobert. The Phils of 1942 proved every bit as bad as the Phillies of 1941. They lost 109 games and compiled a team batting average of .234, the lowest in club history.

The one bright spot in the season was the defensive play of left fielder Danny Litwhiler. He became the first outfielder in major league history (there have been others since) to field 1.000 for 150 games or more. Otherwise, 1942 was not a year to live in the hearts of Philadelphia baseball fans, as the Athletics finished in the cellar as well.

Gerry Nugent's unhappy tenure finally ended in 1943. The club was acquired by New York businessman William D. Cox, who promptly hired Bucky Harris, a major league manager since 1924. If Harris had had a team, that team might have made a showing. As it was, his collection of has-beens and might-have-beens finished seventh.

Schoolboy Rowe (no longer a schoolboy) was picked up from the Brooklyn Dodgers, who thought he was through, and astonished everyone by winning 14 games and losing 8, with a 2.94 ERA. Part way through the season a feud erupted between owner Cox and manager Harris. When the dust cleared, both were gone.

The wealthy Carpenter family of Wilming-ton, Delaware, became the new owners. Freddie Fitzsimmons, Harris's midseason replacement, stayed on as manager. The Carpenters decided that the name "Phillies" carried such unhappy connotations that they offered a $100 savings bond in a name-the-Phillies contest. The name chosen was the "Blue Jays." It made no imprint.

The 1944 and 1945 Phillies continued to occupy the cellar, their rosters a revolving door, their records a study in futility. Ron Northey led the 1944 team in batting with a .288 average, closely followed by first baseman Tony Lupien at .283. Lefthander Ken Raffensberger lost 20 games but had a respectable 3.06 ERA.

The 1945 team featured first baseman/out-fielder Jimmy Wasdell batting .300 and center fielder Vince DiMaggio hitting 15 home runs and driving in 88 runs. It featured no pitchers worth mentioning, although 19 different ones were used.

With the war over in 1946, major league baseball began to return to normal. Surprisingly enough, the Phillies, instead of returning to normal, began to get better. They finished in fifth place in 1946 with a mostly new lineup consisting of seasoned veterans, young prospects, and a few wartime Phillies' players such as Ron Northey, Ken Raffensberger, and Schoolboy Rowe (who had served two years in the military).

Long-time Phillie catcher Andy Seminick took over behind the plate in 1946. Old pros who were new to the Phillies included Frank McCormick at first base and Jim Tabor at third. A new kid of note was outfielder Del Ennis, who wasted no time in proving himself. In 1946 he batted .313, clubbed 17 homers, and drove in 73 runs. *The Sporting News* named him its National League Rookie of the Year.

The team dipped to seventh in the standings and 1947 and sixth in 1948, but there were plenty of hopeful signs for the future. Harry ("The Hat") Walker joined the team early in the 1947 season in a trade with the Cardinals for Ron Northey. Walker proceeded to have the season of a lifetime, hitting .363 to walk away with the batting crown.

Eighteen-year-old Curt Simmons, signed as a $65,000 bonus baby, pitched on the last day of the

GREAT TEAMS — The Whiz Kids

Between 1915 (and a World Series loss) and 1980 (and a World Series win after 97 years) faithful Phillies fans had only one team to point to as National League champions. They were the Whiz Kids—the average age was 26—of 1950 and the surprise pennant winners that year. Here is a typical lineup.

The leadoff hitter: First baseman **Eddie Waitkus,** still recovering from a gunshot wound suffered in 1949. A deranged fan who claimed she was in love with him had nearly killed him to keep him from other women.

Batting second: **Richie Ashburn,** center field, putting in a typical .300+ year at the plate.

Third hitter: Left fielder **Dick Sisler,** who became the Bobby Thomson of the Phillies when he hit a game-winning home run on the last day of the 1950 season to clinch the pennant.

Batting cleanup: Right fielder **Del Ennis,** a power hitter having his finest of many fine years.

Fifth: **Willie Jones,** third base, a superb fielder who could also hit for distance.

The sixth hitter: Shortstop **Granny Hamner,** who, like most of the other Whiz Kids, had one of his best seasons in 1950.

Batting seventh: **Andy Seminick,** whose .288 that year stood 45 points above his career average.

Batting eighth, in front of the pitcher: Weak-hitting second baseman **Mike Goliat** in his only full season in the majors, who drove in a very respectable 64 runs.

Of course, the Phils needed pitching to win, and they got it from **Robin Roberts, Curt Simmons, Bob Miller, Russ Meyer, Jim Konstanty, Bubba Church,** and **Ken Heintzelman.** The team ERA, 3.50, led the league.

The consensus is that these 1950 Whiz Kids were a good but not a great team. The Phillies of 1899, 1915, 1980—and no doubt some of the late 1970s clubs—were stronger, but, perhaps because expectations for the Whiz Kids were initially lower (or maybe because of the nickname) the 1950 Phillies continue to attract favorable notice from baseball commentators.

1947 season against the New York Giants. The young left-hander won, 3-1, allowing just five hits.

In 1948 the Phillies added a few more future stars, most notably center fielder Richie Ashburn, first baseman-outfielder Dick Sisler, and future Hall of Fame pitcher Robin Roberts. With youngsters Roberts and Simmons and aging hurlers Dutch Leonard and Schoolboy Rowe, the Phillies had quite a pitching staff, although in 1948 two of them were still green and the other two a bit too elderly.

The 1946 and 1947 teams were managed by Ben Chapman, an aggressive ex-Yankee outfielder who helped build the Phillies but often seemed to go looking for trouble. A Southerner, born in Tennessee and raised in Alabama, he was one of the cruelest needlers of Jackie Robinson when major-league baseball's color barrier was breached in 1947.

Chapman was fired in 1948, replaced briefly by Dusty Cooke and then by Eddie Sawyer. Sawyer, a Phi Beta Kappa with a master's degree from Cornell, was reputed to be good at developing young players—and he was. His 1949 Phillies finished third, their highest place in the standings since 1917.

Five newcomers added strength. Three of them were former Cubs—first baseman Eddie Waitkus, outfielder Bill Nicholson, and pitcher Russ Meyer. One came out of the farm system—

highly touted third baseman Willie Jones. And one was a sleeper, 31-year-old Jim Konstanty, a pudgy, bespectacled pitcher that Eddie Sawyer used only in relief. Konstanty, at 33, had labored mostly in the minors.

One grim note in 1949 was the shooting in June of Eddie Waitkus by a young woman in a hotel room in Chicago—the real-life incident that Bernard Malamud fictionalized in *The Natural.* Seriously wounded, Waitkus was out for the season, and there were fears that he might not be ready for the 1950 campaign.

Whiz Kids and Fizz Kids

The Phillies' Whiz Kids of 1950 were a one-season phenomenon. They won the pennant by two games and that was the end of their magic. They lost the World Series in four straight games, dropped to fifth place in 1951, and throughout the 1950s never again came closer to first place than 9½ games out in 1952.

Yet the Whiz Kids were an undeniably fine team. After decades of poor pitching, the Phillies got outstanding performances from starters Robin Roberts, 20-11, and Curt Simmons, 17-8, with able support from rookies Bob Miller, 11-6, and Bubba Church 8-6. Then there was Jim Konstanty, 16-7, so brilliant in relief that he won the National League's Most Valuable Player Award, the first relief pitcher to be so honored.

Only two regulars batted over .300, center fielder Richie Ashburn (.307) and right fielder Del Ennis (.311). But the Whiz Kids, youthful and spirited, were solid at every position.

By the end of August 1950 the Phillies were leading the league by 9½ games and seemed to have the pennant clinched. But no. Their hitters suddenly stopped hitting. In mid-September Curt Simmons was called to active duty with the army. Bubba Church and Bob Miller sustained injuries. The Phillies' lead dropped to seven games, to three games, and then to one game as the Whiz Kids continued to stumble and the second-place Brooklyn Dodgers continued to romp.

The two teams met at Ebbetts Field for the last game of the regular season. A win for the Dodgers would mean a tie and a playoff. The Dodgers called on Don Newcombe as their starting pitcher. The Phillies went with Robin Roberts. With the score tied 1-1 in the bottom of the ninth inning, Brooklyn's Cal Abrams tried to score from second on a Duke Snider single to center. Richie Ashburn fielded the ball on one hop and fired a strike to the plate, catching Abrams by a good 15 feet. The game went into extra innings.

In the top of the 10th inning, Phillies' shortstop Dick Sisler drove a fast ball into the left-field stands, scoring Robin Roberts and Eddie Waitkus ahead of him. The Phillies won 4-1, and pandemonium erupted in Philadelphia. The Whiz Kids had done it.

After a 35-year wait, and more dreary seasons than anyone wanted to remember, the National League pennant was back in Philadelphia. Unhappily for their fans, the Whiz Kids did not repeat their heroics in the World Series. The mighty New York Yankees set them down in four straight games. Although the games were close and exciting, they were all Yankee victories. The Phils still had no World Championship.

The same Phillies' team returned in 1951 (Curt Simmons was still in the army), but the elan of 1950 was gone. The Phils, never contenders, ended the season in fifth place. Robin Roberts had a 21-15 season, but, except for Richie Ashburn and Willie Jones, the offense failed.

Nor was 1952 much better, except for Robin Roberts superb 28-7 showing, which earned him *The Sporting News's* Major League Player of the Year award. Curt Simmons, back again, compiled a 14-8 record. The Phils finished fourth that year, and in midseason Eddie Sawyer departed to make way for a new manager, Steve O'Neill.

Although O'Neill's Phillies played at a .565 clip, other teams in those years—particularly the Dodgers, Giants, and Braves—had powerhouse ball clubs. The Whiz Kids, even with Simmons and Roberts at the top of their form, could not climb above third place.

The 1954 season was memorable mainly for

Transcendental Graphics

Robin Roberts

Roberts' continuing success. He won more than 20 games (21-15) for the fifth straight year. Richie Ashburn hit well as always (.313), and the two Phillie catchers, Stan Lopata and Smokey Burgess, both had good years at the plate as well as behind it.

Each season in the late 1950s began hopefully. Each one ended in disappointment. How could a team with such fine pitching (to which the Phillies were so unaccustomed) not put it all together? Worse, why did they drop from fourth in 1954 and 1955 to fifth in 1956 and 1957, to last in 1958, 1959, and 1960?

During much of this decline the manager was Mayo Smith, a virtual unknown when hired, who oversaw the replacement of the aging Whiz Kids, concentrating too much on pitchers, too little on black ballplayers, and too frequently on aging players from other teams.

Of course, the Phillies had their moments. In 1955 it was Richie Ashburn winning the batting title, his .338 easily topping the .319s of Stan Musial and Jackie Robinson. The 1956 standouts were, as usual, Ashburn, Ennis, and Jones, while

catcher Stan Lopata belted 32 homers and drove in 95 runs.

In 1957 a youth movement paid off with two *Sporting News* Rookies of the Year—first baseman Ed Bouchee (.293) and pitcher Jack Sanford (19-8). But there was little improvement in 1958. In fact, things got worse. The club plunged to the cellar, and old Eddie Sawyer was rehired to manage. By now the Whiz Kids were mostly gone. At the end of the 1959 season the only ones left were Robin Roberts and Richie Ashburn, and both had so-so seasons.

Clearly, something drastic had to be done. The front office considered its options and, at the beginning of the 1960 season, hired a genius to manage the club.

Brilliant Manager, Mixed Results

Gene Mauch, 34, probably *was* a genius. When someone asked him if he had ever heard of an obscure shortstop in the low minors, Mauch nodded. "He's hitting .289." Someone corrected him. "No, it's .306." The disputants checked *The Sporting News* to find the correct answer. It was .289. Still, did that kind of ability make him a genius as a manager? His 23-year managerial career would hardly suggest so, but at the outset with the Phillies Mauch simply lacked the personnel.

Finishing last in 1960 and 1961 was no disgrace, but losing 23 straight games in July and August 1961—an all-time major league record—tended to make Phillies' fans wonder if their team was truly on the road to recovery.

A couple of bright spots in the gloom were outfielders Tony Gonzalez and Johnny Callison, who would play key roles in the 1964 pennant race, as would pitchers Art Mahaffey and Chris Short. Mahaffey had his best season in 1962 when he went 19-14 with a 3.94 ERA.

Short put in all or part of 14 seasons for the Phillies, and he was particularly impressive from 1964 to 1968. Gonzalez reached his peak in 1963 with a .306 batting average and 66 RBIs. Callison had two fine seasons, 1964 and 1965, batting in more than 100 runs and hitting more than 30 homers each time.

The 1964 Phillies were by no means an awesome team. After moving up to seventh place in 1962 and fourth place in 1963, the Phillies expected to do well in 1964 but not to finish first. When they almost did—and then failed—they created expectations that brought only disappointment to their fans for the next few seasons.

The big gun for the 1964 Phillies was third baseman Richie Allen. Allen, who later preferred to be called Dick instead of Richie, hit 351 career home runs in the majors, and had all the tools except self-discipline. In 1969 when short-term manager George Myatt was asked if he could handle Allen, Myatt replied, "God Almighty his self couldn't handle that man." But in 1964 rookie Allen batted .318, cracked 29 home runs, and drove in 91 runs.

Without him in the lineup the Phils might never have challenged at all that season. As it was they executed one of the great swan dives in baseball history. On September 21 they were six and a half games in front, with the magic number being seven. They proceeded to lose 10 straight games, while the Cardinals won eight in a row to capture the pennant, and the Reds won nine in a row to share second place with the hapless Phils.

From 1965 to 1967 players came and went, and the Phils never rose above fourth place. Jim Bunning and Chris Short continued to anchor the pitching staff, although Bunning fared badly in his final year and was dealt to Pittsburgh. Bill White, future president of the National League, took over at first base in 1966, replacing Dick (Dr. Strangeglove) Stuart.

Many of the trades appeared to make sense, but none of them produced the desired results. In 1968, the last year before the league split into two divisions, the Phillies tied the L.A. Dodgers for seventh place. On June 14 of that year the Phillies' front office finally gave up on manager Gene Mauch, replacing him with Bob Skinner, who lasted one year.

Like Mauch, Skinner could not get along with Dick Allen. Skinner led the team to a fifth-place finish (i.e., next-to-last) in the new Eastern Division of the National League.

The 1970 and 1971 seasons were notable mainly for the dealing of Dick Allen to the Cards (1970) and the opening of Veterans Stadium, a bowl-shaped, multi-purpose, green-carpeted arena (1971). The Allen deal had major consequences, because to get him the Cards gave up catcher Tim McCarver and outfielder Curt Flood.

Upset at being traded like a commodity, Flood challenged baseball's reserve clause, winning his case after several years of litigation and opening the floodgates for free agency and escalating salaries.

The manager of these fifth- and sixth-place teams was Frank Lucchesi, a nice guy who did what he could with a weak lineup. Shortstop Larry Bowa, a rookie in 1970, would become one of the mainstays of the Phillies in their prime. Rick Wise, a quality pitcher who had been on the staff since 1964, was traded to the Cardinals after the 1971 season. The Phillies got lefty Steve Carlton in exchange, and McCarver became his personal catcher.

Carlton, Schmidt, and Success

Just how great a trade the Phillies had made—Carlton for Wise—became apparent right away. In 1972 the Phillies' new left-hander won 27 games and lost 10, his 1.97 ERA leading the league. Although Carlton won the Cy Young Award in a unanimous vote, the Phillies finished last in the Eastern Division. Carlton's 27 wins constituted 46 percent of the team's victories.

In midseason 1972 Paul Owens, the Phils' general manager, fired Frank Lucchesi and took over himself as field manager for the rest of the season. In September the Phillies brought up some of their top farm-system players to look at. One was catcher Bob Boone. Another was third baseman Mike Schmidt.

GM Paul Owens and manager Danny Ozark, the new skipper for 1973, realizing that lefty Steve

Courtesy of the Philadelphia Phillies

Mike Schmidt

Carlton would need some help, acquired pitchers Jim Lonborg, Ken Brett, Wayne Twitchell, and Dick Ruthven. Yet even with improved pitching (though Carlton dropped off to 13-20), and with outfielders Greg Luzinski and Bill Robinson providing punch at the plate, the 1973 team did not really gel. The Phils finished last for the third year in a row—their last such humiliation until 1988.

The team began a step-by-step climb, placing third in 1974, second in 1975, and first in 1976, 1977, and 1978. The nucleus of these division-winning teams managed by Ozark consisted of catcher Bob Boone, shortstop Larry Bowa, third baseman Mike Schmidt, outfielders Greg Luzinski, Garry Maddox, and Bake McBride, and, on the mound, Steve Carlton, Jim Lonborg, and Larry Christenson. Attendance at Veterans Stadium rose with the fortunes of the team. The Phillies drew 1,808,648 fans in 1974; 2,583,389 in 1978.

Sluggers Mike Schmidt and Greg ("The Bull") Luzinski hit their stride during these years. Schmidt led the National League in homers for three straight seasons, belting 36, 36, and 38 from 1974 to 1976. Greg Luzinski drove in 120 runs in 1975 and 130 in 1977. Steve Carlton won 20 games in 1976 and 23 in 1977.

These were glory years for the Phillies—with just one glitch. The Phils could not win in league-championship play. They never got into the World Series. In 1976 they lost three straight games to Cincinnati's Big Red Machine. In 1977 they took only one game from the Western Division champion L.A. Dodgers. And in 1978 they repeated their failure of 1977 against Los Angeles. The Phillies' front office could and did claim that they had the best ball club in the history of the franchise. But where were the Phillies when the fall classic opened each year? Back home watching television.

The 1979 Phils were even more potent than those of the preceding years, but success eluded them still. They were stronger for two good reasons: Pete Rose and Manny Trillo. Rose, a long-time Cincinnati Reds' star, was signed as a free agent and installed at first base. He batted .331, second in the league. Manny Trillo, a smooth-fielding second baseman who could also hit, was acquired from the Chicago Cubs.

Nevertheless, 1979 was not the Phillies' year. They finished fourth, behind the Pirates, Expos, and Cardinals. Near the end of the season Dallas Green, the team's blunt and combative farm director, took over as manager from Ozark.

Until 1980 the Phillies had never won a World Series. They had been in a Series only twice, 1915 and 1950, and had won only a single game in those two outings. Since the franchise was nearly a hundred years old, whole generations of Phillies' fans had rooted in vain for a World Championship.

When it finally came to pass, the season's heroes, appropriately enough, were Steve Carlton, who won 24 and lost 9, with a 2.34 ERA, and Mike Schmidt, with 48 home runs and 131 RBIs. In addition, Dick Ruthven had a career year (17-10), Tug McGraw sparkled in relief, and Manny Trillo and Bake McBride had better-than-average seasons.

Even so, the division race was hard-fought—the Phils nosing out the Montreal Expos by one game; and the league championship series was also a squeaker—the Phils edging the Houston Astros three games to two.

The World Series proved a bit easier, as the Phillies topped the Kansas City Royals in six games. Steve Carlton won two of the games, and Mike Schmidt drove in seven runs. Other batting stars were Larry Bowa (nine hits) and Bob Boone and Bake McBride (seven hits each). Reliever Tug McGraw saved the fifth and sixth games, striking out batters with the bases loaded three times.

More Success ... and a Slow Fade

No one speaks positively about the strike-shortened 1981 season, certainly not the Phillies, who were leading their division when the walkout began on June 12. Carlton and Schmidt might well have had their greatest seasons—their truncated stats suggest it. An ad hoc division playoff arrangement pitted the Phillies against the Expos, and the Expos prevailed three games to two.

Expectations were high for 1982, but the Phils finished in second place, three games behind the Cards. Carlton had another great season, 23-11, and Schmidt cracked 35 homers. A new catcher, Bo Diaz, contributed 18 homers and 85 RBIs. But second place was by now a disappointment.

In 1983 the Phillies were back on top. Under manager Pat Corrales, who had taken over in 1982, they beat out the Cardinals by six games, and yet the season was not an especially memorable one. The only .300 hitters were part-time outfielders Jim Lefebvre and Greg Gross. Pete Rose faded to .245. Von Hayes, acquired for five other players, drove in fewer runs than weak-hitting shortstop Ivan DeJesus. Even the usually nonpareil Steve Carlton had a losing record (15-16).

Had it not been for the surprising one-year surge of right-hander John Denny (19-6, ERA 2.37) the Phils would almost surely have been also-rans. As it was, they made it to the World Series, only to lose to the Baltimore Orioles four games to one.

The team dropped to third in 1984, again getting sub-.300 performances from the regulars. Steve Carlton, in his 20th year of major league baseball, won 13, lost 7, and was clearly on a downhill slide. The Phils fell to sixth place in 1985.

They bounced back to second place in 1986 under second-year manager John Felske, but the bounce was misleading, since the Phils were 21½ games back of the first-place New York Mets. Mike Schmidt continued with his usual high home-run and RBI totals, but the trades were not working out. Von Hayes continued to disappoint, while second baseman Juan Samuel, pride of the farm system, showed great promise but proved erratic both in the field and at bat.

In 1987 an unimproved team finished fourth. In 1988 and 1989 the Phils came in dead last ("dead" being an appropriate adjective, because they were far behind even the fifth-place teams). The next two seasons saw some modest improvement, but by 1992 the Phillies were back where they had started in 1883—in the National League cellar.

AP/Wide World Photos

Steve Carlton

Worst to First

The Phillies last-place finish in 1992 just made 1993 all the more surprising. With a number of players reporting to camp healthy after enduring injury-plagued 1992 seasons, the Phillies loomed as an National League East darkhorse.

Led by centerfielder Lenny Dykstra (194 hits, 143 runs scored), first baseman John Kruk (.316), catcher Darren Daulton (105 RBIs), and pitchers Tommy Greene and Curt Schilling (16 wins each), Philadelphia raced to the division lead early in the season and staved off a late charge by the Montreal Expos to capture their first title since 1983, becoming only the third team in major league history to go from last place to first in one year.

Philadelphia's exciting style of play revived fan interest in the franchise; the club played before a record home attendance of over three million. In addition, the grubby look and lunchpail work ethic of players such as Kruk and reliever Mitch "Wild Thing" Williams earned the Phillies nationwide attention. After defeating the favored Atlanta Braves in six games in the National League Championship Series, the Phillies faced the defending champion Toronto Blue Jays in the World Series. The Blue Jays proved too formidable an opponent for the Phillies, capturing their second consecutive world title four games to two.

The Series' turning point came in Game Four, a wild affair that saw the Phillies blow a five-run, eighth-inning lead before losing, 15-14. Despite this disappointment, the team has expressed opt

mism for the future, as almost all of the Phillies' key players look to return to the club in 1994.

Sources

BOOKS

Ashburn, Rich, and Allen Lewis, *Richie Ashburn's Phillies Trivia,* Running Press, 1983.
Baseball Guide: 1992 Edition, The Sporting News Publishing Co., 1992.
Baseball Register: 1992 Edition, The Sporting News Publishing Co., 1992.
Bilovsky, Frank, and Rich Westcott, *The Phillies Encyclopedia,* The Leisure Press, 1984.
Honig, Donald, *The Philadelphia Phillies: An Illustrated History,* Simon and Schuster, 1992.
Ivor-Campbell, Frederick, "Team Histories: Philadelphia Phillies," *Total Baseball,* edited by John Thorn and Pte Palmer, Warner Books, 1989.
Lewis, Allen, *The Philadelphia Phillies,* Simon and Schuster, 1982.
Lieb, Frederick G., and Stan Baumgardner, *The Philadelphia Phillies,* G.P Putnam's Sons, 1953.
Lowry, Philip J., *Green Cathedrals,* Cooperstown, NY: Society for American Baseball Research, 1986.
Reichler, Joseph L., editor, *The Baseball Encyclopedia,* 7th edition, Macmillan, 1988.

PERIODICALS

Baseball America, September 10-24, 1992.
Baseball Digest, April 1946; July 1972.
Saturday Evening Post, October 4, 1941; September 10, 1949.
Sports Illustrated, October 13, 1980.

—Gerald Tomlinson for Book Builders, Inc.

PITTSBURGH PIRATES

Major league baseball arrived in Pittsburgh in 1882. The city's ball club, called "Allegheny" rather than "Pittsburgh," became a charter member of the new American Association (AA). This league lacked the prestige of the older and more stable National League (NL), and in 1887 Pittsburgh became the first city to desert the AA in favor of the National League. Among the early stars of the Allegheny team was future Hall of Famer Pud Galvin, a pitcher whose 28-21 won-lost record paced Pittsburgh in 1887. The team finished sixth in the eight-team NL under manager "Hustling" Horace Phillips.

After losing most of their players to the rival Pittsburgh club of the Players League in 1890, the Allegheny organization regrouped in 1891, combining with the other Pittsburgh team, and hired back many of their former players. When they signed a new second baseman, Lou Bierbauer, from the the Brooklyn club of the Players League— stole him away, claimed his prior owners—they

gained their lasting nickname, the Pirates.

Generally mediocre in the nineteenth century, the Pirates, in 1900, merged with the failing Louisville Colonels and became a National League power in the first decade of the twentieth century. Among the players Pittsburgh acquired in the Louisville merger were a couple of outfielders, Honus Wagner (who achieved his greatest fame as a shortstop) and Fred Clarke (who managed the Pirates for 16 years).

Pittsburgh won the National League pennant in 1901, 1902, 1903, and 1909. In late June 1909, the Pirates moved into their new ballpark, Forbes Field, which would be their home for the next 60 years. Between 1899 and 1913 the team never suffered a losing season, finishing second five times and third three times.

The Pirates' victory in the 1909 World Series marked the team's high point, and thereafter the team began losing ground to Frank Chance's Chicago Cubs and John McGraw's New York

Giants. Pittsburgh staged a brief revival under managers Bill McKechnie in 1925 and Donie Bush in 1927, but throughout the 1930s, 1940s, and 1950s, no pennant flew at Forbes Field.

Not until 1960, with shortstop Dick Groat, outfielder Roberto Clemente, and pitchers Bob Friend and Vern Law (all of them long-time Pirates), did Pittsburgh again rise to the top. Under manager Danny Murtaugh they won 95 games that year, lost 59, took the World Series from the favored New York Yankees, and drew 1,705,828 fans, the most ever in a single season at Forbes Field.

For the rest of the 1960s the Pirates were also-rans. Then came the golden seventies, during which Pittsburgh won six National League East division titles—1970, 1971, 1972, 1974, 1975, and 1979. They also won two World Championships, 1971 and 1979, and probably would have won more but for the presence of Cincinnati's Big Red Machine in the National League West.

Attendance at Pittsburgh's new Three Rivers Stadium was disappointing, however, in this era of such slugging superstars as Willie Stargell, Dave Parker, and until his tragic death in December 1972, Roberto Clemente.

Attendance got even worse as the Pirates crumpled in the 1980s, occupying the cellar for three consecutive seasons, 1984, 1985, and 1986. But just as the 1970s had ushered in a rebirth of pennant hopes, so did the 1990s under manager Jim Leyland. The Pittsburgh stars of the day included outfielders Barry Bonds, Andy Van Slyke, and Bobby Bonilla, along with pitchers Doug Drabek and Randy Tomlin.

The Pirates won the division title in 1990, 1991, and 1992 but lost the league championship each time. By 1993 they had also lost, via free agency, Bonds, Bonilla, and Drabek.

Allegheny, Innocents, and Pirates

The Pittsburgh baseball club that joined the new major league American Association in 1882 went by the name of Allegheny, the name of the

Transcendental Graphics

Pud Galvin

county rather than the city. Old records show pitcher James (Pud) Galvin hurling for Allegheny of the American Association in 1885 and 1886, then for Pittsburgh when the reorganized team entered the National League.

Whatever its name, the Allegheny club was not especially memorable, with the exception of Pud Galvin and another, even more successful pitcher from 1885-86, Ed (Cannonball) Morris, who went 39-24 and then 41-20. Allegheny finished third in 1885 and second in 1886.

TEAM INFORMATION AT A GLANCE

Founding date: April 30, 1887 [National League]

Home stadium: Three Rivers Stadium
600 Stadium Circle
Pittsburgh, PA 15212

Dimensions: Left-field line—335 feet
Center field—400 feet
Right-field line—335 feet
Seating capacity: 58,729

Team uniforms: Home—base color white with black and gold trim;
Road—base color gray with word "Pittsburgh" across chest
Team nickname: Allegheny in American Association;
Alleghenies, 1887-1890; Pirates, 1891—
Team logo: gold diamond-shaped box with head of a pirate in black in lower section,
and above it the stylized printed word "Pirates" in gold outlined in black

Franchise record	Won	Lost	Pct.
(1887-1993)	8,426	7,852	.518

World Series wins (5): 1909, 1925, 1960, 1971, 1979
National League championships (9): 1901, 1902, 1903, 1909, 1925, 1927, 1960, 1971, 1979
National League East division first-place finishes (9): 1970, 1971,
1972, 1974, 1975, 1979, 1990, 1991, 1992
League/division last-place finishes (11): 1890, 1891, 1917, 1950,
1952, 1953, 1954, 1955, 1984, 1985, 1986

In 1887 Pittsburgh took the place of ousted Kansas City in the National League NL, and in the tougher competition of the NL the team sank in the standings, finishing in the second division from 1887 through 1889. Then came a truly horrendous season. The Players League (PL) of 1890 (a one-year phenomenon) fielded eight teams, one of them in Pittsburgh.

Worse, they lured away a number of players from the NL team, including pitcher Pud Galvin and first baseman Jake Beckley. The bereft Allegheny club finished not merely in the second division but in the depths of the National League basement, with a record of 23-113, the worst in the history of the franchise. They came in 66½ games behind pennant-winning Brooklyn.

When the Players League folded, the two Pittsburgh ball clubs, from the PL and the NL, combined to form the Pittsburgh Athletic Company. This gave the new team the pick of both rosters and offered Pittsburgh a fighting chance to leave the NL cellar. To strengthen the club further, they

Transcendental Graphics

Jake Beckley

signed second baseman Lou Bierbaur, who had jumped from the Philadelphia team of the American Association to the Brooklyn entry in the Players League.

Brooklyn, of course, had no further use for Beirbaur, but the American Association, fighting for its existence, was incensed. "The action of the Pittsburgh club in signing Bierbaur is piratical," it said in a formal statement to a board of arbitration. The board ruled in favor of Pittsburgh—and also provided the ball club with its nickname, the Pirates.

Neither Bierbaur nor the reclaimed players lifted Pittsburgh out of the slump in 1891, but better days were coming.

In 1892 they struggled to sixth place. The next year, under manager Al Buckenberger, they finished second. Left-handed pitcher Frank Killen had the best year of his career, 34-10, while first baseman Jake Beckley, a future Hall of Famer, led

the team with 106 RBIs. There was no encore. The Pirates sank to seventh and eventually eighth place before the turn of the century.

Connie Mack, the skipper of the Philadelphia Athletics for half a century, began his managerial duties with the Pittsburgh Pirates in 1894, taking the reins from Al Buckenberger near the end of the season. Connie Mack, born Cornelius McGillicuddy, was a playing manager, a catcher who had already put in time with Washington in the National League and Brooklyn in the Players League. His Pirate teams of 1894-96 had winning records but finished far down in the standings.

Six Guys from Louisville

After the 1899 season Louisville (along with Cleveland, Washington, and Baltimore) were dropped from the National League, reducing the number of franchises from 12 to eight. The Louisville Colonels, 75-77 that year, had several first-rate ballplayers on their roster. The Colonels' astute owner, Barney Dreyfuss, and the Pirates owner, Bill (Captain) Kerr effected a merger between the two clubs.

Dreyfuss, a German immigrant who had developed a fondness for baseball in his adopted hometown of Paducah, Kentucky, did well in the brewery business and even better in the baseball business. A year after the Louisville-Pittsburgh merger, Dreyfuss acquired full ownership of the Pirates.

The merger brought not only the talented Dreyfuss to Pittsburgh but also five excellent players. Fred Clarke, an outfielder, had been the playing manager of the Colonels, and in 1900 he became the playing manager of the Pirates. Honus Wagner, best known as a shortstop, played various positions in his early years, always hitting for a high average. In 1900, "The Flying Dutchman's" first year with Pittsburgh, he led the league in batting at .381, in doubles with 45, and in triples with 22. He also stole 38 bases and drove in 100 runs. Another arrival from Louisville was a young left-handed pitcher named Rube Waddell, whose

8-13 record in 1900 was less indicative of his future greatness than was his league-leading 2.37 ERA. Clarke, Wagner, and Waddell were all destined for the Hall of Fame.

The Louisville Colonels supplied two other, lesser-known stars to the Pirates. One was Tommy Leach, a five-foot-six-and-a-half-inch third baseman who played for the Pirates from 1900 through 1911. The other was pitcher Deacon Phillippe, who turned in four 20-win seasons for Pittsburgh between 1901 and 1905.

In the first year of the merged Pirates and Colonels, Barney Dreyfuss's team, managed by Fred Clarke, rose to second place in the National League. Deacon Phillippe had an 18-15 record with a 2.84 ERA. But Philippe was by no means the only noteworthy pitcher on the Pirates' staff. Left-hander Jesse Tannehill, with Pittsburgh since 1897, posted a 20-6 mark, and future Hall of Famer Jack Chesbro, an 1899 arrival, went 14-13.

Starting in 1901, the Pirates won the pennant three straight times. Favored with brilliant pitching from Phillippe and Sam Leever (whose lifetime winning percentage of .676 puts him ninth on the all-time list), the Pittsburgh Pirates contended for the pennant—or won it—in every season of the first decade of the new century. In 1901 Phillippe and Chesbro were 20-game winners, while Tannehill at 18-10 led the league with a 2.18 ERA. Leever posted a 14-5 mark. The big gun on offense was Wagner, who hit .353 and drove in 126 runs.

In 1902 Jack Chesbro paced the all-but-invincible Pirate pitching staff with a 28-6 record, after which he, along with Tannehill, jumped to the New York Highlanders of the fledgling American League. Pittsburgh outfielder Ginger Beaumont outhit Wagner that year, with a league-leading .357 to Wagner's .329, but The Flying Dutchman took league honors in RBIs with 91.

The first World Series between the National and American Leagues was played in 1903, and the Pirates were in it, having taken the NL title once again. The mound aces this time were Sam Leever, 25-7, with a league-leading 2.06 ERA, and Deacon Phillippe, 24-7. Honus Wagner led all NL hitters at .355 and drove in 101 runs. Outfielders Fred Clarke and Ginger Beaumont both had fine seasons, Beaumont hitting .351 and Clarke .341.

Meanwhile, over in the American League, the Boston Pilgrims, under manager Jimmy Collins, breezed to victory. The owners of the two pennant-winning teams, Barney Dreyfuss of Pittsburgh and Henry Killilea of Boston, agreed to stage a postseason best-of-nine playoff for the "world championship." The upstart American Leaguers from Boston triumphed, five games to three.

Pittsburgh, under playing-manager Fred Clarke, fielded solid, exciting ball clubs from 1904 through 1908, but the New York Giants and the Chicago Cubs were a shade stronger, dividing NL pennants between them. Then in 1909 the Pirates again broke loose, winning 110 games, losing 42, and beating out the Cubs by 6½ games.

The Pirates pitching remained as superb as

Transcendental Graphics

Honus Wagner

ever, although the faces had changed. Only Deacon Phillippe (8-3) and Sam Leever (8-1) hung on from the 1903 staff. The new moundsmen included Howie Camnitz (25-6), Vic Willis (22-11), and Lefty Leifield (19-8). Rookie Babe Adams turned in a 12-3 record with a 1.11 ERA and went on to dominate the World Series. Adams would be a familiar face in Pittsburgh for a long time—until 1926, in fact—but in the pennant-winning year of 1909 he was just getting started.

Honus Wagner, now firmly established at shortstop, led all NL hitters for the fourth year in a row, batting .339 and driving in 100 runs. Fred Clarke put up respectable but non-Wagnerian numbers, batting .287 with 68 RBIs, while rookie second baseman Dots Miller checked in at .279 with 87 RBIs.

This time the Pirates' World Series opponents were the Detroit Tigers, featuring superstar Ty Cobb. The best-of-seven Series went down to the wire, with the Pirates winning it four games to three. Pitcher Babe Adams, going the distance

Transcendental Graphics

Fred Clarke

each time, won three games for the Pirates. Honus Wagner collected eight hits, drove in six runs, and stole six bases. Fred Clarke drove in seven runs, and Dots Miller added four. The seventh and deciding game was never in doubt, as the Pirates piled up an 8-0 lead behind Babe Adams's six-hit pitching.

Decline and Fall

After their World Series victory of 1909 the Pirates began to fade. Although Babe Adams was just coming into his own, the rest of the team, and particularly the pitchers, were nearing the end of the road. Howie Camnitz had a couple of 20-win seasons left, 1911 and 1912, and Deacon Phillippe enjoyed a remarkable 14-2 record in 1910 (much of it in relief) before calling it quits.

Few of the hurlers who replaced them were of equal caliber. One exception was left-hander Wilbur Cooper, who joined the staff in 1912. Over the next 13 seasons Cooper won 20 or more games four times and 16 or more games nine times. Honus Wagner stayed on through 1917, but his batting average dropped below .300 for the last four seasons—the first time in his 21-year career that had happened. Fred Clarke, after a fine 1911 season in which he hit .324, ceased being an active player. Following the 1916 season he was replaced as Pittsburgh's manager.

The upshot of all this was that the Pirates began to slide downhill. Through 1912 the situation was tolerable as they finished in second or third place. But in 1914 the Pirates finished seventh and in 1917 they fell into the cellar. Wilbur Cooper pitched well, but few others did.

Burleigh Grimes, a future Hall of Famer, went 3-16 in 1917 during his second year in the majors, and was traded to Brooklyn for second baseman George Cutshaw and outfielder Casey Stengel. One bright note on offense during this lean period was Max Carey, a speedy outfielder who first appeared in a Pirates' uniform in 1910 and last appeared in 1926.

Transcendental Graphics

Kiki Cuyler

As the team floundered, first under Fred Clarke, then under his successors, among whom were Hugo Bezdek and George Gibson, there seemed little to be hopeful about. But in 1921, after three years in fourth place, the Pirates made a run for the flag. Wilbur Cooper won more games than any other NL pitcher, recording 22 wins and 14 losses, while Whitey Glazner (in the one winning season of his brief career) and Babe Adams posted identical 14-5 records.

George Cutshaw batted .340 and Max Carey .309. Outfielder Carson Bigbee, a Pirate veteran, hit .323, and even the generally weak-hitting Rabbit Maranville, approaching the midpoint in his long, Hall-of-Fame career at shortstop, rose to .294. The Pirates held the NL lead through much of the summer, but when the curtain fell they were in second place, four games out. Even so, a runner-up finish was better than they were accustomed to, and Pirate fans began to take heart.

The Roaring Twenties

Throughout the 1920s the Pirates won more games each year than they lost. Yet their usual finish was third or fourth place. Only in 1925 and 1927 did they capture the National League pennant. The 1925 ball club, under manager Bill McKechnie, posted a team batting average of .307, led by a trio of hard-hitting outfielders—Kiki Cuyler (.357), Max Carey (.343), and Clyde Barnhart (.325).

Cuyler, in his second full season, collected 220 hits and led the league in triples with 26, and runs scored with 144. Barnhart drove in 114 runs, fifth highest in the NL. The infield had some punch, too, with shortstop Glenn Wright batting .308 and driving in 122 runs to lead the Pirates in that category.

First baseman George Grantham, acquired from the Cubs in late 1924, hit .326, and Pie Traynor, one of the greatest third basemen ever, hit exactly his career average, .320, and knocked in 106 runs.

With this kind of hitting, about all that was needed from the mound staff was adequacy, and the 1925 pitchers were more than adequate. Unlike the hitters, though, they are not household names: Lee Meadows (19-10), Ray Kremer (17-8), Emil Yde (17-9), Johnny Morrison (17-14), and Vic Aldridge (15-7).

An awesome ball club, the 1925 Pirates took over first place in late July and held it the rest of the way, leaving the second-place Giants 8½ games back. In the World Series the Washington Senators seemed to have victory wrapped up, winning three of the first four games.

No team had ever come back from a three-to-one deficit in a seven-game series—but the Pirates did. They won the fifth game, 6-3, behind Vic Aldridge. Then they won the sixth game, 3-2, behind Ray Kremer on a fifth-inning solo homer by second baseman Eddie Moore, breaking a 2-2 tie. In the seventh game all seemed to be lost when the Senators scored four runs in the first inning. With the great, though aging, Walter Johnson on the mound for Washington, the outlook was bleak.

Transcendental Graphics

Max Carey

But this was not Johnson's day. The Pirate hitters rocked him for 15 hits and won the game, 9-7. A bases-loaded double by Kiki Cuyler in the eighth inning was the deciding blow.

The Pirates should have won the pennant easily in 1926, particularly since they had purchased still another fence-busting outfielder, Paul Waner, from San Francisco of the Pacific Coast League. But the team was torn by dissension, which came to a head over ex-manager Fred Clarke's second-guessing manager Bill McKechnie from the bench.

Clarke, by that time part-owner of the ball club, had come out of retirement to "assist' McKechnie, an arrangement objected to by Babe Adams and others. Adams was unceremoniously fired. "I am 18 years in baseball without ever opening my mouth," he said, "and then when I answer a question, I find myself chucked off the club."

Adams was not alone. Veteran outfielder Carson Bigbee was released, then first baseman Stuffy McInnis, and finally manager Bill McKechnie. After the season, Clarke sold his stock in the Pirates and retired for good.

This upheaval did not slow down the team. The Pirates, under their new manager, Donie Bush, edged out the Cardinals and Giants to take the NL pennant. Unfortunately for the Bucs and their fans, the AL pennant-winner was perhaps the greatest team of all time—the 1927 Yankees. In the World Series, Pittsburgh folded, dropping four straight games, with Babe Ruth and Lou Gehrig driving in 12 runs between them.

The 1927 Pirates, while no match for the Yankees in the Series, were an outstanding ball club, featuring three of the league's five top hitters. Paul (Big Poison) Waner, playing left field, led the NL at .380. His brother, center-fielder Lloyd

Transcendental Graphics

Pie Traynor

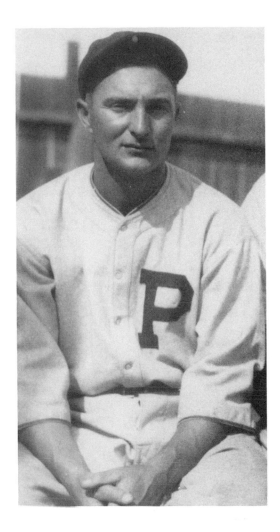

Both photos: *Transcendental Graphics*

The Waner Brothers: Paul "Big Poison" (left) and Lloyd "Little Poison"

(Little Poison) Waner, batted .355, and third baseman Pie Traynor hit .342. The team as a whole posted a .305 batting average.

Few Pittsburgh fans who saw the 1927 Pirates in action could have imagined that their ball club would not win another pennant for 33 years. The Pirates finished fourth in 1928 and second, to the Chicago Cubs, in 1929. The stock market crashed that fall, and the fortunes of the Pirates were scarcely better than the fortunes of Wall Street in the 1930s.

From So-So to the Cellar

In 1930 Pittsburgh still had the Waners in the outfield and Traynor at third base, all of whom hit .360-plus. Pitcher Ray Kremer won 20 games while losing 12, but his 5.02 ERA showed how much he needed those potent Pirate bats in order to win.

The team took fifth place in 1930, but they were a better ball club than the standings indicated. In 1932 and 1933, under returnee manager George

Transcendental Graphics

Arky Vaughn

Gibson, the Pirates stayed tenaciously in the pennant race, finishing second both years, then faded a bit until the late 1930s.

In 1938, Pie Traynor's fourth season as Pittsburgh's skipper, the team appeared to have the pennant in their grasp. Their star hitter was an outfielder, though not one of the Waner brothers. He was rookie Johnny Rizzo, enjoying his one and only great season, batting .301, belting 23 homers, and driving in 111 runs. Also impressive was veteran shortshop Arky Vaughn, a future Hall of Famer, although Vaughan's .322 battng average was well below his league-leading .385 of three years earlier.

Pittsburgh held a seven-game lead at the beginning of September, and even as late as September 23 the Pittsburgh Press could trumpet, "Bucs Home to Put 'Clincher' on Flag." But the 1938 Bucs suffered one of the great late-season collapses in major league history, as the Cubs won ten games in a row—including three crucial games against the Pirates—and the Bucs wound up two games back.

They did not recover. Fourth-place to eighth-place finishes became the norm for the Pirates in the 1940s and 1950s, although in wartime 1944, led by manager Frankie Frisch, they won 90 games, lost 63, and finished second. Their wartime stars were third baseman Bob Elliott, draft-deferred because of head injuries, and blooper-pitcher Rip Sewell.

Elliott drove in more than 100 runs in 1943, 1944, and 1945, while Sewell posted records of 21-9, 21-12, and 11-9 for these years that author Richard Goldstein called "spartan seasons." (To avoid long-distance travel, the Pirates set up their wartime spring-training headquarters in chilly Muncie, Indiana.)

The postwar Pirates were a team with one redeeming quality—Ralph Kiner. A heavy-hitting outfielder and future Hall of Famer, Kiner led the National League in home runs year after year, from 1946 through 1952, without a break. Hitting one homer for every 7.1 official times at bat, he was second only to the legendary Babe Ruth in percentage of homers per 100 times at-bat. But Kiner could not carry the team alone, and the postwar Pirates languished in the second division with the exception of a modest fourth-place effort in 1948.

Until the arrival of manager Danny Murtaugh in late 1957, the 1950s had been an unrelieved disaster for the Bucs. They spent 1950 in last place, moved up to seventh in 1951, then holed up in the cellar for four straight seasons, 1952 through 1955. A few good players came and went, traded away by Branch Rickey, who became the Pirates' general manager at the start of the 1950s.

In his five years at Pittsburgh Rickey did not repeat his earlier successes with the Cardinals and Dodgers. He dealt outfielders Wally Westlake to the Cardinals, Gus Bell to the Reds, and, in 1953, Ralph Kiner to the Cubs.

These were not astute deals. But he also signed a few of the key players in the Pirates' future, notably second baseman Bill Mazeroski and Roberto Clemente. When Rickey stepped

Ralph Kiner: "... With One Swing"

Fans came to the ballpark to see Ralph Kiner. At a time when the Pirates were mired in the nether reaches of the National League—the late 1940s and early 1950s—attendence at Forbes Field soared. There was just one reason: the hitting of Ralph Kiner. Frankie Gustine, a Pirate teammate of Kiner's, said, "It was amazing. If Ralph batted in the eighth, it seemed like the whole place would get up and leave. But if there was a chance he would bat in the ninth, no one left."

The fans came to see Kiner hit home runs, and quite often he obliged them. From his rookie season, 1946, until his last full year in a Pirates' uniform, 1952, Ralph Kiner led the league in home runs (or tied for the lead) every year. His low of 23 as a rookie was just enough to beat out the Giants' Johnny Mize, while his 54 in 1949 is the second highest total ever in the National League.

He also hit 51 In 1947 (to tie Johnny Mize that year) and 47 in 1950. Traded away after only seven seasons, Kiner, with 301 career homers for the Pirates—an average of 43 per season—ranks number two on the Pirates' all-time list of career home run hitters. Willie Stargell with 475 Pirate homers over a 20-year span stands number one.

Kiner was an adequate fielder, a slow runner, and a .279 lifetime hitter. He could do just one thing supremely well—hit home runs. But as Warren Spahn said, "Kiner can wipe out your lead with one swing." He was a valuable asset on a team that was going nowhere, doubly valuable to the franchise because fans crowded into ballpark for the specific purpose of seeing him at bat. He was a drawing card, the most compelling one in the long history of the Pirates. Author Bob Smizik in his recent history of the Pirates observes, "Ralph Kiner drew enough people to Forbes Field during the grim years after World War II to enable the franchise to survive."

Photo: *Transcendental Graphics*

aside in 1955, he was replaced by Joe L. Brown (son of comedian Joe E. Brown), a successful minor league general manager. Brown was determined to build a championship team, and he succeeded.

In 1956 the Pirates finished seventh. The big news for Pittsburgh that year was the hitting of first baseman Dale Long. In his second major league season, Long hit eight home runs in eight consecutive games (a record later tied by the Yankees' Don Mattingly). In 1957, with the Pirates lan-

guishing in last place, Joe Brown fired manager Bobby Bragan and replaced him with the Pirates' first base coach, Danny Murtaugh.

Relaunching the Pirate Ship

Despite their last-place finish in 1957 the Pirates had some promising talent other than Mazeroski and Clemente. At shortstop Dick Groat figured in their plans for the future, as did outfield-

After three games between the Pirates and the New York Yankees, the 1960 World Series looked like a mismatch. The Yanks had scored 30 runs to the Bucs nine. Pittsburgh won the opener, 6-4, behind Vern Law at Forbes Field, as Pirate second baseman Bill Mazeroski hit a key two-run homer. Reliever Roy Face pitched the last two innings to record a save. But then the Mantle-Maris-Berra machine started hitting on all cylinders. New York took game two in a 16-3 rout and game three in a 10-0 whitewash. The Pirates came back with Vern Law, the NL Cy Young Award-winner in 1960, to pitch game four. With relief help from Roy Face and a two-run single in the fifth inning by center fielder Bill Virdon, the Pirates won, 3-2, to even the Series at two games apiece.

Art Ditmar, the Yanks' losing pitcher in game one, started game five for New York. Bill Mazeroski's two-run double in the second inning drove him from the mound and capped a rally that led ultimately to a 5-2 Pirate win, with Roy Face picking up another save. The underdog Pirates were now ahead in the Series, three games to two, and returned to their home ballpark to try to wrap up the World Championship in game six.

Instead, the New York Yankees pulverized the Bucs once more, this time 12-0, tying the Series at three games apiece. At this point the Yanks had outscored the Bucs 38 to 3 in the games New York won, while the Pirates held a modest 14-8 edge in their own three victories. But that was history, for the outcome of the Series now hung on game seven.

Game seven was an action-packed finale to an improbable World Series. Once again behind Vern Law, the Pirates took an early 4-0 lead but blew it. The Yanks had built up a 5-4 edge going into the eighth inning. Pirate reliever Roy Face ran into trouble at last. Two more Yankee runners scored, and the score stood 7-4 when the Bucs came to bat in the last of the eighth. Pittsburgh closed the gap to 7-6—and they still had two runners on base with backup catcher Hal Smith at the plate. Smith delivered a three-run homer to put the Pirates ahead, 9-7. It still wasn't over.

The Yanks came back to tie the game in the top of the ninth, 9-9. Then in the bottom of the ninth, with Ralph Terry on the mound for New York, leadoff hitter Bill Mazeroski took the first pitch for a ball. Finding the second pitch more to his liking, Maz sent it over the left-field wall for a home run. The Pirates won the game, 10-9, and took the Series, four games to three. Outscored 55-27, the Bucs were World Champions.

---

er Bob Skinner and third-baseman-outfielder Frank Thomas. On the mound they had several fine pitchers with middling won-lost records: Bob Friend, Vern Law, Roy Face, and, one who got away (to the Reds) in 1958, Bob Purkey. Murtaugh brought his 1958 Pirates home in second place, eight games behind the Milwaukee Braves. Frank Thomas cracked 35 homers and drove in 109 runs, while Bob Friend went 22-14 to lead the league in wins.

After a fourth-place finish in 1959—during which lefthander Harvey Haddix pitched a 12-inning perfect game for the Pirates, only to lose it, 1-0, in the 13th inning—the Pirates rose to the top in 1960. The 1960 Pirates drew more than 1.7 million fans to Forbes Field. Shortstop Dick Groat led all NL hitters at .325. Roberto Clemente batted .314 and drove in 94 runs for the team's highest RBI total.

Vern Law, 20-9, was the Bucs' only 20-game winner, but Bob Friend posted an 18-12 record. Ace reliever Roy Face recorded 24 saves, although his 10-8 won-lost mark was far below the astonishing 18-1 he had achieved the year before.

The Pirates went into the 1960 World Series against the Yankees as distinct underdogs, but when it was all over—and Bill Mazeroski had blasted his ninth-inning home run in the seventh game—the Pittsburgh Pirates were World Champions. It had been a long, long wait since 1925.

These 1960 heroes were overachievers, however, and it became apparent the very next season as the Pirates slid all the way to sixth place, four games under .500. Even with outfielder Roberto Clemente hitting .351 to lead the league and first baseman Dick Stuart, nicknamed "Dr. Strangeglove" for his fielding foibles, belting 35 homers and driving in 117 runs, the Bucs could not get started.

After a fourth-place finish in 1962 (despite a solid 93-68 record), Joe Brown went into a trading frenzy. Some of the deals he made were unwise, but he did have the good sense to keep rookie outfielder Willie Stargell, along with Clemente, Mazeroski, and Law. Nevertheless, the team struggled through the 1960s.

Even when they put up good numbers, as in 1965 (90-72) and 1966 (92-70), at least two other teams put up better ones. Attendance dropped below a million except in 1966, but the new, carpeted Three Rivers Stadium, which opened on July 16, 1970—and, more importantly, the on-field resurgence of the Pirates—brought new hope and enthusiasm to the Steel Town.

Willie Stargell's Family

The Pirates of the 1970s were in constant contention for the NL East title, winning it no fewer than six times. At the beginning of the decade, before the untimely death of superstar Roberto Clemente, Pittsburgh took three straight division championships—1970, 1971, and 1972. In those three years Willie Stargell, Roberto Clemente, and sometimes Al Oliver and Vic Davalillo patrolled the outfield. Richie Hebner held down third base, and Manny Sanguillan did the catching.

The mainstays of the mound staff were Dock Ellis, whose best year was 1971 at 19-9; Steve

Blass, who peaked at 19-8 in 1972; and reliever Dave Giusti, who saved between 22 and 30 games in each of the three seasons.

In 1970 and 1972 the Pirates won the NL East championship but lost the National League Championship Series (NLCS) to the Cincinnati Reds. But in between was a triumphant year—1971, when Stargell, Clemente, and company mowed down the San Francisco Giants in the NLCS and went on to edge out the Baltimore Orioles, four games to three, in the World Series.

An unlikely batting star of the postseason games was first baseman Bob Robertson, a powerful but erratic hitter, who smashed four home runs in the NCLS—three in one game—and added two more in the World Series. A much more likely star was Roberto Clemente, who collected 12 hits in the World Series, good for a .414 average, and played right field brilliantly. Sportswriter Dick Young of the New York Daily News rhapsodized, "The best player in the World Series 1971, maybe in the whole world, is Roberto Clemente." On the mound the standout was Steve Blass, who, after losing game one of the NLCS, came on to win two games in the World Series—one a three-hitter, one a four-hitter.

Roberto Clemente died in a plane crash on New Year's Eve 1972 while transporting relief supplies to earthquake victims in Nicaragua. [see sidebar] He seemed irreplaceable in 1973, as the Pirates faded to third place. Midway through the season, though, the Pirates called up Dave Parker from the Triple-A International League in Charleston, West Virginia.

Parker saw limited service that year and the next, but in 1974 the Pirates won the NL East title again. Then in 1975, playing regularly, Parker batted .308, hit 25 homers, and drove in 101 runs. Once again the Pirates topped the NL East but failed to advance to the World Series. In 1974 the L.A Dodgers defeated Pittsburgh in the NLCS, while in 1975 Cincinnati's "Big Red Machine" rolled over the Bucs in three straight games.

The late 1970s were years of NL East dominance by the Philadelphia Phillies. The Phillies won the division championship in 1976, 1977, and

Roberto Clemente

Roberto Clemente was born in rural Puerto Rico on August 18, 1934, and died, an internationally known superstar, in a plane crash following take-off from the airport at San Juan, Puerto Rico, on December 31, 1972. He was on a four-engine DC-7 cargo plane carrying relief supplies to earthquake-stricken Nicaragua.

Clemente, the first Hispanic to be elected to baseball's Hall of Fame, posted a .317 career batting average, collected an even 3,000 hits, won the NL batting title four times, and was one of the great outfielders of his era, with a throwing arm that intimidated—and often cut down—base runners. He led the league in assists five times, a National League record.

Proud and temperamental, sensitive to perceived slights or criticisms, he reached the height of his fame in the 1971 World Series, televised throughout the world, in which, as Roger Angell wrote, he played "a kind of baseball that none of us had ever seen before—throwing and running and hitting at something close to the level of absolute perfection...."

Photo: *Transcendental Graphics*

Pittsburgh fans *had* seen it before, of course, but after that ill-fated New Year's Eve flight to Nicaragua, they would not see it again. Waiving the usual five-year rule, the Hall of Fame inducted Roberto Clemente in 1973.

1978, with the Pirates finishing a strong second each year. Chuck Tanner, the manager of the Oakland A's for a number of years, took over as the Bucs' skipper in 1977.

By this time Willie Stargell had moved from the outfield to first base, Al Oliver and Bill Robinson were in the outfield with Dave Parker, and among the Pirate pitchers of note were John Candaleria, 20-5 with a 2.34 ERA in 1977; Don Robinson, 14-6 as a rookie in 1978; and sidearm reliever Kent Tekulve, chalking up 31 saves in 1978. Parker, Clemente's replacement in right field, led the league in batting in 1977 (.338) and in both batting and slugging in 1978 (.334 and .585).

Attendance at Three Rivers Stadium jumped by half a million from 1978 to 1979, and no wonder. The 1979 Pirates seemed destined for glory. Willie Stargell had emerged as the clubhouse leader, an inspirational veteran passing out stars for the players to put on their caps for good performances. Stargell led the team with 34 homers, while Parker led in RBIs with 94. Third baseman Bill Madlock, a midseason acquisition from San Francisco, batted .328 to pace the hitters.

Among the Pirate hurlers, six won in double figures (John Canadleria's 14 being the highest number) and none lost in double figures (although Candaleria with nine came close). The '79 Pirates were a well balanced team, with everyone contributing. They adopted as their theme song the popular "We Are Family," and no one doubted that the patriarch, the Big Daddy of "The Family" was Willie Stargell. In fact, they started calling him "Pops."

The Pirates captured the division title in 1979 after a close, hard-fought race, fending off the Montreal Expos and hanging on to win by two games. They then breezed past the Cincinnati Reds, three games to none, in the NLCS. Their World Series opponents were the Baltimore Orioles of Earl Weaver. It was another tough fight, and, as in 1925, the Bucs had to come back from a deficit of three games to one. Pirate hurlers Jim Rooker and Bert Blyleven combined for a 7-1 victory in game five. Then John Candelaria and reliever Kent Tekulve turned in a 4-0 shutout to tie the Series. Finally, in the decisive seventh game, Baltimore took a 1-0 lead, but in the sixth inning Willie Stagell homered with a runner on, and the Pirates went on to win the game, 4-1, and the series, four games to three.

Transcendental Graphics

Willie Stargell

Up from the Grim Eighties

The Pirates had never repeated as World Champions since 1902, and 1980 was no exception. Chuck Tanner's team won 15 fewer games in 1980 than they had the year before, finishing third in the NL East. Pitcher Jim Bibby, a much-traveled veteran, had a career year, winning 19 and losing only six. But Stargell was nearing retirement, and Parker began to tail off before being signed as a free agent by the Cincinnati Reds after the 1983 season.

The Pirates finished second to the Phillies in 1983. Third baseman Bill Madlock led the league in hitting at .323, while John Candelaria and Larry McWilliams, both lefties, turned in identical 15-8 records. After that, the roof caved in, and the Pirates retreated to the NL East cellar for three straight years.

Attendance slid to a dismal 735,900 in 1985 and there was talk of moving the franchise. The Galbreath family, owners of the ball club for decades, wanted out. A new ownership group took over in 1985 and hired little-known Syd Thrift to rebuild the team. Thrift soon became famous in baseball circles for his successful handling of the Pirate restructuring.

Manager Chuck Tanner lost his job after the bleak 1985 season, giving way to Jim Leyland, recently a coach for the White Sox and before that a minor league catcher and manager. Leyland and the new owners could not produce an instant winner, but the team began to show improvement. In 1988 the Bucs finished above .500 for the first time in five years, taking second place (a distant second place) 15 games behind the New York Mets. In 1989 they drifted back down to fifth place.

Then came the 1990s. Suddenly, the Pirates became the team to beat—and no other team in the NL East was able to beat them. They won the division championship three times in a row: 1990, 1991, 1992. Their standout performers came mostly from the immediate post-Galbreath period.

Outfielder Barry Bonds, son of former Giants' star Bobby Bonds, was signed in the June 1985 free-agency draft. Outfielder Bobby Bonilla came over from the White Sox in a July 1986 trade. Veteran outfielder Andy Van Slyke and pitcher Doug Drabek were obtained for the 1987 season via trades with the Cardinals and Yankees.

The team thus assembled hit its stride in 1990, with Drabek posting a 22-6 record, while Bonds (.301, 33 homers, 114 RBIs, 52 stolen bases) and Bonilla (.280, 32 homers, 120 RBIs) vied for MVP honors. Good as the Pirates were in 1990, they lost to Cincinnati in the NLCS, four games to two.

In 1991 and 1992 the Pirates, after winning in their division, went down to defeat both times at the hands of the Atlanta Braves in the NL playoffs. Bonds, Van Slyke, and Drabek continued to star. Bonilla defected to the Mets in the 1991 free agency draft, and Bonds and Drabek departed in the same way after the 1992 season.

A Pirates' youth movement brought guarded optimism. "If these kids can play like everyone thinks," said manager Jim Leyland, "then we'll be all right. The "kids" Leyland referred to struggled to a fifth place finish at 75-87. Inexperience played a role in the team's demise; over twenty rookies appeared during the year. But pitching was the primary reason for the club's downfall; the Pirates' staff recorded a 4.77 team ERA.

On the positive side, Van Slyke enjoyed another strong season, as did Orlando Merced (.313), veteran infielders Jay Bell (.310) and Jeff King (.295, 98 RBIs), and rookies Al Martin (18 homers, 64 RBIs) and Blas Minor. If Pittsburgh is to regain its status as a contender, however, the club's pitching, particularly its starting pitching, needs to improve.

SOURCES

BOOKS

Baseball Guide: 1987, 1992 Editions, The Sporting News Publishing Co., 1987, 1992.

Baseball Register: 1980, 1983, 1987, 1991, 1992 Editions, The Sporting News Publishing Co., 1980, 1983, 1987, 1991, 1992.

The Complete Handbook of Baseball, 1992, 23rd edition, edited by Zander Hollander, Signet, 1992.

Goldstein, Richard, *Spartan Seasons: How Baseball Survived the Second World War,* Macmillan, 1980.

Hoppel, Joe, *The Series: An Illustrated History of Baseball's Postseason Showcase,* The Sporting News Publishing Co., 1989.

Ivor-Campbell, Frederick, "Team Histories: Pittsburgh Pirates," *Total Baseball,* edited by John Thorn and Pete Palmer, Warner Books, 1989.

Lieb, Frederick G., *The Pittsburgh Pirates,* G. P. Putnam's Sons, 1948.

Reichler, Joseph L., editor, *The Baseball Encyclopedia,* 7th edition, Macmillan, 1988.

Reidenbaugh, Lowell, *Cooperstown: Where Baseball's Legends Live Forever,* The Sporting News Publishing Co., 1983.

Selzer, Jack, *Baseball in the Nineteenth Century: An Overview,* Cooperstown, NY: Society for American Baseball Research, 1986.

Smizik, Bob, *The Pittsburgh Pirates: An Illustrated History,* Walker & Company, 1990.

Voigt, David Quentin, *American Baseball: From the Gentleman's Sport to the Commissioner System,* University Park: The Pennsylvania State University Press, 1983.

Wagenheim, Kal, *Clemente!,* Praeger, 1973.

—*Gerald Tomlinson* for Book Builders, Inc.

NATIONAL LEAGUE WEST

ATLANTA BRAVES

Although Atlanta did not become a major league city until 1966, the Braves' franchise goes back to the beginning of professional baseball. A power in the National Association from 1871 to 1875, the Boston team, then called the Red Stockings, joined the National League (NL) as a charter member in 1876.

Sparked by ace pitcher Tommy Bond, the team won pennants in 1877 and 1878, another pennant in 1883, and then put together an outstanding, near-dynastic team under manager Frank Selee in the 1890s. The Beaneaters, as they were called by then, included such stars as pitcher Kid Nichols, who won 30 or more games for seven straight seasons, and outfielder Hugh Duffy, whose .438 batting average in 1894 remains the major league record.

After the turn of the century the Beaneaters (renamed the Braves in 1911) experienced scant success for nearly half a century. A notable exception occurred in 1914, when in July the Braves rose from last place—a familiar position for them—all the way to first, winning the pennant by 10½ games and the World Series in four straight over the favored Philadelphia A's. This 1914 team, immortalized as the "Miracle Braves," provided the ball club's last pennant until 1948. The various teams throughout that long stretch were seldom contenders. Usually, they were in the second division. Often they were last or next to last.

As on most losing teams, however, there were a few standout players. Hall-of-Fame first baseman George Sisler closed out his major league career with three fine seasons for the Braves in the years 1928 to 1930. Shortstop Rabbit Maranville also played his last professional years with the Braves from 1929 to 1935. Outfielder Wally Berger, a Brave from 1930 to 1937, was a bona fide star who led the league in homers and RBIs in 1935.

But only with the end of World War II did the Braves emerge from their dysfunction as a team. In 1948, with Warren Spahn and Johnny Sain on the mound, the Braves under manager Billy South-worth won the NL pennant, but lost the World Series to Cleveland. The Braves then went into another decline in the standings, a drop that cost them dearly in attendance and ended in Boston losing its National League franchise to Milwau-kee.

The 1953 Milwaukee Braves were an imme-diate hit. In the former home of the minor league Brewers, attendance skyrocketed, the team fin-ished second, and the franchise move—the first change in the list of NL cities since 1900—made owners of other National League ball clubs start studying their maps.

One Brave who debuted in Boston and be-came a superstar in Milwaukee was slugging third baseman Eddie Mathews. An outfielder who be-gan in Milwaukee and later moved on to star for Atlanta was baseball's all-time home run king, Hank Aaron. For 12 of the Braves' 13 years in Milwaukee, Hank Aaron and Eddie Mathews, shoo-ins for the Hall of Fame, anchored the team's offense.

In the pennant-winning seasons of 1957 and 1958, the main pitching chores were shared by Warren Spahn and Lew Burdette, strongly aided the first year by Bob Buhl. When the Braves faded somewhat in the early 1960s attendance dropped just as it had in Boston. By 1965 the Milwaukee Braves were in fifth place, and barely half a million fans showed up at County Stadium. A new group of owners imposed the old Boston-to-Milwaukee solution, moving the franchise to Atlanta.

It worked again—at the gate, if not in the standings. The Atlanta Braves remained in fifth place, but attendance nearly tripled over the previ-ous year. For their first 16 years in Atlanta the Braves were generally mediocre, the exception being 1969, the first year of division play, when they edged out the Giants and the Reds for the NL West title.

The "amazin'" Mets stopped them cold, how-ever, taking three straight games in the National League Championship Series (NLCS) to wrest the pennant away from the Braves, who were stronger on offense but weaker on defense than the Mets.

After another decade-plus in the depths, the Braves rose suddenly to take the division title by one game in 1982, but again lost out in three straight games in the NLCS, this time to the St. Louis Cardinals.

After a second-place finish in 1983, the Braves drooped again, but roared back in 1991, 1992, and 1993 with three straight pennants. Among the stars of the 1991-93 Braves were third baseman Terry Pendleton, outfielders Ron Gant and Dave Justice, and pitchers Tom Glavine and John Smoltz.

Red Stockings and Beaneaters

The history of the Braves begins with the National Association, the first professional base-ball league. From 1871 to 1875 the Boston Red Stockings (*not* the present-day Red Sox) rode roughshod over the opposition, winning four pen-nants in five years, led by pitcher Al Spalding, shortstop George Wright, and George's talented brother Harry, the team's manager as well as an outfielder.

When the National League began business in 1876, the Boston Red Stockings became one of the eight original teams. Pitcher Al Spalding deserted to the Chicago White Stockings, leading his team, now the Cubs, to the first NL pennant. Boston, with the renowned Wright brothers of baseball, finished fourth.

In their second season, 1877, the Red Caps (as they were sometimes called), having acquired pitcher Tommy Bond from Hartford, swept to victory, as they did again in 1878. Bond, a pitcher whose fireball delivery was thought by some to "ruin" catchers, won 40 games each year (40-17 in 1877 and 40-19 in 1878).

He did even better in 1879 (43-19), but Bos-ton fell to second place and did not recover until 1883 when, paced by pitchers Grasshopper Jim Whitney and Charlie Buffinton, they again claimed the pennant. Once more, though, they dropped to second place the following year, then fell out of contention for a while.

TEAM INFORMATION AT A GLANCE

Founding date: April 22, 1876 (Boston) [National League]
April 15, 1953 (Milwaukee)
April 12, 1966 (Atlanta)

Home stadium: Atlanta-Fulton County Stadium
521 Capitol Avenue
Atlanta, GA 30312

Dimensions: Left-field line—330 feet
Center field—402 feet
Right-field line—330 feet
Seating capacity: 52,007

Team uniforms: Home—base color white with scarlet braid and navy blue trim
Road—base color gray with word "Atlanta" across chest
Team nickname: Unofficially called various names—Red Stockings, Red Caps, Beaneaters, Nationals,
Doves, and Rustlers, 1876-1911 (commonly Beaneaters in 1890s); Braves, 1911-present
Team logo: Scarlet tomahawk with navy blue border.

Franchise record	Won	Lost	Pct.
Boston (1876-1952)	5118	5,598	.478
Milwaukee (1953-1965)	1,146	890	.547
Atlanta (1966-1993)	2,134	2,307	.481

World Series wins (2): 1914, 1957
National League championships (14): 1877, 1878, 1883, 1891, 1892,
1893, 1897, 1898, 1914, 1948, 1957, 1958, 1991, 1992
National League West division first-place finishes (4): 1969, 1982, 1991, 1992, 1993
League/division last-place finishes (17): 1906, 1909, 1910, 1911, 1912, 1922,
1924, 1929, 1935, 1976, 1977, 1978, 1979, 1986, 1988, 1989, 1990

In 1890 the Beaneaters, as they had come to be called, got a new manager, Frank Selee. An excellent judge of players, or so knowledgeable people said, Selee had just won successive pennants in the minors at Oshkosh and Omaha. Along with Selee came a rookie pitcher, future Hall-of-Famer Charles (Kid) Nichols. The Beaneaters already had on their staff another future Hall-of-Fame pitcher, John Clarkson, who had won 49 games while losing 19 in 1889.

But the Beaneaters, like other ball clubs, had a problem in 1890. There were suddenly not just two major leagues but three: the National League, the American Association (in its ninth season), and the brand-new Players' League (which lasted for just one year, 1890).

This situation redistributed the talent and muddled the 1890 season. The Beaneaters finished fifth. When the Players' League folded, Selee regained a few of his lost players—Boston's entry in the defunct Players' League had won the pennant—and in 1891 the strengthened Beaneaters topped Anson's Chicago Colts to take the NL crown. Two 30-game winners sparked Boston, John Clarkson (33-19) and Kid Nichols (30-17), along with a 20-game winner, Harry Staley (20-8).

When the American Association closed up shop after the 1891 season—Boston's entry in that league also had captured the pennant—Frank Selee, fine judge of talent that he was, assembled what historian David Q. Voigt has called "a team of superstars."

Among Boston's elite players were catchers King Kelly and Charlie Ganzel, pitcher Jack Stivetts (added to the three great hurlers already on the staff), first baseman Tommy Tucker, second baseman Bobby Lowe, shortstop Herman Long, and third baseman Billy Nash. In the outfield were Hall-of-Famers Hugh Duffy and Tommy McCarthy and career .321 hitter Harry Stovey. The 1892 and 1893 Beaneaters took the flag in the National League, now simply called the "big league," with all competitors thwarted for the time being.

In 1894 the team faded to third place, as Boston's pitchers ran into trouble while their hitters went wild. This was the year Hugh Duffy hit .438, belted 18 homers (it was the dead ball-era), and drove in 145 runs—all league-leading totals. **[see sidebar]** After three more years below the pinnacle, Frank Selee's men recovered and captured two more pennants: 1897 and 1898. His 1892 and 1898 teams each won 102 games, the most season wins in the history of the franchise.

By 1897-98 the roster had changed somewhat, but a few of the new players were stars in their own right, especially Jimmy Collins at third base and Billy Hamilton in the outfield, both Hall of Famers. In 1899 the Beaneaters finished second to Ned Hanlon's Brooklyn Superbas.

Boston first baseman Fred Tenney, a Beaneater from 1894 through 1907 and a lifetime .295 hitter, posted the highest average of his career in 1899—.347—while outfielder Chick Stahl hit .351. This was still a solid ball club, but the turn of the century marked an unhappy turn in the fortunes of the Boston Beaneaters.

Transcendental Graphics

Kid Nichols

From a Quagmire to a Miracle

Frank Selee did not oversee a disaster in 1900, but he did see his team struggle though a losing season, 66-72, and finish 17 games behind Brooklyn, Pittsburgh, and Philadelphia. Shortstop Harry Long led the league in home runs with 12, and third baseman Jimmy Collins ranked fourth in RBIs with 95. But this was not the powerhouse team of the 1890s, and in 1901 a fifth-place finish marked the end of Frank Selee's managerial reign.

Under managers Al Buckenberger, 1902-04, and Fred Tenney, 1905-07, the roof caved in. After finishing third in 1902 (but 29 games behind pennant-winning Pittsburgh), the Beaneaters plunged to sixth in 1903 and seventh in 1904. The great pitchers of the nineties were gone. The infielders had unremembered names such as Ed Abbaticchio, Harvey Aubrey, and Fred Raymer,

PROFILE	Hugh Duffy, .438

In 1894, at the age of 27, a little five-foot-seven outfielder for the Boston Beaneaters set a record that remains unbroken. In 539 times at bat that year Hugh Duffy collected 236 hits for a batting average of .438. Among his hits were 50 doubles and 18 home runs, both league-leading figures. He also led in runs batted in (145), total bases (366), and slugging average (.679). Duffy was not a consistent high-average hitter like others such as Ty Cobb, Rogers Hornsby, or Ted Williams. His career batting average, .328, puts him well below the all-time top 20—in fact, it ties him with Rod Carew. But for that one season, 1894, Hugh Duffy was an opposing pitcher's worst nightmare.

True, high batting averages were more common in those days than they are now. Duffy was not the only .400 hitter in 1894. Joining him in the charmed circle were three Phillies: Tuck Turner (.416), Big Sam Thompson (.404), and Ed Delahanty (.400). Another player on that remarkable fourth-place Phillies' team just missed the mark: Sliding Billy Hamilton, at .399. As Duffy said half a century later, "No one thought much of averages in those days. I didn't realize I had hit that much until the official averages were published four months later."

Photo: *Transcendental Graphics*

and the outfield was making do with similarly unknown and unproductive players. Worse was yet to come.

In 1905 the Beaneaters lost 103 games to finish seventh, 54½ games back. The next year they lost 102 and fell to the cellar, trailing first-place Chicago by 66½ games. Fred Tenney managed the team and played first base through these disastrous campaigns (and another seventh-place finish in 1907) before being fired as Boston's skipper and traded to the New York Giants.

After struggling up to sixth place in 1908 under one-year manager Joe Kelly, the team suffered total impotence for the next four years—four consecutive years in the cellar, four straight 100-loss seasons. The nadir was reached the first year, in 1909, when the ball club lost 108 games (a .295

percentage), when their hottest hitter, outfielder Ginger Beaumont, batted .263 and drove in 60 runs (a low RBI total that even so was 24 runs higher than the Beaneater runner-up, third baseman Bill Sweeney).

It was the year that starting pitcher George Furguson went 5-23, although the ace of the staff, Al Mattern, did surprisingly well—16-20 with a 2.85 ERA. Still, all in all, it was a very bad year. So were 1910, 1911, and 1912.

Then the Braves, as they were called from 1911 onward, hired George Stallings to manage. Stallings, a veteran skipper, had already seen duty with the Phillies, Tigers, and Highlanders (Yankees) before signing on with the Braves. His managerial record at these previous stops was hardly scintillating, but he soon became known to

Transcendental Graphics

Rabbit Maranville

pennant for the Braves in 1914.

The New York Giants took an early lead in 1914. With Christy Mathewson, Rube Marquard, and Jeff Tesreau all throwing well, neither the Braves nor anyone else seemed to have much of a chance. Then the Giants (and especially Marquard) faltered.

On July 19 the race was close, with even the usually hapless Braves only 11 games out, although still in the cellar. Manager Stallings had brought a couple of veteran infielders to the club: shortstop Rabbit Maranville in 1913 and second baseman Johnny Evers in 1914.

With these additions, and with two pitchers having their best seasons ever—Dick Rudolph and Bill James—the Braves climbed steadily upward. Rudolph won 27 games to lead the league; James won 26. A third pitcher, Lefty Tyler, chipped in with a 16-14 record. The fired-up Braves won

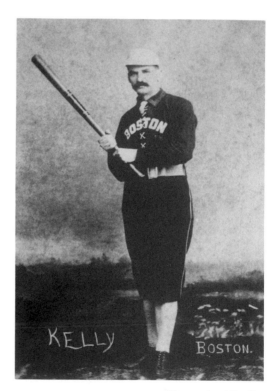

Transcendental Graphics

King Kelly

the baseball world as "The Miracle Man." And for good reason. The 1913 Braves rose to fifth place.

Rookie pitcher Dick Rudolph and two-year veteran Hub Perdue fashioned winning seasons, 14-13 and 16-13 respectively. Rookie hurler Bill James went only 6-10, but his 2.79 ERA held promise. Of course, no one was calling manager George Stallings a miracle man yet. The 1913 Boston Braves finished 31-1/2 games behind John McGraw's formidable New York Giants. Only the most optimistic fan would have predicted a

Transcendental Graphics

Tommy McCarthy

between them. Catcher Hank Gowdy collected six hits, five of them for extra bases, and drove in three runs. In the wake of this triumph George Stallings got a five-year contract, Johnny Evers a new Chalmers automobile, and the team a new ballpark—Braves Field, a one-million-dollar, 40,000-seat facility, completed in August 1915.

The Futile Years

The miracle was, however, just that—a one-time phenomenon. Not that the Braves rolled over and played dead. They put on an exciting drive for the flag in 1915, but no one seemed to have quite the same mastery as in 1914. Dick Rudolph, despite a fine 2.37 ERA, dropped to 22-19, losing more games than any other NL pitcher. Bill James won a mere five games, his career essentially over. The Braves finished second in 1915, then in 1916, after another good race, they came in third, just four games back with an 89-63 won-lost record.

In 1917 the Braves began one of the most extended periods of futility in baseball history. Between World War I and the end of World War II in 1945, the Braves never finished higher than fourth—and finished that high only three times, in 1921, 1933, and 1934.

In 1933 and 1934 the team, under manager Bill McKechnie, featured outfielder Waller Berger, a superstar among journeymen. In 1933 Berger batted .313 with 27 homers and 106 RBIs. In 1934 his stats included a .298 batting average, 34 homers, and 134 runs batted in. No one else on the Braves came close to Berger's power totals.

The most consistent pitcher for Boston in this glum era was southpaw Ed Brandt who, after a shaky 9-21 debut in 1928, put in four winning seasons between 1931 and 1934. Brandt's best year was 1931 when he went 18-11 with a 2.92 ERA. In the Braves' two years in fourth place he posted won-lost records of 18-14 and 16-14.

In the long dry stretch from 1917 to 1945 the Braves ended up in seventh place no fewer than 11 times. Had it not been for the ill-starred Phillies, who claimed the cellar all but two of those times,

60 of their last 76 games to overtake the Giants and win the pennant going away.

They finished 10½ games in front and the Boston fans went wild. They loved their "Miracle Braves." On Labor Day they nearly mobbed Giants' outfielder Fred Snodgrass when he thumbed his nose at their revered pitcher Lefty Tyler.

As if to confirm that the events of 1914, however awesome, were no fluke, the Braves went on to stifle the Philadelphia Athletics in the World Series, four games to none. The regular season stars were again the heroes. Dick Rudolph and Bill James won two games apiece. Rabbit Maranville and Johnny Evers drove in five runs

Boston would have had a truly depressing skein of last-place finishes. As it was, they hit bottom four times, in 1922, 1924, 1929, and 1935.

The 1935 ball club epitomized the futility of it all. Wally Berger, a pearl among swine, led the league with 34 home runs and 130 RBIs. Boston's next highest homer total was that of Babe Ruth, a "crumbling monument" in historian Marshall Smelser's words, who had six round-trippers in this, his final year. The next highest RBI total was third baseman Pinkey Whitney's 60.

Pitching? Bill Cantwell, a 20-game winner in 1933, chalked up a 4-25 mark, leading the league in losses. Ed Brandt, reliable for the previous four years, went 5-19 and was released. The team lost 115 games, their all-time high, and finished 61½ games behind the pennant-winning Chicago Cubs. Manager Bill McKechnie gave way to Casey Stengel, but the Old Professor had no better luck. The wartime Braves landed in sixth place three times, the last two, 1945-46, under new skipper Bob Coleman.

Transcendental Graphics

Warren Spahn

Spahn and Sain ... and So Long, Boston

The postwar Braves bore little resemblance to their predecessors. A new owner, promoter Lou Perini, took over the ball club and installed Billy Southworth as manager. Southworth had led the Cardinals to three pennants and two World Championships. He arrived in Boston at the perfect time, because two promising pitchers who had been rookies in 1942 were returning from the war. They were Warren Spahn and Johnny Sain.

With Sain winning 20 games in 1946 (20-14, 2.21 ERA) the Braves moved up to fourth place. Spahn came into his own in 1947, and, with the addition of third baseman Bob Elliott from the Pirates, the Braves edged up to third place. Spahn and Sain each won 21 games in 1947, while Bob Elliott hit .317, belted 22 homers, and drove in 113 runs. Rookie first baseman Earl Torgeson contributed 16 homers, and outfielder Tommy Holmes batted .300+ for the fourth straight year (.309). A

pennant seemed imminent.

It came in 1948. Rookie Alvin Dark took over at shortstop and had a banner year, hitting .322. Johnny Sain led all NL pitchers with 24 wins, losing 15, while Warren Spahn dropped off to 15-12. Spahn and Sain were backed up on the mound by rookie Vern Bickford, 11-5, and a veteran hurler from the Giants, Bill Voiselle, 13-13.

The Boston Braves took the league lead in June and held on to prevail against three strong contenders, the Dodgers, Cardinals, and Pirates. Bob Elliott had another fine year, batting .283, homering 23 times, and driving in 100 runs. Tommy Holmes upped his batting average to .325.

Two other outfielders hit .300 as well—Jeff Heath (.319) and Frank McCormick (.303). Both were aging veterans who had starred in the thirties and early forties for other ball clubs: Heath for the Indians and McCormick for the Reds. League-leading hitting and pitching, along with above-average fielding, brought the Braves a deserved pennant in 1948. It was no miracle this time.

But the World Series was a disappointment. The Cleveland Indians of Bob Feller, Bob Lemon, and Gene Bearden took the measure of Boston, four games to two. Feller pitched a two-hitter in the opening game but lost it to Johnny Sain's four-hitter, 1-0, the run coming on a Tommy Holmes single in the eighth inning, which scored Phil Masi from second base.

Feller also lost game five as Bob Elliott slammed a three-run homer in the first inning and a solo shot in the third. But Lemon and Bearden stymied the Braves, Lemon winning two games. In game six the Braves, down 4-1, staged a comeback in the eighth inning when catcher Phil Masi doubled home two runs to make it 4-3. But Gene Bearden, in relief of Lemon, retired the next four batters, and the Indians were World Champions.

In 1949 Johnny Sain fell on hard times (10-17, 4.81 ERA), and the Braves tumbled to fourth in the standings. No one could blame Warren Spahn, who posted a 21-14 mark with a 3.07 ERA. But Vern Bickford, despite a 16-11 record, gave up more hits than innings pitched and registered more bases on balls than strikeouts. The hitting fell off.

Bob Elliott drove in only 77 runs, high for the team, and Eddie Stanky's .285 batting average set the pace for the Braves' regulars. Unhappily for the fans at Braves Field, 1949 was more than just a downward blip. It was part of a pattern. The Braves finished fourth in 1950 and 1951 as well.

Billy Southworth resigned midway through the 1951 season, and Tommy Holmes took the helm. Holmes lasted only 35 games into 1952 before Charlie Grimm supplanted him. Nothing helped, not even the arrival of a rookie third baseman named Eddie Mathews. The youngster slammed 25 homers, which naturally attracted some attention. But veteran outfielder Sid Gordon hit the same number, and Gordon's .289 batting average and 75 RBIs overshadowed Mathews's .242 and 58.

Warren Spahn had a terrible year, 14-19,

despite a 2.98 ERA. Fans stayed away in droves. The Braves finished seventh—and soon they were no longer in Boston. Owner Lou Perini, who had initially been the savior of the Boston Braves, now became their executioner. The franchise moved to Milwaukee in 1953.

Heyday in Milwaukee

The Milwaukee Brewers (not the current American League [AL] team) had held a franchise in the minor league American Association since 1902. Eddie Mathews, in fact, had come to bat nine times for the AA Brewers at the end of the 1951 season. In his first at-bat he blasted a grand-slam home run. Mathews moved up to Boston in 1952 for a good but not Rookie-of-the-Year season. Now he was back in Milwaukee, playing third base for the major league Milwaukee Braves, and both the Braves and their third baseman had a season worth remembering.

Transcendental Graphics

Eddie Mathews

During the regular season the 1957 Milwaukee Braves drew 2,215,404 fans, a National League record at the time. The team won 95 games, lost 59, and captured the pennant with relative ease. Manager Fred Haney's men, facing the Yankees in the World Series, split the first two games in New York. The Yanks, behind Whitey Ford, won the opener, 3-1. The Braves, behind Lew Burdette, came back to take game two, 4-2. Two days later, in the first World Series contest played in County Stadium, the Yanks clobbered the Braves, 12-3, as Tony Kubek, a young Milwaukee native playing for New York, slammed two home runs, one with two teammates aboard, the other with the bases empty.

Game four was crucial to the Braves chances, and they almost lost it. After building a 4-1 lead behind Warren Spahn, they watched in dismay as Yankee catcher Elston Howard cracked a three-run homer in the top of the ninth to give New York a 5-4 lead. The Braves had one more chance. Braves' pinch hitter Nippy Jones was awarded first base after proving to umpire Augie Donatelli that he had been hit on the foot. (He showed Donatelli a smudge of shoe polish on the ball.) A sacrifice bunt sent Felix Mantilla, running for Jones, to second base, and shortstop Johnny Logan brought him home with a double. That tied the score, 5-5. It did not stay tied long. The next hitter was third baseman Eddie Mathews, and he sent the crowd home happy by blasting a two-run homer, giving the Braves a 7-5 victory and a 2-2 tie in the Series.

In game five Lew Burdette took the mound again for the Braves. He allowed no runs, seven singles, struck our five, and walked nobody in besting Whitey Ford, 1-0. Milwaukee's left fielder Wes Covington saved the shutout, and perhaps the game, by making a spectacular catch in the fourth inning that robbed Gil McDougald of a home run. The Braves scored the game's only run in the sixth inning on successive singles by Eddie Mathews, Hank Aaron, and Joe Adcock.

After a 3-2 loss to the Yankees in game six, which tied the series at three games apiece, the Braves went once more with Lew Burdette. The Yanks countered with Don Larsen, a year and two days after his perfect World Series game against the Brooklyn Dodgers. Larsen was far from perfect this time, however, as the Braves erupted for four runs in the third inning, knocking him out of the box and going on to win, 5-0. It was Burdette's second straight shutout and gave the Milwaukee Braves their first and only World Championship.

The Braves were definitely welcome in Milwaukee. Attendance jumped to more than six times over the previous years' turnout at Braves Field, Boston. The Milwaukee Braves vaulted into second place. Warren Spahn had a great year, 23-7, with a league-leading 2.20 ERA. His number of strikeouts dropped a bit (he had led the NL in whiffs for the last four years), but only pennant-winning Brooklyn's Carl Erskine topped Spahn's winning percentage.

Eddie Mathews showed Milwaukee fans what to expect from him in the future as he batted .302, belted a league-leading 47 homers, and drove in 135 runs. Pitcher Lew Burdette, only 6-11 in

Boston, also served notice of what was to come, going 15-5. Burdette's won-lost mark included 8-0 in relief, but henceforth he would be primarily a starter.

The Milwaukee Braves did not ascend to the heights immediately. They finished third in 1954, then second in 1955 and 1956. The 1956 season saw a tough three-way race that Milwaukee seemed to be winning. But a few Braves' losses late in the season brought the decision down to the final day. When the Brooklyn Dodgers' "Boys of Summer" defeated the Pittsburgh Pirates, the Braves finished one game back. Cincinnati, the other contender, came in two games behind.

Milwaukee's young outfielder Hank Aaron, in his third season with the team, led the National League in batting at .328, although he trailed Mathews in homers, 37 to 26. First baseman Joe Adcock copped the team high for home runs with 38.

The year 1957 brought the Milwaukee Braves a pennant. Fred Haney had replaced Charlie Grimm as manager part way through the 1956 campaign, and now it was Haney's job to see that the talented Braves fulfilled their potential. They did. The team got off to a fast start in 1957, fought off a late-season challenge by the Cardinals, and won the pennant by eight games. The mid-June acquisition of a new second baseman, old pro Red Schoendienst from the Giants, bolstered the one weak position on the squad. Warren Spahn, Lew Burdette, and Bob Buhl won a total of 56 games while losing only 27. Spahn's 21 victories paced the NL.

On offense—except for the brief flurry of excitement caused by Bob (Hurricane) Hazle, a utility outfielder who blew into town and hit .403 in 134 times at bat—the year belonged to Hank Aaron. For the first time Aaron led the league in home runs (44) and RBIs (132). He also paced the NL in runs scored with 118, and his .322 batting average was exceeded only by Stan Musial's .351 and Willie Mays's .333.

The 1957 World Series marked the high point in the history of the Milwaukee Braves, as the Braves defeated the proud New York Yankees of Mickey Mantle and Whitey Ford, four games to three. Lew Burdette pitched and won three complete games, the last two of them shutouts, and Hank Aaron hit for a .393 average with three homers and seven RBIs. This Yankee-thrashing triumph of 1957 brought the franchise its first World Championship in 43 years.

The Braves repeated as NL pennant-winners in 1958 with basically the same team. The power, as usual, came from Eddie Mathews and Hank Aaron, ably supported by third-year outfielder Wes Covington, who hit .330 and slammed 24 home runs. Two other long-ball threats were catcher Del Crandall and Joe Adcock, who in 1958 divided his time between first base and the outfield.

Warren Spahn (22-11) and Lew Burdette (20-10) were the mound aces.

It was a great ball club, but Hank Aaron noted in his autobiography that "somehow there wasn't quite the atmosphere that we'd enjoyed the season before.... 1957 was a once-in-a-lifetime experience." The Braves lost the World Series, four games to three. They took the first two games, then lost the third game. Spahn pitched a two-hitter in game four, winning 3-0. But Yankee pitcher Bob Turley shut out the Braves 4-0 in New York, after which the Braves dropped the final two games at County Stadium, becoming the first team since 1925 to blow a three-game-to-one lead.

A tied National League finish in 1959 was decided by a best-of-three playoff between the Braves and the Los Angeles Dodgers. In this crucial series, which could have given Milwaukee its third straight pennant, only 19,000 people showed up at County Stadium for the first game. "I suppose that should have told us something about our future in Milwaukee," Aaron observed later. No doubt it should have.

The Braves lost the playoff to the Dodgers, finished second in 1960, fourth in 1961, and attendance slipped and slipped. In their final four years in Milwaukee the Braves finished fifth three times—1962, 1964, and 1965—and sixth once, 1963. The record crowds of the 1950s gave way to sparse, unprofitable turnouts in the sixties. After 13 seasons in Milwaukee, the franchise owners gave up and moved on.

Atlanta: From Chumps to Champs

The Braves' ball club that moved into Atlanta Stadium (now Atlanta-Fulton County Stadium) in 1966 still had some pizazz. Hank Aaron, at 32, was as dangerous a hitter as ever. In his first year at Atlanta he belted 44 homers and drove in 130 runs. Eddie Mathews, however, was nearing the end of his career and would play only one so-so season for Atlanta before being traded.

The team still had plenty of power at the plate, though, particularly in catcher Joe Torre, who in

"Hammerin' Hank" Aaron

Hank Aaron was a thoroughgoing professional, a steady, hard-working ballplayer who hit with power and consistency for 23 major league seasons. He played 12 of those seasons for the Milwaukee Braves (1954-65) and nine for the Atlanta Braves (1966-74). These two cities were not big media centers in those days, and Aaron's remarkable achievements attracted surprisingly little attention until he began closing in on Babe Ruth's career home run record of 714. "Hammerin' Hank" (his autobiography is titled *I Had a Hammer*) ended the 1973 season with 713 homers—one short of Ruth's total.

Fans eagerly (or fearfully, if they were diehard Ruth fans) awaited the opening of the 1974 season. They did not have long to wait. Hank Aaron tied Ruth's record with a homer on opening day. Then on April 8, before 53,775 fans in Atlanta, he replaced the Babe as the all-time home run king by lofting an Al Downing pitch into the seats. Eventually, he ran his career total to 755, leaving that as the mark for some great, yet-to-emerge power hitter with consistency and longevity to challenge in days to come.

Aaron never crossed the 50-home-run plateau in a season, although he connected for 40 or more homers eight times and 30 or more 15 times. Moreover, unlike many home run hitters, he maintained an excellent lifetime batting average of .305, leading the league twice in hitting: .328 in 1956 and .355 in 1959. He drove in 100 or more runs in 11 of his 23 seasons, accomplishing it five times in a row between 1959 and 1963. In short, Hank Aaron, who was elected to the Hall of Fame in 1982 and is now a senior vice president in the Atlanta Braves organization, was an awesomely efficient ballplayer.

Photo: *Transcendental Graphics*

1966 hit .315 with 36 homers and 101 RBIs, and first baseman-outfielder Felipe Alou, whose 218 hits led the league and whose .327 batting average led the Braves by just a whisker over outfielder Rico Carty's .326.

What the Atlanta Braves lacked was the old Braves' great pitching. Tony Cloninger and Ken Johnson each won 14 games in 1966, Denny Lemaster won 11, and no one else won in double figures. The Braves finished fifth in 1966, seventh in 1967, and fifth again in 1968. Lum Harris, an ex-Houston skipper, took over the reins in 1968. He

lasted longer in the job than anyone since Billy Southworth, 1946-51.

The team's performance in 1969, the first year of divisional play, was one reason for Harris's tenure. To the surprise of nearly everyone, the Braves finished with a flourish in 1969, winning 93 games, beating out the Giants in a close race. This brought them face to face with the Amazin' Mets, who won the new best-of-five National League Championship Series in three straight games. Hank Aaron homered in each game, driving in seven runs, nearly half of the Braves' total.

Atlanta's ace pitcher, Phil Niekro, had gone 23-13 in the regular season, with a 2.37 ERA, but he got roughed up in the NLCS—although not as badly as Ron Reed, 18-10 for the year, who started game two, lasted just 1-2/3 innings, and exited the fray with a 21.60 ERA.

The 1970 season provided no happy memories for Atlanta fans. The Braves fell to fifth place that year, rose to third in 1971, then dropped back to fourth and fifth the next two years. Phil Niekro stayed on, winning consistently in double figures. In 1974, when the Braves took 88 games to finish third, though far behind Los Angeles and Cincinnati, Niekro won 20 games to tie for the league lead with a 20-13 record and a 2.38 ERA.

Outfielder Ralph Garr, one of the lesser-known .300 career hitters (lifetime .306), batted .353 in 1974 to outdistance the league's number two hitter, Pittsburgh's Al Oliver, by 32 percentage points. Garr's 214 hits and 17 triples also led the league. But the Braves as a team had become unimpressive and were getting worse. When Hank Aaron was traded to the American League's Milwaukee Brewers in November 1974, it was truly the end of an era.

For four straight years, 1976 through 1979, the Aaronless and spiritless Braves occupied the NL West basement, losing 101 games in 1977, the most for the franchise since the abysmal Boston Braves of 1935 lost 115. In 1980, under third-year manager Bobby Cox (who would later lead Toronto and Atlanta to pennants), the Braves rejoined the ranks of winners by the narrowest of margins, 81-80, and finished fourth. In split-season 1981 they finished fourth the first half of the season, fifth the second half, and then in 1982, led by manager Cox's replacement, ex-Brave and Cardinal star Joe Torre, they held on in a very tight race to nose out the Dodgers by a single game.

By then the Braves had a new superstar. He was Dale Murphy, a tall, rangy outfielder who had come up through the Braves' farm system as a catcher, arriving in Atlanta via Savannah and Richmond in 1977. Switched to the outfield and occasionally first base, Murphy struck out a lot, but he also hit a lot of home runs—33 in 1980, 36

in 1982. An All-Star and the National League MVP in 1982, he drove in 109 runs to tie for the league lead.

The Braves' third baseman Bob Horner had plenty of power, too, contributing 32 home runs and 97 RBIs to Atlanta's first-place effort. On the mound, old reliable Phil Niekro posted a remarkable 17-4 record and seemed a good bet to win at least one of the NLCS games against St. Louis, winner in the NL East. But neither the veteran knuckleballer nor anyone else could keep the Cards from taking three straight games to advance to the World Series.

In a repeat of their post-1969 history, the Braves hung in there for a couple of years after winning the division title. They finished second in 1983, tied for second in 1984, but then collapsed to fifth and sixth place from 1985 through 1990, trailing the division leader by anywhere from 20-1/2 games (1987) to 39-1/2 games (1988).

With a 65-97 record, the 1990 Braves ranked last in the NL in pitching and fielding, and third from last in hitting. The *1991 Baseball Guide* summed up the season with this headline: "Braves Are Bad, Knowhutimean?" And so they were, except for outfielder and Rookie-of-the-Year Dave Justice and catcher Greg Olson, the Braves' only All-Star representative. At that, Justice starred mainly in the second half of the season and Olson in the first half. Could such a team show progress in 1991?

Could it ever. The 1991 Braves, having added free-agent third baseman Terry Pendleton, rocketed to the top of the NL West with 94 wins and 68 losses, neatly reversing both the won-lost record and the standing of the prior year. Sportswriters credited Bobby Cox, who as general manager since 1986 had put the pieces in place and then, taking over as field manager in 1991, played them to perfection.

Pendleton, who had been on a downward slide at St. Louis, came back with a vengeance, batting .319, hitting 22 homers (the most of his career), and driving in 86 runs. Outfielders Dave Justice, Ron Gant, and Lonnie Smith all had fine seasons—Gant, in particular, with 32 homers, 105

AP/Wide World Photos

Tom Glavine

Tom Glavine won the first game, 3-1, on a four-hitter, the big blow for Atlanta being catcher Damon Berryhill's three-run homer in the sixth inning. After losing the next three games, each by a one-run margin, the Braves won game five on a five-run fifth inning. Designated hitter Lonnie Smith delivered a three-run homer to cap the rally as the Braves prevailed, 7-2. But in the sixth game the Blue Jays won again by a one-run margin, 4-3, and made off with the World Championship. As the curtain came down on postseason play, the Braves could take pride in having come close in both 1991 and 1992, but at that point the team had still not triumphed in a World Series since 1957.

The Braves entered the 1993 season with great expectations. During the offseason the team added 1992 National League Cy Young Award-winner Greg Maddux to an already formidable pitching staff. But offensive woes contributed to a slow start, and in July, the Braves found themselves trailing the red-hot San Francisco Giants by ten games.

Atlanta's front office went looking for a strong bat to bolster the lineup and acquired slugger Fred McGriff from the San Diego Padres. With McGriff inserted into the batting order, the Braves immediately went on a tear, narrowing the gap between the Giants and them heading into a home-and-home showdown with San Francisco. Atlanta won five of the six games during the two series and eventually moved into first place in September.

The club was unable to clinch an early pennant, however, for in a memorable stretch drive the Giants rebounded and tied the Braves for the division lead heading into the season's final game. After pounding the Colorado Rockies to finish with an incredible 104-58 record, the Braves watched the Giants fall to Los Angeles and began celebrating their third consecutive National League West title. The season ended disappointingly, though, as the Braves lost the National League Championship Series to the Philadelphia Phillies, four games to two.

Still, several players had remarkable seasons: Maddux finished with 20 wins, a 2.36 ERA, and captured his second consecutive Cy Young Award;

RBIs, and 34 stolen bases.

But the real story of 1991 was the Braves' young pitching staff. Lefthander Tom Glavine (20-11 with a 2.55 ERA) earned the Cy Young Award. Steve Avery, another lefty, went 18-8 in the regular season and won the MVP Award in the NLCS. John Smotz started dismally but rebounded to post a 14-13 record. Atlanta fought off the Pittsburgh Pirates, four games to three, in the NLCS but succumbed in seven games to the AL champion Minnesota Twins.

The Braves repeated as National League pennant-winners in 1992, with Tom Glavine turning in a 20-8 year, John Smoltz 15-8, and Charlie Leibrandt 15-7. Terry Pendleton again led Braves' hitters at .311 with 21 homers and 105 runs batted in. Atlanta made it past Pittsburgh in the NLCS, four games to three, but could win only two games from the Toronto Blue Jays in the World Series.

Glavine and Avery won 22 and 18 games, respectively; Justice hit 40 home runs with 120 RBIs; McGriff pounded 37 homers and 101 RBIs; and Gant added 36 homers and 117 RBIs. Though the Braves didn't win it all in 1993, they again proved they are one of the premier teams in baseball.

SOURCES

BOOKS

Aaron, Hank, with Lonnie Wheeler, *I Had a Hammer: The Hank Aaron Story,* Harper-Collins, 1991.

Baseball Guide, The Sporting News Publishing Co., 1980, 1991, and 1992 editions.

Baseball Register, The Sporting News Publishing Co., 1945, 1965, 1980, and 1992 editions.

Carter, Craig, editor, *Daguerreotypes,* 8th edition, The Sporting News Publishing Co., 1990.

Hollander, Zander, editor, *The Complete Handbook of Baseball, 1992,* 23rd edition, Signet, 1992.

Hoppel, Joe, *The Series: An Illustrated History of Baseball's Postseason Showcase,* The Sporting News Publishing Co., 1989.

Ivor-Campbell, Frederick, "Team Histories: Atlanta Braves," *Total Baseball,* edited by John Thorn and Pete Palmer, Warner Books, 1989.

Kaese, Harold, *The Boston Braves,* G. P. Putnam's Sons, 1948.

Kaese, Harold, and Russell G. Lynch, *The Milwaukee Braves,* G. P. Putnam's Sons, 1954.

Lowry, Philip J., *Green Cathedrals,* Society for American Baseball Research, 1986.

Reichler, Joseph L., editor, *The Baseball Encyclopedia,* 7th edition, Macmillan, 1988.

Reidenbaugh, Lowell, *Cooperstown: Where Baseball's Legends Live Forever,* The Sporting News Publishing Co., 1983.

Selzer, Jack, *Baseball in the Nineteenth Century: An Overview,* Society for American Baseball Research, 1986.

Voigt, David Quentin, *American Baseball: From the Gentleman's Sport to the Commissioner System,* Pennsylvania State University Press, 1983.

Voigt, David Quentin, *American Baseball: From the Commissioners to Continental Expansion,* Pennsylvania State University Press, 1983.

PERIODICALS

Baseball America, February 21, 1993; March 21, 1993.

Baseball Digest, October, 1964.

Baseball Research Journal, 1978.

The National Pastime, 1983.

—*Gerald Tomlinson* for Book Builders, Inc.

COLORADO ROCKIES

The Colorado Rockies have brought major league baseball to the vast mountainous region of America as the newest franchise in the National League West. To citizens throughout the Mountain Time Zone—long starved for a big-league team—the Rockies represent a hard-fought victory in recognition of the area's solid baseball tradition and widespread fan support.

Rockiesmania has swept far and wide through Colorado and its neighboring states. The team sold more than 24,000 season tickets before it even took the field, then drew a record one million fans in its first 17 home appearances. On Opening Day 1993 in Denver, a phenomenal crowd of 80,227 packed Mile High Stadium to the rafters to cheer a franchise whose presence in the city was nothing less than a dream come true.

The history of the Colorado Rockies is a reflection of how major league baseball is solicited and financed in these times of staggering costs and high expectations. Luring the team to Denver

required the efforts of the region's politicians, business leaders, and citizenry, from the fabulously wealthy Coors family of brewing fame to the members of a sandlot Little League team.

The search for investors willing to gamble on Denver's relatively small baseball market almost proved the region's undoing, but the ordinary taxpayers saved the day by approving additional taxes to construct a new ballpark. Unlike South Florida, where dynamic D. Wayne Huizenga stepped up as the principal driving force behind the Marlins, Colorado's acquisition of an expansion franchise required a team effort from many hands—and a timely reminder that Denver had been promised a major league entry decades ago.

The quest for the Rockies properly begins with Denver entrepreneur Bob Howsam. Shortly after World War II, Howsam bought a controlling interest in the Denver Bears of the Class A Western League. Denver had long enjoyed an off-again-on-again relationship with professional baseball—

pro games had been played in the region as early as the 1880s, but most teams had folded as interest waned.

Howsam felt the time was ripe in 1948 for a permanent baseball presence in Denver. He raised the cash for a new, lighted ballpark constructed over an old city dump, and moved the team there late in 1948. The following year the Bears set attendance records for Class A baseball with a total of 463,039 fans paying to see the games.

Howsam is remembered fondly in Denver for his "strike zone" uniforms. Bears players wore garb that was white between the knees and on the chest and dark elsewhere, so umpires could judge the strike zone better. The experiment was popular with the referees but hated by the team and the fans. Reluctantly Howsam retired the idea.

In 1955 the Philadelphia Athletics moved to Kansas City. Major league baseball had finally advanced past the Mississippi, but it was still some 800 miles from Denver. Fortunately, Howsam was able to acquire the Kansas City Blues, a Triple-A farm team for the Yankees that had been upstaged by the Athletics. Howsam moved the Blues to his stadium in Denver and dubbed them the Bears.

He might have found success with this endeavor, but televised baseball games began to cut into his profits. Attendance at Bears games declined despite the exciting play offered by the likes of Marv Throneberry and Whitey Herzog as Yankee farm hands.

Howsam decided that if he couldn't beat major league baseball he would somehow join it. He and his father-in-law, a prominent Colorado politician, teamed with baseball executive Branch Rickey and potential owners in Houston and Buffalo to form a whole new league. The Continental League was born in 1959, with charter franchises in Denver, Houston, Minneapolis-St. Paul, New York, Toronto, Atlanta, Buffalo, and Dallas-Fort Worth. Rickey served as league commissioner.

Sensing a threat from the upstart league, the established major leagues announced in 1960 that they would each expand by two teams, with further expansion possible in the future. That expansion brought teams to Minneapolis, Los Angeles, Houston, and New York. Thereafter, most of the Continental League cities obtained teams by one means or another. Atlanta won the Braves when that franchise left Milwaukee in 1966. Dallas-Fort Worth got the Rangers in 1972 from Washington, D.C. In 1977, the last time baseball expanded before the 1990s, Toronto acquired the Blue Jays. Denver was left in the lurch.

Howsam claimed that major league baseball's ownership had promised in writing to satisfy every Continental League city. He pored through his files looking for the pertinent documentation, but he never found it. In the meantime, financial losses forced him to sell the Bears to Denver developer Gerald Phipps.

Howsam moved away from Denver, working as general manager for the St. Louis Cardinals and the Cincinnati Reds. Little did he know that his work on behalf of the Continental League—and the venture's eventual failure under pressure from the established leagues—would lend power to Denver's case for expansion in the 1990s.

In the late 1960s and early 1970s, Bears Stadium underwent a transformation. It was expanded to hold the 76,000 fans it can seat today, principally to satisfy the needs of the Broncos football team. The city of Denver bought the facility in 1968 and renamed it Mile High Stadium.

During those years a minor league Bears team still drew modest attendance there. The major league expansion in 1969 passed over Denver because no qualified buyer arose to foot the steep costs of franchise acquisition and start-up.

The great tease began in the mid-1970s. Billionaire oil man Marvin Davis of Denver made several attempts to purchase an existing franchise for his city. He tried to buy the Chicago White Sox in 1976 and the Baltimore Orioles in 1977. When those deals fell through, he spent years trying to obtain the Athletics from Oakland owner Charlie Finley. The A's deal fell through finally in 1985.

By that time, baseball in Denver had found a new champion in Mayor Federico Peña. Peña took office in 1984, at a time when Denver's economy

TEAM INFORMATION AT A GLANCE

Founding date: July 5, 1991
First major league game played April 5, 1993.

Home stadium: Mile High Stadium
2755 W. 17th St.
Denver, CO 80204
Phone: (303) 292-0200

Dimensions: Approximately 125,000 square feet.
Seating capacity: 50,000.

Team colors: Purple, black, and silver.
Team nickname: Rockies.
Logo: Baseball superimposed over purple mountains.

Franchise record	Won	Lost	Pct.
(1993)	67	95	.414

was reeling. The mayor commissioned a study concluding that major league baseball would pump millions of dollars into the local economy each year. Then Peña created the Denver Baseball Commission (DBC), a panel empowered to try to bring a big-league team to town.

The DBC went right to work in 1984, inviting the two league presidents and a dozen baseball executives to Denver for a tour and a lavish party. A "Challenge the Majors" baseball game timed to coincide with the visit attracted 32,926 fans to see the Bears at Mile High Stadium.

The hype and hoopla did not move major league baseball. The owners did not plan to expand and were not required to, because their enterprise was not subject to antitrust legislation. As the 1980s drew to a close, further expansion seemed unlikely, even though a number of cities had expressed strong interest in winning a team. Peña must have been flabbergasted when the taxpayers of St. Petersburg, Florida voted to build a state-of-the-art domed ballpark on just the *hope* of luring a franchise to the area.

Those who wanted baseball in Denver realized they would have to widen the net. In the late 1980s the DBC was replaced by the Colorado Baseball Commission, an 18-member statewide board created to lobby baseball's owners for a team. At approximately the same time, Colorado senator Tim Wirth formed the Senate Task Force on the Expansion of Major League Baseball. Over time the task force attracted more than a dozen powerful senators—including Dan Quayle and Al Gore—whose constituencies wanted a shot at major league baseball.

At first baseball commissioner Peter Ueberroth proved intractable during interviews with the task force. Later, as the senators flexed political muscle and provided plenty of publicity, Ueberroth and his successors gave ground. Baseball's owners did not want to alienate nineteen members of the U.S. Senate, so on June 14, 1990, the National League released a timetable allowing for the introduction of two expansion franchises by the 1993 season.

More than a year later, when Denver had finally won its team, then-commissioner Fay Vincent told the city fathers: "I think the citizens of Colorado should know that if it hadn't been for Tim Wirth and his task force there probably wouldn't have been any expansion. The political pressure played a significant role in the process." Vincent's remarks were reprinted in a book entitled *Playing Hardball: The High-Stakes Battle for Baseball's New Franchises.*

Once the National League announced its intention to expand, the push was on in Colorado. The league owners made it clear that they wanted prospective cities to provide a first-class facility for baseball—preferably *just* for baseball.

With that in mind, the Colorado legislature brought the matter to the taxpayers: would the citizens be willing to pay an extra 0.1 percent sales tax (a penny on a ten-dollar purchase) to raise funds for a new stadium *if* Denver won a franchise?

The matter went to the polls on August 14, 1990, and was approved by 54 percent of the voters. Ground was broken on the new facility—named Coors Field—in 1992. Until it was ready for occupation, the team would play at Mile High Stadium.

In *Playing Hardball,* David Whitford wrote: "For three decades, ever since Bob Howsam's near-miss with the Continental League in 1961, Denver had been doing everything in its power to prove itself worthy of major league baseball. Year after year, fans packed Mile High Stadium, civic boosters flirted with the owners, politicians offered up concessions, and millionaires jostled for the privilege of buying. More than any other city in North America, Denver professionalized the art of franchise seeking. But now with expansion finally on the agenda, and with the funds in place to build a beautiful new stadium, the only thing missing was the one crucial ingredient—a buyer."

The task of lining up an ownership group fell to Denver lawyer Paul A. Jacobs. Jacobs had to find enough interested and able investors to fund the staggering $95 million franchise fee plus at least $20 to $30 million in start-up costs. With just days remaining before the franchise application deadline in the summer of 1990, a group was assembled that included five general partners who pledged $30 million and agreed to take an active role in running the team, as well as a number of limited partners pledging up to a maximum of $63.5 million. The deal was complicated with so many individuals involved, but it had one advantage: it was the only ownership effort for Colorado. Other regions—including South Florida—had competing ownership interests.

Jacobs saw clearly that the potential baseball owners in Colorado needed incentive to invest in a team that would play in a relatively small market. So he negotiated an extremely generous lease arrangement with Denver's Stadium District Board. In essence, the stadium board agreed to build a ballpark with taxpayer money but then allow the baseball team's ownership to pocket *all* of the revenues generated by the stadium, from concessions and advertising, to luxury boxes, right down to the naming rights. Rent was free through the year 2000.

The terms of the lease made investment in Denver's major league baseball effort very attractive indeed. More limited partners stepped up, and those already committed—including Jerry D. McMorris of the NW Transport Service and Peter Coors—increased their contributions. By the time Denver made the "short list" of potential sites for a team, sufficient funds had been raised—and a brand-new baseball park was part of the package.

Denver Wooed the Expansion Committee

The National League Expansion Committee placed six metropolitan regions on the short list as possible franchise sites. Then the committee visited each of the six locations to examine the baseball facilities and other local amenities. The committee arrived in Denver on March 26, 1991, having warned civic leaders ahead of time not to overdo preparations for the visit. Still, this was one test Denver did not plan to fail.

When the committee arrived at Mile High Stadium, the electronic scoreboard showed a game in progress. The soft sounds of contented crowd noise were piped through the public address system. In the home team locker room, freshly-pressed baseball uniforms hung in cubicles, and a full team meal was laid out on tables. Outside the park, church bells pealed "Take Me Out to the Ballgame." A flight over the site of the future Coors Field ballpark revealed a sandlot game in process, featuring local Little Leaguers.

After a luncheon with Colorado first lady Bea Romer and Wyoming governor Mike Sullivan, the committee members were whisked to a rally in downtown Denver where 3,000 hysterical fans chanted "BASEBALL! BASEBALL! BASE-BALL!" The hoopla ran counter to the committee's rules for the visit, but it was impressive nonetheless. The committee members were visibly moved by the spectacle.

Shortly after the Expansion Committee left Denver that day, snow began to fall. By midafternoon the following day more than two feet blanketed the entire region. It seemed as if even Mother Nature had done her part to secure baseball for Denver, holding her fury in check until the visit was well over.

The obvious regional fan support for baseball, the "sweetheart" lease on the stadium, the plans to erect a new ballpark, and, yes, the long-standing feeling that Denver deserved a nod after its abortive Continental League experiment, all stood in the region's favor.

On June 10, 1991, the Expansion Committee recommended Denver and South Florida as the sites for the two expansion franchises. The major league owners unanimously approved the choice on July 5, 1991, and the Colorado franchise was born. That same day, the Colorado Baseball Partnership announced that the team would be called the Rockies and that the logo would be a baseball superimposed over majestic purple mountains.

The general partnership that would guide the fledgling Rockies included McMorris as chairman, president, and chief executive officer on behalf of NW Transport; Coors Brewing Company, who provided the name for the new ballpark; and Charles Monfort and Oren Benton. Jacobs became general counsel for the new team.

The group named Bob Gebhard, a former vice president of the Minnesota Twins, as general manager. Working on a much smaller budget than his counterparts in South Florida, Gebhard managed to scout all 26 established major league clubs in 1992 in preparation for the November, 1992, expansion draft.

The Rockies' first-ever manager was Don Baylor, an 18-year veteran major leaguer who played his entire career in the American League. Baylor's vast playing experience includes three visits to the World Series, including a winning trip in 1987 when he batted .385 in five games with the Twins. Baylor was recognized as an able leader among his peers before he retired from play in 1988.

Among those who felt Baylor had potential as a manager was Gebhard, who worked with Baylor in Minnesota. Baylor had never managed in the majors before being asked to skipper the Rockies. His first staff included Larry Bearnarth as pitching coach, Ron Hassey as first base coach, Amos Otis as batting coach, and Jerry Royster as third base coach. Former manager Don Zimmer also joined the squad as bench coach.

In 1992 a Rockies farm team was established at Bend, Oregon (Class A). Rockies players also appeared with the Visalia Oaks in the California League and with the Mesa, Arizona Cubs. A total of 50 players were selected in the June 1992 Free Agent Draft, of which 40 signed with the team and reported to the minor leagues. The Rockies' first-ever first-round pick in that draft fell upon pitcher John Burke from the University of Florida.

Throughout the summer of 1992, Gebhard and his staff prepared for the all-important Expansion Draft. This draft would allow the Rockies, and their counterpart, the Florida Marlins, to select unprotected players from each of the existing major league franchises. For the first time in history, the expansion teams were allowed to draw talent from both leagues. The established clubs protected 15 players for the first round of the draft, then 18 players (National League) and 19 players (American League) in the second round.

The draft was held on November 17, 1992. The Rockies won the coin toss for first pick and chose right-handed pitcher David Nied from the Atlanta Braves. For seven-and-a-half hours the expansion draft continued. It was broadcast in its entirety on cable television, and cheers could be heard from Denver pubs each time Gebhard made a choice.

Top Rockies draft selections included third baseman Charlie Hayes from the Yankees, right-handed pitcher Darren Holmes from the Brewers, outfielder Jerald Clark from the Padres, outfielder Kevin Reimer from the Rangers, infielder Eric Young from the Dodgers, and infielder Jody Reed from the Red Sox. Later the Rockies traded Reimer to the Brewers for outfielder Dante Bichette and sent Reed to the Dodgers for pitcher Rudy Seanez. Free agents Daryl Boston, Andres Galarraga, and Jeff Parrett signed during the winter of 1992-93.

The Rockies opened the 1993 baseball season on April 5 at Shea Stadium, where Dwight Gooden and the Mets beat them, 3-0. Four days later they took the field in Denver for their home opener, where a dangerously-packed Mile High Stadium hosted 80,227 fans. Some souvenir stands had to close because the mobs of people around them caused fire hazards.

Scores of politicians from several states were on hand, and the team fielded nearly 400 requests for press credentials. The game was broadcast to 48 countries worldwide, including Japan and Venezuela. And the Colorado Rockies won big, 11-4 over the Montreal Expos.

Bob Howsam observed the first pitch from his seat in the first row behind home plate. It was somehow fitting that Howsam should have the satisfaction of watching the first Colorado major league baseball game in the stadium he built for that purpose. A senior consultant to the Rockies, Howsam was finally content that a goal had been reached and a faithful fan pool satisfied at last. "You never forget the fans," he told the *Rocky Mountain News*, "and now we can finally pay them back for all of their support."

The Rockies first season was phenomenally successful; the team set a record for victories by an expansion club with 67 and drew almost four and a half million fans to Mile High Stadium, the most ever by any ballclub. Gallarraga led the National League with a .370 batting average, becoming the first player from a first-year expansion club to win a batting crown. Bichette and Hayes posted strong numbers, and the Rockies' bullpen, which had failed them so often early in the season, was a strongpoint by year's end.

Though Colorado struggled at times, as all expansion teams do, the club has assembled a solid nucleus of players, and with McMorris promising to pursue big-name talent through both trades and the free agent market, the future looks sky-high for the Rockies.

Sources

BOOKS

Whitford, David, *Playing Hardball: The High-Stakes Battle for Baseball's New Franchises,* Doubleday, 1993.

PERIODICALS

Philadelphia Inquirer, May 28, 1993.
Rocky Mountain News, April 6, 1993; April 9, 1993; April 10, 1993.

—Anne Janette Johnson

LOS ANGELES DODGERS

Baseball in Brooklyn dates back to the pre-Civil War era. In the 1850s there were four well-known amateur baseball clubs in Brooklyn—the Atlantics, Eckfords, Excelsiors, and Putnams. The players were young men of high social standing who agreed to uphold strict standards of gentlemanly conduct.

From 1859 to 1862 Jim Creighton, a pitcher, starred for the Excelsiors. His death at the age of 21, caused by "an internal injury occasioned by strain" while batting, moved his teammates to erect a monument to him in Brooklyn's Greenwood Cemetery. Carved in the granite were crossed bats, a baseball cap, a base, and a scorebook.

By the late 1860s Candy Cummings, a pitcher for the Excelsiors, had become the star of Brooklyn. He snapped his wrist as he made the then-standard underhand delivery to the plate, producing baseball's first curve ball. Because of the increasing popularity of the sport, gentlemanly amateurs gradually gave way to hard-nosed pros.

The National League (NL) came into being in 1876, at first without a team in Brooklyn. In 1883 Brooklyn, then an independent city, joined professional baseball with an entry in the minor Inter-State League. The next year the club moved up to the majors, joining the American Association (AA), which fielded 13 teams that season. Brooklyn finished ninth. The number of teams dropped to eight in 1885, with Brooklyn remaining in the AA.

After fair-to-middling finishes in their first five years, the Brooklyn Bridegrooms, as they were called, won the pennant in 1889, led by pitcher Bob Caruthers (40-11). The Bridegrooms transferred from the American Association to the National League for the 1890 season—and won the year's pennant.

Thus, the franchise that was to become the Brooklyn Dodgers (and later the Los Angeles Dodgers) was an immediate success in the National League.

The Brooklynites did not repeat as champions for another decade, however. In 1899 and 1900, under new manager Ned Hanlon, the club (now called the Superbas) won two straight pennants, then trailed off again. The team came to life once more after moving to Ebbets Field in 1913 and hiring manager Wilbert Robinson in 1914. The rejuvenated Dodgers—so named until the success of Uncle Robbie transformed them for a while into the Robins—won pennants in 1916 and 1920, with Zack Wheat starring in the outfield and Jeff Pfeffer and Rube Marquard on the mound.

A drought that lasted two decades followed the 1920 regular-season triumph and the subsequent loss of the World Series to Cleveland. (Brooklyn had also lost the 1916 series to the Boston Red Sox.) From 1921 through 1938 the Robins/Dodgers finished second only once (1924) and third only once (1932). Mostly they finished sixth or seventh.

Then along came Leo "The Lip" Durocher. A scrappy shortstop since the late 1920s, Durocher emerged as an aggressive and successful manager for the Dodgers, starting in 1939. That year the team moved up from seventh place to third. A year later they placed second. A year after that, in 1941, with young outfielder Pete Reiser tearing up the league, they captured the pennant.

The Dodgers, minus many stars, did moderately well during World War II, but it was the postwar era that really saw the team blossom. Under managers Burt Shotton, Charlie Dressen, and Walter Alston, the Brooklyn Dodgers won six pennants. They even won a World Series, at long last, in 1955.

These postwar Dodgers were strengthened by owner Branch Rickey's decision to recruit black players into the major leagues. Jackie Robinson's appearance in a Brooklyn uniform in 1947 is one of the landmark events in baseball history. By the time the Dodgers won the pennant in 1955, their star pitcher, Don Newcombe, was black. So was their catcher, Roy Campanella, along with Jim Gilliam, Jackie Robinson's replacement at second base.

The world ended for Brooklyn baseball fans

Transcendental Graphics

Candy Cummings (left)

after the 1957 season. Dodger owner Walter O'Malley foresaw a huge potential market for major league baseball on the West Coast. The Triple-A Pacific Coast League had tried to become a third major league in the 1940s, but organized baseball—which is to say the owners— would have none of it. Franchise shifting, and later expansion of the two existing leagues, was to be the answer.

Consequently, in 1958 the Dodgers moved to Los Angeles, at first into the gigantic Memorial Coliseum. The Dodgers, still managed by Walt Alston, continued to win their share of pennants and, after 1969, division championships.

The L.A. Dodgers won the World Championship in their second season on the West Coast, nosing out the Milwaukee Braves (an earlier franchise shift) for the National League pennant and then defeating the Chicago White Sox in the World Series.

TEAM INFORMATION AT A GLANCE

Founding date: April 19, 1890 (Brooklyn)
April 15, 1958 (Los Angeles)

Home stadium: Dodger Stadium
1000 Elysian Park Avenue
Los Angeles, CA 90012
Phone: (213) 224-1500
FAX: (213) 224-1459

Dimensions: Left-field line—330 feet
Center field—400 feet
Right-field line—330 feet
Seating capacity: 56,000

Team colors: Dodger blue and white
Team nickname: Bridegrooms, 1890-1898; Superbas, 1899-1910; Dodgers, 1911-present
Unofficially called Robins during tenure of Wilbert Robinson, 1915-1931
Team logo: Word "Dodgers" in blue script slanting upward with tail of letter "s" drawn back through
descender of letter "g"; baseball outlined in blue rising above the name, with flight lines shown.

Franchise record	Won	Lost	Pct.
Brooklyn (1890-1957)	5,214	4,926	.514
Los Angeles (1958-1993)	3,095	2,621	.541

World Series wins (6): 1955, 1959, 1963, 1965, 1981, 1988
National League championships (21): 1890, 1899, 1900, 1916, 1920, 1941, 1947, 1949,
1952, 1953, 1955, 1956, 1959, 1963, 1965, 1966, 1974, 1977, 1978, 1981, 1988
National League East division first-place finishes (7): 1974, 1977, 1978, 1981, 1983, 1985, 1988
League/division last-place finishes (2): 1905, 1992

When Alston retired after 23 years at the helm of the Dodgers—four seasons in Brooklyn and 19 in Los Angeles—his place was taken by one of his coaches, ex-pitcher Tommy Lasorda. "It's like inheriting the Hope Diamond," exulted Lasorda. And it was. With the rock-solid infield of Steve Garvey, Davey Lopes, Bill Russell, and Ron Cey, not to mention excellent pitching and an adequate outfield, the L.A. Dodgers finished first in Lasorda's initial two seasons as manager, 1977 and 1978, and won the World Series in 1978.

After that the Dodgers finished first in 1983, 1985, and 1988. They lost the pennant to the NL East team in 1983 and 1985, but won both the National League pennant and the World Series in 1988. In 1992, however, they finished last in their division—the Dodgers' first last-place finish since way back in 1905.

A Strong Beginning

By 1890 professional baseball was well established in Brooklyn. The Brooklyn *Eagle* newspaper had boasted a year earlier, "We have the biggest Bridge, the biggest Burying Ground, and the biggest Base Ball club in this blessed land of big things." The city's Bridegrooms won the pennant in the American Association in 1889, then defected to the increasingly strong National League.

That left a weakened AA to compete with the new Players League, a third major league that failed after a single season, 1890. The American Association folded a year later. (The present American Association, a Triple-A minor league circuit, was founded in 1902.)

Brooklyn entered the National League in 1890 and debuted by edging out Cap Anson's Chicago White Stockings for the pennant. Brooklyn manager Bill McGunnigle's Bridegrooms featured three fine pitchers: Tom Lovett, 30-11, in his best season ever; Adonis Terry, 26-16, a six-year veteran with Brooklyn's AA team; and Bob Caruthers, 23-11, whose lifetime won-lost percentage of .692 (218-97) is the highest in baseball history (.002 higher than Whitey Ford's).

Playing first base for the Bridegrooms was Dave Foutz, a former pitcher (lifetime 147-66) whose career won-lost percentage is the same as Ford's. In 1890 the versatile Foutz batted .303, drove in 98 runs, and stole 42 bases. Right fielder Oyster Burns led the league in RBIs with 128.

Meanwhile, in the Brooklyn front office, young Charles Ebbets was learning the business side of baseball. Ebbets had been a draftsman, a small-press publisher, and a New York State Assemblyman. But baseball was his first love, and by 1890 he had been working for the Brooklyn ball club for six years.

When the Players League failed after one season, the manager of its second-place Brooklyn team, Monte Ward, took over as skipper of the

Transcendental Graphics

Big Dan Brouthers played for Brooklyn during the 1890s

Bridegrooms. Ward, a Hall of Famer, was even more multi-talented than Dave Foutz. A pitcher, shortstop, lawyer, and baseball executive, John Montgomery Ward led the Bridegrooms to a sixth-place finish in 1891 and bettered that to third place in 1892. Foutz then took over for four seasons.

The team faded through the 1890s, falling to tenth place (in a 12-team league) in 1898, with Charlie Ebbets managing the club at the end of the season, his only stint as a manager. The Superbas (as the Bridegrooms were renamed in 1899) rebounded startlingly in 1899 and 1900 as a result of the self-interested actions of a Baltimore brewer named Harry Von der Horst, the owner of the Orioles, then in the National League.

Von der Horst, impressed by Charlie Ebbets' know-how and the team's success at the gate, made a deal with the Superbas' organization whereby he gained a controlling interest in the Brooklyn ball club. To protect his new investment, he moved manager Ned Hanlon from the Orioles to the Superbas—along with shortstop-first baseman Hughie Jennings, outfielders Wee Willie Keeler and Joe Kelley, and star pitchers Doc McJames and Jim Hughes.

In 1900, after Baltimore had dropped out of the National League, Brooklyn also inherited pitcher Iron Man McGinnity and outfielder Jimmy Sheckard. With this infusion of talent, it was hardly surprising that the Brooklyn Superbas waltzed home with the pennant both years.

Their success might have continued except that the new American League (AL), established in 1901, began raiding the National League clubs and cut deeply into the Superbas' roster. Brooklyn lost McGinnity to the new league immediately and Kelley and Keeler within the next two years. Wild Bill Donovan, a right-handed pitcher, had a great 1901 season for Brooklyn (25-15) and a good year in 1902 (17-15) before defecting to the Detroit Tigers.

The Superbas finished third in 1901, second in 1902 (although 27½ games behind Pittsburgh), fifth in 1903 (19 games back), and then dropped completely out of contention for more than a decade. They finished in last place in 1905.

Few players from this period are familiar names today. Even the better ones, such as left-handed pitcher Nap Rucker, labored mostly in vain. Rucker posted a mundane .500 lifetime won-lost mark, 134 wins, 134 losses, all for Brooklyn from 1907 through 1916, despite a fine 2.42 ERA.

A brighter ray of hope shone through in 1909 when Charlie Ebbets purchased a young outfielder named Zack Wheat from Mobile for $1,200. Wheat, who became a fan favorite, put in his entire 18-year-major-league career with Brooklyn. For years a sign on the wall at Ebbets Field carried the message, "Zack Wheat caught 317 flies last year [the number changed each season]; Tanglefoot fly paper caught 10 million." A hard-hitting, smooth-fielding right-hander who batted from the left side, Wheat, a Hall of Famer, was a lifetime .317 hitter with no discernible flaws.

Two other players of distinction joined the club in 1910: first baseman Jake Daubert, a classy fielder and sharp hitter, brought up from Memphis; and catcher Otto Miller, who stayed with the club for 13 seasons.

During the years in the wilderness, from just after the turn of the century until the outbreak of the First World War in Europe, Brooklyn fans could, and did, cheer for Nap Rucker, Jake Daubert, and Zack Wheat.

Transcendental Graphics

Zack Wheat

The Brooklyn Dodgers, or Trolley Dodgers, played their first league game at Ebbets Field on April 9, 1913. The Bedford Avenue ballpark, a handsome showplace of brick and concrete, stood in the Pigtown district of Flatbush. On opening day someone forgot to bring the key to the bleacher gates, and fans stood waiting until the key arrived. Someone else had forgotten to bring the flag for the center-field flagpole, and that caused another delay.

Worst of all, the architects had forgotten to include a press box in their plans. Two rows of seats in the front of the upper deck had to be ripped out to make way for members of the fourth estate, but it was not until 1929 that a permanent press box was installed. On the outfield fence Abe Stark, a haberdasher located at 1514 Pitkin Avenue, Brooklyn, advertised, "Hit Sign, Win Suit." Much later the Schaefer Beer Company put up sign on the scoreboard in right-center field that flashed the "H" in the company name for a hit, and an "E" for an error.

The antics of the Daffiness Boys of the 1920s led Brooklynites to begin calling their team "dem Bums." (One fan says, "The Dodgers have three on base." Another replies, "Yeah, which base?"). Cartoonist Willard Mullin picked up the nickname, and it became part of American folklore. One of the best-known fans at Ebbets Field was Hilda Chester, a bleacherite who clanged a cowbell at appropriate moments in the game. Also legendary was the Dodger Sym-Phony Band, which entertained fans with loud and cacophonous music.

Of course, the main show was on the field, where "dem Bums" often put on memorable performances. Casey Stengel, who broke in with Brooklyn and became a favorite there, was playing at Ebbets Field one day in 1918 after being traded to the Pirates. When he came to bat for the first time, the fans howled their greetings. Casey responded by doffing his cap. As he did, a bird flew off the top of his head and winged its way out of the park.

Ebbets Field did not survive the Dodgers' franchise move to Los Angeles. On February 23, 1960, a two-ton wreckers' ball, painted white with stitches like a baseball, began its work of demolition. Today a middle-income housing development stands on the spot where Babe Herman once doubled into a double play and where Cookie Lavagetto slammed a two-run double with two outs in the ninth inning of a World Series game to ruin Yankee pitcher Bill Bevans' no-hitter and win the game for the Dodgers.

Starting in 1911, they could also cheer for the Dodgers by name, for in that year the Superbas became the Dodgers (for "Trolley Dodgers").

The Dodgers needed more than a name change, however, to improve their game. They needed an infusion of both spirit and skill. Their seventh-place finish in 1912, 46 games back, was typical of the years under managers Patsy Donovan (1906-1908), Harry Lumley (1909), and Bill Dahlen (1910-1913).

During the 1912 season a brand-new ballpark for the Dodgers was constructed on a city block in the Flatbush section of Brooklyn. This new stadium would replace Washington Park in the Red Hook section as the home of the Dodgers. The Brooklyn Rapid Transit Company provided convenient transportation to the new ballpark.

Ebbets Field and Uncle Robbie

Twenty-five-thousand fans jammed Ebbets Field for the season opener on April 9, 1913. The lineup was not much different from the year before, with a couple of exceptions. The new center fielder for the Dodgers was young Charles

Dillon (Casey) Stengel, up from Montgomery of the Southern Association.

Stengel had appeared briefly at Washington Park the year before and in his Dodger debut went four-for-four, hitting all singles. The other notable newcomer was pitcher Ed Reulbach, acquired from the Chicago Cubs, where he had won in double figures for eight seasons. He would stay in Brooklyn for only one season.

Notwithstanding the inspiration of their new ballpark, the Dodgers finished sixth in 1913, and manager Bill Dahlen departed. His replacement was Wilbert Robinson, who for years had been one of John McGraw's coaches with the Giants. Robinson, or "Uncle Robbie" as he came to be known, thought he had the nucleus of a pennant-winning team. He did, but it would take three seasons to get there.

A crucial addition to the 1914 Dodgers was Jeff Pfeffer, a right-handed pitcher, who turned in a 23-12 record. Pfeffer had appeared briefly the year before, and he would pitch effectively in the two pennant-winning seasons to come. Three other noteworthy pitchers came on board in 1915. One was right-hander Jack Coombs from the Philadelphia A's. In his first stint as a Dodger, Coombs posted a 15-10 mark, but his best years were behind him.

Another pitcher, picked up in mid-season from the Giants, was future Hall of Famer Rube Marquard, already an established star. And, finally, the Dodgers acquired left-hander Sherry Smith, who went 14-8 for the Dodgers in 1915. The improving team finished fifth in 1914 and third in 1915. Their 80 wins in 1915 were the team's highest total since 1900.

It takes consistently good pitching to finish on top, and to their solid staff of Pfeffer, Coombs, Smith, and Marquard, the Dodgers added a proven 20-game winner, Larry Cheney, acquired from the Cubs in a late-season trade in 1915. Reliable Jake Daubert still held down first base, and patroling the outfield were Zack Wheat (catching 333 flies and hitting .312) along with Casey Stengel and newcomer Jimmy Johnston.

In 1916 manager Wilbert Robinson's ball club (unofficially called the Robins in his honor, but herein referred to as the Dodgers for clarity and continuity) edged out the Philadelphia Phillies in a tight pennant race.

Jeff Pfeffer won 25 games for Brooklyn and lost only 11, with an impressive 1.92 ERA. Larry Cheney, 18-12, matched Pfeffer's ERA, and Rube Marquard, 13-6, beat it at 1.58. At that, the Dodgers needed all this superb pitching in order to defeat the Phillies's Grover Cleveland Alexander (33-12) and Eppa Rixey (22-11).

As good as they were, the 1916 Brooklyn Dodgers could not defeat the Boston Red Sox for the World Series. The ace of the Red Sox staff, none other than the great Babe Ruth, pitched for a win in the series, while Ernie Shore won two and Carl Mays took one for Boston. The Dodgers managed a single victory, the third game, as Jeff Pfeffer retired all eight men he faced, after replacing starter Jack Coombs in the seventh inning, to preserve a 4-3 lead.

With much the same team in 1917, the Dodgers fell all the way to seventh place. Even the arrival of young spitballer Burleigh Grimes in 1918 (his previous season's record at Pittsburgh, 3-16, made him expendable) failed to improve the team's statistics.

Even though the Dodgers climbed to fifth place, they actually won 13 fewer games than in 1917. The club fared about the same in 1919, although the personnel changed somewhat. Gone to Cincinnati was Jake Daubert. Aging Ed Konetchy took Gentleman Jake's place at first base. Stengel had left for Pittsburgh in 1918 in a trade that also sent veteran Dodgers' second baseman George Cutshaw to the Pirates. Outfielder Hy Myers, who had been up and down with the club since 1909, put in a fine year in 1919, batting .307 and driving in 73 runs to lead the league in that department.

The pitching staff now included Pfeffer, Grimes, Smith and Al Mamaux (who came from Pittsburgh, with Grimes, in the Stengel-Cutshaw trade). Mamaux was past his prime, but Burleigh Grimes ("Boily" in Brooklynese) was just embarking on a Hall-of-Fame career. The 1919 Dodgers finished fifth, 27 games behind the first-place Reds. Despite the team's adequate pitching, only an extreme optimist would have predicted a pennant for Brooklyn the next year.

From First Place to Depression

That extreme optimism prevailed, however, as the Dodgers won the pennant in 1920. Although the club finished seven games ahead of the second-place Giants, the race was close. Until mid-September the pennant was up for grabs. Then the Dodgers reeled off 16 victories in their last 18 games, leaving the rest of the league lagging behind. Zack Wheat, Ed Konetchy, and Hy Myers all hit above .300. Even old Otto Miller, a lifetime .245 hitter, came through with a .289 season.

As usual, the mound staff was tough and balanced. Burleigh Grimes led with 23 wins and 11 losses, while Steve Smith had the best ERA, 1.85. Six pitchers won in double figures. As a whole the 1920s Dodgers won 93 games, a total they would not surpass for the next two decades.

As in 1916, the Dodgers struggled in World Series play. This time they faced the Cleveland Indians, and once more they could not maintain their momentum in post-season competition. In this best-of-nine series, the Indians took five games to the Dodgers' two, with Cleveland's Stan Coveleski winning three times.

The most memorable incident of the series occurred in the fifth inning of the fifth game when Cleveland second baseman Bill Wambganss made an unassisted triple play. Brooklyn was mounting a threat that inning. With the Dodgers' second baseman Pete Kilduff on second, catcher Otto Miller on first, and no outs, the batter, Clarence Mitchell, smashed a line-drive toward second. Wambganss caught it, stepped on second to double off Kilduff, and tagged out Miller arriving from first. It was, and continues to be, the only unassisted triple play in World Series history.

Of the two series games that Brooklyn won, the first (game two) was a 3-0 shutout by Burleigh Grimes, the second (game three) a 2-1 three-hitter

Transcendental Graphics

Burleigh Grimes

by Sherry Smith. Overall, the Dodgers' bats were fairly silent. Only Zack Wheat, with nine hits, and shortstop Ivy Olson, with eight, were productive.

The rest of the 1920s saw the Dodgers, still under Uncle Robbie, with a virtual lock on sixth place. After finishing fifth in 1921, they ended in sixth place in 1922, 1923, 1925, 1926, 1927, 1928, and 1929. They found much more success, however, in 1924. They started slowly that year but came on strong in September, finishing only a game and a half behind John McGraw's Giants.

A number of players turned in some sparkling performances, both veterans and new arrivals alike. Two years earlier Wilbert Robinson had signed Arthur (Dazzy) Vance, a right-handed, fireball pitcher who had been bouncing around the minors for ten years. After an 18-12 season for Brooklyn in 1922 and an 18-15 record in 1923, Vance paced the second-place Dodgers in 1924 with a 28-6 mark. He led the league in strikeouts with 262.

Dazzy Vance PROFILE

Although Arthur Charles "Dazzy" Vance is now in the Baseball Hall of Fame, he was not an overnight success. The tall right-hander with a blazing fast ball and an explosive curve spent ten years in the minors before he landed a spot with the Brooklyn Dodgers in 1922.

By then he had pitched just 30 innings in the majors—for the Pirates and Yankees—after having labored for Red Cloud, Superior, and Hastings in the Nebraska State League and St. Joseph in the Western League. Then it was back to the minors—Columbus, Toledo, Memphis, Rochester.

Finally, at the age of 31, Vance put in a full season for Brooklyn. He won 18 games, lost 12, and struck out 134 batters to lead the league in that department, thus proving he was definitely ready for the majors. Starting in 1922, he led the National League in strikeouts seven years in a row. In 1924 he led the league in just about everything else, too, with a 28-6 won-lost record, a 2.16 ERA, and 262 strikeouts.

There are many tales of Vance's mastery of the art of pitching. One concerns a post-season all-star game in which Dazzy was pitching to Baby Doll Jacobson of the St. Louis Browns. The third of three sharp-breaking curves left Jacobson lying flat on his back. "Strike three, you're out," bellowed the umpire. Jacobson glared up at him. "And damn glad of it," he said.

Photo: *Transcendental Graphics*

His performance was so stellar, in fact, that he was voted the National League MVP in 1924. Among Vance's competition for the award was the Cardinals' Rogers Hornsby who batted .424 that year, the highest single-season batting average of the twentieth century.

Another major contributor to the success of the 1924 Dodgers was first baseman Jack Fournier. Although Fournier was nearly as old as Dazzy Vance, his time, unlike Vance's, had been spent in the major leagues, with the White Sox, Yankees, and Cardinals. Fournier's 27 homers for Brooklyn led the league. The "big bang" style of baseball had begun; Babe Ruth hit 46 homers in the AL that year. Fournier's 116 RBIs led the team. For the Dodgers, Fournier's .324 batting average was topped only by Zack Wheat's .375, which, while a distant second to Hornsby's, tied Wheat's own career best.

Another new face was that of second baseman Andy High, a rookie in 1922, who had a career year in 1924, batting .328. Center fielder Eddie Brown, formerly of the Giants, arrived in 1924 and, at .308 with 74 RBIs, helped the Dodgers stay close to their Bronx rivals throughout the season.

The Roaring Twenties may not have produced any truly great Dodger teams, but those euphoric years did beget the Daffiness Boys. The name comes from the supposedly hilarious antics of Dazzy Vance, Babe Herman, and lesser flakes such as Ivy Olson and Chick Fewster.

Whether these players were any daffier than many other ballplayers (and funny or not, Vance and Herman were outstanding athletes), they, or the press that reported their antics, helped create what Donald Honig calls "the popular perception of the Dodgers—of clowns, buffoons, traffic jams on the basepaths, madcap fans rooting zealously for chronic losers."

First baseman (later outfielder) Babe Herman, born in Buffalo, arrived in Brooklyn in 1926 after impressive minor league deeds in Edmonton, Omaha, Atlanta, San Antonio, Little Rock, Seattle, and elsewhere. He began strong at Ebbets Field with a .316 batting average and 131 RBIs.

In 1930 his batting stats were impressive: 241 hits, 48 doubles, 11 triples, 35 home runs, 143 runs scored, 130 runs batted in, a .393 batting average, and a .678 slugging average. His fielding percentage that year, .978, matched Joe DiMaggio's lifetime mark (for purposes of comparison), so the Brooklyn Babe can hardly be considered a stumblebum in the outfield.

Jokes about him, such as, "Baseball wouldn't be any fun if they had only one base and he couldn't throw to the wrong one," are amusing but misleading. He was an all-around ballplayer, a capable fielder and baserunner, and one of the better hitters in the history of the game.

Yet the Daffiness Boys *were* part of a struggling team. Vance and Herman could not carry the whole ball club. An occasional strong addition, such as first baseman Del Bissonette in 1928, catcher Al Lopez in 1930, and outfielder Lefty O'Doul in 1931, pleased the fans but brought only modest improvement in the standings. The Dodgers moved up to fourth place in 1930 and 1931.

A pleasant surprise in 1930 was shortstop Glenn Wright, obtained from Pittsburgh in a trade. Wright spent five seasons with the Dodgers, his first year being his best. He batted .321, hit 22 home runs, and drove in 126 runs. Catcher Al Lopez, too, enjoyed a fine rookie season in 1930,

batting .309 with 57 RBIs (both career highs).

Considering that 1930 was also Herman's phenomenal .393 year, it is easy to see why the Dodgers, though finishing fourth, were only six games out. In fact, they were in first place for part of that summer, and the fans responded, setting a new attendance record of 1,100,000.

Left-handed pitcher Watty Clark had a few good seasons for the Dodgers. One of them was 1931, when, with the backing of Babe Herman, Lefty O'Doul, Del Bissonette, and Al Lopez, he won 14 games, lost 10, and posted a 3.20 ERA. Again, the Dodgers had a winning season, 79-63, but finished behind the Cardinals, Giants, and Cubs.

By this time Wilbert Robinson had spent 18 years managing the ball club, and the owners decided it was time for a change. The Dodgers replaced bluff, rotund Uncle Robbie with tough, leathery Max Carey, an ex-outfielder who had put in all or part of 17 seasons with the Pirates before ending his playing days as a Dodger flychaser.

Waiting for Durocher

Max Carey's Dodgers finished third in 1932. Vance, nearing the end of his career, had a so-so season, but Watty Clark had a career year, 20-12. Joining these two old pros on the mound was a tall, hard-throwing, right-handed rookie named Van Lingle Mungo. The youngster had made five appearances in 1931, and 1932 marked his first full season.

Although he won 13 games and lost 11, he walked a league-leading 115 batters. Wildness would continue to plague the pitcher. By 1933 Vance was gone and Mungo was the ace of a nondescript staff that included newcomers Boom Boom Beck (12-20) and Ray Benge (10-17).

The lean years of the Great Depression saw little improvement in the Dodgers' fortunes. For a few years following 1932, they finished no higher than fifth—and never had another winning season until 1939. When the team under Max Carey fell to sixth place in 1933, the manager was replaced at the helm by Casey Stengel. The firing of Carey took place in February, prompting his classic remark to the press, "What the hell were they expecting me to do, win the pennant over the winter?"

Stengel had no more success than Carey. Billy Herman, Del Bissonette, and Lefty O'Doul were gone. Pitchers Van Lingle Mungo, Ray Benge, and rookie Dutch Leonard both won and lost in double figures. Manager Stengel, not yet the colorful "Old Professor," could do little to spark interest in a basically ordinary ball club. Attendance fell. Stengel led the Dodgers to three second-division finishes, 1934-1936, before giving way to Burleigh Grimes, who fared no better.

Help was on the way, however. It came not in a baseball uniform but in a business suit. The savior was a new general manager (GM), Larry MacPhail, appointed in 1938. MacPhail was a forceful builder and innovator.

He was also a free spender. One of his first moves was to install lights at Ebbets Field, which increased the gate, but made life a little tougher for the batters on both sides. On the night of June 15, 1938, Cincinnati's Johnny Vander Meer, pitching under the new Ebbets Field lighting, threw his second straight no-hitter to defeat Brooklyn and enter the record books.

Another MacPhail move that paid off was his decision to convert veteran shortstop Leo Durocher, new to the Dodgers in 1938, into Brooklyn's manager. Durocher was a hard case, scrappy, loud-mouthed, but driven to succeed. "Nice guys finish last" was his credo. He gambled, fought with owner MacPhail, got fired, then rehired. Although Leo "The Lip" was tough, there was a new sense of purpose among the Dodgers. The nation was coming out of the Great Depression, and so was the team in Flatbush. Durocher brought the Dodgers in third in 1939, second in 1940, and first in 1941.

The ascent of the Dodgers paralleled the assembling of a core of first-rate ballplayers to replace the journeymen of the mid-thirties. Among the few holdovers were infielder Cookie Lavagetto and pitchers Luke Hamlin and Freddie Fitzsim-

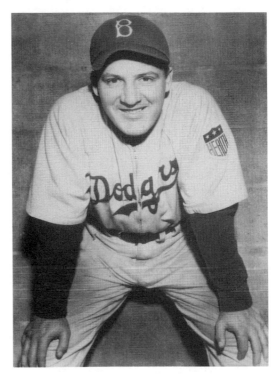

Transcendental Graphics

Joe "Ducky" Medwick

mons. These players had been with the Dodgers for a year or so when Durocher arrived, as the team's regular shortstop, from the St. Louis Cardinals. First baseman Dolf Camilli signed on the same year as Durocher.

By 1941, with these exceptions, the starting lineup was virtually new. So was the pitching staff. Larry and The Lip's new outfield consisted of Dixie Walker in right, Pete Reiser in center, and Joe Medwick in left. In the infield, joining Dolf Camilli at first and Cookie Lavagetto at third was rookie shortstop Pee Wee Reese, up from Louisville.

Veteran second sacker Billy Herman was the last to arrive, coming from the Cubs in a trade in early 1941. The new catcher, Mickey Owen, was also a 1941 arrival. The pitching improved, but not spectacularly. Whit Wyatt and Hugh Casey came aboard in 1939, and Curt Davis in 1940.

"Wait till next year," had been a popular saying in Brooklyn for two decades. Finally, in 1941, it was next year. They had a new pitcher, Kirby Higbe from the Phillies, who tied Whit Wyatt for the National League lead in victories. Each won 22 games, with Higbe losing nine and Wyatt ten.

On offense the Dodgers were dominant. Reiser won the batting crown at .343. He led the league in other categories as well, including doubles (39), triples (17), total bases (299), and slugging average (.558). Camilli had the most home runs (34) and RBIs (120). Three Dodgers were among the top five National Leaguers in slugging average and total bases—Reiser, Camilli, and Medwick. In total bases they stood one, two, three.

And yet this was not an unbeatable team. The Cardinals battled Durocher's men for supremacy throughout the season. When the Dodgers finally clinched the pennant, there were just two games remaining. In 1941 the Brooklyn team won an even 100 games, the most since 1899. The American League champion New York Yankees won 101.

The World Series promised to be a classic, but turned into a disappointment. The first three games were close but rather routine, except for the third matchup in which Brooklyn pitcher Freddie Fitzsimmons, who had a shutout going, took a line drive on the knee in the seventh inning and had to leave the game. Hugh Casey relieved him, gave up two runs, and the Yanks won, 2-1. That gave the Yankees a two-to-one margin in the series.

Then came the killer, game four, which found the Dodgers leading 4-3 in the top of the ninth with two men out. Casey had taken the mound in relief. The count had gone to three-and-two on the Yankee's Tommy Henrich, when Casey threw a curve—possibly a spitter—that broke sharply down. Henrich swung and missed for strike three. But, alas, catcher Mickey Owen missed the ball, too. It rolled off to the right, and Henrich took off for first base and made it safely.

Casey, upset, gave up a single to Joe DiMaggio, a double to Charlie Keller, a walk to Bill Dickey, and a double to Joe Gordon. That left the score 7-4 in favor of the Yankees, which is how it remained. The dazed Dodgers, down three games to one, went quietly the next day as Whit Wyatt lost a 3-1 decision to the Yanks' Ernie Bonham. The Dodgers at their half-century mark still lacked a world championship.

Two months later the Japanese bombed Pearl Harbor, signalling the United States' entrance into World War II. Within a year's time rosters were decimated as players left for the military. It was too soon for the war to have much effect on the 1942 season, though. The Dodgers' immediate problem was not war but rather St. Louis.

Brooklyn had only a few changes in personnel. Most notably, Arky Vaughan took over third base from Cookie Lavagetto who had enlisted in the Navy. The team had an exceptional season, even better than the previous year, winning 104 games while losing only 50. But the Cards claimed 106 victories with just 48 losses to take the pennant.

After 1942 much of the Dodger lineup went to war. Even Larry MacPhail, Brooklyn's dynamic GM, heeded the call, entering the Army as a commissioned officer. The man who replaced him was Branch Rickey. By the 1943 season the Dodgers were without Reese, Reiser, and Casey. They also lost Larry French, a veteran pitcher acquired late in 1941, who had led the league in won-lost percentage for them (15-4) in 1942, with an ERA of 1.83.

Hobbled as they were by the demands of war, so were all the other teams, and the Dodgers finished third. Then they lost Billy Herman and Kirby Higbe to the service, Arky Vaughan to retirement, and Joe Medwick to the Giants. The Dodgers fell to seventh place in 1944, but rebounded to third in 1945.

Dixie Walker ("The People's Cherce") played through the war, fattening his batting average to .357 in 1944 to lead the league at the expense of the kids, has-beens, and 4-Fs who were pitching to him.

A few of the Dodgers' wartime players, notably second baseman Eddie Stankey and outfielder Augie Galan, had enough talent to survive the

Branch Rickey is one of the great figures in American baseball. He is the man mainly responsible for establishing the farm system, breaking the color barrier, and (because of his threat of starting a third major league) forcing the National and American leagues to expand. This seems like quite a record for a farm boy from Lucasville, Ohio, whose baseball skills were minimal but whose inventive mind and tireless work wrought such far-reaching changes in the national pastime.

Rickey started the modern farm system while an administrator with the St. Louis Cardinals. Although he insisted "it was not a stroke of genius, it was necessity," given the high purchase price of star players, the fact is he built a system that everyone copied, and for good reason—it brought a succession of pennant-winning teams to St. Louis.

When Rickey joined the Brooklyn Dodgers as president-general manager during World War II, he transferred his farm-system expertise to Flatbush, and it paid off for Brooklyn as it had for St. Louis.

Three years after joining the Dodgers Rickey announced that a black ballplayer, Jackie Robinson, would be signed to play in organized baseball, specifically to play for Triple-A Montreal in 1946. Today that sounds hardly revolutionary, but it was. A kind of gentlemen's agreement had barred blacks from major league baseball (and, by extension, minor league baseball) from the very beginning. A great player, a sure Hall of Fame candidate such as Josh Gibson, Buck Leonard, or Satchel Paige, could play only in the old Negro Leagues. Once Robinson joined the Brooklyn Dodgers, however, other blacks followed and baseball apartheid ended.

Rickey, known as "The Mahatma," made one more insurgent move. The National and American League owners of the 1950s were entirely happy with their monopoly on franchises and had no desire to see more cities gain access to major league baseball. Rickey banded together with a group of wealthy would-be franchise owners to establish the Continental League—a third major league. To head off this threat, the owners of the day moved to allow new franchises that would expand the two existing major leagues. There was never a functioning Continental League, but in time, thanks in part to Branch Rickey, there were big league teams in Houston, Kansas City, and on and on through Miami and Denver.

"Mahatma" refers to someone who is wise and held in high regard or reverence. Given Branch Rickey's vast influence on present-day baseball, it was a fitting sobriquet.

return of the major leaguers from the military, but most were not. Also managing to survive and prosper was Dodger boss Branch Rickey, who was about to change the face of baseball in a most dramatic way.

The Glory Years

From 1947 until they packed their bags for Los Angeles in late 1957, the Dodgers won six pennants, finished second three times (once in 1951, when they lost the playoff game that would have given them the title), and placed third twice. These postwar Brooklyn Dodgers became quite famous, "The Boys of Summer" as acknowledged in Roger Kahn's book title.

A *New York Times* reviewer called the club "a team so extraordinary that Marianne Moore wrote poems to it." And yet there was usually frustration mingled with the triumph, for, except in 1955, the Dodgers could not win the World Series. Five times they lost to the hated New York Yankees.

In 1947 Branch Rickey handed the managerial reins to 63-year-old Burt Shotton. An experienced skipper, though with a mediocre record mostly with the Phillies in the late twenties and early thirties, Shotton inherited a superb ball club. He also found himself involved in one of the pivotal events in American baseball history—the introduction of a black ballplayer to the major leagues.

That recruit was Jackie Robinson, who had been educated at UCLA where he starred in football. After playing for the all-black Kansas City Monarchs, he was signed by Rickey to a Montreal contract—a move that shook the baseball establishment. Robinson stayed at Triple-A Montreal of the International League for one year, 1946, where he led the league in hitting at .349. He was

Transcendental Graphics

Pee Wee Reese

28 years old in 1947 when he first appeared in a Brooklyn Dodgers' uniform.

Robinson promised Rickey that he would ignore insults, knockdown pitches, spikings, and any other difficulties that came his way in breaking baseball's long-standing color barrier. Not only did he succeed in doing so, he also had a fine season, batting .297 and gaining Rookie of the Year honors.

Robinson joined the Dodgers as a first baseman, although he would move over to second a year later. The 1947 team also included shortstop Pee Wee Reese, rifle-armed outfielder Carl Furillo, injury-prone Pete Reiser in his last good year, and old veteran Dixie Walker, who would be dealt to Pittsburgh at the end of the season.

The Dodgers won the pennant by a five-game margin and battled the Yankees all the way to the seventh game of an exciting World Series. In the final matchup, Yankee relief ace Joe Page shut the Dodgers down for the last five innings. The Yanks won, 5-2, and the world championship once again eluded Brooklyn.

In 1948 the Dodgers slipped to third place, but fielded some new players who would gain popularity. Gil Hodges, after coming up as a catcher from Newport News, switched to first base, and Jackie Robinson moved to second. Billy Cox, acquired from the Pirates, took over at third. Behind the plate, after spending a season at Montreal, was catcher Roy Campanella.

Duke Snider appeared in the outfield for 53 games after being brought up from Montreal. In 1949 he would become the Dodgers' regular center fielder, while Furillo patrolled right field.

The mound staff included Ralph Branca, Rex Barney, Preacher Roe, Joe Hatten, and Erv Palica. Rookie right-hander Don Newcombe arrived in 1949, enhancing the Dodgers' pennant hopes considerably and winning Rookie of the Year honors with a 17-8 record. Brooklyn finished first that year, but only after a tight pennant race with the Cardinals. Again the Dodgers lost the World Series, this time four games to one, to those seemingly invincible Yankees. Preacher Roe pitched a six-hit shutout in the second game to

Transcendental Graphics

Duke Snider

register the Dodgers' only win, 1-0.

The Dodgers lost out, quite surprisingly, to Philadelphia's Whiz Kids in 1950, but tied the Giants for first place in 1951 after blowing a 13½ game lead in August. They lost the playoffs when the Giants' Bobby Thomson hit a three-run homer off Ralph Branca in the bottom of the ninth—the "shot heard round the world"—to give the Giants a 5-4 playoff win and the pennant.

The Dodgers fared better in 1952 and 1953, finishing first both years. But still the team folded against the Yanks in both World Series. Meanwhile, the team underwent a number of managerial changes. First, Burt Shotton gave way to Chuck Dressen in 1951. Dressen, after tying the Giants in 1951, then winning two straight pennants, asked Walter O'Malley, the Dodgers' new president and principal owner, for a two-year contract.

O'Malley turned him down, hiring in his place Walter Alston, a long-time minor league first baseman who fanned in his only plate appearance in the majors. Alston was willing to settle for a one-year contract, not only then but for many years thereafter, and in 1954, his first year at the helm, he led the Dodgers to a second-place finish, behind Leo Durocher's Giants.

By 1955 the Dodgers' lineup still included Hodges, Reese, Robinson, Furillo, Snider, and Campanella. Jim Gilliam had taken over at second base, and Sandy Amoros was the left fielder. Newcombe and Erskine were on the mound, joined now by Clem Labine, Billy Loes, and Johnny Podres.

This 1955 ball club under Walter Alston was the most successful of all the great teams of the glory years, winning the pennant by 13½ games—but, more important, finally defeating the New York Yankees in the World Series, four games to three. Brooklyn Dodgers fans were unaware that this was to be their first and last world championship.

The Dodgers won the pennant again in 1956 with the same basic team, plus pitcher Sal Maglie who came over early in the season from Cleveland and compiled a 13-5 won-lost record. But this time, even with Sal the Barber, they could not vanquish the mighty Yankees. The series went to seven games, with the Yanks' Johnny Kucks hurling a three-hit shutout in the deciding game.

Unfortunately for Brooklyn fans, the 1957 Dodgers did not win the pennant. Despite the fine showing of its new ace pitcher Don Drysdale, who went 17-9 with a 2.69 ERA, the team was not to participate in any more World Series games at Ebbets Field. Pee Wee Reese, nearing the end of his long career, batted only .224. Don Zimmer, touted as his successor at the shortstop position, did even worse, batting .219. Milwaukee won the flag, St. Louis finished second, and Brooklyn ended up third.

Although the shifting of major league franchises did not originate with Walter O'Malley and Brooklyn, it probably hit harder in Brooklyn than anywhere else. As Neil J. Sullivan wrote in *The Dodgers Move West,* "The Dodgers were more than a business, more even than a sports franchise. They represented a cultural totem, a tangible sym-

Transcendental Graphics

Walter Alston (right)

bol of the community and its values." That symbol was now hightailing its way out of town.

At the Dodgers last game at Ebbets Field on September 24, 1957, the team's Danny McDevitt pitched a 2-0 shutout against the Pirates. Organist Gladys Gooding played some farewell dirges, and a faithful contingent of 6,702 fans said goodbye to the team that had loomed so large in the history of Brooklyn.

On to Los Angeles

The Angels of Los Angeles had a proud history of their own, albeit a minor league history in the Triple-A Pacific Coast League. They finished their 1957 season in sixth place in the PCL, with veteran Monte Irvin in the outfield, power-hitting Steve Bilko at first base, and young Sparky Anderson at second base.

The minor-league Angels' home ballpark was Wrigley Field, built in 1925 and capable of seating just over 20,000 fans. By 1958 Wrigley Field was as deserted as Ebbets Field. The Los Angeles Dodgers decided to play at the huge Memorial Coliseum—in which some of the seats were more than 700 feet from home plate—until a new Dodger Stadium in Chavez Ravine was ready to occupy.

Fans poured through the turnstiles that first year—78,672 witnessed the Dodgers' home opener against the new San Francisco Giants. The opening three-game series drew 170,000 customers. For the entire season the L.A. Dodgers drew 1,845,556, beating in their first year the all-time Brooklyn attendance record. Those bereft Dodger

fans back east reviled Walter O'Malley, but in a business sense the brash owner had gambled correctly in moving his team to the West Coast. Nothing in the performance of the 1958 L.A. Dodgers quite justified the enthusiasm of the fans, though.

The Alston-led club posted a 71-83 record to finish seventh, just a shade above the last-place Phillies. No Dodger team had done that poorly since wartime 1944. Duke Snider (batting .312) and Carl Furillo (83 RBIs) paced the Dodger attack. Don Drysdale (12-13) and Johnny Podres (13-15) were hardly at peak form, nor was Sandy Koufax (11-11), who would not really come into his own until the 1960s. Only rookie right-hander Stan Williams (9-7) had more wins than losses.

Transcendental Graphics

Roy Campanella

Transcendental Graphics

Don Drysdale

An important Dodger who was unable to make the transition from Brooklyn to Los Angeles was Roy Campanella. One of the finest catchers in baseball, Campy was involved in an auto accident during the off-season and suffered permanent paralysis. His place was taken by John Roseboro, a capable catcher who put in 11 seasons behind the plate for the Dodgers but lacked Campanella's batting power and charisma.

Despite the dismal 1958 season, O'Malley signed manager Walter Alston to another one-year contract—in all, Alston would sign 23 such contracts, straight through 1976. The owner's faith in his skipper this time was repaid. The Dodgers won the NL pennant in 1959.

The team still bore a clear resemblance to the one that had moved from Brooklyn two years earlier. Gil Hodges held down first base, and Duke Snider roamed the outfield. Jim Gilliam had moved to third base to make room for Charlie Neal at second. Don Zimmer and Maury Wills shared shortstop duties.

In the outfield, along with Snider, were Wally Moon, acquired from the Cardinals, and young Don Demeter. On the mound loomed the old standbys: Don Drysdale, Sandy Koufax, Johnny Podres, Stan Williams, and Roger Craig. Drysdale led the staff in wins with 17, while Craig had the best ERA, 2.06. The 1959 pennant was not easily won, however. The race involved all three new NL franchise cities—Los Angeles, San Francisco, and Milwaukee. The Giants faded at the very end, but the Dodgers and Braves finished in a dead heat, requiring a three-game playoff.

Milwaukee had a couple of 21-game winners, Warren Spahn and Lew Burdette, but neither was rested enough to start the first game at County Stadium in Milwaukee. The Braves went with Carl Willey, lost the game 3-2, and started Lew Burdette in game two against the Dodgers' Drysdale. Although neither pitcher was around at the finish, L.A. won the game, 6-5, with a dramatic come-from-behind rally to take the pennant.

In the World Series against the Chicago White Sox, the L.A. Dodgers quickly showed that Brooklyn's post-season jinx did not necessarily apply to them. The Dodgers' new relief ace Larry Sherry got credit for two of L.A.'s four wins and registered saves in the other two. The batting star for the Dodgers was second baseman Charlie Neal, who collected ten hits, including two doubles and two homers, and drove in six runs. Big Ted Kluszewski had ten RBIs for Chicago in a losing cause, the White Sox winning only the first and fifth games.

That fifth game set an all-time World Series attendance record. Played in the mammoth Los Angeles Coliseum, it drew a crowd of 92,706. But the matchup, while disappointing for L.A. fans,

was something of a series oddity. Bob Shaw, Chicago's starting pitcher in the 1-0 contest, was relieved by Billy Pierce in the eighth inning, who in turn was relieved by Dick Donovan—three pitchers to fashion a five-hit shutout.

After the 1959 championship season, 1960 was a disappointment. With basically the same team, the Dodgers finished in fourth place, 13 games behind the pennant-winning Pirates. There were a few bright spots. First baseman Norm Larker had his best year at the plate, batting .323 to lead the Dodger regulars. Tommy Davis, a star of the future, arrived via the farm system and played much of the season in center field.

This was also the year that big Frank "Hondo" Howard (six-feet-seven-inches tall, weighing 250 pounds) came up from the minors, and the year Maury Wills took over full time at shortstop. Wills stole 50 bases in 1960, the most in the National League since Max Carey stole 51 in 1923, launching a new base-stealing era in major league baseball.

In 1961 the Dodgers climbed to second place. Rookie Willie Davis joined Tommy Davis in the outfield. Ron Fairly, a young outfielder-first baseman, came through with a .322 batting average and 48 RBIs in 111 games. The pitching staff, strong as it was, continued to lack a 20-game

The House That O'Malley Built

Aging Brooklyn fans will never come to love Walter O'Malley, the man who packed the Dodgers off to La La Land and consigned Ebbets Field to the wreckers' ball. But O'Malley, to whom baseball was a business, period, did have a keen appreciation of what would appeal to fans. He could have built a multipurpose stadium, a "concrete ashtray."

What actually arose in Chavez Ravine was a baseball-only, grass-surfaced, modern-yet-traditional stadium. Of course, not everyone was pleased with the project, certainly not some residents in Chavez Ravine. In his book *Green Cathedrals,* Philip J. Lowry notes under the heading "Former Us" that the area was once "used by squatters and goats. On August 21, 1957, Mr. Manuel Arechiga, his wife, and four granddaughters were evicted from their house but not before inflicting bites and bruises on sheriff's deputies."

Twenty-five years later, 3,608,881 paying customers trekked to the site of the Arechigas' demolished home to watch the L.A. Dodgers just miss winning the National League West championship. Wags could call the stadium Taj O'Malley or O'Malley's Golden Gulch, but the audacious, hard-headed Irish businessman had created a ballpark (albeit without water fountains in the beginning) that appealed to both casual entertainment-seekers and dedicated baseball fans.

winner, although two Dodgers came close. Johnny Podres posted an 18-5 record and Sandy Koufax, 18-13. Next year, 1962, the biggest news was perhaps the April opening of Dodger Stadium, a new but traditional baseball-only ballpark in Chavez Ravine that attracted a record 2,755,184 paid admissions its first year.

The 1962 Dodgers finished in a tie for first place with the San Francisco Giants, both teams at 101-61. This was the fourth tie in National League history, and the Dodgers were involved in all of them.

This time the three-game playoff ended in a Brooklyn-style disaster. In the decisive third game the Dodgers led 4-2 going into the top of the ninth, three outs from the pennant. But relievers Ed Roebuck and Stan Williams could not restrain the Giant attack, and when the game was over, San Francisco had earned a 6-4 victory plus the National League pennant.

This bitter ending took away from the fact that a number of L.A. players had outstanding seasons. Don Drysdale won 25 games and struck out 232 batters to lead the league, receiving the Cy Young Award for his efforts. Sandy Koufax, after years of showing great promise but erratic performance, turned in the second of six seasons in which he seemed all but unhittable. His 14-7 won-lost record in 1962 went along with a league-leading 2.54 ERA, and he struck out 216 batters that year, just 16 below Drysdale's total and good for second in the league.

Koufax—about whom Alston said, "All at once ... they just stopped hitting him"—was actually a bit down from his league-leading, record-setting 269 fannings the previous year. Clearly, these two pitchers, backed up by Johnny Podres and three solid relievers—Ed Roebuck, Ron Perranoski, and Larry Sherry—would become formidable foes in the future.

Tommy Davis hit for a .346 average with 230 hits and 153 RBIs, all league-leading totals. Maury Wills stole a record-shattering 104 bases. All in all, the 1962 season was a memorable one in L.A. Dodger history. "Wait till next year" seemed more like a promise than an excuse.

Highs and Lows

Great pitching made the difference in 1963. Although Tommy Davis won the batting title again, he finished with a 20-point lower average, .326, than in 1962, and his RBI total fell from 153 to 88. Frank Howard's batting average dropped 23 points from .296 to .273 and his RBI production fell from 119 to 64. Maury Wills upped his batting average a few points, but he stole 40 bases (to lead the league), rather than the 104 he had swiped in 1962.

The pitchers, especially Sandy Koufax, made up for the deficit. Koufax, the left-handed, Brooklyn-born fireballer, had a dazzling 25-5 season. He led the league with a 1.88 ERA, setting National League records for strikeouts with 306 (erasing his own previous record) and for shutouts with 11. Drysdale fanned 251 batters in the course of a 19-17 season, while Johnny Podres had more modest stats, winning 14 and losing 12. The other major force on the mound that pennant-winning year was Ron Perranoski, who posted a 13-3 record, all in relief. His 1.67 ERA was a career best.

The Dodgers won four fewer games in 1963 than they had the previous year, but they finished six games ahead of the second-place Cardinals. Then came a World Series that would have been a Brooklyn fan's dream come true. The Dodgers took four straight games from the New York Yankees. Koufax won two, with Drysdale and Podres claiming one victory each.

The Yankees had a team series batting average of .171. The Dodgers' own batting average, .214, testified to the dominance of pitching in this particular fall classic. Whitey Ford and Jim Bouton were effective for the Yankees, but the Koufax-Drysdale-Podres trio was simply overwhelming, posting World Series ERAs of 1.50, 0.00, and 1.08 respectively.

The Dodger dominance of 1963 appeared to end immediately. The team finished with a losing record, in a tie for sixth place, in 1964. The Dodgers roared back in 1965 and 1966 to win the pennant both years, however. In 1965 Maury Wills stole 94 bases, but otherwise the L.A. of-

Transcendental Graphics

Sandy Koufax

fense was relatively moderate.

Pitching carried the day, particularly the talents of Koufax (26-8, ERA 2.08) and Drysdale (23-12, ERA 2.77). Koufax struck out 382 batters—another new record—and Drysdale fanned 210. In the 1965 World Series the Dodgers defeated the Minnesota Twins four games to three. Koufax won the final game, shutting out the Twins, 2-0, on a three-hitter.

A three-way race in 1966 became a two-way race late in the season as the Pirates faltered. That left the Dodgers and Giants to fight it out, and the L.A. club finished with a flourish as Koufax won his 27th game (to only nine losses with an ERA of 1.73) on the last day of the season to clinch the pennant.

A new pitcher also appeared in Dodger blue that year, a player who would not depart until after the 1980 season, by which time he had erased some of the all-time Dodger records being set by Koufax and Drysdale. His name was Don Sutton.

After mowing down minor league hitters at Santa Barbara and Albuquerque in 1965, Sutton moved directly to the big show, where in his first year for the Dodgers he won 12, lost 12, and struck out 209 batters. He did not figure in the 1966 World Series, but neither, figuratively speaking, did most of the other Dodgers.

The series against the Baltimore Orioles was as much of a disaster for Walter Alston's men as the previous one against the Yankees had been a triumph. Los Angeles succumbed in four straight. Koufax started the second game, losing 6-0 to Jim Palmer, abetted by Willie Davis's three straight errors in the outfield in the fifth inning. He was never to pitch in the majors again, retiring at the age of 30 with arthritis in his pitching elbow.

The Dodgers seemed comatose in the series, batting for an average of .142. They scored two runs in the entire four-game rout, both of them in the first game, which Drysdale lost, 5-2. Some believe this World Series performance and Sandy Koufax's departure were bad omens, for in 1967 the Dodgers plummeted to eighth place in the ten-team National League.

Veteran left-hander Claude Osteen, who had performed well for the pennant-winning Dodgers of '65 and '66, became the ace of the staff with a 17-17 record. Drysdale sank to 13-16, and sophomore Sutton was 11-15. As a team they struggled and failed to improve much in 1968, finishing in a tie for seventh place, 21 games back.

Division play started in 1969, which made it impossible to finish lower than sixth. Although the Dodgers landed in fourth in the National League West that year, the team was on the mend. In this first year of divisional play, the Dodgers won 85 and lost 77. Claude Osteen and Bill Singer won 20 games apiece, and Don Sutton chipped in with 17.

Singer, a tall right-hander and a native Angeleno, had been shuttling back and forth between Los Angeles and Triple-A Spokane for some time before putting in his first full season for the Dodgers in 1967. The club held on to Singer until 1972, then traded him to the California Angels, for whom he promptly won 20 games again. From 1970 through 1975 the Dodgers finished second four times, third once, and first once (1974). Their second-place finish in 1970 was not at all close, as the Sparky Anderson-managed Cincinnati Reds dominated the division.

Dodger first baseman Wes Parker had a career year, batting .319, driving in 111 runs, and leading the league in fielding at .996. Three other Dodgers topped .300—second baseman Ted Sizemore (.306) and outfielders Willie Davis (.305) and Manny Mota (.305). None of the pitchers put up impressive numbers, not even Claude Osteen (16-14) or Don Sutton (15-13).

The 1971 Dodgers' won-lost record improved only marginally, but nonetheless they almost caught the pennant-winning Giants down the stretch, finishing just one game back. Willie Davis and Manny Mota repeated as .300 hitters, but the real batting power that season came from the much-traveled Dick Allen, spending his only year at L.A.

Allen played third base, first base, and the outfield. He batted .295, hit 23 home runs, drove in 90 runs, but was traded during the winter to the White Sox for left-handed pitcher Tommy John. Al Downing, a left-hander new to the club in 1971, won 20 games and lost 9, his finest season in the majors. Don Sutton had his best year to date, 17-12, with a 2.55 ERA.

The 1972 season started with a 13-day players' strike. It ended with the Cincinnati Reds atop the NL West, the Dodgers in third place, and a new Dodger lineup beginning to take shape. Although slick-fielding Wes Parker was still at first base, the roster now held two possible successors to him. One was Steve Garvey, who played third base, though on a part-time basis, in 1972. The other was Bill Buckner, also a part-timer, who played the outfield and occasionally substituted for Parker at first base.

Bill Russell, who like Garvey and Buckner had come up through the Dodger farm system, took over at shortstop from veteran Maury Wills. Although the Dodgers finished third, Sutton and Claude Osteen both had outstanding seasons. Sutton was 19-9 and Osteen finished at 20-11, each with the lowest ERA of his career.

The 1973 Dodgers won 95 games, but the increasingly powerful Cincinnati Reds, soon to be called the "Big Red Machine," won 99 games. Two more regulars joined the infield—Davey Lopes at second base and Ron Cey at third. These players were also products of the Dodger farm system. Fans of the club's minor league teams in Spokane and Albuquerque were getting yearly previews of the L.A. Dodgers to come.

In 1973 Buckner and Garvey alternated at first base. Another potential first baseman, Tom Paciorek, was on the roster, too. Up from Spokane and Albuquerque, Paciorek was placed primarily in the outfield by Walter Alston. With the addition of Andy Messersmith to the mound staff, the second-place Dodgers were a strong contender in 1973 and clearly would be in the pennant race in 1974.

The Dodgers took the flag in 1974, winning 102 games, and also introduced an infield that would remain remarkably stable over many seasons. Steve Garvey, as fine a fielder as Wes Parker and a much more consistent and powerful hitter, had finally nailed down first base. Davey Lopes was at second, Bill Russell at shortstop, and Ron Cey at third. Behind the plate was Steve Yeager, who first came up from Albuquerque in 1972, and would outlast all but Ron Cey at his position. The outfield, considerably more changeable, featured Jimmy Wynn, acquired from Houston; Bill Buckner, a left fielder until traded to the Cubs; and Willie Crawford, a long-time Dodger nearing the end of his playing days.

Dodger pitching excelled in 1974, even though reliever Mike Marshall, a peripatetic right-hander, appeared in an astounding 106 games, an all-time record, posting a 15-12 won-lost mark. Starter Andy Messersmith won 20 games and lost only 6, while Don Sutton came in at 19-9 and Tommy John at 13-3. This solid, well-balanced Dodger team breezed past Pittsburgh in the NL Championship Series, then went on to face the formidable Oakland A's in the World Series.

Every game of the series was decided by a 3-2 score except game five, which Oakland won 5-2. Don Sutton, with some help from Mike Marshall, who picked off pinch runner Herb Washington (a world-class sprinter) in the ninth inning, won the second game. That was the Dodgers' only victory in a series filled with costly errors and weak hitting. Steve Garvey's eight hits and .381 average led both teams. But no Dodger had more than two RBIs.

The 1975 Dodgers were a strong team. Indeed, they were essentially the same team, except for the arrival of pitcher Burt Hooton from the Cubs and the one-year loss of Tommy John for surgery on the elbow of his pitching arm. But the Big Red Machine had clicked into high gear, and the Reds rode home with a 108-54 record. The Dodgers finished second, 20 games out.

Matters improved only slightly in 1976, as Cincinnati again proved too potent, winning 102 games against the Dodgers' 92. Dusty Baker appeared in the L.A. outfield for the first time that season, and Don Sutton finally became a 20-game winner (21-10) for the only time in his 15 years with L.A. At the very end of the 1976 season, after 23 years on the job, Walter Alson retired, turning over the managerial duties to one of his coaches, Tommy Lasorda.

Winning with Lasorda

"Although many people aren't aware of it," wrote Tommy Lasorda in *The Artful Dodger,* "I served a thirty-year apprenticeship as an extremely active player, a minor league and major league coach, a traveling secretary, a scout, and a minor league manager." In fact, Lasorda had managed many of his Dodgers already, but at the minor league level. Now he, like they, were playing on a wider stage. Lasorda was ready, and so were the Dodgers.

After two years in the shadow of Sparky Anderson's Cincinnati steamroller, the Dodgers went on a roll of their own. They, like the Reds, won two straight pennants, 1977 and 1978, leaving Cincinnati in second place both times. The Dodgers had few superstars. Only outfielder Reggie Smith, acquired from St. Louis, hit above .300, although Steve Garvey (.297) drove in 115 runs

and Ron Cey (.241) drove in 110. Garvey, Cey, Smith, and Dusty Baker all collected 30 or more homers. Tommy John, fully recovered from surgery, turned in a 20-7 year with a 2.78 ERA.

After dispatching the Phillies three games to one in the NL Championship Series, the Dodgers ran into Brooklyn's old nemesis, the New York Yankees, in the World Series, and came up short. The series lasted six games. In the final matchup the Yanks' Reggie Jackson staked his claim to the title of "Mr. October" by slamming three consecutive homers off three different Dodger pitchers, each on the first pitch. Five of Jackson's nine hits in the series were home runs.

In 1978 the race for the division title was closer, but the Dodgers prevailed. They went on to defeat the Phillies once more in the divisional playoffs, again three games to one. Once more they faced the Yankees in the World Series, and again they went down to defeat, four games to two. Davey Lopes had a fine series, cracking three home runs (one more than "Mr. October"), two of them in the first game, which the Dodgers won 11-5. Ron Cey drove in all four runs in the second game to give Burt Hooton the victory.

The Yankees then swept the next four games. Dodger pitching, usually reliable, fell apart. The Yanks as a team batted .302, and an unheralded New York shortstop, Bucky Dent, got ten hits, drove in seven runs, and was named series MVP.

The Cincinnati Reds resurfaced in 1979 to finish first, and an increasingly strong Houston Astros ball club, featuring pitching by J. R. Richard and Joe Niekro, took second place. The Dodgers finished third, led by Steve Garvey at the plate (.315 and 110 RBIs) and rookie Rick Sutcliffe on the mound (17-10). In 1980 a nip-and-tuck divisional race between the Dodgers and the Astros ended in a tie. A one-game playoff (reduced from three games to match American League practice) gave the Astros the National League West championship.

The strike-shortened 1981 season saw the Los Angeles debut of a new pitching phenomenon named Fernando Valenzuela. A chubby left-hander from Sonora, Mexico, he had an odd habit of

| PROFILE | Tommy Lasorda: Bleeding Dodger Blue |

When Tommy Lasorda took over as manager of the Los Angeles Dodgers, he had already managed 17 of the 25 players on the roster when they were in the minor leagues. In 1968, for example, Lasorda, then in his fourth year as a skipper in the Dodger organization, was in charge of the Ogden, Utah, ball club in the Pioneer League, a Rookie classification, which is the lowest rung of the ladder in professional baseball.

His first baseman that year was 18-year-old Bill Buckner, whose .344 batting average led the league. His third baseman was 19-year-old Steve Garvey, whose 20 home runs set the pace in that category. In the outfield were Tom Paciorek and Bobby Valentine, both future major leaguers. The Ogden pitching was not quite so promising, but the Rookie Dodgers won the pennant handily for Lasorda. It was their third straight first-place finish.

Lasorda, a native of Norristown, Pennsylvania, followed the usual Dodger rookie's path to the top, with stops at Spokane and Albuquerque, where his Dodger farm teams never finished lower than third place. He then took a coaching job on Walter Alston's L.A. staff. It was like old home week, because Lasorda, as a young pitcher, had played for Alston at Montreal, then the Dodgers' top farm club.

A left-hander, he had won 66 games and lost only 30 during a five-year stretch in the Canadian city. Lasorda was originally drafted from the Philadelphia Phillies' organization by Nashua, New Hampshire, a Class A team in the Brooklyn Dodgers' organization, way back in 1948. Except for brief interludes with the Kansas City Athletics and New York Yankees, he wore Dodger blue, in one capacity or another, for nearly half a century thereafter.

Tommy Lasorda used to tell people that when he died he wanted to be buried under the pitcher's mound at Dodger Stadium. One year in spring training, owner Peter O'Malley called his gung-ho manager into the office and presented him with a tombstone that had Dodger blue blood dripping from it. Wrote Lasorda, "Naturally, I was overwhelmed by this outstanding present. After accepting it, I said, 'Mr. O'Malley, I want to tell you that I love the Dodgers so much that I want to keep working for you even after I'm dead and gone."

glancing straight up at the sky just before he delivered a pitch. Valenzuela won 13 games, with 7 losses, in 1981 and was named NL Rookie of the Year.

The Dodgers, in a complicated playoff arrangement, won the NL pennant and went on to defeat the Yankees, four games to two, in the World Series. Steve Garvey collected ten hits, but the real batting stars for the Dodgers were Pedro Guerrero, an outfielder just beginning to work his way into the regular lineup, and third baseman Ron Cey. Guerrero drove in seven runs, five of them in the final game, and Cey drove in six. Four Dodger pitchers shared the victories—Burt Hooton, Fernando Valenzuela, Jerry Reuss, and reliever Steve Howe.

From 1982 through 1992 the Dodgers skipped up and down in the standings. They finished first in the NL West in 1983, 1985, and 1988. They missed by a whisker, a mere one game, in 1982 and again in 1991. They also took second place, five games back, in 1990. But in 1984, 1987, and 1989 they ended up fourth; in 1986 they were fifth; and in 1992 they came in dead last. The 1983 and 1985 Dodgers failed to get past their NL East rivals in the championship series, falling to the Phillies in 1983 and the Cardinals in 1985.

In 1988 it was a different story. The New York Mets, who had beaten the Dodgers ten times out of 11 in the regular season, apparently tried to even things out in postseason play, losing four games (while winning three) to give the NL pen-

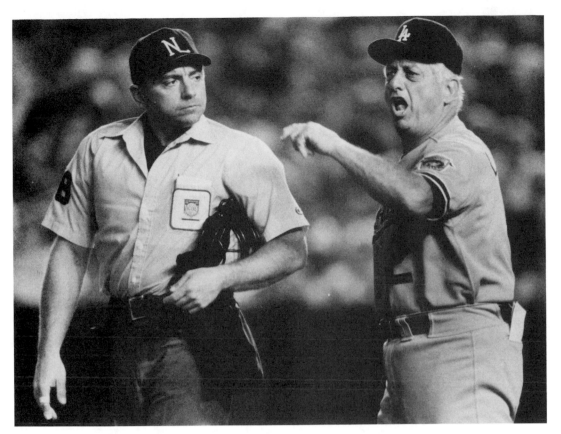

AP/Wide World Photos

Tommy Lasorda

nant to the Dodgers. The L.A. standouts in the playoff games were ace pitcher Orel Hersheiser and rookie Tim Belcher, along with ailing outfielder Kirk Gibson, who had only four hits in 26 times at bat, but whose homers in games four and five were decisive.

Few people expected to see the Dodgers get to the World Series at all, let alone win it against Oakland's power-laden A's. But win it they did, with Hersheiser and Belcher once more sharing three of the four victories. Outfielder Mickey Hatcher emerged as a surprising hero of the series, belting a two-run, first-inning home run in game one and another two-run, first-inning homer in game five—the final game, as the A's eked out just one victory against the weak-hitting, injury-plagued Dodgers. Kirk Gibson, who could barely walk from the training room to home plate, delivered a dramatic home run to win the first game of the series. Catcher Rick Dempsey, substituting for the injured Mike Scosia, doubled home the last run in the Dodgers' 5-2 victory in the final game.

After a disappointing fourth-place finish in 1989, the Dodgers improved in 1990. They took second place that year, five games behind Cincinnati. Then in 1991 Atlanta edged them out by a single game. After that came the sudden, thudding crash to the cellar in a season that was Tommy Lasorda's 17th straight year as manager, and perhaps his most painful.

The Dodgers rebounded to an 81-81 record in 1993 as NL Rookie of the Year Mike Piazza, an old family friend of Lasorda's, set new major-league records for a rookie catcher with 35 home runs and 112 RBIs, and Brett Butler continued his steady play in center field.

Changes are coming in 1994, as evidenced by the hiring of coaches Reggie Smith and Bill Russell, the leading candidates to replace Lasorda when he retires. Obviously, Lasorda would like to leave the team in good hands. The L.A. ball club is, after all, the jewel in the organizational crown for which he says he "bleeds Dodger blue."

SOURCES

BOOKS

Alston, Walter, and Si Burick, *Alston and the Dodgers*. Garden City, NY: Doubleday & Company, 1966.

Baseball Guide: 1992 Edition. St. Louis: The Sporting News Publishing Co., 1992.

Baseball Register: 1945, 1965, 1980, 1992 Editions. St. Louis: The Sporting News Publishing Co., 1945, 1965, 1980, 1992.

Beverage, Richard E. *The Angels: Los Angeles in the Pacific Coast League, 1919-1957*. Placentia, CA: The Deacon Press, 1981.

Golenbock, Peter. *Bums: An Oral History of the Brooklyn Dodgers*. New York: G. P. Putnam's Sons, 1984.

Graham, Frank. *The Brooklyn Dodgers: An Informal History*. New York: G. P. Putnam's Sons, 1945.

Holway, John B., and Bob Carroll. "Lives of the Players: Leo 'The Lip' Durocher." *Total Baseball*, edited by John Thorn and Pete Palmer. New York: Warner Books, 1989.

Honig, Donald. *The Brooklyn Dodgers: An Illustrated Tribute*. New York: St. Martin's Press, 1981.

Honig, Donald. *The Los Angeles Dodgers: The First Quarter Century*. New York: St. Martin's Press, 1983.

Ivor-Campbell, Frederick. "Team Histories: Los Angeles Dodgers." *Total Baseball*, edited by John Thorn and Pete Palmer. New York: Warner Books, 1989.

Kahn, Roger. *The Boys of Summer*. New York: Harper & Row, Publishers, 1971.

Lasorda, Tommy, and David Fisher. *The Artful Dodger*. New York: Arbor House, 1985.

Lowry, Philip J. *Green Cathedrals*. Cooperstown, NY: Society for American Baseball Research, 1986.

Mann, Arthur. *Branch Rickey: American in Action*. Boston: Houghton Mifflin Company, 1957.

Reichler, Joseph L., ed. *The Baseball Encyclopedia*, 7th ed. New York: Macmillan Publishing Company, 1988.

Reidenbaugh, Lowell. *Cooperstown: Where Baseball's Legends Live Forever*. St. Louis: The Sporting News Publishing Co., 1983.

Reidenbaugh, Lowell. *Take Me Out to the Ball Park*. St. Louis: The Sporting News Publishing Co., 1983.

Schoor, Gene. *The Complete Dodgers Record Book*. New York: Facts on File, 1984.

Selzer, Jack. *Baseball in the Nineteenth Century: An Overview*. Cooperstown, NY: Society for American Baseball Research, 1986.

Sullivan, Neil J. *The Dodgers Move West*. New York: Oxford University Press, 1987.

Voigt, David Quentin. *American Baseball: From The Gentleman's Sport to the Commissioner System*. University Park: The Pennsylvania State University Press, 1983.

Voigt, David Quentin. *American Baseball: From the Commissioners to Continental Expansion*. University Park: The Pennsylvania State University Press, 1983.

Voigt, David Quentin. *American Baseball: From Postwar Expansion to the Electronic Age*. University Park: The Pennsylvania State University Press, 1983.

Whittingham, David. *The Los Angeles Dodgers: An Illustrated History*. New York: Harper & Row, Publishers, 1982.

PERIODICALS

Baseball Digest, October 1973.
New York Times Magazine, February 26, 1956.
Sports Illustrated, April 1, 1957.

—*Gerald Tomlinson* for Book Builders, Inc.

SAN DIEGO PADRES

Organized baseball in San Diego dates back only to 1936, when the owner of the Hollywood Stars of the Pacific Coast League (PCL) moved the franchise from Tinseltown to San Diego. From the beginning the new ball club was known as the Padres, and the nickname never changed. The Padres finished the 1968 season in the PCL, then moved on without a break to the expanded National League (NL) in 1969. The only difference was that while the Padres had been a power in the PCL they were a doormat in the NL.

As the new entry in the six-team National League West, the Padres finished last in each of their first six seasons. Their 52-110 record in 1969 was their worst, but San Diego lost 100 or more games in 1971, 1973, and 1974. Not until 1978, their tenth year, did they have a winning season. The team's most consistently productive player during their first five years was first baseman Nate Colbert, who belted 38 homers in a couple of those seasons and drove in 111 runs in 1972, the first

Padre to top 100. Managers Preston Gomez, Don Zimmer, and John McNamara oversaw the skein of last-place finishes.

When the Padres left the cellar in 1975, they did not rise very far or very fast, although Randy Jones, a young left-handed pitcher, turned in two superb seasons, going 20-12 in 1975 and 22-14 in 1976. The Padres signed Dave Winfield, a promising outfielder off the University of Minnesota campus in June of 1973. Winfield joined the small and select group of outfielders that never played in the minors. Starting right off at San Diego, he quickly established himself as one of the Padres' key players. Not until 1978, however, under manager Roger Craig, did San Diego have a winning season. They finished fourth that year with an 84-78 record, as Dave Winfield batted .308 with 24 homers and 97 RBIs. Veteran spitballer Gaylord Perry won 22 games for the Padres, lost only six, and posted a 2.72 ERA.

The success of 1978 was not repeated for

some time. San Diego dropped back in the standings and stayed there, playing no better than .500 ball, until 1984 when, managed by Dick Williams, they vaulted into first place and won the National League pennant. The Padres lost the World Series to the Detroit Tigers, four games to one, but their remarkable rise from nowhere gave their fans hope for the future.

Although their dreams of winning another pennant were dashed, they played consistently better in the late 1980s than they had before—with the exception of 1987. In that year they skidded to the cellar, despite the league-leading .370 batting average of outfielder Tony Gwynn and the .313 average, with 20 homers and 91 RBIs, of first baseman John Kruk.

Sixth Place Six Times

As late as 1967 the San Diego Padres of the Pacific Coast League played in tiny Westgate Park, a facility in Mission Valley with a seating capacity of 8,200. But San Diego longed for major league baseball, and in August of 1967 a 50,000-seat, $27.75 million-dollar stadium opened in Mission Valley near the San Diego River. The first game played in San Diego Stadium, as it was then called, was a football game between the San Diego Chargers and Detroit Lions. The next year, 1968, the San Diego Padres of the PCL played there, drawing 203,000 fans, not a very good turnout for a second-place Triple-A team in an imposing new stadium. It was a harbinger of things to come.

The Padre team that took the field in 1969, an expansion ball club in the new six-team National League West (this being the first year of division play) was not likely to finish second, nor did it. The Padres came in last, and miserably last, 41 games behind first-place Atlanta—but, worse than that, 29 games behind fifth-place Houston. The Padres lost 110 games.

Although rookie pitcher Clay Kirby was a 20-game loser, a couple of fairly good hitters brightened up the generally leaden lineup. First baseman Nate Colbert belted 24 homers and hit .255, while

outfielder Ollie Brown contributed 20 homers with a .264 batting average. Not great, but a lot better than, say, shortstop Tommy Dean's .176. Colbert and Brown sparked the San Diego offense, what little there was of it, in the early years. Brown put in three seasons for the last-place Padres; Colbert served six.

The team improved to 63-99 in 1970. Nate Colbert upped his home run total to 38, while a young outfielder, Clarence "Cito" Gaston, had a career year, batting .318, hitting 29 homers, and driving in 93 runs. Clay Kirby pitched eight innings of no-hit ball against the New York Mets on July 21, 1970, but, needing a run or two, manager Preston Gomez lifted Kirby for a pinch-hitter.

The Padre reliever quickly gave up a couple of runs, and the Mets won the game. It was that kind of season. Although the Padres slipped a bit to 61-100 in 1971, Colbert and Brown had their usual good, but not terrific, years. On the mound Kirby seemed to be repaying the team's confidence in him as he posted a 15-13 record with a fine 2.83 ERA.

Nate Colbert was the standout performer for San Diego in 1972, the Padres' fourth straight last-place effort. His 38 homers were second in the league to Johnny Bench's 40, and his 111 RBIs put him fourth. Clay Kirby continued to pace the mound staff at 12-14 with an ERA of 3.13. Early in the season the Padres fired Preston Gomez, and Don Zimmer got the first of his many opportunities to manage.

But since Gomez wasn't the team's problem, Zimmer wasn't the solution. The Padres remained in the cellar in 1972 and 1973. Attendance at San Diego Stadium, never robust, showed few signs of improvement. Early in 1974 the Padres' owner, C. Arnholt Smith, decided to sell out to some buyers who wanted to move the franchise to Washington, D.C.

At the last minute—new Washington uniforms had already been designed and manufactured—Ray Kroc, founder of the McDonald's hamburger chain, bought the ball club and kept it in San Diego. Local fans showed their appreciation at the box office. Even though the Padres

TEAM INFORMATION AT A GLANCE

Founding date: April 8, 1969

Home stadium: San Diego Jack Murphy Stadium
9449 Friars Road
San Diego, CA 92108
Phone: (619) 283-7294
FAX: (619) 282-8886

Dimensions: Left-field line—327 feet
Center field—405 feet
Right-field line—327 feet
Seating capacity: 59,022

Team colors: Blue, orange, and gray
Team nickname: Padres, 1969-present
Team logo: Word "Padres" in navy blue lettering outlined in white with orange

Franchise record	Won	Lost	Pct.
(1969-1993)	1,783	2,203	.447

National League championships (1): 1984
National League West first-place finishes (1): 1984
League/division last-place finishes (9): 1969, 1970, 1971,
1972, 1973, 1974, 1980, 1981, 1987, 1993

shuffled home in last place for the sixth consecutive year under new manager John McNamara, attendance surged, topping one million for the first time. Fans even forgave the burger magnate's gaffe at the Padres' home opener, when he grabbed the public address microphone and snarled, "This is the most stupid ball playing I've ever seen."

If Kroc wasn't much of a diplomat, he was a good businessman. His timing with the Padres, as it had been with McDonald's, was perfect. The 1974 team, with outfielder Dave Winfield playing his first full season, and second-year pitcher Randy Jones ready to break loose, was about to vacate the basement, although neither Winfield nor Jones became a star in 1974. The big outfielder hit .275 with 20 homers and 75 RBIs—not bad, but not the stuff of legend. And Jones looked dreadful, winning only eight games while losing 22 (to lead the league) and posting a swollen 4.46 ERA.

Getting Respectable

Dave Winfield made no spectacular progress from 1974 to 1975, but Randy Jones's turned suddenly great. He went 20-12, with a league-leading 2.24 ERA, and won the NL Cy Young Award. No other Padre pitcher won in double figures, though, and at the plate only the Padres' aging first baseman, future Hall-of-Famer Willie McCovey, showed power comparable to Winfield's. McCovey led the team in home runs with 23 to Winfield's 15. But "Stretch" McCovey's great years were behind him; Winfield's lay ahead. The 1975 Padres finished in fourth place, ahead of Atlanta and Houston.

Jones enjoyed another brilliant year in 1976, going 22-14 with a 2.74 ERA. The Padres sold Willie McCovey to Oakland in late August. Mike Ivie, a product of the San Diego farm system, played first base most of the season and led the team with a batting average of .291. Ivie edged out Winfield in RBIs, 70 to 69. The Padres, clearly better than before but still no match for the strong

Cincinnati Reds and L.A. Dodgers, came in fifth in the NL West, three games ahead of the last-place Atlanta Braves.

Over the next three seasons Dave Winfield improved markedly. Despite his lack of minor league seasoning, he put up solid stats from the beginning. Only with experience, however, did he begin to show his true potential. His yearly RBI totals rose from 92 to 97 and then to a league-leading 118. His home run totals rose from 25 and 24 to 34, third in the league, in 1979.

Unhappily for the Padres, Winfield's progress was not matched by that of pitcher Randy Jones, who fell on hard times after 1976 and never had another winning season. Nor did the Padres show much improvement in the standings, finishing

AP/Wide World Photos

Steve Garvey

fifth, fourth, and fifth between 1977 and 1979.

A couple of new arrivals attracted attention in 1978. One was a rookie, shortstop Ozzie Smith, who had spent a single year in the minors at Walla Walla in the Northwest League. His batting was adequate, his base running outstanding, and his fielding brilliant.

The other acquisition was a veteran pitcher, Gaylord Perry, a spitball artist who had already made his mark with San Francisco, Cleveland, and Texas. He did not disappoint, chalking up a 21-6 record for the Padres in 1978 with a 2.72 ERA, good for the Cy Young award.

Roger Craig, once a pitcher for the Dodgers, Mets, and other teams, made his managerial debut for the Padres that year. It went well. For the first time since San Diego moved up to the majors, the Padres won more games than they lost—84 wins, 78 losses, to finish 11 games behind the pennant-winning L.A. Dodgers.

But just when things appeared to be getting better for the Padres, the team tumbled back down again, to fifth place in 1979 and then to the cellar under a new manager, Jerry Coleman, who stepped from the team's broadcast booth to the dugout (and back again after one year). Split-season 1981 produced no better results as the Padres finished last in both halves of play. After 13 years in the National League West, San Diego had finished in the basement eight times, never rising higher than fourth place.

Williams and a World Series

Padres' owner Ray Kroc and general manager Jack McKeon persuaded Dick Williams to lead the ball club in 1982. Williams, a hard-nosed motivator who made enemies but got results, had gained quite a reputation for his managerial stints with the Red Sox, A's, Angels, and Expos.

With the Padres he faced one of his toughest challenges: taking a team that had never finished higher than fourth and trying to mold a winner. "And so," wrote Dick Williams in his autobiography, "began the McNightmare chapter of my

life.... My lineup was awful."

Williams soon made changes, replacing Ozzie Smith at shortstop with Garry Templeton and installing Tim Flannery as the regular second baseman. But his best moves involved players already in the organization. Outfielder Tony Gwynn came up from Hawaii of the Pacific Coast League to become the Padres' all-time all-star hitter, replacing Nate Colbert in everything but the power categories.

Pitchers Eric Show and Dave Dravecky also arrived from Hawaii. Other players improved markedly. Young left-hander Tim Lollar, acquired from the Yankees, had suffered through a 2-8 season in 1981 with a 6.08 ERA but in 1982 he went 16-9 with a 3.13 ERA.

After a fast start in 1982 that made them look like contenders, the Padres slumped, broke even at 81-81, and finished fourth, eight games back. In this—only their second .500-or-better campaign—the Padres attracted 1,607,516 paying customers, the second-highest total ever in the ballpark that in 1981 had been renamed Jack Murphy Stadium in honor of the late San Diego *Union* sports editor who had pushed hard for the stadium and for major league baseball in San Diego.

In December of 1982 the Padres signed first baseman Steve Garvey as a free agent. Garvey, a longtime .300-hitting veteran from the L.A. Dodgers, replaced Broderick Perkins, a pretty good first sacker who was dealt to Cleveland.

The 1983 season was a replay of 1982—81 wins, 81 losses, and a fourth-place finish, 10 games back. In preparation for 1984 the Padres acquired two veterans from the Yankees: Graig Nettles, a classy-fielding, power-hitting third baseman, and flamethrowing relief pitcher "Goose" Gossage.

A December trade with the Chicago Cubs brought outfielder-first baseman Carmelo Martinez to the Padres, while up from the Triple-A Las Vegas farm team came another outfielder, a highly touted power hitter, Kevin McReynolds, the 1983 PCL Player of the Year.

Manager Williams observed, "With veterans (Garvey and Templeton), hot kids (McReynolds

AP/Wide World Photos

Tony Gwynn

and Martinez), and plain great players (Gwynn), our team's future was now." He neglected to mention his pitching staff, but it, too, was impressive. Eric Show, Ed Whitson, Mark Thurmond, Tim Lollar, Dave Dravecky, Andy Hawkins, "Goose" Gossage, and Craig Lefferts would all have good years.

In 1984 the Padres took over first place in the National League West in early June. They faded a bit in the second half of the season, but their 92-70 won-lost mark was the only winning record in the weak NL West division. The Padres finished 12 games ahead of deadlocked second-place Atlanta and Houston.

Tony Gwynn was San Diego's brightest star, batting .351 to lead the league. Most of the other regulars came through in 1984, too—Steve Garvey batting .284 and driving in 87 runs; Kevin McReynolds hitting 20 homers and driving in 75 runs; and Graig Nettles contributing 20 round-trippers along with 65 RBIs. It was a solid team effort. Still, few

but the San Diego faithful expected the Padres to defeat the Chicago Cubs in the National League Championship Series.

The Cubs pulverized the Padres, 13-0, in the first game of the NLCS. In a game umpired by college and former pro umps—because of a strike by the major league arbiters—the Cubs unloaded five home runs off Eric Show and his ineffective relievers. The Cubs won the second game, 4-2, against Mark Thurmond, Andy Hawkins, Dave Dravecky, and Craig Lefferts.

At this point the outlook wasn't brilliant for the Padre nine. But San Diego kept it alive with a 7-1 victory in game three, the big blows being Garry Templeton's two-run double in the fifth inning and Kevin McReynolds' homer in the sixth. Ed Whitson pitched eight innings of five-hit ball, and "Goose" Gossage shut down the Cubs in the ninth.

Down two games to one, the Padres pulled out a squeaker in game four. They took a 2-0 lead, lost it, took a 5-3 lead, lost it, and went into the bottom of the ninth with the must-win game tied 5-5. Tony Gwynne singled. Steve Garvey, already three-for-four on the day, picked out a Warren Brusstar pitch that he liked and socked it for a two-run homer, giving the Padres the game, 7-5, and an even chance to win the pennant the next day. If they won game five, they would become the first team to come back from a two-games-to-none deficit in the NLCS.

They won it. Although the Cubs took an early 3-0 lead in game five, the Padres closed the gap to 3-2 in the last of the sixth. Then in the seventh they wrapped it up on an error and a bad bounce. The error came on a Tim Flannery grounder that skipped between the legs of the Cubs' first baseman, Leon Durham. The bad hop came on a Tony Gwynn double-play grounder that skipped past Cub second baseman Ryne Sandberg for a two-run single. All told, the Padres scored four runs in the inning, won the game, 6-3, and went on to the World Series, where a tough Detroit Tiger team lay in wait.

The Tigers made short work of Dick Williams's men, taking the Series four games to one.

Only the second game, an Andy Hawkins win, went San Diego's way. In that game the much-traveled Kurt Bevacqua, the Padres' designated hitter, blasted a three-run homer in the fifth inning to give San Diego a 5-3 victory.

Down from the Mountaintop

In 1985 the Padres, with essentially the same roster, eked out a tie for third place, finishing 12 games behind the L.A. Dodgers, after building a 49-39 record by the All-Star break. The combative Williams was replaced as skipper by Steve Boros, who was later succeeded by Larry Bowa. Neither of the two had much success.

Tony Gwynn continued to terrorize NL pitchers, but Kevin McReynolds slipped to .234 in 1985 and was traded to the Mets after the 1986 season. Steve Garvey, his skills clearly eroding, retired in 1987. The pitching became progressively worse. In 1987 only one staffer, Ed Whitson, won in double figures, and his record, 10-13 with a 4.73 ERA, was hardly a Cy Young-level performance.

The Padres did feature a few first-rate ballplayers during these years. First baseman-outfielder John Kruk, a farm-system product, looked like an oversized munchkin, but he played like a pro, batting .309 in 1986 and .313 in 1987 before being dealt to the Phillies. Infielder Randy Ready showed promise as well, but was also shipped off to the Phillies after a couple of seasons. The Padres finished fourth in 1986 and last in 1987. Tony Gwynn enjoyed a career year in 1987, as his team floundered, batting .370 to lead the league by a country mile. A newcomer, catcher Benito Santiago, won NL Rookie of the Year honors.

Early in the 1988 season Jack McKeon, who Williams believed had been angling for the job for years, took over as field manager. The Padres improved under him, finishing third that year and second the next. Their 1989 record, 89-73, was the third best in their history, and they finished only three games behind the San Francisco Giants.

Gwynn, batting .336, led the league for the third straight year. Also impressive were a couple of infielders up from Las Vegas, second-year utility man Bip Roberts (.301) and rookie second baseman Roberto Alomar (.295). Ed Whitson was back in form, recording a 16-11 mark with a 2.66 ERA, and Bruce Hurst, a veteran hurler acquired from the Red Sox, went 15-11 with a 2.69 ERA. Reliever Mark Davis chalked up 44 saves and a glittering 1.85 ERA.

The Padres were picked as preseason favorites for 1990, but they failed to deliver. A new ownership group took over early in the season, ending the Kroc era. Jack McKeon resigned as manager and returned to the front office. He was replaced by Greg Riddoch, who had last managed in the Class A Northwest League in 1981. The situation deteriorated throughout the season.

Bip Roberts and Tony Gwynn shared team batting honors in 1990 at .309 each, which pleased Roberts but not Gwynn. Outfielder Joe Carter, playing his first (and only) year for the Padres, hit 24 homers and drove in 115 runs.

First baseman Jack Clark, in his second (and last) season with the Padres, hit 25 homers but missed a number of games because of injuries. Catcher Benito Santiago broke his forearm in three places when he threw up his hand to ward off a pitch. All in all, it was not a good season. The Padres finished in a tie for fourth place, 16 games off the pace.

Sparked by sluggers Fred McGriff and Gary Sheffield, they moved up to third in 1991 and 1992. But wholesale changes in personnel made it unclear just where the Padres were headed. To help reduce the club's payroll, McGriff and Sheffield were traded during the 1993 season, and a number of other high-priced veterans were let go. Not surprisingly, the Padres struggled to a 61-101 record, 43 games out of first place, their worst showing ever.

Gwynn again proved himself to be one of baseball's top hitters, batting .358, second best in the league. Newcomers Phil Plantier and Derek Bell added home-run punch to the lineup, and pitchers Andy Benes and Gene Harris had strong years. But the rest of the club is weak, and the team plans to give its young (and inexpensive) players every opportunity to fill the holes left by the departed veterans. The rebuilding program could take years to pay off.

SOURCES

BOOKS

Baseball Guide, 1980, 1983, 1985, 1987, 1991, and 1993 editions, *The Sporting News* Publishing Co., 1980, 1983, 1985, 1987, 1991, and 1993.

Baseball Register, 1980, 1983, 1987, 1991, and 1993 editions, *The Sporting News* Publishing Co., 1980, 1983, 1987, 1991, 1993.

Complete Baseball Record Book, 1993 edition, *The Sporting News* Publishing Co., 1993.

Ivor-Campbell, Frederick, "Team Histories: San Diego Padres," *Total Baseball,* edited by John Thorn and Pete Palmer, Warner, 1989.

Lowry, Philip J., *Green Cathedrals,* Society for American Baseball Research, 1986.

Reichler, Joseph L., editor, *The Baseball Encyclopedia,* 7th edition, Macmillan, 1988.

Reidenbaugh, Lowell, *Take Me Out to the Ball Park, The Sporting News* Publishing Co., 1983.

Who's Who in Baseball, 55th edition and 60th edition, Who's Who in Baseball Magazine Co., 1970 and 1975.

Williams, Dick, and Bill Plaschke, *No More Mr. Nice Guy: A Life of Hardball,* Harcourt Brace Jovanovich, 1990.

PERIODICALS

Baseball America, February 21, 1993; April 4, 1993.

Sports Illustrated, April 16, 1984.

—*Gerald Tomlinson* for Book Builders, Inc.

SAN FRANCISCO GIANTS

Since their founding in 1883 the Giants, first in New York and later in San Francisco, have won 19 league championships. That total falls far short of the New York Yankees' 33 but compares favorably with the Brooklyn/Los Angeles Dodgers' 21. Unlike the Yanks and Dodgers, however, the Giants enjoyed most of their success early in the team's history and then tailed off. By the mid-1920s they had already won a dozen pennants—three in a row from 1911 through 1913 and four in a row from 1921 through 1924.

The great stars of those first three seasons were pitchers Christy Mathewson and Rube Marquard, joined in the last two seasons by the lesser-known Jeff Tesreau. From 1921 to 1924 the standouts were infielders Frankie Frisch and Dave (Beauty) Bancroft plus outfielders Ross Youngs and Irish Meusel. John McGraw managed all seven of these championship teams.

After 1924 the Giants won only seven pennants over the next seven decades. Three first-

place finishes in the 1930s (in the days of Mel Ott, Bill Terry, and Carl Hubbell) were followed by a drought in the 1940s. Then Willie Mays, Monte Irvin, and Sal Maglie, among others, brought them back to life under manager Leo Durocher in the early 1950s.

Following their move to San Francisco in 1958, the Giants won only two isolated pennants. The first came in 1962 on some fine pitching by Jack Sanford, Juan Marichal, Billy Pierce, and Billy O'Dell along with powerful hitting by Willie Mays, Orlando Cepeda, Felipe Alou, and Willie McCovey. 27 years later, long after divisional play had begun, the Giants finally captured another National League (NL) pennant, this time led by sluggers Kevin Mitchell and Will Clark and pitchers Rick Reuschel and Scott Garrelts.

Troy, New York, and Worcester, Massachusetts, had franchises in the National League in 1882. Their teams finished seventh and eighth, and at the winter meetings that year the two ball clubs were persuaded to "resign" from the league. The cities were simply too small to support major league baseball. On the last day of the 1882 season the Troy Haymakers drew just 25 fans.

As soon as Troy and Worcester were gone, John B. Day, a well-to-do Manhattan tobacco merchant and the owner of the independent New York Metropolitans (called Mets for short), applied for one of the franchises. Upon receiving it, Day surprised the baseball world by announcing that the Mets would play in the rival American Association (AA), and he would enter a brand-new team in the National League.

The defunct Troy Haymakers had a number of top players, whom Day signed to New York "Nationals" contracts. Among there were three future Hall of Famers: Buck Ewing, a versatile, rifle-armed catcher; Roger Connor, a power-hitting first baseman; and Smiling Mickey Welch, a

Trancendental Graphics

Buck Ewing

young right-handed pitcher. But since Day owned another team he had to stock with players, he acquired a few of the Trojan standouts for the Mets, among them future Hall of Fame pitcher Tim Keefe and catcher Bill Holbert.

The New York Nationals opened their season on May 1, 1883—at the Polo Grounds. Actually, there have been four New York City ballparks called the Polo Grounds. This first one stood at West 110th Street, just north of Central Park. On opening day, 1883, it held more than 12,000 fans, including former U.S. President Ulysses S. Grant. The size of the turnout must have made quite an impression on the ex-Haymaker players.

These 1883 Nationals had another Hall-of-Famer in the lineup in addition to the three already named. He was John Montgomery Ward, who played center field that day, although he became better known as a pitcher and a shortstop. Monte Ward, a star player, manager, lawyer, labor organizer, and baseball executive, was an important figure in baseball history. He was just another ballplayer in 1883, however, posting a 12-14 pitching record and batting .255.

The Nationals won their opener, 7-5, to get the season off to a good start. Later they faded. Despite Connor's .357 batting average, Ewing's 10 home runs (to lead the league), and Welch's 27-21 won-lost record, the team finished sixth. Although John Day's Mets won the AA championship in 1884, and went on to oppose the NL's Providence Grays in a kind of prototype World Series, the Mets were not making money.

At the end of the 1884 season Day decided to shift his best Mets' players to the Nationals. He signed pitcher Tim Keefe (37-17 for the Mets in 1884) and third baseman Dude Esterbrook (.314 batting average) to contracts with the Nationals. He also invited the Mets' manager, Jim Mutrie, to take over the management of his NL ball club.

The thus-strengthened New York Nationals of 1885 won 85 games and lost only 27. Astonishingly, this performance was not good enough for the pennant. Cap Anson's Chicago White Stockings won 87 games and lost 25, consigning New York to second place. The National's two pitchers,

TEAM INFORMATION AT A GLANCE

Founding date: May 1, 1883 (New York)
April 15, 1958 (San Francisco)

Home stadium: Candlestick Park
Candlestick Point, State Route 1
San Francisco, CA 94124

Dimensions: Left-field line—335 feet
Center field—400 feet
Right-field line—335 feet
Seating capacity: 58,000

Team uniforms: Home—base color white with black and orange trim
Road—base color gray with black and orange trim
Team nickname: Nationals or Gothams, 1883-1885; Giants, 1885—
Team logo: Outlined word "Giants," all capitals with oversized "G" and "S,"
printed in an arch between stitching across outlined baseball

Franchise record	Won	Lost	Pct.
New York (1883-1957)	6,067	4,898	.553
San Francisco (1958-1993)	2,967	2,775	.517

World Series wins (5): 1905, 1921, 1922, 1933, 1954
National League Championships (19): 1888, 1889, 1904, 1905, 1911, 1912, 1913,
1917, 1921, 1922, 1923, 1924, 1933, 1936, 1937, 1951, 1954, 1962, 1989
National League West division first-place finishes (3): 1971, 1987, 1989
League/division last-place finishes (7): 1900, 1902, 1915, 1943, 1946, 1984, 1985

"Smiling Mickey" Welch and "Sir Timothy" Keefe posted records of 44-11 and 32-13 respectively, while slugging first baseman Roger Connor led the league in hitting at .371.

In center field that year, and for a number of years thereafter, was Orator Jim O'Rourke, a future Hall of Famer, who in 1885 batted an even .300 and led the league in triples with 16. Manager Jim Mutrie had begun to refer to the team as his "big fellows," later changing it to "my giants." A

sportswriter picked it up and from that day forward the home-team players at the Polo Grounds were not the nondescript "Nationals" but the classy and distinctive "Giants." (John Day sold his Mets' franchise to a Staten Island entrepreneur, who soon disbanded the ball club.)

Powerful as this Giants' team was, it did not advance immediately to the summit. In 1886 and 1887, with the same strong pitching and Hall of Fame lineup, the club dropped to third and then

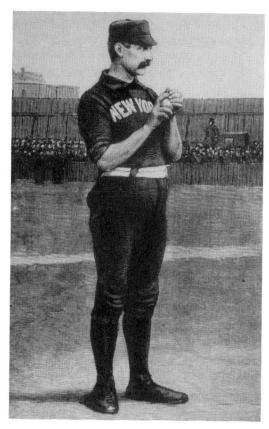

Transcendental Graphics

Tim Keefe

eryone learned a basic lesson: Play only the number of games required to win. After the sloppy and meaningless final games, Giant manager Jim Mutrie said disgustedly, "If I ever engage in another World Series, the ball will stop rolling just as soon as the series is decided."

In 1889 the Giants played their home games after July 8 in the club's "new" Polo Grounds, a horseshoe-shaped wooden stadium at 155th Street and Eighth Avenue. The pennant race was quite close that year, with a tough Boston Beaneaters' team—featuring right fielder King Kelly and pitchers John Clarkson and Old Hoss Radbourn—finishing in second place.

For the Giants, first baseman Roger Connor drove in 130 runs to lead the league; outfielder Mike Tiernan led the Giants with a .335 batting average; and two pitchers—Cannonball Crane and Hank O'Day—assisted Welch and Keefe, the Giant aces, on the mound. In postseason play the AA champion Brooklyn Bridegrooms fell to the Giants in nine games and, as Mutrie had vowed, there was no extraneous tenth game. The Giants had now won back-to-back championships, and the future looked promising. But 1890 proved to be a tumultuous year for baseball. The New York Giants were caught in the maelstrom and badly buffeted.

Every star player on the Giants ball club except Mickey Welch and Mike Tiernan defected to John Montgomery Ward's new Players League. Worse yet, the Players League had a franchise in New York whose stadium, Brotherhood Park, was a stone's throw from the Polo Grounds.

The new team—with Buck Ewing, Roger Connor, Tim Keefe, Orator Jim O'Rourke, Cannonball Crane, and other New York favorites—called itself the "Big Giants." The badly weakened "real Giants" finished in sixth place in the National League. Their ace pitcher was 18-year-old rookie Amos Rosie, destined, like so many other early Giants, for the Baseball Hall of Fame.

The Players League ended after one season, having cost owners in all three major leagues many millions of dollars. Members of the players' Brotherhood drifted back to their original teams,

fourth place. The White Stockings took the flag in 1886, the Detroit Tigers in 1887. But in 1888 and 1889 New York climbed to the top of the heap.

A preview of things to come occurred on May 9, 1888, when first baseman Roger Connor slammed three home runs in one game, an almost unbelievable feat in that dead ball era, when a dozen home runs a season were sometimes enough to lead the league. The Giants coasted to the championship in 1888, even though their 84-47 record was far less glittering than that of the 1885 team. In the 10-game post season series they faced the St. Louis Browns of the AA.

The Giants won the series in eight games, but the teams played the final two as scheduled. Ev-

and the Giants turned in a winning season in 1891, although finishing third. The "real" Giants moved into their ex-rivals' ballpark, renamed it the Polo Grounds (number three), and played there until it burned in 1911.

At the end of 1891 the AA folded, leaving the NL as the only major league left. The National League added four ball clubs, creating a cumbersome 12-team circuit that lasted through the rest of the century.

Transcendental Graphics

John McGraw

Having 12 teams in the league—Baltimore, Louisville, St. Louis, and Washington were the additions—made it harder than ever to finish first. In 1894 the Giants, under playing-manager Monte Ward, came in a strong second, as pitchers Amos Rosie and Jouett Meekin each won 36 games to tie for the league lead. A number of players batted over .300, and two of them, first baseman Jack Doyle and center fielder George Van Haltren, drove in 100 or more runs.

Second place was the best the Giants could do, however, until after the first of the century. Part of the problem had to do with the ownership of the club. Financier Edward Talcott, who had bought the Giants from founder John Day in the wake of the players' revolt, sold out to Andrew Freedman, a Tammany Hall politico. Freedman alienated everyone in sight, went through a succession of managers, and generally ran the franchise into the ground.

In 1900, with the National League down to eight teams again, the Giants skidded to the cellar. They moved up a notch in 1901, then dropped back to the basement in 1902. The hapless Giants won 48 games in 1902 and lost 88, finishing 53½ games behind league-leading Pittsburgh, their worst finish ever. Clearly, something drastic needed to be done.

McGraw, Mathewson, Marquard

The turnaround in 1903 was spectacular. It began in mid-1902 when John T. Brush, owner of the Cincinnati Reds (one of the NL magnates at war with the upstart American League [AL]), sold his Reds franchise and bought the Baltimore Orioles of the AL. He promptly eviscerated the O's. John McGraw, the Baltimore manager, was signed by the Giants. McGraw, "Little Napoleon," would become the very symbol of the rejuvenated Giants, staying with the team for the next 30 years.

Nor was McGraw the only acquisition from the stricken Orioles. Two other future Hall of Fame pitchers, Joe (Iron Man) McGinnity and catcher Roger Bresnahan, came over from Baltimore. Already on the Giants' pitching staff was a young right-hander with obvious potential: Christy Mathewson.

Matty had won 20 games in 1901, his first full season in the majors, posting a 2.11 Earned Run Average (ERA) in 1902 with a league-leading eight shutouts for his last-place team. With McGinnity and Mathewson on the mound in 1903, and Bresnahan behind the plate, the Giants of John McGraw rose phoenix-like from the cellar to contention.

The 1903 Giants finished second to the Pittsburgh Pirates, their 84-55 record showing how impressively they had climbed. It augured well for the future. Iron Man McGinnity won more games, 31, than anyone else in the National League. Christy Mathewson came in right behind him with 30 victories. Roger Bresnahan, playing mostly in the outfield, batted .350, while outfielder Sam Mertes drove in 104 runs to lead the league. Although 1903 was a good season for the Giants, it was just a warm-up for what was to come.

By 1904 John McGraw had "the man I've wanted ever since I've had charge of this team"—shortstop Bill Dahlen, who endeared himself to the fans of Brooklyn (where he had been playing) by saying, "Brooklyn is all right, but if you're not with the Giants, you might as well be in Albany." It was certainly great being with the Giants in 1904. They won the pennant by a 13-game margin over Chicago.

McGinnity had a 35-8 season with a league-leading 1.61 ERA. Mathewson, nicknamed "Big Six" after a famous New York fire engine, was not far behind at 33-12 with a 2.02 ERA. And a third and fourth pitcher turned in fine years: Luther (Dummy) Taylor, a deaf mute from Kansas, at 21-15 with a 2.34 ERA, and George (Hooks) Wiltse, a rookie, at 13-3 with a 2.84 ERA. The Giants led the league not only in team pitching but also in team batting and fielding.

Over in the new American League the Boston Pilgrims (later the Red Sox) took the flag, but John McGraw had already announced that the Giants would not play a World Series with the American League champions as Pittsburgh had in 1903.

McGraw dismissed the AL as a "minor league," perhaps forgetting that the AL's Boston Pilgrims had won the World Series the previous year.

The Giants came back stronger than ever in 1905, with another fine new pitcher putting up impressive numbers. He was Red Ames, 22-8,

Transcendental Graphics

Joe "Iron Man" McGinnity

Christy Mathewson's Three Shutouts

There are few unbeatable records in baseball. For a long time many fans thought that Babe Ruth's one-season home run record (60) and certainly his lifetime home run record (714) would never be topped. But Roger Maris (61) broke the Babe's first record and Hank Aaron (755) broke the second. Then Pete Rose shattered a few of Ty Cobb's "unbeatable" marks.

But one record that probably never will be beaten (although it might be matched) is Christy Mathewson's string of three shutouts in the seven-game 1905 World Series. To top it would require an almost inconceivable set of circumstances, perhaps something akin to the time lapse caused by the 1989 San Francisco earthquake after two games had been played.

Christy Mathewson pitched the opening game of the World Series on October 9 against Eddie Plank of the Philadelphia Athletics. Matty allowed just four hits and no walks as the Giants won 3-0. Joe McGinnity (nicknamed "Iron Man") started the second game against the A's Chief Bender. McGinnity and the Giants lost, 3-0. On October 12 Giants' manager John J. McGraw started Mathewson again, this time against 20-game winner Andy Coakley. Once more Matty shut down the A's on four hits, the Giants winning 9-0.

Photo: *Transcendental Graphics*

At this point Mathewson had won two of the four games needed to take the Series. The next day, October 13, McGraw came back with Iron Man McGinnity. (It is worth noting that the Giants were not struggling under the burden of a two-man mound staff. Red Ames had compiled a 22-8 record that season, Dummy Taylor 15-9, and Hooks Wiltse 15-6.) McGinnity won, 1-0, as his five-hitter bested Eddie Plank's four-hitter on the strength of an unearned run.

The Giants were now one game from the World Championship, and McGraw decided to go with his ace again, Christy Mathewson. For the third time Matty, again facing Chief Bender, tossed a shutout, 2-0, allowing just six hits. In this unusual World Series every game was a shutout, Mathewson winning three, McGinnity one, and the A's Bender one.

joining Christy Mathewson, 31-8, and Iron Man McGinnity, 21-15. Mathewson's sparkling 1.27 ERA led the league.

Turkey Mike Donlin, a hard-hitting, curfew-breaking outfielder, who had been acquired from Cincinnati in mid-1904, paced all Giant hitters at .356. Roger Bresnahan, "The Duke of Tralee," ceased playing various positions and became mostly a full-time catcher. He hit .302 in 1905, the Giants' second straight pennant-winning year.

But if the 1905 season was sweet for McGraw's men, the World Series (back again after the one-year hiatus) was sweeter still—especially for Christy Mathewson. Matty set a World Series record unlikely ever to be broken when he pitched three shutouts in six days as the Giants defeated Connie Mack's Philadelphia Athletics four games to one.

Nothing went quite right in 1906, or, indeed, for the next few seasons. Of course, with the Chicago Cubs winning 116 games in 1906 and 107 games in 1907, the Giants would have needed a couple of phenomenal seasons to top them. As it was, the Giants finished second in 1906, fourth in 1907.

When the Cubs of "Tinker-to-Evers-to-Chance" (along with Three Finger Brown and Ed Reulbach) faded to just 99 wins in 1908, the Giants and Pirates stayed in contention all the way, finishing in a tie for second place, one game behind Chicago. This was the year of Fred Merkle's famous "bonehead" play, a mistake that many New York fans (but not John McGraw) felt cost the Giants the pennant.

The third-place Giants of 1909 were a talented ball club, as were the second-place finishers of 1910. On the mound, Hooks Wiltse, Red Ames and, especially, Christy Mathewson continued their winning ways. By 1910 the Giants were poised for a streak of pennant-winning seasons.

What was needed for success, as it turned out, was the emergence of young left-hander Rube Marquard as a consistent winning pitcher. Marquard had been with the team since 1908, but had a spotty record until 1911. In fact, in 1909 the future Hall of Famer had a 5-13 won-lost mark despite a 2.60 ERA. This would change dramatically in 1911.

The 1911 season belonged to the Giants. As Marquard blossomed into a 24-7 pitcher, Christy Mathewson rolled right along with a 26-13 record and a league-leading 1.93 ERA. First baseman Fred Merkle and second baseman Larry Doyle had fine years, as did outfielders Fred Snodgrass and Red Murray.

This was a team with tremendous speed, stealing a dazzling total of 347 bases. Said John McGraw, "The 1911 team stole the pennant." The leading pilferers were Josh Devore, an outfielder, with 61 stolen bases, Fred Snodgrass with 51, Fred Merkle with 49, Red Murray with 48, and Larry Doyle with 38. Although catcher Chief Meyers, utility infielder Art Fletcher, and Larry Doyle were the only regulars to hit better than .300, the team as a whole had a league-leading batting average of .279.

In 1911 the Giants played most of their early-season home games at Hilltop Park, home of the

Transcendental Graphics

Rube Marquard

Highlanders (soon to be the Yankees), because the wooden Polo Grounds (number three in Giants' history) burned to the ground in mid-April. A new concrete-and-steel stadium arose on the site. It was slated to be called Brush Stadium, after the Giants' ailing owner, but the name Polo Grounds was too firmly entrenched. The final Polo Grounds (number four), with its distant center-field wall, would be the home ballpark of the Giants until the

Transcendental Graphics

Ross Youngs

franchise moved to San Francisco in 1958.

Although the years 1911, 1912, and 1913 were golden ones for the Giants, the three straight pennants they won, all under manager John McGraw, did not overawe their American League postseason rivals. In 1911 the Philadelphia A's bested the Giants in the World Series, four games to two, as Mathewson lost two close games and Marquard one. The final game was a 13-2 rout that Red Ames started and lost.

In 1912 the Giants fell victim to the Boston Red Sox and Smoky Joe Wood, a pitcher at his peak, who got credit for three of Boston's four victories. Marquard won two games for the Giants. The Series went the limit—and more. After nine innings of the seventh game (with the Series tied three games to three) the score stood 1-1. New York scored a run in the top of the 10th inning to take a 2-1 lead, but in the bottom of the 10th Snodgrass dropped a fly ball, Merkle missed a pop foul, and the Red Sox went on to score twice, winning the game and the Series.

The 1913 World Series was a repeat of 1911, the Philadelphia A's winning it in six games. The big gun for the A's in the 1913 fall classic was third baseman Frank (Home Run) Baker, who, appropriately enough, slammed key homers in games two and three.

War and Four Straight Pennants

The years immediately preceding World War I were memorable for Giants' fans. Author Harry Golden remembered, "a lady with a very large black picture hat sitting in the front row of the center field bleachers ... and just as the Giants took the field you could hear her battle cry in every corner of the Polo Grounds—'Come on, Artie!'—and the shortstop Arthur Fletcher would wave his glove at her, everybody would applaud, and then the first visiting batter would step up to the plate."

But the war in Europe—not to mention the upstart Federal League of 1914 and 1915—would change everything. Before the war was over, many of the great Giant players of 1911, 1912, and 1913 were gone: Mathewson, Marquard, Meyers, Snodgrass, Merkle, and Doyle. The fans at the Polo Grounds turned nasty when the Giants, after finishing second in 1914, crashed to the cellar in 1915. Mathewson's arm was gone; he won 8 games and lost 14. Snodgrass hit an anemic .194 and was sold to the Braves. Marquard, struggling at 9-8, tangled with McGraw and wound up in Brooklyn.

Fortunately for the Giants there were some quality players to take their places. Right-hander

Jeff Tesreau, who had joined the club in 1912, continued to compile winning records. Right-handed pitcher Pol Perritt and veteran left-hander Rube Benton did well. The Giants climbed to fourth place in 1916, then vaulted into first place in wartime 1917.

This was the year that McGraw punched out umpire Bill (Lord) Byron at home plate, then compounded the error by calling National League President John K. Tener (who had fined him $500) a "tool of the Phillies"—inviting the scribes to quote him—then repudiated his statement, which left the sportswriters looking like liars. John McGraw's fiery temper, which sometimes inspired lagging ballplayers, this time cost him $1,000 (on top of the $500) when the New York Chapter of the Baseball Writers' Association brought suit against him and won.

Nevertheless, the Giants kept right on playing great baseball, winning the pennant by 10 games, but once again losing the World Series, this time to Pants Rowland's Chicago White Sox. When the magnanimous Rowland tried to shake hands with

Transcendental Graphics

Frankie Frisch

McGraw after a series of Giant errors had cost New York the sixth and final game of the Series, McGraw met the White Sox manager with a snarled, "Get away from me, you goddamned busher." Nobody ever called John J. McGraw a nice guy.

McGraw was a good manager, though. Between 1903 and 1925 his Giants finished first or second 19 times and third or lower only four times. Three of these second-place finishes occurred in 1918, 1919, and 1920—in preparation, as it were, for four consecutive first-place finishes. Pol Perritt, in his last good year, was the most consistently effective Giant pitcher in 1918, with an 18-13 record and a 2.74 ERA.

The Giants' solid outfield consisted of George Burns (not to be confused with the comedian; batting .290), Benny Kauff (.315), and Ross Youngs (.302). Burns, acquired from Utica of the New York State League, had been with the Giants since 1911. Benny Kauff came over in 1916 from the Federal League, where he had twice led the league in hitting. Youngs, a rookie up from Rochester, was a lifetime .322 hitter in his 10 seasons with the Giants.

One of the pitching stars of 1919 and 1920 was Jesse Barnes, whose 25 victories in 1919 led the league, but whose 20-15 record in 1920 was slightly overshadowed by lefty Art Nehf's 21-12 and Fred Toney's 21-11. All three pitchers were veterans of other major league ball clubs, and all three would contribute to the 1921 pennant-winning Giants, helping to launch the third and longest of John McGraw's pennant-winning sequences— 1904-05, 1911-13, and 1921-24.

In late August, 1921, the Pittsburgh Pirates, 7½ games ahead of the Giants, came to the Polo Grounds for a five-game series. The Pirates, supremely confident when they arrived, were badly shaken when they left. McGraw, in a blistering clubhouse meeting, called the Pirates a "bunch of banjo-playing, wisecracking humpty-dumpties," and the Giants set out to prove him right.

Behind pitchers Art Nehf and Shufflin' Phil Douglas, a tall, hard-drinking, much-traveled Georgian, the Giants won five straight games,

Transcendental Graphics

Dave Bancroft

opening up the pennant race and serving notice that the Pittsburgh banjo-players were not going to walk over the team that McGraw considered the best in baseball.

By season's end the Giants led the Pirates by four games. They would now attempt to do to the New York Yankees of Babe Ruth and Carl Mays what they had done to the Pittsburgh Pirates. They succeeded. In the best-of-nine World Series, the Giants triumphed, five games to three, as their pitchers followed McGraw's ernest advice concerning Babe Ruth: "Don't give that big baboon anything but low curves." Ruth connected for one homer anyway. Little Napoleon, after nearly two decades at the helm of the Giants, could finally claim a second World Championship for the Giants.

The Giants of that day were what the New York Yankees would later become. In the words of Noel Hynd, author of *The Giants of the Polo Grounds,* they were "the most famous team in America, the most loved, the most hated, the most feared, and the most imitated." Who were the players who made the Giants of the early 1920s so formidable? Among the best known of the regu-

lars were first baseman George Kelly, second baseman Frankie Frisch, shortstop Dave (Beauty) Bancroft, third baseman Heinie Groh, and outfielders Ross Youngs and Irish Meusel.

Of these six players, Ross Youngs had the highest lifetime batting average, .322, and Dave Bancroft the lowest, .279. In 1922 an 18-year-old shortstop, Travis Jackson from Waldo, Arkansas, joined the club. His lifetime batting average would be .291, and his plaque would eventually hang at the Hall of Fame. Small wonder that for the four pennant-winning years in the early 1920s the team batting average of the Giants never dropped below .295.

The end of the dead-ball era was tough on pitchers, though, and there were no ERAs (nor any individual won-lost records) to match those of the Mathewson-Marquard era. The most effective Giant pitchers of the day were Art Nehf, Rosy Ryan, and Jack Bentley. Although Shufflin' Phil Douglas put in his best season in 1922, going 11-4, he was declared permanently ineligible in mid-August of that year by Commissioner Kenesaw Mountain Landis.

It seems that Douglas had written a letter to a Cardinal player, perhaps while drunk, suggesting that he was willing to sit out the rest of the season if the Cardinals would make it worth his while. Presumably, this would help St. Louis win the pennant. What it did was to speed Douglas into early retirement.

The Giants won the pennant by seven games over Cincinnati and went on once more to engage Miller Huggins' Yankees in the World Series. This time (with the Series changed back to a best-of-seven contest) the powerful Giants swept past their local rivals four games to none. Actually, five games were played, the second one ending in a 3-3 tie at the end of the tenth inning, called "on account of darkness," even though the sun was still high in the sky. The fans were baffled. Judge Landis, disgusted, donated the game's proceeds to charity.

Of the other four games, Art Nehf won one, Rosy Ryan won one, and two mid-season new-comers—Jack Scott and Hugh McQuillan—won a game apiece. Scott, a Cincinnati castoff, pitched the Series' only shutout, besting the Yanks' great Waite Hoyt, 3-0, in game three. The Giant batting stars were Irish Meusel, who drove in seven runs, and Heinie Groh and Frankie Frisch, who collected 17 hits between them.

Close National League pennant races in 1923 and 1924 ended each time with the Giants on top. In 1923 they edged out Cincinnati again. In 1924 the second-place team was Brooklyn. For the third straight year the Giants' World Series opponents were the New York Yankees, and this time the McGraw men did not polish off the Yanks with ease. Quite the contrary. The Yanks took the series four games to two, and they might have won it in four straight except for the heroics of Giant outfielder Casey Stengel.

In the first game Stengel, picked up from the Phillies in 1921, hit a ninth-inning inside-the-park home run to give the Giants a 5-4 victory. In the third game Stengel provided Art Nehf with the only run he needed when he blasted a seventh-inning homer into the right field bleachers to give the Giants a 1-0 victory.

In 1924 the Washington Senators under playing manager Bucky Harris won the American League pennant, giving Hall-of-Fame pitcher Walter Johnson his first World Series start after 18 years in the majors. "The Big Train" struck out 12 Giants, but a 12th-inning single by Ross Youngs with the bases loaded gave New York a 5-4 win. The winning Giants pitcher, Art Nehf, collected three hits off Johnson, an achievement he later claimed was his proudest in baseball.

The Series went to seven games, by which time Johnson had lost his second start. But in the final contest The Big Train, in relief of Firpo Marberry, at last got credit for a victory when in the 12th inning the Senators' Earl McNeely hit a grounder toward rookie Giant third baseman Freddie Lindstrom. The ball took a bad hop over Lindstrom's head, Muddy Ruel scored from second, and the Washington Senators won their only World Championship in the history of the ball club. Giant pitcher Jack Bentley was philosophical: "Cheer up, boys," he said. "It just looks as though the Good Lord couldn't stand seeing Walter Johnson get beat again."

From the 1920s to Manager Bill Terry

For 31 years the New York Giants were John J. McGraw's ball club, all the way from the turn of the century to the Great Depression. The Giants were nearly always competitive. Yet 1924 marked the end of their dominance in the National League. They would always finish first in the division, except in 1926, when they had to settle for fifth, and in 1932, McGraw's final, abbreviated season, when they sank to sixth (and stood eighth when he stepped down).

During those years they fielded very good teams but not great ones. They got competent but seldom outstanding pitching except from Freddie Fitzsimmons, Carl Hubbell, and, for two seasons, Larry Benton. Fitzsimmons, arriving in 1925 after six years in the minors, won consistently as a Giant.

Hubbell came up from Beaumont of the Texas League in 1928. King Carl succeeded from the start, but his best seasons followed the departure of McGraw. Benton's two fine seasons were 1927 and 1928. Acquired from the Boston Braves early in the 1927 season, Benton ended with a 13-5 record that year and a 25-9 mark the next, leading the league in victories.

One of the premier newcomers to the post-pennant Giants was first baseman Bill Terry. The tall left-hander appeared in three games in 1923 and 77 games in 1924, but it was not until 1925 that he displaced George Kelly at first base. It is a measure of Terry's potential (originally a pitcher, Memphis Bill was still an unsure first baseman) that George Kelly, himself a Hall-of-Famer, had to move over to second base to make room for the rookie.

Terry's lifetime batting average of .341 is impressive enough, but his .401 mark in 1930 is a staple of baseball history. Terry was the last National Leaguer to reach the .400 plateau. (Ted

Williams hit .406 for the Red Sox in 1941—the last American Leaguer to scale the height.) Terry's 254 hits in 1930 are also an NL record, one he shares with the Phillies' Lefty O'Doul.

Bill Terry was not the only key acquisition during McGraw's last years at the helm. In 1927 three short-termers came aboard. Rogers Hornsby, the great Cardinal infielder, played a single season for the Giants, batting a Hornsbyesque .361 before moving on to the Braves and then the Cubs. Edd Roush, an ex-Cincinnati Red, joined the Giants in 1927 and played through 1929. Roush, like Hornsby, was nearing the end of a brilliant Hall of Fame career. Burleigh Grimes, the famous spitball pitcher, was the third arrival in 1927. He played just one year for the Giants, posting a 19-8 record, then went to Pittsburgh.

Transcendental Graphics

Bill Terry

More important than any of these stars to the future of the Giants, however, was Mel Ott, a 17-year-old kid from Gretna, Louisiana. In 1926 McGraw refused to send the teenager to the minors. "Ott stays with me!" he yelled at Toledo Mudhens' manager Casey Stengel, who wanted Ott at Toledo. "No minor league manager is going to ruin him." McGraw's worry was that the left-handed hitting Ott, who raised his right foot high before striding into the pitch, would be taught a more conventional style of hitting—and that it would be a mistake.

Ott remained with the Giants, and before he was 20 he had a permanent position in the Giant outfield, so permanent, in fact, that he stayed through World War II and into 1947. With Bill Terry, Mel Ott, and Travis Jackson in the regular lineup and Carl Hubbell and Freddie Fitzsimmons on the mound, the Giants were near the top (but not at the top) of the National League through the late 1920s and into 1930 and 1931.

But in 1932 the team got off to a slow 17-23 start. On June 3 John McGraw summoned Bill Terry to his office. The two had not spoken for two years, and Terry remembered the occasion: "I was expecting to be notified I was traded." Not so. He was told he could have the managerial job if he wanted it. He did. His tenure would last through 1941, and in the early years, through 1937, he enjoyed considerable success.

With essentially the same team that McGraw had led, plus veteran Cardinal catcher Gus Mancuso and young right-handed pitcher Hal Schumacher in the starting rotation, Terry guided the Giants to a pennant in his first full season at the reins. And while John McGraw had had limited success in postseason play, Bill Terry's 1933 Giants defeated the Washington Senators convincingly in the World Series, four games to one. Carl Hubbell won two of the games, allowing no earned runs. The batting standout for the Giants was Mel Ott, with two homers, four Runs Batted In (RBIs), and a .379 batting average.

The Cardinals, under their sophomore manager Frankie Frisch, nosed out the Giants for the pennant in 1934. Ott led the league in home runs with 35 and RBIs with 135, while Carl Hubbell posted the league's best ERA, 2.30, in winning 21 games and losing 12. Hal Schumacher had a 23-10 record and Freddie Fitzsimmons 18-14.

In 1935 the Giants fell to third, 8½ games back of the Chicago Cubs and four behind the Cards. Then in 1936 everything clicked once more. Carl Hubbell won a career high 26 games, while losing only six, with a league-leading 2.31 ERA. But the World Series proved a disappointment, as the Giants faced their formidable Bronx foes, the Yankees, in a Subway Series.

The Yankee team included Lou Gehrig, Bill Dickey, Red Rolfe, and rookie Joe DiMaggio, not to mention Lefty Gomez and Red Ruffing on the mound. Although Carl Hubbell baffled the Yankee hitters in game one, winning 6-1, the Bronx Bombers lived up to their nickname in game two, pounding out 17 hits against Hal Schumacher and

a succession of relievers, winning the game 18-4. The Yanks took the next two contests by closer scores, with Gehrig connecting for a homer in each game.

The Giants eked out a 5-4 win in game five, but then ran into another slaughter, as the Yanks broke open a 6-5 game in the ninth inning, scoring seven times to make the final score 13-5. "They're the toughest club I've ever faced," Bill Terry admitted ruefully.

Terry's men had to go up against them again in 1937, for once more the Giants battled their way to the National League pennant, while the potent Yankees were breezing to the American League flag. Carl Hubbell won 22 games to lead the league, losing only eight. A pleasant surprise for the Giants was rookie pitcher Cliff (Mountain Music) Melton, who broke in as a 20-game winner (20-9), with a better ERA than Hubbell's. It was

Transcendental Graphics

Mel Ott

Melton's first and last great season.

Mel Ott again led the National League in home runs, this time with 31. Fans looking toward the Giant-Yankee match up in the World Series might have noted that on the Yankee squad Joe DiMaggio had cracked 46 homers, Lou Gehrig 37, and Bill Dickey 29. A World Championship for the Giants would not be easy.

It was impossible. The Yanks won the first two games by identical 8-1 scores. They won game three, 5-1, then ran into trouble, as pitcher Bump Hadley got pummelled for six runs in the second inning of game four, and Carl Hubbell hung on to win, 7-3. It was the only bright spot for the Giants. In game five the Yankees, behind Lefty Gomez, won, 4-2, as Cliff Melton took his second loss. It was a disappointing World Series for Giant fans and not a particularly exciting one for followers of the powerhouse Yankees.

In Search of Success

The team Bill Terry headed in 1938 had some weaknesses, and time would only make them worse. Hal Schumacher and Carl Hubbell had ailing arms. Their big winning seasons were behind them. Cliff Melton could not, then or ever, match the performance of his rookie year. Mel Ott was still in his prime, and at a lower level so were outfielder Jo-Jo Moore and infielder Burgess Whitehead.

But the rest of the starting lineup soon became an exercise in musical chairs. First base, for instance, passed from Johnny McCarthy (1938) to Zeke Bonura (1939) to Babe Young (1940-41) to Johnny Mize (1942)—and then the wartime instability set in. Bill Terry's impressive managerial start stalled. The Giants fell to third place in 1938 and then into the second division in 1939, 1940, and 1941.

Five days before the bombing of Pearl Harbor plunged the United States into World War II, Mel Ott arrived at the hotel suite of Horace Stoneham, the Giants' young owner, in Jacksonville, Florida. Stoneham, with Bill Terry present, asked Ott to

Transcendnetal Graphics

Carl Hubbell

manage the Giants. "I guess a fellow couldn't refuse a chance like this, could he?" said the high-kicking batsman, not realizing the grim days that lay ahead. He accepted. Mel Ott became just the third manager of the Giants since 1902.

Ott inherited an already weakened team, not to mention the effects of the Second World War. Everybody who was anybody (and not 4-F, too young, or disabled) went off to the military. Remaining behind were such players as Joe Orengo, Johnnie Wittig, Ace Adams, and Rube Fischer. Who? Right. And then there were the old-timers, past their prime but able to handle most wartime diamond duties.

Ernie Lombardi and Joe Medwick, to name two, added a little class and even a little punch to the Giants' wartime lineup. But Mel Ott's charges finished last in 1943 and never climbed out of the second division until 1947, finishing fifth in the last two wartime years and last again in postwar 1946.

Willie Mays could do it all. He was one of the finest center fielders in the history of the game. In fact, early in his career sportswriters and other ballplayers were often more impressed by his spectacular catches and his strong, accurate throwing arm than they were by his hitting. In the majors he won eleven straight Gold Gloves. But it soon became clear that he could hit, too.

His .353 batting average at Trenton of the Inter-State League and his .477 at Minneapolis of the American Association demonstrated his promise at the plate, even if his dismal 1-for-22 start with the Giants cast brief doubts. In 1955, while still in his early 20s, he hit 51 home runs for the New York Giants. When he retired after 22 years in the majors, he stood third on the all-time home-run list with 660 career blasts, trailing only Hank Aaron and Babe Ruth. He could also run. For four years in a row he led the National League in stolen bases, and his 77 percent success ratio on steals puts him high on that list. "If he could cook," said manager Leo Durocher, "I'd marry him."

Photo: *Transcendental Graphics*

By 1947 the veterans were back. Johnny Mize held down first base for the Giants, belting 51 homers and driving in 138 runs to lead the league. Willard Marshall was back in the outfield, batting .291, hitting about 37 homers, and driving in 107 runs. Catcher Walker Cooper, an exception to the wartime-klutz stereotype (he had starred for the Cardinals in those dark days), batted .305, cracked 35 homers, and drove in 122 runs. Rookie pitcher Larry Jansen racked up a 21-5 record, and Dave Koslo, back from the front, went 15-10.

The biggest news in 1947, though, was the arrival in New York of "The Hondo Hurricane," Clint Hartung, described as "an entire ball club in himself." A tall, powerful, good-natured kid from Hondo, Texas, he had talent, but he was not quite the "half-Feller, half-Foxx" he was touted as be-

ing. Giants' publicist Garry Schumacher told the New York press, tongue in cheek, that Hartung "should go straight to Cooperstown."

In fact, Hartung went straight into the Giants' outfield, where he bobbled grounders and misplayed fly balls until Mel Ott decided to check out his pitching skills. Hartung finished the season with a 9-7 record, a 4.57 ERA, and a .309 batting average. He did show promise, which unfortunately was never realized. "The Hondo Hurricane" had one last moment in the sun, however.

Neither the Giants collectively nor Clint Hartung individually showed much improvement in 1948, and halfway through the season owner Horace Stoneham threw caution to the winds and hired Leo (The Lip) Durocher to manage his team. Stoneham could not have chosen a manager more hated by Giant fans. The Lip, cocky and pugnacious, had managed the rival Dodgers for nine and a half seasons. He had just returned to the Brooklyn ball club after a year's suspension for associating with unsavory characters. And now he was going to manage the Giants? He was, and he was going to do it his way. When Horace Stoneham asked Leo to write a report on which members of the team were not contributing and should be let go, Durocher allegedly scrawled the message, "Back up a truck."

Fireworks at the Polo Grounds

Leo Durocher intended to build a winning team, and he did. The Giants climbed from fifth place in 1948 to first in 1951. Despite their antipathy, Giant fans were quick to spot signs of Durocher's expertise. They noted that in 1948 the Dodgers under Leo the Lip went 8-4 against the Giants, but after he switched teams in midseason, the Giants proceeded to go 7-3 against the Dodgers. That impressed them.

So did the Giants' rise to third place in 1950, as the lineup was transformed from one of lethargic sluggers (in The Lip's view) to one of scrappy Durocher types "who came to kill you," such as second baseman Eddie Stanky, shortstop Alvin Dark, and third baseman Hank Thompson.

An important addition to the pitching staff came in the menacing figure of Sal "The Barber" Maglie, available after a flirtation with the outlaw Mexican League. Maglie turned in an 18-4 record with a 2.71 ERA.

In midseason the Giants acquired a little-used pitcher, Jim Hearn, from the Cardinals, and Hearn, rejuvenated, went 11-4 in New York, with a league-leading 2.49 ERA (1.94 as a Giant). The Philadelphia "Whiz Kids" beat out the Giants for the NL pennant in 1950, while the talent-laden Brooklyn Dodgers finished second. The stage was set for 1951.

All the high hopes harbored by Giant fans faded quickly as the team went into an early tailspin. At the end of April they were in the cellar.

Bobby Thomson, the center fielder, was not hitting. By mid-May his batting average stood at .229. Right fielder Don Mueller was doing even worse, hitting below .200. Wrote Arthur Daley in *New York Times,* "It will take a miracle for the Giants to win the championship now."

One element of that miracle was playing center field for the Minneapolis Millers of the American Association. His name was Willie Mays, and he was batting .477. On May 12, 1951, Durocher phoned Mays in Minneapolis and told him to report to the Giants. Mays was not an instant star in New York.

Failing to get a hit in his first 12 at-bats, he expected to be sent back to the minors. When Mays was 1-for-22, Durocher told the discouraged youngster, "You're my center fielder. You're here to stay." Eventually, Mays started to hit—his fielding was superb from the outset—and he finished the season at .274, with 20 homers and 68 RBIs.

The Dodgers held a solid lead through mid-August, but then the Giants began to close the gap. "We're gonna win—we're gonna win—we're gonna win," Durocher kept telling his players on the train to New York after a discouraging loss to the Reds. But the season ended in a tie between the Giants and the Dodgers, forcing a three-game playoff series. The Giants won the first game, the Dodgers the second, and it all came down to the final game at the Polo Grounds.

With the Giants behind 4-1 in the last of the ninth inning, Alvin Dark got an infield hit, and Don Mueller sent him to third with a single. After Monte Irvin popped out, first baseman Whitey Lockman drove a double into the left field corner, scoring Dark and sending Mueller to third. Mueller, having sprained his ankle sliding into third base, was replaced by a pinch runner—Clint Hartung. Yes, The Hondo Hurricane was still on the roster. He had appeared in 21 games that season and had scored three runs.

Bobby Thomson came to the plate for the Giants. Ralph Branca faced him from the mound. As Russ Hodges, the voice of the Dodgers announced it on radio: "Branca throws again ...

Transcendental Graphics

Monte Irvin

Field celebration by taking the pennant. This was the year in which pitcher Johnny Antonelli, acquired from the Braves, finally lived up to his potential, posting a 21-7 record and a league-leading 2.30 ERA. It was also the year in which Don Mueller, a lifetime .296 hitter, batted .342, with 212 hits.

Mays led the league at .345, with 33 doubles, 13 triples, and 41 homers. The Say Hey Kid had arrived. It was also the year in which part-time outfielder Dusty Rhodes became "The Colossus of Rhodes," a reliable pinch-hitter with considerable power. The Giants won the pennant by five games. The New York Yankees, like the Dodgers, had been done in by an unexpected show of force in 1954—by the Cleveland Indians, who won a hard-to-beat 111 games. The Giants had won only 97, but they promptly won four more games in the World Series, walking off with the World Championship, four games to none.

Though no one knew it at the time, it was the New York Giants' last hurrah. They finished third in 1955, sixth in 1956 (under their new manager Billy Rigney), and sixth again in 1957. Then they were gone, the Polo Grounds deserted, the saga of the New York Giants ended.

there's a long fly ... it's gonna be ... I believe ... *the Giants win the pennant ... the Giants win the pennant ... the Giants win the pennant...."* Hartung scored his fourth run of the season, Lockman scored behind, and Bobby Thomson, instantly and incredibly a Giant immortal, completed his circuit of the bases.

Then it was back to reality, as the Yankees defeated the Giants four games to two in the World Series. Monte Irvin collected 11 hits and Alvin Dark 10 in the losing cause. After 1951 the "Boys of Summer," those great Dodger teams of Reese, Robinson, Furillo, and Campanella dominated the National League, winning pennants in 1952, 1953, 1955, and 1956.

But in 1954, the year of Willie Mays' emergence as a superstar, the Giants under Leo Durocher once again interrupted the annual Ebbets

On to San Francisco

New York City baseball took a crushing one-two punch when the Dodgers moved to Los Angeles and the Giants to San Francisco. But there was understandable joy on the West Coast. In 1958 the San Francisco Giants played their home games in Seals Stadium, which sportscaster Russ Hodges called a "beautiful little watch-charm ball park, all green and cozy and freshly painted."

The San Francisco Giants had a number of new faces in the lineup—rookies Orlando Cepeda at first base, Jim Davenport at third, Bob Schmidt behind the plate, and Willie Kirkland and Felipe Alou in the outfield.

The pitching staff still featured Johnny Antonelli, Ruben Gomez, Stu Miller, Mike McCor-

Candlestick Park: Cave of the Winds

"San Francisco has always been a city of giants," said Governor Pat Brown of California. "Now we have a home for them." The year was 1960, the home was Candlestick Park, named for the jagged rocks and trees that rise like candlesticks on Hunters Point overlooking San Francisco Bay. Its location, picturesque but windy, created problems for players and fans alike. In the 1961 All-Star game, Stu Miller, a Giant hurler, was blown off the mound by a gust of wind. The plate umpire ruled it a balk. That same year a disaffected fan brought suit against the Giants, charging them with breach of warranty for selling him a radiant-heated box seat that "froze" his feet during ball games, forcing him to leave and miss the high points of the game. He settled for $1,597.

A major renovation of Candlestick Park attempted to correct the wind problem and succeeded to some extent. Synthetic turf replaced natural grass. Seven years later the Giants tore out the carpet and reinstalled the grass. But the biggest disturbance at Candlestick Park was neither a spongy infield nor a gale-force wind. It was an earthquake. A quarter of an hour before the start of game three of the 1989 World Series between the Giants and the Oakland A's, a tremor that registered 6.9 on the Richter scale rocked the Bay area. The game was postponed. Fifty-nine people died in the disaster, part of the Nimitz Freeway collapsed, but the ballpark suffered no major structural damage.

A more serious threat to Candlestick Park came three years later when the Giants' ownership proposed to give it the Polo Grounds treatment—a franchise move to St. Petersburg, Florida. The transfer seemed to be in the bag, but then the National League owners nixed the deal, and the Giants remained, for the time being at least, in their windswept home by the Bay.

---

mick, and Al Worthington. This first edition of the San Francisco Giants finished a respectable third, behind the Milwaukee Braves (recently of Boston) and the Pittsburgh Pirates. Unfortunately for San Francisco fans, third place, along with second and fourth, became a familiar niche for the West Coast Giants.

Although they were a strong, winning ball club in the late 1950s and early 60s, they finished third in 1959 and 1961, fifth in 1960—the year the Giants moved into their permanent home, Candlestick Park—and then, in a burst of good fortune and fine performances, they edged out the co-expatriate L.A. Dodgers by one game in 1962.

By that time the team was distinctly San Franciscan, with only a few holdovers, most notably Willie Mays, from the New York days. One of the popular new stars was first baseman (and part-time outfielder) Willie McCovey, who first arrived in 1959 after blistering Pacific Coast League

pitching for the Phoenix Giants. McCovey, unlike Mays, took off like a rocket in the majors, batting .354 in his first year, but then settling into a home-run-hitting pattern that put him tenth on the all-time career list for round-trippers but left him with a modest .270 lifetime batting average.

Four pitchers, none of them ex-Polo Grounders, won in double figures on the pennant-winning 1962 Giants' team. The ace was Jack Sanford, 24-7, acquired from the Phillies in 1959. Then there were Juan Marichal, 18-11, up from Tacoma two years earlier; Billy O'Dell, 19-14, an ex-Oriole; and Billy Pierce, 16-6, a long-time veteran of the White Sox.

The leading hitters on the '62 ball club were Willie Mays, .304 with 49 homers and 141 RBIs; Orlando Cepeda, .306 with 35 homers and 114 RBIs; and Felipe Alou, .316 with 25 homers and 98 RBIs.

This impressive aggregation, managed by

Alvin Dark, who had taken over the year before, won 103 games, the most for any Giant ball club since 1912. An optimist might have seen the prospect of another pennant or two, but none was forthcoming.

Good Teams, No Flag

The San Francisco Giants never finished with a won-lost percentage below .500 for any of their first 14 seasons. They came in third in 1963 and fourth in 1964, but that fourth-place finish, which sounds mediocre, occurred in a tight four-way race. The Giants were just three games behind pennant-winning St. Louis at the end of the season. From 1965 through 1969 they finished second every year, often a close second. They came very near to a pennant in 1965, closing just 1½ games behind the L. A. Dodgers. Willie Mays blasted 52 home runs that year, and Juan Marichal won 22 games.

But this was in the days of Sandy Koufax and Don Drysdale, who won 26 and 23 games respectively for the Dodgers. On August 22, 1965, Marichal was batting against Sandy Koufax, one of whose pitches brushed him back from the plate. "You better not hit me with that ball," he warned Dodger catcher John Roseboro.

Roseboro, however, whizzed the ball back to Koufax on the mound, barely missing Marichal's ear on the way. "The Dominican Dandy," furious, turned and brought his bat down on Roseboro's skull. The blow gashed the Dodger catcher's head and raised a lump on his hand. The home plate umpire ejected Marichal from the game, and the Giant ace was subsequently suspended for nine days and fined $1,750, the stiffest penalty in league history at that time.

Many of the Giants' regulars during these seasons were of star quality. Orlando Cepeda played first base for the first couple of years, after which Willie McCovey took over. Willie Mays patrolled the outfield the entire time, joined in 1968 by Bobby Bonds. Jim Ray Hart was at third

Transcendental Graphics

Willie McCovey

base. On the mound were Juan Marichal and Gaylord Perry. In 1967 Mike McCormick returned from a four-year sojourn in Baltimore and Washington, winning 22 games for the Giants to lead the league.

Alvin Dark managed the team through 1964, then gave way to Herman Franks, who was replaced by Clyde King in 1969. Early in the 1970 season, with the Giants apparently going nowhere, Charlie Fox, an ex-catcher with a lifetime .429 batting average in the majors (on the basis of going 3-for-7 for the Yankees in 1942), took over as manager and guided the team to a third-place finish. Gaylord Perry's 23 wins for the Giants led the league. Willie McCovey paced the team in home runs with 39 and RBIs with 126, while catcher Dick Dietz had a career year, batting .300, hitting 22 homers and driving in 107 runs.

In 1971, the third year of division play, the Giants finished first in the National League West.

After having led all the way, they barely held on at the end to thwart Walter Alston's Dodgers by a single game.

In the National League Championship Series, the Giants, behind the pitching of Gaylord Perry, defeated the Pirates in the first game but then dropped the next three. First baseman Bob Robertson of the Pirates belted four home runs, three of them in game two, while third baseman Richie Hebner hit a key home run in each of the last two games. For the Giants, Willie McCovey was the big hitter, with two homers and six RBIs.

Futility

The Giants failed to improve through the 1970s. In 1972 the team suffered its first losing season. Attendance dropped and continued to decline through much of the decade. Willie Mays was dealt to the New York Mets in 1972. Willie McCovey and Juan Marichal, both past their prime, were let go in 1974 (although McCovey returned in 1977). Bobby Bonds departed for the New York Yankees in 1975.

In the mid-1970s a discouraged Horace Stoneham was prepared to sell the franchise to a Canadian brewery that hoped to move the team to Toronto. But a pair of U.S. buyers were found— San Francisco realtor Robert Lurie and Arizona cattleman Arthur (Bud) Herseth—and the Giants stayed in the City by the Bay.

After four sub-.500 seasons in a row the team made a strong run in 1978 under second-year manager Joe Altobelli. One of the bona fide Giant stars of the late 70s and early 80s, outfielder Jack Clark, had a fine year in 1978, batting .306 with 25 home runs and 98 runs batted in. On the mound lefty Bob Knepper went 17-11 with an ERA of 2.63. Another left-hander, Vida Blue, after a decade at Oakland, joined the Giants and finished 18-10 with a 2.79 ERA. This was a team worth watching, and attendance rose by more than a million over the previous year.

But in 1979 the Giants regressed to their old losing ways, as the team won 71 and lost 91 to finish fourth, 19½ games back. Joe Altobelli was fired late in the season and replaced by Dave Bristol.

It made little difference that season or in 1980. Frank Robinson, who had managed for two years and part of another at Cleveland, took over at the start of the strike-shortened 1981 split season. The Giants finished fifth and third, seemingly trapped in the middle of the pack.

It appeared to be the same old story in 1982. The Giants opened with a revamped but elderly lineup, putting Reggie Smith, 37, at first base and Joe Morgan, 38, at second. For quite a while it looked as if the Giants were going nowhere. On August 2, the day after Frank Robinson's induction into the Hall of Fame, they were 50-55, trailing the Braves by 13 games. Although veteran Jack Clark (after a slow start) and rookie outfielder Chili Davis were doing well, the Giants as a team were not. Then things changed.

Transcendental Graphics

Juan Marichal

The Giants put together a 10-game winning streak, caught their breath, stumbled for a few games, but roared back with a 20-7 September to finish 87-75, two games behind Atlanta. The wholly new starting rotation had its problems all year, but the bullpen, especially Greg Minton, was brilliant down the stretch. Minton recorded 30 saves and posted a 10-4 won-lost record with a 1.83 ERA. Reggie Smith batted .284, and old Joe Morgan was named the team's MVP.

Success never seemed to follow success for the Giants, however. They fell to fifth place in 1983, and to the cellar in 1984 and 1985. Manager Frank Robinson received his walking papers in mid-1984, to be replaced by Danny Ozark, who in turn was replaced in 1985 by Jim Davenport, who also was replaced near the end of the '85 season by Roger Craig, a one-time pitcher who had managed the Padres with modest results for two seasons.

Roger Craig at the Helm

In 1985 the Giants drew only 816,697 fans, in contrast to the division-champion Dodgers' 3,264,593. San Francisco not only had a failing ball club but a failing franchise. For a new manager to turn that around was no small order, yet Roger Craig did it. With a few good acquisitions— among them outfielder Candy Maldonado from the Dodgers and pitcher Mike LaCoss from the Royals—and a infusion of spirit, the Giants looked like winners throughout 1986. Rookies Will Clark at first base and Robby Thompson at second had fine years, and pitcher Mike Krukow, who had gone 8-11 in 1985, went 20-9 for his best season in the majors. The Giants won the close games, attendance nearly doubled to 1,528,748, and confidence in the future returned.

The Giants finished in first place in 1987,

AP/Wide World Photos

Barry Bonds

winning 90 and losing 72, almost reversing the totals of two years earlier. Pitcher Dave Dravecky and third baseman-outfielder Kevin Mitchell joined the Giants via a shrewd trade with San Diego. Will Clark hit .306, slammed 35 homers, and drove in 91 runs; Candy Maldonado hit .308, with 20 homers and 85 RBIs; and Chili Davis cracked 24 homers and drove in 76 runs.

Pitchers Mike LaCoss, Kelly Downs, Scott Garrelts, and Atlee Hammaker won in double figures. The Giants won their division by six games but could not get past St. Louis in the National League Championship Series, losing four games to three. The Cardinals' Danny Cox shut out the Giants 6-0 in the final game.

The Giants fell to fourth place in 1988 but rebounded to first in 1989, a year in which Kevin Mitchell and Will Clark finished first and second in the MVP voting. Mitchell batted .291, blasted 47 homers, and drove in 125 runs. Clark hit .333, with 23 homers and 111 RBIs.

Veteran right-hander Rick Reuschel, in his third year with the Giants, had a 17-8 record and a 2.94 ERA. Scott Garrelts went 14-5 with a 2.28 ERA. Relievers Steve Bedrosian and Craig Lefferts chalked up 43 saves between them. In the National League Championship Series the fired-up Giants breezed past the Chicago Cubs four games to one to capture their first pennant since 1962.

And thus it happened that, after the Oakland A's had won two games of the 1989 World Series from the Giants, the two teams were in Candlestick Park on the evening of October 17 when a major earthquake struck the Bay area. The capacity crowd at the ballpark had to be evacuated and the Series postponed. When play resumed, the Giants were still no match for the powerful Oakland A's, who proceeded to wrap up the Series in two more games.

After 1989 the Giants went on a downhill slide, falling to third in 1990, though cheered by the emergence of third baseman Matt Williams as a likely star of the future. Williams led the league in RBIs with 122 (the third Giant in a row to do so, Will Clark having done it in 1988 and Kevin Mitchell in 1989). In 1991 the team slipped to fourth, 19 games behind, and in 1992 the skid put them in fifth, 26 games back. An announcement late in 1992 that the Giants would be moving to St. Petersburg, Florida, caused consternation in San Francisco. Not long afterward, however, the proposed move was rescinded by Major League Baseball.

The Giants then made news by signing superstar free-agent Barry Bonds, a two-time MVP award winner. The acquisition of Bonds, the emergence of closer Rod Beck, and strong performances from pitchers Bill Swift and John Burkett, second baseman Robby Thompson, Williams, and rookie manager Dusty Baker, who was selected as the NL's Manager of the Year, propelled the Giants into first place for much of the 1993 season. After the club opened a ten-game lead over Atlanta in July, however, the Braves went on a tear, taking five out of six games from San Francisco in one stretch and eventually passing the Giants with just a few weeks to go.

In a stirring pennant race, San Francisco battled back and found themselves tied for the division lead heading into their season finale with Los Angeles. But a Dodger victory, coupled with an Atlanta win, spoiled the Giants' title hopes. Still, the team ended with a remarkable 103-59 record. Added to Baker's post-season honor was Bond's third NL MVP award in the last four years; he batted .336 with 46 homers and 123 runs batted in and led the league in six offensive categories. Whether the Giants can contend again in 1994 remains to be seen, but the front office hopes to keep the heart of the lineup intact for the future.

SOURCES

BOOKS

Allen, Lee, *The Giants and the Dodgers: The Fabulous Story of Baseball's Fiercest Feud,* Putnam, 1964.

Baseball Guide, Sporting News, 1983, revised edition, 1987, revised edition, 1992.

Baseball Register, Sporting News, 1945, revised edition, 1992.

Durocher, Leo, with Ed Linn, *Nice Guys Finish Last,* Simon & Schuster, 1975.

Durso, Joseph, *The Days of Mr. McGraw,* Prentice Hall, 1969.

Einstein, Charles, *Willie's Time: A Memoir,* Lippincott, 1979.

Graham, Frank, *The New York Giants: An Informal History,* Putnam, 1952.

Hodges, Russ, and Al Hirshberg, *My Giants,* Doubleday, 1963.

Honig, Donald, *The National League: An Illustrated History,* Crown, 1983.

Hynd, Noel, *The Giants of the Polo Grounds,* Doubleday, 1988.

Ivor-Campbell, Frederick, "Team Histories: San Francisco Giants," *Total Baseball,* edited by John Thorn and Pete Palmer, Warner Books, 1989.

Lowry, Philip J., *Green Cathedrals,* Society for American Baseball Research, 1986.

Reichler, Joseph L., editor, *The Baseball Encyclopedia,* 7th edition, Macmillan, 1988.

Reidenbaugh, Lowell, *Take Me Out to the Ball Park,* Sporting News, 1983.

Stein, Fred, *Under Coogan's Bluff,* Chapter & Cask, 1978.

Voight, David Quentin, *American Baseball: From Postwar Expansion to the Electronic* Age, Pennsylvania State University Press, 1983.

PERIODICALS

Baseball Digest, April 1954.
Baseball (magazine), April 1922.
Life, October 11, 1954.
Sports Illustrated, August 11, 1958; June 4, 1962.

—*Gerald Tomlinson* for Book Builders, Inc.

THE NEGRO LEAGUES

Essay by Gerald Tomlinson
By arrangement with Book Builders, Inc.

Baseball enjoyed great popularity with both the Northern and Southern armies during the Civil War. When the war ended in 1865, the game that had spread so rapidly in army camps and military prisons made great strides as a civilian pastime. Among the growing population of the United States were 4.5 million new citizens, blacks that had formerly been slaves, some of whom were talented ballplayers. Many of these freedmen played in communities throughout the South and, later, in larger northern cities on all-black teams, such as the Uniques and Monitors of Brooklyn and the Excelsiors and Pythians of Philadelphia.

In 1867 the black Pythians sent a representative to the annual meeting of the National Association of Base Ball Players (NABBP), an organization founded in 1858 to consolidate the rules and establish guidelines for the new ball clubs that were springing up throughout the East and Midwest.

The Pythians were rebuffed. The NABBP nominating committee voted unanimously to exclude "any club which may be composed of one or more colored persons." That same principle was adopted in 1876 by the new National League (NL)—the NABBP having disbanded a few years earlier—although the NL did it by a "gentleman's agreement" rather than on paper.

These rules did not entirely prevent black participation in organized baseball. The minor leagues, especially the low minors, were essentially autonomous in the late 19th century, and gifted black ballplayers sometimes found work. John W. "Bud" Fowler, born in Cooperstown, New York, and Moses Fleetwood "Fleet" Walker, from Mount Pleasant, Ohio, were among the first black professionals. In 1887 Bud Fowler played second base for Binghamton, New York, and Fleet Walker caught for Newark, New Jersey, both in the International League. The Newark Eagles had an all-black battery when left-hander George W. Stovey was on the mound.

In a notorious incident in July of 1887, however, Cap Anson of the Chicago White Stockings refused to take the field in a scheduled exhibition game against the Newark Eagles if George Stovey and Fleet Walker were to play. That September the International League owners, concerned by what they saw as the growing furor over "the colored element," banned any future contracts with black ballplayers.

Over the winter of 1887-88, every black player in the top five minor leagues was told that his contract would not be renewed for the next season. Thus, nine years before the U.S. Supreme Court allowed "separate but equal" public schools, organized baseball created a separate but unequal pattern for professional baseball. Both major and minor leagues would henceforth be for whites only—except for the occasional Hispanic with light skin.

At first the all-black professional and semipro teams played informally. Rivalries developed within cities and between cities, and in 1887 the League of Colored Base Ball Clubs—a professional circuit with teams in Baltimore, Boston, Cincinnati, Louisville, New York, Philadelphia, Pittsburgh, and Washington, D.C.—was founded.

Prior to 1920, however, few black leagues, including the League of Colored Base Ball Clubs, were more than short-lived, ad hoc ventures. The teams played in leased ballparks, and players jumped from one ball club to another with little regard for contracts. Barnstorming, which soon became the lifeblood of black professional baseball, made it all but impossible to do accurate long-term scheduling.

Andrew "Rube" Foster, an outstanding pitch-

Transcendental Graphics

Rube Foster (back row, third from left) with the Royal Ponciana Baseball Club, c. 1905

er who had spent many years on independent black teams, proposed in 1919 that one all-black team be allowed to join the National League and another all-black team to join the American League. After being turned down, Foster, who by then was managing the Chicago American Giants, formed the Negro National League. This was the first of the great Negro Leagues and the one that ushered in the golden age—1920 to 1946—of black baseball.

All but two of the teams in the Negro National League were based in Midwestern cities, with Chicago represented twice (American Giants and Giants). Other teams included the Cuban Stars of Cincinnati, Dayton Macros, Detroit Stars, Indianapolis ABCs, Kansas City Monarchs, and St. Louis Giants. In the East were the Bacharach Giants of Atlantic City and Hilldale, a team based in Darby, Pennsylvania, a suburb of Philadelphia.

The Eastern Colored League, established in 1923, absorbed the Atlantic City and Hilldale teams, joining them with the Baltimore Black Sox and three New York City entries—the Brooklyn Royal Giants, Lincoln Giants, and Cuban Stars. The League lasted five years. The Negro American League, established in 1937, survived until the 1960s.

Among the great teams in black baseball (all of them with Negro League affiliations at one time or another) were the Baltimore Elite Giants, Birmingham Black Barons, Chicago American Giants, Cleveland Buckeyes, Detroit Stars, Homestead Grays, Kansas City Monarchs, Newark Eagles, New York Black Yankees, New York Cuban Stars, Philadelphia Stars, and Pittsburgh Crawfords.

The Indianapolis Clowns were one of the legendary black comic teams, of which there were many, and even some of the straight teams had players with comic routines. The best of the black players were very good indeed, a fact that the National Baseball Hall of Fame began to recognize in 1969.

Among the Hall-of-Fame black stars who never appeared in the major leagues because of organized baseball's long-standing "gentleman's

Transcendental Graphics

John Henry "Pop" Lloyd

agreement" were James "Cool Papa" Bell, Oscar Charleston, Martin Dihigo, Andrew "Rube" Foster, Josh Gibson, William "Judy" Johnson, Walter "Buck" Leonard, and John Henry (Pop) Lloyd.

A few outstanding players from the Negro Leagues, such as Satchel Paige and Monte Irvin, ended their playing days in the majors, while several contemporary major league superstars, including Hank Aaron, Ernie Banks, Roy Campanella, Willie Mays, and Jackie Robinson, got their start on all-black ball clubs. One of the finest third basemen ever, Ray Dandridge, closed out his 21-year baseball career at the Triple-A level.

Branch Rickey, general manager of the Brooklyn Dodgers, was the driving force behind the post-World War II integration of organized baseball. Rickey's signing of the Kansas City Monarchs' Jackie Robinson to a professional contract signaled the end of segregated baseball. Robinson played for the Montreal Royals in the Triple-A International League in 1946, and moved up to the Brooklyn Dodgers in 1947.

This signing immediately opened the door for other blacks, including Roy Campanella, Don Newcombe, Larry Doby, and Hank Thompson. Yet complete integration did not occur overnight, and the Negro Leagues struggled through the 1950s with diminishing popularity and profits.

Increasingly, the best black players—some of them from all-black teams, others directly from the newly-integrated minor leagues—went to the majors. Both the Negro and minor leagues suffered from the televising of major league baseball. By the end of the 1950s the violent and discriminatory era of "blackball," as author John B. Holway called it, was over.

"Gentleman's Agreement"

Undoubtedly there were black baseball players in the United States since the game's inception. The commercial possibilities for baseball were not readily apparent, however, because of the sport's lack of formal organization. Two years after the Civil War, when the all-black Excelsiors of Philadelphia came to Brooklyn to play the local Uniques and Monitors, the *Brooklyn Daily Union* announced, "these organizations are composed of very respectable colored people, well-to-do in the world ... and include many first-class players."

Also in 1867, the all-black Pythians of Philadelphia tried to join the National Association of Base Ball Players (NABBP) but were rejected. The nominating committee foresaw discord if black teams were accepted, "whereas by excluding them no injury could result to anyone."

This ban on black players and ball clubs continued as the game changed from an amateur sport to a professional calling (at least for the highly skilled). Gentlemen's ball clubs gave way to commercial baseball teams, and, as historian David Q. Voigt noted, "clubs changed some of their class-bound policies and invited husky yeomen into the ranks."

Of course, these husky yeomen were overwhelmingly white, although occasionally a black player would be admitted—but not at the highest level. The National League, founded in 1876, excluded black teams and players by a "gentleman's agreement."

Conversely, among the many struggling minor league organizations, a talented black player was sometimes accepted. One such player was John W. "Bud" Fowler. Born in 1858, Fowler—whose name at birth was John Jackson—is variously reported as having broken in with a local team in Chelsea, Massachusetts, a semipro team in Newcastle, Pennsylvania, or with the Mutuals of Washington (such is the factual haze surrounding early black ballplayers). Regardless, he appeared with independent, otherwise all-white barnstorming teams throughout the country, from Massachusetts to Colorado. He pitched, caught, and played the outfield, but his ideal position was second base.

Between 1884 and 1887 he played for Stillwater, Keokuk, Pueblo, Topeka, and Binghamton in the Northwest, Western, Colorado, and International Leagues. *Sporting Life* commented in 1885, "The poor fellow's skin is against him. With his splendid abilities he would long ago have been on some good club had his color been white instead of black." Fowler eventually became one of the best known of the several dozen black ball-players who performed on professional or semipro white teams before the turn of the century.

Another of the minor league's black stars was Frank Grant, a native of Pittsfield, Massachusetts, and a classy second baseman. After starring briefly for Meriden, Connecticut, in the Eastern League, Grant moved on to Buffalo, where he played for three seasons (1886 through 1888), batting .344, .353, and .346. The *Buffalo Express* identified the light-skinned Grant as a "Spaniard." (Later Fowler wrote, "If I had not been quite so black, I might have caught on as a Spaniard or something of that kind.") But the way was not easy for Grant; in 1888 the Buffalo Bison players refused to pose for a team photograph if it included Grant, the team's star second baseman and leading hitter.

THE NEGRO LEAGUES

Moses Fleetwood Walker PROFILE

Moses Fleetwood Walker, the son of a physician in Mt. Pleasant, Ohio, was born on October 7, 1857. He attended Oberlin College, where he studied, among other things, Greek, Latin, French, and German. In 1881, his last year at Oberlin, he and his brother, Welday Wilberforce Walker, played varsity baseball. Fleet was the team's catcher, while Welday patroled right field.

The team played three games and won them all, including a game against the University of Michigan. Fleet must have impressed the men from Ann Arbor, because the next year he transferred to Michigan, where he played in 1882 and 1883. Then, without earning a degree, he signed a professional baseball contract with Toledo of the Northwestern League. Toledo won the pennant in 1883, with Walker catching 60 games and batting .251.

The next year Toledo joined the 13-team American Association, recognized as a major league, although it was hardly as strong a circuit as the eight-year-old National League. Walker, the first black major leaguer, batted .263 in 42 games. His brother, Welday, appeared in five games for Toledo, making him the second black in the majors.

Boos and hisses met Fleet Walker in Louisville, one of the league's two Southern cities. A threat of physical violence came by letter from Richmond, but before the trip east, Walker suffered a broken rib from a foul tip (there were no chest protectors in those days), and he did not play in the former capital of the Confederacy.

Toledo released him at the end of the season, notwithstanding his "fine, gentlemanly deportment," and Walker dropped back to the minors, playing for Cleveland, Ohio, in the Western League and Waterbury, Connecticut, in the Southern New England and Eastern Leagues in 1885 and 1886. He then moved up to Newark, New Jersey, in the International League, where he caught in 69 games in 1887 and batted .264. Fleet Walker ended his career at Syracuse, also in the International League, playing with little distinction in 1888 and 1889.

In 1883, while at Toledo, Moses Fleetwood Walker, a journeyman catcher but a pioneer in integrated professional baseball, figured in an incident involving Adrian (Cap) Anson of the Chicago White Stockings. Anson declared his team would not play if Walker caught for Toledo in an exhibition game between the two clubs. Manager Charlie Morton of Toledo said there would be no game if Walker was forced to ride the bench. Anson backed down, and Walker caught. Ironically, Walker was not scheduled to catch that day. He had a sore hand, and Morton put him in the game only because of Anson's ultimatum.

Two other black players who gained prominence in the 1880s were pitcher George W. Stovey and catcher Moses Fleetwood "Fleet" Walker. Stovey, a left-hander, compiled a 16-15 record for Jersey City in the Eastern League in 1886, with a dazzling 1.13 earned run average (ERA). The next season he got more support at the plate from his new Newark teammates and posted a 34-14 mark with a 2.46 ERA.

Fleet Walker has a distinction that many people assume belongs to Jackie Robinson. In 1884 the American Association was a major league in which Toledo, Ohio, fielded a team. Fleet Walker was the catcher on that team, thus becoming the first black to play in organized baseball at the major league level.

At the beginning of the 1887 season, the future of black players in professional baseball looked promising. Eight blacks, among them Fowler, Grant, Stovey, and Walker, were on rosters in the International League. Moreover, the League of Colored Base Ball Players had won recognition as a minor league under the National Agreement, a pact among baseball owners to honor each others' player contracts.

Two players, Fleet Walker and his brother Welday Walker, had already played at the major league level in the American Association. All of these hopeful signs faded during the 1887 campaign, and by the end of the year the status of black players in professional baseball was tenuous and deteriorating.

The League of Colored Baseball Players folded before the 1887 season opened. This failure dimmed the prospect of having a number of all-black minor league ball clubs serve as stepping stones to the majors. *Sporting Life* reported on racial incidents on various International League teams and asked, "how far will this mania for engaging colored players go?"

In May of 1887 the Syracuse club signed Bob Higgins, a 19-year-old black pitcher whose presence angered several of his teammates—two of whom refused to pose with him for a team photo. On July 14, 1887 the International League owners took notice of this controversy. According to *Sporting Life,* "Several representatives declared that many of the best players in the League were anxious to leave on account of the colored element, and the board finally directed Secretary White to approve no more contracts with colored men."

This was devastating for black ballplayers in the minors, but more bad news awaited. On July 19, George Stovey was scheduled to pitch an exhibition game against Cap Anson's Chicago White Stockings. Stovey withdrew before the game got underway, saying he was ill. The real reason he bowed out, however, was that Anson threatened to remove his team from the field if Newark's star black hurler appeared. Anson, a native of Marshalltown, Iowa, had made the same threat four years earlier against Toledo and Fleet Walker, but Toledo's manager had defied him by playing Walker.

The Newark Eagles released George Stovey at the end of the 1887 season, despite his having set an all-time International League record for wins

with 34. Binghamton likewise let Bud Fowler go, despite his .350 batting average. Only the low minors or the many all-black teams that were being formed remained as career options for such players as Stovey and Fowler. By the end of the 19th century, even the low minors had closed their doors to black players. Henceforth, for 50 years organized baseball was a Jim Crow operation.

The Cuban Giants and Chief Tokohama

No one knows for sure when black professional baseball was born. In 1882 the *Cincinnati Enquirer* reported, "Philadelphia has a nine of colored professionals." And in 1885 Frank P. Thompson, headwaiter at the Argyle Hotel in Babylon, New York, on Long Island's South Shore, formed an all-black team from among his waiters. The waiters seem to have been chosen mostly for their baseball ability, because when they went up against the National League's New York Metropolitans they played competitively, despite losing 11-3. A white entrepreneur, John F. Lang, turned the Argyle's black waiters—at first called the Athletics—into a professional barnstorming ball club.

Another white businessman, Walter Cook of Trenton, New Jersey, supplied both capital and a new name, the Cuban Giants. Cook hoped that the supposed, though spurious, Cuban connection would raise the team's status in the eyes of white fans.

Instead, the rapidly improving quality of the team brought it acclaim. Except for several blacks still struggling to survive in the virtually all-white minor leagues, the Cuban Giants attracted the best black ballplayers available. By 1886 only two former Argyle waiters remained on the club, and by 1887—the year Cap Anson kept George Stovey out of that exhibition game—the Cuban Giants were a definite success.

Their games against major and minor league teams, college and university nines, and semipro outfits were well attended, and the "Giants" nickname was adopted by black teams throughout the country.

In a game against the National League pennant-winning Detroit Wolverines, the Cuban Giants led 4-2 in the eighth inning before four Giant errors gave the game to Detroit. The Giants even had a brief fling in organized baseball. In 1889 the Middle States League invited the Giants and the all-black Gorhams of New York to join the league, and both teams obliged.

The next season the league became the Eastern Interstate League, with the Cuban Giants still as members. When the Eastern Interstate League disbanded, the Cuban Giants joined the Connecticut State League, which failed in mid-1891. The Giants subsequently resumed full-time barnstorming.

By the turn of the century there were a number of all-black traveling baseball teams besides the Cuban Giants, among them the Columbia Giants of Chicago (formerly the Page Fence Giants, founded by Bud Fowler in Adrian, Michigan, in 1895), the Red Stockings of Norfolk, Virginia, and the Cuban X Giants of New York. Although the leagues and teams in organized baseball began maintaining records and statistics at about this time, the black traveling teams kept little factual information about themselves.

Yet because the black barnstormers played throughout the country against varying levels of competition, any records would have meant little. The majority of black ballplayers of that era, and even later, have to be judged mainly by the recollection of other players and spectators—both black and white. However, one early black player, Sol White, "a tremendous long ball hitter," according to black sportswriter Art Rust, Jr., did write a book in 1906 titled *The History of Colored Baseball* that looks at the pre-league days of black baseball and presents an overview of blacks in the minors.

Even without detailed stats or thorough press coverage (the white press concentrated on major league baseball and the local minor league teams), many knowledgeable baseball people realized that black players represented a great untapped source of talent. In 1901 John J. McGraw attempt-ed to sign black second baseman Charlie Grant to a major league contract by masquerading him as a Native American. McGraw managed and played third base for the Baltimore Orioles in the new American League. The Orioles trained in Hot Springs, Arkansas, and stayed at the Eastland Hotel. One of the Eastland bellboys was Charlie Grant, a light-skinned black who had played for the Columbia Giants, an all-black team based in Chicago.

McGraw observed Grant playing ball on the hotel grounds and realized that the youthful second baseman had major league ability. Hoping to circumvent the American League's ban on blacks, McGraw, noticed the name "Tokohama Creek" on a wall map at the Eastland Hotel and announced that he planned to sign infielder Charlie Tokohama, a full-blooded Cherokee, to a Baltimore contract. *Sporting Life* called Tokohama "a phenomenal fielder ... between 21 and 23 years of age.... He is, moreover, a good batter."

But Charlie Comiskey, president of the Chicago White Sox, saw through the ruse. "Somebody told me," Comiskey said, "that the Cherokee of McGraw's is really Grant, the crack Negro second baseman from Cincinnati, fixed up with war paint and a bunch of feathers." Confronted with the evidence, McGraw backed off, and Charlie Grant, who was never actually signed by Baltimore despite the preseason publicity, returned to the all-black Columbia Giants.

In 1902 Sol White and two Philadelphia sportswriters organized the Philadelphia Giants, a powerful all-black team of the early 1900s. In 1905 a white Brooklyn cafe owner, J. W. Connor, formed the Brooklyn Royal Giants. Cuba, a hotbed of baseball for years, produced two strong teams that played extensively in the United States, the Cuban Stars and the Havana Stars. (These two teams are not to be confused with the already established Cuban Giants and Cuban X Giants, composed of American blacks, or with the various American-based "Cuban Stars" that later sprang up.) Although the two authentic Cuban ball clubs had both black and white players, they played in the United States as black teams.

In 1906, when an attempt was made to operate an integrated league (not under the auspices of organized baseball, however), the Cuban Stars and Havana Stars joined it. So did the all-black Cuban X Giants and the Quaker Giants of New York, along with two white teams from Pennsylvania, the Philadelphia Professionals and the Riverton-Palmyra Athletics.

This pioneering circuit, called the International League of Professional Base Ball Clubs, lasted one season. Sol White's formidable Philadelphia Giants entered the league in August and somehow—mathematical probability notwithstanding—won the pennant.

A great many all-black teams were organized after the turn of the century. Most of the better-known teams resided in northern cities even though the majority of blacks still lived in the South. The business side of black baseball remained haphazard as player contracts were often verbal (and generally meaningless), and players moved freely from team to team, even during a single season. Professional black players might appear in as many as 200 games a year, but the loose organization of the enterprise caused even the black press, such as the *Chicago Defender,* to refer to the ball clubs as semipro teams.

Rube Foster and His Era

As black teams proliferated and the profit potential of the national pastime became more evident, the black baseball enterprise clearly needed administrative leadership, someone with business acumen and executive skills. Such a person appeared in the form of Andrew "Rube" Foster, a man whom historian Robert W. Peterson has called "an unlettered genius who combined generosity and sternness, the superb skills of a dedicated athlete and an unbounded belief in the future of the black baseball player."

Foster came from Calvert, Texas, a village southeast of Waco, where his father was an elder in the black Methodist Episcopal church. In 1897, 17-year-old Foster, who dropped out of school after eighth grade, was pitching for the black barnstorming team the Waco Yellow Jackets when he caught the eye of Frank C. Leland, the owner of the Chicago Union Giants. Leland signed Foster but warned him of the challenge he would face in playing the top white ball clubs in the nation. Undaunted, Foster replied, "It will be a case of Greek meeting Greek. I fear nobody." In his first game for the Union Giants he hurled a shutout.

In 1902 Foster pitched and won an exhibition game against the Philadelphia Athletics. Since his mound opponent that day was future Hall-of-Famer Rube Waddell, Foster's teammates hung the nickname Rube on him too. Rube Foster was an imposing, charismatic figure, six foot four and weighing over 200 pounds. Honus Wagner called him "one of the greatest pitchers of all time. He was the smartest pitcher I have ever seen in all my years of baseball." In 1902 Foster won four games out of his teams' five victories for the Philadelphia Cuban X Giants against the Philadelphia Giants in a playoff to determine the "Colored Championship of the World."

In 1905 Foster reportedly won 51 of 55 exhibition games against all levels of competition, including major league teams. Nevertheless, Foster achieved his most lasting fame as a manager, an organizer, and a baseball administrator. By 1907 he was the playing manager—and part owner—of the Leland Giants.

Dave Malarcher, a noted black third baseman of the day, remarked that Foster was "an absolute genius at handling men, in devising strategies of defense and attack.... His philosophy of the 'big inning' paralleled the later American League gospel—the winning team will score more runs in one inning than the losing team will score in the whole game." The strategy seemed to work for Foster. In 1910 his Leland Giants won 123 games and lost only six, with a lineup that included shortstop John Henry "Pop" Lloyd and outfielder Pete Hill—considered two of the greatest black ballplayers of all time.

In 1911 Foster and John M. Schorling, a white tavern owner, formed the Chicago American Giants and agreed on an even split of gate receipts.

Transcendental Graphics

Oscar Charleston

from a trip East in 1919, Foster began campaigning in the pages of the *Chicago Defender* for an organization of black ball clubs, a Negro league. He wanted to curb the raiding of players by opposing teams. Apparently on the American Giants' 1919 barnstorming tour, the eastern teams—many of them partly owned by white booking agent Nat Strong—had tried to pluck some of Foster's best players from his roster. In addition to protecting his players, Foster hoped that the pennant-winning team in his new Negro League would be able to play the major league championship team in a kind of post-World Series.

In 1920 Foster created the National Association of Professional Baseball Clubs, commonly known as the Negro National League. This effort won him the sobriquet "The Father of Black Baseball." This association of eight Midwestern barnstorming teams was the first successful all-black league in baseball history. A second such circuit, the Eastern Colored League, began operating in 1923. Both leagues survived the 1920s but fell on hard times during the Great Depression.

Blackball Stars of the 1920s

The Negro National League and Eastern Colored League were not truly parallel to the all-white National League and American League. The all-black teams, still mainly independent enterprises, received most of their income from barnstorming rather than from league play. The number of league games played each season varied from team to team. For example, in 1922 the Chicago American Giants won the Negro National League pennant with a record of 36 wins and 23 losses—a total of 59 games. The Indianapolis ABCs finished second in the league with a 46-33 record—a total of 79 games—while the Pittsburgh Keystones, in sixth place, went 16-21, playing only 37 games.

A black roster typically contained no more than 17 or 18 players as opposed to the 25 players on most major league rosters. Because of the

The American Giants acquired most of the Leland Giants' players, a move that immediately made the new, independent team a powerhouse in the Midwest. Foster continued to play regularly as well as manage, book games, and direct the ball club until 1915, after which he appeared on the field only occasionally, often as a first baseman.

The Chicago American Giants, featuring such stars as pitcher Smokey Joe Williams, first baseman Ben Taylor, second baseman Bingo DeMoss, and outfielders Oscar Charleston and Christobel Torrienti, traveled throughout the country. For long trips they rented a private railroad car.

After the Chicago American Giants returned

When the Eastern Colored League was founded in 1923, the stage was set for a Colored World Series between the pennant winner in the ECL and top team in the older Negro National League. A Colored World Series seemed a sure bet to be profitable and popular. The first one was played in 1924 between the Kansas City Monarchs and Hilldale. The Monarchs prevailed, five games to four, with one tie.

Attendance, surprisingly, was mediocre. The games were exciting and well played, but the average crowd was only 4,500 per game. It dropped to 4,000 in 1925 as Hilldale triumphed over Kansas City, and then fell to fewer than 2,000 a game in 1926 when the Chicago American Giants beat the Atlantic City Bacharachs. After Chicago won again in 1927, the Colored World Series was abandoned. It did not resume again until 1942.

Nonetheless, the Colored World Series came back in 1942, when interest in Negro League baseball was at an all-time high. The Kansas City Monarchs won that year, just as they had in the first Series in 1924. The Homestead Grays took the crown in 1943 and 1944. The popularity of the Series faded as the Negro Leagues began to crumble.

In the 1948 Series, with the end of black baseball in sight, a few fans got their first glimpse of Willie Mays, a 17-year-old rookie outfielder playing for the Birmingham Black Barons. Of course, that same year, in the World Series between the Cleveland Indians and the Boston Braves, fans could watch Cleveland outfielder Larry Doby, late of the Newark Eagles, crack out seven hits in the Indians' victory over the Braves. Also on the Cleveland roster was black baseball's great pitcher, Satchel Paige.

relatively small number of players, there were some remarkably versatile black ballplayers. An outstanding pitcher, Martin Dihigo could also play capably and even brilliantly at nearly any position—second base in particular—and was a lifetime .304 hitter.

During the 1920s two additional all-black leagues were formed in the South—the Southern Negro League and the Texas-Oklahoma-Louisiana League. The Southern Negro League, in which the Birmingham Black Barons were the premier ball club, developed some outstanding players. The teams in the league faced an intractable problem, as did those in the Texas-Oklahoma-Louisiana League; they could not play against white ball clubs as their northern counterparts could.

This and the fact that the cities themselves were smaller, kept gate receipts much lower than in the North, making it impossible for teams to match the salaries that the two northern leagues paid. The top players—pitcher Satchel Paige being a prime example—almost inevitably ended up

on teams in the Negro National League or the Eastern Colored League.

Despite Foster's hope, none of the Negro League clubs had much control over their players. Contract violations remained as common as they had been prior to the league structure. Players jumped teams almost at will, and few black ball clubs owned their own stadiums, which made them dependent on rentals from major and minor league operators. Inadequate training led to some distinctive styles of play but at times also revealed a shaky grasp of fundamentals. In addition, the salaries of black ballplayers were not commensurate with those of their white counterparts. Some teams remained staunchly independent, and a few were purely entertainment troupes, or "clowning" teams.

What the best of the Negro League teams had in common with the majors were a number of highly gifted individual ballplayers. The most talented of these were clearly of major league caliber, and remarks to that effect by notable major leaguers dot the pages of books about black baseball. Hall-of-Fame shortstop Honus Wagner commented: "They called John Henry Lloyd 'The Black Wagner,' and I was anxious to see him play. Well, one day I had an opportunity to go see him play, and after I saw him I felt honored that they would name such a great player after me."

Hall-of-Fame second baseman Frankie Frisch said, "I can still recall [Cristobal] Torriente.... He could hit a ball! Pretty good? In those days Torriente was a hell of a ballplayer. Christ, I'd like to whitewash him and bring him up." Hall-of-Fame manager Connie Mack told Dick Lundy and Bunny Downs that "if you could speak another language, you'd be my second base combination." And Hall-of-Fame pitcher Dizzy Dean observed, "I know who's the best pitcher I ever did see ... and it's old Satchel Paige, that big lanky colored boy."

Those four players were all active in the 1920s, with Satchel Paige the youngster and John Henry "Pop" Lloyd the oldest. An established star as early as 1910, Lloyd, like many black players, performed for various teams, often as a playing manager in his later years. Among the ball clubs featuring Lloyd at shortstop were the Macon Acmes, Cuban X Giants, Philadelphia Giants, Leland Giants, Lincoln Giants, Chicago American Giants, Brooklyn Royal Giants, Columbus Buckeyes, Atlantic City Bacharach Giants, Philadelphia Hilldales, and New York Black Yankees.

In 1932, at the age of 48, the smooth-fielding, hard-hitting shortstop retired as an active traveling player (although he still played semipro ball for a team in Atlantic City). A left-handed place-hitter, Lloyd batted cleanup on Foster's great Chicago American Giants' teams and was at his peak until the early 1920s. One white sportswriter, Ted Harlow of St. Louis, called him "the greatest player of all time, including Ty Cobb and Babe Ruth." As an indication of his talent, Lloyd was named to the Baseball Hall of Fame in 1977.

Most experts rank Cristobal Torriente among the three best Negro League outfielders. Torriente, a native of Cuba, was a left-handed long-ball hitter who played for the Chicago American Giants from 1920 through 1925. In 1920 he appeared in a postseason exhibition game in Havana, Cuba, against the New York Giants. Babe Ruth, who had hit 54 homers that year for the Yankees, was the star attraction on the otherwise all-Giant team. Ruth went hitless in three official trips to the plate, while Torriente, wielding a considerably hotter bat, blasted three home runs off Giant pitching (including a two-run double off the Babe himself who, perhaps in frustration, had gone in to pitch to the torrid Torriente).

Dick Lundy was a superb fielder and consistent hitter who, like Lloyd, hailed from northern Florida. Lundy starred for the Bacharach Giants through most of the 1920s. When recalling the play of Lundy, black ballplayers generally used the word "graceful." Although he had a reputation as a hard-nosed competitor, he was pure poetry at shortstop. Unlike many of the black stars of the 1920s, he became the popular hero of a single team, the Atlantic City Bacharach Giants. Unfortunately, that team—and the Eastern Colored League—failed after the 1928 season, and Lundy moved on to the Baltimore Black Sox, Philadelphia Stars, and Newark Eagles. He retired in 1940.

The most famous of the great Negro League stars was the unparalleled pitcher Satchel Paige. Born in 1905, Paige first played professionally in 1926 with the Chattanooga Black Lookouts. When the color barrier fell after World War II, he pitched in the majors for the Cleveland Indians. By then Paige had already toiled in the Negro Leagues for 22 years.

A legend who bridged the worlds of black and white baseball, Paige was a favorite of fans from coast to coast, gaining his greatest notice while hurling for the Pittsburgh Crawfords and the Kansas City Monarchs. Paige had blazing speed, and although there were several black pitchers who threw harder—Joe Williams and Dick Redding—none threw with greater accuracy.

Paige's pinpoint control, coupled with his speed, was such that he could—and often did—call in his outfielders, sit them down, and proceed to strike out the side. Whether Paige was the greatest pitcher in black baseball history is a matter of conjecture. A 1952 *Pittsburgh Courier* poll of knowledgeable blackball observers gave the edge to Smokey Joe Williams by a razor-thin margin.

But Paige, the tall, thin right-hander with the matchstick legs, was for many years the biggest gate attraction in the Negro Leagues. His barnstorming tours demonstrated to countless white fans that the exclusion of blacks from major league baseball was merely based on race, not ability. As an ancient major league rookie in 1948, Paige won six games for the Cleveland Indians, lost one, and posted a 2.47 ERA. He was named to the Baseball Hall of Fame in 1971.

Other standouts of the 1920s make up a potent all-star lineup. Mule Suttles, a power-hitting but somewhat awkward first baseman, broke in as a 17-year-old with the Birmingham Black Barons. Suttles played until he was 42, observing, "Don't worry about the Mule going blind; just load the wagon and give me the lines." Another was Newt Allen of the Kansas City Monarchs, a smooth-fielding, switch-hitter with fine bat control who said, tongue-in-cheek, that he played not by the Queensberry rules but by "the coonsberry rules—that's just any way you think you can win."

Shortstop Willie Wells starred for the St. Louis Stars beginning in 1925, though he is most often remembered for his play over the next two decades. When author James Riley named his All-Time All-Stars of Black Baseball, he put Wells on the second team, just behind the peerless John Henry Lloyd.

The hot corner in the 1920s belonged to William "Judy" Johnson, a student of the game and one of the best-fielding third basemen in the history of black baseball. A star for Hilldale and later for the Pittsburgh Crawfords, Judy Johnson had a talent for stealing signs and for assessing players' strengths and weaknesses and sizing up the situation in a game. Teammates thought he would have made a first-rate major league manager.

An outfielder of the 1920s—and for all time—was the lightning-fast "Cool Papa" Bell, who starred for the St. Louis Stars, Pittsburgh Crawfords, and Homestead Grays. A favorite saying was that Bell was so fast he could switch off the

Transcendental Graphics

Martin Dihigo

light and be in bed before the room was dark. Turkey Stearnes, a left-hander like Bell, was a powerful, long-ball-hitting outfielder for the Detroit Stars throughout most of the 1920s. Rounding out an all-lefty, all-star outfield was Chino Smith, a mite-sized slugger for the Lincoln Giants, who hit two homers and a triple in the first Negro League game played in Yankee Stadium.

One of the top catchers of the 1920 was Biz Mackey, who was outstanding on both offense and defense. The switch-hitting Mackey put in some fine seasons for Hilldale of the Eastern Colored League. In 1923, the league's first year, Mackey belted 20 homers and posted a .698 slugging percentage in 49 league games.

There were many fine black pitchers in the 1920s. Among them was Wilbur "Bullet Joe" Rogan, a player nearly as versatile as Martin Dihigo. Rogan could play any position except catcher, although his fame came through his pitching efforts for the Kansas City Monarchs. A U.S. soldier for nearly a decade, he joined the Monarchs at the age of 26 and pitched regularly for them from 1920 to 1930. So capable a hitter was he that the potent Monarchs often batted him fourth, fifth, or sixth.

The Negro Leagues and the Great Depression

Rube Foster, the powerful organizing force behind Negro League baseball, died in 1930, having spent his last four years in a mental hospital; he was sorely missed. Two years earlier the Eastern Colored League had disbanded, and less than a year later the Negro National League failed. Thus the organizational structure of black baseball collapsed at the onset of the Great Depression. Money, always scarce among black Americans, became scarcer still as jobs disappeared and bread lines formed. The popular, firmly established institution of black baseball needed an infusion of funds. It had always been cash poor, but now it was nearly broke.

Into the breach stepped Gus Greenlee, referred to in Donn Rogosin's *Invisible Men* as "Pittsburgh's most prominent black racketeer." Greenlee, the numbers czar of Pittsburgh's black ghetto, was the force behind two important events in 1933: the founding of the Pittsburgh Crawfords

Transcendental Graphics

**Members of the Pittsburgh Crawfords c. 1935, including (left to right)
Oscar Charleston, Josh Gibson, (unidentified), and Judy Johnson**

and the reorganization of the Negro National League.

The new and powerful Crawfords banded together with the Baltimore Black Sox, Chicago American Giants, Columbus Blue Birds, Detroit Stars, and Nashville Elite Giants in the revamped six-team circuit. In 1935 the Homestead Grays, one of the outstanding barnstorming teams of the era, also joined the new Negro National League. Homestead, Pennsylvania, a steel town near Pittsburgh, later shared the Grays' base of operations with Washington, D.C.

Despite the Depression, the Negro National League prospered, and in 1937 the Negro American League was formed, restoring the National-American League parallel to white professional baseball and making a revived Negro World Series possible. Owned by white entrepreneur J. L. Wilkinson, the Kansas City Monarchs were the crown jewel in the new eight-team Negro American League.

Both circuits, however, saw teams come and go. Among the noteworthy arrivals in the Negro National League were the Newark Eagles, New York Black Yankees, New York Cuban Stars, and Philadelphia Stars. The Chicago American Giants and Detroit Stars, formerly mainstays in the Negro National League, switched over to the Negro American League.

Greenlee seemed to be doing well in both the numbers game and in baseball. So did the other black racketeer-owners of Negro National League teams—Tom Wilson of the Baltimore Elite Giants, Abe Manley of the Newark Eagles, Ed "Soldier Boy" Semler of the New York Black Yankees, Alex Pompez of the New York Cubans, and Ed Bolden of the Philadelphia Stars.

Looming larger than any of these men, at times was Mrs. Effa Manley, wife and co-owner with Abe Manley of the Newark Eagles. For 15 years the shrewd and beautiful Effa Manley was a powerful force in the operation of the Negro National League, the Newark Eagles, and the New Jersey NAACP. Mrs. Manley was a dynamic, take-charge person whose decisions were sometimes more personal than strategic. She once told the Eagles' manager to put Terris McDuffie in a game he was not scheduled to pitch so that her girlfriends in the stands could see how handsome McDuffie was.

When Greenlee arrived on the black baseball scene in the early 1930s, there was another more conventional entrepreneur already there. He was Cumberland "Cum" Posey, the long-time man behind the Homestead Grays. A gifted, light-skinned black athlete, Posey had been named to manage the Grays in 1917. As time went by, he gained ownership of the club.

This proved such a successful venture that when the Eastern Colored League was formed in 1923, the Grays remained independent. Shrewd and allegedly greedy, Posey often raided the league teams for ballplayers. He acquired two aging superstars, Smokey Joe Williams and Oscar Charleston, that way. In 1931 he picked up Satchel Paige from the failed Cleveland Cubs.

An educated man, Posey had little use for the younger, former beer-truck hijacker Greenlee. Nonetheless, most people in black baseball—including the Negro League managers and players—got along well with Greenlee and the other gangster owners of the Depression era. Although Negro League baseball was never a very profitable enterprise, the 1930s were part of its golden age. Many of the stars of the 1920s were still active, and a number of all-time greats also debuted in the 1930s. One such player was superstar catcher Josh Gibson.

Born in Buena Vista, Georgia, Gibson came north as a child to join his father, who worked in a Pittsburgh steel mill. As a teenage catcher, Gibson attracted the attention of Posey, and when the Homestead Grays regular catcher split a finger playing a white semipro team, Gibson was pressed into service. One of the most powerful hitters of all time, Gibson caught for the Grays in 1930 and 1931, gaining immediate popularity for his moon-shot home runs.

Capable behind the plate, Gibson became famous even among white fans for hitting the ball farther in many major league parks than any of the famous American or National League sluggers.

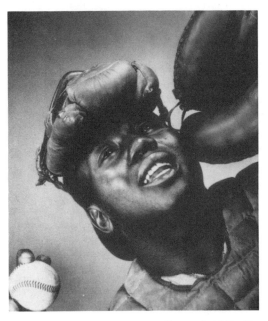

Transcendental Graphics

Josh Gibson

Gibson and Mickey Mantle were the only two batters ever to hit the facade in fair territory in Yankee Stadium.

When the Depression deepened in 1932 and Posey found himself hard-pressed for cash, Gibson jumped to Greenlee's Pittsburgh Crawfords. Although the Negro Leagues were defunct that year, barnstorming continued, and Greenlee proceeded to acquire players. He signed the Homestead Grays' Judy Johnson and Oscar Charleston.

By mid-season of 1932, Greenlee's team featured Paige on the mound, Gibson behind the plate, Judy Johnson at third base, and Oscar Charleston in the outfield. Two years later Greenlee added outfielder "Cool Papa" Bell from the St. Louis Stars. With these five future Hall of Famers on the roster, the 1934-36 Pittsburgh Crawfords have been regarded as one of the great teams in Negro League history.

Besides molding the Pittsburgh Crawfords into a powerhouse, building the 5,000-seat Greenlee Field stadium, and establishing the Negro

National League, Greenlee made another great contribution to black baseball. He and Tom Wilson organized the first East-West All-Star Game, a contest that soon became the biggest event of the Negro League season. Played in Chicago's Comiskey Park (hoome of the White Sox), the game attracted 20,000 fans the first year, 1933, in the midst of the Great Depression. Each year thereafter until 1950, the East-West All-Star Game brought fans by the thousands—51,000 in 1943—to Comiskey Park to see the best players, as voted by the fans, in Negro League baseball.

Because the game was heavily promoted by the *Chicago Defender* and *Pittsburgh Courier,* there was a certain bias toward the local teams, including the Chicago American Giants, Pittsburgh Crawfords, and Homestead Grays. Among the East All-Stars in 1933 were Cool Papa Bell, Oscar Charleston, Biz Mackey, Josh Gibson, Judy Johnson, and Dick Lundy.

The West All-Stars included Turkey Stearnes, Willie Wells, Mule Suttles, and Willie Foster. This well-attended annual event may have contributed to the demise of the Negro Leagues; it demonstrated dramatically to major league owners how many black fans there were—and pointed up how few of those fans were attending all-white major league games.

In the early 1930s, Posey, owner of the independent Homestead Grays, found himself in deep financial trouble. Greenlee's raids had decimated his ball club, which in 1934 was down to about six players. At this juncture Smokey Joe Williams, by then retired and tending bar in Harlem, called his old boss to suggest a new recruit; the kid's name was Buck Leonard. In John B. Holway's *Blackball Stars,* Leonard is quoted as saying, "I was wondering why he picked me up. I guess it was because he didn't have any money to pay us. I got $125 a month, plus 60 cents a day on which to eat—sixty cents!"

Even so, Leonard, like the other Grays, admired the quiet, serious owner of the Homestead team. And everyone liked Buck Leonard, probably the most popular star ever to play in the Negro Leagues. He was a first baseman who could do it

Comedy routines in black baseball started in the 19th century. In *Black Manhattan* James Weldon Johnson wrote that the Cuban Giants "often staged a comic pantomime for the benefit of the spectators." But the Cuban Giants were not a clown team; they played serious baseball. The comedy acts were so popular, however, that clown teams soon began to appear.

In the 1920s the Tennessee Rats, a clown team, barnstormed the Midwest. In the early 1930s the Zulu Cannibals performed in the East, booked by promoter Syd Pollock. In a team photo the Zulu Cannibals wore long hair, grass skirts, no shirts, and war-painted faces. "They positively appear as illustrated," promised Pollock.

Many blacks objected to the demeaning racial stereotyping this kind of entertainment represented, no matter how talented some of the clowning players were, both as ballplayers and comedians. The Negro Leagues at first wanted no part of the clown teams either in their circuits or in their cities. But the teams were popular. "Book the Zulus and pack your park," Pollock advertised, and it was more than just puffery.

In the 1930s another clown team became even more successful than the Zulus—the Ethiopian Clowns, later the Indianapolis Clowns, owned by Abe Saperstein (who also owned the Harlem Globetrotters). The Clowns' biggest star beginning in 1942 was first baseman Goose Tatum, an outstanding ballplayer but also a comedic genius.

Another star, Pepper Bassett, "The Rocking Chair Catcher" alternated between the Clowns and a number of strong Negro League teams, including the Philadelphia Stars and Birmingham Black Barons. As a Clown, Bassett did his catching from a rocking chair and threw out embarrassed runners without bothering to get up. The Clowns had pitchers who could throw strikes from behind their backs or between their legs. In fact, they were a very good team apart from their "Spec Bebop and King Tut" comedy routines.

The Clowns joined the Negro National League in 1943. In 1952, when black baseball was falling apart, they signed a shy rookie named Henry Aaron, but the Milwaukee Braves' organization quickly picked him up. The next year, 1953, the Clowns hired the first woman to play professional baseball in the United States: second baseman Toni Stone. She did all right, too, batting .267 for the Clowns and moving on to the Kansas City Monarchs.

Ironically, the wonderfully theatrical Clowns outlasted the serious and once-mighty Monarchs. By then, of course, black ballplayers had proved they were anything but Stepin Fetchits, as they had begun making an indelible mark in the integrated major leagues.

---

all. Leonard, whose first name was actually Walter, hit for both power and percentage. He was also a talented fielder—adept at handling bunts and at scooping errant throws out of the dirt. Leonard was the catalyst in rebuilding the Homestead Grays as a formidable team in the Negro National League, which, after a long stint of independence, the Grays decided to join in 1935.

Another force in rebuilding the Homestead team was Rufus "Sonnyman" Jackson, a Pittsburgh racketeer whom Posey enlisted in the struggle against the rapacious Greenlee. Buck Leonard noted, "We weren't doing much until Rufus Jackson came in there with some fresh money." Then they regained the services of Josh Gibson, a move that led the black press to hail the power duo of Gibson and Leonard as the "Thunder Twins." Managing the revived Homestead ball club was Vic Davis, an old pro with the Grays' organization and a scrappy, spray-hitting outfielder who was also the team's manager, beginning in 1935.

With Gibson and Leonard leading the way by batting third and fourth in the lineup, Vic Harris's Homestead Grays won nine straight Negro Na-

Transcendental Graphics

Buck Leonard

Teams such as the Homestead Grays, Kansas City Monarchs, and Newark Eagles became famous nationwide. The annual East-West All-Star Game was the "highlight in the affairs of the elite," according to the *Chicago Defender,* and the Union-Pacific railroad added extra cars to carry fans to Chicago for the big game.

The fans were not solely black; the East-West All-Star Game, more than the league games, attracted whites in large numbers. "It was more than just the athletic contest," commented Max Manning, a pitcher for the Newark Eagles. "It was good to look up and see 50,000 up there screaming for you. The game made us big time, just like the major-leaguers. The crowds were always mixed, with many whites, and it was terrific."

From Jim Crow to Jackie Robinson

In 1942, three million fans saw Negro League teams play, and the popularity of black baseball was never higher. The awareness of inequity was heightened during the war. "How do you think I felt," black pitcher Chet Brewer asked later, "when I saw a one-armed outfielder [Pete Gray of the St. Louis Browns]?" Even though blacks served in the military, they still could not play in the major leagues. In 1942 Negro League pitcher Nate Moreland and Jackie Robinson, an All-American football star at UCLA, asked for a tryout at a White Sox training camp in Pasadena, California. Manager Jimmy Dykes granted the request and was impressed, at least with young Robinson, but it ended there.

Commissioner Kenesaw Mountain Landis later rebuked Brooklyn manager Leo Durocher for saying he was willing to sign black players. Nonetheless, talk of integration increased and in 1943 the Los Angeles Angels of the Pacific Coast League announced tryouts for three black players, but other PCL owners killed the idea. In 1943 Bill Veeck, Jr., a 29-year-old minor league owner, came up with a radical scheme to rejuvenate the hapless Philadelphia Phillies by buying the team and stocking it with players from the Negro

tional League pennants between 1937 and 1945. During this period, the Kansas City Monarchs were the dominant team in the Negro American League. Powerful as they were, the Monarchs were less consistently successful in league play than the Grays.

Teams in the Negro Leagues typically played about 200 games a year, only a third of which counted in the final standings. When the Pittsburgh Crawfords won the pennant in 1935, for instance, their won-lost record in the Negro National League was 39-15. All their other games were exhibitions, barnstorming contests against a wide variety of both black and white professional and semipro teams. These events generated much of the revenue for the Negro League ball clubs. They also brought top baseball talent to towns and cities across America, allowing local ball clubs to test themselves against the black professionals.

Leagues. "I had not the slightest doubt," Veeck wrote in his autobiography, "that ... the Phils would have leaped from seventh place to the pennant." Learning of the plan, Landis, a foe of integration (despite his statements to the contrary), thwarted Veeck's purchase.

At baseball's winter meetings in 1943, actor Paul Robeson, who a quarter of a century earlier had played on integrated baseball and football teams at Rutgers University, addressed the owners and asked that major league baseball accept black players. The owners applauded Robeson but did nothing. At this time, Commissioner Landis remarked that there was no law preventing blacks from participating in organized baseball.

Indeed, in 1938 Clark Griffith, the owner of the Washington Senators, had said, "the time is not far off when colored players will take their places beside those of other races in the major leagues." In the midst of World War II, Griffith invited Josh Gibson and Buck Leonard to come to his office to discuss the possibility of playing for the Senators. They expressed their willingness to do so, "but he never did make us an offer," said Leonard.

During World War II the Brooklyn Dodgers trained at Bear Mountain, New York. In April of 1945 sportswriter Joe Bostic appeared at the training camp with two Negro League ballplayers in tow—pitcher Terris McDuffie and first baseman Dave "Showboat" Thomas. Branch Rickey, the president of the Dodgers, had an agenda of his own that did not include McDuffie and Thomas. He let them stay in camp, but made no effort to sign them.

Ten days later the Boston Red Sox, under pressure from a local white politician and Boston sportswriter Dave Egan, offered tryouts to three Negro League players—shortstop Jackie Robinson of the Kansas City Monarchs, second baseman Marvin Williams of the Philadelphia Stars, and outfielder Sam Jethroe of the Cleveland Buckeyes. All three did well. The Red Sox coach running the event (neither the Boston players nor their manager was present) said, "you boys look like pretty good players. I hope you enjoyed the workout." The three black stars never heard from the Red Sox again.

There was apparently a lack of determination to integrate major league baseball. But at least one person in the game was earnest about the prospect of signing black players—Branch Rickey, "The Mahatma," a man already enshrined in baseball's pantheon for his development of the farm system.

After assuming control of the Brooklyn Dodgers in 1942, Rickey began slowly and cautiously breaking baseball's color barrier. In *Baseball's Great Experiment,* Jules Tygiel concluded that a combination of factors, "geographic, moral, competitive, and financial—coupled with Rickey's desire for a broader role in history," probably persuaded Rickey to press forward on the project.

Under the guise of attacking what he called the "rackets" represented by the Negro Leagues, Rickey proposed to establish a new all-black "United States League," with regular schedules and standard, enforced contracts. His purpose in suggesting this segregated circuit was not to perpetuate all-black teams but to do precisely the opposite, while camouflaging the reason for his club's active and obvious scouting of black ballplayers.

Rickey knew it would take an extraordinary individual to don a Dodger uniform and take the field with (and against) a wholly white baseball establishment. His painstaking search settled finally on the rookie shortstop of the Kansas City Monarchs, Jackie Robinson. Robinson had been the first four-letter man at UCLA, starring in football, basketball, baseball, and track. He had served as a lieutenant in the U.S. Army and had risked a dishonorable discharge at Fort Hood, Texas, for refusing to sit in the back of a local bus. In his first and only year with the Kansas City Monarchs he had been chosen as the West's All-Star shortstop.

Robinson seemed an ideal choice. He was young, intelligent, articulate, neither a drinker nor a smoker, and one of the better players in the Negro Leagues. Indeed, several sportswriters had identified the Monarchs' shortstop as a possible black pioneer in the majors. But they, like Rickey, had one serious reservation: Robinson was aggressive and had a quick temper. Rickey told the young

Jackie Robinson

Jackie Robinson was no kid when he broke baseball's color line. In 1947, his first year in the majors, he was 28 years old, a college graduate, an Army veteran, a one-year Negro League star, and a one-year minor league star. No one considered him the best black ballplayer of his time. Branch Rickey of the Brooklyn Dodgers choose him for a variety of reasons—his education and his experience in playing on integrated college teams among them.

Robinson was named Rookie of the Year in 1947. A daring baserunner, he led the league in stolen bases that season. Still, Rickey said, "You haven't seen Robinson yet. Maybe you won't really see him until next year. You'll see something when he gets to bunting and running as freely as he should."

It took two years. Jackie Robinson's greatest season was 1949, when he batted .342 to lead the league. He drove in 124 runs that year, stole 37 stolen bases, and was named the National League's Most Valuable Player. Here was clear statistical confirmation of the quality of black ballplayers.

If Robinson, a man some Negro Leaguers thought would fail in the majors, could turn in that kind of performance, the future seemed bright indeed for others on the way up. He finished his career with a .311 batting average. Yet, as with many Negro Leaguers and ex-Negro Leaguers, Robinson contributed more than glittering statistics to his team. He was a pressure player. On base, he could break the concentration of the best pitchers in the business. He stole home 19 times, five times in one season. He played what the Negro Leaguers called "tricky baseball," which emphasized using a whole bagful of baseball tools, not just power hitting. He ignited the Dodgers of the late 1940s and early 1950s. The "Boys of Summer," with Robinson in the lineup, won six pennants in ten years.

Robinson made a believer out of opponents and teammates alike. After an exhibition game against the Dodgers, manager Casey Stengel told his Yankee players, "All of you guys, when you get into the locker room I want you to check your lockers. He [Robinson] stole everything out there he wanted today, so he might have stolen your jocks as well." And Leo Durocher, managing the Dodgers, observed: "This guy didn't just come to play. He came to beat ya."

Photo: *Transcendental Graphics*

black star in graphic detail of the hostility he would face in organized baseball. Robinson listened to the litany of slights and insults he could expect, finally asked, "Mr. Rickey, do you want a ball player who's afraid to fight back?" Rickey answered, "I want a player with guts enough not to fight back."

At the end of the interview Robinson signed a contract to play for the Montreal Royals in the Triple-A International League. If he succeeded at Montreal, he would be promoted to the Brooklyn Dodgers. Rickey's announcement on October 23, 1945, shook the baseball world, even though rumors and predictions of the move had been circulating for some time. A number of observers of black baseball questioned the choice of Robinson, doubting that he was good enough to play in the majors. They feared that the "great experiment" would fail and result in the continued exclusion of blacks.

Playing second base for Montreal in 1946, Robinson led the league in batting at .349 and stole 40 bases. His tenure was not free from incident, however. Several Baltimore Oriole players threatened to boycott their game against the Montreal Royals. International League president Frank Shaughnessy telegraphed that if this happened, he would arrange their lifetime suspensions from organized baseball. They played. Still, the harassment Robinson was subjected to was every bit as rough as Rickey had predicted.

Robinson survived and held his temper in check. Montreal won the pennant, and in 1947 the Royals' black second baseman—who had switched over to first base—was ready to move up to the majors. Thereafter, Jackie Robinson's story in professional baseball becomes a part of the history and tradition of the Brooklyn Dodgers.

Meanwhile, Rickey had been signing other black players from the Negro Leagues, most notably catcher Roy Campanella from the Baltimore Elite Giants and pitcher Don Newcombe from the Newark Eagles. Cleveland Indians' owner Bill Veeck plucked second baseman Larry Doby from the Newark Eagles, making Doby the first black to play in the American League. The St. Louis Browns signed two players from the Kansas City Monarchs, but only infielder Hank Thompson did well in the majors. These and subsequent acquisitions posed an urgent threat to the well-being of the Negro Leagues and the future of independent black barnstorming teams.

Integration, Disintegration

Effa Manley, co-owner of the Newark Eagles, was furious when her star players began their exodus to the majors. Big-league owners, so recently disdainful of black athletes, were now raiding Negro League rosters and scouting unsigned black prospects. J. L. Wilkinson, owner of the Kansas City Monarchs, received no compensation when Jackie Robinson was taken from his team and then saw fans desert Blues Stadium in Kansas City to ride 245 miles by train to watch Robinson play for the Dodgers against the St. Louis Cardinals.

Although supporters of integration complained that Major League owners had moved too slowly, Negro League club owners were quickly and negatively impacted. In 1948 both the Newark Eagles and New York Black Yankees disbanded. The Homestead Grays went back to full-time barnstorming, and the Negro National League fell apart. Reorganized as a ten-team circuit, it struggled through the early 1950s, but its future was in peril.

The Negro American League lasted into the 1960s as a weak, four-team circuit, but folded along with its marquis team, the Kansas City Monarchs. Only the Indianapolis Clowns, themselves integrated and strictly vaudeville, remained, hanging on until the 1970s. Organized, integrated baseball simply engulfed professional black baseball. Thirty years after integration, Effa Manley told an interviewer, "Every time I see the Dodgers get beat, I say they don't deserve to win for what they did to Negro baseball."

What they did was to diminish the appeal of all-black competition and to hire away the most gifted young players. For a time the Negro Leagues and independent black teams furnished talent to the majors. Many black ballplayers began their careers on all-black teams and then moved into organized baseball, sometimes at the major league level, sometimes not. Several of the brightest of these transitional black stars now have plaques at the Baseball Hall of Fame. Among them are Satchel Paige, Monte Irvin, Roy Campanella, Ernie Banks, Willie Mays, Hank Aaron, and trailblazer Jackie Robinson.

Although Rickey's Dodgers and Veeck's Indians moved swiftly to integrate every level in their organizations, they were not immediately joined by the other 14 ball clubs. It took the

| QUOTES | Voices of Negro League Players | QUOTES |

"We used to play four in one day just about every Fourth of July. I'd pitch two and catch two. The way I made it was to sleep 35 minutes between each game." —**Double Duty Radcliffe,** Pittsburgh Crawfords

"In the majors you couldn't throw spitters. We could. In the majors you didn't see a lot of knock-down pitches. We saw them all the time. We had to hit balls doctored up so bad you'd think carpenters worked on them." —**Mahlon Duckett,** Philadelphia Stars

"That was our game—run, steal, make them make mistakes.... Baseball is like everything else: You got to study every angle to win." —**Judy Johnson,** Hilldale

"Satchel Paige and Josh Gibson got more publicity in the Negro League, but Buck Leonard was just as good." —**Monte Irvin,** Newark Eagles

"Well, it wasn't left up to me to put him in there ... but most of the black ballplayers thought Monte Irvin should have been the first black in the major leagues. Monte was our best young ballplayer at the time.... He could do everything." —**Cool Papa Bell,** Homestead Grays

"I've enjoyed it, and I think I've been a lucky fellow. Didn't make no money, but I think I went a long ways. I have no regrets. None at all." —**Ray Dandridge,** Newark Eagles

"The major leagues were easy. I learned baseball the hard way; the Negro Leagues made me." —**Willie Mays,** Birmingham Black Barons

Transcendental Graphics

Ray Dandridge

Philadelphia Phillies and the Boston Red Sox 12 years to sign their first black players. Bill Cash, a catcher for the Philadelphia Stars, was signed by the Chicago White Sox and sent to Davenport, Iowa. "I hit .340 there, hit everybody, but the White Sox never moved me up and refused to trade me to another team. Reserve clause. The majors had enough blacks, I guess."

Yet many of the players who spent some or all of their careers in the Negro Leagues remained philosophical. Pat Scantlebury, a pitcher for the New York Cubans in the late 1940s remarked, "I was never bitter about the segregation. That was the way it was in those days. I wanted to play, and I could only play in black leagues, so I played in black leagues. I always felt, after integration, that our efforts, all those games and all those bus rides, made it possible for Jackie Robinson and those who followed. Yes sir, we paved the way."

SOURCES

BOOKS

Aaron, Hank, with Lonnie Wheeler, *I Had a Hammer: The Hank Aaron Story,* Harper-Collins, 1991.

Benson, Michael, *Ballparks of North America: A Comprehensive Historical Reference to Baseball Grounds, Yards and Stadiums, 1845 to Present,* McFarland & Company, 1989.

Chadwick, Bruce, *When the Game Was Black and White: The Illustrated History of the Negro Leagues,* Abbeville Press, 1992.

Daguerreotypes, 8th Edition, edited by Craig Carter, The Sporting News Publishing Co., 1990.

DiClerico, James M., *The Jersey Game: The History of Modern Baseball from Its Birth to the Big Leagues in the Garden State,* Rutgers University Press, 1991.

Holway, John B., *Blackball Stars: Negro League Pioneers,* Meckler Books, 1988.

Minor League Baseball Stars, edited by Robert L. Davids, Society for American Baseball Research, Volume 1, 1978; Volume 2, 1985.

O'Neal, Bill, *The International League: A Baseball History, 1884-1991,* Eakin Press, 1992.

Peterson, Robert W., *Only the Ball Was White,* Prentice Hall, 1970.

Riley, James A., *The All-Time All-Stars of Black Baseball,* TK Publishers, 1983.

Rogosin, Donn, *Invisible Men: Life in Baseball's Negro Leagues,* Atheneum, 1983.

Rust, Art, Jr., *"Get That Nigger Off the Field!,"* Delacorte Press, 1976.

Total Baseball, edited by John Thorn and Pete Palmer, Warner Books, 1989.

Tygiel, Jules, *Baseball's Great Experiment: Jackie Robinson and His Legacy,* Oxford University Press, 1983.

Voigt, David Quentin, *American Baseball: From the Gentleman's Sport to the Commissioner System,* Pennsylvania University Press, 1983.

PERIODICALS

Baseball Research Journal, 1972, 1973, 1982, 1983, 1986.

Baseball Historical Review, 1981.

The National Pastime, 1990.

ALL-TIME ALL-STARS OF BLACK BASEBALL

This list comes from James A. Riley's *The All-Time All Stars of Black Baseball*. Riley based his selections on a survey of more than 80 people who had either played black baseball or have studied it extensively.

	First Team	Second Team	Third Team
1b	Buck Leonard	Ben Taylor	Mule Suttles
2b	Martin Dihigo	Bingo DeMoss	Newt Allen
ss	John Henry Lloyd	Willie Wells	Dick Lundy
3b	Ray Dandridge	Judy Johnson	Oliver Marcelle
of	Oscar Charleston	Monte Irvin	Sam Jethroe
of	Cool Papa Bell	Turkey Stearnes	Willard Brown
of	Cristobal Torriente	Pete Hill	Clint Thomas
c	Josh Gibson	Biz Mackey	Roy Campanella
p	Satchel Paige	Smokey Joe Williams	Willie Foster
mgr	Rube Foster	C. I. Taylor	Vic Harris

Index

A

Aaron, Hank 16, 22, 24, 79, 81, 85, 96, 201, 440, 449, 450, 523, 540
Abbaticchio, Ed 442
Abbott, Glenn 261, 262
Abbott, Jim 210, 239
Abrams, Cal 132
Adair, Jerry 133
Adams, Ace 511
Adams, Babe 426, 427, 428
Adamson, Joel 376
Adcock, Joe 232, 449
Agee, Tommie 391, 392, 393
Agganis, Harry 153
Aguilera, Rick 118, 397, 398
Aikens, Willie Mays 69, 70, 236
Aldridge, Vic 427
Alexander, Doyle 220
Alexander, Grover Cleveland 195, 293, 332, 346, 347, 349, 403, 408, 409
Alle, Neil 397
Allen, Dick 28, 40, 360, 417, 482
Allen, Johnny 53, 196
Allen, Mel 204
Allen, Newt 543
Allen, Richie 417
Allison, Bob 18, 114, 115, 116
Alomar, Roberto 224, 225
Alomar, Sandy 59
Alou, Felipe 384, 449, 497, 514
Alou, Matty 360, 361
Alou, Moises 384
Alston, Walter 19, 475, 476, 477, 482, 483
Altobelli, Joe 517
Altrock, Nick 289
Alvis, Max 81
Ames, Red 342, 504
Andersen, Richard 375
Anderson, Craig 388

Anderson, John 48
Anderson, Sparky 163, 178, 179, 180, 181, 182, 314, 315, 317, 476
Andrews, Mike 40, 252
Andujar, Joaquin 364
Angus, Samuel F. 166
Anson, Adrian 285, 286, 288
Anson, Cap 6, 522, 526
Antonelli, Johnny 18, 514
Aparicio, Luis 38, 39, 133
Appier, Kevin 75
Appling, Luke 36, 37
Argyros, George 263, 264
Arias, Alex 375
Armas, Tony 255
Armour, Bill 167, 168
Arnovich, Morrie 412
Arroyo, Luis 357
Ashburn, Richie 388, 389, 414, 415, 416
Ashby, Alan 326, 327
Aspromonte, Bob 393
Aspromonte, Ken 58
Aubrey, Harvey 442
August, Don 95, 96
Augustine, Jerry 86, 88
Auker, Eldon 129
Ault, Doug 214
Autry, Gene 231, 232, 233, 235
Averill, Earl 52, 53, 232
Avery, Steve 224, 451, 452

B

Backman, Wally 396, 397, 398
Baerga, Carlos 59, 60
Bagby, Jim 12, 49, 51, 52
Bagwell, Jeff 328
Bahnsen, Stan 28
Bailey, Bill 125

E

F

H

Haas, Moose 86, 88, 89, 90, 91, 92
Haas, Mule 36, 37, 246
Haas, Walter 255, 257
Hack, Stan 13, 294
Haddix, Harvey 356, 357
Hadley, Bump 511
Hafey, Chick 12, 309, 347, 348
Haines, Jesse 345, 346, 347
Hall, George 5
Hall, Jimmie 115, 116
Hallahan, Bill 349
Hamilton, Billy 7, 405, 406, 407, 442
Hamilton, Darryl 98, 99, 100
Hamlin, Luke 471
Hammaker, Atlee 518
Hands, Bill 298
Haney, Fred 128, 449
Hanlon, Ned 7, 462, 465
Hansen, Ron 39
Hanson, Erik 268
Harazin, Al 401
Harder, Mel 52, 53
Hardin, Jim 135
Hargrove, Mike 275, 276
Harkness, Tim 390
Harlow, Larry 236
Harmon, Bob 341
Harnisch, Pete 140, 328
Harper, George 409
Harper, Jack 338, 339
Harper, Tommy 80, 81, 82
Harrah, Toby 275, 276, 279
Harrelson, Bud 391, 392, 395, 399,
Harridge, Will 132
Harrington, John 158, 161
Harris, Bob 129
Harris, Bucky 110, 112, 113, 170,
  176, 199, 413
Harris, Vic 543
Hart, Jim Ray 516
Hartnett, Gabby 13, 286, 295
Hartsfield, Roy 215
Hartung, Clint 512, 513
Harwell, Ernie 173

Hassamaer, Bill 108
Hassey, Ron 459
Hatcher, Billy 327
Hatcher, Mickey 484
Hatten, Joe 475
Hawkes, Chicken 409
Hawkins, Andy 494
Hawley, Pink 306
Hayes, Charlie 460
Hayes, Von 419
Hazle, Bob 449
Hearn, Jim 513
Heath, Jeff 53, 446
Hebner, Richie 433
Heep, Danny 398
Hegan, Jim 54
Hegan, Mike 80, 81, 85
Heidrick, Emmett 339
Heidrick, John 338
Heilbronner, Louie 338
Heilmann, Harry 35, 169, 170, 173
Heise, Bob 83
Hemond, Roland 40
Hemus, Solly 357
Henderson, Dave 158, 159, 260,
  262, 263, 265
Henderson, Rickey 22, 209, 225,
  226, 242, 254, 255, 256, 258
Henderson, Steve 265, 396
Hendrick, George 363, 364
Hendrick, John 337
Hendricks, Jack 309, 342
Henke, Tom 213, 222, 225, 280
Henrich, Tommy 15, 198, 199, 200,
  472
Henry, Doug 98, 99
Herman, Babe 469, 470
Herman, Billy 12, 153, 286, 294, 471,
  472
Hernandez, Keith 363, 364, 397, 398,
  400
Hernandez, Roberto 43
Hernandez, Willie 180
Herndon, Larry 180
Herr, Tommy 365
Herrmann, Garry 9, 306, 307

J

K

375

LaCoss, Mike 518
Ladd, Pete 92
LaGrow, Lerrin 252
Lahoud, Joe 82
Lajoie, Nap 8, 45, 46, 47, 48, 49, 125, 242, 243, 406
Lamont, Gene 28, 42
Lamp, Dennis 220
Landis, Kenesaw 11, 507, 537
Lane, Frank 37, 38, 82, 249
Lang, John F. 526
Langford, Rick 255
Langston, Mark 264, 265, 266
Lanier, Hal 326
Lanier, Max 15
Lankford, Ray 367
Lannin, Joseph J. 146
Lansford, Carney 235, 236, 257
LaPoint, Dave 89
Larkin, Barry 319
LaRoche, Dave 235, 236
Larsen, Don 132, 201, 248
LaRussa, Tony 23, 28, 41, 42, 258
Lasorda, Tommy 23, 463, 483, 484, 485
Lau, Charley 65
Laudner, Tim 117, 118
Lavagetto, Cookie 114, 471, 472
Law, Vance 384
Law, Vern 422, 431, 433
Lazzeri, Tony 12, 192, 194
Lea, Charlie 383
Leach, Terry 398
Leach, Tommy 425
Leary, Tim 94
Lee, Bill 13, 286, 294, 382
Lee, Hal 410
Lee, Thornton 36
Leever, Sam 425, 426
Lefebvre, Jim 266, 301, 419
Lefferts, Craig 494, 519
LeFlore, Ron 382
Leibrandt, Charlie 73, 224, 452
Leifield, Lefty 426
Lemanczyk, Dave 215

Lemaster, Denny 450
Lemon, Bob 41, 54, 55, 56, 57, 64, 207, 208, 209
Lemon, Chet 41
Lemon, Jim 114, 115, 271, 273
Leon, Jeff 95
Leonard, Buck 523, 535, 536, 537, 538, 543
Leonard, Dennis 65, 66, 68, 69, 74
Leonard, Dutch 10, 148, 414, 470
Lerch, Randy 89
LeRoux, Edward G. 158
Lewis, Duffy 146
Lewis, Ed 144
Leyland, Jim 422, 435, 436
Lezcano, Sixto 86, 88, 89, 96
Lillis, Bob 326
Lindell, Johnny 199
Lindstrom, Freddie 508
Lippy, Leo 310
Litwhiler, Danny 413
Livingston, Mickey 296
Lloyd, Graeme 99
Lloyd, Pop 523, 531, 543
Lockman, Whitey 299
Lockwood, Skip 80, 82
Loes, Billy 475
Lofton, Kenny 59, 60
Loftus, Tom 109, 306
Lolich, Mickey 176, 177
Lollar, Sherm 38, 39
Lollar, Tim 493, 494
Lombardi, Ernie 311, 511
Lombardozzi, Steve 117, 118
Lonborg, Jim 84, 417, 418
Long, Dale 272, 431
Long, Harry 442
Long, Tom 342
Lopat, Ed 17
Lopat, Eddie 199, 201
Lopata, Stan 416
Lopes, Davey 256, 327, 463, 482, 483
Lopez, Al 27, 38, 39, 40, 45, 56, 58, 470
Lopez, Aurelio 327

Lopez, Hector 204, 248
Lovett, Tom 464
Lowe, Bobby 167, 442
Lucas, Gary 159
Lucas, Henry 335
Lucas, John 334
Lucchesi, Frank 275, 276, 417
Luderus, Fred 408
Luecken, Rick 265
Lumley, Harry 466
Lundgren, Carl 289, 290
Lundy, Dick 531, 535, 543
Lupien, Tony 413
Lurie, Robert 517
Luzinski, Greg 41, 42, 417, 418
Lyle, Sparky 205, 207
Lynch, Jerry 312
Lynn, Fred 140, 154, 155, 158, 231
Lyons, Ted 35, 37

M

Maas, Kevin 210
MacDougald, Gil 58
Mack, Connie 1, 10, 13, 35, 62, 192,
  241, 242, 244, 245, 246, 247, 248,
  424
Mack, Denny 333
Mackey, Biz 535, 543
MacPhail, Andy 105, 119
MacPhail, Larry 199, 471, 472
MacPhail, Lee 71, 205
MacPhail, Lee Jr. 133
Maddox, Elliott 396
Maddox, Garry 418
Maddux, Greg 301, 452
Madlock, Bill 275, 434, 435
Magadan, Dave 376, 400
Maglie, Sal 17, 497, 513
Magrane, Joe 366
Mahaffey, Art 416
Mahoney, Jim 272
Malarcher, Dave 528
Maldonado, Candy 224, 518
Mallon, Les 410

Malone, Pat 294
Mamaux, Al 467
Mancuso, Frank 129
Mancuso, Gus 348, 509
Manley, Abe 534
Manley, Effa 534, 540
Mann, Les 343
Manno, Bruce 98
Mantilla, Felix 388, 389
Mantle, Mickey 17, 18, 19, 186, 201,
  202, 203, 204
Manush, Heinie 127
Mapes, Cliff 199
Maranville, Rabbit 293, 427, 439,
  444, 445
Marberry, Firpo 112
Marcelle, Oliver 543
Marichal, Juan 497, 515, 516, 517
Mariner, Jonathan 375
Marion, Marty 15, 27, 352, 353,
  354, 355, 356
Maris, Roger 18, 19, 202, 203, 204,
  248, 359
Marquard, Rube 10, 189, 462, 467,
  497, 504, 505
Marshall, Jim 254
Marshall, Mike 378, 379, 482
Martin, Al 436
Martin, Billy 71, 84, 115, 177, 200,
  206, 207, 208, 209, 248, 254, 255,
  256, 275
Martin, Jerry 70
Martin, Pepper 13, 348, 349, 350, 351
Martinez, Buck 64
Martinez, Carmelo 494
Martinez, Dennis 137, 378, 384
Martinez, Edgar 268, 269
Martinez, Jose 375
Masi, Phil 447
Mathews, Eddie 79, 201, 440, 447,
  448, 449
Mathewson, Christy 9, 10, 14, 24,
  189, 307, 308, 348, 497, 502, 503,
  504, 505
Matlack, Jon 276, 393, 394, 395
Mattern, Al 443

N

O

T